LAND FORCES
OF THE WORLD

This 1990 edition is published by Crescent Books
Distributed by Crown Publishers, Inc.

Copyright © Brian Trodd Publishing House Limited 1990

ISBN 0-517-69128-0

h g f e d c b a

Printed in Portugal

LAND FORCES
OF THE WORLD

CHRISTOPHER CHANT

CRESCENT BOOKS
New York

CONTENTS

TAMSE/Thyssen Henschel TAM

(Argentina/West Germany)

Type: main battle tank

Crew: 4

Combat weight: 30,500 kg (67,240 lb)

Dimensions: length, gun forward 8·23 m (27·0 ft) and hull 6·775 m (22·23 ft); width 3·12 m (10·24 ft); height to turret top 2·42 m (7·94 ft)

Armament system: one 105-mm (4·13-in) Rheinmetall Rh-105-30 rifled gun with 50 rounds, two 7·62-mm (0·3-in) FN-MAG machine-guns (one co-axial and one AA) with 6,000 rounds, and four smoke-dischargers on each side of the turret; the turret is electro-hydraulically powered, the main gun is stabilized in elevation (−7° to +16°) and azimuth (360°), and an optical fire-control system is fitted

Armour: welded steel

Powerplant: one 537-kW (720-hp) MTU MB 833 Ka-500 diesel engine with 650 litres (143 Imp gal) of internal fuel and provision for two 200-litre (44-Imp gal) auxiliary tanks carried at the rear

Performance: speed, road 75 km/h (46·6 mph); range, road 550 km (342 miles) on internal fuel and 900 km (559 miles) with auxiliary fuel; fording 1·4 m (4·6 ft) without preparation, 2·25 m (7·4 ft) with preparation and 4·0 m (13·1 ft) with snorkel; gradient 60%; side slope 30%; vertical obstacle 1·0 m (39·4 in); trench 2·5 m (8·2 ft); ground clearance 0·44 m (17·3 in)

Variants

TAM: this is the baseline medium tank model developed in West Germany to Argentine requirements, using the hull of the Marder MICV as the structural and automotive basis, and built in Argentina; the same basis has been used for the VCTP infantry fighting vehicle, designed to operate with this Tanque Argentino Mediano; it is not known with certainty whether the main armament is the Rh-105 as stated above or the British ROF L7A3 of the same calibre; Argentina is also developing the same basic chassis for a self-propelled howitzer, using the turret and ordnance of the OTO Melara Palmaria 155-mm (6·1-in) equipment on a chassis lengthened from six to seven roadwheels; this equipment has a combat weight in the order of 45,000 kg (99,206 lb), so it is possible that a more powerful engine has been installed to maintain performance at the level of the lighter tank version

VCRT: armoured recovery vehicle based on the chassis of the TAM tank and VCTP armoured personnel carrier; the basic chassis is fitted with a rear-mounted dozer blade, which also doubles as a stabilizer for winch and crane operations, plus superstructure and recovery rig designed by Krupp MaK, and comprising a 30,000-kg (66,128-lb) capacity winch in the glacis and a 22,000-kg (48,501-lb) capacity crane; the latter is located on the right of the superstructure, and has traverse through 213·5°

TH 301: improved prototype produced by Thyssen Henschel with upgraded 560-kW (751-hp) powerpack and superior fire-control system with laser rangefinder and low-light-level TV; this private-venture development weighs 31,000 kg (68,342 lb) and is 8·455 m (27·74 ft) long with the gun forward; Thyssen Henschel is also developing a version of this tank with a 120-mm (4·72-in) gun and the same fire-control system as the TH-301

ENGESA EE-T1 Osorio

(Brazil)

Type: main battle tank

Crew: 4

Combat weight: 40,400 kg (89,065 lb)

Dimensions: length, gun forward 9·36 m (30·71 ft) and hull 7·13 m (23·39 ft); width 3·256 m (10·68 ft); height to turret top 2·37 m (7·78 ft)

Armament system: one 105-mm (4·13-in) ROF L7A3 rifled gun with 45 rounds, and two 7·62-mm (0·3-in) FN-MAG machine-guns (one co-axial and one AA) with 5,000 rounds or one 7·62-mm FN-MAG co-axial machine-gun with 3,000 rounds and one 0·5-in (12·7-mm) AA Browning machine-gun with 900 rounds, and six smoke-dischargers on each side of the turret; the turret is electrically powered, the main gun is stabilized in elevation (−10° to +20°) and azimuth (360°), and an O IP optical fire-control system is fitted; this last includes stabilized optics and a laser rangefinder

Armour: bi-metallic plate and composite

Powerplant: one 775-kW (1,039-hp) MWM TBD 234-V12 diesel engine with an unrevealed quantity of internal fuel

Performance: speed, road 70 km/h (43·5 mph); range, road 550 km (342 miles); fording 1·2 m (3·9 ft) without preparation and 2·0 m (6·6 ft) with preparation; gradient 60%; side slope 40%; vertical obstacle 1·15 m (45·3 in); trench 3·0 m (9·8 ft); ground clearance 0·46 m (18·1 in)

Variants

EE-T1 Osorio: this is the basic MBT model, developed in the early 1980s and first seen in prototype form during 1984, and its optional features are full NBC protection, a simple fire-control system (day/night sights with a laser rangefinder and ballistic computer), an automatic fire-extinguishing system, and a land navigation system; the ammunition for the main armament is stowed as 33 in the hull and 12 in the turret

EE-T2 Osorio: upgunned model, the main armament being a GIAT 120-mm smooth-bore gun with 38 rounds (26 in the hull and 12 in the turret); this model has a more sophisticated fire-control system with a ballistic computer and stabilized optics, a combat weight of 43,700 kg (96,340 lb) and lengths of 10·10 m (33·14 ft) with the gun forward and 9·30 m (30·51 ft) for the hull; the manufacturer is also considering the possibility of using the same basic hull for a 155-mm (6·1-in) self-propelled howitzer, a self-propelled AA mounting with two 30- or 35-mm cannon, an armoured bridgelayer and an armoured recovery vehicle

Bernardini MB-3 Tamoio

(Brazil)

Type: main battle tank

Crew: 4

Combat weight: 30,000 kg (66·138 lb)

Dimensions: length, gun forward 8·77 m (28·77 ft) and hull 6·50 m (21·325 ft); width over skirts 3·22 m (10·56 ft); height to top of commander's cupola 2·50 m (8·20 ft)

Armament system: one 90-mm (3·54-in) Bernardini rifled gun with 68 rounds, and two 7·62-mm (0·3-in) FN-MAG machine-guns (one co-axial and one AA) with 5,000 rounds or one 7·62-mm FN-MAG co-axial machine-gun with 3,000 rounds and one 0·5-in (12·7-mm) AA Browning machine-gun with 600 rounds, and four smoke-dischargers on each side of the turret; the turret is electrically powered, the main gun is stabilized in elevation (−6° to +16°) and azimuth (360°), and an optical fire-control system is fitted; this last includes a laser rangefinder and ballistic computer

Armour: composite and spaced

Powerplant: one 375-kW (503-hp) Saab-Scania DSI-14 diesel engine with 700 litres (154 Imp gal) of internal fuel

Performance: speed, road 67 km/h (41·6 mph); range, road 550 km (342 miles); fording 1·3 m (4·3 ft) without preparation; gradient 60%; side slope 30%; vertical obstacle 0·71 m (28 in); trench 2·4 m (7·9 ft); ground clearance 0·5 m (19·7 in)

Variants

MB-3 Tamoio: produced as a private venture, the Tamoio (also spelled Tamoyo) was developed in the early 1980s on the basis of the X-30 experimental tank evolved from the Brazilian version of the US M41 light tank; though the X-30 was not built in armed form, it was planned to offer the type with a choice of 90- or 105-mm (3·54- or 4·13-in) main armament, and this option is retained in the MB-3; the Tamoio began trials in 1984, and is offered with the locally built Saab-Scania diesel or alternatively the 736-hp (549-kw) Detroit Diesel 8V-92TA diesel

MB-3 Tamoio III: again produced as a private venture, the Tamoio III appeared in 1987, and is a simple tank with useful capabilities through the use of the powerful ROF L7 rifled gun (with 50 rounds carried as 32 in the hull and 18 in the turret) and a capable Ferranti Falcon fire-control system with stabilized optics; the Tamoio III weighs 31,000 kg (68,342 lb), and its dimensions include lengths of 8·90 m (29·20 ft) with the gun forward and 6·30 m (20·67 ft) for the hull, a width of 3·20 m (10·50 ft) over the skirts, and a height of 2·65 m (8·69 ft) to the top of the commander's cupola; the maximum speed is again 67 km/h (41·6 mph), but range is 600 km (373 miles)

Type 80

(China)

Type: main battle tank

Crew: 4

Combat weight: 38,000 kg (83,774 lb)

Dimensions: length, gun forward 9·328 m (30·60 ft) and hull 6·325 m (20·75 ft); width over skirts 3·372 m (11·06 m); height to top of AA machine-gun 2·874 m (9·43 ft)

Armament system: one 105-mm (4·13-in) rifled gun with 44 rounds, one 7·62-mm (0·3-in) Type 59T co-axial machine-gun with 2,250 rounds, one 12·7-mm (0·5-in) Type 54 AA machine-gun with 500 rounds, and four smoke-dischargers on each side of the turret; the turret is electro-hydraulically powered, the main gun is stabilized in elevation (−4° to +18°) and azimuth (360°), and

Below: Chinese Type 80 Twin 57-mm self-propelled Anti-Aircraft Gun system.

an Image-Stabilized Fire-Control System 212 fire-control system is fitted; this last includes stabilized optics, a laser rangefinder, gun and vehicle sensors and a ballistic computer; the type can also generate smoke by injecting fuel into the exhaust system

Armour: cast and welded steel

Powerplant: probably one 545-kW (731-hp) Type 12150L-7BW turbocharged diesel engine with 1400 litres (308 Imp gal) of internal fuel, plus provision for external fuel

Performance: speed, road 60 km/h (37·3 mph); range, road 430 km (267 miles); fording 0·8 m (2·6 ft) without preparation and 5·0 m (16·4 m) with preparation; gradient 60%; side slope 40%; vertical obstacle 0·8 m (31·5 in); trench 2·7 m (8·9 ft); ground clearance 0·48 m (18·9 in)

Variants

Type 80: this new Chinese MBT was known during development as the Type 69-III and entered production in the late 1980s as the mainstay of the growing armour force fielded by the Chinese into the next century; the type has a wholly new hull, a turret modelled on that of the Type 69, and a 105-mm (4·13-in) rifled gun with an advanced fire-control system; standard equipment includes an NBC system and night vision equipment, and the comparatively high power-to-weight ratio offers better cross-country performance than that of earlier Chinese MBTs

Type 85-II: revealed in 1989, this appears to be a variant of the Type 80 with a welded rather than cast turret; the new turret is fitted with the standard 105-mm (4·13-in) gun, but the turret's shape and construction allow easy addition of extra armour; the glacis can also be fitted with a panel of composite armour to improve protection in the frontal arc

Type 85-IIA: exactly how this Type 85-II subvariant differs from the baseline vehicle has not been revealed, though the Type 85-IIA is slightly shorter and, at a combat weight of 39,500 kg (87,082 lb), slightly heavier

Type 69-II

(China)
Type: main battle tank
Crew: 4
Combat weight: 36,500/37,000 kg (80,467/81,570 lb)
Dimensions: length, gun forward 8·657 m (28·40 ft) and hull 6·243 m (20·48 ft); width 3·298 m (10·82 ft); height with AA gun at full elevation 3·909 m (12·825 ft)
Armament system: one 100-mm (3·94-in) rifled gun with an unrevealed number of rounds, two 7·62-mm (0·3-in) Type 59T machine-guns (one bow and one co-axial) with an unrevealed number of rounds, and one 12·7-mm (0·5-in) Type 54 AA machine-gun with an unrevealed number of rounds; the turret is electro-hydraulically powered, the main gun is stabilized in elevation (an unrevealed arc) and azimuth (360°), and a TFSCS-L (Tank Simplified Fire-Control System - Laser) is fitted, this last including stabilized optics, a laser rangefinder and a ballistic computer; an optional fit for export models is the TSFCS-C which adds sensors for variables such as cross wind, ambient temperature and propellant-charge temperature; the type can also generate smoke by injecting fuel into the exhaust system
Armour: cast and welded steel varying in thickness from 20 to 203 mm (0·79 to 8 in)

Powerplant: one 435-kW (583-hp) Model 12150L-7BW diesel engine with an unrevealed quantity of internal fuel

Performance: speed, road 50 km/h (31·1 mph); range, road 440 km (273 miles); fording 1·4 m (4·6 ft); gradient 60%; side slope 40%; vertical obstacle 0·8 m (31·5 in); trench 2·7 m (8·9 ft); ground clearance 0·425 m (16·75 in)

Variants

Type 69-I: introduced in the early 1980s, the Type 69-I is in essence an improved Type 59 MBT with superior 100-mm (3·94-in) smooth-bore armament allied to a new fire-control system and night vision equipment; the type also features a slightly more powerful diesel powerplant; standard features are NBC protection and an engine compartment fire-suppression system

Type 69-II: further improved model optimized for the export market and fitted with a rifled rather than smooth-bore main armament, and possessing a number of options in the fire-control system

Type 69-II Mk B: command version of the Type 69-II with an additional radio set; a further development with two radios of the same type is the
Type 69-II Mk C

Type 69-IIM: under this designation Pakistan is developing, with Chinese aid, an upgrade package for its Type 69-II MBTs; the package comprises a 105-mm (4·13-in) main gun, a laser rangefinder and a number of other modernization features

Type 79: revealed in 1987, this is a version of the Type 69-II with the turret revised to allow the mounting of a 105-mm (4·13-in) rifled main gun fitted with a thermal sleeve; this increases weight to 37,500 kg (82,672 lb), and the tank has a TSFCS (possibly the TSFCS-L model including a laser rangefinder), and a series of five removable skirts along the upper portion of the tracks

Type 653: armoured recovery vehicle model of the Type 69 with a welded superstructure, 70,000-kg (154,321-lb) capacity winch, dozer blade and hydraulic crane; the type has a five-man crew and a combat weight of 38,000 kg (83,774 lb)

Type 80: self-propelled twin 57-mm AA mounting based conceptually on the Soviet ZSU-57-2 but using the hull of the Type 69-II MBT; the type has a combat weight of 31,000 kg (68,342 lb) and has a 433-kW (580-hp) diesel, and is limited to clear-weather operations by its lack of anything but optical sights; the Chinese have also developed a twin 37-mm AA mounting on the same chassis,

though the designation for this useful system remains unknown; the two-man power-operated turret has an optical fire-control system for the twin P793 Type B cannon, each with a cyclic rate of 380 rounds per minute and muzzle velocity of 1000 m (3,281 ft) per second; the effective AA range is 4000 m (4,375 yards), and the practical surface-to-surface range 3500 m (3,830 yards); combat weight is 34,200 kg (75,397 lb)

Type 84: armoured vehicle-launched bridge variant of the Type 69, with the turret replaced by a hydraulically operated folding bridge able to span a gap of 16·0 m (52·5 ft); the type's combat weight is 38,500 kg (84,876 lb)

Type 59

(China)
Type: main battle tank
Crew: 4
Combat weight: 36,000 kg (79,365 lb)
Dimensions: length, gun forward 9·00 m (29·53 ft) and hull 6·04 m (19·82 ft); width 3·27 m (10·73 ft); height overall 2·59 m (8·50 ft) and to turret top 2·40 m (7·87 ft)
Armament system: one 100-mm (3·94-in) Type 59 rifled gun with 34 rounds, two 7·62-mm (0·3-in) Type 59T machine-guns (one co-axial and one in glacis) with 3,500 rounds, and one 12·7-mm (0·5-in) Type 54 AA machine-gun with 200 rounds; the turret is electro-hydraulically powered, the main gun is stabilized in elevation (−4° to +17°) but not in azimuth (360°), and an optical fire-control system is fitted though the type can be retrofitted with the TSFCS-C fire-control system (see Type 69-II); the type can also generate smoke by injecting fuel into the exhaust system
Armour: cast and welded steel varying in thickness between 20 mm (0·79 in) and 203 mm (8 in)
Powerplant: one 388-kW (520-hp) Model 12150L V-12 diesel engine with 815 litres (179 Imp gal) of internal fuel, plus provision for 400 litres (88 Imp gal) of auxiliary fuel
Performance: speed, road 50 km/h (31·1 mph); range, road 440 km (273 miles) on internal fuel and 600 km (373 miles) with auxiliary fuel; fording 1·4 m (4·6 ft) without preparation and 5·5 m (18·0 ft) with preparation; gradient 60%; side slope 40%;

The derivation of the Type 59 from the Soviet T-54 is clear in this scene at an amphibious exercise.

vertical obstacle 0·79 m (31 in); trench 2·7 m (8·86 ft); ground clearance 0.425 m (16.7 in)

Variants

Type 59: this is the Chinese derivative of the Soviet T-54, and is currently the main gun tank fielded by the armies of China, though the model has also been exported to Albania, Cambodia (latterly Kampuchea), Congo, North Korea, Pakistan, Sudan, Tanzania and Vietnam; early models of the Type 59 were very similar to the basic T-54, but the development of the Soviet series was then mirrored in Chinese models that thus sported gun stabilization, a fume extractor, and night vision devices of the active and passive varieties; recently many tanks have been upgraded with Western guns (the 105-mm/4·13-in ROF L7A3), laser rangefinders and night vision devices, the American designation for this version being **Type 59 M1984**; a similar retrofit package is also offered by Royal Ordnance in the UK, and other Western manufacturers have proposed basic improvements to the Type 59's systems, most notably the fire-control and night vision systems, for which the Belgian OIP LRS-5 and British IR18 respectively have been proposed

Type 59 (Improved): upgraded Type 59 version offered by the Chinese from 1986; the variant offers a 545-kW (731-hp) diesel for much improved performance, new APFSDS-T ammunition for the 100-mm (3·94-in) smooth-bore gun which is stabilized in azimuth and elevation, a new fire-control system, and provision for an NBC system

CRIS/GIAT Type 59: announced in 1987, this is a joint Chinese and French improvement package for Type 59 tanks with an upgraded turret containing a GIAT 105-mm (4·13-in) main gun firing standard NATO ammunition types, a much improved fire-control system, and a Halon engine and crew compartment fire-extinguishing system

Type 59 ARV: simple development of the Type 59 as a basic armoured recovery vehicle; the type has no turret, is fitted with a single 12·7-mm (0·5-in) local defence machine-gun, and is limited to towing operations by its lack of a winch; it is possible that further developments of the Type 59's chassis will follow, and the type has been evaluated with a Marconi Marksman turret (two 35-mm cannon and a radar fire-control system) as a British-led suggestion for a self-propelled AA equipment with superior capabilities to the Chinese army's current optically controlled equipment with two 37-mm cannon on a Type 59 chassis

China National Machinery & Equipment Import and Export Corporation/Cadillac Gage Textron Jaguar: announced late in 1988 as a joint Chinese and private-enterprise US venture, this four-man main battle tank is based on a lengthened version of the Type 59's chassis with five road wheels, rear drive sprocket and front idler, two track-return rollers and Chinese torsion-bar suspension (with Cadillac Gage hydropneumatic suspension possibly to be adopted for the definitive vehicle); the type has a 675/750-hp (503/559-kW) Detroit Diesel engine driving a fully automatic transmission to provide a maximum road speed of at least 50 km/h (31·1 mph); the hydraulically powered turret accommodates a 105-mm (4·13-in) Royal Ordnance Low Recoil Force gun, a 7·62-mm (0·3-in) co-axial machine-gun, and a 12·7-mm (0·5-in) AA machine-gun; systems include two-axis gun stabilization, a Marconi digital fire-control system, and automatic fire suppression in the engine and crew compartments; options will include night vision devices and NBC protection

GIAT AMX-48 Leclerc

(France)

Type: main battle tank
Crew: 3
Combat weight: 50,000/53,000 kg (110,229/ 116,843 lb)
Dimensions: length, gun forward not revealed and hull 6·60 m (21·65 ft); width 3·30 m (10·83 ft); height 2·30 m (7·55 ft)
Armament system: one 120-mm (4·72-in) GIAT CN-120 smooth-bore gun with 40 rounds (18 rounds in the hull and 22 rounds in a Creusot-Loire automatic loader), one co-axial 20-mm GIAT M693 (F2) cannon with an unrevealed number of rounds or one 0·5-in (12·7-mm) Browning M2HB heavy machine-gun with an unrevealed number of rounds, one 7·62-mm (0·3-in) NF1 AA machine-gun with an unrevealed number of rounds, and three smoke-dischargers on each side of the turret; the turret is electro-hydraulically powered, the main gun is stabilized in elevation (an unrevealed arc) and azimuth (360°) , and a Sagem/ESD digital fire-control system is fitted; this last includes stabilized optics, a low-light-level TV sight, various sensors, a laser rangefinder and a ballistic computer
Armour: welded steel with superimposed layer of combined laminate and reactive armour
Powerplant: one 1120-kW (1,502-hp) Unidiesel (Poyaud) V8X-1500 Hyperbar diesel engine with an unrevealed quantity of internal fuel
Performance: not revealed

Variant

Leclerc: this is planned as the main French MBT for the 1990s and beyond; the prototype appeared early in 1987, and is characterized by its low overall height, very high power-to-weight ratio (offering the real probability of excellent cross-country performance) and the latest reactive armour, which is a layer of small explosive plates over the basic steel armour, designed to detonate and so snuff out the hypervelocity gas jet of incoming HEAT rounds; the type has full NBC protection, and is provided with a snorkel kit for deep wading

---

Though it has secured no orders, the AMX-40 has been an invaluable development vehicle.

GIAT AMX-40

(France)

Type: main battle tank
Crew: 4
Combat weight: 43,700 kg (96,340 lb)
Dimensions: length, gun forward 10·05 m (32·97 ft) and hull 6·80 m (22·31 ft); width over skirts 3·35 m (10·99 ft); height to turret top 2·38 m (7·81 ft) and to commander's sight 3·10 m (10·17 ft)
Armament system: one 120-mm (4·72-in) GIAT CN-120 smooth-bore gun with 40 rounds, one 20-mm GIAT M693 (F2) co-axial cannon with 578 rounds, one 7·62-mm (0·3-in) NF1 AA machine-gun with 2,170 rounds, and three smoke-dischargers on each side of the turret; the turret is electro-hydraulically powered, the main gun is stabilized in elevation (−8° to +20°) and azimuth (360°) , and a COTAC fire-control system is fitted; this last includes stabilized optics, a low-light-level TV sight, various sensors, a laser rangefinder and a ballistic computer
Armour: welded and laminate
Powerplant: one 970-kW (1,301-hp) Poyaud V12X diesel engine with 1100 litres (242 Imp gal) of internal fuel plus provision for two jettisonable long-range tanks
Performance: speed, road 70 km/h (43·5 mph); range, road 600 km (373 miles) on standard fuel or 850 km (528 miles) with auxiliary fuel; fording 1·3 m (4·3 ft) without preparation, 2·3 m (7·5 ft) with preparation and 4·0 m (13·1 ft) with snorkel; gradient 70%; side slope 30%; vertical obstacle 1·0 m (39·4 in); trench 3·2 m (10·5 ft); ground clearance 0·45 m (17·7 in)

Variant

AMX-40: this is a French development vehicle serving primarily as an export type but also as prototype for a new-generation of French MBTs, which are obsolescent in terms of protection and fire-control compared with American, British and West German MBTs; the type appeared in 1983 and has full NBC protection; amongst its features are an assisted loading system for the main armament, independent elevation of the co-axial armament between −8° and +40°, and the versatile external stowage system; this last allows the use of two fuel tanks for long-range missions, or the mix of one fuel tank and one container with 12 rounds of 105-mm (4·13-in) ammunition, or even

two containers for 24 additional rounds of main armament ammunition

GIAT AMX-30B2

(France)
Type: main battle tank
Crew: 4
Combat weight: 37,000 kg (81,570 lb)
Dimensions: length, gun forward 9·48 m (31·1 ft) and hull 6·59 m (21·62 ft); width 3·10 m (10·17 ft); height to turret top 2·29 m (7·51 ft)
Armament system: one 105-mm (4·13-in) GIAT CN-105 (F1) rifled gun with 47 rounds (28 in the hull and 19 in the turret), one 20-mm GIAT M621 (F1) co-axial cannon with 480 rounds, one 7·62-mm (0·3-in) GIAT NF1 cupola-mounted AA machine-gun with 2,050 rounds, and two smoke-dischargers on each side of the turret; the turret is electro-hydraulically powered, the main gun is stabilized in elevation (−8° to +20°) and azimuth (360°), and a COTAC fire-control system is fitted; this last includes optical sights, a low-light-level TV, various sensors, a laser rangefinder and a ballistic computer
Armour: welded and cast steel varying in thickness between 20 mm (0·79 in) and 80·8 mm (3·18 in)
Powerplant: one 540-kW (724-hp) Hispano-Suiza HS 110 multi-fuel engine with 900 litres (198 Imp gal) of internal fuel
Performance: speed, road 65 km/h (40·4 mph); range, road 450 km (280 miles); fording 1·3 m (4·27 ft) without preparation, 2·2 m (7·2 ft) with preparation and 4·0 m (13·1 ft) with snorkel; gradient 60%; side slope 30%; vertical obstacle 0·93 m (36·6 in); trench 2·9 m (9·5 ft); ground clearance 0·44 m (17·3 in)

Variants

AMX-30: this is the baseline French MBT introduced in the mid-1960s with a 520-kW (697-hp) Hispano-Suiza HS 110 engine plus 970-litre

The AMX-30 is the basic model of this French MBT.

(213-Imp gal) fuel capacity for a road range of 600 km (373 miles), a combat weight of 36,000 kg (79,365 lb) when carrying the alternative co-axial armament (one 0·5-in/12·7-mm Browning machine-gun with 1,050 rounds), and a less sophisticated optical fire-control system
AMX-30B2: improved model introduced in 1979 with the COTAC integrated fire-control system (featuring a laser rangefinder, a low-light-level TV and a ballistic computer), a new gearbox and many detail improvements; the result of these developments is a considerable enhancement of combat capability, though the use of a slightly more powerful engine with reduced fuel capacity results in a marked decrease in range
AMX-30S: higher-powered version designed for desert operations and fitted with appropriate special equipment (sand shields etc); the type is operated only by Saudi Arabia, whose vehicles are fitted with a 460-kW (617-hp) engine driving through a gearbox with lower ratios for a maximum speed of 60 km/h (37·3 mph)
AMX-30 (Spain): Spanish AMX-30 tanks are being upgraded by Santa Barbara with an 635-kW (852-hp) MTU diesel and automatic transmission, a new fire-control system (including a laser rangefinder), and possibly reactive armour; Spain has also decided to retrofit some of its AMX-30 MBTs to AMX-30R standard as launchers for Roland SAMs
AMX-30 (Venezuela): Venezuelan AMX-30s are being upgraded with a Belgian SABCA fire-control system (including a laser rangefinder and provision for full weapon stabilization), and there is also the possibility that such vehicles will subsequently be retrofitted with a 908-hp (677-kW) Teledyne Continental Motors AVDS-1790 diesel with fully automatic transmission and increased fuel capacity for a range of 720 km (447 miles)
AMX-30D: 38,000-kg (83,774-lb) armoured recovery vehicle based on the chassis of the AMX-30 with a spare engine carried over the rear of the hull, a dozer blade, a crane, a 35,000-kg (77,160-lb) capacity main winch and a 3500-kg (7,716-lb) capacity auxiliary winch; there are three models of the ARV, the AMX-30D with its crane able to lift only 12,000 kg (26,455 lb) except

directly to the front of the vehicle, the **AMX-30D1** with its crane able to lift 15,000 kg (33,069 lb) through an arc of 240° , and the **AMX-30D(S)** desert version based on the AMX-30S
AMX-30R: SAM version designed for the battlefield engagement of low-level targets ranging from stationary helicopters to supersonic attack aircraft; the twin-tube launcher (for Roland 1, 2 or 3 missiles) and associated radar arrangement are similar to those of the West German Roland/ Marder system, but French IFF equipment is fitted
AMX-30 VLB: vehicle-launched bridge version able to span a gap of some 20 m (65·6 ft) with a 22-m (72·2-ft) scissors-type bridge launched from the rear of the turretless vehicle
AMX-30 EBG: combat engineer tractor version of the AMX-30 with a dozer blade, a 20,000-kg (44,092-lb) capacity winch, an auger, a 142-mm (5·59-in) demolition gun, four mine-launcher tubes (each with five anti-tank mines) and self-protection capability in the form of one 7·62-mm (0·3-in) machine-gun and four smoke-dischargers
Shahine: SAM version of the AMX-30 series, developed in parallel with the AMX-30 SA AA gun system during the later 1970s; there are two components to the system, an acquisition unit with Thomson-CSF pulse-Doppler radar able to detect targets at a range of 18·5 km (11·5 miles) and handle simultaneously 18 of the 40 computer-registered targets, and a fire unit with three ready-to-fire Matra R.460 SAMs on each side of the 17-km (10·6-mile) range fire-control/missile-control radar; each type of unit has back-up TV sensors for fair-weather operation in the event of radar failure; reload missiles are carried on a separate vehicle and loaded with the aid of a crane
Super AMX-30: under this designation an AMX-30 upgrade package is being offered by a consortium of West German companies; the main change is the adoption of a new powerpack (comprising an MTU MB 833 Ka-501 and automatic transmission) and greater fuel capacity for 20% greater range, a new NBC system, electric rather than hydraulic turret functions, and the Krupp-Atlas Modular Laser Fire-Control 30 system

Krauss-Maffei/Krupp MaK Leopard 2

(West Germany)

Type: main battle tank
Crew: 4
Combat weight: 55,150 kg (121,583 lb)
Dimensions: length, gun forward 9·668 m (31·72 ft) and hull 7·722 m (25·33 ft); width over skirts 3·70 m (12·14 ft); height to turret top 2·46 m (8·07 ft)
Armament system: one 120-mm (4·72-in) Rheinmetall Rh-120 smooth-bore gun with 42 rounds, two 7·62-mm (0·3-in) MG3A1 machine-guns (one co-axial and one cupola-mounted) with 4,750 rounds, and eight smoke-dischargers on each side of the turret; the turret is electro-hydraulically powered, the main gun is stabilized in elevation (−9° to +20°) and azimuth (360°), and an EMES 15 fire-control system is fitted; this last includes stabilized optics, thermal sights, a laser rangefinder, various sensors for ambient factors conditions, and a ballistic computer
Armour: spaced multi-layer type
Powerplant: one 1120-kW (1,502-hp) MTU MB 873 Ka-501 diesel engine with 1200 litres (264 Imp gal) of internal fuel
Performance: speed, road 72 km/h (44·7 mph); range, road 550 km (342 miles); fording 1·0 m (3·3 ft) without preparation, 2·25 m (7·4 ft) with preparation and 4·0 m (13·1 ft) with snorkel; gradient 60%; side slope 30%; vertical obstacle 1·1 m (43·3 in); trench 3·0 m (9·8 ft); ground clearance 0·63 m (24·8 in)

Variants

Leopard 2: this is the baseline MBT in service with the West German army since 1979 and ordered by several other nations; the type is an extremely capable MBT with a host of advanced features, and is characterized by such modern systems as NBC protection, passive night vision equipment and automatic fire-extinguishing; the main armament is exceptionally powerful and used in conjunction with a capable fire-control system
Leopard 2 AEV: armoured engineer vehicle derivative of the basic type currently under development
Bergepanzer 3: armoured recovery vehicle derivative of the basic type currently under development
Leopard 2 (Netherlands): version for Dutch service with FN-MAG machine-guns and various items of Dutch equipment
Leopard 2 (Switzerland): version for Swiss service with detail modifications and items of Swiss equipment

Krauss-Maffei/Krupp MaK Leopard 1A4

(West Germany)

Type: main battle tank
Crew: 4
Combat weight: 42,400 kg (93,474 lb)
Dimensions: length, gun forward 9·543 m (31·31 ft) and hull 7·09 m (23·26 ft); width over skirts 3·37 m (11·06 ft); height to top of commander's periscope 2·764 m (9·07 ft)
Armament system: one 105-mm (4·13-in) ROF/Rheinmetall L7A3 rifled gun with 60 rounds, two 7·62-mm (0·3-in) MG3A1 machine-guns (one co-axial and one cupola-mounted) with 5,500 rounds, and four smoke-dischargers on each side of the turret; the turret is electro-hydraulically powered, the main gun is stabilized in elevation (−9° to +20°) and azimuth (360°), and an EMES 12 fire-control system is fitted; this last includes stabilized optics, a computer-controlled rangefinder and a ballistic computer
Armour: cast and welded steel varying in thickness from 10 mm (0·39 in) to 70 mm (2·76 in)
Powerplant: one 620-kW (831·5-hp) MTU MB 838 Ca-M500 multi-fuel engine with 985 litres (217 Imp gal) of internal fuel
Performance: speed, road 65 km/h (40·4 mph); range, road 600 km (373 miles); fording 1·2 m (3·9 ft) without preparation, 2·25 m (7·4 ft) with preparation and 4·0 m (13·1 ft) with snorkel; gradient 60%; side slope 30%; vertical obstacle 1·15 m (45·3 in); trench 3·0 m (9·8 ft); ground clearance 0·44 m (17·3 in)

Variants

Leopard 1: this is the baseline West German MBT which entered service in 1965; since that time these early vehicles have been upgraded to **Leopard 1A1** standard with a thermal sleeve on the gun, a gun-stabilization system, rubber skirts etc and then to **Leopard 1A1A1** standard with additional spaced armour on the turret and mantlet, plus detail improvements
Leopard 1A2: version similar to the Leopard 1A1A1 without spaced mantlet and turret armour but with an improved NBC system, a turret of improved steel, passive night sights and other detail modifications
Leopard 1A3: version based on the Leopard 1A1 and Leopard 1A2 but with a new turret of welded spaced armour with a wedge-shaped mantlet
Leopard 1A4: version based on the Leopard 1A3 but fitted with an integrated fire-control system; the type has full NBC protection and night vision devices
Leopard 1A5: all older Leopard variants in service with the West German army are being upgraded to this standard with the EMES 18 fire-control system (developed by Krupp-Atlas and

Above: Leopard 1 MBTs of the Dutch army.
Below: The Leopard 2 is a formidable MBT with potent firepower and protection.

incorporating a Carl Zeiss thermal imaging system for continued operability under battle-field conditions of smoke and haze even at night), additional armour and a number of survivability features such as an explosion-suppression system; elements of this standard are offered by Krauss-Maffei as optional retrofits for Leopard 1 tanks in service with other countries, the features most popular being additional armour, the EMES 18 fire-control system, the PBZ 200 low-light-level TV sight system, an add-on dozer blade, and modification of the main armament to allow the firing of APFSDS projectiles
Leopard AS 1: variant of the Leopard 1A3 for Australia with tropical kit and a SABCA integrated fire-control system with laser rangefinder and seven sensors delivering data to an analog computer; the Australians operate the Leopard as a tank, medium armoured recovery vehicle, armoured vehicle-launched bridge and armoured dozer, and plan to use the type as an armoured mineclearer
Leopard 1 (Belgium): Belgian version with

FN-MAG machine-guns, detail modifications and SABCA fire-control system

Leopard 1 (Canada): Canadian version of the Leopard 1A3 with SABCA fire-control system

Leopard 1 (Denmark): Danish version of the Leopard 1 with only very small differences from the West German model

Leopard 1 (Greece): Greek version of the Leopard 1A3 with only very small differences from the West German model

Leopard 1 (Italy): Italian version produced by OTO Melara with only small differences from the West German model

Leopard 1 (Netherlands): Dutch model with different radios, machine-guns, smoke-dischargers etc

Leopard 1 (Norway): Norwegian model with only very small differences from the West German model

Leopard 1 (Turkey): Turkish model with only very small differences from the West German Leopard 1A3 model

Leopard 1 ARV: 39,800-kg (87,743-lb) armoured recovery vehicle variant with a front-mounted dozer blade, a crane, a 35,000-kg (77,160-lb) capacity winch and other equipment; the type has two 7·62-mm (0·3-in) MG3 machine-guns for local and AA defence, and is also fitted with smoke-dischargers; there is also a product-improved variant with a more powerful crane and a hydraulically operated jack mounted on the right-hand side of the hull at the rear

Leopard 1 AEV: armoured engineer vehicle variant derived from the Leopard 1 ARV, but has an auger instead of the spare powerpack, a dozer blade fitted with scarifiers for the ripping-up of roads, a stock of explosives, and a heat exchanger system

Leopard 1 AVLB: 45,300-kg (99,867-lb) armoured vehicle-launched bridge variant able to span a gap of some 20 m (65·6 ft) with a 22-m (72·2-ft) bridge

---

Israeli Ordnance Corps Merkava Mk 1

(Israel)
Type: main battle tank
Crew: 4
Combat weight: 60,000 kg (132,275 lb)
Dimensions: length, gun forward 8·63 m (28·31 ft) and hull 7·45 m (24·44 ft); width 3·70 m (12·14 ft); height to turret top 2·64 m (8·66 ft) and to commander's cupola 2·75 m (9·02 ft)
Armament system: one 105-mm (4·13-in) Israel Military Industries M68 rifled gun with 85 rounds, one optional 0·5-in (12·7-mm) Browning M2HB heavy machine-gun over the main armament with an unrevealed number of rounds, three 7·62-mm (0·3-in) FN-MAG machine-guns (one co-axial and two roof-mounted) with 10,000 rounds, and one 60-mm (2·36-in) Soltam Commando mortar with 30 rounds; the turret is electro-hydraulically powered, the main gun is stabilized in elevation (−8·5° to +20°) and azimuth (360°), and an Elbit Matador Mk 1 fire-control system is fitted; this last includes stabilized optics, various sensors for ambient conditions, a laser rangefinder and a digital ballistic computer
Armour: cast and welded steel
Powerplant: one 900-hp (671-kW) Teledyne Continental Motors AVDS-1790-6A diesel engine with 900 litres (198 Imp gal) of internal fuel
Performance: speed, road 46 km/h (28·6 mph); range, road 400 km (249 miles); fording 1·38 m (4·5 ft) without preparation and 2·0 m (6·6 ft) with

preparation; gradient 60%; side slope 38%; vertical obstacle 0·95 m (37·4 in); trench 3·0 m (9·8 ft); ground clearance 0·47 m (18·5 in)

Variants
Merkava Mk 1: this extremely capable MBT began to enter service with the Israeli army in 1979, and features full NBC protection, an explosion-suppression system and night vision equipment; the type was designed in the light of Israel's enormous experience of combat operations with and against several types of tank, and is optimized for the particular conditions faced by the Israeli Armoured Corps: great emphasis is therefore placed on protection of the crew (especially over the frontal arc), a low silhouette without sacrifice of good gun depression, and a power-to-weight ratio intended to provide battlefield mobility rather than outright speed

Merkava Mk 2: entering service in 1983, this version of the Merkava has stabilized optics (Matador Mk 2 fire-control system) with slaved main armament, modifications to ease maintenance, Blazer reactive armour (as a retrofit) and improved fire-suppression equipment; the 60-mm (2·36-in) mortar is located in a compartment in the rear of the turret, and in the Merkava Mk 2 can be loaded and fired from inside the vehicle; it is believed that the original engine has been retained, but that the combination of this diesel with a new and highly efficient transmission has allowed a 25% increase in range with only modest enlargement of the fuel supply; some sources claim, however, that the Merkava Mk 2 has a 980-hp (731-kW) Teledyne Continental Motors AVDS-1790 engine and a Hughes thermal sight for the gunner; Merkava Mk 1 tanks are being brought up to Mk 2 standard

Merkava Mk 3: entering service in 1989, the Merkava Mk 3 has armour 100% improved over that of the Mk 1, the Matador Mk 3 fire-control system to control an Israeli Military Industries 120-mm (4·72-in) smooth-bore gun with 50 rounds of IMI ammunition, and a 1,200-hp (895-kW) Teledyne Continental AVDS-1790-9AR powerpack for much enhanced performance and mobility as combat weight has increased only slightly to 61,000 kg (134,480 lb); although the tank is similar in appearance to its predecessors, every major component but the transmission has been improved; the advanced 'special armour' is attached in sections for ease of replacement, and this modular protection also makes simple the replacement of the whole protection when improved armour becomes available; other features of the Merkava Mk 3 are the threat-warning

system (believed to offer 360° coverage), the carriage of ammunition in individual containers for a high level of protection against fire or internal explosion, an electric turret/gun-control system, and independent coil spring suspension for the six roadwheels on each side, of which four on each side are provided with hydraulic rotary dampers

---

OTO Melara/IVECO Fiat C1 Ariete

(Italy)
Type: main battle tank
Crew: 4
Combat weight: 48,000 kg (105,820 lb)
Dimensions: length, gun forward 9·669 m (31·72 ft) and hull 7·595 m (24·92 ft); width over skirts 3·545 m (11·63 ft); height to turret top 2·46 m (8·07 ft)
Armament system: one 120-mm (4·72-in) OTO Melara OTO 120 smooth-bore gun with about 40 rounds, two 7·62-mm (0·3-in) MG3 machine-guns (one co-axial and one hatch-mounted AA) with about 2,500 rounds, and four smoke-dischargers on each side of the turret; the turret is electro-hydraulically powered, the main gun is stabilized in elevation (−9° to +20°) and azimuth (360°), and an Officine Galileo TURMS OG14L3 fire-control system is fitted; this last includes stabilized optics, various sensors for ambient conditions, a laser rangefinder and a ballistic computer
Armour: welded steel and composite
Powerplant: one 895-kW (1,201-hp) Fiat V-12 MTCA diesel engine with an unrevealed quantity of internal fuel
Performance: speed, road more than 65 km/h (40·4 mph); range, road more than 550 km (342 miles); fording 4·0 m (13·1 ft) with preparation; gradient 60%; side slope 30%; vertical obstacle not revealed; trench not revealed; ground clearance 0·44 m (17·3 in)

Variant
C1 Ariete: appearing in prototype form in 1987 for service by 1990, the C1 Ariete (battering ram) is a joint development by OTO Melara and IVECO in a programme designed to produce this tank and an 8 × 8 wheeled tank destroyer, with the former company primarily responsible for this tracked weapon

The design of the excellent Merkava 1 reflects the lessons of Israel's short but war-torn history.

OTO Melara/Fiat OF-40 Mk 1

(Italy)
Type: main battle tank
Crew: 4
Combat weight: 45,500 kg (100,309 lb)
Dimensions: length, gun forward 9·222 m (30·26 ft) and hull 6·893 m (22·61 ft); width over skirts 3·51 m (11·52 ft); height to turret top 2·42 m (7·94 ft) and to top of sight 2·76 m (9·06 ft)
Armament system: one 105-mm (4·13-in) OTO Melara OTO 105/52 rifled gun with 57 rounds (42 in the hull and 15 in the turret), two 7·62-mm (0·3-in) FN-MAG machine-guns (one co-axial and one hatch-mounted AA) with 5,700 rounds, one optional 0·5-in (12·7-mm) Browning M2HB heavy machine-gun with an unrevealed number of rounds in place of the 7·62-mm (0·3-in) AA machine-gun, and four smoke-dischargers on each side of the turret; the turret is electro-hydraulically powered, the main gun has optional stabilization in elevation (−9° to +20°) and azimuth (360°), and an Officine Galileo fire-control system is fitted; this last includes stabilized optics, various sensors for ambient conditions, a laser rangefinder and a ballistic computer
Armour: welded steel
Powerplant: one 620-kW (832-hp) MTU MB 838 Ca-M500 multi-fuel engine with 1000 litres (220 Imp gal) of internal fuel
Performance: speed, road 65 km/h (40·4 mph); range, road 600 km (373 miles); fording 1·2 m (3·9 ft) without preparation, 2·25 m (7·4 ft) with preparation and 4·0 m (13·1 ft) with snorkel; gradient 60%; side slope 30%; vertical obstacle 1·1 m (43·3 in); trench 3·0 m (9·8 ft); ground clearance 0·44 m (17·3 in)

Variants

OF-40 Mk 1: this is the baseline MBT introduced in 1980 with such standard features as NBC protection and passive night vision devices; the type was designed for the export market, and uses several components of the Leopard 1 tank, which is built under licence in Italy by OTO Melara and Fiat
OF-40 Mk 2: improved model with improved reliability, main armament stabilization as standard and the upgraded Officine Galileo OG14L2 fire-control system with laser rangefinder and low-light-level TV; the fire-control system is available as the OG14L2A with gun stabilization and the OG14L2B with gun and line-of-sight optical stabilization
OF-40 Mk 3: upgraded model based on the Mk 2 but carrying a 120-mm (4·72-mm) OTO Melara OTO 120 smooth-bore gun and powered by a 745-kW (999-hp) Fiat V-12 MTCA diesel engine
OF-40 ARV: 45,000-kg (99,206-lb) armoured recovery vehicle using the standard OF-40 chassis, and fitted with a spade, an 18,000-kg (36,683-lb) capacity crane and a 35,000-kg (77,160-lb) capacity winch

---

Mitsubishi Type 89

(Japan)
Type: main battle tank
Crew: 3
Combat weight: 50,000 kg (110,229 lb)
Dimensions: (estimated) length, gun forward 9·70 m (31·82 ft) and hull 7·50 m (24·61 ft); width 3·40 m (11·15 ft); height 2·30 m (7·55 ft)
Armament system: one 120-mm (4·72-in) Rheinmetall Rh-120 smooth-bore gun with an unrevealed number of rounds in the hull and in the automatic loader, one 7·62-mm (0·3-in) co-axial machine-gun with an unrevealed number of rounds, one 0·5-in (12·7-mm) Browning M2HB AA machine-gun with an unrevealed number of rounds, and three smoke-dischargers on each side of the turret; the turret is electro-hydraulically powered, the main gun is stabilized in elevation (an unrevealed arc) and azimuth (360°), and an advanced fire-control system is fitted; this last includes stabilized optics, a low-light-level TV, various sensors for ambient conditions, a laser rangefinder and a digital ballistic computer
Armour: multiple-layer steel with ceramic pockets
Powerplant: one 1125-kW (1,509-hp) Mitsubishi 10ZG diesel engine with an unrevealed quantity of internal fuel
Performance: speed, road 70 km/h (43·5 mph); range, road 500 km (311 miles); fording 2·0 m (6·6 ft); gradient not revealed; side slope not revealed; vertical obstacle not revealed; trench not revealed; ground clearance variable between 0·2 and 0·6 m (7·9 and 23·6 in)

Variant

Type 89: due to enter service in the early 1990s, this Japanese main battle tank was developed as the TK-X as successor to the Type 74; it was originally proposed that a smooth-bore gun developed by Japan Iron Works be used, but this failed to meet requirements and the West German ordnance was adopted in its place, together with an automatic loading device that has allowed the crew to be reduced to three

---

Mitsubishi Type 74

(Japan)
Type: main battle tank
Crew: 4
Combat weight: 38,000 kg (83,774 lb)
Dimensions: length, gun forward 9·41 m (30·87 ft) and hull 6·70 m (21·98 ft); width 3·18 m (10·43 ft); height to turret top 2·48 m (8·14 ft)
Armament system: one 105-mm (4·13-in) ROF L7A1 rifled gun with 55 rounds, one 7·62-mm (0·3-in) Type 74 co-axial machine-gun with 4,500 rounds, one 0·5-in (12·7-mm) Browning M2HB roof-mounted heavy machine-gun with 660 rounds, and three smoke-dischargers on each side of the turret; the turret is electrically powered, the main gun is stabilized in elevation (−12·5° to +15° using the suspension, or −6·5° to +9·5° mechanically) and azimuth (360°), and a Mitsubishi fire-control system is fitted; this last includes optical sights, a laser rangefinder and a ballistic computer
Armour: cast and welded steel
Powerplant: one 560-kW (751-hp) Mitsubishi 10ZF Type 22 WT diesel engine with 950 litres (209 Imp gal) of internal fuel
Performance: speed, road 53 km/h (33·0 mph); range, road 300 km (186 miles); fording 1·0 m (3·3 ft) without preparation and 2·0 m (6·6 ft) with preparation; gradient 60%; side slope 40%; vertical obstacle 1·0 m (39·4 in); trench 2·7 m (8·9 ft); ground clearance adjustable from 0·2 to 0·65 m (7·9 to 25·6 in)

Variants

Type 74: this baseline Japanese MBT entered service in 1974 after a chequered development history designed initially to produce a vehicle whose ordnance was fitted with an automatic loader; the type has interesting variable-height hydro-pneumatic suspension that permits the crew not only to vary the type's ground clearance in accordance with the dictates of the terrain, but also to incline the vehicle up/down and sideways; an NBC system is standard, and it is believed that the maximum speed is higher than officially admitted; in the late 1980s the Japanese started a modernization programme for the Type 74, this including a thermal sleeve for the main gun, additional armour on top and front of the turret, and the addition of passive night vision equipment; the chassis of the Type 74 is used for the Type 97 (AW-X) self-propelled AA system fitted with two 35-mm cannon and radar
Type 78 ARV: based on the chassis of the Type 74 MBT, this armoured recovery vehicle has a dozer blade and a side-mounted crane

Below: Japan's Type 74 MBT can most charitably be described as an indifferent fighting machine.

Left: The OF-40 Mk 2 is similar to the Mk 1 in virtually everything but its fire-control system, which is the OG14L2 system with a low-light-level TV (on the turret front to the right of the newly stabilized main gun) and a laser rangefinder.

Mitsubishi Type 61

(Japan)
Type: main battle tank
Crew: 4
Combat weight: 35,000 kg (77,160 lb)
Dimensions: length, gun forward 8·19 m (26·87 ft) and hull 6·30 m (20·67 ft); width 2·95 m (9·68 ft); height to turret roof 2·49 m (8·17 ft)
Armament system: one 90-mm (3·54-in) Type 61 rifled gun with an unrevealed number of rounds, one 0·3-in (7·62-mm) Browning M1919A4 co-axial machine-gun with an unrevealed number of rounds, and one 0·5-in (12·7-mm) Browning M2HB cupola-mounted machine-gun with an unrevealed number of rounds, and three smoke-dischargers on each side of the turret; the turret is hydraulically powered, the main gun lacks stabilization in elevation (an unrevealed arc) and azimuth (360°), and an optical fire-control system is fitted
Armour: cast and welded steel varying in thickness from 15 mm to 64 mm (0·59 in to 2·52 in)
Powerplant: one 450-kW (604-hp) Mitsubishi Type 12 HM 21 WT diesel engine with an unrevealed quantity of internal fuel
Performance: speed, road 45 km/h (28·0 mph); range, road 200 km (124 miles); fording 0·99 m (3·25 ft) without preparation; gradient 60%; side slope not revealed; vertical obstacle 0·685 m (27 in); trench 2·489 m (8·17 ft); ground clearance 0·4 m (15·75 in)

Variants

Type 61: this type first saw service in 1962; it is now obsolete as a result of its poor performance and armament, and its lack of any adequate fire-control capability and even NBC protection
Type 67 AVLB: armoured vehicle-launched bridge using the chassis of the Type 61 MBT and able to span a 10-m (32·8-ft) gap with a 12-m (39·4-ft) bridge
Type 67 AEV: armoured engineer vehicle again using the chassis of the Type 61 MBT and equipped with a dozer blade and a light-capacity crane
Type 70 ARV: armoured recovery vehicle also developed on the chassis of the Type 61 MBT and equipped with an A-frame, a dozer blade and a winch

Seen here during a firing exercise, the Type 61 is an obsolete MBT that reflects a very strong American influence in its overall design with a high turret and relatively small-calibre main gun fitted with a simple T-shaped muzzle brake. The vehicle also has poor ballistic protection and no NBC protection at all.

Hyundai/General Dynamics Type 88

(South Korea/USA)
Type: main battle tank
Crew: 4
Combat weight: 52,000 kg (114,638 lb)
Dimensions: length overall 9·58 m (31·43 ft) and hull 7·39 m (24·25 ft); width 3·594 m (11·79 ft) over skirts; height to top of turret 2·248 m (7·375 ft)
Armament system: one 105-mm (4·13-in) M68A1 rifled gun with 47 rounds, one 0·5-in (12·7-mm) Browning M2HB AA heavy machine-gun with 1,000 rounds, two 7·62-mm (0·3-in) machine-guns (one co-axial and one AA) with 11,400 rounds, and one bank of six smoke-dischargers on each side of the hull; the gun is stabilized in elevation (an unrevealed arc) and azimuth (360°), and an advanced fire-control system is fitted; this last includes stabilized optics, thermal imaging sight, laser rangefinder, various sensors for ambient conditions and a digital ballistic computer
Armour: welded steel and laminate
Powerplant: one 895-kW (1,200-hp) MTU MB 871 Ka-501 diesel engine with an unrevealed quantity of internal fuel
Performance: speed, road 65 km/h (40·4 mph); range, road 500 km (311 miles); fording 1·2 m (3·9 ft) without preparation and 1·8 m (5·9 ft) with preparation; gradient 58%; side slope not revealed; vertical obstacle 1·0 m (39·4 in); trench 2·74 m (9·0 ft); ground clearance 0·46 m (18 in)

Variant

Type 88: introduced to service in 1987 after evolution as the **XK-1**, this is a useful MBT developed by General Dynamics to the particular requirements of the South Korean army; the tank is characterized by classified (but highly effective) protection, a basically West German powerplant and drive system, a kneeling suspension that allows a large gun elevation arc, and a largely American vision and fire-control system for the US armament system, which is matched to that of South Korea's M48 tanks for logistic interoperability; in early vehicles the fire-control system was based on the Hughes VSG-X thermal imaging system developed for the M1A1 Abrams, though in later vehicles it is centred on the Texas Instruments Gunner's Primary Tank Thermal Sight developed for the M1A2 version of the Abrams; the type is fitted as standard with an NBC system and night vision equipment, and is notable for its low silhouette; there have been serious delivery delays with the production version, South Korean industry finding it difficult to assemble the Texas Instruments thermal imaging sight system

Bofors Stridsvagn 103B

(Sweden)
Type: main battle tank
Crew: 3
Combat weight: 39,700 kg (87,522 lb)
Dimensions: length overall 8·99 m (29·49 ft) and hull 7·04 m (23·10 ft); width 3·63 m (11·91 ft); height to top of cupola 2·14 m (7·02 ft)
Armament system: one 105-mm (4·13-in) Bofors L74 (ROF L7) rifled gun with 50 rounds in an automatic loader with 10 racks of five rounds, three 7·62-mm (0·3-in) FFV ksp58 machine-guns (two co-axial and one AA) with 2,750 rounds, and four smoke-dischargers on each side of the hull; the gun lacks stabilization for its elevation arc of −10° to +20° and is fixed in azimuth (0°), and an optical fire-control system is fitted; this last includes stabilized optics
Armour: welded steel
Powerplant: one 240-hp (179-kW) Rolls-Royce K60 multi-fuel engine and one 490-shp (365-kW) Boeing 553 gas turbine with 960 litres (211 Imp gal) of internal fuel
Performance: speed, road 50 km/h (31 mph); range, road 390 km (242 miles); fording 1·5 m (4·9 ft) without preparation and with preparation amphibious; gradient 58%; side slope 70%; vertical obstacle 0·9 m (35·4 in); trench 2·3 m (7·5 ft); ground clearance 0·4 m (15·75 in)

Variants

Strv 103B: designation of the full-production model delivered from 1966 with permanent dozer blade and flotation collar; some vehicles have twin Lyran flare launchers; the type is not fitted with an NBC system, and its primary claims to fame are its exceptionally low silhouette and radical main armament installation with the gun fixed in azimuth and thus laid by traversing the whole vehicle
Strv 103C: improved standard to which all Strv 103Bs are being brought after development with the designation **Strv 103B (Modernized)**; this has a 275-hp (205-kW) Detroit Diesel 6V-53T engine in place of the Rolls-Royce unit, and a Bofors Aerotronics fire-control system with a laser rangefinder and ballistic computer

Federal Construction Pz 68

(Switzerland)
Type: main battle tank
Crew: 4
Combat weight: 39,700 kg (87,522 lb)
Dimensions: length, gun forward 9·49 m (31·14 ft) and hull 6·98 m (22·90 ft); width 3·14 m (10·30 ft); height to top of cupola 2·75 m (9·02 ft)
Armament system: one 105-mm (4·13-in) PzKan 61 (ROF L7A1) rifled gun with 56 rounds, two 7·5-in (0·295-in) MG-51 machine-guns (one co-axial and one AA) with 5,400 rounds, and three smoke-dischargers on each side of the turret; the turret is electro-hydraulically operated, the main gun is stabilized in elevation (−10° to +21°) and azimuth (360°), and an optical fire-control system is fitted
Armour: cast steel varying in thickness from 20 to 60 mm (0·79 to 2·36 in)
Powerplant: one 490-kW (657-hp) MTU MB 837 Ba-500 diesel engine with 710 litres (156 Imp gal) of internal fuel
Performance: speed, road 55 km/h (34 mph); range, road 350 km (217 miles); fording 1·1 m (3·6 ft) without preparation and 2·3 m (7·5 ft) with preparation; gradient 70%; side slope 30%; ver-

The Pz 61 is an obsolescent Swiss MBT whose powerful gun gives it a modest tactical value.

tical obstacle 1·0 m (39·4 in); trench 2·6 m (8·5 ft); ground clearance 0·41 m (16 in)

Variants

Pz 68: this is an improved version of the Pz 61 with gun-stabilization system, ammunition resupply hatch, upgraded powerplant and better tracks; after the development of enhanced derivatives this variant was redesignated **Pz 68 Mk 1**

Pz 68 Mk 2: improved Pz 68 Mk 1 with thermal sleeve for main armament

Pz 68 Mk 3: improved Pz 68 Mk 2 with larger turret

Pz 68 Mk 4: product-improved Pz 68 Mk 3

Bruckenlegepanzer 68: armoured vehicle-launched bridge based on the Pz 68 chassis with an 18·23-m (59·8-ft) bridge

Federal Construction Pz 61

(Switzerland)

Type: main battle tank

Crew: 4

Combat weight: 38,000 kg (83,774 kg)

Dimensions: length, gun forward 9·43 m (30·94 ft) and hull 6·78 m (22·24 ft); width 3·06 m (10·04 ft); height to top of cupola 2·72 m (8·92 ft)

Armament system: one 105-mm (4·13-in) PzKan 61 (ROF L7A1) rifled gun with 56 rounds, two 7·5-mm (0·295-in) MG-51 machine-guns (one co-axial and one AA) with 5,400 rounds, and three smoke-dischargers on each side of the turret; the turret is electro-hydraulically powered, the main gun lacks stabilization in elevation (−10° to +21°) and azimuth (360°) , and an optical fire-control system is fitted

Armour: cast steel varying in thickness from 20 to 60 mm (0·79 to 2·36 in)

Powerplant: one 470-kW (630-hp) MTU MB 837 Ba-500 diesel engine with 760 litres (167 Imp gal) of internal fuel

Performance: speed, road 50 km/h (31 mph); range, road 300 km (186 miles); fording 1·1 m (3·6 ft) without preparation; gradient 70%; side slope 30%; vertical obstacle 0·75 m (29·5); trench 2·6 m (8·5 ft); ground clearance 0·42 m (16·5 in)

Variants

Pz 61: this was the first indigenously designed Swiss tank to reach the production stage, and entered service in 1965; the initial models had a 20-mm co-axial cannon, but survivors have been modified to the **Pz 61 AA9** standard described above; the tank has an NBC system but only an optical fire-control system

Entpannungspanzer 65: armoured recovery vehicle based on the Pz 61, and fitted with a 15,000-kg (33,069-kg) A-frame and a 25,000-kg (55,115-lb) winch; the crew is five, and combat weight 38,000 kg (83,774 lb)

Below: In original form, as seen here, the Pz 61 had a co-axial 20-mm cannon in the turret front.

T-80

(USSR)

Type: main battle tank

Crew: 3

Combat weight: 42,000 kg (92,593 lb)

Dimensions: length, gun forward 9·90 m (32·48 ft) and hull 7·40 m (24·28 ft); width over skirts 3·40 m (11·155 ft); height without AA machine-gun 2·20 m (7·22 ft)

Armament system: one 125-mm (4·92-in) D-81TM (2A46 Rapira 3) smooth-bore gun/missile-launcher with 40 rounds (including AT-8 'Songster' missiles), one 7·62-mm (0·3-in) PKT co-axial machine-gun with 2,000 rounds, one 12·7-mm (0·5-in) NSVT AA machine-gun with 500 rounds, and between 8 and 12 smoke-dischargers generally including four on the right and five on the left of the main armament; the turret is electrically powered, the main gun is stabilized in elevation (−6° to +18°) and azimuth (360°) , and an advanced fire-control system is fitted; this last includes stabilized optics, a laser rangefinder, various sensors for ambient conditions, and a ballistic computer

Armour: cast and composite

Powerplant: one 735-kW (986-hp) gas turbine with 1000 litres (220 Imp gal) of internal plus provision for 400 litres (88 Imp gal) of external fuel in two jettisonable tanks

Performance: speed, road 75 km/h (46·6 mph); range, road 400 km (249 miles) on internal fuel and 600 km (373 miles) with external fuel; fording 1·4 m (4·6 ft) without preparation and 5·5 m (18·0 ft) with snorkel; gradient 60%; side slope 40%; vertical obstacle 0·9 m (35·4 in); trench 2·9 m (9·5 ft); ground clearance 0·38 m (15 in)

Above: The T-80 is basically the T-64B with the latter's most troublesome features rectified.

Variants

T-80: this important tank serves with the Soviet forces stationed in East Germany, and is in essence a much improved version of the T-64B with the mechanical problems eliminated and (probably) provision for the 'Songster' tube-launched missile in only a small proportion of the overall total strength; perhaps the most important modifications are the replacement of the T-64's troublesome five-cylinder diesel with a gas turbine engine (driving through a manual or possibly semi-automatic gearbox), the readoption of conventional rubber-rimmed road wheels in place of the T-64's resilient steel wheels, and the use of torsion-bar rather than hydro-pneumatic suspension; the type is fitted mostly with conventional armour (the Soviets having apparently opted for the manufacturing ease and cheapness of this type over more capable yet considerably more expensive and weighty composite armour) though a laminate glacis plate and an interior layer of 'special armour' are fitted; since 1984 the T-80 tanks in Soviet service have been retrofitted with reactive armour; this consists of flat panels of plastic explosive attached to the turret and hull fronts, and is designed to disrupt the formation of an effective cutting jet by incoming hollow-charge warheads; other modifications include an improved laser rangefinder; the T-80 is fitted as standard with an NBC system and passive night vision devices

M1989: designation in the US system of terminology for a new version of the T-80 with additional armour protection, an improved fire-control system, and propulsion by a diesel rather than gas turbine

T-72M1

(USSR)
Type: main battle tank
Crew: 3
Combat weight: 41,000 kg (90,388 lb)
Dimensions: length, gun forward 9·53 m (31·27 ft) and hull 6·67 m (21·69 ft); width over skirts 3·72 m (12·20 ft); height to top of cupola 2·39 m (7·84 ft)
Armament system: one 125-mm (4·92-in) D-81TM (2A46 Rapira 3) smooth-bore gun with 42 rounds (20 in the hull and 22 in the autoloader), one 7·62-mm (0·3-in) PKT co-axial machine-gun with 2,000 rounds, one 12·7-mm (0·5-in) NSVT AA machine-gun with 500 rounds, and 12 smoke-dischargers (five on the right of the turret and seven on the left); the turret is electrically operated, the main gun is stabilized in elevation

(−6° to +14°) and azimuth (360°), and an advanced fire-control system is fitted; this last includes stabilized optics, a laser rangefinder, various sensors for ambient conditions, and a ballistic computer; the type can also generate smoke by injecting fuel into the exhaust
Armour: cast, welded and composite to a maximum thickness of 250+ mm (9·84 in)
Powerplant: one 585-kW (785-hp) Model V-46 diesel engine with 1190 litres (262 Imp gal) of internal fuel plus provision for 400 litres (88 Imp gal) of external fuel in two jettisonable tanks
Performance: speed, road 60 km/h (37·3 mph); range, road 480 km (298 miles) on internal fuel and 700 km (435 miles) with auxiliary fuel; fording 1·2 m (3·94 ft) without preparation and 5·0 m

(16·4 ft) with snorkel; gradient 60%; side slope 40%; vertical obstacle 0·85 m (33·5 in); trench 2·8 m (9·2 ft); ground clearance 0·43 m (16·9 in)

Variants
T-72A: this is the baseline model of one of the Soviets' most important current MBTs, believed to have entered troop trials service in 1971 after evaluation of the **T-72** prototype series; the basic vehicle is thought to be a development of the T-64 with probably the same combination of 125-mm (4·92-in) D-81T (2A26) gun and basket autoloader (with the projectiles horizontal on the turret floor and the propellant casings vertical round the base of the turret) but with simplified systems, torsion-bar rather than hydro-mechanical suspension, and a different powerplant; all versions have an NBC system and night vision devices; the T-72A may have been the pre-production model with an IR searchlight left of the main armament
T-72B: full-scale production model with the IR searchlight to the right of the D-81TM (2A46) main armament and the IR searchlight relocated from the left to the right of the main armament; another modification from the T-72A model (and thus the T-64 series) is the use of a cassette rather than basket autoloading system with the projectiles and propellant casings in a two-row horizontal arrangement on the turret floor; the type remained in production into the late 1970s, and was the first model to be exported; the command version of this model is the **T-72K**
T-72B(M): improved version of the T-72 with a panel of appliqué armour on each side of the turret front
T-74G: licence-production version built initially in Czechoslovakia as the **Stredni Tank T-72G**, in Poland as the **Sredni Czolg T-72G** and in Yugoslavia as the **Tenk M-84**; this type is also built in Iraq as the **Assad Babyle** (Babylon lion) with modifications suiting it to desert operations
T-72M: in the mid-1970s the Soviets started development of an improved T-72 built with pockets of laminate ceramic armour let into the front of the steel turret; other improvements include a laser rather than optical rangefinder as part of the gunner's sight, two fire-extinguishers carried externally on the turret, plastic armour side skirts covering the suspension and upper part of the tracks, and other improvements; in US terminology the tank is known as the **T-72 M1980/1**; the command version of this model is the **T-72MK**
T-72M1: the T-72M was followed quickly onto the production lines by this variant, known in the US terminology as the **T-72 M1980/1**, with a number

Left and below: The T-64B is the full-production variant of one of the USSR's most important MBTs, offering high firepower and good protection.

of internal improvements including a better engine cooling system; the model also has 20-mm (0·79-in) appliqué armour on the glacis and smoke-dischargers on the turret; the variant known only by its US designation **T-72 M1981/2** has a horizontal panel of armour spaced about 130 mm (5·12 in) above the engine decking, presumably as a hindrance to top attack; the **T-72 M1981/3** has a bank of six smoke-dischargers on each side of the turret frontal armour; the **T-72 M1984** has the snorkel stowage position relocated from the left to the rear of the turret and is fitted with additional overhead armour plus anti-radiation cladding material to reduce the effects of enhanced-radiation (neutron) weapons and of electro-magnetic pulse
T-72M2: introduced in the mid-1980s, this improved MBT resembles the late-production T-72M1 with a revised turret of thicker construction to allow the incorporation of a new generation of laminate ceramic armour pockets; early examples have six smoke-dischargers on each side of the turret front, while later vehicles have a bank of eight smoke-dischargers sited well back on the left side of the turret; this variant has the designation **T-72 M1986** in the US terminology, and the designation **T-72 M1988** is used for the same model with provision for ERA (explosive reactive armour) of the type likely to be fitted on many tanks of the T-72M series to defeat the gas/vaporized metal jets of hollow-charge warheads
T-72MS: very little has been revealed about this latest member of the T-72 series, which is apparently reconfigured in significant respects, and has a new engine and suspension; the gun of this variant fires a projectile with laser guidance rather than the radio guidance of the AT-8 'Songster', though it is not clear if this weapon is a gun-fired projectile or a missile with its own propulsion; it is possible that the export version of this tank is designated **T-72S**
BREM-1: armoured recovery vehicle variant of the T-72 series with a front-mounted dozer blade, a 12,000-kg (26,455-lb) capacity hydraulic crane at the front of the hull on the left, a 25,000-kg (55,115-lb) capacity main winch, an auxiliary winch and a wide assortment of tools
IMR: combat engineer vehicle variant of the T-72 series with a front-mounted dozer blade and a multi-role crane that can be fitted with pincers for the uprooting of trees and similar obstacles
TR-125: Romanian development of the T-72 generally equivalent to the T-72M1 with a combat weight of 48,000 kg (105,820 lb) due mainly to the provision of considerably thicker armour over the frontal arc, on each side seven road wheels of a different type, one-piece skirts, and a 655-kW (878-hp) diesel engine for a road speed of 60 km/h (37·3 mph) and a road range of 540 km (336 miles)

T-64B

(USSR)
Type: main battle tank
Crew: 3
Combat weight: 42,000 kg (92,593 lb)
Dimensions: length, gun forward 9·90 m (32·48 ft) and hull 7·40 m (24·28 ft); width over skirts 4·64 m (15·22 ft); height to top of cupola 2·20 m (7·22 ft)
Armament system: one 125-mm (4·92-in) D-81TM (2A46 Rapira 3) smooth-bore gun/missile-launcher with 40 rounds (including AT-8 'Songster' missiles), one 7·62-mm (0·3-in) PKT co-axial machine-gun with 3,000 rounds, and one 12·7-mm (0·5-in) NSVT AA machine-gun with 500 rounds; the turret is electrically powered, the main gun is stabilized in elevation (−5° to +18°) and azimuth (360°), and an optical fire-control system is fitted; this last includes stabilized optics, various sensors for ambient conditions, and a ballistic computer; the type can generate smoke by injecting fuel into the exhaust system
Armour: cast steel and composite to a maximum thickness of 200 mm (7·87 in)
Powerplant: one 560-kW (751-hp) five-cylinder diesel engine with 1000 litres (220 Imp gal) of internal fuel plus provision for 400 litres (88 Imp gal) of external fuel in two jettisonable tanks
Performance: speed, road 75 km/h (46·6 mph); range, road 400 km (249 miles) on internal fuel and 600 km (373 miles) with auxiliary fuel; fording 1·4 m (4·6 ft) without preparation and 5·5 m (18·0 ft) with snorkel; gradient 60%; side slope 40%; vertical obstacle 0·915 m (36 in); trench 2·72 m (8·9 ft); ground clearance 0·377 m (14·8 in)

Variants

T-64: this is the baseline variant of the Soviet army's current mainstay MBT, which began to enter service in 1968 and is armed, according to some analysts, with a 115-mm (4·53-in) U-5TS (2A20 Rapira 1) main gun or, according to others, with a short-barrel version of the 125-mm (4·92-in) 2A46 Rapira 3 gun; standard equipment includes NBC protection and night vision devices; the type has suffered from numerous mechanical problems, but is nonetheless significant for its advanced capabilities and high-quality fire-control system

T-64A: first definitive model with a 125-mm (4·72-in) Rapira 3 main gun and automatic loader, and a bank of six smoke-grenade dischargers mounted on each side of the turret front; the type is also designated **T-64 M1981/1** in the US terminology, and it is believed that the type has suffered severe powerplant, transmission and hydro-pneumatic suspension problems; this may explain why, in conjunction with its advanced capabilities, it has never been exported and then rapidly complemented by the T-72 series; there are several variants within the T-64A series, these including the **T-64 M1980** with revised stowage and flexible side skirts over the upper portion of the running gear, the **T-64 M1980/2** with an enlarged gunner's optical sight incorporating a laser rangefinder, and the **T-64K** command tank model; internally, one of the most important features of the T-64A is the provision of a carousel-type autoloader for the main armament, with the semi-combustible propellant casings arranged in a circular arrangement round the inside of the turret ring and the projectiles in a ring arrangement in trays on the turret floor

T-64B: variant of the T-64 M1980/2 complete with a laser rangefinder and the same main armament as the T-80 in the form of a combined gun/missile-launcher for standard smooth-bore ammunition and the tube-launched AT-8 'Songster' guided missile; this latter is probably in the same 125-mm calibre as the standard projectiles, and is fired with a muzzle velocity of 150 m (492 ft) per second before the solid-propellant rocket motor ignites to boost cruise speed to 1800 km/h (1118 mph) for a 3000-m (3,280-yard) flight of 7 seconds; the missile has a maximum effective range of 4000 m (4,375 yards) and radio command to line of sight guidance; since 1984 the T-64B tanks in Soviet service have been retrofitted with explosive reactive armour, resulting in the Western designation **T-74B-R**; this ERA consists of flat panels of plastic explosive attached to the turret and hull fronts, and as skirts along the forward portion of the tracks, designed to disrupt the formation of an effective cutting jet by incoming hollow-charge warheads

In tactical terms the most valuable T-64 variant, the T-64B has a powerful smooth-bore gun and an advanced fire-control system.

T-62A

(USSR)
Type: main battle tank
Crew: 4
Combat weight: 40,000 kg (88,183 lb)
Dimensions: length, gun forward 9·335 m (30·63 ft) and hull 6·63 m (21·75 ft); width 3·30 m (10·83 ft); height 2·395 m (7·86 ft)
Armament system: one 115-mm (4·53-in) U-5TS (2A20 Rapira 1) smooth-bore gun with 40 rounds (16 in the hull and 24 in the turret), one 7·62-mm (0·3-fin) PKT co-axial machine-gun with 2,500 rounds, and one 12·7-mm (0·5-in) DShKM AA machine-gun with 250 rounds; the turret is electro-hydraulically powered, the main gun is stabilized in elevation (−4° to +17°) and azimuth (360°), and an optical fire-control system is fitted; the type can generate smoke by injecting fuel into the exhaust system
Armour: cast and welded steel varying in thickness from 14 to 242 mm (0·59 to 9·53 in)
Powerplant: one 430-kW (577-hp) Model V-55 diesel engine with 675 litres (148 Imp gal) of internal fuel plus provision for 285 litres (63 Imp gal) of external fuel and additional provision for 400 litres (88 Imp gal) of supplementary external fuel in two jettisonable tanks
Performance: speed, road 50 km/h (31 mph); range, road 450 km (280 miles) on internal fuel and 650 km (404 miles) with external fuel; fording 1·4 m (4·6 ft) without preparation and 5·5 m (18·0 ft) with snorkel; gradient 60%; vertical obstacle 0·8 m (31·5 in); trench 2·85 m (9·35 ft); ground clearance 0·43 m (17 in)

Variants

T-62: this is the baseline MBT developed from the T-54/T-55 series and introduced to service from 1962; this initial model lacks the 12·7-mm (0·5-in) AA machine-gun but, like all other T-62 variants, has NBC protection and a fire-suppression system; the tank has a notably low silhouette, but to a certain extent this limits the type's tactical capabilities by restricting the elevation arc of the main armament, which can be loaded only with the turret trained straight to the front

T-62A: improved T-62 with revised turret shape and 12·7-mm (0·5-in) AA machine-gun; the type can also be fitted with mineclearing equipment; later in the type's operational career many examples were updated with more modern equipment such as a laser rangefinder and ballistic computer for the fire-control system, a better IR searchlight, and passive night vision equipment for the commander and gunner; in service the T-62A has clearly proved somewhat deficient in protection, and in Afghanistan many such tanks have been revised in the field to accommodate additional protection (of the conventional passive variety) over the frontal arc as well as along the sides; the T-62A has been widely exported, and in an effort to capitalize on the refit market for these vehicles, Royal Ordnance is offering a new 115-mm (4·53-in) barrel, or alternatively the turret reworked to accommodate the standard L7 weapon in 105-mm (4·13-in) calibre

T-62K: command variant of the T-62 series with a land navigation system and additional communications gear

T-62M: T-62A fitted with the track and drive sprocket of the T-72

T-62 Flamethrower: this has a flame gun fitted co-axially with the main armament; the flame gun has a range of 100 m (110 yards)

M1977 ARV: armoured recovery vehicle based on the chassis of the T-62; it is a limited-capability vehicle restricted to towing operations

The T-62 baseline model lacks the 12·7-mm (0·5-in) AA machine-gun of its later variants.

T-55

(USSR)
Type: main battle tank
Crew: 4
Combat weight: 36,000 kg (79,365 lb)
Dimensions: length, gun forward 9·00 m (29·53 ft) and hull 6·45 m (21·16 ft); width 3·27 m (10·73 ft); height to turret top 2·40 m (7·87 ft)
Armament system: one 100-mm (3·94-in) D-10T2S rifled gun with 43 rounds, one 7·62-mm (0·3-in) SGMT co-axial machine-gun with 3,500 rounds, and one 12·7-mm (0·5-in) DShKM AA machine-gun with 250 rounds; the turret is electro-hydraulically powered, the main gun is stabilized in elevation (−4° to +17°) and azimuth (360°), and an optical fire-control system is fitted; the type can generate smoke by injecting fuel into the exhaust system
Armour: cast and welded steel varying in thickness from 20 to 203 mm (0·79 to 8 in)
Powerplant: one 430-kW (577-hp) Model V-55 diesel engine with 960 litres (211 Imp gal) of internal fuel and provision for 200 litres (44 Imp gal) of external fuel in two jettisonable tanks
Performance: speed, road 50 km/h (31 mph); range, road 500 km (311 miles) on internal fuel and 600 km (373 miles) with external fuel; fording 1·4 m (4·6 ft) without preparation and 4·546 m (14·9 ft) with snorkel; gradient 58%; vertical obstacle 0·8 m (31·5 in); trench 2·7 m (8·85 ft); ground clearance 0·425 m (16·7 in)

Variants
T-55: the T-55 is modelled closely on the T-54, and entered service in the late 1950s; compared with the T-54 the T-55 lacks the loader's hatch and associated 12·7-mm (0·5-in) DShKM AA machine-gun but has a more powerful engine and features a main gun stabilized in elevation and azimuth; the type was later retrofitted with the AA machine-gun, and then designated **T-55(M)**; an NBC system is standard, having been retrofitted to this model but incorporated from scratch in later models
T-55A: upgraded 1963 version of the T-55 eliminating the 7·62-mm (0·3-in) machine-gun in the glacis plate and replacing the SGMT co-axial

machine-gun with a more modern PKT weapon of the same 7·62-mm calibre; when retrofitted with the 12·7-mm (0·5-in) AA machine-gun this model is known as the **T-55A(M)**
TO-55: flamethrower tank with a short-barrelled flame gun located co-axially with the main armament, and able to project its flame to a range of some 150/200 m (165/220 yards); the vehicle carries 460 litres (101 Imp gal) of flame fuel but the volume required for this additional tankage means that the ammunition capacity for the main armament is less than in the standard gun tank
BTS-2: 32,000-kg (70,547-lb) armoured recovery vehicle based on the T-55 and known in the West as the **T-55-TK**, with a rear platform to accommodate a spare engine; other items fitted on this model are a rear spade and a jib able to lift 1000 kg (2,205 lb); the Czechs produced a basically similar model with improved protection for the commander plus an armament of one 7·62-mm (0·3-in) machine-gun; the Polish version of the same basic model is **WZT-1**, and the Poles have also developed a more advanced model, basically similar to the BREM-1 on the chassis of the T-72, with the designation **WZT-2**
KAM-1: Finnish armoured recovery vehicle variant based on the chassis of the T-55 but fitted with a dozer blade and winch, as well as a new super-

Though obsolescent, the T-55 series remains in widespread service and differs from the T-54 mainly in its more powerful engine.

structure accommodating a crane
MTU-20: 37,000-kg (81,570-lb) Soviet armoured vehicle-launched bridge version of the T-55 capable of spanning a gap of 18 m (59·1 ft) with a 20-m (65·6-ft) bridge
MT-55: 37,000-kg (81,570-lb) Czech armoured vehicle-launched bridge model able to span a gap of 16 m (52·5 ft) with an 18-m (59·1-ft) scissors bridge; the same designation is used, somewhat confusingly, for a Czech-developed armoured recovery vehicle with a jib crane and provision for a roller mineclearing system
BLG-60: 37,000-kg (81,570-lb) East German armoured vehicle-launched bridge model able to span a gap of 20 m (65·6 ft) with a 21·6-m (70·9-ft) scissors bridge
IMR: combat engineer vehicle derivative of the T-55 with the turret replaced by a hydraulically operated crane that can be traversed through 360° and additionally fitted with pincers for the uprooting of trees and other battlefield obstacles; the vehicle has a front-mounted dozer blade
T-55 Mineclearer: developed for Soviet operations in Afghanistan, this vehicle is turretless and fitted with a new type of mineclearing roller system, replacement rollers for which are carried on the rear of the hull; the type has a new raised superstructure accommodating the driver and, to his side, a cupola-mounted 12·7-mm (0·5-in) machine-gun; T-55s are also in service with a number of older plough and roller systems, while a more recent development is a version fitted with rocket-propelled explosive charges fired across a minefield and detonated once they have landed
T-55 (Egypt): the T-55s operated by the Egyptian army are being regunned with the ROF L7A3 105-mm (4·13-in) rifled gun, and other items of Western equipment are being fitted at the same time; the Egyptian vehicles are already fitted with a West German IR searchlight and Yugoslav laser rangefinder
T-55 (India): these have a 0·5-in (12·7-mm) Browning M2HB machine-gun in the AA role
T-55 (Iraq): Iraq has considerably upgraded its T-55 MBTs with the 125-mm (4·92-in) gun and automatic loading system of the T-72 MBT; the turret has been considerably reworked with a higher roof and an ejection port in the rear for the stub of the semi-combustible cartridge case, and other modifications undertaken during the rebuild programme include passive night vision equipment, side skirts, and a bank of four smoke-dischargers on each side of the turret; Iraq is also offering the type for export with the same type of multi-layer frontal and skirt armour as used on Egypt's upgraded T-55s

T-55 (Israel): of the numerous T-55s captured by the Israelis, many have been revised with the 105-mm (4·13-in) M68 rifled main gun, 0·3-in (7·62-mm) Browning co-axial machine-gun and 0·5-in (12·7-mm) Browning AA machine-gun; the vehicles have been considerably modified with Israeli and US equipment, especially in the communications and fire-control fields, and are now designated **TI-67**; Israel has also produced a considerably enhanced variant with the designation **T-55 Model S** and incorporating, in addition to the complete range of TI-67 modifications, a 609-hp (454-kW) General Motors 8V-71T diesel with a semi-automatic hydro-mechanical transmission, new air cleaners, a fire-suppression system, Blazer reactive armour, a Cadillac Gage weapon-stabilization system, an El-Op Matador fire-control system, IR detectors, and passive night vision devices for the commander, gunner and driver

T-55 (Romania): these modified vehicles have six rather than five roadwheels, new sideskirts, and a revised 12·7-mm (0·5-in) AA machine-gun armament; it is believed that these vehicles have the designation **TR-77**

T-55 Upgrade: the widespread use of the T-55 in many countries has led to the development of several update packages and items of equipment for these vehicles by Western companies; amongst the more important of these are revised armament and associated fire-control system, revised propulsion (engine, transmission and suspension), and revised protection (armour, fire-suppression and NBC)

T-54

(USSR)

Type: main battle tank
Crew: 4
Combat weight: 36,000 kg (79,365 lb)
Dimensions: length, gun forward 9·00 m (29·53 ft) and hull 6·45 m (21/16 ft); width 3·27 m (10·73 ft); height to turret top 2·40 m (7·87 ft)
Armament system: one 100-mm (3·94-in) D-10T rifled gun with 34 rounds, two 7·62-mm (0·3-in) SGMT machine-guns (one co-axial and one in glacis plate) with 3,000 rounds, and one 12·7-mm (0·5-in) DShKM AA machine-gun with 500 rounds;

the turret is electro-hydraulically powered, the main gun lacks stabilization in either elevation (−4° to +17°) or azimuth (360°), and an optical fire-control system is fitted; the type can generate smoke by injecting fuel into the exhaust system
Armour: cast and welded steel varying in thickness from 20 to 203 mm (0·79 to 8 in)
Powerplant: one 390-kW (523-hp) Model V-54 diesel engine with 812 litres (179 Imp gal) of internal fuel, plus provision for 280 litres (61·6 Imp gal) of external fuel and additional provision for external fuel in two jettisonable tanks
Performance: speed, road 48 km/h (30 mph); range, road 400 km (249 miles) on internal fuel and 600 km (373 miles) with external fuel; fording 1·4 m (4·6 ft) without preparation and 4·55 m (14·9 ft) with snorkel; gradient 58%; vertical obstacle 0·8 m (31·5 in); trench 2·7 m (8·85 ft); ground clearance 0·425 m (16·7 in)

Variants

T-54: the initial T-54 series entered service in 1948, and appeared in two basic forms; the earlier of these had two turret cupolas, could not be fitted with a snorkel for deep wading, and possessed an oddly shaped rear to the turret; the later model still has two cupolas (that on the right being fitted with a 12·7-mm/0·5-in DShKM AA machine-gun), but the turret was more normally shaped and could be fitted with a snorkel; when retrofitted with IR driving lights the type is designated **T-54(M)**, and the model is also built in China as the Type 59; standard features of current examples of the T-54 series are night vision devices and NBC protection, but a major tactical disadvantage is the lack of gun depression so requiring the type to use hull-up positions where the benefits of its low silhouette and good ballistic shape are fully needed; the original 100-mm (3·94-in) D-10T gun is stabilized in neither elevation nor azimuth
T-54A: mid-1950s variant with a bore evacuator for the D-10TG main armament, which is also stabilized in elevation; the retrofitting of IR driving lights results in the designation **T-54A(M)**
T-54B: 1957/8 variant built as standard with IR driving lights; the main armament is the D-10T2S gun stabilized in both elevation and azimuth

The initial model of the elderly T-54 has no bore evacuator on the barrel of the main gun.

T-54C: basically the T-54B with the gunner's cupola replaced by a hatch without the machine-gun; the variant is also known as the **T-54X**
T-54-T: 32,000-kg (70,547-lb) armoured recovery vehicle derivative of the basic T-54, and has a rear platform for the carriage of a spare engine, a rear spade and a small jib capable of lifting 1000 kg (2,205 lb)
T-54(A): armoured recovery vehicle developed in East Germany on the basis of the T-54, and apart from a full range of specialist tools the type has a push/pull bar and a dismountable crane with a lifting capacity of 1000 kg (2,205 lb); chemical and nuclear agent detectors are fitted, but the type's capabilities are limited by lack of a winch or spade
T-54(B): essentially the T-54(A) with attachment points for tow ropes, and weighs 32,000 kg (70,547 lb)
T-54(C): another East German armoured recovery vehicle, in this instance weighing 34,000 kg (74,956 lb) complete with a rear platform for a spare engine, a rear spade, a front-mounted dozer blade and a jib crane able to lift 20,000 kg (44,092 lb)
WZT-1: armoured recovery vehicle developed in and used by Poland on the basis of the T-54
MTU: Soviet armoured vehicle-launched bridge based on the T-54 chassis, and able to span a gap of 11 m (36·1 ft) with a 12·3-m (40·35-ft) bridge
T-54 (India): Indian T-54s have received the same basic modifications as the T-55s operated by the Indian army
T-54 (Israel): T-54s captured by the Israelis have undergone the same type of modification programme as Israel's T-55 tanks, including a complete package of modernization to produce the **T-54 Model S**
Ramses II: under this designation the Egyptian army is evaluating a total upgrade package for the T-54, designed in the USA under the leadership of Teledyne Continental Motors; the package includes total revision of the T-54's propulsion, armament and fire-control systems; the propulsion system now comprises a 908-hp (677-kW) Teledyne Continental Motors AVDS-1790-5A diesel driving a West German automatic transmission, new hydro-pneumatic suspension and American tracks; the armament system comprises a 105-mm (4·13-in) M68 series rifled gun with a Cadillac Gage two-axis stabilization system; and the fire-control system is the SABCA Titan Mk 1 with laser rangefinder and digital computer; a comparable upgrade is also offered by Royal Ordnance of the UK on the basis of a 600-hp (447-kW) Perkins diesel driving a revised version of the current transmission, Krauss-Maffei shock absorbers, a 105-mm (4·13-in) Royal Ordnance L7 series gun, a Wallop Industries gunner's sight with laser rangefinder incorporated into a new Marconi fire-control and gun-control system, and additional protection in the form of extra armour and a fire-suppression system

T-34/85

(USSR)

Type: medium tank
Crew: 5
Combat weight: 32,000 kg (70,547 lb)
Dimensions: length, gun forward 8·076 m (26·5 ft) and hull 6·19 m (20·31 ft); width 2·997 m (9·83 ft); height 2·743 m (9·0 ft)
Armament system: one 85-mm (3·35-in) ZIS-S53 rifled gun with 56 rounds, and two 7·62-mm (0·3-in) DTM machine-guns (one co-axial and one

in glacis plate) with 2,394 rounds; the turret is electrically or manually powered, the main gun lacks stabilization in either elevation ($-5°$ to $+25°$) or azimuth (360°), and an optical fire-control system is fitted; the type can generate smoke by injecting fuel into the exhaust system

Armour: cast and welded steel varying in thickness from 18 to 90 mm (0·71 to 3·54 in)

Powerplant: one 375-kW (503-hp) Model V-2-34 or V-2-34M diesel engine with 590 litres (130 Imp gal) of internal fuel plus additional provision for external fuel in two jettisonable tanks

Performance: speed, road 55 km/h (34 mph); range, road 300 km (186 miles); fording 1·32 m (4·33 ft); gradient 60%; vertical obstacle 0·73 m (28·75 in); trench 2·5 m (8·2 ft); ground clearance 0·38 m (15 in)

Variants

T-34/85: introduced in 1943 as an upgunned version of the original T-34/76 with a 76-mm (3-in) main gun, the T-34/85 was produced in vast numbers during and after World War II; many thousands were remanufactured in the 1960s, and these still constitute an important part of the arsenals of many smaller clients of the USSR; there were numerous variants on the basic chassis, but the only ones still in substantial service are various armoured recovery vehicles such as the **T-35-T(A)** turretless towing vehicle, the **T-34-T(B)** turretless armoured recovery vehicle with a spare engine on an aft platform plus a small crane and winch, the **SKP-5** crane vehicle able to lift 5000 kg (11,023 lb) and the **WPT-34** with a large forward superstructure, a platform-mounted spare engine and rear-mounted spade and winch

Type 63: Chinese conversion of the T-34/85 into a self-propelled AA gun mounting, the turret being removed and the ring plated over to provide a mounting for a high, open-topped, slab-sided armoured mounting for two 37-mm AA guns; the mounting can traverse through 360°, and the guns can be elevated between $-5°$ and $+85°$; each barrel has cyclic and practical fire rates of 170 and 80 rounds per minute fed from five-round clips carried in boxes attached to the sides of the hull; FRAG-T and AP-T rounds are carried, and the effective surface and AA ranges are 9500 m (10,390 yards) and 3000 m (9,845 ft) respectively; overall length is 6·432 m (21·10 ft) and height including the sight 3·268 m (10·72 ft)

Vickers Defence Systems (ROF Leeds) FV4030/4 Challenger

(UK)

Type: main battle tank
Crew: 4
Combat weight: 136,685 lb (62,000 kg)
Dimensions: length, gun forward 37·93 ft (11·56 m) and hull 27·53 ft (8·39 m); width over skirts 11·54 ft (3·518 m); height to top of commander's sight 9·68 ft (2·95 m)
Armament system: one 120-mm (4·72-in) ROF L11A5 rifled gun with up to 64 rounds, two 7·62-mm (0·3-in) machine-guns (one co-axial L8A2 and one AA L37A2) with 4,000 rounds, and five smoke-dischargers on each side of the turret; the turret is electrically powered, the main gun is

The angular external appearance of the Challenger is dictated by the use of Chobham armour, which cannot be produced in curved panels.

stabilized in elevation ($-10°$ to $+20°$) and azimuth (360°), and a Marconi Improved Fire-Control System is fitted; this last includes stabilized day/night optics, a laser rangefinder, various sensors and a ballistic computer

Armour: steel and laminate

Powerplant: one 1,200-hp (895-kW) Rolls-Royce Condor 12V 1200 diesel engine with 395 Imp gal (1796 litres) of internal fuel

Performance: speed, road 35 mph (56·3 km/h); range, road not revealed; fording 3·5 ft (1·07 m) without preparation; gradient 58%; side slope 27%; vertical obstacle 36 in (0·91 m); trench 10·33 ft (3·15 m); ground clearance 19·7 in (0·5 m)

Variants

FV4030/4 Challenger: this is an evolutionary development of the Chieftain MBT via the FV4030/3 Shir 2 ordered by Iran but then cancelled after the fall of the Shah in 1979; the type began to enter British service in 1983 and is fitted with full NBC protection and night vision devices; late-production vehicles were delivered with the Barr & Stroud TOGS (Thermal Observation and Gunnery System), which has also been retrofitted to older vehicles; this forms part of the Challenger Improvement Programme package, and other elements are probably the L30 Modern Technology Gun, and several improvements to the gun-control system, the IFCS and the commander's cupola; it is also possible that a number of automotive improvements will be made in the future

Challenger ARRV: 136,685-lb (60,000-kg) Armoured Repair and Recovery Vehicle derivative of the Challenger main battle tank retaining the basic combination of hull and powerplant with a new superstructure and a recovery rig that includes an Atlas AK 6000 M8 hydraulic crane with extending jib, hydraulic main and separate auxiliary winches, and a front-mounted blade used as an earth anchor, stabilizer and conventional dozer blade; a crew of five (plus two passengers) is carried, and the defensive armament of one 7·62-mm (0·3-in) machine-gun is supplemented by no fewer than 20 smoke-dischargers (12 at the front and eight at the rear)

Challenger 2 Mk 2: as a private venture Vickers Defence Systems has produced a radically

updated and improved turret that can be retrofitted to the existing hull to create the Challenger 2, the original Mk 1 concept having been superseded by the current Mk 2 concept for a turret with better integration of the weapon and fire-control systems than in the baseline Challenger with its externally mounted TOGS; the proposed main weapon is the 120-mm (4·72-in) Royal Ordnance Nottingham L30 rifled gun, with fire-control entrusted to an updated version of the TOGS using a Computing Devices of Canada digital computer, Marconi gun-control system, a commander's SFIM stabilized panoramic sight (with a laser rangefinder, thermal imaging and a separate thermal imager for surveillance), and a gunner's Sagem/Barr & Stroud stabilized sight (with day optics, a laser rangefinder, thermal imaging and a separate thermal imager for surveillance); secondary armament is a pair of 7·62-mm (0·3-in) machine-guns, one mounted co-axially with the main gun and the other on the loader's hatch; Vickers is now working on a production-standard version of this concept to meet the British army's requirement for a Challenger 'successor'

Vickers Defence Systems (ROF Leeds) FV4201 Chieftain Mk 5

(UK)

Type: main battle tank
Crew: 4
Combat weight: 121,250 lb (55,000 kg)
Dimensions: length, gun forward 35·42 ft (10·795 m) and hull 24·67 ft (7·518 m); width over skirts 11·50 ft (3·504 m); height overall 9·50 ft (2·895 m)

Armament system: one 120-mm (4·72-in) ROF L11A5 rifled gun with 64 rounds, one co-axial 0·5-in (12·7-mm) L21A1 ranging machine-gun with 300 rounds (not fitted in vehicles with the IFCS with laser rangefinder), two 7·62-mm (0·3-in) machine-guns (one co-axial L8A1 and one AA L37A1) with 6,000 rounds, and six smoke-dischargers on each side of the turret; the turret is electrically powered, the main gun is stabilized in

Though low in mobility, the Chieftain is well protected and fields a powerful gun whose capabilities are unexploited to the full because the fire-control system is not fully integrated.

elevation (− 10° to + 20°) and azimuth (360°), and a Barr & Stroud Tank Laser Sight Unit or Marconi Improved Fire-Control System is fitted; this last includes stabilized day/night optics, a laser rangefinder, various sensors and a ballistic computer

Armour: cast and welded steel; all in-service Chieftains are being retrofitted with the Stillbrew appliqué armour system (an outer layer of steel over an inner laminate layer) over the most vulnerable sections of the frontal arc

Powerplant: one 750-hp (559-kW) Leyland L60 No·4 Mk 8A multi-fuel engine with 210 Imp gal (955 litres) of internal fuel

Performance: speed, road 30 mph (48 km/h); range, road 310 miles (499 km); fording 3·5 ft (1·07 m) without preparation; gradient 70%; side slope 30%; vertical obstacle 36 in (0·91 m); trench 10·33 ft (3·15 m); ground clearance 20 in (0·51 m)

Variants

Chieftain Mk 1: numerically the most important British main battle tank, the Chieftain was conceived on the basis of the Centurion, but fitted with the 120-mm (4·72-in) rifled main gun; the first prototype ran in 1961, and the type began to enter service in 1965; the Chieftain Mk 1 is the training model, of which 40 were built in 1965/1966 with a 585-hp (436-kW) engine; of these vehicles most were later upgraded, the **Chieftain Mk 1/2** being the Mk 1 brought up to Mk 2 standard, the **Chieftain Mk 1/3** having a new powerpack, and the **Chieftain Mk 1/4** being the Mk 1 with a new powerpack and modified 0·5-in (12·7-mm) ranging machine-gun

Chieftain Mk 2: initial service model, which began to enter British army regimental use in 1967 with a 650-hp (485-kW) engine and a complement of 600 rounds for its ranging machine-gun

Chieftain Mk 3: second service model, essentially an improved Mk 2 with improved auxiliary power unit and main engine plus a number of detail modifications to the secondary armament and trackwork

Chieftain Mk 3/S: development of the Mk 3 with turret air-breathing and other modifications (including a commander's firing switch) pioneered in the **Chieftain Mk 3/G** and **Chieftain Mk 3/2** prototypes

Chieftain Mk 3/3: basically the Mk 3 fitted with a farther-reaching ranging machine-gun, provision for a Barr & Stroud laser rangefinder, a low-loss air-cleaning system, turret air-breathing, a new NBC pack and 720-hp (537-kW) Leyland L60 No·4 Mk 6A engine; this important variant weighs 119,270 lb (54,101 kg) but is dimensionally similar to the Mk 5; the export version for Iran was the **Chieftain Mk 3/3P**

Chieftain Mk 4: experimental model with greater fuel capacity

Chieftain Mk 5: improved version of Mk 3/3 with a better engine and improved transmission system, and detail modifications to the fire-control system etc; the export models were the **Chieftain Mk 5/2K** for Kuwait and the **Chieftain Mk 5/5P** for Iran; in common with all Chieftain marks in British service, this variant has been retrofitted with the Barr & Stroud Thermal Observation and Gunnery System; future improvement is centred on the possible retrofit of the L30 Modern Technology Gun, a high-pressure rifled weapon

Chieftain Mk 6: Mk 2 with a modified ranging machine-gun and new powerpack

Chieftain Mk 7: Mk 3 and Mk 3/S with modified ranging machine-gun and powerpack

Chieftain Mk 8: Mk 3/3 with Mk 7 modifications

Chieftain Mk 9: Mk 6 with the Improved Fire-Control System

Chieftain Mk 10: Mk 7 with IFCS

Chieftain Mk 11: Mk 8 with IFCS

Chieftain Mk 12: Mk 5 with IFCS

Chieftain 800: private-venture export variant developed by Royal Ordnance with an 800-hp (596-kW) Rolls-Royce CV12 TCE diesel and improved transmission

Chieftain 900: comparable to the Chieftain 800 but with a 900-hp (671-kW) 671-kW) version of the same CV12 engine (Rolls-Royce Condor 900E) and fitted with Chobham laminate armour for a considerably higher standard of protection; the combat weight is 123,450 lb (55,997 kg)

Chieftain ARRV: based on the Chieftain main battle tank chassis and hull, the Chieftain Armoured Recovery and Repair Vehicle was designed specifically for operations in support of the Challenger main battle tank, whose powerpack is too heavy for the standard FV434 armoured repair vehicle used with the Chieftain

Chieftain AVRE: there was to have been an FV4203 Chieftain Assault Vehicle Royal Engineers, but when this was cancelled some 12 Chieftain main battle tanks were converted at the Willich engineer workshops of the British Army of the Rhine to fulfil a comparable role; the turret of the main battle tank is replaced by a sheet metal superstructure fitted with rails for the carriage of three fascines or five rolls of trackway, and other features of this extemporized vehicle are a front-mounted dozer blade and provision for mine ploughs; a fully engineered vehicle may come from industry sources in the 1990s

FV4204 Chieftain ARV: based on the chassis and hull of the Chieftain Mk 5, the Chieftain Armoured Recovery Vehicle has two winches and a crane, the main winch being rated at 90,000 lb (40,824 kg) when used with the front-mounted dozer blade, and the crane at 12,800 lb (5806 kg)

FV4205 Chieftain AVLB: the Chieftain Armoured Vehicle-Launched Bridge can span gaps of up to 75 ft (22·86 m) with the 80-ft (24·38-m) No·8 Tank Bridge, or 40 ft (12·19 m) when fitted with the 44-ft (13·41-m) No·9 Tank Bridge

Chieftain Mk 6 AVLB: this improved Armoured Vehicle-Launched Bridge is based on the chassis and hull of the Chieftain Mk 1/4 gun tanks and fitted with the Mk 8 Bridge and Pierson mine plough system

Khalid: built for Jordan, this vehicle was originally developed for Iran as the **FV4030/2 Shir 1**, in essence a Chieftain Mk 5 with improved fire-control and automotive features; the Shir 1, of which 125 had been ordered, was cancelled in 1979 together with the much improved **FV4030/3 Shir 2** (1,225 ordered); the Khalid is the Shir 1 with detail modifications to suit the type to Jordanian requirements, and the powerplant is a 1,200-hp (895-kW) Rolls-Royce Condor 12V 1200 diesel; the Khalid weighs 127,865 lb (58,000 kg), and its dimensions include a hull length of 27·53 ft (8·39 m), a width of 11·54 ft (3·52 m) and a height of 9·88 ft (3·01 m)

ROF Leeds/ROF Woolwich/ Leyland/Vickers FV4017 Centurion Mk 13

(UK)
Type: main battle tank
Crew: 4
Combat weight: 114,240 lb (51,819 kg)
Dimensions: length, gun forward 32·33 ft (9·85 m) and hull 25·67 ft (7·82 m); width over skirts 11·12 ft (3·39 m); height to top of cupola 9·87 ft (3·01 m)
Armament system: one 105-mm (4·13-in) ROF L7A2 rifled gun with 64 rounds, one 0·5-in (12·7-mm) L21A1 co-axial ranging machine-gun with 600 rounds, two 7·62-mm (0·3-in) machine-guns (one co-axial L8A1 and one AA L37A1) with 4,750 rounds, and six smoke-dischargers on each side of the turret; the turret is electrically powered, the main gun is stabilized in elevation (−10° to +20°) and azimuth (360°), and an optical fire-control system is fitted
Armour: cast and welded steel varying in thickness from 0·66 to 6 in (17 to 152 mm)
Powerplant: one 650-hp (485-kW) Rolls-Royce Meteor Mk IVB petrol engine with 228 Imp gal (1037 litres) of internal fuel
Performance: speed, road 21·5 mph (34·6 km/h); range, road 118 miles (190 km); fording 4·75 ft (1·45 m) without preparation and 9·0 ft (2·74 m) with preparation; gradient 60%; side slope 30%; vertical obstacle 36 in (0·91 m); trench 11·0 ft (3·35 m); ground clearance 20 in (0·51 m)

Variants

Centurion Mk 5: the Centurion series entered service in the period immediately after World War II, but the Mk 5 is the earliest model to remain in service, and was designed by Vickers; it differs from earlier models primarily in having a 20-pdr (3·28-in/83·4-mm) main gun with 65 rounds in place of the original 17-pdr (3-in/76·2-mm) weapon; there is no ranging machine-gun, and the main and secondary armament ammunition capacities are 65 and 4,250 rounds respectively; this variant weighs 111,835 lb (50,728 kg), and its dimensions include lengths of 32·25 ft (9·829 m) with the gun forward and 24·79 ft (7·556 m) for the hull, and a height of 9·65 ft (2·94 m) without the AA machine-gun; this model has a fuel capacity of only 100 Imp gal (455 litres), limiting road range to a mere 65 miles (105 km); developments of the Mk 5 are the uparmoured **Centurion Mk 5/1** and the upgunned **Centurion Mk 5/2** with the 105-mm (4·13-in) L7 gun
Centurion Mk 6: uparmoured Mk 5 with L7 gun and additional fuel capacity; developments are the **Centurion Mk 6/1** with IR night vision equip-

In Sweden, the ageing Centurion has been upgraded simply yet effectively for improved performance and better offensive firepower.

ment and stowage basket on the turret rear, and the **Centurion Mk 6/2** with a ranging machine-gun
Centurion Mk 7: Leyland-developed **FV4007** model with 20-pdr gun and 61 rounds plus a fume extractor; developments are the **FV4012 Centurion Mk 7/1** with thicker armour and the **Centurion Mk 7/2** with the 105-mm gun
Centurion Mk 8: essentially the Mk 7 with improved main gun mounting and contra-rotating commander's cupola; developments are the uparmoured **Centurion Mk 8/1** and the upgunned **Centurion Mk 8/2** with the 105-mm gun
Centurion Mk 9: upgunned and uparmoured Mk 7 fitted with the 105-mm gun and designated **FV4015**; developments are the **Centurion Mk 9/1** with IR driving lights and stowage basket on the turret rear, and the **Centurion Mk 9/2** with a ranging machine-gun for the main armament
Centurion Mk 10: Mk 8 with improved armour and the 105-mm gun with 70 rounds, and designated **FV4017**; developments are the **Centurion Mk 10/1** with IR driving lights and a stowage basket on the turret rear, and the **Centurion Mk 10/2** with a ranging machine-gun for the main armament
Centurion Mk 11: Mk 6 with ranging machine-gun, IR driving lights and stowage basket on turret rear
Centurion Mk 12: Mk 9 with ranging machine-gun, IR driving lights and stowage basket on turret rear
Centurion Mk 13: Mk 10 with ranging machine-gun and IR driving lights
FV4002 Centurion AVLB: based on the chassis and hull of the Centurion Mk 5, the Centurion Armoured Vehicle-Launched Bridge can span a gap of 45 ft (13·72 m)
FV4003 Centurion AVRE: based on the chassis of the Centurion Mk 5, the 114,220-lb (51,810-kg) Centurion Armoured Vehicle Royal Engineers has a turret-mounted 165-mm (6·5-in) demolition gun, and also a front-mounted dozer blade; the vehicle is designed to tow a trailer carrying the Giant Viper mineclearing equipment, and can also be fitted with mineclearing ploughs; this variant is sometimes designated the **Centurion 165 AVRE** to distinguish it from the later **Centurion 105 AVRE**, which is the standard gun tank modified for the AVRE role with provision for mine ploughs and a tow point for the Giant Viper equipment
FV4006 Centurion ARV Mk 2: the Centurion Armoured Recovery Vehicle Mk 2 is a standard gun tank with its turret replaced by a welded superstructure for the commander; the vehicle weighs 110,880 lb (50,295 kg), and the use of rear-mounted spades gives a winch capacity of 68,340 lb (31,000 kg)
FV4018 Centurion BARV: 89,600-lb (40643-kg) Centurion Beach Armoured Recovery Vehicle with a revised superstructure allowing the vehicle to operate in water 9·5 ft (2·90 m) deep

Centurion (Austria): Austria has bought 120 Centurion tanks from the Netherlands for use in the static defence role
Centurion (Denmark): these are currently to Mk 5 and Mk 5/2 standard (20-pdr and 105-mm L7A3 guns respectively), with a 0·5-in (12·7-mm) Browning AA machine-gun; they are to be fitted with an Ericsson gunner's sight with laser range-finder, plus a number of other important updating features
Centurion (Israel): Israel operates a substantial fleet of Centurion tanks, and most of these vehicles have been very substantially improved to **Upgraded Centurion** standard with a 750-hp (559-kW) Teledyne Continental Motors AVDS-1790-2A diesel and automatic gearbox, additional fuel capacity, redesigned ammunition stowage for the 105-mm M68 rifled gun (allowing the carriage of 72 rounds), and a 0·5-in (12·7-mm) Browning M2HB machine-gun mounted over the barrel of the main armament and fired by remote control; the result began to enter service in 1970, and is basically a Centurion Mk 5 with usefully increased ammunition capacity, a road speed of 48 km/h (26·7 mph) and the markedly improved road range of 600 + km (373 + miles); other modifications developed and adopted by the Israelis are appliqué active armour of the Blazer type, an advanced fire-control system, and provision for a dozer blade or mineclearing equipment (either plough or roller types modelled on Soviet equipments); Israel has also converted a number of Centurions into armoured personnel carriers with the turret removed and the hull sides increased in height; this open-topped vehicle can be fitted with a variable number of 7·62- and/or 12·7-mm (0·3- and/or 0·5-in) machine-guns
Centurion (Jordan): like the Israeli Centurion Mk 5s, these vehicles are being re-engined with the AVDS-1790 diesel, and are being fitted with an advanced SABCA fire-control system imported from Belgium, a Cadillac Gage gun-stabilization system, revised hydro-pneumatic suspension, and a Graviner explosion-suppression system; the revised tanks are designated **Tariq** in local service
Centurion (South Africa): South African Centurion tanks are being remanufactured with a new 750-hp (559-kW) V-12 diesel plus automatic transmission, a locally produced L7A1 105-mm (4·13-in) rifled gun with 72 rounds, two 7·62-mm (0·3-in) machine-guns with 5,600 rounds, and six smoke-dischargers on each side of the turret; the name **Olifant** has been given to these much improved tanks, which have a weight of 56,000 kg (123,457 lb), a length of 8·61 m (28·25 ft), a road speed of 45 km/h (28 mph), and a range of 500 km (311 miles) on 1240 litres (273 Imp gal) of fuel
Centurion (Sweden): in Swedish service the Centurion has the designation **Strv 101** and **Strv 102**, and these vehicles are being modified with a new Bofors Aerotronics fire-control system with laser rangefinder, a new gun-control system, the AVDS-1790-2DC diesel coupled to an automatic transmission, a commander's cupola imported from Israel (in which country it is fitted to the M48A5 and M60A1), a twin launcher for Lyran illuminating flares, and passive night vision equipment; thus modified the vehicles are designated **Strv 104**, which may be further enhanced with FFV reactive armour, a thermal sleeve for the 105-mm (4·13-in) gun, a muzzle reference system, further additions to the passive night vision equipment and, possibly, a retrofitted 120-mm (4·72-in) gun
Centurion (Switzerland): Swiss Centurions are designated **Pz 55** (Mk 5) and **Pz 57** (Mk 7), and are essentially similar to the British versions

Vickers Defence Systems Main Battle Tank Mk 7

(UK)

Type: main battle tank
Crew: 4
Combat weight: 120,460 lb (54,641 kg)
Dimensions: length, gun forward 35·92 ft (10·95 m) and hull 25·33 ft (7·72 m); width without appliqué armour 11·25 ft (3·42 m); height to top of commander's sight 9·83 ft (2·99 m)
Armament system: one 120-mm (4·72-in) ROF L11A5 rifled gun or GIAT CN-120 smooth-bore gun with 40 rounds, one co-axial 7·62-mm (0·3-in) RSAF Chain Gun with 2,000 rounds, one optional 7·62-mm (0·3-in) AA machine-gun with an unrevealed number of rounds, and six smoke-dischargers on each side of the turret; the turret is electrically powered, the main gun is stabilized in elevation (− 10° to + 20°) and azimuth (360°), and a Marconi Centaur 1 fire-control system is fitted; this last includes stabilized optical/thermal sights, a laser rangefinder, various sensors and a ballistic computer
Armour: welded steel and appliqué laminate
Powerplant: one 1120-kW (1,501-hp) MTU MB 873 Ka-501 diesel engine with 265 Imp gal (1200 litres) of internal fuel
Performance: speed, road 45 mph (72 km/h); range, road 310 miles (500 km); fording 2·6 ft (0·8 m) without preparation and 5·6 ft (1·7 m) with preparation; gradient 60%; side slope 30%; vertical obstacle 43 in (1·1 m); trench 9·85 ft (3·0 m); ground clearance 18 in (0·457 m)

Variant

Main Battle Tank Mk 7: originally known as the **Vickers Valiant** when first offered unsuccessfully with a Vickers-designed hull, the Main Battle Tank Mk 7 was developed in response to Middle Eastern requirements by Vickers in association with Krauss-Maffei, the former supplying the universal turret and overall design/integration control, and the latter the hull and automotive components based very closely on those of the Leopard 2; the type was completed in prototype form in 1985 and is now ready for production should orders be forthcoming; standard equipment includes a fire-suppression system and NBC protection

Below: A model here conveys the essence of the Vickers MBT Mk 7 with the Leopard 2's hull.

Vickers Defence Systems Main Battle Tank Mk 3(I)

(UK)

Type: main battle tank
Crew: 4
Combat weight: 90,390 lb (41,001 kg)
Dimensions: length, gun forward 31·17 ft (9·50 m) and hull 23·92 ft (7·29 m); width over skirts 10·63 ft (3·24 m); height without AA machine-gun 9·74 ft (2·97 m)
Armament system: one 105-mm (4·13-in) ROF L7A1 rifled gun with 50 rounds, one 0·5-in (12·7-mm) Browning M2HB co-axial ranging machine-gun with 1,000 rounds, two 7·62-mm (0·3-in) machine-guns (one co-axial L37A2 and one optional L8A2 AA) with 5,000 rounds, and five smoke-dischargers on each side of the turret; the turret is electrically powered, the main gun is stabilized in elevation (− 10° to + 20°) and azimuth (360°), and a Marconi EFCS 600 fire-control system is fitted; this last includes day/night optical sights, a laser rangefinder and a ballistic computer

Above: The Vickers MBT Mk 1 is a cost-effective tank sold to Kuwait and licence-built in India.

Armour: welded steel varying in thickness from 0·67 to 3·15 in (17 to 80 mm)
Powerplant: one 850-hp (634-kW) Perkins (Rolls-Royce) CV12 TCE diesel engine with 220 Imp gal (1000 litres) of internal fuel
Performance: speed, road 36·7 mph (59 km/h); range, road 340 miles (550 km); fording 3·6 ft (1·1 m); gradient 60%; side slope 30%; vertical obstacle 34·6 in (0·88 m); trench 9·85 ft (3·00 m); ground clearance 18 in (0·457 m)

Variant

Main Battle Tank Mk 3(I): appearing in prototype form in 1986, this is a much developed version of the Main Battle Tank Mk 3, with considerable improvement to the ride of the tank through the adoption of a new suspension system with rotary dampers, which also increases the ground clearance of the vehicle and improves trench-crossing capability; the interior of the tank has been much revised to improve operability and maintenance, and while the armament has been left substantially unaltered, the fire-control system has been improved

Vickers Defence Systems Main Battle Tank Mk 3

(UK)

Type: main battle tank
Crew: 4
Combat weight: 85,120 lb (36,610 kg)
Dimensions: length, gun forward 32·11 ft (9·79 m) and hull 24·81 ft (7·56 m); width 10·4 ft (3·17 m); height to turret top 8·12 ft (2·48 m)
Armament system: one 105-mm (4·13-in) ROF L7A1 rifled gun with 50 rounds (32 in the hull and 18 in the turret), one 0·5-in (12·7-mm) L7A1 co-axial ranging machine-gun with 700 rounds, one or two 7·62-mm (0·3-in) machine-guns (one co-axial L8A2 and one optional AA) with 2,600 rounds, and six smoke-dischargers on each side of the turret; the turret is electrically powered, the main gun is stabilized in elevation (− 10° to + 20°) and azimuth (360°), and a GEC-Marconi EC620 fire-control system is fitted; this last includes day/night optical sights, a laser rangefinder and a ballistic computer
Armour: welded steel varying in thickness from 0·67 to 3·15 in (17 to 80 mm)

Powerplant: one 720-hp (537-kW) Detroit Diesel 12V-71T diesel engine with 220 Imp gal (1000 litres) of internal fuel
Performance: speed, road 31 mph (50 km/h); range, road 330 miles (530 km); fording 3·6 ft (1·1 m); gradient 60%; side slope 30%; vertical obstacle 23·75 in (0·83 m); trench 9·85 ft (3·0 m); ground clearance 17 in (0·43 m)

Variants

Main Battle Tank Mk 1: this 85,100-lb (38,601-kg) private-venture tank was developed in the early 1960s in response to a request from the Indian army; the resulting Main Battle Tank Mk 1 was accepted for Indian service and placed in production with a 650-hp (485-kW) Leyland L60 Mk 4B multi-fuel engine for a maximum speed of 30 mph (48 km/h) and road range of 300 miles (483 km); the main armament has a maximum depression of −7°, and is used with a Marconi EC517 gun-control system; the main, ranging and secondary armament ammunition capacities are 44, 600 and 3,000 rounds respectively; the Main Battle Tank Mk 1 has lengths of 31·92 ft (9·728 m) with gun forward and 26·0 ft (7·93 m) for the hull, and a height of 8·67 ft (2·64 m) without the AA machine-gun; the Main Battle Tank Mk 1 was built under licence in India as the **Vijayanta**, and this differs in some important respects from the Main Battle Tank Mk 1 otherwise operated only by Kuwait; the Vijayanta weighs 40,000 kg (88,183 lb), and its principal dimensions include a length of 9·788 m (32·11 ft) with the gun forward, a width of 3·168 m (10·39 ft) over the skirts and a height of 2·711 m (8·89 ft); the variant is powered by a 535-hp (399-kW) variant of the Leyland L60 diesel, giving a road range of 350 km (217·5 miles); some Indian-produced models are being fitted with the SFCS 600 fire-control system, and the Indian fleet is being further upgraded with additional armour, a muzzle reference system and new powerplant, probably the 750-hp (559-kW) Perkins (Rolls-Royce) CV12
Main Battle Tank Mk 3: this is the upgraded model with a Detroit Diesel engine for greater range, additional armour and improved fire-control capability; the type is in service with Nigeria as the **Eagle** and with Kenya, while Kuwaiti Mk 1s have been brought up to this standard by the retrofitting of General Motors diesel engines
Armoured Bridgelayer: based on the chassis of the Mk 3, this AVLB carries a 44-ft (13·41-m) bridge
Armoured Recovery Vehicle: based on the chassis of the Mk 3, this ARV has a 55,115-lb (25,000-kg) capacity winch and (on some vehicles only) an 8,820-lb (4000-kg) crane

Above: The Vickers MBT Mk 3 is the Mk 1 with improved armour and a Detroit Diesel engine.

General Dynamics M1A1 Abrams

(USA)
Type: main battle tank
Crew: 4
Combat weight: 126,000 lb (57,154 kg)
Dimensions: length, gun forward 32·24 ft (9·828 m) and hull 25·98 ft (7·918 m); width 12·00 ft (3·657 m); height overall 9·47 ft (2·886 m)
Armament system: one 120-mm (4·72-in) M256 smooth-bore gun with 40 rounds, two M240 7·62-mm (0·3-in) machine-guns (one co-axial and one loader's AA) with 12,400 rounds, one 0·5-in (12·7-mm) Browning M2HB machine-gun (commander's AA) with 1,000 rounds, and six smoke-dischargers on each side of the turret; the turret is electro-hydraulically powered, the main gun is stabilized in elevation (−10° to +20°) and azimuth (360°), and an advanced fire-control system is fitted; this last includes stabilized day/night optical/thermal sights, a laser rangefinder, various sensors for ambient conditions, and a digital ballistic computer; the type can also generate smoke by injecting fuel into the exhaust system
Armour: steel and laminate
Powerplant: one 1,500-hp (1119-kW) Avco Lycoming AGT-1500 gas turbine with 504 US gal (1908 litres) of internal fuel
Performance: speed, road 41·5 mph (66·8 km/h); range, road 290 miles (467 km); fording 4·0 ft (1·22 m) without preparation and 7·8 ft (2·375 m) with preparation; gradient 60%; side slope 40%; vertical obstacle 42 in (1·067 m); trench 9·0 ft (2·74 m); ground clearance 17 in (0·43 m)

Variants

M1 Abrams: this is the successor to the M60 series as the US Army's main battle tank, and has been designed with the European theatre in mind; the type began to enter service in 1980 with standard features such as an NBC pack and an advanced fire-control system for the fully stabilized main armament, and offers significant improvements over the M60 series in armament,

Below: The American M1 series introduced the gas turbine to the tank propulsion field, but this smooth-running and compact engine is noisy and has a high fuel consumption.

protection, mobility, reliability, availability, maintainability and durability; the M1 Abrams weighs 120,250 lb (54,545 kg), and its principal dimensions include a length of 32·04 ft (9·766 m) with the gun forward, a width of 11·98 ft (3·653 m) and an overall height of 9·465 ft (2·885 m); the armament comprises one 105-mm (4·13-in) M68A1 rifled gun with 55 rounds (eight in the hull and 47 in the turret), one 0·5-in (12·7-mm) machine-gun with 1,000 rounds and two 7·62-mm (0·3-in) machine-guns with 11,400 rounds; the main armament has a maximum depression angle of −9°; the lighter weight of the M1 produces better performance than that of the M1A1, including a maximum road speed of 45 mph (72·4 km/h), a maximum road range of 310 miles (499 km), and a vertical obstacle capability of 49 in (1·24 m); tanks produced between October 1984 and May 1986 are to the upgraded **M1 Improved** standard with additional armour
M1A1 Abrams: much improved model of the Abrams which began to enter service in 1986; the variant differs from the original model principally in its armament, which is the 120-mm (4·72-in) Rheinmetall Rh-120 smooth-bore gun produced in the USA as the M256; 40 rounds of ammunition are provided for this weapon (four in the hull and 36 in the turret bustle), and other improvements to the M1A1 lie in the fields of vision, fire-control, ballistic and NBC protection, refuelling rate, and the provision of three rather than two blow-off panels in the turret roof to mitigate the effect of any ammunition explosion; further improvements are to be a commander's independent thermal viewer, improved 120-mm ammunition, a more advanced laser rangefinder and more durable track links (M1A1 Block II to be designated **M1A2 Abrams** in service) and crew reduced to three by the adoption of an automatic loader for the main armament, improved suspension, rapid-reload capability, rapid-refuel capability, and several other mobility and protection enhancements (M1A1 Block III to be designated **M1A3 Abrams** in service); variants of the M1 series currently under development are a Heavy Assault Bridge (from BMY and Israel Military Industries) to bridge a gap of 100 ft (30·5 m) and an Armored Recovery Vehicle (from General Dynamics); also available for use on the M1 series are a dozer kit and a roller mineclearing kit

General Dynamics M60A3

(USA)

Type: main battle tank
Crew: 4
Combat weight: 116,000 lb (52,618 kg)
Dimensions: length, gun forward 30·96 ft (9·436 m) and hull 22·79 ft (6·946 m); width 11·91 ft (3·631 m); height 10·73 ft (3·27 m)
Armament system: one 105-mm (4·13-in) M68A1 rifled gun with 63 rounds (26 in the hull and 37 in the turret), one 7·62-mm (0·3-in) M240 co-axial machine-gun with 5,950 rounds, one 0·5-in (12·7-mm) M85 AA machine-gun with 940 rounds, and six smoke-dischargers on each side of the turret; the turret is electro-hydraulically powered, the main gun is stabilized in both elevation (−10° to +20°) and azimuth (360°), and an advanced Hughes fire-control system is fitted; this last includes stabilized day/night optics, a laser rangefinder, various sensors for ambient conditions, and a digital ballistic computer; the type can also generate smoke by injecting fuel into the exhaust system
Armour: cast and welded steel
Powerplant: one 750-hp (559-kW) Teledyne Continental Motors AVDS-1790-2C diesel engine with 375 US gal (1420 litres) of internal fuel
Performance: speed, road 30 mph (48·3 km/h); range, road 300 miles (483 km); fording 4·0 ft (1·22 m) without preparation and 7·87 ft (2·4 m) with preparation; gradient 60%; side slope 30%; vertical obstacle 36 in (0·91 m); trench 8·5 ft (2·59 m); ground clearance 17·7 in (0·45 m)

Variants

M60: this initial variant of the US Army's most important tank (in numerical terms) began to supplant the M48 series as the US Army's main battle tank from 1960; while generally comparable in dimensions and performance to later models, it lacks the gun-stabilization system of the M60A1 and M60A3 variants, has a mechanical analog computer for arriving at ballistic solutions and possesses a turret of inferior ballistic qualities; the type has a combat weight of 109,600 lb (49,715 kg), a length of 30·54 ft (9·309 m) with the gun forward and a height of 10·54 ft (3·213 m); the variant is powered by the AVDS-1790-2A diesel, for which 385 US gal (1497 litres) of fuel are provided; the main armament can be depressed to a maximum of -9°, and is provided with 60 rounds of ammunition; full NBC protection is standard

M60A1: 1962 model improved over the M60 in having a sharper-fronted turret of superior ballistic qualities, and stowage for 63 rather than 60 rounds of 105-mm (4·13-in) ammunition; the type has a combat weight of 116,000 lb (52,618 kg), and is dimensionally identical with the subsequent M60A3; the following M60A2 variant with a 152-mm (6-in) combined gun/missile-launcher (for the Shillelagh anti-tank missile) is no longer in service, surviving vehicles being available for rework to other equipment

M60A3: product-improved M60A1 with a superior fire-control (with a laser rangefinder and digital computer), smoke-dischargers, a more reliable engine and an add-on gun-stabilization system; the type began to enter service in 1978, and is now being upgraded with appliqué/reactive armour to defeat modern HEAT warheads

M60A3 TTS: M60A3 development used by the US Army National Guard; as indicated by its designation the model differs from the baseline M60A3 in being fitted with a tank thermal sight; US Army planners are currently investigating the possibility of a product-improved M60A3 TTS, which has the prospective designation **M60A4** to cover enhanced features in the fields of mobility (the 1,050-hp/783-kW AVDS-1790 diesel engine driving an automatic transmission), survivability (appliqué and wrap-around armour upgrades, improved ammunition stowage, spall liners, an automatic fire-extinguisher system, a lower cupola, an engine smoke-generation kit and laser protection) and 'fightability' (improved fire-control system, enhanced main armament stabilization system and upgraded thermal sight/laser rangefinder system)

M60 AVLB: 122,900-lb (55,747-kg) Armored Vehicle-Launched Bridge using the chassis of the M60 and capable of spanning a gap of 60 ft (18·3 m) with its 63-ft (19·2-m) scissors-type bridge

M728 CET: 115,000-lb (52,164-kg) Combat Engineer Tractor armed with a 165-mm (6·5-in) M135 demolition gun, and carrying specialized equipment such as a front-mounted dozer blade, a folding A-frame and a 25,000-lb (11,340-kg) capacity winch

M60 (Israel): Israel has about 1,000 M60A1 and M60A3 tanks, and these have generally been upgraded in two major improvement programmes; in the first vehicles were fitted with Blazer reactive armour, a new commander's cupola with externally mounted 7·62-mm (0·3-in) machine-gun, a remotely fired 0·5-in (12·7-mm) Browning machine-gun attached over the barrel of the main armament, a thermal sleeve over the M68 main gun, the IMI CL-3030 instantaneous self-screening system with mountings on each side of the main armament, and other modifications; in the second programme tanks are fitted with new passive armour (glacis, nose, turret front, turret sides, turret roof and skirts) as additional protection against both chemical- and kinetic-energy attack, a new version of the AVDS-1790 diesel engine (possibly the 600-hp/447-kW AVDS-1790-6A model used in the Merkava Mk 1) driving new tracks, and a revised fire-control system (the Elbit/El-Op Matador already in service in the Merkava series)

The M60A3 is the definitive version of this important MBT, and in common with other US tanks up to the M1 has a notably tall silhouette.

24

Chrysler (General Dynamics) M48A5 Patton

(USA)

Type: main battle tank
Crew: 4
Combat weight: 108,000 lb (48,989 kg)
Dimensions: length, gun forward 30·53 ft (9·306 m) and hull 20·06 ft (6·419 m); width 11·91 ft (3·63 m); height 10·12 ft (3·09 m)
Armament: one 105-mm (4·13-in) M68A1 rifled gun with 54 rounds, three 7·62-mm (0·3-in) M60D machine-guns (one co-axial and two AA) with 10,000 rounds, and smoke-dischargers; the turret is electro-hydraulically powered, the main gun lacks stabilization in either elevation (−9° to +19°) or azimuth (360°), and an optical fire-control system is fitted; the type can also generate smoke by injecting fuel into the exhaust system
Armour: welded and cast steel varying in thickness from 0·5 to 4·72 in (12·7 to 120 mm)
Powerplant: one 750-hp (559-kW) Teledyne Continental Motors AVDS-1790-2A/D diesel engine with 375 US gal (1420 litres) of internal fuel
Performance: speed, road 30 mph (48·3 km/h); range, road 310 miles (499 km); fording 4·0 ft (1·22 m) without preparation and 8·0 ft (2·44 m) with preparation; gradient 60%; side slope 30%; vertical obstacle 36 in (0·91 m); trench 8·5 ft (2·59 m); ground clearance 16·5 in (0.39 m)

Variants

M48: this was the original production model of the Patton tank, and entered service in 1952 as the replacement for the M47 series; the type has a combat weight of 99,000 lb (44,906 kg), is 27·70 ft (8·444 m) long with the gun forward, possesses a main armament of one 90-mm (3·54-in) gun with 60 rounds, a co-axial armament of one 0·3-in (7·62-mm) machine-gun with 5,900 rounds and an AA armament of one 0·5-in (12·7-mm) machine-gun with 180 rounds, and is powered by a 810-hp (604-kW) Continental AVDS-1790 petrol engine with an internal fuel supply of 200 US gal (757 litres) for a range of only 70 miles (113 km); the training version of this initial variant is the M48C with a hull of mild steel
M48A1: improved model remedying some of the M48's lesser failings without real concern for the major problems of a petrol engine and catastrophically short range, though provision is made for jettisonable external tanks; the variant has a weight of 104,000 lb (47,174 m) and a length of 28·64 ft (8·729 m) with the gun forward
M48A2: improved M48A1 with a T-shape muzzle brake to the 90-mm (3·54-in) main armament, internal tankage increased to 335 US gal (1268 litres) for a road range of 160 miles (257 km) and provision for jettisonable external tanks; the ammunition capacities are also modified to 64 90-mm (3·54-in) rounds, 5,590 7·62-mm (0·3-in) rounds and 1,365 0·5-in (12·7-mm) rounds; the variant weighs 106,000 lb (47174 kg), and its length is 28·50 ft (8·686 m) with the hull forward
M48A2C: M48A2 with improved fire-control equipment
M48A3: major model produced by rebuilding M48A1 and M48A2 tanks with the 750-hp (559-kW) AVDS-1790-2A diesel and internal tankage for 375 US gal (1420 litres), track-return rollers reduced in number from five to three, and improved fire-control; the powerplant and fuel system modifications increase range to 290 miles (467 km), and the variant has the same weight and dimensions as the M48A2, though the ammunition capacity is again altered, this time to 62 90-mm (3·54-in) rounds, 6,000 7·62-mm (0·3-in) rounds and 630 0·5-in (12·7-mm) rounds

M48A5: produced from 1975 by conversion of M48A1 and M48A3 tanks, the M48A5 introduces a host of internal and external modifications to improve the basic type's serviceability and habitability, and also sees the introduction of turret-mounted smoke-dischargers and of the 105-mm (4·13-in) main armament plus revised secondary and AA fits; almost identical modifications programmes are being undertaken by Greece, South Korea and Turkey
M48 Armored Vehicle-Launched Bridge: 122,900-lb (55,747-kg) AVLB able to span a gap of 60 ft (18·3 m) with its 63-ft (19·2-m) scissors-type bridge
M48 (Israel): Israel operates numbers of M48 tanks brought up to the basic capability of the M60 series with a 12-cylinder Continental diesel, 105-mm (4·13-in) main armament and an Israeli-designed commander's cupola amongst a number of other improvements and modernizations
M48 (Spain): Spanish M48s have been upgraded considerably in a local modification programme resulting in the addition of the suffix 'E' to the basic designation; these modifications are directed generally to the powerplant (diesel) and to the main armament and its fire-control system; the

M48A3E retains the standard 90-mm (3·54-in) main gun, while the **M48A5E** and upgraded **M48A5E1** have a 105-mm (4·13-in) weapon in the form of either the M68 or the Rheinmetall Rh-105; the M48A5E1 has a more advanced fire-control system with a laser rangefinder, analog electronic computer and a number of vehicle sensors
M48 (West Germany): the West German army uses a number of M48 series tanks brought up to
M48A2GA2 standard with M48A5-type modifications based on the 105-mm (4·13-in) L7A3 gun complete with thermal sleeve and 46 rounds of ammunition, two 7·62-mm (0·3-in) MG3 machine-guns with 4,750 rounds, and four smoke-dischargers on each side of the turret; a similar programme has been applied to the M48s used by the Turkish army, and other modifications offered by Krauss-Maffei are an NBC system, a more advanced fire-control system (with a laser rangefinder and ballistic computer), night-vision equipment, appliqué armour and improved suspension; there are also a number of powerpack improvements offered by one West German and two American companies

A well-decorated M48A2 of the US Marine Corps lands during an amphibious exercise.

Detroit Tank Plant/American Locomotive M47M

(USA)

Type: medium tank
Crew: 4
Combat weight: 103,205 lb (46,814 kg)
Dimensions: length, gun forward 28·06 ft (8·55 m) and hull 20·56 ft (6·27 m); width 11·12 ft (3·39 m); height to turret top 9·69 ft (2·95 m)
Armament system: one 90-mm (3·54-in) M36 rifled gun with 79 rounds (68 in the hull and 11 in the turret), one 0·3-in (7·62-mm) M1919A4 co-axial machine-gun with 4,125 rounds, and one 0·5-in (12·7-mm) M2HB AA machine-gun with 440 rounds; the turret is hydraulically powered, the main gun lacks stabilization in either elevation (−9° to +19°) or azimuth (360°), and an optical fire-control system is fitted
Armour: welded steel varying in thickness from 0·5 to 4 in (12·7 to 102 mm)
Powerplant: one 750-hp (559-kW) Teledyne Continental Motors AVDS-1790-2A diesel engine with 390 US gal (1476 litres) of internal fuel
Performance: speed, road 30 mph (48 km/h); range, road 375 miles (603 km); fording 4·0 ft (1·22 m); gradient 60%; side slope 30%; vertical obstacle 36 in ft (0·91 m); trench 8·5 ft (2·59 m); ground clearance 18·5 in (0·47 m)

Variants

M47: the five-man M47 entered service with the US Army in 1953, but was not judged a great success, largely because it is powered by an 810-hp (604-kW) Teledyne Continental AVDS-1790-5B petrol engine with a mere 231 US gal (875 litres) of internal fuel for a range of only 80 miles (129 km); main armament ammunition amounts to 71 rounds (increased to 105 rounds if the 0·3-in/7·62-mm M1919A4 bow machine-gun is omitted); the M47 weighs 101,785 lb (46,170 kg) and has a length of 27·91 ft (8·508 m) with the gun forward
M47E1: Spanish-developed variant with an AVDS-1790-2A diesel engine, an improved Cadillac Gage turret and a 7·62-mm (0·3-in) MG42 co-axial machine-gun
M47E2: Spanish-developed variant similar to the M47E1 but fitted with 105-mm (4·13-in) M68 or Rheinmetall Rh-105 main armament
M47M: this model was developed as a retrofit package for Iran, and provided the basic M47 with the powerplant, fire-control and fuel tankage of the M60A1 main battle tank
M47 (Israel): known as the **Rhino**, this Israeli-developed model has the powerpack and the 105-mm (4·13-in) M68 rifled gun (plus 63 rounds) of the M60A1
M47 (South Korea): South Korean development has produced an **M47 Armored Recovery Vehicle**, which has a turret-mounted winch in place of the 90-mm (3·54-in) gun, and an A-frame at the front of the hull

Right: An M51 Super Sherman with its 105-mm (4·13-in) gun traversed to the rear, towed by a Sherman-based recovery vehicle.
Below: Even in its improved forms the M47 is an obsolete tank for the modern battlefield.

M4A3E8 Sherman

(USA)

Type: medium tank
Crew: 5
Combat weight: 71,175 lb (32,285 kg)
Dimensions: length, gun forward 24·67 ft (7·5128 m) and hull 20·58 ft (6·273 m); width 8·75 ft (2·667 m); height to turret top 11·25 ft (3·43 m)
Armament system: one 3-in (76-mm) M1A1/2 rifled gun with 71 rounds, two 0·3-in (7·62-mm) Browning M1919A4 machine-guns (one co-axial and one bow) with 6,250 rounds, and one 0·5-in (12·7-mm) Browning M2HB AA machine-gun with 600 rounds; the turret is hydraulically powered, the main gun lacks stabilization in either elevation (−10° to +25°) or azimuth (360°), and optical sights are fitted
Armour: cast and welded steel varying in thickness from 1 to 3 in (25·4 to 76·2 mm)
Powerplant: one 450-hp (336-kW) Ford GAA petrol engine with 168 US gal (636 litres) of internal fuel
Performance: speed, road 30 mph (48 km/h); range, road 100 miles (161 km); fording 3 ft (0·91 m); gradient 60%; vertical obstacle 24 in (0·61 m); trench 7·4 ft (2·26 m); ground clearance 17 in (0·43 m)

Variants

M4: this initial model of the Sherman was introduced in October 1941 and is armed with a 75-mm (2·95-in) gun in a cast turret on a welded hull with a 353-hp (263-kW) Continental R-975-C1 radial engine; many versions of the Sherman remain in service despite their age, most having been upgraded to greater or lesser extent (generally with a diesel powerplant such as the 335-kW/449-hp Poyaud 520 V8S2 or Detroit Diesel 8V-71T) to provide continued utility (as well as greater range and enhanced reliability) in less advanced corners of the world
M4A1: introduced in December 1941 as a derivative of the M4 with a cast hull
M4A2: introduced in December 1941 as a version of the M4 powered by the 375-hp (280-kW) General Motors 6046 coupled powerplant
M4A3: introduced in January 1943 as a derivative of the M4 with the 450-hp (336-kW) Ford GAA-III powerplant
M4A4: introduced in February 1942 with welded hull and turret, and powered by a 375-hp (280-kW) Chrysler five-bank engine
M4A6: version of the M4A4 with the 450-hp (336-kW) Caterpillar RD-1820 diesel
M4 (76 mm): unofficial designation of earlier M4s retrofitted with the 76-mm (3-in) M1 gun and some 70 rounds (fired at a muzzle velocity of 2,600 ft/792 m per second) instead of the 75-mm M3 with some 90 rounds (fired at a muzzle velocity of 2,030 ft/619 m per second); the slightly larger gun offers significantly enhanced armour-penetration capabilities (4 in/102 mm rather than 3·15 in/80 mm at 1,000 yards/914 m)
Sherman Firefly: designation of M4A3 chassis fitted with the British 17-pdr anti-tank gun and 42 rounds; the gun has a muzzle velocity of 2,900 ft (884 m) per second, allowing its projectile to penetrate 4·72 in (120 mm) of armour at 500 yards (457 m)
M32: armoured recovery vehicle developed in World War II and based on the Sherman chassis with an A-frame and 60,000-lb (27,216-kg) capacity winch
M74: armoured recovery vehicle developed after World War II and based on the M4A3 with a dozer blade, A-frame and 90,000-lb (40,824-kg) capacity winch

Steyr SK105/A1 Kürassier

(Austria)
Type: light tank
Crew: 3
Combat weight: 17,500 kg (38,580 lb)
Dimensions: length, gun forward 7·763 m (25·47 ft) and hull 5·582 m (18·31 ft); width 2·50 m (8·20 ft); height to top of commander's cupola 2·53 m (8·30 ft)
Armament system: one 105-mm (4·13-in) GIAT CN-105-57 rifled gun with 44 rounds (32 in the hull and six in each of the two revolving cylinders of the semi-automatic loading system), one 7·62-mm (0·3-in) MG74 co-axial machine-gun with 2,000 rounds, and three smoke-dischargers on each side of the turret; the turret is hydraulically powered, the main gun lacks stabilization in either elevation (−8° to +12°) or azimuth (360°), and an optical fire-control system is fitted; this last includes day/night optical/thermal sights and a laser rangefinder
Armour: welded steel varying in thickness from 8 to 40 mm (0·31 to 1·57 in)
Powerplant: one 240-kW (322-hp) Steyr 7FA diesel engine with 400 litres (88 Imp gal) of internal fuel
Performance: speed, road 65·3 km/h (40·6 mph); range, road 520 km (323 miles); fording 1·0 m (3·3 ft); gradient 75%; side slope 40%; vertical obstacle 0·8 m (31·5 in); trench 2·41 m (7·9 ft); ground clearance 0·4 m (15·75 in)

Variants

SK105/A1 Kürassier: based on the chassis of the Saurer 4K 7FA APC with a Steyr development of the FL-13 oscillating turret of the French AMX-13 light tank, the Kürassier was developed mainly as a tank destroyer in the second half of the 1960s and entered production in 1971; the type has individual NBC protection, and the ordnance has recently been modified (with a retrofit kit available) to fire a more devastating APFSDS round
SK105/A2 Kürassier: improved model of the Kürassier with a fully stabilized upper turret, completely automatic loader and ballistic computer
SK105/A3 Kürassier: developed in the early 1980s to provide continued capability against the latest main battle tanks carrying multi-layer or laminated armour, this is a variant of the Kürassier fitted with the US M68 105-mm (4·13-in) gun firing APFSDS ammunition; the same type of oscillating turret is retained, though this welded-armour construction (with bolt-on top plate to allow it to

blow off without difficulty in the event of an explosion inside the turret) has been enlarged to accommodate the greater recoil distance and other requirements of the more powerful gun, including the two six-round automatic-loading magazines for the larger ammunition, of which 32 rounds are carried; the gun can be elevated between −8° and +12·5°, and the maximum rate of fire is eight rounds per minute; the oscillating upper portion of the turret is fully stabilized, and the gun is used in association with the new digital fire-control system; the complete tank weighs 20,700 kg (45,635 lb), and with the 265-kW (360-hp) Steyr 9FA diesel driving through a ZF automatic gearbox this results in a maximum speed of 67 km/h (41·6 mph) and range of 500 km (311 miles) on 420 litres (92·4 Imp gal) of fuel; the SK105/A3's dimensions include an overall length of 8·729 m (28·64 ft) with the gun forward, a width of 2·50 m (8·2 ft) and a height of 2·76 m (9·06 ft) to

the gunner's sight
4K 7FA SB 20 Bergepanzer Greif: 19,800-kg (43,651-lb) armoured recovery vehicle development of the Kürassier using the same hull fitted in this application with a 6000-kg (13,228-lb) capacity crane, a 20,000-kg (44,092-lb) capacity winch and a front-mounted dozer blade
4KH 7FA-Pi Pionierpanzer: 19,000-kg (41,887-lb) armoured engineer vehicle development of the Kürassier, basically similar to the Greif apart from having a larger dozer blade, an 8000-kg (17,637-lb) capacity winch and an excavator instead of the crane

Above: The type's air-portability is shown by this AMX-13/105 disembarking from a Transall C.160.
Below: An AMX-13/105 (right) with the related AMX VCI APC and a modified combat engineer vehicle.

Bernardini X1A2

(Brazil)
Type: light tank
Crew: 3
Combat weight: 19,000 kg (41,887 lb)
Dimensions: length, gun forward 7·10 m (23·29 ft) and hull 6·50 m (21·33 ft); width 2·60 m (8·53 ft); height to turret top 2·45 m (8·04 ft)
Armament system: one 90-mm (3·54-mm) Cockerill/ENGESA rifled gun with 66 rounds, one 7·62-mm (0·3-in) co-axial machine-gun with 2,500 rounds, one 0·5-in (12·7-mm) Browning M2HB AA heavy machine-gun with 750 rounds, and three smoke-dischargers on each side of the turret; the turret is hydraulically powered, the main gun lacks stabilization in either elevation (−8° to +17°) or azimuth (360°), and an optical fire-control system (with optional laser rangefinder) is fitted
Armour: welded steel
Powerplant: one 225-kW (302-hp) Saab-Scania DS-11 diesel engine with 600 litres (132 Imp gal) of internal fuel
Performance: speed, road 55 km/h (34·2 mph); range, road 600 km (373 miles); fording 1·3 m (4·3 ft); gradient 70%; side slope 30%; vertical obstacle 0·7 m (27·6 in); trench 2·1 m (6·9 ft); ground clearance 0·5 m (19·7 in)

Variants

X1A: developed in the early 1970s, this Brazilian light tank was based on the chassis of the M3A1 Stuart light tank (built during World War II by the USA) but fitted with a 209-kW (280-hp) Saab-Scania diesel and a new turret accommodating the French 90-mm (3·54-in) GIAT CN-90 (F1) rifled gun; the vehicle weighs 15,000 kg (33·069 lb)
X1A1 Carcara: development of the X1A with a hull increased in length (by an extra suspension group) to 5·3 m (17·39 ft) for an overall length of 6·36 m (20·87 ft) with the gun forward; the vehicle weighs 17,000 kg (37,478 lb), and with 305 litres (67 Imp gal) of fuel has a range of 520 km (323 miles)
X1A2: full-production version of the X1A1 with new rather than rebuilt chassis
XLP-10: armoured vehicle-launched bridge derivative of the X1A series able to span a gap of 10 m (32·8 ft)

Early-production X1A2 light tanks reveal this Brazilian type's similarity to the M3 Stuart.

Type 63

(China)
Type: light tank
Crew: 4
Combat weight: 18,700 kg (41,225 lb)
Dimensions: length, gun forward 8·437 m (27·68 ft) and hull 7·15 m (23·46 ft); width 3·20 m (10·50 ft); height including AA machine-gun 2·522 m (8·27 ft)
Armament system: one 85-mm (3·35-in) rifled gun with 47 rounds, one 7·62-mm (0·3-in) co-axial machine-gun with 1,000 rounds, and one 12·7-mm (0·5-in) Type 54 AA machine-gun with 500 rounds; the turret is hydraulically powered, the main gun lacks stabilization in either elevation (an unrevealed arc) or azimuth (360°), and an optical fire-control system is fitted
Armour: cast and welded steel varying in thickness from 10 to 14 mm (0·39 to 0·55 in)
Powerplant: one 300-kW (402-hp) Model 12150-L diesel engine with 545 litres (120 Imp gal) of internal fuel
Performance: speed, road 64 km/h (39·8 mph) and water 12 km/h (7·5 mph) driven by two water-jets; range, road 370 km (230 miles); fording amphibious; gradient 60%; side slope 30%; vertical obstacle 0·87 m (34·25 in); trench 2·9 m (9·5 ft); ground clearance 0·4 m (15·75 in)

Variant

Type 63: this is a derivative of the Soviet PT-76 amphibious light tank, which was probably built in China in small numbers as the Type 60 and identical with the PT-76 other than provision for a pintle-mounted 12·7-mm (0·5-in) AA machine-gun; the Type 63 uses the same armament and similar automotive components as the T-62 light tank, and is propelled in the water by twin water-jets; the tank lacks NBC protection and night vision capability; some examples have been upgraded with a laser rangefinder

Type 62

(China)
Type: light tank
Crew: 4
Combat weight: 21,000 kg (46,296 lb)
Dimensions: length, gun forward 7·90 m (25·92 ft) and hull 5·55 m (18·21 m); width 2·86 m (9·38 ft); height 2·55 m (8·37 ft)

Armament system: one 85-mm (3·35-in) rifled gun with 47 rounds, one 7·62-mm (0·3-in) co-axial machine-gun with 1,750 rounds, one 7·62-mm (0·3-in) bow machine-gun with an unrevealed number of rounds, and one 12·7-mm (0·5-in) Type 54 AA machine-gun with 1,250 rounds; the turret is hydraulically powered, the main gun lacks stabilization in either elevation (−4° to +20°) or azimuth (360°), and an optical fire-control system is fitted
Armour: cast and welded steel
Powerplant: one 320-kW (429-hp) diesel engine with 730 litres (160·6 Imp gal) of internal fuel
Performance: speed, road 60 km/h (37·3 mph); range, road 500 km (311 miles); fording 1·3 m (4·25 ft); gradient 60%; side slope 30%; vertical obstacle 0·7 m (27·6 in); trench 2·55 m (8·4 ft); ground clearance 0·42 m (16·5 in)

Variant

Type 62: this is little more than a scaled-down Type 59 MBT intended for operations in adverse terrain; the type lacks an NBC system, amphibious capability and night vision devices

Creusot-Loire AMX-13/90

(France)
Type: light tank
Crew: 3
Combat weight: 15,000 kg (33,069 lb)
Dimensions: length, gun forward 6·36 m (20·87 ft) and hull 4·88 m (16·01 ft); width 2·50 m (8·20 ft); height to commander's hatch 2·30 m (7·55 ft)
Armament system: one 90-mm (3·54-in) GIAT CN-90 (F3) rifled gun with 34 rounds (13 in the hull and six in each of the two revolver cylinders of the automatic loading system), two 7·5- or 7·62-mm (0·295- or 0·3-in) machine-guns (one co-axial and one AA) with 3,600 rounds, and two smoke-dischargers on each side of the turret; the turret is hydraulically powered, the main gun lacks stabilization in either elevation (−5° to +12·5°) or azimuth (360°) , and an optical fire-control system is fitted
Armour: welded steel varying in thickness from 10 to 25 mm (0·39 to 1 in)
Powerplant: one 185-kW (248-hp) SOFAM 8Gxb petrol engine with 480 litres (105·6 Imp gal) of internal fuel
Performance: speed, road 60 km/h (37·3 mph); range, road 400 km (249 miles); fording 0·6 m (23·6 in); gradient 60%; side slope 30%; vertical obstacle 0·65 m (2·1 ft); trench 1·6 m (5·25 ft); ground clearance 0·37 m (14·6 in)

Variants

AMX-13 modèle 51/75: this first production model of one of the world's most successful light tanks appeared in 1952, and is armed with a 75-mm (2·95-in) main gun fed from two six-round revolving magazines in the bustle of the oscillating turret; overall ammunition capacities are 37 75-mm (2·95-in) rounds and 3,600 machine-gun rounds; the version currently in service with the French army is also fitted with a pair of SS.11 wire-guided anti-tank missiles, one on each side of the turret; a version of the same basic concept is available for export with six HOT anti-tank missiles, three on each side of the turret
AMX-13/75: designed during the 1950s for North African operations, this variant has a manually-loaded 75-mm (2·95-in) gun in an FL-11 turret
AMX-13/90: upgunned variant of the early 1960s,

and similar to the modèle 51/75 apart from its main armament, a 90-mm (3·54-in) GIAT CN-90 (F3) rifled weapon in the same FL-10 turret; the same loading system is used, but whereas the modèle 51/75 has 37 75-mm (2·95-in) rounds for use in the two manually replenished revolving cylinders, the AMX-13/90 carries 34 90-mm (3·54-in) rounds for the same loading system

AMX-13/105: upgunned export derivative with a 105-mm (4·13-in) GIAT CN-105-57 (F1) gun in an FL-12 turret, and a choice between the SOFAM petrol engine and 280-hp (209-kW) Detroit Diesel 6V-53T diesel engine, the latter boosting speed to 64 km/h (40 mph) and range to 550 km (342 miles)

Char de Dépannage modèle 55: 15,300-kg (33,730-lb) armoured recovery variant of the AMX-13 series with two winches (the main one having a pull of 15,000 kg/33,069 lb), an A-frame and four rear-mounted spades

Char Poseur de Pont AMX-13: 19,700-kg (43,430-lb) armoured vehicle-launched bridge derivative carrying a 14·01-m (45·96-ft) folding bridge

AMX-13 Update: given the fact that the AMX-13 is still in widespread service (and likely to remain so in those areas where light protection, modest firepower and compact size are more important than the massive capabilities of more advanced tanks), it is hardly surprising that a number of protective, mobility and firepower update packages have been offered by several manufacturers; in Argentina some AMX-13s have been locally produced from knock-down kits with the 195-kW (260-hp) KHD V-8 diesel, and both Peru and Venezuela are refitting their AMX-13 fleets with this powerplant; in Belgium Cockerill Mechanical Industries offer a revised AMX-13 with the 75-mm (2·95-in) main gun replaced by a 90-mm

(3·54-in) Cockerill Mk IVA3 gun and revised automatic loading system; in France Creusot-Loire offers a 650-kg (1,433-lb) package of appliqué armour to increase protection levels significantly, while CIT offers a laser rangefinder; in West Germany GLS, a Krauss-Maffei subsidiary, offers a mobility update package centred on new tracks and running gear; in Israel NIMDA offers a total refit package with new Detroit Diesel engine, armament and fire-control system; in the Netherlands ex-Dutch army AMX-13s have been refurbished entirély by RDM and sold to Indonesia; and in Singapore the AMX-13 is being refitted

with the Detroit Diesel 6V-53T engine and an automatic transmission, hydro-pneumatic suspension, improved protection, electric rather than hydraulic turret functions and other modernizations; several other companies are in the field with offers of powerpack modification, the two most commonly promoted engines being the Detroit Diesel 6V-53T and Baudouin 6 F 11 SRY

Above: The Char Poseur de Pont AMX-13 with its bridge in the folded (stowed) position.
Below: The oscillating nature of the AMX-13/90's upper turret is evident in this illustration.

North Korean light tank

(North Korea)
Type: light tank
Crew: 4
Combat weight: 20,000 kg (44,092 lb)
Dimensions: length, gun forward not revealed and hull 7·00 m (22·97 ft); width 3·20 m (10·50 ft); height 2·60 m (8·53 ft)
Armament system: one 85-mm (3·35-in) rifled gun with an unrevealed number of rounds, one 7·62-mm (0·3-in) co-axial machine-gun with an unrevealed number of rounds, and one 12·7-mm (0·5-in) AA machine-gun with an unrevealed number of rounds
Armour: cast and welded steel
Powerplant: one diesel engine of unrevealed power with an unrevealed quantity of internal fuel
Performance: not revealed

Variant

North Korean light tank: first revealed in 1987, this is a North Korean development, though it is not known if it is based on the Chinese Type 63 to which it is similar in dimensions and armament; the details above are speculative rather than definitive

---

PT-76

(USSR)
Type: light tank
Crew: 3
Combat weight: 14,000 kg (30,864 lb)
Dimensions: length, gun forward 7·625 m (25·02 ft) and hull 6·91 m (22·67 ft); width 3·14 m (10·30 ft); height, early model 2·255 m (7·40 ft) and late model 2·195 m (7·20 ft)
Armament system: one 76·2-mm (3-in) D-56T rifled gun with 40 rounds, one 7·62-mm (0·3-in) SGMT co-axial machine-gun with 1,000 rounds, and in some vehicles one 12·7-mm (0·5-in) DShKM AA machine-gun with an unrevealed number of rounds; the turret is electrically powered, the main gun lacks stabilization in either elevation (−4° to +30°) or azimuth (360°), and an optical fire-control system is fitted; the type can generate smoke by injecting fuel into the exhaust system
Armour: welded steel varying in thickness from 5 to 17 mm (0·2 to 0·67 in)

PT-76 light tanks reveal their natural buoyancy in their primary amphibious role.

Powerplant: one 180-kW (241-hp) Model V-6 diesel engine with 250 litres (55 Imp gal) of internal fuel plus provision for 180 litres (40 Imp gal) of external fuel
Performance: speed, road 44 km/h (27·3 mph) and water 10 km/h (6·2 mph) driven by two water-jets; range, road 450 km (280 miles) with maximum fuel and water 65 km (40 miles); fording amphibious; gradient 70%; vertical obstacle 1·1 m (43·3 in); trench 2·8 m (9·2 ft); ground clearance 0·37 m (14·6 in)

Variants

PT-76 Model 1: introduced in 1952, this is the main light tank used by the Soviet forces (army and naval infantry) for reconnaissance despite its small size, very thin armour, and lack of NBC protection and night-fighting capability; this initial model is apparently no longer in service, and was distinguishable by its multi-baffle muzzle brake and lack of bore evacuator
PT-76 Model 2: version with a double-baffle muzzle brake and forward-located bore evacuator; it is thought that the Indonesian marine corps is upgrading its PT-76 light tanks with a 90-mm (3·54-in) rifled main gun of Belgian (probably Cockerill) origin
PT-76 Model 3: version similar to the Model 2 but without a bore evacuator
PT-76B: version with a fully-stabilized D-56TM main armament; the NATO reporting designation is **PT-76 Model 4**
Type 60: Chinese-built copy of the PT-76

Vickers/FMC VFM 5

(UK/USA)
Type: light tank
Crew: 4
Combat weight: 43,540 lb (19,750 kg)
Dimensions: length, gun forward 28·25 ft (8·61 m) and hull 20·33 ft (6·20 m); width 8·83 ft (2·69 m); height to turret roof 8·60 ft (2·62 m)
Armament system: one 105-mm (4·13-in) M68 rifled gun with 41 rounds (22 in the hull and 17 in the turret), one 7·62-mm (0·3-in) L8A2 co-axial machine-gun with 1,000 rounds, one 0·5-in (12·7-mm) Browning M2HB AA heavy machine-gun with 5,000 rounds, and six smoke-dischargers on each side of the turret; the turret is electrically powered, the main armament in stabilized in elevation (−10° to +20°) and azimuth (360°), and a Marconi fire-control system is fitted; this last includes stabilized optical/thermal sights, a laser rangefinder and a ballistic computer

Armour: cast and welded aluminium with steel overpanels
Powerplant: one 552-hp (412-kW) Detroit Diesel 6V-92TA6 diesel engine with 150 US gal (568 litres) of internal fuel
Performance: speed, road 44 mph (70 km/h); range, road 300 miles (483 km); fording 4·33 ft (1·32 m) without preparation; gradient 60%; side slope 40%; vertical obstacle 2·5 ft (0·76 m); trench 7·0 ft (2·13 m); ground clearance 16 in (40·6 cm)

Variants

Battle Tank Mk 5: introduced in 1986, this is the export derivative of the CCVL and developed jointly by Vickers (turret, armament, fire-control system) and FMC (hull and automotive system); the result is a tank with the weight of a light tank but the armament and protection of a main battle tank; the protective capability of the type is enhanced by its low silhouette
FMC Close Combat Vehicle Light: this is a competitor in the US Army's Armored Gun System competition for a light combat vehicle needed by its newly organized light divisions; the FMC turret of the purely US model has a 105-mm (4·13-in) M68A1 rifled gun with a low-recoil system produced by Rheinmetall and an automatic loader plus 19-round magazine; another 24 rounds are stowed in the hull to replenish the loader; the secondary armament comprises a 7·62-mm (0·3-in) M240 co-axial machine-gun with 5,000 rounds, and the turret also sports a bank of 16 smoke-dischargers on each side; the gunner has a stabilized day/night sight plus laser range-finder and ballistic computer; the CCVL has a combat weight of 42,800 lb (19,414 kg), and its principal dimensions are lengths of 30·75 ft (9·37 m) with the gun forward and 20·33 ft (6·20 m) for the hull, a width of 8·83 ft (2·69 m) and a height of 7·75 ft (2·36 m); the CCVL is powered by a 575-hp (429-kW) Detroit Diesel 6V-92TA engine for a maximum road speed of 43·5 mph (70 km/h), and the fuel capacity of 150 US gal (568 litres) provides a road range of 300 miles (483 km)

Cadillac Gage Stingray

(USA)
Type: light tank
Crew: 4
Combat weight: 44,600 lb (20,231 kg)
Dimensions: length, gun forward 30·67 ft (9·35 m) and hull 20·67 ft (6·229 m); width 8·92 ft (2·71 m); height overall 8·33 ft (2·55 m)
Armament system: one 105-mm (4·13-in) ROF L7A3 rifled Low Recoil Force Gun with 36 rounds (28 in the hull and eight in the turret), one 7·62-mm (0·3-in) M240 co-axial machine-gun with 2,400 rounds, one 0·5-in (12·7-mm) Browning M2HB AA heavy machine-gun with 1,100 rounds, and four smoke-dischargers on each side of the turret; the turret is electro-hydraulically operated, the main gun is stabilized in elevation (−7·5° to +20°) and azimuth (360°), and a Marconi Digital Fire-Control System is fitted; this last includes stabilized OEC day/night optical/thermal sights, a laser range-finder, various sensors for ambient conditions, and a Cadillac Gage ballistic computer
Armour: welded steel
Powerplant: one 535-hp (399-kW) Detroit Diesel 8V-92TA diesel engine with 200 US gal (757 litres) of fuel
Performance: speed, road 41·5 mph (67 km/h); range, road 300 miles (483 km); fording 4·0 ft (1·22 m); gradient 60%; side slope 40%; vertical obstacle 30 in (0·76 m); trench 7·0 ft (2·13 m); ground clearance 18 in (0·46 m)

Variant

Stingray: produced as a private venture and first revealed in prototype form in 1984, the Stingray is Cadillac Gage's complement to the Commando series of wheeled armoured fighting vehicles, offering good firepower and mobility though only slight protection; this last is apparently a disincentive to export sales, and the company is investigating the possibility of additional protection through the use of appliqué ceramic or reactive armour, and further improvement in overall capability is promised by the adoption of a more advanced combination of primary optical sensors as well as a thermal imager; the vehicle can be supplied with chemical-resistant paint and individual NBC protection

Right: The Stingray (seen here in prototype form) was designed to offer its operators MBT firepower with light tank protection for a high level of strategic portability and tactical mobility.

Cadillac (General Motors) M41A3 Walker Bulldog

(USA)
Type: light tank
Crew: 4
Combat weight: 51,800 lb (23,496 kg)
Dimensions: length, gun forward 29·94 ft (8·212 m) and hull 19·09 ft (5·819 m); width 10·50 ft (3·20 m); height to top of cupola 8·94 ft (2·73 m)
Armament system: one 76-mm (3-in) M32A1 rifled gun with with 65 rounds, one 0·3-in (7·62-mm) M1919A4 co-axial machine-gun with 5,000 rounds, and one 0·5-in (12·7-mm) M2HB AA heavy machine-gun with 2,175 rounds; the turret is electro-hydraulically powered, the main gun lacks stabilization in either elevation (−9·5° to +19·5°) or azimuth (360°), and an optical fire-control system is fitted
Armour: cast and welded steel varying in thickness from 0·35 to 1·25 in (9·25 to 31·75 mm)
Powerplant: one 500-hp (373-kW) Avco Lycoming AOSI-895-5 petrol engine with 140 US gal (530 litres) of internal fuel
Performance: speed, road 45 mph (72·4 km/h); range, road 100 miles (161 km); fording 40 in (1·02 m); gradient 60%; side slope 30%; vertical obstacle 2·33 ft (0·71 m); trench 6·0 ft (1·83 m); ground clearance 17·75 in (0·45 m)

Variants

M41: this successor to the M24 Chaffee entered service in 1951, and is powered by the 500-hp (373-kW) Teledyne Continental Motors AOS-895-3 petrol engine; 76-mm (3-in) ammunition stowage is 57 rounds
M41A1: improved M41

Below: The M41's outmoded concept shows obsolete features such as a bow machine-gun.

M41A2: M41A1 with simplified gun and turret control systems, stowage for 65 rounds of 76-mm (3-in) ammunition, and fuel-injected AOSI-895-5 engine

M41A3: improved M41A2

M41 (Brazil): the Brazilian army is converting its M41 tanks to **M41Bro and M41C** standards in an extensive modernization programme run by Bernardini; for the M41B this involves the replacement of the original engine with a 300-kW (402-hp) Saab-Scania DS-14A 04 diesel for a maximum road speed of 70 km/h (43·5 mph), and the revision of the fuel tankage and electrical system; in the first 20 M41Bs the original 76-mm (3-in) gun was retained, but subsequent vehicles had their ordnances bored out from the original 76-mm (3-in) gun to 90-mm (3·54-in) calibre under the revised designation Ca 76/90 M32 BR1 so that Cockerill 90-mm (3·54-in) ammunition can be fired; other modifications include the provision of four smoke-dischargers on each side of the turret, and the incorporation of a night vision system; the M41C for the Brazilian marine corps is similar to the M41B but is powered by a DS-14 OA diesel engine and has a new fire-control system for the Ca 76/90 M32 BR1 gun able to fire an APFSDS round

M41 (Denmark): Danish vehicles are being upgraded by the installation of the 465-hp (347-kW) Cummins VTA-903T diesel for a range of 350 miles (563 km), a fire-suppression system, side skirts, a laser rangefinder, night vision devices, an NBC system, four smoke-dischargers on each side of the turret, and a 7·62-mm (0·3-in) DISA AA machine-gun in place of the original 0·5-in (12·7-mm) weapon

M41 (Spain): Spanish vehicles are being modified to **M41E** standard with the 400-hp (298-kW) Detroit Diesel 8V-71T diesel engine for a range of 300 miles (483 km) and, for a possible later retrofit, a 90-mm (3·54-in) gun

M41 (Thailand): the M41 light tanks operated by the Thai army are being upgraded to **M41GTI** (German Tank Improvement) standard by two West German concerns; this programme involves the replacement of the original petrol engine with a 330-kW (442-hp) MTU MB 833 Aa-501 diesel engine, the enlarging of the fuel capacity to 800 litres (176 Imp gal), the fitting of a fire-suppression system and the incorporation of many suspension improvements; the revised vehicle has a maximum road speed of 60 km/h (37·3 mph) and a range of 600 km (373 miles); the original main armament is retained, but the secondary armament now comprises two 7·62-mm (0·3-in) Heckler und Koch HK21E machine-guns, and other modifications are a stabilized gun-control system used in conjunction with the MOLF 41 fire-control system (including thermal imaging capability and a laser rangefinder), the addition of an NBC system, and the incorporation of dual-role dischargers for smoke and anti-personnel grenades; the combat weight of this variant is 24,500 kg (54,012 lb)

M41/Cockerill: the Belgian company Cockerill is supplying kits by which M41s can be retrofitted with a 90-mm (3·54-in) Cockerill Mk IV gun

M41 Upgrade: several upgrade packages are available for the improvement of in-service M41 light tanks; several of these centre on the power-pack, offering the Cummins VTA-903T, Detroit Diesel 8V-71T or Perkins (Rolls-Royce) Condor CV-8 diesels with improved transmission; Cadillac Gage offers its Turret Modernization System for the M41, this providing lighter weight, greater reliability, and considerably enhanced tracking and aiming for a greater probability of securing a first-round hit; there is also a new

APFSDS round for the M32 gun

Type 64: Taiwanese reworking of the M41A2/A3 with stronger armour (including a bolt-on outer layer of laminate steel), a Taiwanese development of the original main armament with higher performance, and upgraded secondary armament; further improvements may include a modern fire-control system (with laser rangefinder and ballistic computer), night vision equipment and (possibly) a new main gun

Cadillac (General Motors) M24 Chaffee

(USA)
Type: light tank
Crew: 5
Combat weight: 40,500 lb (18,371 kg)
Dimensions: length, gun forward 18·00 ft (5·49 m) and hull 16·50 ft (5·03 m); width 9·67 ft (2·95 m); height to top of commander's cupola 8·08 ft (2·46 m)
Armament system: one one 75-mm (2·95-in) M6 rifled gun with 48 rounds, two 0·3-in (7·62-mm) M1919A4 machine-guns (one bow and one co-axial) with 3,750 rounds, and one 0·5-in (12·7-mm) M2HB AA machine-gun with 440 rounds; the turret is hydraulically powered, the main gun lacks stabilization in either elevation (−10° to +15°) or azimuth (360°), and an optical fire-control system is fitted
Armour: cast and welded steel varying in thickness from 0·5 to 1·5 in (12·7 to 38·1 mm)
Powerplant: two 110-hp (82-kW) Cadillac 44T24 petrol engines with 110 US gal (416 litres) of internal fuel
Performance: speed, road 34 mph (55 km/h);

range, road 175 miles (281 km); fording 3·33 ft (1·02 m); gradient 60%; side slope 30%; vertical obstacle 36 in ft (0·91 m); trench 8·0 ft (2·44 m); ground clearance 18·0 in (0·46 m)

Variants
M24: the initial production model of this replacement for the M3 and M5 series was delivered in 1944, but the type is no longer in service in its original form
M24 (Norway): the Norwegians have converted a number of M24s to a more advanced standard, under the designation **NM-116**, with a 250-hp (186-kW) Detroit Diesel 6V-53T engine and a new armament layout, comprising a French 90-mm (3·54-in) GIAT D-925 main gun with 41 rounds (requiring the elimination of the bow machine-gun to provide additional ammunition-stowage volume), two 0·5-in (12·7-mm) M2HB machine-guns (one co-axial and one AA) with 500 rounds, and four smoke-dischargers on each side of the turret; other modifications have been made to the safety and fire-control systems, including the addition of a laser rangefinder; the performance of the NM-116 includes a maximum road speed of 57 km/h (35·4 mph) and a road range of 400 km (249 miles); the Norwegians have also developed an armoured recovery vehicle variant, the **BK 710** with an 11,000-kg (24,250-lb) capacity crane replacing the turret and with a 19,000-kg (41,887-lb) capacity winch
M24 (Taiwan): this is essentially similar to the Norwegian model, but the Taiwanese have also developed a flamethrower version in which the flame gun replaces the bow machine-gun

Used by some smaller countries, the M24 has a 75 mm (2·95-in) gun but lacks protection for anything but the reconnaissance role.

Henschel/Hanomag (Thyssen Henschel) Jagdpanzer Jaguar 1

(West Germany)
Type: tracked tank destroyer (missile)
Crew: 4
Combat weight: 25,500 kg (56,217 lb)
Dimensions: length, hull 6·61 m (21·69 ft); width 3·12 m (10·24 ft); height to hull top 1·98 m (6·50 ft) and including missiles 2·54 m (8·33 ft)
Armament system: one Euromissile K3S single-tube launcher with 20 HOT anti-tank missiles, two 7·62-mm (0·3-in) MG3 machine-guns (one bow and one AA) with 3,200 rounds, and eight smoke-dischargers on the hull roof
Armour: welded and spaced steel varying in thickness from 12 to 50 mm (0·47 to 1·97 in)
Powerplant: one 375-kW (503-hp) MTU MB 837 Aa diesel engine with 470 litres (103 Imp gal) of internal fuel
Performance: speed, road 70 km/h (43·5 mph); range, road 400 km (249 miles); fording 1·4 m (4·6 ft) without preparation and 2·1 m (6·9 ft) with preparation; gradient 58%; side slope 30%; vertical obstacle 0·75 m (29·5 in); trench 2·0 m (6·6 ft); ground clearance 0·44 m (17·3 in)

Variant

Jagdpanzer Jaguar 1: this vehicle is based on the same chassis as the Jagdpanzer Kanone tank destroyer and Marder mechanized infantry combat vehicle, and the type was built from 1967 with the designation **Jagdpanzer Rakete** and a primary armament of two SS.11 wire-guided missile launchers; between 1978 and 1983 316 of the 370 vehicles were rebuilt to Jaguar 1 standard with the HOT system; the type has also been evaluated with a four-tube Euromissile HCT launcher for HOT missiles, but no orders have been placed for this variant; standard equipment includes an NBC system and night vision devices

Its low silhouette and missile system make the Jagdpanzer Jaguar 1 an effective tank destroyer.

Henschel/Hanomag (Thyssen Henschel) Jagdpanzer Kanone (JPz 4-5)

(West Germany)
Type: tracked tank destroyer (gun)
Crew: 4
Combat weight: 27,500 kg (60,626 lb)
Dimensions: length, overall 8·75 m (28·71 ft) and hull 6·238 m (20·47 ft); width 2·98 m (9·78 ft); height without machine-gun 2·085 m (6·84 ft)
Armament system: one 90-mm (3·54-in) rifled gun with 51 rounds, two 7·62-mm (0·3-in) MG3 machine-guns (one co-axial and one AA) with 4,000 rounds, and eight smoke-dischargers on

In concept the Jagdpanzer Kanone dates back to World War II, but it is still a useful vehicle.

the hull roof; the gun is manually controlled and lacks stabilization in either elevation (−8° to +15°) or azimuth (15° left and 15° right of the centreline), and an optical fire-control system is fitted
Armour: welded and spaced steel varying in thickness from 12 to 50 mm (0·47 to 1·97 in)
Powerplant: one 375-kW (503-hp) MTU MB 837 Aa diesel engine with 470 litres (103 Imp gal) of internal fuel
Performance: speed, road 70 km/h (43·5 mph); range, road 400 km (249 miles); fording 1·4 m (4·6 ft) without preparation and 2·1 m (6·9 ft) with preparation; gradient 58%; side slope 30%; vertical obstacle 0·75 m (29·5 in); trench 2·0 m (6·6 ft); ground clearance 0·44 m (17·3 in)

Variants

Jagdpanzer Kanone: this is basically the same vehicle as the Jaguar 1 but armed with a 90-mm (3·54-mm) rifled gun rather than with a missile system, World War II experience having convinced the Germans that low-silhouette gun-armed vehicles were and still are highly effective tank-killers; 750 vehicles were produced between 1965 and 1967, and some thought has

been given to converting at least some of the survivors to mount a 105-mm (4·13-in) rifled or 120-mm (4·72-mm) smooth-bore gun; standard equipment includes an NBC system and night vision devices

Jagdpanzer Jaguar 2: produced by conversion of JPZ vehicles between 1983 and 1985, these 162 vehicles are similar to the Jaguar 1 but have a TOW anti-tank missile launcher and TAS-4 night sight rather than the main gun

JPK 90: Belgian variant of the Jagdpanzer Kanone differing in having the power train, suspension and tracks of the Marder mechanized infantry combat vehicle, a simplified version of the SABCA fire-control system used in the Leopard 1 main battle tank, Lyran flare launchers, passive night vision devices, and FN-MAG rather than MG3 machine-guns

IVECO Fiat/OTO Melara B1 Centauro

(Italy)
Type: wheeled tank destroyer (gun)
Crew: 4
Combat weight: 21,000 kg (46,296 lb)
Dimensions: length with gun forward not revealed and hull 7·00 m (22·97 ft); width 3·04 m (9·97 ft); height to turret roof 2·53 m (8·30 ft)
Armament system: one 105-mm (4·13-in) OTO Melara OTO 105/52 rifled gun with 40 rounds, one 7·62-mm (0·3-in) MG3 co-axial machine-gun with an unrevealed number of rounds, one 7·62-mm (0·3-in) MG3 AA machine-gun with an unrevealed number of rounds, and three smoke-dischargers on each side of the turret; the turret is power operated and the gun lacks stabilization in either elevation (− 6° to + 15°) or azimuth (360°), and an Officine Galileo fire-control system is fitted; this last includes stabilized optics, a laser rangefinder and ballistic computer
Armour: welded steel
Powerplant: one 390-kW (523-hp) IVECO (Fiat) MTCA V-6 diesel engine with an unrevealed quantity of internal fuel, driving an 8 × 8 layout
Performance: speed, road 100 km/h (62·1 mph); range, road 800 km (497 miles); other details not revealed

Variant
B1: this wheeled tank destroyer is being developed in parallel with the C1 main battle tank by the same partners, though primary responsibility for the B1 rests with IVECO rather than OTO Melara because of the former's greater experience with wheeled rather than tracked vehicles; the first prototypes of the B1 were revealed in 1986 after development on the basis of the Tipo 6636 AVH, a 6 × 6 armoured personnel carrier, and the type is expected to enter service by 1990; gun stabilization is not required because the Italian army expects to use its B1 equipments in stationary fire positions, but a more advanced turret is envisaged for export vehicles

Komatsu Type 60 Model C

(Japan)
Type: tracked tank destroyer (recoilless rifle)
Crew: 3
Combat weight: 8000 kg (26,247 lb)
Dimensions: length overall 4·30 m (14·11 ft); width 2·23 m (7·32 ft); height 1·59 m (5·22 ft)
Armament system: two 106-mm (4·17-mm) Type

60 recoilless rifles with eight rounds and one 0·5-in (12·7-mm) ranging machine-gun with an unrevealed number of rounds; the recoilless rifles are located on a manually powered mounting capable of elevation between − 20° and + 15° and traverse of 30° left and 30° right of the centre-line, and optical sights are fitted
Armour: welded and riveted steel to a maximum thickness of 12 mm (0·47 in)
Powerplant: one 110-kW (147·5-hp) Komatsu SA4D105 diesel engine with 77 litres (17 Imp gal) of internal fuel
Performance: speed, road 55 km/h (34 mph); range, road 130 km (81 miles); fording 1·0 m (3·3 ft); gradient 60%; side slope 30%; vertical obstacle 0·55 m (21·7 in); trench 1·8 m (5·9 ft); ground clearance 0·35 m (13·8 in)

Variants
Type 60 Model A: initial production model from 1960 with an 89-kW (120-hp) Komatsu 6T 120-2 diesel and a maximum speed of 45 km/h (28 mph)
Type 60 Model B: 1967 development with stronger construction
Type 60 Model C: definitive production model from 1975 to 1979 with more powerful engine; none of the variants has NBC protection

Talbot Cazador M41E TUA

(Spain)
Type: tracked tank destroyer (missile)
Crew: 4
Combat weight: 23,000 kg (50,705 lb)
Dimensions: length overall 5·84 m (19·16 ft); width 3·27 m (10·73 ft); height to hull top 1·91 m

(6·27 ft) and to top of extended launcher 3·46 m (11·35 ft)
Armament system: one Emerson Electric Improved TUA (TOW Under Armor) elevating launcher for 12 BGM-71 TOW anti-tank missiles, one 7·62-mm (0·3-in) machine-gun or 0·5-in (12·7-mm) Browning MB2HB heavy machine-gun with 2,000 rounds mounted on the launcher for local protection, and eight smoke-dischargers mounted on the glacis plate; smoke can also be generated by injecting fuel into the exhaust system
Armour: welded steel varying in thickness between 9·25 and 31·75 mm (0·36 and 1·25 in)
Powerplant: one 450-hp (336-kW) Detroit Diesel 8V-71T diesel engine with 850 litres (187 Imp gal) of internal fuel
Performance: speed, road 80 km/h (49·7 mph); range, road 560 km (348 miles); fording 1·016 m (40 in); gradient 60%; vertical obstacle 0·71 m (28 in); trench 1·828 m (6·0 ft); ground clearance not revealed

Variant
Cazador M41E TUA: produced as a private venture, this is a comparatively straightforward development of the Spanish-modernized M41E light tank chassis to accommodate the TUA launcher with two powerful TOW missiles plus 10 reload missiles inside the hull; a version with the HCT turret and four ready-to-fire Euromissile HOT anti-tank missiles has also been proposed.

The elevating missile launcher/sight system allows the hull and crew of Cazador M41E TUA to remain under cover while the missiles do their work. The launcher is retracted for travel and reloading from the 10 spare rounds carried in the hull.

Hagglund & Soner Infanterikanonvagn 91

(Sweden)
Type: tracked tank destroyer (gun)
Crew: 4
Combat weight: 16,300 kg (35,935 lb)
Dimensions: length, gun forward 8·84 m (29·00 ft) and hull 6·41 m (21·03 ft); width 3·00 m (9·84 ft); height to top of commander's cupola 2·32 m (7·61 ft)
Armament system: one 90-mm (3·54-in) Bofors KV 90 S 73 rifled gun with 59 rounds (43 in the hull and 16 in the turret), two 7·62-mm (0·3-in) machine-guns (one co-axial and one AA) with 4,250 rounds, two Lyran flare launchers on the turret roof, and six smoke-dischargers on each side of the turret; the turret is electro-hydraulically powered, the main gun lacks stabilization in either elevation (−10° to +15°, except over the rear arc where the figures are +1° to +15°) or azimuth (360°), and an optical fire-control system is fitted; this last includes optical sights, a laser rangefinder and a ballistic computer
Armour: welded steel
Powerplant: one 245-kW (329-hp) Volvo-Penta TD 120 A diesel engine with 400 litres (88 Imp gal) of internal fuel
Performance: speed, road 65 km/h (40·4 mph) and water 6·5 km/h (4 mph) driven by its tracks; range, road 500 km (311 miles); fording amphibious; gradient 60%; side slope 30%; vertical obstacle 0·8 m (31·5 in); trench 2·8 m (9·2 ft); ground clearance 0·37 m (14·6 in)

Variants
Ikv 91: developed in the later 1960s by Hagglund & Soner for service entry in 1975, this is a powerful tank destroyer with a capable fire-control system, and produced for the Swedish army between 1975 and 1978; the type is designed for arctic conditions and has NBC protection, but lacks night vision capability

Ikv 91-105: much improved version developed as a private venture on the basis of the Ikv 91 but fitted with the 105-mm (4·13-in) Rheinmetall Rh-105-11 low-impulse rifled gun and stowage for 40 rounds (under special circumstances the ammunition capacity can be increased to 50 rounds); the type has a weight of 18,000 kg (39,683 lb) but is still amphibious (with waterborne performance boosted when the two optional propellers are fitted), and its length is 9·72 m (31·89 ft) with gun forward; the type is also provided with a choice of two passive fire-control systems, one based on a low-light-level TV camera plus an IR scanner, and the other on a thermal imaging sight; the Ikv 91-105 is powered by a 270-kW (362-hp) Volvo TD 121 G diesel, and extra power and weight provide basically the same performance as in the Ikv 91

The Ikv 91-105 is lightly armoured, but the needle-nosed design of the turret front and mantlet provide adequate hull-down protection.

Hagglund & Soner Pvrbv 551

(Sweden)

Type: tracked tank-destroyer (missile)
Crew: 4
Combat weight: 9700 kg (21,384 lb)
Dimensions: length overall 4·81 m (15·78 ft); width 2·54 m (8·33 ft); height over raised missile launcher 2·98 m (9·78 ft)
Armament system: one single-tube TOW elevating launcher with an unrevealed number of missiles
Armour: welded steel
Powerplant: one 136-hp (101-kW) Ford Model 2658E petrol engine with 260 litres (57 Imp gal) of internal fuel
Performance: speed, road 41 km/h (25·5 mph); range, road 350 km (217 miles); fording 0·9 m (2·95 ft); gradient 60%; vertical obstacle not revealed; trench 1·5 m (4·9 ft); ground clearance 0·33 m (13 in)

Variant

Pvrbv 551: this vehicle has been produced by conversion of obsolete Ikv 102 and Ikv 103 infantry cannons, the whole powerplant and transmission being changed, the hull being extended to the rear, the protection and communications being upgraded and, perhaps most importantly of all, the glacis-mounted gun being removed (and the gap plated over) in favour of an elevating launcher for TOW anti-tank missiles stowed inside the hull

Above right: the Pvrbv 551 is another lightly armoured Swedish anti-tank vehicle, in this instance with a TOW launcher as primary weapon.

ASU-85

(USSR)

Type: airborne tracked tank destroyer (gun)
Crew: 4
Combat weight: 15,500 kg (34,171 lb)
Dimensions: length, overall 8·49 m (27·85 ft) and hull 6·00 m (19·69 ft); width 2·80 m (9·19 ft); height without AA machine-gun 2·10 m (6·89 ft)
Armament system: one 85-mm (3·35-in) D-70 rifled gun with 40 rounds, one co-axial 7·62-mm (0·3-in) SGMT machine-gun with 2,000 rounds, one 12·7-mm (0·5-in) DShKM AA heavy machine-gun with an unrevealed number of rounds, and (on some vehicles only) smoke-dischargers on the hull rear; the main gun is manually operated and lacks stabilization in either elevation (−4° to +15°) or azimuth (12°), and optical sights are fitted
Armour: welded steel varying in thickness from 8 to 40 mm (0·315 to 1·57 in)
Powerplant: one 180- or 210-kW (241- or 282-hp) Model V-6 diesel engine with 250 litres (55 Imp gal) of internal fuel
Performance: speed, road 45 km/h (28 mph); range, road 260 km (162 miles); fording 1·1 m (3·6 ft); gradient 70%; vertical obstacle 1·1 m (43·3 in); trench 2·8 m (9·2 ft); ground clearance 0·4 m (15·75 in)

Variant

ASU-85: developed in the late 1950s as the primary self-propelled tank destroyer of the Soviet airborne forces, the ASU-85 is based on the chassis and automotive system of the PT-76 light tank; standard equipment includes an NBC system and night vision devices

Above: Because of its airborne forces role, the ASU-85 has only very light protection.

ASU-57

(USSR)

Type: airborne tracked tank destroyer (gun)
Crew: 3
Combat weight: 3350 kg (7,385 lb)
Dimensions: length overall 4·995 m (16·39 ft) and hull 3·48 m (11·42 ft); width 2·086 m (6·84 ft); height 1·18 m (3·87 ft)

Armament system: one 57-mm Ch-51 or Ch-51M rifled gun with 40 rounds, and (some vehicles) one 7·62-mm (0·3-in) machine-gun with an unrevealed number of rounds; the main gun is manually operated and lacks stabilization in either elevation (an unrevealed arc) or azimuth (an unrevealed arc), and optical sights are fitted
Armour: welded steel to a maximum thickness of 6 mm (0·24 in)
Powerplant: one 41-kW (55-hp) Model M-20E petrol engine with 140 litres (31 Imp gal) of internal fuel
Performance: speed, road 45 km/h (28 mph);

range, road 250km (155miles); fording 0·7m (2·3ft); gradient 60%; side slope 30%; vertical obstacle 0·5m (19·7in); trench 1·4m (4·6ft); ground clearance 0·2m (8in)

Variant
ASU-57: developed in the early 1950s, the ASU-57 is a small and very low light assault gun/tank transporter designed for use by the Soviet airborne forces; the vehicle is very simple in concept and operation, and lacks modern features such as night vision devices and NBC protection

Right: The ASU-57 'tank destroyer' has capability now only against light AFVs and strongpoints.

American Locomotive/ Grand Blanc Tank Arsenal/ Massey Harris/Montreal Locomotive M36 Jackson

(USA)
Type: tracked tank destroyer (gun)
Crew: 5
Combat weight: 61,000 lb (27,670 kg)
Dimensions: length, gun forward not revealed and hull 19·50 ft (5·94 m); width 10·00 ft (3·05 m);

Below: The M36 Jackson is totally obsolete and only in very limited operational service.

height 10·33 ft (3·15 ft)
Armament: one 90-mm (3·54-mm) M3 rifled gun with 45 rounds and one 0·5-in (12·7-mm) Browning M2HB AA heavy machine-gun with 1,050 rounds; the turret is hydraulically powered, the main gun lacks stabilization in either elevation (−10° to +30°) or azimuth (360°), and optical sights are fitted

Armour: cast and welded steel up to a maximum thickness of 1·5 in (38·1 mm)
Powerplant: one 450-hp (336-kW) Ford GAA petrol engine with 192 US gal (727 litres) of internal fuel
Performance: speed, road 26 mph (42 km/h); range, road 155 miles (249 km); fording 3·0 ft (0·91 m); gradient 60%; vertical obstacle 18 in (0·46 m); trench 7·5 ft (2·23 m); ground clearance 17·4 in (0·44 m)

Variant
M36: a development of the legendary M4 Sherman medium tank, the M36 was introduced into service during 1943, and some examples remain in limited service to this day

General Motors Corporation (Buick) M18 Hellcat

(USA)
Type: tracked tank destroyer (gun)
Crew: 5
Combat weight: 37,577 lb (17,036 kg)
Dimensions: length, gun forward 21·83ft (6·65m) and hull 17·50ft (5·33m); width 9·42ft (2·87m); height 8·42ft (2·57m)
Armament system: one 76-mm (3-in) M1A rifled gun with 45 rounds and one 0·5-in (12·7-mm) Browning M2HB AA heavy machine-gun with 800 rounds; the turret is hydraulically powered, the main gun lacks stabilization in either elevation (−10° to +20°) or azimuth (360°), and optical sights are fitted
Armour: cast and welded steel varying in thickness from 0·3 to 1 in (7·9 to 25·4 mm)
Powerplant: one 400-hp (298-kW) Continental R-975-C4 petrol engine with 169 US gal (640 litres) of internal fuel
Performance: speed, road 55 mph (88 km/h); range, road 105 miles (169 km); fording 4·0 ft (1·22 m); gradient 60%; vertical obstacle 36 in (0·91 m); ground clearance 14·5 in (0·37 m)

Variant
M18: delivered in 1944, the Hellcat was designed round a capable anti-tank weapon and a high-speed chassis with good cross-country performance, and the type remains in limited service to this day

ACEC Cobra

(Belgium)

Type: tracked multi-role armoured fighting vehicle

Crew: 3

Combat weight: 9500 kg (20,944 lb)

Dimensions: length, gun forward 6·86 m (22·51 ft) and hull 4·81 m (15·78 ft); width 2·75 m (9·02 ft); height overall 2·20 m (7·22 ft)

Armament system: one 90-mm (3·54-in) MECAR KEnerga rifled gun with 29 rounds, one 7·62-mm (0·3-in) FN-MAG co-axial machine-gun with 750 rounds, and four smoke-dischargers on each side of the turret; the turret is electrically powered, the gun lacks stabilization in either elevation (−10° to +25°) or azimuth (360°), and an OIP LRS 5 optical fire-control system is fitted; this last includes day/night optical/thermal/image intensification sights, a laser rangefinder and a ballistic computer

Armour: welded steel

Powerplant: one 190-hp (142-kW) Cummins VT-190 diesel engine with 309 litres (68 Imp gal) of internal fuel and powering a diesel/electric drive

Performance: speed, road 75 km/h (46·6 mph); range, road 600 km (373 miles); fording 1·1 m (3·6 ft) without preparation and amphibious with preparation; gradient 60%; side slope 45%; vertical obstacle 0·6 m (23·6 in); trench 1·7 m (5·6 ft), ground clearance 0·4 m (15·75 in)

Variant

Cobra: designed as a private venture, this multi-role armoured fighting vehicle appeared in prototype form in 1987, and uses the hull and chassis of the same company's Cobra armoured personnel carrier; the currently envisaged armament is contained in the two-man ACEC AK90E turret, which can also accommodate the 90-mm (3·54-in) Cockerill Mk 7 gun; an alternative turret is the Cockerill C25 armed with a 25-mm Oerlikon-Bührle KBB cannon with 250 rounds, one 7·62-mm (0·3-in) co-axial machine-gun with 750 rounds, and eight smoke-dischargers (four on each side of the turret)

ENGESA EE-3 Jararaca

(Brazil)

Type: wheeled scout car

Crew: 3

Combat weight: 5800 kg (12,787 lb)

Dimensions: length overall 4·163 m (13·66 ft); width 2·235 m (7·33 ft); height to top of machine-gun 2·30 m (7·55 ft)

Armament system: see Variant (below)

Armour: welded bi-metallic steel

Powerplant: one 90-kW (121-hp) Mercedes-Benz OM 314A diesel engine with 140 litres (30·8 Imp gal) of internal fuel, and driving a 4 × 4 layout

Performance: speed, road 100 km/h (62·1 mph); range, road 700 km (435 miles); fording 0·6 m (2·0 ft); gradient 60%; side slope 30%; vertical obstacle 0·4 m (15·75 in); ground clearance 0·335 m (13·2 in)

Variant

EE-3 Jararaca: this light scout car was designed to partner ENGESA's other armoured fighting vehicles in the export market, and the use of a central tyre pressure-regulation system gives the EE-3 good cross-country mobility under very diverse terrain conditions; the armament installa-

Above: An EE-3 Jararaca scout car in basic form without its optional one-man machine-gun turret.

Below: The EE-3's machine-gun can be replaced by weapons such as this Milan missile launcher.

tion has also been made as wide as possible to attract customers with differing requirements, and pintle-mounted gun options include one 7·62-mm (0·3-in) medium machine-gun, one 0·5-in (12·7-mm) Browning M2HB heavy machine-gun or one 20-mm cannon; the EE-3 can alternatively carry a 60-mm (2·36-in) breech-loaded mortar, or one launcher for the Euromissile Milan anti-tank missile, or two cupola-mounted 7·62-mm (0·3-in) machine-guns, or the ENGESA ET-MD one-man turret with one 7·62-mm (0·3-in) and one 0·5-in (12·7-mm) machine-gun, or the ENGESA ET-20 one-man turret with one 7·62-mm (0·3-in) machine-gun and one 20-mm cannon; the turrets accommodate two smoke-dischargers on each side

ENGESA EE-T4 Ogum

(Brazil)

Type: tracked multi-role armoured fighting vehicle

Crew: 2-3

Combat weight: 4900 kg (10,802 lb)

Dimensions: length overall 3·70 m (12·14 ft); width 2·22 m (7·22 ft); height to top of hull 1·35 m (4·43 ft)

Armament system: see Variant (below)

Armour: welded bi-metallic steel

Powerplant: one 125-hp (93-kW) Perkins QT 20 B4 diesel engine with 160 litres (35·2 Imp gal) of internal fuel

Performance: speed, road 70 km/h (43·5 mph); range, road 450 km (280 miles); fording 0·8 m (2·6 ft); gradient 60%; side slope 30%; vertical obstacle 0·4 m (15·75 in); trench 1·5 m (4·9 ft), ground clearance 0·34 m (13·4 in)

Variant

EE-T4 Ogum: introduced in 1987, this is a very useful light armoured fighting vehicle of the multi-role type and designed specifically for the export market so successfully targeted by ENGESA; in many respects the Ogum bears similarities to the West German Wiesel, but is a more capable machine offered with a number of optional role fits and armaments; as a light armoured personnel carrier the Ogum can carry four infantrymen in its rear compartment, but more aggressive roles are generally planned with a cupola-mounted 0·5-in (12·7-mm) Browning M2HB heavy machine-gun or a turret-mounted 20-mm cannon in the reconnaissance role, or a 120-mm (4·7-in) mortar in the close-range fire-support role; in its last capacity the Ogum stows the mortar horizontally in the rear compartment for travel, the weapon being hinged out through 140° with its baseplate on the ground for action; only a few bombs can be carried in the mortar-fitted Ogum, a larger supply being carried in an accompanying vehicle; it is also anticipated that the Ogum can be developed as an ambulance (with a lengthened hull) or as a command post vehicle

---

ENGESA EE-9 Cascavel Mk IV

(Brazil)

Type: wheeled armoured car

Crew: 3

Combat weight: 13,400 kg (29,541 lb)

Dimensions: length, gun forward 6·20 m (20·34 ft) and hull 5·20 m (17·06 ft); width 2·64 m (8·66 ft); height to top of commander's cupola 2·68 m (8·79 ft)

Armament system: one 90-mm (3·54-in) Cockerill/ENGESA EC-90-III rifled gun with 44 rounds (20 in the hull and 24 in the turret, one 7·62-mm (0·3-in) co-axial machine-gun with 2,400 rounds, one optional 0·5-in (12·7-mm) M2HB or 7·62-mm (0·3-in) AA machine-gun with an unrevealed number of rounds, and two or three smoke-dischargers on each side of the turret; the turret is electrically powered, the main gun lacks stabilization in either elevation (−8° to +15°) or azimuth (360°), and an OIP LRS 5 or Marconi optical fire-control system (with optional laser rangefinder) is fitted

Armour: welded bi-metallic steel

Powerplant: typically one 212-hp (158-kW) Detroit Diesel 6V-53N diesel engine with 390 litres (86 Imp gal) of internal fuel, and driving a 6 × 6 layout

Performance: speed, road 100 km/h (62 mph); range, road 880 km (547 miles); fording 1·0 m (3·3 ft); gradient 60%; side slope 30%; vertical obstacle 0·6 m (23·6 in); ground clearance 0·375 m (14·75 in)

Variants

EE-9 Cascavel Mk I: this was the initial production model of the Cascavel, with deliveries beginning in 1974; armament was a 37-mm gun and the powerplant a Mercedes-Benz diesel; most have been upgraded with the ET-90 turret armed with a 90-mm (3·54-in) gun as described above

EE-9 Cascavel Mk II: export version of the Mk I but with automatic rather than manual transmission and a French-supplied Hispano-Suiza H 90 turret with 90-mm (3·54-in) GIAT CN-90 (F1) rifled gun

EE-9 Cascavel Mk III: upgraded model with Mercedes-Benz diesel plus automatic transmission, and the new ET-90 turret with Brazilian-built Cockerill 90-mm (3·54-in) rifled gun

EE-9 Cascavel Mk IV: improved model with different powerplant; fitted with the ET-90 turret, this was the first variant to have a central tyre pressure-regulation system; an integrated fire-control system is under development to provide the type with the capability of making full use of its powerful main gun

EE-9 Cascavel Mk V: identical with the Mk IV apart from the powerplant, in this instance a 140-kW (188-hp) Mercedes-Benz OM 352A diesel

A front view of the EE-9 Cascavel Mk IV shows its classic armoured car configuration.

GIAT AMX-10RC

(France)
Type: wheeled armoured reconnaissance vehicle
Crew: 4
Combat weight: 15,880 kg (35,009 lb)
Dimensions: length, gun forward 9·15 m (30·02 ft) and hull 6·357 m (20·86 ft); width 2·95 m (9·68 ft); height to turret top 2·215 m (7·27 ft)
Armament system: one 105-mm (4·13-in) GIAT CN-105 (F2 MECA) rifled gun with 38 rounds (26 in the hull and 12 in the turret), one 7·62-mm (0·3-in) co-axial machine-gun with 4,000 rounds, and two smoke-dischargers on each side of the turret; the turret is electro-hydraulically powered, the main gun lacks stabilization in either elevation (−8° to +20°) or azimuth (360°), and a COTAC fire-control system is fitted; this last includes stabilized optics, a low-light-level TV, a laser rangefinder, various sensors for ambient conditions, and a ballistic computer
Armour: welded aluminium
Powerplant: one 195-kW (261-hp) Renault (Hispano-Suiza) HS 115 diesel engine with an unrevealed quantity of internal fuel, and driving a 6 × 6 layout
Performance: speed, road 85 km/h (53 mph) and water 7·2 km/h (4·5 mph) driven by two waterjets; range, road 800 km (497 miles); fording amphibious; gradient 60%; side slope 40%; vertical obstacle 0·7 m (27·6 in); trench 1·15 m (3·8 ft); ground clearance variable between 0·2 and 0·6 m (7·8 and 23·6 in)

Variants
AMX-10RC: this is basically the reconnaissance version of the AMX-10P infantry fighting vehicle, and is fitted with the TK 105 turret; the type began to enter French service in 1979; the vehicle has an NBC system, and the advanced fire-control/observation system permits effective engagements by day or night; the latest production batches have the 225-kW (302-hp) Baudouin 6 F 11 SRX diesel, which is more fuel-efficient than the Hispano-Suiza and thus provides greater range on the same fuel capacity
AMX-10RAC: derivative with a TS 90 turret armed with a 90-mm (3·54-in) GIAT CS Super (F4) rifled gun and 37 rounds
AMX-10 RAA: proposed AA version with the Thomson-CSF/SAMM SABRE turret with two 30-mm cannon and associated fire-control system
AMX-10 RTT: proposed armoured personnel carrier version for a crew of 3 + 10 and armed with a 0·5-in (12·7-mm) Browning M2HB machine-gun or, alternatively, with a GIAT Dragar turret armed with a 25-mm cannon

---

Panhard EBR

(France)
Type: wheeled armoured car
Crew: 4
Combat weight: 13,500 kg (29,762 lb)
Dimensions: length, gun forward 6·15 m (20·18 m) and hull 5·56 m (18·24 m); width 2·42 m (7·94 m); height to turret top (on eight wheels) 2·32 m (7·61 ft)
Armament system: one 90-mm (3·54-in) GIAT CN-90 (F1) rifled gun with 43 rounds, one 7·5-mm (0·295-in) co-axial machine-gun with 2,000 rounds, and two smoke-dischargers on each side of the turret; the turret is hydraulically powered, the main gun lacks stabilization in either elevation

The AMX-10RC has very costly and complex systems, but combines the firepower of an MBT, the protection of a light tank, and the battlefield mobility of an armoured car.

(−10° to +15°) or azimuth (360°), and an optical fire-control system is fitted
Armour: cast and welded steel varying in thickness from 10 to 40 mm (0·39 to 1·57 in)
Powerplant: one 150-kW (201-hp) Panhard 12 H 6000 petrol engine with 380 litres (84 Imp gal) of internal fuel, and driving a 4 × 4 (optional 8 × 8) layout
Performance: speed, road 105 km/h (65·2 mpg); range, road 650 km (404 miles); fording 1·2 m (3·9 ft); gradient 60%; vertical obstacle 0·4 m (15·75 in); trench 2·0 m (6·6 ft); ground clearance on four wheels 0·33 m (13·0 in) and on eight wheels 0·41 m (16·1 in)

Variants
EBR: this heavy armoured car has recently been phased out of service with the French army, and is unusual in having front and rear drivers and alternative 4 × 4 or 8 × 8 drives, the four central tyreless wheels being lifted off the ground unless needed for extra traction in adverse conditions; the main armament system is the same as that of later AMX-13 light tanks, featuring a 90-mm (3·54-in) gun in an FL-11 oscillating turret
EBR ETT: 13,000-kg (28,660-lb) armoured personnel carrier version of the EBR, built in very small numbers; 12 infantry can be carried in addition to the crew of three, and armament comprises a turret-mounted 7·5-mm (0·295-in) machine-gun

The elderly EBR is still in limited service, but only with Mauritania and Morocco.

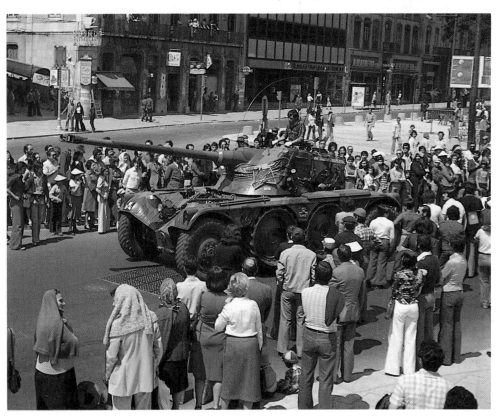

Renault VBC 90

(France)

Type: wheeled armoured car
Crew: 3
Combat weight: 13,500 kg (29,762 lb)
Dimensions: length, gun forward 8·135 m (26·69 ft) and hull 5·63 m (18·47 ft); width 2·50 m (8·20 ft); height to turret top 2·552 m (8·37 ft)
Armament system: one 90-mm (3·54-in) GIAT CS Super (F4) rifled gun with 45 rounds (25 in the hull and 20 in the turret), two 7·62-mm (0·3-in) machine-guns (one co-axial and one AA) with 4,000 rounds, and two smoke-dischargers on each side of the turret; the turret is manually powered with electrical assistance, the main gun lacks stabilization in either elevation (−8° to +15°) or azimuth (360°), and a SOPTAC or simpli-fied COTAC fire-control system is fitted; the SOPTAC type is an optical system with the option of laser rangefinding, and the COTAC type includes optical sights, a laser rangefinder, vari-ous sensors for ambient conditions, and a ballistic computer
Armour: cast and welded steel
Powerplant: one 170-kW (228-hp) Renault VI MIDS 06·20·45 diesel engine with an unrevealed quantity of internal fuel, and driving a 6 × 6 layout
Performance: speed, road 92 km/h (57·2 mph); range, road 1000 km (621 miles); fording 1·2 m (3·9 ft); gradient 50%; side slope 30%; vertical obstacle 0·6 m (23·6 in); trench 1·0 m (3·3 ft); ground clearance not revealed

The VBC 90 has been only a minor export suc-cess but, despite its use of a 90-mm (3·45-in) main gun with capable fire-control system, has been bought by the gendarmerie.

Variant

VBC 90: this is a powerful armoured car normally fitted with the GIAT TS 90 turret as described above; optional turrets are the Hispano-Suiza Lynx 90 with 90-mm (3·54-in) GIAT CN-90 (F1) rifled gun, the Hispano-Suiza MARS turret with a 90-mm rifled gun, the SAMM TTB 190 turret with 90-mm CS Super (F4) gun, the GIAT turret fitted with 81-mm (3·2-in) CL81 breech-loaded smooth-bore mortar, and the ESD TA-20 turret with two 20-mm cannon; optional extras are an NBC system and a front-mounted winch; the type has also been evaluated with the MECAR KEnerga 90/46 Weapons Station, a turreted installation with the 90-mm (3·54-in) KEnerga rifled gun and 50 rounds

LOHR RPX 90

(France)
Type: wheeled armoured car
Crew: 3
Combat weight: 11,000 kg (24,250 lb)
Dimensions: length, gun forward 7·408 m (24·30 ft) and hull 5·20 m (17·06 ft); width 2·65 m (8·69 ft); height to turret top 2·54 m (8·33 ft)
Armament system: one 90-mm (3·54-in) GIAT CN-90 (F1) rifled gun with 50 rounds (29 in the hull and 21 in the turret), one or two 7·62-mm (0·3-in) machine-guns (one co-axial and one optional AA) with 2,000 rounds, and two smoke-dischargers on each side of the turret; the turret is electro-hydraulically powered, the main gun lacks stabilization in either elevation (−8° to +35°) or azimuth (360°), and an optical fire-control system is fitted
Armour: welded steel
Powerplant: one 230-kW (308-hp) diesel engine with an unrevealed quantity of internal fuel, and driving a 6 × 6 layout
Performance: speed, road 110 km/h (82 mph); range, road 1000 km (621 miles); fording 1·4 m (4·6 ft); gradient 60%; side slope 40%; vertical obstacle 0·6 m (23·6 in); trench not revealed; ground clearance 0·5 m (19·7 in)

Variant
RPX 90: developed as a private venture and first tested in 1987, this is a small armoured reconnaissance vehicle notable for its powerful armament and good cross-country mobility, the latter conferred by the type's high power-to-weight ratio plus large low-pressure tyres; the prototype was fitted with the MARS 90 two-man turret, but as this has been taken off the market before entering production, the RPX 90 is now probably offered with the Lynx 90 turret; this turret can be fitted with the GIAT 90-mm (3·54-in) rifled gun as quoted in the specification above, but can also be fitted with the 90-mm (3·54-in) Cockerill Mk III rifled gun, whose maximum elevation is limited to +30°; other turret options include the Hispano-Suiza Serval fitted with a 60-mm (2·36-in) breech-loaded smooth-bore mortar, the GIAT TS 90 with GIAT 90-mm (3·54-in) CS Super (F4) rifled gun, a unit with six Matra Mistral SAMs, and other installations with 7·62-mm (0·3-in) machine-guns and/or 20-mm cannon

The RPX 90 can be fitted with the 90-mm (3·54-in) Lynx 90 turret or (right) the Serval unit with 60-mm mortar, 20-mm cannon and 7·62-mm machine-gun.

Panhard ERC 90 F4 Sagaie 2

(France)
Type: wheeled armoured car
Crew: 3
Combat weight: 10,000 kg (22,046 lb)
Dimensions: length, gun forward 7·97 m (26·15 ft) and hull 5·57 m (18·27 ft); width 2·70 m (8·86 ft); height 2·30 m (7·55 ft)
Armament system: one 90-mm (3·54-in) GIAT CS Super (F4) rifled gun with 32 or 33 rounds (13 in the hull and 20 in the turret), two 7·62-mm (0·3-in) machine-guns (one co-axial and one AA) with 2,500 rounds, and two or four smoke-dischargers on each side of the turret; the turret is electrically powered, the main gun lacks stabi-

Right: The ERC 90 F4 Sagaie 1 has the TS 90 turret and a single petrol engine by comparison with the Sagaie 2's twin diesel engines.

lization in either elevation (−8° to +15°) or azimuth (360°), and an optical fire-control system is fitted

Armour: welded steel

Powerplant: two 75-kW (101-hp) Peugeot XD 34T diesel engines, or two 108-kW (145-hp) Peugeot PVR petrol engines with 350 litres (77 Imp gal) of internal fuel, and driving a 4 × 4 (optional 6 × 6) layout

Performance: speed, road 110 km/h (68·4 mph) and water 7·2 km/h (4·5 mph) driven by two waterjets; range, road 600 km (373 miles); fording amphibious (standard version with foam-filled side boxes) or 1·2 m (3·9 ft) without preparation (desert version); gradient 50%; side slope 30%; vertical obstacle 0·8 m (31·5 in); trench 0·8 m (31·5 in); ground clearance 0·35 m (13·8 in)

Variant

ERC 90 F4 Sagaie 2: this is basically an improved version of the Sagaie 1 with an uparmoured SAMM TTB 90 turret in place of the Sagaie 1's TS 90 type; other improvements are an uprated twin-engined powerplant with greater fuel capacity, and a hull enlarged in length and width; a wide diversity of optional equipment can be installed; as on the Sagaie 1, the central pair of wheels can be lifted for road travel; on vehicles designed for desert operations the waterjets and foam filling for the side boxes can be omitted, and optional equipment includes air conditioning and an NBC system

Panhard ERC 90 F4 Sagaie 1

(France)

Type: wheeled armoured car

Crew: 3

Combat weight: 8100 kg (17,857 lb)

Dimensions: length, gun forward 7·693 m (25·24 ft) and hull 5·098 m (16·73 ft); width 2·495 m (8·19 ft); height 2·254 m (7·40 ft)

Armament system: one 90-mm (3·54-mm) GIAT CS Super (F4) rifled gun with 20 rounds (all in the turret), two 7·62-mm (0·3-in) machine-guns (one co-axial and one AA) with 2,000 rounds, and two smoke-dischargers on each side of the turret; the turret is manually powered, the main gun lacks stabilization in either elevation (−8° to +15°) or azimuth (360°), and an optical fire-control system is fitted

Armour: welded steel

Powerplant: one 115-kW (154-hp) Peugeot petrol engine with 242 litres (53 Imp gal) of internal fuel, and driving a 4 × 4 (optional 6 × 6) layout

Performance: speed, road 100 km/h (62 mph) and water 9·5 km/h (5·9 mph) driven by two waterjets or 4·5 km/h (2·8 mph) driven by its wheels; range, road 800 km (497 miles); fording amphibious (standard version with foam-filled side boxes) or 1·2 m (3·9 ft) without preparation

The ERC 90 F1 Lynx has the same basic ERC hull as the Sagaie 1, but carries the simpler, lighter but less well protected Lynx 90 turret.

(desert version); gradient 60%; side slope 30%; vertical obstacle 0·8 m (31·5 in); trench 1·1 m (3·6 ft); ground clearance 0·344 m (13·5 in)

Variants

ERC 90 F4 Sagaie 1: this is the baseline model of a potent armoured reconnaissance vehicle that began to enter service from 1979; optional extras are an NBC system, waterjet propulsion, air conditioning, land navigation system, and extra ammunition capacity (10 rounds for the main armament and 1,000 rounds for the secondary armament); like the other ERC models, this variant is now available with an 85-kW (114-hp) Mercedes-Benz OM 617A diesel, which boosts range to 1000 km (621 miles)

ERC 90 F4 Sagaie TTB 90: similar to the standard model, this variant has a TTB 190 rather than TS 90 turret, though the CS Super (F4) gun is retained together with 23 rounds of ammunition; gun stabilization, powered turret functions and a better fire-control system are also available as extras

ERC 90 F1 Lynx: similar to the standard model but fitted with a Hispano-Suiza Lynx 90 turret with 90-mm (3·54-in) GIAT CN-90 (F1) gun and 21 rounds; optional extras are the same as those of the Sagaie 1; this version weighs 7700 kg (16,975 lb) and has lengths of 6·115 m (20·06 ft) with the gun forward and 5·30 m (17·39 ft) for the hull

ERC 60-20 Serval: fitted with a revised turret, this 7000-kg (15,432-lb) model has a primary arma-

ment of one 60-mm (2·36-in) LR breech-loaded mortar with 50 rounds and one 20-mm cannon with 300 rounds

ERC 60/12 Mangouste: similar to the Serval, this model has a 60-mm (2·36-in) LR mortar with 60 rounds and one 0·5-in (12·7-mm) machine-gun with 1,200 rounds

EMC 81: mortar-carrier variant fitted with an open-topped turret and 81-mm (3·2-in) breech-loaded mortar, for which 78 rounds are provided

ERC Lanza: variant fitted with a SAMM TTB 125 turret armed with a 25-mm Hughes Chain Gun and 7·62-mm (0·3-in) co-axial machine-gun

ERC S 530 A: AA variant with a SAMM S 530 A turret with twin 20-mm cannon

ERC TA-20: AA variant with ESD TA-20 turret with twin 20-mm cannon

ERC 20 Kriss: AA variant fitted with SAMM TAB 220 turret with twin 20-mm cannon

Panhard AML H 90

(France)
Type: light wheeled armoured car
Crew: 3
Combat weight: 5500 kg (12,125 lb)
Dimensions: length, gun forward 5·11 m (16·77 ft) and hull 3·79 m (12·43 ft); width 1·97 m (6·46 m); height overall 2·07 m (6·79 m)
Armament system: one 90-mm (3·54-in) GIAT CN-90 (F1) rifled gun with 21 rounds, two 7·62-mm (0·3-in) machine-guns (one co-axial and the other AA) with 2,000 rounds, and two smoke-dischargers on each side of the turret; the turret is manually powered, the main gun lacks stabilization in either elevation (−8° to +15°) or azimuth (360°), and an optical fire-control system is fitted
Armour: welded steel varying in thickness from 8 to 12 mm (0·315 to 0·47 in)
Powerplant: (original models) one 65-kW (87-hp)

Panhard Model 4HD air-cooled petrol engine or (current models) one 75-kW (101-hp) Peugeot XD 3T diesel engine with 156 litres (34 Imp gal) of internal fuel, and driving a 4 × 4 layout
Performance: speed, road 90 km/h (56 mph); range, road (original models) 600 km (373 miles) or (current models) 800 km (497 miles); fording 1·1 m (3·6 ft) and with preparation amphibious; gradient 60%; side slope 30%; vertical obstacle 0·3 m (11·8 in); trench 0·8 m (2·6 ft) with one channel or 3·1 m (10·2 ft) with four channels; ground clearance 0·33 m (13 in)

Variants

AML H 90: the AML series began to enter service in 1961, and has since then been produced in large numbers for the domestic and export markets; the H 90 version is fitted with a powerfully armed Hispano-Suiza turret, which originally had provision for two SS.11 or ENTAC wire-guided anti-tank missiles, one located on each side of the turret

AML Lynx 90: successor to the H 90 version, the Lynx 90 variant is the current production model, and features a more advanced turret with provision for passive night vision equipment, laser rangefinder and powered traverse

AML HE 60-7: the HE 60 turret has twin 7·62-mm machine-guns on the left and a breech-loaded 60-mm (2·36-in) HB 60 mortar on the right, with 3,800 rounds and 53 rounds respectively, though these numbers are altered to 3,200 and 32 when additional radio equipment is fitted for the command role

AML HE 60-20: variant of the HE 60-7 type with a 20-mm cannon and 500 rounds in place of the twin 7·62-mm (0·3-in) machine-gun installation

AML HE 60-20 Serval: improved version of the HE 60-20 type with powerful M693 or KAD-B16 cannon with 300 rounds

AML S 530: AA version carrying the S 530 turret with two M621 (F1) 20-mm cannon and 600 rounds

AML TG 120: the TG 120 turret has a 20-mm cannon with 240 rounds and a co-axial 7·62-mm (0·3-in) machine-gun

EPR: this is the scout car model, basically the AML with its turret replaced by a ring-mounted 12·7-mm (0·5-in) heavy machine-gun; variants currently proposed are the **ERA** raider vehicle (one 20-mm cannon and two 7·62-mm/0·3-in machine-guns, or one 20-mm cannon and two lateral 7·62-mm/0·3-in machine-guns, one Milan anti-tank launcher with six missiles plus two lateral 7·62-mm/0·3-in machine-guns), the **EPF** border vehicle (one 0·5-in/12·7-mm or two 7·62-mm/0·3-in machine-guns plus a searchlight) and the **EPA** airfield protection vehicle (three 7·62-mm/0·3-in machine-guns and a searchlight)

AML 20: model with open-top TL 20 SO turret carrying one 20-mm M693 cannon and 1,000 rounds

AML Eclairage: scout car model with open-top turret fitted with one M693 20-mm cannon and one 7·62-mm (0·3-in) machine-gun plus 1,050 and 2,000 rounds respectively

Eland Mk 1: South African licence-built version of the AML HE 60-7 with a 60-mm mortar and two 7·62-mm (0·3-in) machine-guns

Eland Mk 2: improved version of the Eland Mk 1 with better engine and detail modifications

Eland Mk 5: Eland Mk 1 upgraded to the latest standard

Eland Mk 6: Eland Mk 2 upgraded to the latest standard

Eland Mk 7: current model produced with either the HE 60-7 turret or a more powerful turret featuring one 90-mm (3·54-in) GIAT CN-90 (F1) rifled gun and two 7·62-mm (0·3-in) machine-guns (one co-axial and one AA); other improvements are a quick-change engine, better suspension and transmission, and upgraded protection; this version is also known as the **Eland 90**

The four-wheel drive AML has powerful armament in its 90-mm (3·45-in) gun.

Panhard VBL

(France)

Type: wheeled reconnaissance/anti-tank vehicle
Crew: 2 (reconnaissance) or 3 (anti-tank version)
Combat weight: 3590 kg (7,914 lb) with NBC system
Dimensions: length overall 3·70 m (12·14 ft) or 3·82 m (12·53 ft) with additional fuel; width 2·02 m (6·63 ft); height overall 2·14 m (7·02 ft)
Armament system: one 7·62-mm (0·3-in) pintle-mounted machine-gun with 3,000 rounds, or one 0·5-in (12·7-mm) pintle-mounted machine-gun with 1,200 rounds, or one 7·62-mm machine-gun with 3,000 rounds plus one Milan anti-tank launcher with six missiles
Armour: welded steel varying in thickness from 5 to 11 mm (0·2 to 0·43 in)
Powerplant: one 80-kW (107-hp) Peugeot XD 3T diesel engine with an unrevealed quantity of internal fuel, and driving a 4 × 4 layout
Performance: speed, road 100 km/h (62·1 mph) and water 4 km/h (2·5 mph) driven by a single propeller; range, road 750 km (466 miles) with standard fuel or 1000 km (621 miles) with onboard fuel cans; fording 0·9 m (2·95 ft) and with preparation amphibious; gradient 50%; side slope 30%; vertical obstacle not revealed; trench not revealed; ground clearance 0·37 m (14·6 in)

Variants

VBL: the VBL was designed to a French requirement and first appeared in 1983; the French army is to use the VBL as a two-seat front-line intelligence gathering and reconnaissance vehicle, and as a three-man anti-tank machine; Panhard has proposed at least 22 derived models for a host of roles; the same chassis has been adopted for the Mygale/Aspic SAM system (both radar and missile vehicles), and is being evaluated with an alternative air surveillance radar for use with self-propelled mountings such as the VCR carrying RBS 70 Rayrider SAMs or the ERC Kriss with two 20-mm cannon

ULTRAV M11: 4000-kg (8,818-lb) version of the VBL optimized for jungle operations, 3·85 m (12·63 ft) long and carrying a SAMM BTM 208 one-man turret armed with two machine-guns (one 0·5-in/12·7-mm and one 7·62-mm/0·3-in weapon); the same basic vehicle has been proposed to meet a US requirement, with a weight of 3930 kg (8,664 lb) and an overall length of 3·82 m (12·53 ft) plus an armament of one 0·5-in (12·7-m) Browning M2HB heavy machine-gun with 600 rounds, plus an unspecified number of 40-mm grenade-launchers; another variant is a small armoured personnel carrier, with a capacity of 2 + 4 in a vehicle weighing 3900 kg (8,598 lb) and overall length increased to 3·91 m (12·83 ft) by increasing the wheelbase from 2·45 to 2·75 m (8·04 to 9·02 ft)

Below: A VBL prototype with a Milan anti-tank missile launcher.

LOHR RPX 6000

(France)

Type: wheeled scout car
Crew: between 2 and 4
Combat weight: 6300 kg (13,889 lb)
Dimensions: length overall 4·585 m (15·04 ft); width 2·164 m (7·10 ft); height without armament 1·65 m (5·41 ft)
Armament system: see Variant (below)
Armour: welded steel
Powerplant: one 135-kW (181-hp) BMW petrol engine with an unrevealed quantity of internal fuel, and driving a 4 × 4 layout
Performance: speed, road 110 km/h (68·4 mph); range, road 600 km (373 miles); fording 0·95 m (3·1 ft); gradient 60%; side slope 30%; vertical obstacle 0·4 m (15·75 in); trench not revealed; ground clearance 0·4 m (15·75 in)

Below: RPX 6000 with SAMM BTM turret, 60-mm grenade-launcher and 0·5-in machine gun.

Variant

RPX 6000: designed as a private venture and first tested in 1981, this is a light scout car notable, in common with other LOHR vehicles, for its good cross-country performance; the type can be fitted with a variety of turrets such as the Euromissile MCT with two ready-to-fire Milan medium anti-tank missiles, the Euromissile HCT with three ready-to-fire HOT heavy anti-tank missiles and one 7·62-mm (0·3-in) machine-gun, the one-man SAMM BTM 208 with two machine-guns (one 0·5-in/12·7-mm and one 7·62-mm/0·3-in weapon), the GIAT Capre with a 20-mm cannon plus 500 rounds and a 7·62-mm (0·3-in) machine-gun plus 2,000 rounds, a Helio installation with one 0·5-in (12·7-mm) heavy machine-gun and various grenade-launchers, as well as a number of other installations; the RPX 6000 is offered with a number of options such as amphibious capability, NBC protection and night vision devices; the type can also be fitted with a diesel powerplant, in the form of the 95-kW (127-hp) BMW unit for greater range and a maximum road speed of 90 km/h (55·9 mph), and in this form is designated **RPX 6000D**

LOHR VPX 5000

(France)

Type: tracked multi-role armoured vehicle
Crew: between 2 and 4
Combat weight: between 4600 and 5800 kg

(10,141 and 12,787 lb) depending on specific configuration

Dimensions: length overall 4·20 m (13·78 ft); width 2·00 m (6·56 ft); height without armament 1·60 m (5·25 ft)

Armament system: see Variants (below)

Armour: welded steel

Powerplant: one 135-kW (181-hp) BMW petrol engine with an unrevealed quantity of internal fuel

Performance: speed, road 80 km/h (49·7 mph); range, road 350 km (217 miles); fording 0·95 m (3·1 ft); gradient 60%; side slope 30%; vertical obstacle 0·5 m (19·7 in); trench not revealed; ground clearance 0·35 m (13·8 in)

Variants

VPX 5000: designed as a private venture and first tested in 1981, this is a light multi-role vehicle notable for the variety of turrets and installations that can be used to create a role-specific model; among these are the Euromissile MCT with two ready-to-fire Milan medium anti-tank missiles, the Euromissile HCT with three ready-to-fire HOT heavy anti-tank missiles and one 7·62-mm (0·3-in) machine-gun, the remotely controlled GIAT Mascot with one 7·62-mm (0·3-in) machine-gun (complemented by an infantry launcher for Milan anti-tank missiles over the hatch at the rear of the hull), and the one-man SAMM BTM 208 with two machine-guns (one 0·5-in/12·7-mm and one 7·62-mm/0·3-in weapon); the type can alternatively be fitted for air surveillance with any of several specialized radars with their antennae on elevating masts, or for battlefield surveillance with the RASIT radar, or as a mortar vehicle with one 81-mm (3·2-in) Thomson-Brandt mortar

VPX 40 M: dedicated 120-mm (4·72-in) mortar carrier based on the VPX 5000, but weighing 4500 kg (9,921 lb) and powered by a 95-kW (127-hp) petrol engine for a maximum road speed of 80 km/h (49·7 mph) and a maximum road range of 400 km (249 miles); the armament comprises one Thomson-Brandt MO-120-RT-61 rifled mortar with 20 rounds

LOHR RPX 3000

(France)

Type: wheeled multi-role armoured vehicle

Crew: 2 + 2

Combat weight: 3500 kg (7,716 lb)

Dimensions: length overall 3·75 m (12·30 ft); width 2·00 m (6·56 ft); height without armament 1·65 m (5·41 ft)

Armament system: see Variant (below)

Armour: welded steel

Powerplant: one 95-kW (127-hp) BMW diesel with an unrevealed quantity of internal fuel, and driving a 4 × 4 layout

Performance: speed, road 110 km/h (68·4 mph); range, road 600 km (373 miles); fording not revealed; gradient 60%; side slope 30%; vertical obstacle not revealed; trench not revealed; ground clearance 0·35 m (13·75 in)

Variant

RPX 3000: designed as a private venture and first tested in 1985, this is a light scout car and multi-role wheeled vehicle notable, in common with other LOHR vehicles, for its good cross-country performance; the type is generally fitted with one 7·62-mm (0·3-in) machine-gun at the front, for use by the commander or driver, and above the rear compartment either a machine-gun (7·62-mm/0·3-in or 0·5-in/12·7-mm type) or an infantry launcher for the Milan medium anti-tank missile

Above: A VPX 5000 with a remotely controlled GIAT Mascot mount for one 7·62-mm (0·3-in) machine-gun.

Below: This RPX 3000 carries a swivel-mounted 7·62-mm (0·3-in) machine-gun and a Milan launcher.

Thyssen Henschel Spahpanzer Luchs

(West Germany)

Type: wheeled reconnaissance vehicle

Crew: 4

Combat weight: 19,500 kg (42,989 lb)

Dimensions: length overall 7·743 m (25·40 ft); width 2·98 m (9·78 ft); height to machine-gun rail 2·905 m (9·53 ft)

Armament system: one 20-mm Rheinmetall MK 20 Rh 202 cannon with 375 rounds, one 7·62-mm (0·3-in) MG3A1 machine-gun with 100 ready-use rounds, and four smoke-dischargers on each side of the turret; the turret is electro-hydraulically powered, the main gun lacks stabilization in either elevation (−15° to +69°) or azimuth (360°), and an optical fire-control system is fitted

Armour: welded steel

Powerplant: one 290-kW (389-hp) Mercedes-Benz OM 403A multi-fuel engine with 500 litres (110 Imp gal) of internal fuel, and driving an 8 × 8 layout

Performance: speed, road 90 km/h (56 mph) and water 9 km/h (5·6 mph) driven by two propellers; range, road 800 km (497 miles); fording amphibious; gradient 60%; side slope 30%; vertical obstacle 0·6 m (23·6 in); trench 1·9 m (6·2 ft); ground clearance 0·44 m (17·3 in)

Variant

Spahpanzer Luchs: the Luchs (lynx) is the West German army's standard amphibious reconnaissance vehicle, and started to enter service in 1975; the type has a full NBC system and passive night vision devices, and can be driven equally rapidly forwards and backwards; it has been proposed that the Luchs could be developed as an air-defence vehicle with Roland SAMs (two in the ready-to-fire position plus reload missiles inside the hull); such a vehicle would be cheaper than a tracked vehicle, and possess an admirable blend of battlefield mobility and weight low enough for easy air portability

Above: With drivers at front and rear, the Spah-panzer Luchs can be driven equally fast in either direction, a distinct tactical advantage.

Below and bottom right: The TH 400 armoured car on trials with a weighted structure simulating the turret; several are available.

Thyssen Henschel TH 400

(West Germany)

Type: wheeled reconnaissance vehicle
Crew: 3-4
Combat weight: 23,000 kg (50,705 lb)
Dimensions: length overall 6·203 m (20·35 ft); width 2·98 m (9·78 ft); height 2·083 m (6·83 ft)
Armament system: see Variant (below)
Armour: welded steel
Powerplant: one 280-kW (375-hp) Mercedes-Benz OM 422 LA 90° diesel engine with 800 litres (176 Imp gal) of internal fuel, and driving a 6 × 6 layout
Performance: speed, road 95 km/h (59 mph); range, road 1000 km (621 miles); fording 1·2 m (3·9 ft); gradient 60%; side slope 30%; vertical obstacle 0·6 m (23·6 in); trench not revealed; ground clearance 0·465 m (18·3 in)

Variant

TH 400: first revealed in 1984, this is a private-venture development based on the company's investigation of a new type of double trailing-arm suspension for markedly improved mobility in adverse terrain; the design is optimized for maximum flexibility of operational equipment, options ranging from recovery gear to weapon turrets as different as the Fives-Cail Babcock FL-20 with a 105-mm (4·13-in) rifled gun and the Thomson-CSF SABRE with two 30-mm cannon

Porsche Wiesel

(West Germany)
Type: airportable tracked armoured vehicle
Crew: 2 (cannon-armed model) or 3 (TOW-armed model)
Combat weight: 2750 kg (6,063 lb)
Dimensions: length, gun forward (20-mm cannon version) 3·469 m (11·38 ft) and hull 3·265 m (10·71 ft); width 1·82 m (5·97 ft); height to hull top 1·252 m (4·11 ft) and overall 1·99 m (6·53 ft) for the TOW version and 1·875 m (6·15 ft) for the cannon version
Armament system: one 20-mm Rheinmetall MK 20 Rh 202 cannon with 400 rounds, or one TOW anti-tank launcher with eight missiles; the turret is manually powered, the cannon lacks stabilization in either elevation (−10° to +60°) or azimuth (50° left and 50° right of the centreline), and an optical fire-control system is fitted
Armour: welded steel
Powerplant: one 75-kW (101-hp) VW-Audi diesel engine with 80 litres (17·6 Imp gal) of internal fuel
Performance: speed, road 80 km/h (49·7 mph); range, road 300 km (186 miles); fording not revealed; gradient 60%; side slope 30%; vertical obstacle 0·4 m (15·75 in); trench 1·2 m (3·9 ft); ground clearance 0·3 m (11·9 in)

Variants

Wiesel MK 20 A1: designed for use by West German airborne units, and thus portable in transport aircraft and medium-lift helicopters, the Wiesel was developed by Porsche in the late 1970s but then cancelled, only to be reinstated for the West German army in the mid-1980s; this cannon-armed model has a one-man Keller und Knappich E6-II-A1 turret with a dual-feed cannon, for which a ready-use supply of 160 rounds is standard

Wiesel TOW A1: derivative of the basic model with a TOW overhead launcher and eight rounds; the launcher is elevated for firing, and has a total traverse angle of 90° (45° left and 45° right of the centreline); a number of other variants have been proposed, including an alternative anti-tank vehicle with the Euromissile HCT turret with two ready-to-use HOT heavy anti-tank missiles (as well as six reload missiles) and one 7·62-mm (0·3-in) machine-gun plus 500 rounds, a command vehicle with additional radio gear and one 7·62-mm (0·3-in) machine-gun plus 500 rounds, a RASIT radar-equipped battlefield surveillance vehicle with its antenna on a hydraulically elevated mast, a 2580-kg (5,688-lb) ammunition resupply vehicle with 14 TOW missiles and an armament of one 7·62-mm (0·3-in) machine-gun plus 500 rounds, a two-man recovery vehicle with a small crane, an anti-aircraft vehicle using a longer hull and fitted with one launcher for 10 RBS 70 Rayrider SAMs as well as one 7·62-mm (0·3-in) machine-gun plus 500 rounds, an alternative AA vehicle fitted with one four-rail launcher for 10 FIM-92 Stinger-POST SAMs as well as one 7·62-mm (0·3-in) machine-gun plus 500 rounds, a reconnaissance vehicle with the Rheinmetall TF 20·15 turret carrying one 20-mm MK 20 Rh 202 cannon plus 420 rounds, an ambulance based on a longer hull for the carriage of two litters and one seated casualty or four seated casualties, and an armoured personnel carrier based on a longer hull for a crew of 2+6

Top right: The Wiesel MK 20 A1 is the basic reconnaissance model with a 20-mm cannon.
Above right: In Czechoslovak service the FUG is known as the OT-65, and is seen here with its radio aerial being erected.

FUG

(Hungary)
Type: wheeled scout car
Crew: 2+4
Combat weight: 7000 kg (15,432 lb)
Dimensions: length overall 5·79 m (12·76 ft); width 2·50 m (8·20 m); height with turret (OT-65A) 2·25 m (7·38 m)
Armament system: one 7·62-mm (0·3-in) SGMB pintle-mounted machine-gun with 1,250 rounds
Armour: welded steel to a maximum thickness of 13 mm (0·51 in)
Powerplant: one 75-kW (101-hp) Csepel D.414·44 diesel engine with 200 litres (44 Imp gal) of internal fuel, and driving a 4 × 4 layout
Performance: speed, road 87 km/h (54 mph) and water 9 km/h (5·6 mph) propelled by two water-jets; range, road 600 km (373 miles); fording amphibious; gradient 60%; side slope 30%; vertical obstacle 0·4 m (15·75 in); trench 1·2 m (3·9 ft); ground clearance 0·34 m (13·4 in)

Variants

FUG: this light scout car entered service with the Hungarian army in 1964, and features a two-man crew with accommodation in the rear for four infantrymen; the type lacks NBC protection, and variants include an ambulance and an NBC reconnaissance vehicle; in Czech service the type is known as the **OT-65**

OT-65A: Czech variant with the turret of the OT-62B armoured personnel carrier installed over the hull; the turret is armed with a 7·62-mm vz 59T machine-gun and (on the outside of the right-hand side of the turret) an 82-mm (3·23-in) recoilless rifle

49

RAMTA RAM V-2L

(Israel)
Type: wheeled multi-role armoured fighting vehicle
Crew: 2+6
Combat weight: 6000 kg (13,228 lb)
Dimensions: length overall 5·50 m (18·04 ft); width 2·03 m (6·66 ft); height overall 2·20 m (7·22 ft)
Armament system: one 0·5-in (12·7-mm) Browning M2HB pintle-mounted heavy machine-gun with 1,500 rounds, or one 40-mm M129 pintle-mounted grenade-launcher with six ammunition boxes, or three 7·62-mm (0·3-in) Browning M1919A4 pintle-mounted machine-guns with 5,000 rounds, or one rocket-launcher with six rounds
Armour: steel to a maximum thickness of 8 mm (0·315 in)
Powerplant: one 100-kW (134-hp) Deutz diesel engine with 160 litres (35 Imp gal) of internal fuel, and driving a 4 × 4 layout
Performance: speed, road 96 km/h (60 mph); range, road 950 km (590 miles); fording 1·0 m (3·3 ft); gradient 60%; side slope 35%; vertical obstacle 0·8 m (31·5 in); trench not revealed; ground clearance 0·31 m (12·2 in)

Variants
RAM V-1: this first model entered service in 1980, and is the 3·4-m (11·15-ft) wheelbase short model of the open-top V-1 series with a crew of two plus four infantrymen, a combat weight of 5400 kg (11,905 lb) and a length of 5·02 m (16·47 ft); the type can be used as a limited-capability infantry fighting vehicle (three 7·62-mm/0·3-in machine-guns with 5,000 rounds and one anti-tank launcher with six rockets), or as an infantry combat vehicle (three 7·62-mm/0·3-in machine-guns with 5,000 rounds, one 52-mm mortar with 36 rounds, and two anti-tank rockets), or as a close-range anti-tank vehicle (one M40 106-mm/4·17-in recoilless rifle with 18 rounds), or as a long-range anti-tank vehicle (one TOW launcher with 16 mis-

siles and two 7·62-mm/0·3-in machine-guns with 2,500 rounds)
RAM V-1L: variant of the V-1 with a 3·8-m (12·47-ft) wheelbase for a crew of 2+6, a combat weight of 5600 kg (12,346 lb) and a length of 5·42 m (17·78 ft); the same armament options as the V-1 are available, together with an AA option carrying two 20-mm cannon and 720 rounds in a TCM-20 installation, or carrying the later TCM Mk 3 installation generally accommodating a pair of 23-mm cannon
RAM V-2: short-wheelbase model of the enclosed variant, with a crew of 2+6 (sometimes 2+8), a combat weight of 5700 kg (12,566 lb) and a length of 5·02 m (16·47 ft); the same type of armament options as the V-1 are available, together with one 0·5-in (12·7-mm) Browning machine-gun plus 1,500 rounds
RAM V-2L: long-wheelbase model of the V-2, with the whole range of armament options available for the V-2

Below: A RAM V-2L with one 0·5-in (12·7-mm) and two 7·62-mm (0·3-in) machine-guns.

RAMTA RBY Mk 1

(Israel)
Type: wheeled scout car
Crew: 2+6
Combat weight: 3600 kg (7,937 lb)
Dimensions: length overall 5·023 m (16·48 ft); width 2·03 m (6·66 ft); height empty without armament 1·66 m (5·45 ft)
Armament system: up to five 0·5-in (12·7-mm) Browning M2HB heavy machine-guns or 7·62-mm (0·3-in) medium machine-guns pintle-mounted round the fighting compartment
Armour: steel to a maximum thickness of 8 mm (0·315 in)
Powerplant: one 120-hp (89-kW) Chrysler 225-2 petrol engine with 140 litres (30·8 Imp gal) of internal fuel, and driving a 4 × 4 layout
Performance: speed, road 100 km/h (62·1 mph); range, road 550 km (342 miles); fording 0·75 m (2·5 ft); gradient 60%; side slope 35%; vertical

Above: An RBY Mk 1 with two 7·62-mm (0·3-in) machine-guns and personal weapons (an M16 rifle and anti-tank rocket-launcher).

obstacle not revealed; trench not revealed; ground clearance 0·27 m (10·6 in)

Variant
RBY Mk 1: announced in 1975, this is a simple but versatile multi-role scout car admirably suited to the Israeli concept of wide-ranging mobile warfare in which deep reconnaissance and attack is a crucial feature; the type can also be configured for the anti-tank role with a main armament of one 106-mm (4·17-in) recoilless rifle plus 16 rounds, and a secondary armament of two 7·62-mm (0·3-in) machine-guns plus 5,000 rounds

IVECO Fiat/OTO Melara Tipo 6616

(Italy)
Type: wheeled armoured car
Crew: 3
Combat weight: 8000 kg (17,637 lb)
Dimensions: length, gun forward not revealed and hull 5·37 m (17·62 ft); width 2·50 m (8·20 ft); height to turret roof 2·035 m (6·68 ft)

The Tipo 6616: very clean lines, 90-mm (3·45-in) Cockerill gun and OTO Melara turret.

The Tipo 6616: very clean lines, 90-mm (3·45-in) Cockerill gun and OTO Melara turret.

Armament system: one 20-mm Rheinmetall MK 20 Rh 202 cannon with 400 rounds (150 in the hull and 250 in the turret), one 7·62-mm (0·3-in) co-axial machine-gun with 1,000 rounds, and three smoke-dischargers on each side of the turret; the turret is electrically powered, the main gun lacks stabilization in either elevation (−5° to +35°) or azimuth (360°), and an optical fire-control system is fitted

Armour: welded steel varying in thickness from 6 to 8 mm (0·24 to 0·315 in)

Powerplant: one 120-kW (161-hp) Fiat modello 8062·24 diesel engine with 150 litres (33 Imp gal) of internal fuel, and driving a 4 × 4 layout

Performance: speed, road 100 km/h (62·1 mph) and water 5 km/h (3·1 mph) driven by its wheels; range, road 700 km (435 miles) and water 20 km (12·5 miles); fording amphibious; gradient 60%; side slope 30%; vertical obstacle 0·45 m (17·7 in); trench not revealed; ground clearance 0·37 m (14·6 in)

Variant
Tipo 6616: derived from the Tipo 6614 armoured personnel carrier, the Tipo 6616 began to enter service in the mid-1970s and has secured small export sales in addition to limited domestic use for paramilitary roles; the type has also been offered with alternative turrets; the two most important of these are the OTO Melara T90 CKL and the OTO Melara T60/70; the former is a two-man turret fitted with a 90-mm (3·54-in) Cockerill Mk III rifled gun plus 36 rounds (20 in the hull and 16 in the turret) and one 7·62-mm (0·3-in) co-axial machine-gun with 2,250 rounds to produce a vehicle with a combat weight of 8200 kg (18,078 lb), while the latter is fitted with a 60-mm (2·36-in) OTO Melara high-velocity gun (firing an APFSDS-T round with a muzzle velocity of 1615 m/5,299 ft per second) and 38 rounds, and two 7·62-mm (0·3-in) machine-guns

OTO Melara OTO R3 Capraia

(Italy)
Type: wheeled reconnaissance vehicle
Crew: 4 or 5
Combat weight: 3200 kg (7,055 lb)
Dimensions: length overall 4·86 m (15·94 ft); width 1·78 m (5·84 ft); height to hull top 1·55 m (5·09 ft)
Armament system: see Variant (below)
Armour: welded aluminium to a maximum thickness of 32 mm (1·26 in)
Powerplant: one 70-kW (94-hp) Fiat modello 8144·81·200 diesel engine with an unrevealed quantity of internal fuel, and driving a 4 × 4 layout
Performance: speed, road 105+ km/h (65·25+ mph) and water 8·5 km/h (5·3 mph) driven by two waterjets; range, road 500 km (311 miles); fording amphibious; gradient 75%; side slope 40%; vertical obstacle not revealed; trench not revealed; ground clearance 0·35 m (13·8 in)

Variant
OTO R3 Capraia: first revealed in 1982, this is a private venture development on a proven chassis to provide the basis for a multi-role reconnaissance vehicle with a crew of four, and a light armoured personnel carrier with a crew of 2 + 3; the reconnaissance variant can be fitted with a wide assortment of turrets such as the T 12·7 FA (with one externally mounted 0·5-in/12·7-mm Browning M2HB heavy machine-gun and 100 rounds), the T 7·62 FA (with one externally mounted 7·62-mm/0·3-in machine-gun and 80 rounds), the T 20 FA-HS (with one externally mounted 20-mm Oerlikon-Bührle KAD-B17 cannon and 120 rounds), the Folgore × 2 FA (with two Breda Folgore anti-tank launchers and one 7·62-mm/0·3-in machine-gun plus 80 rounds), the T 106 × 2 FA (with two externally mounted 106-mm/4·17-in M40 recoilless rifles) and a turret with one launcher for the BGM-71 TOW heavy anti-tank missile

An OTO R3 with the 20-mm cannon of its T 20 FA-HS remotely controlled turret (with external ammunition magazine) in action.

Komatsu Type 87

(Japan)

Type: wheeled reconnaissance and patrol vehicle

Crew: 5

Combat weight: 13,500 kg (29,762 lb)

Dimensions: length overall 5·37 m (17·62 ft); width 2·48 m (8·14 ft); height 2·38 m (7·80 ft)

Armament system: one 25-mm Oerlikon KBA cannon with an unrevealed number of rounds, one 7·62-mm (0·3-in) Type 74 co-axial machine-gun with an unrevealed number of rounds, and three smoke-dischargers on each side of the turret; the turret is electrically powered, the main gun lacks stabilization in either elevation (an unrevealed arc) or azimuth (360°), and an optical fire-control system is fitted

Armour: welded steel

Powerplant: one 227·5-kW (305-hp) Isuzu 10PB1 diesel engine with an unrevealed quantity of internal fuel, and driving a 6 × 6 layout

Performance: speed, road 100 km/h (62·1 mph); range, road not revealed; fording 1·0 m (3·3 ft); gradient 60%; side slope not revealed; vertical obstacle 0·6 m (23·6 in); trench 1·5 m (4·9 ft); ground clearance 0·45 m (17·7 in)

Variants

Type 82: this is a specialist eight-crew command and communications version of the Type 87, weighing 13,600 kg (29,982 lb) and having an overall length of 5·72 m (18·77 ft); the armament comprises one 7·62-mm (0·3-in) and one 0·5-in (12·7-mm) machine-gun, each ring-mounted; the type entered service in the mid-1980s

Type 87: also entering service in the mid-1980s, this is the reconnaissance and patrol version of the Type 82 with a revised superstructure to accommodate the cannon-armed turret

---

Abdallah Al-Faris Dera Al Jazirah 2

(Saudi Arabia)

Type: wheeled armoured car

Crew: 2 + 7

Combat weight: 18,500 kg (40,785 lb)

Dimensions: length overall 6·99 m (22·93 ft); width 2·94 m (9·65 ft); height to hull top 2·05 m (6·73 ft)

Armament system: one 90-mm (3·54-in) Cockerill Mk 7 rifled gun with an unrevealed number of rounds (15 in the turret and an unrevealed number in the hull), one 7·62-mm (0·3-in) co-axial machine-gun with 250 ready-use rounds, one 7·62-mm (0·3-in) optional AA machine-gun with 250 ready-use rounds and four smoke-dischargers on each side of the turret; the turret is electrically powered, the main gun lacks stabilization in either elevation (−9° to +20°) or azimuth (360°), and an optical fire-control system is fitted

Armour: welded steel

Powerplant: one 310-kW (416-hp) KHD diesel engine with an unrevealed quantity of internal fuel, and driving a 6 × 6 layout

Performance: speed, road 105 km/h (65·25 mph) and water unrevealed driven by two propellers; range, road 1000 km (621 miles); fording amphibious; gradient not revealed; side slope not revealed; vertical obstacle not revealed; trench not revealed; ground clearance variable between 0·19 and 0·64 m (7·5 and 25·2 in)

Variant

Al Jazirah 2: this has been developed as a private venture since 1983 on the basis of the Al Jazirah wheeled armoured personnel carrier, and amongst its features are variable suspension, power steering and a central tyre pressure-regulation system; the turret is of the Cockerill LCTS 90 mm type

---

Armscor Rooikat

(South Africa)

Type: wheeled armoured car

Crew: 4

Combat weight: not revealed

Dimensions: not revealed

Armament system: one 76·2-mm (3-in) rifled gun with an unrevealed number of rounds, two 7·62-mm (0·3-in) machine-guns (one co-axial and one AA) with an unrevealed number of rounds, and four smoke-dischargers on each side of the turret; the turret is powered, the main gun is stabilized in elevation (an unrevealed arc) but not in azimuth (360°), and an optical fire-control system is fitted; this last includes stabilized image-intensification optics and a laser range-finder

Armour: welded steel

Powerplant: one diesel engine of unrevealed power with an unrevealed quantity of internal fuel, and driving an 8 × 8 layout

Performance: speed, road 120 km/h (74·6 mph); range, road 1000 km (621 miles); other details not revealed

Variant

Rooikat: under development in the late 1980s by Armscor for production by Sandock-Austral (chassis and system integration) and Lyttleton Engineering (turret and weapons system), the Rooikat (lynx) is designed to replace the Eland 4 × 4 armoured car; the type has a comparatively small-calibre main gun, but this is a high-velocity type firing HE-T and APFSDS ammunition, the former for the support role and the latter for the anti-tank role; the locally developed APFSDS projectile is reckoned capable of defeating Soviet tanks up to the T-62 at any angle of attack out to a theoretical maximum range of 3000 m (3,280 yards); the Rooikat is fitted as standard with a biological/chemical warfare defence system

ENASA VEC

(Spain)

Type: wheeled reconnaissance vehicle

Crew: 5

Combat weight: 13,750 kg (30,313 lb)

Dimensions: length, gun forward not revealed and hull 6·25 m (20·50 ft); width 2·50 m (8·20 ft); height to hull top 2·00 m (6·56 ft)

Armament system: one 25-mm McDonnell Douglas Helicopters M242 Bushmaster cannon with an unrevealed number of rounds (an unrevealed number in the hull and 170 in the turret), one 7·62-mm (0·3-in) co-axial machine-gun with 400 rounds, and three smoke-dischargers on each side of the turret; the turret is electrically powered, the main gun lacks stabilization in either elevation (−10° to +50°) or azimuth (360°), and an optical fire-control system is fitted

Armour: welded aluminium

Powerplant: one 230-kW (308-hp) Pegaso modelo 9157/8 diesel engine with 400 litres (88 Imp gal) of internal fuel, and driving a 6 × 6 layout

Performance: speed, road 106 km/h (65·9 mph) and water 3 km/h (1·86 mph) driven by its wheels or 9 km/h (5·6 mph) driven by two waterjets; range, road 800 km (497 miles); fording amphibious; gradient 60%; side slope 30%; vertical obstacle 0·6 m (23·6 in); trench 1·5 m (4·9 ft); ground clearance 0·4 m (15·75 in)

Variant

VEC: this derivative of the BMR-600 infantry fighting vehicle entered Spanish service in the early 1980s, and is designed as a cavalry scout vehicle with good protection and a 25-mm cannon in a slight modification of the OTO Melara T 25 turret; for export sales a wide diversity of armament fits is offered, such as one 20-mm Rheinmetall MK 20 Rh 202 cannon (in a Fiat/OTO Melara T 20 turret), or one 20-mm Oerlikon-Bührle KAA cannon (in a GAD-BOA turret), or one 25-mm Oerlikon KBA-B cannon (in a GBD-COA or T 25 turret), plus 7·62-mm (0·3-in) and/or 0·5-in (12·7-mm) Browning machine-guns and three smoke-dischargers on each side of the turret; other options include an AA version with turreted cannon, or an anti-tank version with wire-guided missiles, or a fire-support vehicle with a 90-mm (3·54-in) rifled gun; optional equipment includes waterjet propulsion, NBC protection, a 4500-kg (9,921-lb) capacity winch, a land navigation system, and additional communications gear

MOWAG Shark

(Switzerland)

Type: wheeled reconnaissance vehicle and multi-role weapon carrier

Crew: 3 or 4

Combat weight: up to 22,000 kg (48,501 lb) depending on specific weapon installation

Dimensions: length, gun forward dependent on specific weapon installation and hull 7·52 m (24·67 ft); width 3·00 m (9·84 ft); height to top of hull 1·90 m (6·23 ft)

Armament system: see Variant (below)

Armour: welded steel

Powerplant: one 600-hp (448-kW) Detroit Diesel 8V-71TA diesel engine with 400 litres (88 Imp gal) of internal fuel, and driving an 8 × 8 layout

Performance: speed, road 100 km/h (62·1 mph); range, road 500 km (311 miles); fording 1·3 m (4·3 ft); gradient 60%; side slope 35%; vertical obstacle 0·46 m (18·1 in); trench 2·3 m (7·55 ft); ground clearance 0·46 m (18·1 in)

Variant

Shark: developed as a private venture aimed at the export market, the Shark is an advanced type using proved components and assemblies, and designed as a multi-role vehicle depending on the specific armament fit; the prototype first appeared in 1981 with the two-man Oerlikon-Bührle GDD-BOE turret, armed with one 35-mm Oerlikon-Bührle KDE cannon with 151 rounds, one 7·62-mm (0·3-in) co-axial machine-gun with 230 rounds, and six smoke-dischargers on the rear of the turret; this installation featured turret and main armament stabilization, but is no longer offered; current options include the turret developed for the Krauss-Maffei Wildcat self-propelled AA system (a radar-fitted installation with two 30-mm Mauser MK 30 Model F cannon) and three types with a 105-mm (4·13-in) rifled gun; these latter are the Fives-Cail Babcock FL-12 (and upgraded FL-15) with the GIAT CN-105/57 gun and co-axial machine-gun, the Fives-Cail Babcock FL-20 with the GIAT CN-105 (F1) gun and 20-mm GIAT M693 (F2) co-axial cannon, and the Rheinmetall LPTS with the Rh-105-11 super low recoil gun, two 7·62-mm (0·3-in) machine-guns (one co-axial and one AA), and one 76-mm (3-in) grenade-launcher for local defence; the Shark has ample volume for the addition of features such as extra ammunition stowage, an NBC system, and a fire-suppression system; night vision devices are another option; for service further into the future MOWAG is investigating the possibility of armament fits as diverse as the Martin Marietta/Oerlikon-Bührle ADATS installation with dual-role anti-aircraft and anti-tank missiles, the Thomson-CSF Crotale installation with four R.440 SAMs, various anti-tank installations and at least one rocket-launcher installation

MOWAG SPY

(Switzerland)

Type: wheeled reconnaissance vehicle

Crew: 3

Combat weight: 7500 kg (16,534 lb)

Dimensions: length overall 4·52 m (14·83 ft); width 2·50 m (8·20 ft); height to top of hull 1·66 m (5·45 ft)

Armament system: one 0·5-in (12·7-mm) Browning M2HB machine-gun with 3,000 rounds, one co-axial 0·3-in (7·62-mm) Browning M1919 machine-gun with 2,000 rounds, and three smoke-

SPY with Type V 042 turret and remotely controlled 0·5-in (12·7-mm) machine-gun.

dischargers on each side of the turret; the turret is manually powered, the main gun lacks stabilization in either elevation (−10° to +50°) or azimuth (360°), and an optical fire-control system is fitted

Armour: welded steel

Powerplant: one 205-hp (153-kW) Detroit Diesel 8V-71 diesel engine with 200 litres (44 Imp gal) of internal fuel, and driving a 4 × 4 layout

Performance: speed, road 110 km/h (68·4 mph); range, road 700 km (435 miles); fording 1·3 m (4·3 ft); gradient 60%; side slope 35%; vertical obstacle 0·5 m (19·7 in); trench not revealed; ground clearance 0·39 m (15·4 in)

Variant

SPY: using many components of the Piranha armoured fighting vehicle series, the SPY is a light reconnaissance vehicle that began to enter service with an undisclosed Far Eastern country in the mid-1980s; the type is fitted with a MOWAG one-man turret, either the V 041 with manually controlled 7·62-mm (0·3-in) machine-guns, or the V 042 with a remotely controlled 0·5-in (12·7-mm) machine-gun

Left: A Shark weapons carrier with a Crotale quadruple launcher for R.440 SAMs.
Far left: A VEC with an OTO Melara T 25 turret and all hatches open.

BRDM-2

(USSR)

Type: wheeled scout car
Crew: 4
Combat weight: 7000 kg (15,432 lb)
Dimensions: length overall 5·75 m (18·86 ft); width 2·35 m (7·71 ft); height 2·31 m (7·58 ft)
Armament system: one 14·5-mm (0·57-in) KPVT heavy machine-gun with 500 rounds, and one co-axial 7·62-mm (0·3-in) PKT machine-gun with 2,000 rounds; the turret is manually powered, the main gun lacks stabilization in either elevation (−5° to +30°) or azimuth (360°), and an optical fire-control system is fitted
Armour: welded steel varying in thickness from 2 to 14 mm (0·08 to 0·55 in)
Powerplant: one 105-kW (141-hp) GAZ-41 petrol engine with 290 litres (64 Imp gal) of internal fuel, and driving a 4 × 4 (optional 8 × 8) layout
Performance: speed, road 100 km/h (62·1 mph) and water 10 km/h (6·2 mph) driven by one water-jet; range, road 750 km (466 miles); fording amphibious; gradient 60%; vertical obstacle 0·4 m (15·75 in); trench 1·25 m (4·1 ft); ground clearance 0·43 m (16·9 in)

Below: BRDM-2 scout cars on manoeuvres, windscreen armoured shutters raised.

Variants

BRDM-2: developed in the late 1950s as successor to the BRDM-1, the BRDM-2 differs from its predecessor in having enclosed armament and a more powerful engine located at the rear for better road, cross-country and water performance; there are four semi-retractable chain-driven belly wheels (two on each side) for additional traction in difficult going; standard equipment includes an NBC system and waterjet propulsion

BRDM-2-RKh: nuclear and chemical reconnaissance version of the baseline model, distinguishable by the racks for automatically positioned marker poles

BRDM-2U: command version with a hatch in place of the turret, and additional generating capacity for the extra radio equipment carried

BRDM-2 'Swatter': anti-tank version with the turret replaced by an overhead-covered retractable arm launcher for four AT-2 'Swatter-C' IR-homing missiles; four reloads are carried inside the hull; the variant appeared in the early 1970s and, like other missile-equipped variants, has a crew reduced to two or three so that four reload missiles can be accommodated inside the hull

BRDM-2 'Sagger': anti-tank version with the turret replaced by an overhead-covered retractable arm launcher for six AT-3 'Sagger' wire-

guided missiles; eight reloads are carried inside the hull; the variant appeared in the early 1970s

BRDM-2 'Spandrel': anti-tank version with its turret surmounted by five launcher tubes for AT-5 'Spandrel' semi-automatic command to line of sight missiles; another 10 missiles are carried inside the hull; the variant appeared in the mid-1970s

BRDM-2/SA-9 'Gaskin': introduced in 1968, this is a self-propelled SAM system mounted on the chassis of the BRDM-2 reconnaissance vehicle and designed to provide regimental-level short-range defence against low-level air threats; threat detection is entrusted to a battery-level truck-mounted 'Gun Dish' radar, which passes target information to the 'Gaskin' launch vehicles, which each have an erector/launcher in place of the normal turret; this combined erector/launcher carries two missile container/launchers on each side of the central pedestal, and four reload rounds are carried on the outside of the launch vehicle's hull; the engagement envelope for the IR-homing missiles are minimum/maximum ranges of 500/8000 m (550/8,750 yards) and minimum/maximum altitudes of 20/5000 m (65/16,405 ft)

Right: The BRDM-1 is far inferior to its successor, the BRDM-2.

BRDM-1

(USSR)

Type: wheeled scout car
Crew: 5
Combat weight: 5600 kg (12,346 lb)
Dimensions: length overall 5·70 m (18·70 ft); width 2·25 m (7·38 ft); height without armament 1·90 m (6·23 ft)
Armament system: one 7·62-mm (0·3-in) SGMB pintle-mounted machine-gun with 1,250 rounds
Armour: welded steel to a maximum thickness of 10 mm (0·39 in)
Powerplant: one 65-kW (87-hp) GAZ-40P petrol engine with 150 litres (33 Imp gal) of internal fuel, and driving a 4 × 4 (optional 8 × 8) layout
Performance: speed, road 80 km/h (49·7 mph) and water 9 km/h (5·6 mph) driven by one water-jet; range, road 500 km (311 miles); fording amphibious; gradient 60%; vertical obstacle 0·4 m (15·75 in); trench 1·22 m (4·0 ft); ground clearance 0·315 m (12·4 in)

Variants

BRDM-1: this amphibious scout car became standard in Warsaw Pact armies from 1959, and was notable for its four chain-driven semi-retractable belly wheels (for improved performance in adverse conditions), its exposed main armament and its lack of NBC protection

BRDM-U: command version with extra antennae

BRDM-RKh: nuclear and chemical reconnaissance version with racks for the automatic marking of safe lanes with special poles

BRDM-1 'Snapper': anti-tank version with the superstructure extended aft for the location of a fixed triple launcher for AT-1 'Snapper' missiles; reserve missiles are stored in the hull; in this application the crew is reduced to two or three

BRDM-1 'Swatter': anti-tank version with a fixed quadruple launcher for AT-2 'Swatter-A' missiles; crew is reduced to two or three

BRDM-1 'Sagger': anti-tank version with elevating and overhead-covered six-rail launcher for AT-3 'Sagger' missiles; this variant has a crew of two or three, and first appeared in 1965

Alvis FV601(C) Saladin Mk 2

(UK)
Type: wheeled armoured car
Crew: 3
Combat weight: 25,550 lb (11,589 kg)
Dimensions: length, gun forward 17·33 ft (5·284 m) and hull 16·16 ft (4·93 m); width 8·33 ft (2·54 m); height to turret roof 7·19 ft (2·19 m)
Armament system: one 76-mm (3-in) L5A1 rifled gun with 42 rounds (31 in the hull and 11 in the turret), two 0·3-in (7·62-mm) Browning M1919 machine-guns (one co-axial L3A3 and one AA L3A4) with 2,750 rounds, and six smoke-dischargers on each side of the turret; the turret is electrically powered, the main armament lacks stabilization in either elevation (−10° to +20°) or azimuth (360°), and an optical fire-control system is fitted
Armour: welded steel varying in thickness from 0·315 to 1·25 in (8 to 32 mm)
Powerplant: one 170-hp (127-kW) Rolls-Royce B80 Mk 6A petrol engine with 53 Imp gal (241 litres) of internal fuel, and driving a 6 × 6 layout
Performance: speed, road 45 mph (72 km/h); range, road 250 miles (400 km); fording 3·5 ft (1·07 m) without preparation and 7·0 ft (2·13 m) with preparation; gradient 46%; side slope not revealed; vertical obstacle 18 in (0·46 m); trench 5·0 ft (1·52 m); ground clearance 16·75 in (0·43 m)

Variants

FV601C Saladin Mk 2: this British armoured car entered service in 1959, and is still a modestly useful vehicle in areas where its lack of NBC protection or night-vision equipment is not a major disadvantage
FV601(D): used by the West German border police as the **Geschutzer Sonderwagen III (Kfz 93)**, this version of the Saladin lacks the co-axial machine-gun

Below: The short-barrelled gun of the Saladin Mk 2 is a low-velocity type designed to fire the HESH anti-tank/bunker round. This is effective by explosive rather than kinetic energy.

Alvis FV101 Scorpion

(UK)
Type: tracked combat reconnaissance vehicle
Crew: 3
Combat weight: 17,800 lb (8074 kg)
Dimensions: length overall 15·73 ft (4·794 m); width 7·33 ft (2·235 m); height overall 6·90 ft (2·102 m)
Armament system: one 76-mm (3-in) ROF L23A1 rifled gun with 40 rounds, one co-axial 7·62-mm (0·3-in) L43A1 machine-gun with 3,000 rounds, and four smoke-dischargers on each side of the turret; the turret is manually powered, the main gun lacks stabilization in either elevation (−10° to +35°) or azimuth (360°), and a day/night optical fire-control system is fitted
Armour: welded aluminium
Powerplant: one 190-hp (142-kW) Jaguar J60 No·1 Mk 100B petrol engine with 93 Imp gal (423 litres) of internal fuel
Performance: speed, road 50 mph (80·5 km/h) and water 4 mph (6·4 km/h) driven by its tracks; range, road 400 miles (644 km); fording 3·5 ft (1·07 m) without preparation and amphibious with preparation; gradient 60%; side slope not revealed; vertical obstacle 19·75 in (0·5 m); trench 6·75 ft (2·06 m); ground clearance 14 in (0·356 m)

Variants

FV101 Scorpion: baseline model of an extensive family whose models are derived generally from the Spartan armoured personnel carrier derivative of the CVR(T), the Scorpion was designed by Alvis Ltd in the 1950s and 1960s, and began to enter British service in 1972 as the air-transportable **Combat Vehicle Reconnaissance (Tracked)**, a reconnaissance and anti-tank machine to complement the Fox wheeled reconnaissance vehicle; the type is fitted as standard with NBC protection, and amongst the variations found on Scorpions in service with countries other than the UK are a 0·5-in (12·7-mm) Browning M2HB heavy machine-gun on an AA mounting (Irish vehicles), and a number of features optimized for desert warfare (Omani vehicles)

FV107 Scimitar: Scorpion version with a 30-mm RARDEN cannon and 165 rounds instead of the low-velocity 76-mm (3-in) gun; the FV107 weighs 17,195 lb (7800 kg), and its principal dimensions include a length of 16·355 ft (4·985 m) with the gun forward, a width of 7·36 ft (2·242 m) and an overall height of 6·88 ft (2·096 m)

Scorpion 90: private-venture development of the basic Scorpion with a 90-mm (3·54-in) Cockerill Mk III rifled gun and 33 rounds, used in conjunction with the more capable OIP-5 fire-control system incorporating a laser rangefinder; this vehicle has a combat weight of 19,230 lb (8723 kg) and a length of 17·35 ft (5·288 m) with the gun forward; the turret has powered 360° traverse, and the main armament can be elevated between −8° and +30°; initial production vehicles have a Cadillac Gage turret functions system, with an all-electric system available as an option on later vehicles; the first customer for the type was Malaysia, whose vehicles are also fitted with two banks of four 76-mm (3-in) Wegmann dischargers for smoke and/or fragmentation grenades

Improved Scorpion: private-venture development with a 200-hp (149-kW) Perkins T6·3544 diesel; this raises combat weight to 18,210 lb (8260 kg), with consequent degradation of performance with the notable exception of range, which increases to 520+ miles (837+ km); the improvement package has been incorporated in the Scorpion 90s built for Malaysia

Above and below: The CRV(T) Scorpion was evolved as successor to the Saladin, and uses the L23A1 lightened version of its predecessor's L5A1 low-pressure main gun.

ROF Leeds FV721 Fox

(UK)

Type: wheeled combat reconnaissance vehicle
Crew: 3
Combat weight: 13,495 lb (6121 kg)
Dimensions: length, gun forward 16·67 ft (5·08 m) and hull 13·67 ft (4·166 m); width 7·00 ft (2·134 m); height to turret top 6·50 ft (1·981 m) and overall 7·22 ft (2·20 m)
Armament system: one 30-mm ROF L21 RARDEN cannon with 99 rounds, one 7·62-mm (0·3-in) L8A1 co-axial machine-gun with 2,600 rounds, and four smoke-dischargers on each side of the turret; the turret is manually powered, the main gun lacks stabilization in either elevation (−14° to +40°) or azimuth (360°), and a day/night optical fire-control system is fitted
Armour: welded aluminium
Powerplant: one 190-hp (142-kW) Jaguar J60 No·1 Mk 100B petrol engine with 32 Imp gal (145·5 litres) of internal fuel, and driving a 4 × 4 layout
Performance: speed, road 65 mph (104·6 km/h) and water 3·25 mph (5·2 km/h) driven by its wheels; range, road 270 miles (434 km); fording 3·3 ft (1·0 m) without preparation and amphibious with preparation; gradient 58%; side slope not revealed; vertical obstacle 19·75 in (0·5 m); trench 4·0 ft (1·22 m) with channels; ground clearance 12 in (0·3 m)

Variants

FV107 Fox: a development of the Ferret scout car into an all-aluminium light armoured car, the Fox was designed by Daimler in the late 1960s and entered British service in 1973 as the **Combat Vehicle Reconnaissance (Wheeled)**; standard equipment includes night vision devices
Panga: Royal Ordnance, Leeds, export derivative of the Fox whose one-man turret is fitted with a 0·5-in (12·7-mm) Browning M2HB heavy machine-gun with or without a co-axial 7·62-mm (0·3-in) L37A2 machine-gun; other armament options are a 25-mm McDonnell Douglas Helicopters M242 Bushmaster cannon with 250 rounds and a 7·62-mm (0·3-in) machine-gun with 1,500 rounds, or a twin launcher for Milan medium anti-tank missiles coupled with a 7·62-mm (0·3-in) machine-gun

Left and below: The CRV(W) Fox is the wheeled counterpart to the tracked Scorpion, and is an updated Ferret with the 30-mm L21 RARDEN cannon.

Daimler FV711 Ferret Mk 4

(UK)

Type: wheeled scout car
Crew: 2
Combat weight: 11,900 lb (3598 kg)
Dimensions: length overall 13·00 ft (3·96 m);
width 7·00 ft (2·134 m); height 6·67 ft (2·03 m)
Armament system: one 0·3-in (7·62-mm) Browning M1919A4 (L3A4) machine-gun with 2,500 rounds, and three smoke-dischargers on each side of the turret; the turret is manually powered, the gun lacks stabilization in either elevation (−14° to +40°) or azimuth (360°), and an optical fire-control system is fitted
Armour: welded steel varying in thickness from 8 to 16 mm (0·315 to 0·63 in)
Powerplant: one 129-hp (96-kW) Rolls-Royce B60 Mk 6A petrol engine with 21 Imp gal (96 litres) of internal fuel, and driving a 4 × 4 layout
Performance: speed, road 50 mph (80·5 km/h); range, road 190 miles (306 km); fording 3·0 ft (0·91 m) without preparation and amphibious with preparation; gradient 46%; vertical obstacle 16 in (0·41 m); trench 4·0 ft (1·22 m) with channels; ground clearance 17 in (0·43 m)

Variants

FV701(C) Ferret Mk 1: this was the initial two-seat liaison scout car, and entered service in 1953 as the second production model; it lacked the turret and was armed with a 0·303-in (7·62-mm) Bren Gun and 450 rounds; the **FV704 Ferret Mk 1/2** was a three-seat version with an armoured roof

FV701(E) Ferret Mk 2: turret-fitted reconnaissance version of the Mk 1, developed into the **Ferret Mk 2/2** with a collar to raise the turret slightly, the **FV701(H) Ferret Mk 2/3** with detail improvements, the **Ferret Mk 2/4** with extra armour, the **Ferret Mk 2/5 Mk 2** brought up to Mk 2/4 standard, the **FV703 Ferret Mk 2/6** with single launchers (one on each side of the turret) for a maximum of four Vigilant anti-tank missiles, and the **Ferret Mk 2/7** version of the Mk 2/6 without the Vigilant system

Ferret Mk 3: Ferret Mk 1/1 brought up to Mk 4 standard but fitted with a machine-gun turret

FV711 Ferret Mk 4: earlier Ferret upgraded with stronger suspension and a folded flotation screen

FV712 Ferret Mk 5: Mk 4 with Swingfire heavy anti-tank missile system

Alvis Ferret 80: private venture by Alvis, announced in 1982 and designed to maintain the Ferret as a viable reconnaissance vehicle on the modern battlefield; the Ferret 80 uses proved components and assemblies from the standard Ferret, but also features modern refinements for enhanced mobility and protection; the latter includes construction in aluminium armour; the vehicle is 13·88 ft (4·23 m) long and 7·68 ft (2·34 m) wide, and varies in height with the specific armament installation; power is provided by a 156-hp (116-kW) Perkins T6·3544 diesel for a maximum road speed of 60 mph (96·6 km/h) and a maximum road range of 350 miles (563 km) on 35 Imp gal (149 litres) of fuel; a variety of turrets can be installed, the three most commonly associated with the Ferret 80 being the Helio FVT 700 (with two 7·62-mm/0·3-in machine-guns), the Helio FVT 800 (with one 0·5-in/12·7-mm Browning M2HB heavy machine-gun and one 7·62-mm/0·3-in machine-gun), and the Helio FVT 900 (with one 20-mm Oerlikon-Bührle cannon and one 7·62-mm/0·3-in machine-gun); as a two-man reconnaissance vehicle the Ferret 80 weighs 13,225 lb (5999 kg) and is 7·71 ft (2·35 m) high, these figures increasing to 14,330 lb (6500 kg) and 8·27 ft

(2·52 m) in the three-man reconnaissance vehicle, and to 15,650 lb (7099 kg) and 8·00 ft (2·44 m) in the model with the 20-mm cannon

GKN Sankey/GKL Harimau: private-venture development using the Ferret as its basis, though in this application as the starting point for a rebuild retaining the original welded-steel construction over a number of automotive improvements; the engine is a 105-kW (141-hp) VM HR 692 diesel with 20 Imp gal (91 litres) of fuel, giving this 10,580-lb (4799-kg) vehicle a maximum road speed of 62 mph (99·8 km/h), a maximum road range of 250 miles (402 km) and a 60% gradient capability; the standard turret accommodates one 0·5-in (12·7-mm) Browning M2HB heavy machine-gun, but other installations include two 7·62-mm (0·3-in) machine-guns, one 20-mm cannon, one 25-mm cannon, or a launcher for BGM-71 TOW or Milan anti-tank missiles

The Ferret Mk 2/6 was identifiable from its two turret-side launchers for four lightweight but effective Vigilant anti-tank missiles.

Short Brothers Shorland S51 Mk 5

(UK)
Type: wheeled armoured patrol car
Crew: 3
Combat weight: 7,935 lb (3599 kg)
Dimensions: length overall 14·80 ft (4·51 m); width 5·83 ft (1·778 m); height overall 7·50 ft (2·286 m)
Armament system: one 7·62-mm (0·3-in) L7A3 machine-gun with 1,500 rounds, and four smoke-dischargers on each side of the turret; the turret is manually powered, the gun lacks stabilization in either elevation (an unrevealed arc) or azimuth (360°), and an optical fire-control system is fitted
Armour: welded steel
Powerplant: one 114-hp (85-kW) Rover petrol engine with 24·2 Imp gal (110 litres) of internal fuel, and driving a 4 × 4 layout
Performance: speed, road 75 mph (120·7 km/h); range, road 435 miles (700 km); vertical obstacle 9 in (0·23 m); fording not revealed; vertical obstacle not revealed; trench not revealed; ground clearance 12·75 in (0·32 m)

Variants
Shorland S51 Mk 1: derived from the long-wheelbase Land Rover and delivered from 1965 mainly for internal security duties, the Shorland Mk 1 has a 67-hp (50-kW) four-cylinder engine and 7·25-mm (0·29-in) armour
Shorland S51 Mk 2: improved model with four-cylinder 77-hp (57-kW) engine and 8·25-mm (0·32-in) armour
Shorland S51 Mk 3: improved version with V-6 91-hp (68-kW) engine
Shorland S51 Mk 4: improved version with V-8 engine and upgraded armour protection
Shorland S51 Mk 5: improved version of the Mk 4 with more power and better all-round performance
Shorland S52: armoured patrol car derivative based on the superstructure of the Shorland S53 but fitted with the automotive system of the Shorland S51

Shorland S53: mobile air-defence vehicle derivative fitted with a variant of the LML(V) triple launcher for Blowpipe or Javelin short-range SAMs; six missiles are stored in the rear of the vehicle
Shorland S54: anti-hijack derivative for use at airports and fitted with armoured glass rather than the standard glass windows with armoured shutters
Shorland S55: armoured personnel carrier derivative with a complement of 2 + 6; this variant is 13·98 ft (4·26 m) long, and its roof ring can be fitted with a 7·62-mm (0·3-in) machine-gun as well as two banks of four smoke-dischargers mounted one on each side of the machine-gun mount
Shorland S56: command and radar vehicle derivative with additional communications equipment and a surveillance radar with antenna on the roof of the vehicle

A side view shows the derivation of the Shorland armoured patrol car (designed for use by security forces rather than by an army proper) from the Land Rover utility vehicle.

Cadillac Gage V-600

(USA)
Type: wheeled armoured reconnaissance vehicle

Crew: 4

Combat weight: 37,500 lb (17,010 kg)

Dimensions: length, with gun forward not revealed and hull 20·67 ft (6·30 m); width 8·79 ft (2·68 m); height overall 9·00 ft (2·743 m)

Armament system: one 105-mm (4·13-in) ROF Low Recoil Force Gun with 34 rounds (26 in the hull and eight in the turret), one 7·62-mm (0·3-in) M240 co-axial machine-gun with 2,400 rounds, one 7·62-mm (0·3-in) AA machine-gun with 1,200 rounds or 0·5-in (12·7-mm) Browning M2HB AA heavy machine-gun with 100 rounds, and four smoke-dischargers on each side of the turret; the turret is electro-hydraulically powered, the main gun has optional stabilization in elevation (−7·5° to +20°) and azimuth (360°), and a Marconi Digital Fire-Control System is fitted; this last includes day/night sights, a laser rangefinder and a ballistic computer

Armour: welded steel

Powerplant: one 270-hp (201-kW) Cummins VT-504 diesel engine with an unrevealed quantity of internal fuel, and driving a 6 × 6 layout

Performance: speed, road 56 mph (90·1 km/h); range, road 400 miles (644 km); fording not revealed; gradient 60%; side slope not revealed; vertical obstacle 24 in (0·61 m); trench not revealed; ground clearance 21 in (0·53 m)

Variant
V-600: produced as a private venture and first revealed in 1986, the V-600 was initially designated the V-300A1; the vehicle is typical of Cadillac Gage's wheeled armoured fighting vehicles, and amongst the options offered with this powerful vehicle are individual NBC protection, chemical-resistant paint, a fire-suppression system and night vision devices; the vehicle is fitted with the impressive Cadillac Gage Low Recoil Force Turret

Cadillac Gage Commando Scout

(USA)
Type: wheeled scout car

Crew: 1 + 1 or 1 + 2

Combat weight: 16,000 lb (7258 kg)

Dimensions: length overall 16·41 ft (5·003 m); width 6·75 ft (2·057 m); height 7·08 ft (2·16 m)

Armament system: two 7·62-mm (0·3-in) machine-guns with 4,800 rounds, or two 0·5-in (12·7-mm) Browning M2HB heavy machine-guns with 2,200 rounds, or one TOW launcher with six missiles, or one 106-mm (4·17-in) M40 recoilless rifle with 15 rounds; the turret is manually powered, the guns lack stabilization in either elevation (−10° to +55°) or azimuth (360°), and an optical fire-control system is fitted

The Commando Scout command vehicle.

Armour: welded steel

Powerplant: one 149-hp (111-kW) Cummins V-6 diesel engine with 100 US gal (379 litres) of internal fuel, and driving a 4 × 4 layout

Performance: speed, road 60 mph (96·6 km/h); range, road 800 miles (1287 km); fording 3·8 ft (1·17 m); gradient 60%; side slope 30%; vertical obstacle 24 in (0·61 m); trench not revealed; ground clearance not revealed

Variant
Commando Scout: introduced to service in 1983 by Indonesia, the Commando Scout is a very useful light reconnaissance vehicle with extensive armament options suiting it for reconnaissance and light anti-tank operations; the type can also be used in the command role with an extended roof and armament comprising one 7·62-mm (0·3-in) machine-gun; the Commando Scout can be fitted with the Twin/Combination Machine-Gun (1-Metre) Turret for two 7·62-mm (0·3-in) machine-guns, or two 0·5-in (12·7-mm) machine-guns, or one machine-gun of each calibre, or one 7·62-mm (0·3-in) machine-gun and one 40-mm Mk 19 grenade-launcher, and this turret can be provided with PAT (Power-Assisted Traverse); the Twin Machine-Gun (1-Metre) Turret is similar, but carries two 7·62-mm (0·3-in) machine-guns; other options are a launcher for BGM-71 TOW heavy anti-tank missiles or, over the rear of the hull, a Command Pod with vision blocks and a ring mounting for one 7·62-mm (0·3-in) machine-gun and 3,000 rounds

TAMSE/Thyssen Henschel VCTP

(Argentina/West Germany)

Type: tracked armoured personnel carrier
Crew: 2 + 10
Combat weight: 27,500 kg (60,626 lb)
Dimensions: length overall 6·79 m (22·28 ft); width 3·28 m (10·76 ft); height 2·45 m (8·04 ft)
Armament system: one 20-mm Rheinmetall MK 20 Rh 202 cannon with an unrevealed number of rounds and one 7·62-mm (0·3-in) AA machine-gun with an unrevealed number of rounds in the turret, one remotely controlled 7·62-mm (0·3-in) machine-gun over the rear of the troop compartment, and four smoke-dischargers on each side of the hull; the turret is electro-hydraulically powered, the main gun lacks stabilization in either elevation (−17° to +65°) or azimuth (360°), and simple optical sights are fitted
Armour: welded steel
Powerplant: one 535-kW (717-hp) MTU MB 833 Ka-500 diesel engine with 652 litres (143 Imp gal) of internal fuel plus provision for 400 litres (88 Imp gal) of auxiliary fuel
Performance: speed, road 75 km/h (46·6 mph); range, road 570 km (354 miles) on internal fuel or 915 km (569 miles) with auxiliary fuel; fording 1·0 m (3·3 ft); gradient 60%; side slope 30%; vertical obstacle 1·0 m (39·4 in); trench 2·5 m (8·2 ft); ground clearance 0·44 m (17·3 in)

Variants

VCTP: designed for commonality with the TAM tank and therefore based on the same chassis, the Vehiculo de Combate Transporte de Personal is in essence a less refined version of the West German Marder mechanized infantry combat vehicle with a more powerful engine; there is provision for the embarked troops to use their weapons from inside the vehicle via three ports on each side of the troop compartment, and the troop compartment has two centrally-hinged roof hatches; an NBC system is fitted as standard
VCTM: the Vehiculo de Combate Transporte de Mortero is the mortar-carrier version of the VCTP with a three-part roof hatch in place of the VTCP's turret to allow the firing of the 120-mm (4·72-in) 120LR mortar located in the rear compartment; 61 mortar bombs (49 HE and 12 long-range) are carried, and local defence is provided by a single 7·62-mm (0·3-in) pintle-mounted machine-gun; the VCTM has a crew of five, and its overall dimensions differ from those of the VCTP only in width (3·25 m/10·66 ft) and height (1·858 m/6·10 ft)

Steyr 4K 7FA G 127

(Austria)

Type: tracked armoured personnel carrier
Crew: 2 + 8
Combat weight: 14,800 kg (32,628 lb)
Dimensions: length overall 5·87 m (19·26 ft); width 2·50 m (8·20 ft); height without armament 1·61 m (5·29 ft)
Armament system: one 0·5-in (12·7-mm) Browning M2HB cupola-mounted heavy machine-gun with an unrevealed number of rounds, one 7·62-mm (0·3-in) pintle-mounted machine-gun with an unrevealed number of rounds, and four smoke-dischargers mounted on the rear of the cupola; the cupola is manually powered, the main gun lacks stabilization in either elevation (−10° to +35°) or azimuth (360°), and simple optical sights are fitted

Armour: welded steel to a maximum thickness of 25 mm (0·98 in)
Powerplant: one 240-kW (322-hp) Steyr 7FA diesel engine with 360 litres (79 Imp gal) of internal fuel
Performance: speed, road 64 km/h (40 mph); range, road 520 km (323 miles); fording 1·0 m (3·3 ft); gradient 75%; side slope 40%; vertical obstacle 0·8 m (31·5 in); trench 2·1 m (6·9 ft); ground clearance 0·42 m (16·5 in)

Top and centre: Two views of the 4K 7FA G127 with a 7·62-mm (0·3-in) MG74 over the troop compartment.
Above: The 4K 7FA FLA 1/2.20AA vehicle.

Variants

4K 7FA G 127: this is essentially an uparmoured development of the 4K 4FA with automotive components of the SK 105 series; the first production models were completed in 1977, and options include night vision equipment and individual NBC protection; the troop compartment is accessed by twin doors at the rear, there are two outward-opening hatches in the troop compartment roof, and there is provision for the embarked troops' 7·62-mm (0·3-in) MG74 machine-gun to be pintle-mounted above the roof; provision can also be made for the embarked troops to use their personal weapons from inside the vehicle using two ports in each side of the troop compartment, installation of this provision resulting in the designation **4K 7FA KSpZ**

4K 7FA MICV 1/127: mechanized infantry combat vehicle derivative of the basic 4K 7FA with a one-man Steyr SP 1/127 manually/hydraulically powered turret accommodating one 0·5-in (12·7-mm) Browning M2HB heavy machine-gun and co-axial 7·62-mm (0·3-in) machine-gun

4K 7FA MICV 2/30: improved mechanized infantry combat vehicle turning the scales at 15,900 kg (35,053 lb) when fitted with a one-man turret carrying one 30-mm ROF L21A1 RARDEN cannon and one 7·62-mm (0·3-in) co-axial machine-gun

4K 7FA G 20: updated version of the 4K 7FA G 127 with a 20-mm cannon in a one-man Oerlikon-Bührle turret; it is also possible to fit 25- or 30-mm cannon in place of the 20-mm weapon (resulting in the designations **4K 7FA G 25** and **4K 7FA G 30**); options with this type include a full NBC system and automatic fire-suppression equipment

4K 7FA FSCV 90: fire-support variant of the series, a five-man vehicle based on the 4K 7FA MICV 1/127 but fitted with any one of four possible turrets equipped with a 90-mm (3·54-in) rifled gun; the turret options are the GIAT TS 90 turret carrying the 90-mm (3·54-in) GIAT CS Super (F4) gun plus 64 rounds of ammunition including 20 in the turret, two 7·62-mm (0·3-in) machine-guns (one co-axial and the other AA) plus 2,000 rounds of ammunition, and two smoke-dischargers on each side of the turret (resulting in the designation **4K 7FA FSCV 1/90**), the Cadillac Gage 90-mm Turret carrying the 90-mm (3·54-in) Cockerill Mk III gun with an undisclosed number of rounds including eight in the turret, two 7·62-mm (0·3-in) machine-guns (one co-axial and the other AA) with an unrevealed number of rounds including 600 in the turret, and optional smoke-dischargers on each side of the turret (resulting in the designation **4K 7FA FSCV 2/90**), the Cockerill CS 90 turret carrying the 90-mm (3·54-in) Cockerill Mk III gun with an unrevealed number of rounds including 12 in the turret, two 7·62-mm (0·3-in) machine-guns (one co-axial and the other AA) with an unrevealed number of rounds including 600 in the turret, and eight smoke-dischargers on each side of the turret (resulting in the designation **4K 7FA FSCV 3/90**), and the SAMM TTB 190 turret carrying the 90-mm (3·54-in) GIAT CS 90 (F4) gun plus 35 rounds, two 7·62-mm (0·3-in) machine-guns (one co-axial and the other AA) with 3,000 rounds including an unrevealed number in the turret, and four 76-mm (3-in) Wegmann smoke/fragmentation grenade-launchers on each side of the turret (resulting in the designation **4K 7FA FSCV 4/90**)

4K 7FA-FU: command model with a crew of seven and additional radio equipment

4K 7FA-San: ambulance model with a crew of two (driver and medical attendant) plus provision for two litters and four seated casualties

4K 7FA GrW 81: mortar-carrier version with an 81-mm (3·2-in) mortar and 78 bombs, the mortar firing through a hatch in the roof; the crew is five

4K 7FA FLA 1/2·20: AA version fitted with the French TA 20/RA 20 turret carrying two 20-mm cannon

4K 7FA FLA 3/2·30: AA version fitted with the French SABRE turret carrying two 30-mm cannon

Leonidas 1: 4K 7FA built under licence in Greece, and identical in all respects to the Austrian-built model, though the type may be retrofitted with a Greek-designed turret accommodating a 20-mm cannon or 0·5-in (12·7-mm) Browning M2HB heavy machine-gun

Leonidas 2: improved version of the Leonidas 1 with firing ports in the sides of the troop compartment, which is revised with the troops sitting in the centre and facing outwards so as to be able to use the firing ports; the first 100 vehicles are baseline armoured personnel carriers, and subsequent vehicles have the capability to mount a Greek-designed turret mounting a main weapon of up to 30-mm calibre

Steyr (Saurer) 4K 4FA G1

(Austria)

Type: tracked armoured personnel carrier
Crew: 2 + 8
Combat weight: 12,500 kg (27,557 lb)
Dimensions: length overall 5·40 m (17·72 ft); width 2·50 m (8·20 ft); height to top of machine-gun 2·10 m (6·89 ft)
Armament system: one 0·5-in (12·7-mm) Browning M2HB cupola-mounted heavy machine-gun, one 7·62-mm (0·3-in) pintle-mounted machine-gun, and four smoke-dischargers on the rear of the cupola; the cupola is manually powered, the main gun lacks stabilization in either elevation (−10° to +35°) or azimuth (360°), and simple optical sights are fitted
Armour: welded steel varying in thickness from 8 to 35 mm (0·315 to 1·38 in)

Powerplant: one 185-kW (248-hp) Steyr 4FA diesel engine with 184 litres (40·5 Imp gal) of internal fuel
Performance: speed, road 65 km/h (40·4 mph); range, road 370 km (230 miles); fording 1·0 m (3·3 ft); gradient 75%; side slope 50%; vertical obstacle 0·8 m (31·5 in); trench 2·2 m (7·2 ft); ground clearance 0·42 m (16·5 in)

Variants

4K 4FA: this was the main production model of this useful armoured personnel carrier series, and deliveries began in 1961; the family began life as the Oesterreichische Saurer-Werke 3K 3H in 1958 before the company was taken over by Steyr-Daimler Puch in 1970, and was developed in 1959 as the 4K 3H, both variants being powered by a 150-kW (201-hp) Saurer 3H diesel; the design was then recast with a different hull shape and revised running gear to emerge as the 4K 2P with the 185-kW (248-hp) Saurer 2P diesel, and this was placed in production as the **4K 4F** variant followed by the **4K 3FA** with a 170-kW (228-hp) diesel and the 4K 4FA with a more powerful engine; as in the standard version of the later 4K 7FA series, the embarked troops cannot fire their personal weapons from inside the vehicle, but must emerge from roof hatches to fire on the move; the troop compartment is accessed by twin doors in the rear; when fitted with a shield for the protection of its machine-gunner the vehicle is designated **4K 4FA G1**; the type has also been developed as the basis of a self-propelled rocket-launcher carrying two nine-tube banks of tubes for 81-mm (3·2-in) SNORA rockets; the rocket-launcher can be traversed through 360° and elevated between −10° and +50°

The 4K 4FA-G2 is identifiable by its Oerlikon-Bührle GAD turret with a 20-mm cannon and 100 rounds of ready-use ammunition.

4K 4FA-G2: upgunned version with a 20-mm Oerlikon 204 GK cannon and 100 rounds of ready-use ammunition in an Oerlikon-Bührle GAD-AOA turret, a manually powered type offering 360° traverse as well as cannon elevation between -12° and +70°; this version has a combat weight of 15,000 kg (33,069 lb)

4K 3FA-Fu1: brigade commander's command and control vehicle based on the 4K 3FA

4K 3FA-FuA: artillery command vehicle based on the 4K 3FA

4K 3FA-Fu/FlA: AA command vehicle based on the 4K 3FA

4K 3FA-FS: wireless and teleprinter version based on the 4K 3FA

4K 4FA-San: ambulance model with the same crew and casualty parameters as the 4K 7FA San

4K 4FA GrW 81: mortar-carrier version with an 81-mm (3.2-in) mortar

Above right: The 4K 4FA-G1 is more lightly armed with a 0.5-in (12.7-mm) heavy machine-gun.

Steyr Pandur

(Austria)
Type: wheeled armoured personnel carrier
Crew: 2 + 8/10
Combat weight: 12,000 kg (26,455 lb)
Dimensions: length overall 5.697 m (18.69 ft); width 2.50 m (8.20 ft); height to hull top 1.81 m (5.94 ft)
Armament system: see Variants (below)
Armour: welded steel
Powerplant: one 185-kW (248-hp) Steyr WD612.75 diesel engine with 195 litres (42.9 Imp gal) of internal fuel plus provision for an additional 105 litres (23.1 Imp gal), and driving a 6 × 6 layout
Performance: speed, road 105 km/h (65.25 mph) and water 9 km/h (5.6 mph) driven by two propellers; range, road 650 km (404 miles); fording 1.2 m (3.9 ft) or optionally amphibious; gradient 70%; side slope 35%; vertical obstacle 0.5 m (19.7 in);

The reconnaissance Pandur ARSV 25 has a 25-mm Oerlikon-Bührle cannon in a Creusot-Loire T-25 electrically powered turret.

trench 1.2 m (3.9 ft); ground clearance 0.42 m (16.5 in)

Variants
Pandur: this useful wheeled armoured personnel carrier was developed as a private venture and revealed in 1985; access to the troop compartment is provided by two rear-mounted doors, and the embarked troops can use their personal weapons either from two centrally hinged roof hatches on each side, or through two optional firing ports in each side of the troop compartment; a central tyre pressure-regulation system is standard, as are NBC protection and a fire-suppression system; the design team was at great pains to maximize the Pandur's operational flexibility, and for this reason the basic hull can be fitted with a wide assortment of turreted and non-turreted installations up to a maximum weight of 1900 kg (4,189 lb) to produce role-dedicated models; the Pandur MICV 127 is a mechanized infantry combat vehicle fitted with a one-man turret carrying a 0.5-in (12.7-mm) Browning M2HB heavy machine-gun; the **Pandur ARFSV 90** is an armoured reconnaissance fire-support vehicle fitted with a two-man turret carrying a 90-mm (3.54-in) rifled gun; the **Pandur AMC 81** is a mortar-carrier fitted internally with a turntable-mounted 81-mm (3.2-in) mortar and carrying externally a 0.5-in (12.7-mm) machine-gun; the **Pandur ATGMC** is an anti-tank guided-missile

carrier fitted with the Euromissile HCT turret launcher for HOT heavy anti-tank missiles; the **Pandur AAMB** is an unarmed ambulance
Pandur ARSV 25: this more potent version of the Pandur is the Pandur Armoured Reconnaissance Scout Vehicle 25, and it is fitted with the two-man Creusot-Loire T-25 turret armed with one 25-mm Oerlikon-Bührle KBA cannon, one 7.62-mm (0.3-in) co-axial machine-gun, and single bank of three smoke dischargers on each side; turret traverse (360°) and main armament elevation (−10° to +50°) are both powered; the Pandur ARSV 25 has a combat weight of 11,500 kg (25,353 lb) and carries a crew of 3 + 2, and its height is 2.65 m (8.69 ft)
Pandur ARSV 30: it was originally suggested that the version of the Pandur with a 30-mm weapon should carry the turret of the Alvis Fox with its 30-mm L21A1 RARDEN cannon, but the present Pandur Armoured Reconnaissance Scout Vehicle 30 prototype has a different two-man turret armed with a 30-mm Mauser MK 30 cannon, a 7.62-mm (0.3-in) FN-MAG co-axial machine-gun and a bank of three smoke-dischargers on each side of the turret; the same type of electro-hydraulic drive is used as on the Pandur ARSV 25, but in this application with more powerful motors for higher rates of turret traverse (360°) and main armament elevation (−10° to +50°); the variant has a combat weight of 12,500 kg (27,557 lb), a crew of 3 + 2, and a height of 2.689 m (8.82 ft)

BN Constructions SIBMAS

(Belgium)

Type: wheeled armoured personnel carrier
Crew: 3 + 11
Combat weight: 14,500 to 17,500 kg (31,966 to 38,580 lb) depending on role and specific armament
Dimensions: length overall 7·32 m (24·02 ft); width 2·50 m (8·20 ft); height to turret top 2·77 m (9·09 ft)
Armament system: see Variants (below)
Armour: welded steel
Powerplant: one 240-kW (322-hp) MAN D2566 MK diesel engine with 400 litres (88 Imp gal) of internal fuel, and driving a 6 × 6 layout
Performance: speed, road 100 km/h (62 mph) and water 11 km/h (6·8 mph) driven by two propellers or 4 km/h (2·5 mph) driven by its wheels; range, road 1000 km (621 miles); fording amphibious; gradient 70%; side slope 40%; vertical obstacle 0·6 m (23·6 in); trench 1·5 m (4·9 ft); ground clearance 0·4 m (15·75 in)

Variants

SIBMAS: available from the early 1980s, this useful wheeled armoured personnel carrier has good range and payload, and has provision for the embarked troops to use their personal weapons from inside the hull via firing ports in the sides of the troop compartment, which is accessed by a large door in each side of the hull under the turret; the troop compartment roof is fitted with one small and three large hatches; the type is offered with a wide variety of turreted armament options including the **SIBMAS AFSV-90** armoured fire-support vehicle with a two-man Cockerill CSE 90 turret carrying a 90-mm (3·54-in) Cockerill Mk III rifled gun with an unrevealed number of rounds including 12 in the turret, two 7·62-mm (0·3-in) machine-guns (one co-axial and the other AA) with an unrevealed number of rounds including 600 in the turret, and eight smoke-dischargers on each side of the turret; the CSE 90 turret is fitted with an OIP LRS 5 fire-control system that combines optical sights, a laser rangefinder and a ballistic computer; the SIBMAS can also be fitted with a wide variety of other turrets, including an ESD turret with two 20-mm AA cannon, a Hispano-Suiza Lynx 90 turret with 90-mm (3·54-in) GIAT CN-90 (F1) rifled gun and two 7·62-mm (0·3-in) machine-guns (one co-axial and the other AA), a Hispano-Suiza Serval 60/20 turret with a 60-mm (2·36-in) breech-loaded mortar plus a 20-mm cannon and a 7·62-mm (0·3-in) machine-gun, a Vickers turret with two 7·62-mm (0·3-in) machine-guns, a SAMM TG 120 (TTB 120) turret with a 20-mm cannon and a co-axial 7·62-mm (0·3-in) machine-gun, a SAMM S 365 (BTM 208) turret with 0·5-in (12·7-mm) and 7·62-mm (0·3-in) machine-guns, a Helio FVT 800 turret with two 0·5-in (12·7-mm) or 7·62-mm (0·3-in) machine-guns or one of each calibre, and a Helio FVT 900 turret with one 20-mm cannon and one 7·62-mm (0·3-in) machine-gun

SIBMAS ARV: 20,000-kg (44,092-lb) armoured recovery vehicle derivative of the basic vehicle with front- and rear-mounted spades, a 10,500-kg (23,148-lb) capacity crane, a 20,000-kg (44,092-lb) capacity winch and other specialized equipment; other variants on offer are a command post vehicle, an ambulance vehicle for four litters and three seated casualties, and a cargo vehicle with a payload of 4000 + kg (8,818 + lb)

Below: The turret of the SIBMAS ASFV-90 has smoke-dischargers facing forward and backward and a 90-mm (3·54-in) rifled gun.

Beherman Demoen BDX

(Belgium)

Type: wheeled armoured personnel carrier
Crew: 2 + 10
Combat weight: 10,700 kg (23,589 lb)
Dimensions: length overall 5·05 m (16·57 ft); width 2·50 m (8·20 ft); height to top of machine-gun turret 2·84 m (9·32 ft)
Armament system: two 7·62-mm (0·3-in) L7 or MAG machine-guns with 1,000 rounds; the turret is manually powered, the guns lack stabilization in either elevation (−15° to +50°) or azimuth (360°), and simple optical sights are fitted

Left: The boxy Belgian BDX armoured personnel carrier is a significantly improved version of the Timoney APC of Irish design.

Armour: welded steel varying in thickness from 9·5 to 12·7 mm (0·37 to 0·5 in)
Powerplant: one 180-hp (134-kW) Chrysler petrol engine with 248 litres (55 Imp gal) of internal fuel, and driving a 4 × 4 layout
Performance: speed, road 100 km/h (62 mph); range, road 900 km (559 miles); fording amphibious propelled by its wheels or two optional waterjets; gradient 60%; side slope 40%; vertical obstacle 0·4 m (15·75 in); trench not revealed; ground clearance 0·4 m (15·75 in)

Variants

BDX: this is the improved and considerably developed Belgian production version of the Irish **Timoney Mk 5** armoured personnel carrier, and deliveries began in 1978 mainly for paramilitary duties; there is provision for the embarked troops to use their personal weapons from inside the vehicle via three ports (one in each side and one in the rear), and the troop compartment is accessed by three doors (one in each side and one in the rear); the type can be fitted with a Euromissile MCT turret with twin launcher for Milan medium anti-tank missiles, or a Vickers turret for two 7·62-mm machine-guns, or a Vickers turret for one 7·62-mm machine-gun; alternative armament installations include a 48-tube launcher for 50-mm (1·97-in) FIROS rockets, and an 81-mm (3·2-in) mortar in the hull (muzzle loaded) or in a turret (breech loaded); options include air conditioning, NBC protection and a front-mounted dozer blade
BDX Mk 2: version of the BDX with the 180-hp (134-kW) Detroit Diesel 4-53T diesel
Vickers Valkyr: joint prototype by Vickers of the UK and Beherman-Demoen of Belgium to enhance the BDX by improving the driver's position, bettering the ballistic protection, strengthening the suspension so that a greater range of armament installations can be offered, and incorporating a number of detail modifications including the powerplant of the BDX Mk 2

ACEC Cobra

(Belgium)
Type: tracked armoured personnel carrier
Crew: 2 + 10

Combat weight: 8500 kg (18,739 lb)
Dimensions: length overall 4·52 m (14·83 ft); width 2·75 m (9·02 ft); height 2·32 m (7·61 ft)
Armament system: one 0·5-in (12·7-mm) Browning M2HB heavy machine-gun with an unrevealed number of rounds, one 7·62-mm (0·3-in) bow machine-gun with an unrevealed number of rounds, and three smoke-dischargers on each side of the turret; the turret is electrically powered, the gun lacks stabilization in either elevation (−10° to +50°) or azimuth (360°), and simple optical sights are fitted
Armour: welded steel
Powerplant: one 190-hp (142-kW) Cummins VT-190 diesel engine with 309 litres (68 Imp gal) of internal fuel powering an electric drive
Performance: speed, road 75 km/h (46·6 mph) and water 10 km/h (6·1 mph) driven by two waterjets; range, road 600 km (373 miles); fording amphibious; gradient 60%; side slope 45%; vertical obstacle 0·7 m (27·6 in); trench 1·6 m (5·25 ft); ground clearance 0·42 m (16·5 in)

Below: The Cobra is unusual amongst armoured personnel carriers in having a diesel-electric drive, and this view shows the two waterjets.

Variant

Cobra: designed as a private venture and revealed in 1978, the Cobra is an unusual armoured personnel carrier inasmuch as it uses diesel-electric propulsion; the type lacks provision for the embarked troops to use their personal weapons from inside the vehicle, and the only two openings to the troop compartment are the large single door in the rear and one roof hatch; optional equipment includes night vision devices, NBC protection, an air-conditioning system, and alternative armament fits; these last include the Oerlikon-Bührle GAD-AOA turret carrying a 20-mm Oerlikon-Bührle KAA cannon, or a turreted 25-mm cannon, or a Euromissile MCT turret with twin launchers for Milan medium anti-tank missiles, or the Forges de Zeebrugge LAU-97 40-tube launcher for 70-mm (2·75-in) rockets, or a Thomson Brandt 120-mm (4·72-in) mortar carried internally to fire to the rear

Bottom: The Cobra has a bow machine-gun, another unusual feature for a modern APC, and a turret mounting an external 0·5-in (12·7-mm) machine-gun. On the hull front is the trim vane (in the raised position) for waterborne operation.

ENGESA EE-11 Urutu Model V

(Brazil)
Type: wheeled armoured personnel carrier
Crew: 1 + 12
Combat weight: 14,000 kg (30,864 lb)
Dimensions: length overall 6·10 m (20·01 ft); width 2·65 m (8·69 ft); height to top of machine-gun mount 2·90 m (9·51 ft)
Armament system: one 0·5-in (12·7-mm) Browning M2HB heavy machine-gun with an unrevealed number of rounds (but see Variant), and two, three or four smoke-dischargers on the sides of the turret; the turret is manually powered, the gun lacks stabilization in either elevation (−7° to +50°) or azimuth (360°), and simple optical sights are fitted
Armour: welded bi-metallic steel
Powerplant: one 290-hp (216-kW) Detroit Diesel 6V-53T diesel engine with 380 litres (83·6 Imp gal) of fuel, and driving a 6 × 6 layout
Performance: speed, road 105 km/h (65·25 mph) and water 8 km/h (5 mph) driven by two propellers; range, road 850 km (528 miles) and water 60 km (37 miles); fording amphibious; gradient 60%; side slope 30%; vertical obstacle 0·6 m (23·6 in); trench not revealed; ground clearance 0·375 m (14·75 in)

Variant

EE-11 Urutu: featuring great commonality of components with the EE-9 armoured car, the basic Urutu was designed in the early 1970s and

Below: The EE-11 Urutu AFSV has the ET-90 turret with a 90-mm (3·54-in) rifled gun.

entered service with the Brazilian army in 1975 as the **CTRA** (Carro de Transporte Sobre Rodas Anfibio); there is provision for the embarked troops to use their personal weapons from inside the vehicle using either of two systems (five ports comprising two in each side and one in the rear, or 11 ports comprising five in each side and one in the rear); access to the troop compartment is provided by a large rear door, and the compartment has four outward-opening roof hatches; the armament described above is standard for the armoured personnel carrier, but alternatives include a ring-mounted 7·62-mm (0·3-in) machine-gun, a Hagglund & Soner 20-mm cannon turret, a Brandt 60-mm (2·36-in) mortar turret, the turret of the British Scorpion reconnaissance vehicle with 76-mm (3-in) rifled gun, the ENGESA EC-90 turret with 90-mm (3·54-in) rifled gun (producing a variant known as the **Urutu AFSV**), the ENGESA ET-MD turret with 0·5-in (12·7-mm) and 7·62-mm (0·3-in) machine-guns, and the ENGESA ET-20 turret with one 20-mm Oerlikon-Bührle cannon and one 7·62-mm (0·3-in) machine-gun; the EE-11 has so far appeared in five basic models with different engines, the **Urutu Model I** having a 130-kW (174-hp) Mercedes-Benz with manual transmission (and uniquely in the series no central tyre pressure-regulation system), the **Urutu Model II** having a 140-kW (188-hp) Mercedes-Benz with automatic transmission, the **Urutu Model III** having a 212-hp (158-kW) Detroit Diesel 6V-53N diesel with automatic transmission, the **Urutu Model IV** having a 140-kW (188-hp) Mercedes-Benz OM 352A diesel with automatic transmission, and the **Urutu Model V** described above; unnamed variants include an 81-mm (3·2-in) mortar-carrier, an ambulance

model for six to eight sitting wounded or fewer litters, a 2000-kg (4,409-lb) cargo model, a command model, a recovery model with a crane and specialist tools, and a riot-control model

Below: The riot-control EE-11 Urutu has a one-man turret and machine-gun.

Above: An interior view, looking forward, of the command post vehicle of the EE-11 Urutu series.

General Motors Canada Grizzly

(Canada)
Type: wheeled armoured personnel carrier
Crew: 3 + 6
Combat weight: 23,150 lb (10,501 kg)
Dimensions: length, hull 18·69 ft (5·968 m); width 8·30 ft (2·53 m); height overall 8·30 ft (2·53 m)
Armament system: one 0·5-in (12·7-mm) Browning M2HB heavy machine-gun with 1,000 rounds, one 7·62-mm (0·3-in) C1 co-axial machine-gun with 4,400 rounds, and four smoke-dischargers on each side of the turret; the turret is electrically powered, the gun lacks stabilization in either elevation (−8° to +55°) or azimuth (360°), and simple optical sights are fitted
Armour: welded steel varying in thickness from 8 to 10 mm (0·315 to 0·39 in)
Powerplant: one 275-hp (205-kW) Detroit Diesel 6V-53T diesel engine with 54 US gal (204 litres) of internal fuel, and driving a 6 × 6 layout
Performance: speed, road 63 mph (101·5 km/h) and water 4·35 mph (7 km/h) driven by two propellers; range, road 375 miles (603 km); fording amphibious; gradient 60%; side slope 30%; vertical obstacle 15 in (0·38 m); trench 1·33 ft (0·406 m); ground clearance 15·5 in (0·39 m)

Variants

Grizzly: this is the wheeled armoured personnel carrier of the Canadian **Armored Vehicle General Purpose** series, and was derived from the Swiss MOWAG Piranha family to enter service in 1979; the armament is fitted in a Cadillac Gage 1-Metre Turret of the type used on the Commando Scout, and there is provision for the embarked troops to fire their personal weapons from inside the vehicle via ports in the hull sides and rear; access to the troop compartment is provided by two doors in the rear of the hull, and there are also two hatches in the roof of the troop compartment
Cougar: wheeled fire-support vehicle member of the AVGP family, with a crew of three and the turret of the British Scorpion reconnaissance vehicle (one 76-mm/3-in L23A1 rifled gun with 40 rounds including 10 in the turret, one 7·62-mm/0·3-in co-axial machine-gun, and four smoke-dischargers on each side of the turret) and a fire-control system incorporating a laser rangefinder
Husky: wheeled maintenance and recovery vehicle member of the AVGP family, with a crew of three and a 3,850-lb (1746-kg) capacity crane in place of the turret

General Motors Canada Light Armored Vehicle-25

(Canada)
Type: wheeled armoured personnel carrier
Crew: 3 + 6
Combat weight: 28,400 lb (12,882 kg)
Dimensions: length, hull 20·97 ft (6·393 m); width 8·03 ft (2·499 m); height overall 8·83 ft (2·692 m)
Armament system: one 25-mm McDonnell Douglas Helicopters M242 Bushmaster cannon with 630 rounds (420 in the hull and 210 in the turret), one 7·62-mm (0·3-in) M240 co-axial machine-gun with 1,620 rounds (1,200 in the hull and 420 in the turret), one 7·62-mm (0·3-in) M60 AA machine-gun or 0·5-in (12·7-mm) Browning M2HB AA heavy machine-gun with an unrevealed number of rounds, and four smoke-dischargers on each side of the turret; the turret is hydraulically powered, the gun is stabilized in elevation (−10° to +60°) and azimuth (360°), and an optical fire-control system is fitted

Below: The Grizzly armoured personnel carrier is a Canadian development of the Swiss Piranha wheeled vehicle in its 6 × 6 form.

Armour: welded steel varying in thickness from 8 to 10 mm (0·315 to 0·39 in)
Powerplant: one 275-hp (205-kW) Detroit Diesel 6V-53T diesel engine with an unrevealed quantity of internal fuel, and driving an 8 × 8 layout
Performance: speed, road 62 mph (99·8 km/h) and water 6·5 mph (10·5 km/h) driven by two propellers; range, road 415 miles (668 km); fording amphibious; gradient 70%; side slope 30%; vertical obstacle 19·75 in (0·5 m); trench 6·75 ft (2·06 m); ground clearance not revealed

Variants

LAV-25: entering service with the US Marine Corps from 1983, the Light Armored Vehicle-25 is an 8 × 8 derivative of the Armored Vehicle General Purpose series fitted with a two-man Delco turret containing a 25-mm McDonnell Douglas Chain Gun cannon, a 7·62-mm (0·3-in) M240 co-axial machine-gun, and a 7·62-mm (0·3-in) M60 AA medium machine-gun or 0·5-in (12·7-mm) Browning M2HB AA heavy machine-

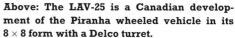

Above: The LAV-25 is a Canadian development of the Piranha wheeled vehicle in its 8 × 8 form with a Delco turret.

gun, and four smoke-dischargers on each side of the turret; the LAV-25 being considered for an upgrade package centred on the use of appliqué armour, to be fitted in the field to avoid increasing the standard vehicle's weight to the degree that it loses its capability for air carriage under the US Marine Corps' Sikorsky CH-53E Sea Stallion helicopter; standard equipment on the LAV-25 includes night vision devices and an NBC system; variants of the LAV are also being produced as the **LAV Logistics Vehicle** (with a higher roof fitted with two hatches for the rapid loading/unloading of supplies with the aid of a rear-mounted crane), the **LAV Mortar-Carrier** (one 81-mm/3·2-in weapon with 94 bombs or perhaps at a later date one 107-mm/4·2-in weapon with 80 bombs), the five-man **LAV Maintenance/Recovery Vehicle** (with a 4,000-lb/1814-kg capacity crane and 30,000-lb/13609-kg capacity winch), the **LAV Anti-Tank Vehicle** (with a retractable Emerson Electric twin launcher for 16 BGM-81 TOW heavy anti-tank missiles), the **LAV Command and Control Vehicle** (with a hull

Above: The LAV-25 was designed for slung carriage under the Sikorsky CH-53 helicopter, and for its weight provides good mobility and protection.

Below: The LAV-25 is also fully amphibious and carries effective armament including a stabilized 25-mm cannon firing hard-hitting projectiles.

similar to that of the logistics version plus additional radio gear), the **LAV Anti-Aircraft Vehicle** (probably with the General Electric Blazer turret carrying one 25-mm GAU-12/U cannon and FIM-92 Stinger SAMs), the **LAV Mobile Electronic Warfare Support System** (with a crew of four and an electronic warfare suite based on the PRD-10 radio direction-finder and VLQ-19 communications jammer) and, for the US Air Force, the **Mobile Armored Reconnaissance Vehicle/Standoff Munition Device** (with equipment for explosive ordnance disposal duties); there is also the possibility that the basic type will be developed as the **LAV Assault Gun Vehicle** with turreted armament to be selected after trials with the 90-mm (3·54-in) MECAR KEnerga, 75-mm (2·95-mm) ARES and 60-mm (2·36-in) Israel Military Industries HMVS weapons, and the **LAV Rocket-Launcher** with a 19-tube launcher for the 2·75-in (70-mm) Hydra 70 multi-role rocket; the LAV Anti-Tank Vehicle has a crew of four, a combat weight of 27,800 lb (12,610 kg), a length of 20·96 ft (6·39 m), a width of 8·2 ft (2·50 m), a height of 10·25 ft (3·125 m), road and water speeds of 62 and 6·5 mph (100 and 10·5 km/h) respectively, and a road range of 410 miles (660 km); the TUA (Tow Under Armor) launcher can be traversed through 360° and elevated between −30° and +34°, and can fire all types of TOW missiles; the 14 spare missiles carried in the hull are loaded into the launchers through a hatch in the hull roof

LAV-APC: ordered in 1989 for Canadian reserve units, this is in essence the US Marine Corps' LAV-25 with its turret replaced by a raised cupola for the commander with provision for a pintle-mounted machine-gun, and the roof over the troop compartment raised and fitted with six hatches (three on each side and two at the rear); the type has a maximum road speed of 62 mph (100 km/h)

Cardoen VTP-1 Orca

(Chile)
Type: wheeled armoured personnel carrier and multi-role vehicle
Crew: 2 + 16
Combat weight: 18,000 kg (39,683 lb)
Dimensions: length overall 7·84 m (25·72 ft); width 2·50 m (8·20 ft); height 2·50 m (8·20 ft)
Armament system: see Variant (below)
Armour: welded steel varying in thickness from 6 to 16 mm (0·24 to 0·63 in)
Powerplant: one 260-hp (194-kW) Detroit Diesel 6V-53T diesel engine with 400 litres (88 Imp gal) of internal fuel, and driving a 6 × 6 layout
Performance: speed, road 120 km/h (74·6 mph); range, road 1000 km (621 miles); fording not revealed; gradient 60%; side slope 30%; vertical obstacle not revealed; trench not revealed; ground clearance not revealed

Variant
VTP-1 Orca: this is a massive but limited vehicle whose embarked troops sit in an open compartment accessed by two doors in the rear; various numbers of 0·5-in (12·7-mm) or 7·62-mm (0·3-in) machine-guns can be pintle-mounted round the upper edge of the troop compartment, and the type has also been proposed for alternative roles (ambulance, AA vehicle, anti-tank vehicle, and maintenance/recovery vehicle) and as an artillery tractor

Above: The VTP-1 Orca is not intended for high-threat battlefields, and therefore has an open topped troop compartment.

Cardoen VTP-2

(Chile)

Type: wheeled armoured personnel carrier
Crew: 2 + 10
Combat weight: 7200 kg (15,873 lb) with 6-mm (0·24-in) armour or 8600 kg (18,959 lb) with 8-mm (0·315-in) armour
Dimensions: length overall 5·37 m (17·62 ft); width 2·32 m (7·61 ft); height 2·22 m (7·28 ft)
Armament system: one 7·62-mm (0·3-in) or 0·5-in (12·7-mm) pintle-mounted machine-gun with an unrevealed number of rounds
Armour: welded steel based on 6- or 8-mm (0·24- or 0·315-in) thickness
Powerplant: one 90-kW (121-hp) Mercedes-Benz OM 352 diesel engine with 150 litres (33 Imp gal) of internal fuel, and driving a 4 × 4 layout
Performance: speed, road 100 km/h (62·1 mph); range, road 600 km (373 miles); fording not revealed; gradient 70%; side slope 30%; vertical obstacle 0·5 m (19·7 in); trench not revealed; ground clearance 0·44 m (17·3 in)

Below: A typical weapon option for the VTP-2 is the Oerlikon-Bührle GAD turret with s single-feed KAA cannon of 20-mm calibre.

Variant

VTP-2: based on the chassis and automotive components of the Mercedes-Benz Unimog high-mobility truck, the VTP-2 was developed in the early 1980s, and is available with open or enclosed bodies, and with armament options that include a 20-mm cannon in an Oerlikon GAD-AOA turret, a mortar, anti-tank missiles and turreted AA cannon; the basic vehicle has provision for the embarked troops to fire their personal weapons from inside the hull; access is provided by a single door in the rear of the troop compartment, which also has two overhead hatches

Cardoen BMS-1 Alacran

(Chile)

Type: halftrack armoured personnel carrier
Crew: 2 + 12
Combat weight: 10,500 kg (23,148 lb)
Dimensions: length overall 6·37 m (20·90 ft); width 2·38 m (7·81 ft); height to hull roof 2·03 m (6·66 ft)
Armament system: one 7·62-mm (0·3-in) or 0·5-in (12·7-mm) pintle-mounted machine-gun with an unrevealed number of rounds
Armour: welded steel
Powerplant: one 225-hp (168-kW) Cummins V-555 diesel engine with 350 litres (77 Imp gal) of internal fuel, and driving a halftrack layout
Performance: speed, road 70 km/h (43·5 mph); range, road 900 km (559 miles); fording 1·6 m (5·25 ft); gradient 70%; side slope 30%; vertical obstacle not revealed; trench not revealed; ground clearance not revealed

Variant

BMS-1 Alacran: first appearing in 1983 as a private venture, the BMS-1 possesses what is now an unusual configuration, and though simple in basic design is still a modestly effective type with provision for the embarked troops to fire their personal weapons from inside the hull via 10 ports (four on each side and two in the rear); the troop compartment is accessed by one large door in the rear, and there are two outward-opening hatches in the roof; the type has provision for turreted armament up to 90 mm (3·54 in) in calibre, and has been proposed for a diversity of armed and unarmed roles

NORINCO/Vickers Defence Systems NVH-1

(China/UK)

Type: tracked mechanized infantry combat vehicle
Crew: 3 + 8
Combat weight: 16,000 kg (35,273 lb)
Dimensions: length overall 6·125 m (20·10 ft); width 3·06 m (10·04 ft); height to turret top 2·77 m (9·09 ft)
Armament system: one 25-mm McDonnell Douglas Helicopter M242 Bushmaster cannon with 520 rounds, one 7·62-mm (0·3-in) McDonnell Douglas EX-34 co-axial machine-gun with 2,000 rounds, and four smoke-dischargers on each side of the turret; the turret is electrically powered, the main gun lacks stabilization in either elevation (an unrevealed arc) or azimuth (360°), and an optical fire-control system is fitted; the last can be simple type or alternatively the OIP LRS 5 type with a laser rangefinder and ballistic computer

Armour: welded steel
Powerplant: one 240-kW (322-hp) Deutz BF8L 413F diesel engine with an unrevealed quantity of internal fuel
Performance: speed, road 65 km/h (40·4 mph) and water 6 km/h (3·7 mph) propelled by its tracks; range, road 500 km (311 miles); fording not revealed without preparation and amphibious with preparation; gradient 60%; side slope 40%; vertical obstacle 0·6 m (23·6 in); trench 2·2 m (7·2 ft); ground clearance 0·48 m (18·9 in)

Variants

NVH-1: first revealed in 1986 after development since 1984, this useful mechanized infantry combat vehicle combines a Vickers two-man turret (with US armament and Belgian fire-control system) and a Chinese hull based on the H-1 development of the YW 531 armoured personnel carrier; the NVH-1 carries a crew of three (commander and gunner in the turret, and driver in the front of the vehicle) and a full squad of infantry, who enter and leave the vehicle using a rear door; the embarked troops also have access to a pair of rearward-opening hatches in the roof, and can use their personal weapons from inside the vehicle via seven firing ports (one in the rear door and three in each side); the NVH-1 has full NBC protection and can be made amphibious by the attachment of side floats in a time of about 20 minutes

NVH-4: slightly longer and naturally amphibious development of the NVH-1, with a crew of 3 + 10 and a combat weight of 17,000 kg (37,478 lb); the type has an overall length of 6·825 m (22·39 ft), which gives a trench-crossing capability of 2·5 m (8·2 ft); in all other respects the NVH-4 is basically similar to the NVH-1

NORINCO YW 531

(China)
Type: tracked armoured personnel carrier
Crew: 4 + 10
Combat weight: 12,600 kg (27,778 lb)
Dimensions: length overall 5·476 m (17·97 ft); width 2·978 m (9·77 ft); height overall 2·563 m (8·41 ft)
Armament system: one 12·7-mm (0·5-in) Type 54 pintle-mounted heavy machine-gun with 1,120 rounds; the mounting is manually powered, pro-

viding weapon elevation from 0° to +90° plus weapon traverse of 360°, and simple optical sights are fitted
Armour: welded steel
Powerplant: one 240-kW (322-hp) Deutz BF8L 413F diesel engine with between 450 and 480 litres (99 and 106 Imp gal) of internal fuel
Performance: speed, road 65 km/h (40·4 mph) and water 6 km/h (3·7 mph) propelled by its tracks; range, road 500 km (311 miles); fording amphibious; gradient 60%; side slope 40%; vertical obstacle 0·6 m (23·6 in); trench 2·0 m (6·6 ft); ground clearance 0·43 m (17 in)

Variants

YW 531: originally described in the West as the **K-63**, **M1967** and **M1970**, the YW 531 is believed to have the formal designation **Type 63** and to be based loosely on the chassis and automotive components of the Type 63 light tank; the model was initially powered by the 195-kW (262-hp) Type 6150L diesel, but later examples and most exported vehicles have the Deutz diesel imported from West Germany; there is only one firing port in each side of the hull, and though the type has very good cross-country performance it lacks such modern features as night-vision equipment and an NBC system; the embarked troops enter and leave the vehicle through a large door in the rear, and have limited capability to fire their personal weapons from inside the vehicle via two ports (one on each side); the vehicle comes in several versions including the **YW 531C**, **YW 531D** and **YW 531E** command variants with differing radio fits; the **YW 531C (Improved)** has a shield for the 12·7-mm (0·5-in) machine-gun, improved vision ports and a superior ventilation system; the YW 531 has also been used as the basis of a psychological warfare vehicle fitted with four loudspeakers, and of an anti-tank vehicle carrying a rear-mounted turret with four Red Arrow 8 tube-launched missiles and associated control equipment, plus reload missiles in the hull

YW 531H: improved version of the YW 531 with the hull increased in length to 5·90 m (19·36 ft) and width to 3·06 m (10·04 ft) for a capacity of 2 + 13, the 240-kW (322-hp) Deutz diesel engine imported from West Germany, a new suspension

The YW 531 is a tracked armoured personnel carrier, used in large numbers and several variants by the Chinese army.

system and a combat weight of 13,600 kg (29,982 lb); the YW 531H is thus very similar in overall parameters and capabilities to the YW 534; there is provision for the embarked troops to fire their personal weapons from inside the vehicle via a varying number of ports – some vehicles have two on the left and three or four on the right, while other vehicles have three on the left and four on the right; the primary armament is a 12·7-mm (0·5-in) machine-gun and 1,120 rounds, fitted in a mounting that provides the gunner with all-round protection

YW 304: 12,800-kg (28,219-lb) self-propelled medium mortar derivative of the YW 531 fitted with an 82-mm (3·2-in) mortar in the erstwhile troop compartment at the rear; the mortar can be traversed through 360° and elevated between +40° and +65°; the mortar can fire to 3040 m (3,325 yards), and 120 mortar bombs are carried; the crew is between six and eight, and local defence is entrusted to a 12·7-mm (0·5-in) machine-gun with 560 rounds

Type 70: self-propelled rocket-launcher derivative of the YW 531 fitted with a 19-tube launcher for 130-mm (5·12-in) rockets; the launcher can be traversed through 180° and elevated from 0° and +50°, allowing the rockets to be fired to a maximum range of 10,370 m (11,340 yards); the 13,400-kg (29,541-lb) Type 70 has a crew of six, and is powered by the 195-kW (262-hp) Type 6150L diesel

Type 82: self-propelled heavy mortar derivative of the YW 531 fitted with a 120-mm (4·72-in) mortar in the erstwhile troop compartment at the rear; the mortar can be traversed a total of 20° (10° left and 10° right of the centreline) and elevated from +45° to +80°; the mortar can fire to 7500 m (8,200 yards), and 50 mortar bombs are carried; the vehicle is 6·125 m (20·10 ft) long, 3·06 m (10·04 ft) wide and 2·593 m (8·51 ft) high

Type 85: 13,800-kg (30,423-lb) armoured command post derivative of the YW 531H with a crew of two plus six command personnel; the vehicle has extensive radio communications equipment, specialist fittings and an armament of one unprotected 12·7-mm (0·5-in) machine-gun backed by two banks of four smoke-dischargers

YW 309: hybrid infantry combat vehicle combining the hull of the YW 531H with the turret (complete with 73-mm/2·87-in low-pressure smooth-bore gun and Red Arrow 73 anti-tank missile launcher) of the WZ 501, the Chinese derivative of the Soviet BMP-1; the YW 309 has a crew of 3 + 8 and a combat weight of 14,700 kg (32,407 lb), while its principal dimensions include a length of 6·27 m (20·57 ft) and an overall height of 2·475 m (8·12 ft); the embarked infantrymen can fire their personal weapons from inside the vehicle, which is fitted with day and night vision equipment

WZ 701: armoured command post derivative of the YW 531 with the original 195-kW (262-hp) Type 6150L diesel; the variant has a crew of three and provision for five command staff, and carries mapboards in the revised rear compartment, together with additional radio equipment; local defence is entrusted to one 7·62-mm (0·3-in) Type 56-1 machine-gun with 1,000 rounds; the upgraded export version is the **YW 701A** powered by the 240-kW (322-kW) Deutz diesel, carrying more advanced communications equipment and fitted with one 12·7-mm (0·5-in) heavy machine-gun plus 560 rounds for local defence

WZ 751: 13,800-kg (30,423-lb) armoured ambulance version of the YW 531H with provision in the rear of the vehicle for two attendants and four litters or eight seated casualties; the vehicle has a defensive armament of one 12·7-mm (0·5-in) unprotected machine-gun with 500 rounds

NORINCO YW 534

(China)

Type: tracked armoured personnel carrier
Crew: 2 + 13
Combat weight: 14,300 kg (31,526 lb)
Dimensions: length overall 6·15 m (20·18 ft); width 3·134 m (10·28 ft); height overall 2·556 m (8·39 ft)
Armament system: one 12·7-mm (0·5-in) Type 54 pintle-mounted heavy machine-gun with 1,100 rounds, and four smoke-dischargers on each side of the hull; the gun mounting is manually operated, providing the weapon with elevation through an unrevealed arc as well as 360° traverse, and simple optical sights are fitted
Armour: welded steel
Powerplant: one 240-kW (322-hp) diesel engine with an unrevealed quantity of internal fuel
Performance: speed, road 65 km/h (40·4 mph) and water 6 km/h (3·7 mph) propelled by its tracks; range, road 500 km (311 miles); fording amphibious; gradient 60%; side slope 40%; vertical obstacle 0·7 m (27·6 in); trench 2·5 m (8·2 ft); ground clearance 0·48 m (18·9 in)

Variants

YW 534: this armoured personnel carrier was developed in parallel with the YW 531H, but has a slightly longer and wider hull than the YW 531H; there is a single rear-mounted door for the embarked troops, who have five ports (two on each side and one in the door) through which to fire their personal weapons; there are also two roof hatches

YW 307: 15,400-kg (33,951-lb) infantry fighting vehicle counterpart to the YW 534, using the same hull but fitted with a one-man turret carrying a 25-mm cannon and co-axial 7·62-mm (0·3-in) machine-gun; a bank of four smoke-dischargers is installed on the front of the power-operated turret, which can traverse through 360°; the guns can be elevated from − 12° to + 52°, and the ammunition capacities are 400 rounds of AP and HE (fired with a muzzle velocity of 1050 m/3,445 ft per second) for the cannon and 1,000 rounds for the machine-gun; the YW 307 has a crew of 3 + 7

NORINCO WZ 551

(China)

Type: wheeled infantry fighting vehicle
Crew: 2 + 9
Combat weight: 15,000 kg (33,069 lb)
Dimensions: length overall 6·65 m (21·82 ft); width 2·80 m (9·19 ft); height overall 2·89 m (9·48 ft)
Armament system: one 25-mm cannon with 400 rounds (200 in the hull and 200 in the turret), one 7·62-mm (0·3-in) co-axial machine-gun with 1,000 rounds, and four smoke-dischargers on each side of the turret front; the turret is electrically powered, the gun lacks stabilization in either elevation (− 8° to + 55°) or azimuth (360°), and an optical fire-control is fitted
Armour: welded steel
Powerplant: one 240-kW (322-hp) Deutz BF8L 413F diesel engine with an unrevealed quantity of internal fuel, and driving a 6 × 6 layout
Performance: speed, road 85 km/h (52·8 mph) and water 7 km/h (4·3 mph) driven by two propellers; range, road 600 km (373 miles); fording amphibious; gradient 60%; side slope 30%; vertical obstacle 0·5 m (19·7 in); trench 1·2 m (3·9 ft); ground clearance 0·41 m (16·1 in)

Variant

WZ 551: this vehicle was revealed late in 1986, and is clearly modelled externally on the Renault VAB series though the Chinese vehicle is longer, wider and heavier than the French design, and has been produced or planned in a number of forms; the baseline version is the 6 × 6 armoured personnel carrier, which has an empty weight of 12,500 kg (27,557 lb) and a crew of 2 + 11; the maximum payload is 7000 kg (15,432 lb) on land and 3500 kg (7,716 lb) on water, and the vehicle is fitted with an externally mounted 12·7-mm (0·5-in) machine gun plus 500 rounds; the embarked troops use a large door in the rear, can fire their personal weapons via seven ports (three on each side and one in the rear) and also have four outward-hingeing roof hatches; standard equip-

Right and below: the WZ 551 wheeled infantry fighting vehicle with external 25-mm cannon.

ment includes an NBC system and night vision systems; from this basic 6 × 6 version have been developed three other versions, namely the infantry fighting vehicle armed with a 25-mm cannon (described above), an infantry fighting vehicle armed with a 73-mm (2·87-in) gun and an ambulance; the 14,200-kg (31,305-lb) infantry fighting vehicle with a 73-mm (2·87-in) gun has the same turret as that fitted on the WZ 501 infantry fighting vehicle, and this turret is essentially that developed by the USSR for the BMP-1 with a low-pressure smooth-bore gun plus 40 rounds, a 7·62-mm (0·3-in) co-axial machine-gun plus 2,000 rounds and (in this Chinese application) one launcher for four Red Arrow 73 anti-tank missiles; the 12,600-kg (27,778-lb) ambulance has a crew of three (one of whom mans the 12·7-mm/0·5-in machine-gun plus 500 rounds) and a raised roof over a rear compartment revised for the carriage of four litters; Chinese thoughts are already turned to the concept of a series of light armoured fighting vehicles based on the WZ 551, including 4 × 4 and 8 × 8 versions for a variety of roles; the 8 × 8 version is already maturing as the basis of a 122-mm (4·8-in) self-propelled howitzer, while the 4 × 4 version has been used for a light anti-tank vehicle; this latter has a crew of four, a weight of 12,500 kg (27,557 lb), and overall dimensions that include a length of 6·05 m (19·85 ft), a width of 2·80 m (9·19 ft) and a height of 2·60 m (8·53 ft) over the quadruple launcher for 12 Red Arrow 8 anti-tank missiles; the vehicle has a maximum road speed of 85 km/h (52·8 mph) and a maximum road range of 600 km (373 miles)

SKOT

(Czechoslovakia/Poland)

Type: wheeled armoured personnel carrier
Crew: 2 + 18
Combat weight: 14,300 kg (31,526 lb)
Dimensions: length overall 7·44 m (24·40 ft); width 2·55 m (8·37 ft); height to hull top 2·06 m (6·76 ft)
Armament system: (SKOT only) one 7·62-mm (0·3-in) PKT pintle-mounted machine-gun with 1,250 rounds; the mounting is manually powered, providing weapon elevation between -6° and +23·5° plus 90° traverse (45° left and 45° right of the centreline), and simple optical sights are fitted
Armour: welded steel to a maximum thickness of 10 mm (0·39 in)
Powerplant: one 135-kW (181-hp) Tatra 928-14 diesel engine with 320 litres (70 Imp gal) of internal fuel, and driving an 8 × 8 layout
Performance: speed, road 94·4 km/h (58·7 mph) and water 9 km/h (5·6 mph) driven by two propellers; range, road 710 km (441 miles); fording amphibious; gradient 60%; side slope 30%; vertical obstacle 0·5 m (19·7 in); trench 2·0 m (6·6 ft); ground clearance 0·46 m (18 in)

SKOT wheeled armoured personnel carrier.

Variants

SKOT: developed from the late 1950s by Czechoslovakia and Poland on the basis of the Tatra 813 8 × 8 cross-country truck, the SKOT entered service in 1964 and is sometimes known in the West by the bogus designation OT-64A; the Czech vehicles are unarmed but the Polish vehicles have a PKT pintle-mounted machine-gun; some SKOTs have been seen with two launchers for four 'Sagger' anti-tank missiles; notable features are the size and capacity of the type, the standard NBC system, full amphibious capability and a central tyre pressure-regulation system; the embarked troops use two doors in the rear of the vehicle, and are also provided with five roof hatches, of which one opens forward and the other four (two on each side) are oblong units opening outwards; there are two firing ports in each side of the troop compartment, giving the embarked troops a limited capability to use their personal weapons from inside the vehicle
SKOT-2: used only by Poland and sometimes known in the West by the bogus designation OT-64B, this model has a pintle-mounted and shielded 7·62-mm PKT or 12·7-mm (0·5-in) DShKM machine-gun, and the roof hatches number three (one forward-opening and two outward-opening)
SKOT-2A: sometimes known in the West by the bogus designation OT-64C(1), this 14,500-kg (31,966-lb) version is armed with a 14·5-mm (0·57-in) KVPT machine-gun (500 rounds) and co-axial 7·62-mm PKT machine-gun (2,000 rounds) in a centrally located and manually powered turret similar to that of the Soviet BRDM-2 and is armoured to a maximum thickness of 14 mm (0·55 in); the turret is capable of 360° traverse and provides gun elevation from −4° to +29°; this variant is 2·50 m (8·20 ft) high to the top of the turret, and is powered by a Tatra 928-18 diesel rated identically with the Tatra 928-14 of the SKOT; there are four hatches in the roof of the troop compartment, the two lateral pairs opening outwards
SKOT-2AP: version used by Poland with a revised turret featuring a curved top; this model is sometimes known in the West by the bogus designation OT-64C(2), and the revised turret allows gun elevation to a maximum of +89·5° to allow the engagement of helicopters; some vehicles also have provision for a single 'Sagger' anti-tank missile on each side of the turret; some export versions have the turret of the OT-62B armoured personnel carrier, the Czech version of the Soviet BTR-50
SKOT R-2: command version of the basic model
SKOT R-3: command version of the basic model
SKOT-WPT: Polish recovery and repair version, fitted with a light crane and armed with a single 7·62-mm (0·3-in) machine-gun

Kadar Fahd

(Egypt)
Type: wheeled armoured personnel carrier
Crew: 2 + 10
Combat weight: 11,250 kg (24,801 lb)
Dimensions: length overall 6·00 m (19·69 ft); width 2·45 m (8·03 ft); height 2·10 m (6·89 ft)
Armament system: see Variant (below)
Armour: welded steel
Powerplant: one 125-kW (168-hp) Mercedes-Benz OM 352A diesel engine with an unrevealed quantity of internal fuel, and driving a 4 × 4 layout
Performance: speed, road 90 km/h (56 mph); range, road 800 km (497 miles); fording 0·7 m (2·3 ft); gradient 75%; side slope 30%; vertical obstacle 0·5 m (19·7 in); trench 0·8 m (31·5 in); ground clearance 0·31 m (12·2 in)

Variant
Fahd: this Egyptian armoured personnel carrier is a comparatively limited type based on the chassis and automotive system of the Daimler-Benz LAP 1117/32 truck; the embarked troops use a door in the rear, and have provision to fire their personal weapons from inside the vehicle via 10 ports, two in the rear and four on each side; there are also two inward-opening hatches over the troop compartment, allowing the location of up to three 7·62-mm (0·3-in) machine-guns for suppressive fire; the Fahd is fitted as standard with a central tyre pressure-regulation system, and options include an NBC system, passive night vision devices, a bank of four smoke-dischargers on each side of the hull, and a 5000-kg (11,023-lb) capacity front-mounted winch; the type can also be fitted with an armament turret for machine-guns or a 20-mm cannon, and can also carry the Milan anti-tank missile system; variants optimized for the command post, recovery, logistics, ambulance and rocket-launcher roles are under development

The XA-180 Pangu is a 6 × 6 wheeled armoured personnel carrier based on the chassis of a 4 × 4 truck, and can be fitted with a one-man turret.

SISU XA-180 Pangu

(Finland)
Type: wheeled armoured personnel carrier
Crew: 2 + 10
Combat weight: 15,000 kg (33,069 lb)
Dimensions: length overall 7·35 m (24·11 ft); width 2·89 m (9·48 ft); height 2·30 m (7·55 ft)
Armament system: one 7·62-mm (0·3-in) PKT pintle-mounted machine-gun with an unrevealed number of rounds, but see Variant (below)
Armour: welded steel
Powerplant: one 180-kW (241-hp) Valmet diesel engine with an unrevealed quantity of internal fuel, and driving a 6 × 6 layout
Performance: speed, road 100 km/h (62·1 mph) and water 10 km/h (6·2 mph) driven by two propellers; range, road 800 km (497 miles); fording amphibious; gradient not revealed; side slope not revealed; vertical obstacle not revealed; trench not revealed; ground clearance 0·4 m (15·75 in)

Variant
XA-180 Pangu: entering service in the mid-1980s, this vehicle is based on the chassis and automotive components of the Valmet SA-150 VK 4 × 4 truck, and can carry a 6500-kg (14,330-lb) payload on roads, or a 3000-kg (6,614-lb) payload across country or swimming; the embarked troops use two doors in the rear and have two inward-opening roof hatches, and the type has seven ports (one in the rear and three on each side) for the use of personal weapons by the embarked troops; it is likely that command, mortar, and 90-mm (3·54-in) fire-support will be developed, and Finland has already selected the type as the basis of its new Crotale NG surface-to-air missile system based on the French Crotale but using the new Vought/Thomson VT-1 missile; in service with Finnish troops on UN service, the type has a one-man turret armed with a single 12·7-mm (0·5-in) DShKM machine-gun and five smoke-dischargers on each side; the turret is manually powered, the gun lacks stabilization in either elevation (an unrevealed arc) or azimuth (360°), and simple optical sights are fitted

GIAT AMX-10P

(France)
Type: tracked mechanized infantry combat vehicle
Crew: 3 + 8
Combat weight: 14,500 kg (31,966 lb)
Dimensions: length overall 5·778 m (18·96 ft); width 2·78 m (9·12 ft); height 2·57 m (8·43 ft)
Armament system: one 20-mm GIAT M693 (F2) cannon with 760 rounds (435 in the hull and 325 in the turret), one 7·62-mm (0·3-in) co-axial machine-gun with 2,000 rounds (1,100 in the hull and 900 in the turret), and two smoke-dischargers on each side of the turret; the turret is electrically powered, the gun lacks stabilization in either elevation (−8° to +50°) or azimuth (360°), and an optical fire-control system is fitted
Armour: welded aluminium
Powerplant: one 210-kW (282-hp) Renault (Hispano-Suiza) HS 115-2 diesel engine with 528 litres (116 Imp gal) of internal fuel
Performance: speed, road 65 km/h (40·4 mph) and water 7 km/h (4·3 mph) driven by two water-jets; range, road 600 km (373 miles); fording amphibious; gradient 60%; side slope 30%; vertical obstacle 0·7 m (27·6 in); trench 2·1 m (6·89 ft); ground clearance 0·45 m (17·7 in)

Variants
AMX-10P: designed from the mid-1960s as replacement for the AMX VCI, the AMX-10P is a useful mechanized infantry combat vehicle rather than a plain armoured personnel carrier, and began to enter French service in 1973; since that time substantial export orders have been received to bolster production swelled by a proliferation of variants; the type has an NBC protection system as standard and is fully amphibious; the embarked troops use a powered ramp at the rear and have two roof hatches that open inwards, and can fire their personal weapons only through a pair of ports in the rear ramp; the standard Toucan II two-man turret can be replaced by a one-man Toucan I or Capre 20 turret, and the M693 cannon can be altered for other 20-mm weapons (typically the Rheinmetall MK 20 Rh 202); there is a driving training version with an observation position in place of the armament turret
AMX-10P 25: upgraded model first shown in 1983, and featuring a one-man Dragar turret with dual-feed 25-mm GIAT 811 cannon plus a ready-use capacity of 220 rounds (175 of HE and 45 of AP), as well as a co-axial 7·62-mm (0·3-in) machine-gun; the turret can be traversed though 360° and the guns elevated between −10° and +45°; the vehicle weighs 14,300 kg (31,526 lb) and has a crew of 3 + 8
AMX-10P Marine: version developed for the Indonesian marines with the 205-kW (275-hp) Baudouin 6 F11 SRX diesel engine and improved waterjet propulsion for a waterborne speed of 10 km/h (6·2 mph); the type is fitted with a rear-mounted GIAT CIBI 50 turret carrying one 0·5-in (12·7-mm) Browning M2HB heavy machine-gun with 120 rounds; the crew is 2 + 13
AMX-10 Sanitaire: unarmed ambulance model with accommodation for a crew of three (driver and two attendants) plus three litters or one litter and four seated casualties
AMX-10 ECH: repair version with Toucan I turret and 6000-kg (13,228-lb) capacity crane
AMX-10 HOT: 14,100-kg (31,085-lb) anti-tank version with a two-man Lancelot turret for four loaded HOT missile launchers, 14 reload missiles being accommodated in the hull; the crew comprises the driver and two loading numbers in the hull, and the commander and gunner in the turret

Above: The AMX-10P is related to the AMX-10RC, and its Toucan II turret has an external 20-mm cannon.

Below: The AMX-10P RATAC has radar for the accurate control of field artillery batteries.

AMX-10PC: Poste de Commandement (command post) version with additional radios and generating capacity for a crew of six (driver, two officers, one NCO and two signallers)

AMX-10P RATAC: radar version with RATAC artillery radar in place of the turret; the crew comprises the driver, commander, two radar operators and radio operator; the vehicle is 2·84 m (9·32 ft) high, and carries a land navigation system

AMX-10 RAV: ammunition resupply version for use with the self-propelled 155-mm (6·1-in) GCT vehicle

AMX-10RC: reconnaissance version (see relevant section)

AMX-10RTT: private-venture development of the AMX-10RC with a complement of 3 + 10; the vehicle has a Dragar turret fitted with a 25-mm GIAT 811 cannon (plus 175 rounds of HE and 45 rounds of APDS ammunition), a 7·62-mm (0·3-in) machine-gun and six Galix grenade-launchers located three on each side of the turret; the troop compartment has four outward-opening roof hatches, a power-operated rear ramp with two firing ports, and three firing ports in each side of the compartment

AMX-10 SAO: artillery observation version with the Toucan II turret replaced by a two-man turret

with long-range laser rangefinder and external 7·62-mm (0·3-in) machine-gun; the five-man crew comprises the driver and two radio operators in the hull, and two artillery specialists in the turret

AMX-10 SAT: artillery survey vehicle with specialist survey equipment and navigation system

AMX-10 TM: tractor version for the 120-mm (4·72-in) Thomson Brandt MO-120-RT-61 rifled mortar, for which the vehicle carries 60 bombs, a crew of six and the Toucan I turret (20-mm cannon and 7·62-mm/0·3-in machine-gun)

AMX-10 VOA: artillery observation version of the AMX-10PC with two-man turret for observation (day and night) and local defence; the four-man crew comprises the driver and radio operator in the hull, and the commander and observer in the turret

AMX-10P/ATILA: the AMX-10P has been developed in three forms with the ATILA automatic artillery fire-control system; the **AMX-10P VFA** is the regimental-level version with the ATILA artillery fire-control system with computer, the **AMX-10P VLA** is the artillery liaison version lacking the computer elements of the ATILA system, and the **AMX-10P SAF** is the high-echelon version of the ATILA artillery fire-control system with an auxiliary power unit, air-

The AMX-10P is fully amphibious, being propelled in the water (after the trim vane has been erected and two bilge pumps have been switched on) by a pair of waterjets at the hull rear.

conditioning systems for the electronics and crew, a multi-role computer and other equipment for its five-man crew

AMX-10 TMC-81: advanced fire-support version with an 81-mm (3·2-in) Brandt CL 81 smooth-bore gun/mortar (with 108 HE and 10 APFSDS rounds) in a 360° traverse turret that provides the ordnance with elevation between −7° and +66°; the type has a crew of four

AMX-10 PAC 90: 14,800-kg (32,628-lb) export fire-support version with the GIAT TS 90 turret carrying the 90-mm (3·54-in) GIAT CS Super (F4) rifled gun plus 30 rounds, a 7·62-mm (0·3-in) co-axial machine-gun plus 2,000 rounds, and a 7·62-mm (0·3-in) or 0·5-in (12·7-mm) AA machine-gun plus 1,200 or 1,000 rounds respectively; this version's principal dimensions include lengths of 7·22 m (23·69 ft) with gun forward and 5·87 m (19·26 ft) for the hull, a width of 2·83 m (9·285 ft) and an overall height of 2·73 m (8·96 ft); advanced sights and/or fire-control systems can be fitted as required, and the crew is 3 + 4

Creusot-Loire AMX VCI

(France)
Type: tracked infantry combat vehicle
Crew: 3 + 10
Combat weight: 15,000 kg (33,069 lb)
Dimensions: length overall 5·70 m (18·70 ft); width 2·67 m (8·76 ft); height to turret top 2·41 m (7·91 ft)
Armament system: see Variants (below)
Armour: welded steel varying in thickness from 10 to 30 mm (0·30 to 1·18 in)
Powerplant: one 185-kW (248-hp) SOFAM 8Gxb petrol engine with 410 litres (90 Imp gal) of internal fuel
Performance: speed, road 60 km/h (37·3 mph); range, road 350 km (217 miles); fording 1·0 m (3·3 ft); gradient 60%; side slope not revealed; vertical obstacle 0·65 m (25·6 in); trench 1·6 m (5·2 ft); ground clearance 0·48 m (18·9 in)

Variants

AMX VCI: this was developed in the early part of the 1950s on the basis of the AMX-13 light tank, and the first production examples appeared in 1957 under the designation **TT 12 Ch modèle 56** (Transport de Troupe Chenillé model 1956), later changed to **AMX VTP** (Véhicule Transport de Personnel) and finally to AMX VCI (Véhicule de Combat d'Infanterie); the AMX VCI can be fitted with a wide diversity of barrelled armament, either pintle- or turret-mounted: the most common fits are a ring/pintle-mounted 7·62-mm (0·3-in) medium machine-gun or 0·5-in (12·7-mm) heavy machine-gun, or a CAFL 38 turret carrying either of the above machine-guns, or various Creusot-Loire turrets carrying a 20-mm cannon, most commonly the GIAT M621 (F1) weapon; there is also provision for the embarked troops to fire their personal weapons from inside the

The VCI can be fitted with the Toucan turret complete with its external 20-mm cannon.

vehicle via 10 firing ports (one in each of the twin rear doors, and two in each of the four two-piece overhead hatches); later examples were fitted as standard with an NBC protection system, and vehicles of this series can be engined (in construction or as a retrofit) with a diesel powerplant, either the 280-hp (209-kW) Detroit Diesel 6V-53T or the 200-kW (268-hp) Baudouin 6 F11 SRY; the use of a diesel engine reduces the fire risk, increases speed marginally to 64 km/h (39·8 mph), and boosts range by some 100 km (62 miles)

VTT/Cargo: battlefield freight model with a payload of 3000 kg (6,614 lb)
VTT/LT: artillery fire-control model of the VTT/PC with a crew of seven and specialist equipment
VTT/PC: Poste de Commandement (command post) model with a crew of six to eight and additional features such as map tables
VTT/PM: Porte Mortier (mortar-carrier) version with an 81-mm (3·2-in) mortar and 128 bombs, or a 120-mm (4·72-in) Thomson Brandt MO-120-LT mortar and 60 bombs, both types firing through a roof hatch; the crew is six
VTT/RATAC: artillery radar vehicle with RAdar de Tir pour Artillerie de Campagne equipment mounted above the roof
VTT/TB: Transport de Blessés (ambulance) model with accommodation for three litters or four seated casualties in addition to the driver, doctor and two attendants
VTT/VCA: Véhicule Chenillé d'Accompagnement (tracked support vehicle) model to accompany the 155-mm (6·1-in) Mk F3 self-propelled gun, carrying part of the gun crew and 25 rounds, and towing a trailer with another 30 rounds
VCG: 17,800-kg (39,242-lb) Véhicule de Combat du Génie (combat engineer vehicle) with a front-mounted dozer blade and A-frame, a 4500-kg (9,921-lb) capacity winch, specialist equipment and a crew of 10

Renault VAB VTT

(France)
Type: wheeled armoured personnel carrier
Crew: 2 + 10
Combat weight: 13,000 kg (28,660 lb)
Dimensions: length overall 5·98 m (19·62 ft); width 2·49 m (8·17 ft); height to hull top 2·06 m (6·76 ft)
Armament system: one 7·62-mm (0·3-in) cupola-mounted machine-gun with an unrevealed number of rounds; the cupola is manually powered, the gun lacks stabilization in either elevation (−15° to +45° with the shield in normal position, or −20° to +80° with the shield in the AA position) or azimuth (360°), and simple optical sights are fitted
Armour: welded steel
Powerplant: one 175-kW (235-hp) MAN D2356 HM72 or 170-kW (228-hp) Renault VI MIDS 06-20-45 diesel engine with 300 litres (66 Imp gal) of internal fuel, and driving a 4 × 4 layout
Performance: speed, road 92 km/h (57 mph) and water 7 km/h (4·3 mph) driven by two waterjets; range, road 1000 km (621 miles); fording amphibious; gradient 60%; side slope 35%; vertical obstacle 0·6 m (23·6 in); trench not revealed; ground clearance 0·4 m (15·75 in)

Variants

VAB VTT: this is the French army's standard wheeled armoured personnel carrier, and was designed in the early 1970s in 4 × 4 and 6 × 6 layouts in response to a requirement for such a vehicle as the primary transport of motorized formations, mechanized formations being allocated the tracked AMX-10P; production began in 1976 for this purpose, the French army opting for the 4 × 4 layout; standard equipment includes NBC protection and active/passive night vision equipment; there is provision for the embarked troops to fire their personal weapons from inside the vehicle via eight windows with armoured shut-

ters (one in each of the two rear doors, and three on each side of the troop compartment); there are also three roof hatches, all of them opening to the front; it is likely that the 6 × 6 version, which is proving successful in the export market, will also be adopted for the French army, this type having a combat weight of 14,200 kg (31,305 lb) and a 1-m (3·3-ft) trench-crossing capability; various alternative armament installations are possible

VAB VCI: Véhicule de Combat d'Infanterie (infantry combat vehicle) development of the VAB currently offered in five forms with different armament turrets; the **VAB VCI Toucan** has a crew of 3 + 8 and is fitted with the one-man GIAT Toucan I turret carrying a 20-mm GIAT M621 (F1) cannon plus 700 rounds, a co-axial 7·62-mm (0·3-in) machine-gun plus 2,000 rounds, and two smoke-dischargers on each side of the turret; this manually powered installation has 360° traverse, and allows elevation of the guns between − 13° and + 50°; the French air force has adopted a 4 × 4 version of the VAB VCI Toucan as the **VIB** (Véhicule d'Intervention sur Base) base intervention vehicle; the **VAB VCI Dragar** is a derivative of the basic version with a crew of eight and fitted with the one-man GIAT Dragar turret carrying a 25-mm GIAT 811 cannon plus 620 rounds, a 7·62-mm (0·3-in) co-axial machine-gun plus 1,400 rounds, and four smoke-dischargers or three Galix grenade-launchers on each side of the turret; the turret functions are electric, and two-axis stabilization can be fitted as an option; the **VAB VCI T 25** is a derivative of the basic version with a crew of eight and fitted with the two-man Creusot-Loire T 25 turret carrying a 25-mm GIAT 811, McDonnell Douglas Helicopters M242 Bushmaster or Oerlikon-Bührle KBA-BO2 cannon plus 530 rounds (including between 215 and 260 in the turret) and a 7·62-mm (0·3-in) co-axial machine-gun with 1,200 rounds (including 200 in the turret); the turret functions are electric, and while the turret can be traversed through 360°, the weapons can be elevated between − 8° and + 55°; the **VAB VCI T 20** is a derivative of the basic version with a crew of 11 and fitted with the one-man Creusot-Loire T 20 turret carrying a 20-mm GIAT M693 (F2), Hispano-Suiza HS 820 or Rheinmetall MK 20 Rh 202 cannon plus 700 rounds (including 130 in the turret) and a 7·62-mm (0·3-in) co-axial machine-gun with 2,200 rounds (including 200 in the turret); the turret functions are electric, and while the turret can be traversed through 360°, the weapons can be elevated between − 8° and + 55°; the **VAB VCI TL 20S** is a derivative of the basic version with a crew of 12 and fitted with the one-man Creusot-Loire TL 20S turret carrying a 20-mm GIAT M693 (F2), Oerlikon-Bührle KAD or Rheinmetall MK 20 Rh 202 cannon plus 900 rounds (including 300 in the turret); the turret functions are manual, and while the turret can be traversed through 360°, the weapons can be elevated between − 8° and + 50°

VAB Bromure: electronic warfare vehicle with a crew of three and a modern electronic warfare suite at the rear

VAB Echelon: repair vehicle with specialized repair equipment and a TLi 52A machine-gun turret

VAB Génie: engineer vehicle with a crew of nine, specialized equipment and stowage on the roof for a rubber dinghy

VAB PC: Poste de Commandement (command post) model for the French army with extra radios and additional mapboards; optional fits produce the **VAB RASIT** with ground-surveillance radar, the **VAB RATAC** with artillery radar, the **VAB FDC** fire-direction centre and the **VAB FOO** forward observation vehicle, the latter two as part of the ATILA automatic artillery fire-control system

VAB Sanitaire: ambulance model with accommodation for four litters or 10 seated casualties

VAB SANTAL: under development in the mid-1980s for the French army is this specialized all-weather low-level air-defence model of the VAB, the HML turret over the hull rear accommodating six ready-to-fire Mistral short-range SAMs (three on each side of the turret) and the surveillance system, which can be an ESD Rodéo pulse-Doppler radar, a Thomson-CSF TRS 2600 pulse-Doppler radar, or a SAT Vipère IR system; six reload missiles are carried in the hull; the turret can also take four smoke-dischargers and a pintle-mounted 7·62-mm (0·3-in) machine-gun for local defence; in 1989 it was decided that the pro-gramme was too expensive and the variant was cancelled

VAB Transmission: communications version fitted with the RITA automatic integrated transmission network and carrying a crew of four

VAB VDAA TA 20: AA gun version of the VAB fitted with the TA 20 turret carrying two 20-mm cannon, one RA-20S radar and the associated fire-control system and ammunition

VAB VDAA TA 25: AA gun version of the VAB fitted with the TA 25 turret carrying two 25-mm Oerlikon-Bührle KBB dual-feed cannon, Contraves Gun King fire-control system with laser rangefinder, and ESD Rodéo or RA-20S radar

VCAC HOT Méphisto: 4 × 4 French army anti-tank version with the Euromissile Méphisto retractable launcher with four ready-to-fire HOT heavy anti-tank missiles plus eight reloads in the hull

VCAC HOT UTM 800: 6 × 6 export anti-tank version with the Euromissile UTM 800 turret for four ready-to-fire HOT heavy anti-tank missiles, another 16 missiles being held in the hull

VCAC MILAN HCT: 4 × 4 anti-tank version with the Euromissile HCT turret with two launchers for Milan medium anti-tank missiles; the vehicle has a crew of eight

VMO: 4 × 4 or 6 × 6 internal-security model with light armament and an obstacle-clearing blade

VTM 120: 6 × 6 Véhicule Tracteur de Mortier de 120 (tractor for the 120-mm mortar) used in conjunction with the 120-mm (4·72-in) Thomson Brandt rifled mortar, with accommodation for 70 bombs and six crew; further development has produced a version with the 120-mm (4·72-in) MO-120-LT mortar turntable-mounted in the vehicle rear, and the **VPM 81** Véhicule Porte Mortier de 81 (81-mm mortar-carrier) has a British 81-mm (3·2-in) mortar in a similar installation

The VAB 6 × 6 wheeled armoured personnel carrier was designed for infantry rather than mechanized formations, and has been produced in substantial numbers. This is an example modified to infantry fighting vehicle standard with a Toucan turret carrying a 20-mm cannon.

Berliet VXB-170

(France)
Type: wheeled armoured personnel carrier
Crew: 1 + 11
Combat weight: 12,700 kg (27,998 lb)
Dimensions: length overall 5·99 m (19·65 ft); width 2·50 m (8·20 ft); height without armament 2·05 m (6·73 ft)
Armament system: one 7·62-mm (0·3-in) cupola-mounted machine-gun with an unrevealed number of rounds, or one 7·62-mm (0·3-in) machine-gun with an unrevealed number of rounds and one 40-mm grenade-launcher with an unrevealed number of rounds, and two smoke-dischargers on each side of the hull; the cupola is manually powered, the gun lacks stabilization in either elevation (− 15° to + 60°) or azimuth (360°), and simple optical sights are fitted
Armour: welded steel to a 7-mm (0·28-in) basis
Powerplant: one 127-kW (170-hp) Berliet V 800 M diesel engine with 220 litres (48 Imp gal) of internal fuel, and driving a 4 × 4 layout
Performance: speed, road 85 km/h (52·8 mph) and water 4 km/h (2·5 mph) driven by its wheels; range, road 750 km (466 miles); fording amphibious; gradient 60%; side slope 30%; vertical obstacle 0·3 in (11·8 in); trench not revealed; ground clearance 0·45 m (17·7 in)

Variant

VXB-170: introduced in the early 1970s, the VXB has secured only limited sales, generally to forces with a paramilitary role; the type has provision for the embarked troops to fire their personal weapons from inside the vehicle via seven ports (two on the left including one in the door, four on the right including one in the door, and one in the rear door); the vehicle has four roof hatches, the single forward unit being used for the pintle- or turret-mounted armament; options include an NBC system, night vision devices, a front-mounted obstacle-clearing blade, and a winch

Above left, left and below: Three views of the VXB-170, a 4 × 4 wheeled armoured personnel carrier based on commercial components and intended for paramilitary rather than first-line military deployment.

Panhard VCR/TT 2

(France)
Type: wheeled armoured personnel carrier
Crew: 2 + 10/12
Combat weight: 9600 kg (21,164 lb)
Dimensions: length overall 6·14 m (20·14 ft); width 2·70 m (8·86 ft); height 2·27 m (7·45 ft)
Armament system: see Variant (below)
Armour: welded steel
Powerplant: two 110-kW (148-hp) Peugeot V6 PRV petrol engines or two 73-kW (98-hp) Peugeot XD 3T diesel engines with an unrevealed quantity of internal fuel, and driving a 6 × 6 layout
Performance: speed, road 110 km/h (68·4 mph) and water 7·2 km/h (4·5 mph) driven by two propellers; range, road 600 km (373 miles) with petrol engines or 1000 km (621 miles) with diesels; fording amphibious; gradient 50+ %; side slope 30%; vertical obstacle 0·8 m (31·5 in); trench 0·8 m (2·6 ft); ground clearance 0·37 m (14·6 in)

Variant

VCR/TT 2: this Véhicule de Combat à Roues/ Transporte de Troupes 2 (wheeled combat vehicle/troop transport Mk 2) was designed as successor to the same company's VCT TT, and uses many components of the Panhard ERC armoured car; the large troop compartment is in the rear of the vehicle, and access is provided by three doors (one on each side and one in the rear); the rear door has two firing ports, and additional capability for the embarked troops to use their personal weapons from inside the vehicle is provided by four upward-opening hatches in each side of the troop compartment; there are also two outward-opening hatches on each side of the roof; provision is additionally made for turreted armament, for example the SAMM BTE 105 carrying one 0·5-in (12·7-mm) Browning M2HB heavy machine-gun, or the SAMM TTB 125 with one 25-mm cannon and one 7·62-mm (0·3-in) coaxial machine-gun; options include a variety of night vision devices, air-conditioning, an NBC system and a front-mounted winch

The **VCR/TT2 is a 6 × 6 armoured personnel carrier seen here with a 0·5-in (12·7-mm) machine-gun on a SAMM BTE 105 turret.**

Panhard VCR/TT

(France)
Type: wheeled armoured personnel carrier
Crew: 3 + 9
Combat weight: 7900 kg (17,416 lb)
Dimensions: length overall 4·875 m (15·99 ft); width 2·478 m (8·13 ft); height including armament 2·56 m (8·40 ft)
Armament system: one 20-mm pintle-mounted cannon with an unrevealed number of rounds, or one 0·5-in (12·7-mm) pintle-mounted machine-gun with an unrevealed number of rounds or one 7·62-mm (0·3-in) pintle-mounted machine-gun with an unrevealed number of rounds, and two smoke-dischargers on each side of the hull; the gun ring is manually powered, the gun lacks stabilization in either elevation (−15° to +65°) or azimuth (360°), and simple optical sights are fitted
Armour: welded steel varying in thickness between 8 and 12 mm (0·315 to 0·49 in)
Powerplant: one 115-kW (154-hp) Peugeot 6V PRV petrol engine with 242 litres (53 Imp gal) of internal fuel, and driving a 4 × 4 (optional 6 × 6) layout
Performance: speed, road 100 km/h (62·1 mph) and water 4 km/h (2·5 mph) driven by its wheels; range, road 800 km (497 miles); fording amphibious; gradient 60%; side slope 30%; vertical

obstacle 0·8 m (31·5 in); trench 1·1 m (3·6 ft); ground clearance 0·315 m (12·4 in)

Variants

VCR/TT: this series of wheeled fighting vehicles has been developed from the basis of the ERC 6 × 6 armoured car, and features a retractable central pair of wheels for improved road performance without compromise of cross-country mobility; the VCR/TT (Véhicule de Combat à Roues/Transporte de Troupes, or wheeled combat vehicle/troop transport) is the standard armoured personnel carrier and can be fitted with a wide range of armament (including some turreted weapons, generally causing a reduction in embarked troop accommodation to six) and optional equipment such as a winch and an NBC system; there is limited provision for the embarked troops to fire their personal weapons from inside the vehicle via one port in the rear door and two hatches on each side of the troop compartment
VCR/AT: 8200-kg (18,078-lb) ATelier (repair) model with specialist equipment
VCR/IS: 8100-kg (17,857-lb) Intervention Sanitaire (medical intervention) ambulance model with accommodation for three crew and four litters or two litters and six seated casualties
VCR/PC: 7900-kg (17,416-lb) Poste de Commandement (command post) model with a crew of six and special fittings in the hull for radios, mapboards etc
VCR/TH: 7800-kg (17,196-lb) Tourelle HOT (HOT turret) anti-tank version with the Euromissile UTM 800 launcher for four ready-to-launch HOT missiles, another 10 missiles being accommodated in the hull; this variant has a remotely-controlled 7·62-mm (0·3-in) machine-gun on the roof for local protection, and a crew of four

The VCR/IS is the battlefield ambulance version of the VCR series with a raised rear hull, special equipment and an orderly for the care of wounded soldiers. A tent, stowed in boxes on the hull sides, can be erected at the rear.

Panhard VCR (4 × 4)

(France)

Type: wheeled armoured personnel carrier
Crew: 3 + 9
Combat weight: 7800 kg (17,196 lb)
Dimensions: length overall 4·875 m (15·99 ft); width 2·478 m (8·13 ft); height to hull top 2·13 m (6·99 ft)
Armament system: see Variant (below)
Armour: welded steel varying in thickness from 8 to 12 mm (0·315 to 0·47 in)
Powerplant: one 115-kW (154-hp) Peugeot V6 PRV petrol engine with 242 litres (53 Imp gal) of internal fuel, and driving a 4 × 4 layout
Performance: speed, road 100 km/h (62·1 mph) and water 7·2 km/h (4·5 mph) driven by two waterjets; range, road 800 km (497 miles); fording amphibious; gradient 60%; side slope 30%; vertical obstacle 0·4 m (15·75 in); trench not revealed; ground clearance 0·315 m (12·4 in)

Variant

VCR (4 × 4): this is a simple development of the VCR 6 × 6 series with two rather than three axles, and can be used in a similar diversity of roles with modified armament fits and interior configurations; the type has provision for the embarked troops to fire their personal weapons from inside the vehicle via one port in the large rear door and two hatches on each side of the troop compartment; the optional armament installations are basically similar to those of the 6 × 6 version of the VCR, and include a number of simple ring mounts (with or without shield) for a 0·5-in (12·7-mm) or 7·62-mm (0·3-in) machine-gun, or a Creusot-Loire CB 20 gun ring with a 20-mm cannon, or a Creusot-Loire gun ring for a 60-mm (2·36-in) Thomson Brandt breech-loaded mortar, or a Euromissile MCT turret with two launchers for the Milan medium anti-tank missile, or the Euromissile Méphisto turret with four launchers for the HOT heavy anti-tank missile

A VCR (4 × 4) with its Mephisto launcher raised and four HOT anti-tank missile containers visible.

Panhard Buffalo

(France)

Type: wheeled armoured personnel carrier
Crew: 2 + 10
Combat weight: 6200 kg (13,668 lb)
Dimensions: length overall 4·60 m (15·09 ft); width 2·40 m (7·87 ft); height to hull top 2·00 m (6·56 ft)
Armament system: see Variant (below)
Armour: welded steel varying in thickness from 8 to 12 mm (0·315 to 0·47 in)
Powerplant: one 110-kW (148-hp) Peugeot V6 PRV petrol engine or 70-kW (94-hp) Peugeot XD 3T diesel engine with an unrevealed quantity of internal fuel, and driving a 4 × 4 layout
Performance: speed, road 100 km/h (62·1 mph) and water 3·6 km/h (2·2 mph) driven by its wheels; range, road 900 km (559 miles); fording amphibious; gradient 60%; side slope 30%; vertical obstacle 0·4 m (15·75 in); trench not revealed; ground clearance 0·35 m (13·8 in)

Variant

Buffalo: this is the M3 reworked with better stowage and a choice between a petrol or diesel engine, and was first revealed in 1985 as a private-venture development for the export market; the troop compartment is located in the rear of the vehicle, and access is provided by four doors (one in each side and two in the rear); the vehicle has two roof hatches, either of which can be fitted with a gun ring; the embarked troops can fire their personal weapons from inside the vehicle via a port in each rear door and three hatches on each side of the troop compartment; a variety of armament installations is possible along the lines of the M3 series, and options for the fully amphibious vehicle include a front-mounted winch and air conditioning; the basic model can also be outfitted as an internal security vehicle, ambulance, mortar carrier and command vehicle

A VCR (4 × 4) armoured personnel carrier with windowed trim boards in amphibious mode.

Panhard M3

(France)

Type: wheeled armoured personnel carrier
Crew: 2 + 10
Combat weight: 6100 kg (13,448 lb)
Dimensions: length overall 4·45 m (14·60 ft); width 2·40 m (7·87 ft); height to top of turret 2·48 m (5·47 ft)
Armament system: see Variants (below)
Armour: welded steel varying in thickness from 8 to 12 mm (0·315 to 0·47 in)
Powerplant: one 67-kW (90-hp) Panhard 4 HD petrol engine with 165 litres (36 Imp gal) of internal fuel, and driving a 4 × 4 layout
Performance: speed, road 90 km/h (55·9 mph) and water 4 km/h (2·5 mph) driven by its wheels; range, road 600 km (373 miles); fording amphibious; gradient 60%; side slope 30%; vertical obstacle 0·3 m (11·8 in); trench not revealed; ground clearance 0·35 m (13·8 in)

Variants

M3: designed in the late 1960s, the M3 has sold successfully in Africa, some Moslem countries and elsewhere since the type entered production in 1971; the automotive components are almost identical with those of the AML armoured car series; the type has provision for the embarked troops to fire their personal weapons from inside the vehicle via a port in each of the two rear doors (supplemented for access by a door on each side of the troop compartment) and three hatches on each side of the vehicle; a large range of light and medium armament fits, of both turreted and ring-mounted types, is possible; typical are a number of Creusot-Loire ring mounts (with or without shield) for a 0·5-in (12·7-mm) or 7·62-mm (0·3-in) machine-gun, or a Creusot-Loire CB 20 for a 20-mm cannon, or a Creusot-Loire ring mounting for a 60-mm (2·36-in) Thomson Brandt breech-loaded mortar, or a Euromissile MCT turret with two launchers for Milan medium anti-tank missiles

M3/VAT: Véhicule ATelier (repair vehicle) with specialist equipment and a crew of four

M3/VDA: Véhicule de Défense Anti-aérienne (air-defence vehicle) with a turret mounting two 20-mm Hispano-Suiza 820 SL cannon (plus 600 rounds), RA-20 radar and a fire-control system; the guns can be elevated from −5° to +85° and the turret can be traversed through 360°; the cyclic rate is either 200 or 1,000 rounds per minute per barrel, and effective AA altitude 1500 m (4,920 ft) with a variety of ammunition types; this model weighs 7200 kg (15,873 lb) and has a crew of three

M3/VLA: engineer version with a front-mounted dozer blade and a crew of six

M3/VPC: Véhicule Poste de Commandement (command post vehicle) with mapboards and extra radios

M3/VSB: radar vehicle carrying either the RASIT battlefield surveillance radar or the RA 20S air surveillance radar

M3/VTS: Véhicule de Transport Sanitaire (medical transport vehicle) with a crew of three (driver and two attendants) plus six sitting wounded, or four litters, or two litters and three seated casualties

Below: The twin rear doors of the M3 are complemented by two more doors in the hull sides in line with the turret ring.

Above: The M3 has armament options such as a Creusot-Loire ring shield and breech-loaded Thomson-Brandt 60-mm mortar.

ACMAT TPK 4·20 VSC

(France)

Type: wheeled armoured personnel carrier
Crew: 2+8/10
Combat weight: 7300 kg (16,094 lb)
Dimensions: length overall 5·98 m (19·62 ft); width 2·10 m (6·89 ft); height to hull top 2·205 m (7·23 ft)
Armament system: one 0·5-in (12·7-mm) pintle-mounted machine-gun with an unrevealed number of rounds or 7·62-mm (0·3-in) pintle-mounted machine-gun with an unrevealed number of rounds, or one 81-mm (3·2-in) mortar with an unrevealed number of bombs
Armour: welded steel 5·8 mm (0·23 in) thick
Powerplant: one 125-hp (93-kW) Perkins 6·3544 diesel engine with 360 litres (79 Imp gal) of internal fuel, and driving a 4 × 4 layout
Performance: speed, road 95 km/h (59 mph); range, road 1600 km (994 miles); fording 0·8 m (2·6 ft); gradient 60%; side slope not revealed; vertical obstacle not revealed; trench not revealed; ground clearance 0·27 m (10·75 in)

Variants

TPK 4·20 VSC: introduced in 1980 and based on the VLRA reconnaissance vehicle but fitted with an armoured body, the VSC is notable for its very great range; there is no provision for the embarked troops to fire their personal weapons from inside the vehicle, which has an open-topped configuration
TPK 6·40 VBL: 8600-kg (18,959-lb) armoured car/armoured personnel version of the VSC with a fully enclosed troop compartment surmounted by a one-man turret for a variety of light armament fits (typically one 0·5-in/12·7-mm and/or one 7·62-mm/0·3-in machine-gun); the VBL has a crew of 2+16 and its principal dimensions include a length of 7·00 m (22·97 ft)

Thyssen Henschel/Krupp MaK Schützenpanzer Neu M-1966 Marder

(West Germany)

Type: tracked mechanized infantry combat vehicle
Crew: 4+6
Combat weight: 30,000 kg (66,138 lb)
Dimensions: length overall 6·79 m (22·28 ft); width 3·24 m (10·63 ft); height to hull top 1·90 m (6·23 ft) and to turret top 2·86 m (9·38 ft)
Armament system: one 20-mm Rheinmetall MK 20 Rh 202 cannon with 1,250 rounds (830 in the hull plus 345 HE and 75 AP in the turret), two 7·62-mm (0·3-in) MG3 machine-guns (one co-axial and the other in a remotely controlled podded installation at the rear of the hull) with 5,000 rounds, one Milan anti-tank launcher, and three smoke-dischargers on each side of the turret; the turret is electro-hydraulically powered, the main gun lacks stabilization in either elevation (−17° to +55°) or azimuth (360°), and a day/night optical fire-control system is fitted
Armour: welded steel
Powerplant: one 440-kW (590-hp) MTU MB 833 Ea-500 diesel engine with 652 litres (143 Imp gal) of internal fuel
Performance: speed, road 75 km/h (46·6 mph); range, road 520 km (323 miles); fording 1·5 m (4·9 ft) without preparation and 2·5 m (8·2 ft) with preparation; gradient 60%; side slope 30%; vertical obstacle 1·0 m (3·3 ft); trench 2·5 m (8·2 ft); ground clearance 0·45 m (17·7 in)

Variants

Marder: designed by Henschel and then built from 1969 by Rheinstahl (which had taken over Henschel) and MaK, the Marder (marten) is the West German army's standard mechanized infantry combat vehicle and a pioneering vehicle of its type; the Marder was at first built without the Milan anti-tank system, which was later added on the right-hand side of the cannon turret; standard systems include an NBC protection system and night vision equipment, and there is provision for the embarked troops to fire their personal weapons from inside the vehicle via two ports in each side of the troop compartment, to which access is provided by a rear ramp
Marder A1: 30,000-kg (66,138-lb) upgraded version produced by retrofit of 670 vehicles from 1982; modifications include a double-belt feed for the cannon, improved night vision capabilities and better habitability; this model has accommodation for only five infantrymen
Marder A1A: upgraded version produced by retrofit of 1,466 vehicles from 1982 to a standard similar to the Marder A1 but without improved passive night vision capability
Marder 25: version with the 20-mm cannon replaced by a 25-mm Mauser MK 25 Model E cannon, which will be retrofitted from the late 1980s
Radarpanzer TUR: 32,000-kg (70,547-lb) battlefield surveillance version with a turret replaced by a hydraulically extending arm supporting the antenna of the 30-km (18·6-mile) range Siemens surveillance radar at a height of about 10 m (32·8 ft); the vehicle has a crew of four and is 7·20 m (23·62 ft) long; the armament comprises two 7·62-mm machine-guns, and four smoke-dischargers are located on each side of the hull rear

Right: The Marder is highly capable, with a turreted 20-mm cannon (and co-axial machine-gun) main weapon and rear machine-gun.
Below: A TPK 4.20 VSC with the two armoured visors and the sides of the troop compartment raised.

Thyssen Henschel Transportpanzer 1 Fuchs

(West Germany)
Type: wheeled armoured personnel carrier
Crew: 2 + 10
Combat weight: 17,000 kg (37,478 lb)
Dimensions: length overall 6·76 m (22·19 ft); width 2·98 m (9·78 ft); height to hull top 2·30 m (7·55 ft)
Armament system: one 20-mm Rheinmetall MK 20 Rh 202 ring-mounted cannon with 150 rounds or 7·62-mm (0·3-in) MG3 ring-mounted machine-gun with an unrevealed number of rounds, and six smoke-dischargers on the left of the hull; the ring mounting is manually powered, the gun lacks stabilization in either elevation (−15° to +75° for the cannon or +45° for the machine-gun) or azimuth (360°), and simple optical sights are fitted
Armour: welded steel
Powerplant: one 240-kW (322-hp) Mercedes-Benz OM 402A diesel engine with 390 litres (86 Imp gal) of internal fuel, and driving a 6 × 6 layout
Performance: speed, road 105 km/h (65 mph) and water 10·5 km/h (6·5 mph) driven by two propellers; range, road 800 km (497 miles); fording amphibious; gradient 70%; side slope 30%; vertical obstacle not revealed; trench not revealed; ground clearance 0·41 m (16 in)

Variants

Transportpanzer 1: deliveries of the Fuchs (fix) as the West German army's standard wheeled armoured personnel carrier began in 1979, and the type is designed for maximum operational flexibility; when cargo is being carried, the normal load is 4000 kg (8,818 lb) reducing to 2000 kg (4,409 lb) when swimming; standard equipment includes an NBC protection system and night vision equipment, but there is no provision for the embarked troops to fire their personal weapons from inside the vehicle; access to the rear compartment is provided by two doors in the rear, and the troop compartment has three roof hatches, of which the forward unit is designed for the optional armament installation; the basic version can also be configured as an engineer vehicle (for the carriage of mines, demolition charges and other specialist kit), as a supply carrier (for the battlefield movement of

Below: An unarmed Transportpanzer 1.

front-line supplies) and as an ambulance for four litters or two litters and four seated casualties
TPz 1 Eloka: electronic warfare version fitted with the EK 33 jamming equipment; unlike other TPz 1 variants this model is not amphibious
TPz 1 FuFu: command and communications version with mapboards and extra radio equipment
ABC Erkundsgruppe: NBC reconnaissance version with specialist sampling and analysis equipment
Panzeraufklarungsradargerat: battlefield surveillance version with RASIT radar on a hydraulically elevating arm above the front of the hull

Thyssen Henschel Condor

(West Germany)
Type: wheeled armoured personnel carrier
Crew: 3 + 9
Combat weight: 12,400 kg (27,337 lb)
Dimensions: length overall 6·47 m (21·23 ft); width 2·47 m (8·10 ft); height to hull top 2·18 m (7·15 ft) and to turret top 2·79 m (9·15 ft)
Armament system: one 20-mm Oerlikon-Bührle KAA cannon with an unrevealed number of rounds (220 in the turret and an unrevealed number in the hull), one 7·62-mm (0·3-in) co-axial machine-gun with an unrevealed number of rounds (500 in the turret and an unrevealed number in the hull), and three smoke-dischargers on each side of the turret; the turret is

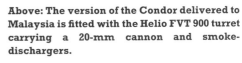

manually operated, the gun lacks stabilization in either elevation (−7° to +60°) or azimuth (360°), and an optical fire-control system is fitted
Armour: welded steel
Powerplant: one 125-kW (168-hp) Mercedes-Benz OM 352A diesel engine with 280 litres (62 Imp gal) of internal fuel, and driving a 4 × 4 layout
Performance: speed, road 100 km/h (62·1 mph) and water 8 km/h (5 mph) driven by a single propeller; range, road 900 km (559 miles); fording amphibious; gradient 60%; side slope 30%; vertical obstacle 0·55 m (21·7 in); trench not revealed; ground clearance 0·475 m (18·7 in)

Variant

Condor: designed as a successor to the highly successful UR-416 series and revealed in prototype form during 1978, the Condor is a versatile type capable of serving as an armoured personnel carrier, ambulance, command post and recovery vehicle with a light crane; the armament above (the one-man Helio FVT 900 turret used in Malaysian vehicles) can be varied to a turret for two 7·62-mm (0·3-in) machine-guns or the Euromissile HCT with two launchers for HOT heavy anti-tank missiles; optional equipment includes an NBC protection system, a winch and habitability items; the type has provision for the embarked troops to fire their personal weapons from inside the vehicle via seven ports (one in the rear door and three on each side of the troop compartment), and access is provided by the rear door and two side doors

Above: The version of the Condor delivered to Malaysia is fitted with the Helio FVT 900 turret carrying a 20-mm cannon and smoke-dischargers.

Thyssen Henschel TM 170

(West Germany)
Type: wheeled armoured personnel carrier
Crew: 2 + 10
Combat weight: 11,200 kg (24,691 lb)
Dimensions: length overall 6·12 m (20·08 ft); width 2·45 m (8·04 ft); height to hull top 2·32 m (7·61 ft)
Armament system: a wide diversity of armament fits is available, including a 7·62-mm (0·3-in) pintle-mounted machine-gun with an unrevealed number of rounds, twin turret-mounted 7·62-mm (0·3-in) machine-guns with an unrevealed number of rounds, a turret-mounted 20-mm cannon with an unrevealed number of rounds, or twin turret-mounted launchers for an unrevealed number of anti-tank missiles

The internal security TM 170 has a one-piece windscreen and obstacle-clearing blade.

Armour: welded steel
Powerplant: one 125-kW (168-hp) Mercedes-Benz OM 352A diesel engine with 175 litres (38·5 Imp gal) of internal fuel, and driving a 4 × 4 layout
Performance: speed, road 100 km/h (62·1 mph) and water 9 km/h (5·6 mph) driven by two water-jets; range, road 700 km (435 miles); fording amphibious; gradient 80%; side slope not revealed; vertical obstacle 0·6 m (23·6 in); trench not revealed; ground clearance 0·48 m (18·9 in)

Variants
TM 170: this vehicle is the largest Thyssen Henschel armoured personnel carrier, and is designed for internal security rather than front-line duties; as such it can be fitted with a wide assortment of armament fits and optional extras, and there is provision for the embarked troops to fire their personal weapons from inside the vehicle via 15 ports (three in the rear door, one in each of the two side doors, and five on each side of the troop compartment)
Armoured Special Vehicle TM 170 Hardliner: updated version of the TM 170 with a number of improvements and a lighter structure; the model has an overall length of 6·14 m (20·14 ft) and a width of 2·47 m (8·10 ft); the vehicle is not amphibious, but can ford to a depth of 1·2 m (3·9 ft) without any preparation, and its 200-litre (44-Imp gal) fuel capacity gives a road range of 870 km (541 miles)
Armoured Special Vehicle TM 170 Hardliner Patrol: version with an enclosed cab but open-topped troop compartment

---

Thyssen Henschel TM 125

(West Germany)
Type: wheeled armoured personnel carrier
Crew: 2 + 10
Combat weight: 7600 kg (16,755 lb)
Dimensions: length overall 5·54 m (18·18 ft); width 2·46 m (8·07 ft); height to hull top 2·02 m (6·61 ft)
Armament system: a wide diversity of armament fits is available, including a 7·62-mm (0·3-in) pintle-mounted machine-gun with an unrevealed number of rounds, twin turret-mounted 7·62-mm

(0·3-in) machine-guns with an unrevealed number of rounds, a turret-mounted 20-mm cannon with an unrevealed number of rounds, or twin turret-mounted launchers for an unrevealed number of anti-tank missiles
Armour: welded steel
Powerplant: one 95-kW (127-hp) Mercedes-Benz OM 352 diesel engine with 175 litres (38·5 Imp gal) of internal fuel, and driving a 4 × 4 layout
Performance: speed, road 85 km/h (52·8 mph) and water 8 km/h (5 mph) driven by two propellers; range, road 700 km (435 miles); fording amphibious; gradient 80%; side slope 40%; vertical obstacle 0·55 m (21·7 in); trench not revealed; ground clearance 0·46 m (18·1 in)

Variant
TM 125: like the larger TM 170, the TM 125 is based on a commercial chassis and powerplant for maximum cost effectiveness and reliability, and is designed for internal security rather than front-line duties; there is provision for the embarked troops to fire their personal weapons from inside the vehicle

---

Thyssen Henschel UR-416

(West Germany)
Type: wheeled armoured personnel carrier
Crew: 2 + 8
Combat weight: 7600 kg (16,755 lb)
Dimensions: length overall 5·21 m (17·09 ft); width 2·30 m (7·55 ft); height with turret 2·52 m (8·27 ft)
Armament system: one 7·62-mm (0·3-in) pintle-mounted machine-gun with an unrevealed number of rounds
Armour: welded steel
Powerplant: one 90-kW (121-hp) Mercedes-Benz OM 352 diesel engine with 150 litres (33 Imp gal) of internal fuel, and driving a 4 × 4 layout
Performance: speed, road 85 km/h (52·8 mph); range, road 700 km (435 miles); fording 1·4 m (4·6 ft); gradient 70%; side slope not revealed; vertical obstacle 0·55 m (21·7 in); trench not revealed; ground clearance 0·44 m (17·3 in)

Variants
UR-416: the basic armoured personnel carrier can be fitted with a variety of armaments ranging from a single pintle-mounted machine-gun to a single turret-mounted 20-mm cannon, and there is provision for the embarked troops to fire their personal weapons from inside the vehicle via 10 ports (three in each side of the troop compartment, one in each of the two side doors, and one in each of the two rear doors); but the UR-416 is optimized for the internal security role in guises such as an ambulance vehicle (eight seated casualties or two litters and four seated casualties in addition to the two crew), an anti-tank vehicle with a Bofors PV-1110 90-mm (3·54-in) recoilless rifle, a command and communications vehicle, a recon-naissance vehicle, and a workshop vehicle
UR-416M: updated production standard with an overall length of 5·10 m (16·73 ft) and a width of 2·25 m (7·38 ft); the type's maximum road speed is 81 km/h (50·3 mph), and its fording capability is 1·0 m (3·3 ft)

Below: The UR-416 is often kept for second-line tasks, but can be given significant armament as shown by this model with a Rheinmetall TF 20 15 turret and 20-mm cannon.

PSZH-IV

(Hungary)

Type: wheeled armoured personnel carrier
Crew: 3 + 6
Combat weight: 7600 kg (16,755 lb)
Dimensions: length overall 5·695 m (18·68 ft); width 2·50 m (8·20 ft); height 2·308 m (7·57 ft)
Armament system: one 14·5-mm (0·57-in) KPVT heavy machine-gun with 500 rounds and one co-axial 7·62-mm (0·3-in) PKT machine-gun with 2,000 rounds; the turret is manually powered, the guns lack stabilization in either elevation (−5° to +30°) or azimuth (360°), and simple optical sights are fitted
Armour: welded steel up to a maximum thickness of 14 mm (0·55 in)
Powerplant: one 75-kW (101-hp) Csepel D.414·44 diesel engine with 200 litres (44 Imp gal) of internal fuel, and driving a 4 × 4 layout
Performance: speed, road 80 km/h (49·7 mph) and water 9 km/h (5·6 mph) driven by two water-jets; range, road 500 km (311 miles); fording amphibious; gradient 60%; side slope not revealed; vertical obstacle 0·4 m (15·75 in); trench 0·6 m (2 ft) with channels; ground clearance 0·42 m (16·5 in)

Variant

PSZH-IV: this small Hungarian wheeled armoured personnel carrier appeared in the mid-1960s, and is used by other Warsaw Pact armed forces (Czechoslovakia and East Germany) mainly for internal security and border patrol; the Czech designation is **OT-66**; standard equipment includes IR driving lights, an NBC protection system and a central tyre pressure-regulation system; access to the troop compartment is pro-

vided by a door on each side, and the embarked troops can fire their personal weapons from inside the vehicle via two ports in each side

Above: The Timoney Mk 5 is built under licence in Belgium. The Mk 6 is much refined.

Below: The PSZH-IV is usually employed on second-line duties such as border patrol.

Timoney Mk 6 Fire-Support Vehicle

(Ireland)

Type: wheeled armoured personnel carrier
Crew: 3 + 9
Combat weight: 22,000 lb (9979 kg)
Dimensions: length overall 16·25 ft (4·593 m); width 8·20 ft (2·50 m); height to turret top 9·00 ft (2·746 m)
Armament system: one 90-mm (3·54-in) GIAT CN-90 (F1) rifled gun with an unrevealed number of rounds (21 in the turret and an unrevealed number in the hull), two 7·62-mm (0·3-in) machine-guns (one co-axial and one AA) with an unrevealed number of rounds (2,000 in the turret and an unrevealed number in the hull), and two, three or four smoke-dischargers or smoke/fragmentation grenade-launchers on each side of the turret; the turret is electro-hydraulically powered, the main gun lacks stabilization in either elevation (−8° to +35°) and azimuth (360°), and an optical fire-control system is fitted
Armour: welded steel varying in thickness from 10 to 14 mm (0·39 to 0·55 in)
Powerplant: one 180-hp (134-kW) Detroit Diesel 4-53T diesel engine with 300 litres (66 Imp gal) of internal fuel, and driving a 4 × 4 layout
Performance: speed, road 60 mph (96·6 km/h) and water unrevealed driven by its wheels; range, road 625 miles (1006 km); fording amphibious; gradient 70%; side slope 50%; vertical obstacle 0·4 m (15·75 in); trench 0·6 m (2 ft); ground clearance 16 in (0·41 m)

Variants

Timoney Mk 6: this is a developed version of the Timoney Mk 5 (produced in Belgium as the BDX) with improved armour, lengthened wheelbase and a Detroit Diesel 4-53T engine boosting range as well as reducing the fire risk; there are many armament options, the most common being the Creusot-Loire TLi turret with one 0·5-in (12·7-mm) Browning M2HB heavy machine-gun and one 7·62-mm (0·3-in) machine-gun
Timoney Mk 6 Fire-Support Vehicle: standard Mk 6 armoured personnel carrier fitted with the Hispano-Suiza Lynx 90 turret

NIMDA Shoet II

(Israel)

Type: wheeled armoured personnel carrier
Crew: 2 + 10
Combat weight: 9700 kg (21,384 lb)
Dimensions: length overall 6·64 m (21·78 ft); width 2·20 m (7·22 ft); height 2·08 m (6·82 ft)
Armament system: up to four 0·5-in (12·7-mm) or 7·62-mm (0·3-in) machine-guns with an unrevealed number of rounds pintle-mounted round the top of the vehicle
Armour: welded steel varying in thickness from 8 to 14 mm (0·315 to 0·44 in)
Powerplant: one 172-hp (128-kW) Detroit Diesel 6V-53N diesel engine with 170 litres (37·4 Imp gal) of internal fuel, and driving a 6 × 6 layout
Performance: speed, road 90 km/h (56 mph); range, road 400 km (249 miles); fording not revealed; gradient 60%; side slope 30%; vertical obstacle not revealed; trench not revealed; ground clearance not revealed

Variants

Shoet II: developed as a private venture, the Shoet II has an open-topped troop compartment which allows the vehicle to be transformed rapidly into an anti-tank vehicle (106-mm/4·17-in recoilless rifle or anti-tank missile launcher), an AA vehicle (guns or missiles), a mortar carrier (81-mm/3·2-in mortar and machine-guns), a reconnaissance vehicle (61-mm/2·4-in light mortar and machine-guns), an ambulance and a recovery vehicle; standard equipment includes night vision devices, a central tyre pressure-regulation system, and fuel tank protection
Shoet III: improved version with more advanced operational features and other significant modifications including the 300-hp (224-kW) Detroit Diesel 6V-53T turbocharged diesel engine

OTO Melara/IVECO (Fiat) VCC-80

(Italy)

Type: tracked infantry armoured fighting vehicle
Crew: 3 + 6
Combat weight: about 19,000 kg (41,887 lb)
Dimensions: length overall 6·705 m (22·00 ft); width 2·98 m (9·78 ft); height overall 2·60 m (8·53 ft)
Armament system: one 25-mm Oerlikon-Bührle KBA-BO2 cannon with an unrevealed number of rounds, two 7·62-mm (0·3-in) MG42/59 machine-guns (one co-axial and the other AA) with an unrevealed number of rounds, and three smoke-dischargers on each side of the turret; the turret is electrically powered, the main gun is stabilized in elevation (−10° to +60°) and azimuth (360°), and an advanced optical fire-control system is fitted; this last includes day/night optical/thermal sights, a laser rangefinder and a ballistic computer
Armour: welded aluminium with additional steel over the front and sides
Powerplant: one 360-kW (483-hp) IVECO (Fiat) diesel engine with an unrevealed quantity of internal fuel
Performance: speed, road 70 km/h (43·5 mph); range, road 600 km (373 miles); fording 1·5 m (4·9 ft) without preparation; gradient 60%; side slope 40%; vertical obstacle 0·85 m (31·5 in); trench 2·5 m (8·2 ft); ground clearance 0·4 m (15·75 in)

Variant

VCC-80: this interesting infantry fighting vehicle resulted from an Italian army requirement of 1982, and resulted in the appearance of the first prototype in 1985; the VCC-80 is notable for its low silhouette and powerful armament, the latter combined with a singularly advanced fire-control

system to allow accurate fire with the vehicle on the move; standard equipment includes an NBC protection system and night vision devices, and there is provision for the embarked troops to use their personal weapons from inside the vehicle via five ports (two in each side and one in the rear door) and there are three hatches over the troop compartment: the circular hatch in the centre opens to the rear, and the two oblong hatches open outwards

OTO Melara C13

(Italy)

Type: tracked infantry armoured fighting vehicle
Crew: 3 + 9
Combat weight: 14,650 kg (32,297 lb)
Dimensions: length overall 5·65 m (18·54 ft); width 2·71 m (8·89 ft); height including machine-gun 2·475 m (8·12 ft)
Armament system: one 0·5-in (12·7-mm) Browning M2HB machine-gun with 800 rounds and four smoke-dischargers on each side of the cupola; the cupola is manually powered, the gun lacks stabilization in either elevation (an unrevealed arc) or azimuth (360°), and simple optical sights are fitted
Armour: welded aluminium with additional steel over the front and sides
Powerplant: one 270-kW (362-hp) Isotta-Fraschini ID 38 SS diesel engine with 400 litres (88 Imp gal) of internal fuel
Performance: speed, road 70 km/h (43·5 mph); range, road 500 km (311 miles); fording not revealed or amphibious with optional kit; gra-

The C13 family was designed for export, and is seen here in the form of the potent C-13/90 model.

dient 60%; side slope 30%; vertical obstacle 0·7 m (27·6 in); trench 1·8 m (5·9 ft); ground clearance 0·4 m (15·75 in)

Variants

C13: this armoured personnel carrier was designed as a private venture mainly for the export market, but by comparison with other such vehicles makes no sacrifices in terms of protection, low silhouette and mobility; the C13 uses a new type of armour developed by OTO Melara, and this armour is also being used on other vehicles in the OTO Melara range; the light armament is fitted in a simple cupola that provides the gunner with side and rear protection through the use of armour sheets, and there is provision for the embarked troops to fire their weapons from inside the vehicle via five ports (two in each side and one in the large rear door); there are three hatches in the roof of the troop compartment, the circular unit in the centre opening to the rear and the two lateral oblong units opening outwards; standard equipment includes a fire-suppression system, and optional items include an NBC protection system, night vision devices, an air-conditioning system, and an amphibious kit

C13/20: 15,500-kg (34,171-lb) infantry fighting vehicle derivative with the OTO Melara TPT Mk 4 cupola replaced by a two-man OTO Melara T 20 turret; this is an electrically powered unit carrying a 20-mm Rheinmetall MK 20 Rh 202 cannon with an unrevealed number of rounds (including 250 in the turret), a 7·62-mm (0·3-in) co-axial machine-gun with an unrevealed number of rounds (including 400 in the turret), and three smoke-dischargers on each side of the turret; the gun lacks stabilization in either elevation (−5° to +35°) or azimuth (360°), and simple optical sights are fitted; the C13/20 has a crew of 3+6

C13/25: 15,700-kg (34,612-lb) infantry fighting vehicle derivative with the OTO Melara TPT Mk 4 cupola replaced by a two-man OTO Melara T 25 turret; this is an electrically powered unit carrying a 25-mm Oerlikon-Bührle KBA cannon with an unrevealed number of rounds (including 135 HE and 35 AP in the turret), a 7·62-mm (0·3-in) co-axial machine-gun with an unrevealed number of rounds (including 400 in the turret), and three smoke-dischargers on each side of the turret; the gun lacks stabilization in either elevation (−10° to +50°) or azimuth (360°), and simple optical sights are fitted

C13/60: 18,000-kg (39,683-lb) infantry fighting vehicle derivative with the OTO Melara TPT Mk 4 cupola replaced by a two-man OTO Melara T 60/70 turret; this is an electrically powered unit carrying a 60-mm (2·36-in) OTO Melara high-velocity gun with an unrevealed number of rounds (including 38 in the turret), a 7·62-mm (0·3-in) co-axial machine-gun with an unrevealed number of rounds (including 200 in the turret), and four smoke-dischargers on each side of the turret; the gun lacks stabilization in either elevation (−6° to +50°) or azimuth (360°), and an optical fire-control system is fitted; the T 60/70A variant of the turret has an automatic loader and is offered with the choice of either the FCS Model 60 Mk 1 or FCS Model 60 Mk 2 fire-control systems, the former being designed for daylight use with magnifying optics, a laser rangefinder, various sensors for ambient conditions, and a ballistic computer, and the latter being designed for all-weather day/night use with stabilized optical/thermal sights, a laser rangefinder, various sensors for ambient conditions, and a ballistic computer; the T 60/70M variant of the turret uses a manual loading system; the C13/60 has a crew of 3+4

C13/90: 16,000-kg (35,273-lb) infantry fighting vehicle derivative with the OTO Melara TPT Mk 4 cupola replaced by a two-man OTO Melara 90 CKL turret; this is an electrically powered unit carrying a 90-mm (3·54-in) Cockerill Mk III rifled gun with an unrevealed number of rounds (including 16 in the turret), a 7·62-mm (0·3-in) co-axial machine-gun with an unrevealed number of rounds (including 1,000 in the turret), and three smoke-dischargers on each side of the turret; the gun lacks stabilization in either elevation (−9° to +30°) or azimuth (360°), and an optical fire-control system is fitted; this last can include night sights, a laser rangefinder and a ballistic computer; the C13/90 has a crew of 3+6

C13/4: 16,500-kg (36,376-lb) AA vehicle derivative with the OTO Melara TPT Mk 4 cupola replaced by a one-man OTO Melara SIDAM 25 turret; this is an electrically powered unit carrying four Oerlikon-Italiana (Oerlikon-Bührle) KBA-B cannon with an unrevealed number of rounds (including 600 in the turret); the guns lack stabilization in either elevation (−5° to +87°) or azimuth (360°), and an advanced optronic fire-control system is fitted; this last combines a low-light-level TV with autotrack capability, a laser rangefinder, a digital ballistic computer and provision for external cuing and/or thermal night sights; the C13/4 has a crew of three

C13 TUA: 15,000-kg (33,069-lb) anti-tank vehicle derivative with the OTO Melara TPT Mk 4 cupola replaced by an Emerson TUA (TOW Under Armor) turret with two launchers and 12 BGM-71 TOW heavy anti-tank missiles; the C13 TUA has a crew of four

C13 Ambulance: 14,650-kg (32,297-lb) ambulance version with a crew of three (driver and two attendants) plus provision for three litters, or one litter and two seated casualties, or six seated casualties

C13 Cargo: 19,000-kg (41,887-lb) cargo carrier version with a crew of two and a revised hull/suspension combination to allow the carriage of 6500 kg (14,330-lb) of freight; the type can be fitted with a 0·5-in (12·7-mm) machine-gun, and can also be used as a minelayer; optional equipment includes a 10,000-kg (22,046-lb) capacity winch or a hydraulic crane

AV 90: development of the basic C13 by OTO Melara in conjunction with Krupp MaK; the type is essentially similar to the C13 in all but its power-pack (engine and transmission), which comprises a 275-kW (369-hp) MTU 8V 183 TA22 diesel (otherwise known as the Mercedes-Benz OM 442A) driving a ZF LSG 1500 automatic gear/steering transmission; the AV 90 is planned in a number of variants analogous to those of the C13 series, and has the advantage of its engine being able to operate effectively in temperatures up to 55°C (131°F)

OTO Melara VCC-1 Camillino

(Italy)

Type: tracked infantry armoured fighting vehicle
Crew: 2+7
Combat weight: 11,600 kg (25,573 lb)
Dimensions: length overall 5·041 m (16·54 ft); width 2·686 m (8·81 ft); height including machine-gun 2·552 m (8·37 ft)
Armament system: one 0·5-in (12·7-mm) Browning M2HB cupola-mounted heavy machine-gun with 1,050 rounds, and one 7·62-mm (0·3-in) MG3 pintle-mounted machine-gun with 1,000 rounds;

the cupola is manually powered, the gun lacks stabilization in either elevation (an unrevealed arc) or azimuth (360°), and simple optical sights are fitted
Armour: welded aluminium with additional steel over the front and sides
Powerplant: one 215-hp (160-kW) Detroit Diesel 6V-53T diesel engine with 360 litres (79 Imp gal) of internal fuel
Performance: speed, road 64·4 km/h (40 mph) and water 5 km/h (3·1 mph) driven by its tracks; range, road 550 km (342 miles); fording amphibious; gradient 60%; side slope 30%; vertical obstacle 0·61 m (24 in); trench 1·68 m (5·5 ft); ground clearance 0·41 m (16 in)

Variants

VCC-1 Camillino: also known as the **Infantry Armoured Fighting Vehicle Mk 1**, this is an Italian upgrading of the US M113A1 armoured personnel carrier with additional armour (a layer of steel over the original aluminium), improved firepower (a forward-mounted cupola with lateral and rear protection for the gunner), the capability for the embarked troops to fire their personal weapons from inside the vehicle (via five ports located as two on each side and one in the large rear ramp), and better seating; improved versions are the **AIFV Mk 2** with a remotely controlled 0·5-in (12·7-mm) machine-gun, and the **AIFV Mk 3** with a turreted 20-mm cannon; standard equipment includes IR driving lights, but no NBC protection system is fitted
VCC-1/TOW: version for Saudi Arabia with an Emerson TOW turret; this is an elevating and armoured launcher/sight unit with two ready-to-fire missiles; another 10 missiles can be held in the hull
VCC-2: improved VCC-1 with appliqué armour on the front and sides

Right: A VCC-1 Camillino for Saudi Arabia with its Emerson Improved TOW System in the raised ready-to-fire position above the roof.

IVECO (Fiat) Tipo 6634

(Italy)

Type: wheeled armoured personnel carrier
Crew: 1+5
Combat weight: 8000 kg (17,637 lb)
Dimensions: length overall 4·70 m (15·42 ft); width 2·00 m (6·56 ft); height to hull top 1·60 m (5·25 ft)
Armament system: one 0·5-in (12·7-mm) Browning M2HB pintle-mounted heavy machine-gun with an unrevealed number of rounds, and three smoke-dischargers on each side of the hull
Armour: welded steel
Powerplant: one 90-kW (121-hp) IVECO (Fiat) 8140 TCA diesel engine with 150 litres (33 Imp gal) of internal fuel, and driving a 4 × 4 layout
Performance: not revealed

Variants

Tipo 6634: this is the original version of a family of wheeled combat vehicles developed on the basis of Fiat commercial vehicles; the Tipo 6634 is the **Armoured Vehicle Light** member of the series, designed as a simple personnel carrier or as the platform for the installation of weapon installations such as the Matra SATCP turret for Mistral SAMs or the Euromissile MCT turret with two launchers for Milan medium anti-tank missiles; the troop compartment has forward-opening sides doors (each fitted with a firing port) and an

upward-opening rear door

Tipo 6633: 10,000-kg (22,046-lb) **Armoured Vehicle Medium** member of the series with a crew of 2+10/11 and principal dimensions that include an overall length of 6·098 m (20·01 ft), a width of 2·50 m (8·20 ft) and a hull height of 1·90 m (6·23 ft); this version is powered by a 150-kW (201-hp) IVECO (Fiat) 8060 TCA diesel with 270 litres (59·4 Imp gal) of fuel, and has a ground clearance of 0·43 m (16·9 in); the type is fully

amphibious, being propelled in the water by two waterjets, and the troop compartment has two additional firing ports; the type can be fitted with turreted armament up to 25-mm calibre

Tipo 6636: 16,500-kg (36,376-lb) **Armoured Vehicle Heavy** member of the series with a crew of 2+10/12 and principal dimensions that include an overall length of 6·70 m (21·98 ft), a width of 2·90 m (9·51 ft) and a hull height of 1·90 m (6·23 ft); this version is powered by a 315-kW (422-hp)

IVECO (Fiat) 8620 TCA diesel and 6 × 6 configuration, and is provided with 400 litres (88 Imp gal) of fuel for a road range of 800 km (497 miles); the model has a ground clearance of 0·4 m (15·75 in); the type is fully amphibious, being propelled in the water by two waterjets, and the troop compartment has two additional doors each with a firing port; the type can be fitted with turreted armament up to 25-mm calibre, or be used as a mortar-carrier

TANGRAM TILOS VTL

(Italy)

Type: wheeled personnel carrier and logistics vehicle

Crew: 1 + 16

Combat weight: 10,500 kg (23,148 lb)

Dimensions: length overall 5·96 m (18·37 ft); width 2·48 m (8·14 ft); height 2·40 m (7·87 ft)

Armament system: none

Armour: none

Powerplant: one 150-kW (201-hp) IVECO (Fiat) diesel engine with 310 litres (68 Imp gal) of internal fuel, and driving a 4 × 4 layout

Performance: speed, road 98 km/h (60·9 mph); range, road 1020 km (634 miles); fording not revealed; gradient 60%; side slope 30%; vertical obstacle 0·6 m (23·6 in); trench not revealed; ground clearance 0·47 m (18·5 in)

Variant

TILOS VTL: this is the tractor unit of the TANGRAM Integrated LOgistic System, designed to tow a six-wheel trailer unit of any length between 6·0 and 12·5 m (19·69 and 41·01 ft) and weighing 14500 kg (31,966 lb) fully laden; the tractor unit can also be used as a separate load-carrier without its trailer

Below: The VTL towing unit of the TILOS logistic system without its large TU freight trailer.

IVECO (Fiat)/OTO Melara Tipo 6614

(Italy)

Type: wheeled armoured personnel carrier

Crew: 1 + 10

Combat weight: 8500 kg (18,739 lb)

Dimensions: length overall 5·86 m (19·23 ft); width 2·50 m (8·20 ft); height including machine-gun mounting 2·18 m (7·15 ft)

Armament system: one 0·5-in (12·7-mm) Browning M2HB pintle-mounted heavy machine-gun with an unrevealed number of rounds

Armour: welded steel varying in thickness from 6 to 8 mm (0·24 to 0·315 in)

Powerplant: one 120-kW (161-hp) IVECO (Fiat) 8062.24 diesel engine with 142 litres (31·25 Imp gal) of internal fuel, and driving a 4 × 4 layout

Performance: speed, road 100 km/h (62·1 mph) and water 4·5 km/h (2·8 mph) driven by its wheels; range, road 700 km (435 miles); fording amphibious; gradient 60%; side slope 30%; vertical obstacle 0·4 m (15·75 in); trench not revealed; ground clearance 0·37 m (14·6 in)

Variants

Tipo 6614: designed as a private venture by IVECO (Fiat) and OTO Melara, this is a very useful second-line type with provision for the embarked troops to use their personal weapons from inside the hull via 10 firing ports (four on each side, including one in each of the two side doors, and one on each side of the large rear ramp); in place of the 0·5-in (12·7-mm) machine-gun, single or twin 7·62-mm (0·3-in) turreted gun(s) can be carried, and optional equipment includes night vision equipment, air conditioning, smoke-dischargers and a front-mounted winch

KM900: Tipo 6614 built under licence in South Korea

KM901: role-specific variants (ambulance, command post, mortar-carrier etc) of the KM900

Mitsubishi Type 88

(Japan)

Type: tracked mechanized infantry combat vehicle

Crew: 3 plus an unrevealed number of infantrymen

Combat weight: not revealed

Dimensions: not revealed

Armament system: one 35-mm Oerlikon-Bührle KDE cannon with an unrevealed number of rounds, one co-axial 7·62-mm (0·3-in) Type 74 machine-gun with an unrevealed number of rounds, and one launcher for an unrevealed number of Chyu-MAT anti-tank missiles on each side of the turret; the turret is powered, the main gun lacks stabilization in either elevation (an unrevealed arc) or azimuth (360°), and an optical fire-control system is fitted; this last includes optical/thermal sights, a laser rangefinder and designator, and a ballistic computer

Armour: welded aluminium

Powerplant: one Mitsubishi diesel engine of unrevealed power with an unrevealed quantity of internal fuel

Performance: not revealed

Variant

Type 88: this useful machine has been designed as Japan's standard mechanized infantry combat vehicle for introduction in the later 1980s; the type has provision for the embarked troops to fire their personal weapons from inside the vehicle (via three ports on each side), access to the troop compartment is provided by a large rear ramp, and there are two outward-opening hatches in the roof of the troop compartment; standard equipment includes an NBC protection system and night vision equipment, though the type lacks amphibious capability

Below: Personal weapons can be seen in the firing ports of this Tipo 6614 4 × 4 wheeled APC.

Mitsubishi Type 73

(Japan)
Type: tracked armoured personnel carrier
Crew: 3 + 9
Combat weight: 13,300 kg (29,321 lb)
Dimensions: length overall 5·80 m (19·03 ft); width 2·80 m (9·19 ft); height including machine-gun 2·20 m (7·22 ft)
Armament system: one 0·5-in (12·7-mm) Browning M2HB cupola-mounted heavy machine-gun with an unrevealed number of rounds, one 0·3-in (7·62-mm) Browning M1919A4 bow-mounted machine-gun with an unrevealed number of rounds, and three smoke-dischargers on each side of the hull rear; the cupola is manually powered, the gun lacks stabilization in either elevation (−10° to +60°) or azimuth (360°), and simple optical sights are fitted
Armour: welded aluminium
Powerplant: one 225-kW (302-hp) Mitsubishi 4ZF diesel engine with 450 litres (99 Imp gal) of internal fuel
Performance: speed, road 70 km/h (43·5 mph) and water 7 km/h (4·3 mph) driven by its tracks; range, road 300 km (186 miles); fording not revealed without preparation and amphibious with a kit; gradient 60%; side slope not revealed; vertical obstacle 0·7 m (27·6 in); trench 2·0 m (6·6 ft); ground clearance 0·4 m (15·75 in)

Variants

Type 73: this is the main Japanese armoured personnel carrier and is an unexceptional vehicle with modest armament and short range; it was designed in the late 1960s as successor to the Type SU 60, and entered production in 1973; the embarked infantry can fire their personal weapons from inside the vehicle via six ports (two on each side and one in each of the two rear doors), and standard equipment includes IR driving lights and an NBC protection system; the type lacks amphibious capability
Type 75: variant used for measuring ground wind, and used in conjunction with the Type 75 self-propelled rocket-launcher

Below: The Type 73 has three smoke-dischargers on each side of the hull rear, as visible here.

Mitsubishi Type SU 60

(Japan)
Type: tracked armoured personnel carrier
Crew: 4 + 6
Combat weight: 11,800 kg (26,014 lb)
Dimensions: length overall 4·85 m (15·91 ft); width 2·40 m (7·87 ft); height including machine-gun 2·31 m (7·58 ft)
Armament system: one 0·5-in (12·7-mm) Browning M2HB cupola-mounted heavy machine-gun with an unrevealed number of rounds, and one 0·3-in (7·62-mm) Browning M1919A4 bow-mounted machine-gun with an unrevealed number of rounds; the cupola is manually powered, the gun lacks stabilization in either elevation (an unrevealed arc) or azimuth (360°), and simple optical sights are fitted
Armour: welded steel
Powerplant: one 165-kW (221-hp) Mitsubishi 8 HA 21 WT diesel engine with an unrevealed quantity of internal fuel
Performance: speed, road 45 km/h (28 mph); range, road 230 km (143 miles); fording 1·0 m (3·3 ft); gradient 60%; side slope not revealed; vertical obstacle 0·6 m (23·6 in); trench 1·82 m (6 ft); ground clearance 0·4 m (15·75 in)

Below: The SU-60 is an obsolescent APC with the outmoded feature of a bow machine-gun.

Variants

SU 60: designed in the late 1950s, this was the Japanese army's primary armoured personnel carrier until the advent of the Type 73, and amongst its features are modest armament (including the same type of unusual bow machine-gun mounting as found in the Type 73) and complete lack of night vision devices, an NBC protection system and amphibious capability; there is no provision for the embarked troops to fire their personal weapons from inside the vehicle, whose troop compartment is fitted with two rear doors; the standard model has been converted in small numbers to produce NBC reconnaissance vehicles, dozer vehicles and a few training vehicles adapted to resemble the Soviet BMD

SV 60: 12,100-kg (26,675-lb) mortar-carrier version with an 81-mm (3·2-in) mortar and 24 bombs, and a crew of five

SX 60: 12,900-kg (28,439-lb) mortar-carrier version with a 107-mm (4·2-in) mortar and eight bombs, and a crew of five

DAF YP-408

(Netherlands)

Type: wheeled armoured personnel carrier
Crew: 2 + 10
Combat weight: 12,000 kg (26,455 lb)
Dimensions: length overall 6·23 m (20·44 ft); width 2·40 m (7·87 ft); height including machine-gun 2·37 m (7·78 ft)
Armament system: one 0·5-in (12·7-mm) Browning M2HB cupola-mounted heavy machine-gun with an unrevealed number of rounds, and three smoke-dischargers on each side of the hull front; the cupola is manually powered, the gun lacks stabilization in either elevation (−8° to +70°) or azimuth (360°), and simple optical sights are fitted
Armour: welded steel varying in thickness from 8 to 15 mm (0·315 to 0·59 in)
Powerplant: one 125-kW (168-hp) DAF DS 575 diesel engine with 200 litres (44 Imp gal) of internal fuel, and driving a 6 × 8 layout
Performance: speed, road 80 km/h (49·7 mph); range, road 500 km (311 miles); fording 1·2 m (3·9 ft); gradient 60%; side slope 70%; vertical obstacle 0·7 m (27·6 in); trench 1·2 m (3·9 ft); ground clearance 0·52 m (20·4 in)

Variants

PWI-S(GR): this is the Dutch army designation of the basic armoured personnel carrier version of the **YP-408**, which was developed in the late 1950s, and produced in the mid- and late 1960s; the type lacks amphibious capability and an NBC protection system, but can be fitted with night vision devices; only the rear doors have provision for the embarked infantry to fire their personal weapons from inside the vehicle

PWI-S(PC): command vehicle similar to the PWI-S(GR) and designed for use by platoon commanders; it is fitted with additional radios and vision equipment

PWCO: command vehicle for company and battalion commanders with some of the seats removed to make room for mapboards; this model also has provision for the erection of a tented extension to the rear

PW-GWT: ambulance vehicle for two litters and four seated casualties

PW-V: cargo model with a payload of 1500 kg (3,309 lb)

PW-MT: mortar tractor for the 120-mm (4·72-in) Thomson Brandt mortar and carrying the seven-man mortar crew plus 50 bombs

Above and below: The YP-408 **PWI-S(GR)** armoured personnel carrier with a 0·5-in (12·7-mm) machine-gun on the overhead mounting, and six firing ports in the hull sides.

PWAT: basic vehicle modified to carry the TOW anti-tank system

PWRDR: battlefield surveillance vehicle with ZB 298 radar

Above: The PW-GWT battlefield ambulance model of the YP-408 can carry a total of six casualties (four seated and two on litters) under the care of two medical attendants.

BRAVIA Chaimite V-200

(Portugal)
Type: wheeled armoured personnel carrier
Crew: 2 + 9
Combat weight: 7300 kg (16,093 lb)
Dimensions: length overall 5·606 m (18·39 ft); width 2·26 m (7·41 ft); height including turret 2·26 m (7·41 ft)
Armament system: the BRAVIA-designed turret can accommodate one 0·5-in (12·7-mm) Browning M2HB heavy machine-gun with an unrevealed number of rounds and one co-axial 7·62-mm (0·3-in) machine-gun with an unrevealed number of rounds, or two 7·62- or 5·56-mm (0·3- or 0·219-in) machine-guns with an unrevealed number of rounds; the turret is manually powered, the gun lacks stabilization in either elevation (−15° to +50°) or azimuth (360°), and simple optical sights are fitted
Armour: welded steel varying in thickness from 6·35 to 7·94 mm (0·25 to 0·313 in)
Powerplant: one 155-kW (208-hp) Model M75 petrol engine or V-6 diesel engine with 300 litres (66 Imp gal) of internal fuel, and driving a 6 × 6 layout
Performance: speed, road 99 km/h (61·5 mph) and water 7 km/h (4·3 mph) driven by its wheels; range, road 965 km (600 miles) with petrol engine or 1530 km (951 miles) with diesel; fording amphibious; gradient 65%; side slope 40%; vertical obstacle 0·9 m (35·4 in); trench not revealed; ground clearance 0·41 m (16·1 in)

Variants

Chaimite V-200: designed in the 1960s for the Portuguese army, and very similar to the Cadillac Gage Commando, the V-200 is the baseline armoured personnel carrier of this useful series, and the optional equipment includes a number of armament additions (a multi-role grenade-launcher and four 3·5-in/88·9-mm recoilless rifles) and night vision devices; standard equipment includes a front-mounted winch, and the embarked troops can fire their personal weapons from inside the vehicle

Chaimite V-300: upgunned model with a crew of four or five and able to carry a one-man Oerlikon-Bührle GAD-AOA turret with a 20-mm KAA-001 cannon, or any of several two-man turrets armed with two machine-guns or one 20-mm cannon and one machine-gun
Chaimite V-400: upgunned model with a MECAR or GIAT 90-mm (3·54-mm) gun
Chaimite V-500: command and communications model
Chaimite V-600: mortar-carrying model with an 81- or 120-mm (3·2- or 4·72-in) mortar, crew and ammunition
Chaimite V-700: anti-tank model with HOT or Swingfire guided missiles
Chaimite V-800: ambulance model
Chaimite V-900: crash rescue model
Chaimite V-1000: riot-control model with a diversity of armament options

Below: The Chaimite V-200 wheeled APC can be fitted with any of several BRAVIA weapon installations on the roof.

BRAVIA Commando Mk III

(Portugal)
Type: wheeled armoured personnel carrier
Crew: 3 + 5
Combat weight: 4855 kg (10,703 lb)
Dimensions: length overall 4·975 m (16·32 ft); width 1·93 m (6·33 ft); height including turret 2·42 m (7·94 ft)
Armament system: the BRAVIA-designed turret can accommodate one 0·5-in (12·7-mm) Browning M2HB heavy machine-gun with an unrevealed number of rounds and one co-axial 7·62-mm (0·3-in) machine-gun with an unrevealed number of rounds, or two 7·62- or 5·56-mm (0·3- or 0·219-in) machine-guns with an unrevealed number of rounds; the turret is manually powered, the gun lacks stabilization in either elevation (− 15° to + 60°) or azimuth (360°), and simple optical sights are fitted
Armour: welded steel varying in thickness from 6·35 to 7·94 mm (0·25 to 0·313 in)
Powerplant: one 81-hp (60-kW) Perkins 4-cylinder diesel engine or 150-hp (112-kW) Dodge H225 petrol engine with 160 litres (35 Imp gal) of internal fuel, and driving a 4 × 4 layout
Performance: speed, road 90 km/h (55·9 mph) with diesel or 110 km/h (68·4 mph) with petrol engine; range, road 800 km (497 miles) with diesel or 600 km (373 miles) with petrol engine; fording not revealed; gradient 70%; side slope not revealed; vertical obstacle not revealed; trench not revealed; ground clearance 0·21 m (8·3 in)

Variant
Commando Mk III: this light armoured personnel carrier is based on a cross-country truck design, and is unexceptional; production began in 1977, and the type has entered service mainly with paramilitary forces

MLI-84

(Romania)
Type: tracked infantry fighting vehicle
Crew: 2 + 9
Combat weight: 16,600 kg (36,596 lb)
Dimensions: length overall 7·32 m (24·02 ft); width 3·15 m (10·33 ft); height to turret top 1·97 m (6·46 ft)
Armament system: one 73-mm (2·87-in) 2A28 smooth-bore gun with 40 rounds, one 7·62-mm (0·3-in) PKT co-axial machine-gun with 2,000 rounds, one 12·7-mm (0·5-in) DShKM AA heavy machine-gun with 250 rounds, and one launcher with four AT-3 'Sagger' anti-tank missiles; the turret is electrically powered, the main gun lacks stabilization in either elevation (− 4° to + 33°) or azimuth (360°), and an optical fire-control system is fitted
Armour: welded steel
Powerplant: one 270-kW (362-hp) Model 8V-1240 DT-S diesel engine with an unknown quantity of internal fuel
Performance: not revealed

Variant
MLI-84: this is in essence the Soviet BMP-1 infantry fighting vehicle built in Romania with slightly greater dimensions and weight, but the original performance levels retained in most respects by the incorporation of a more powerful engine; the main external difference is the location of an AA machine-gun over the troop compartment

Above: The Commando Mk III is seen with the commander's and driver's hatches opened.

MLVM

(Romania)
Type: tracked armoured personnel carrier/limited infantry combat vehicle
Crew: 2 + 7
Combat weight: 9800 kg (21,605 lb)
Dimensions: length overall 5·85 m (19·19 ft); width 2·75 m (9·02 ft); height to turret top 1·95 m (6·40 ft)
Armament system: one 14·5-mm (0·57-in) KPVT heavy machine-gun with an unrevealed number of rounds, and one 7·62-mm (0·3-in) PKT co-axial machine-gun with an unrevealed number of rounds; the turret is manually powered, the guns lack stabilization in either elevation (− 4° to + 84°) or azimuth (360°), and simple optical sights are fitted
Armour: welded steel
Powerplant: one diesel engine of unrevealed power with an unrevealed quantity of internal fuel
Performance: speed, road 48 km/h (29·8 mph); range, road 740 km (460 miles); fording not revealed; gradient 60%; side slope not revealed; vertical obstacle not revealed; trench not revealed; ground clearance 0·38 m (15 in)

Variants
MLVM: this Romanian armoured personnel carrier, or rather limited infantry combat vehicle, was first revealed in 1989 and resembles the Soviet BMP-1 with the crew at the front of the hull on the left with the powerpack to their right, the one-man turret (resembling that of the Czech/Polish SKOT-2A but with a high elevation angle for the main gun to provide improved anti-helicopter capability) in the centre, and the troop compartment at the rear; the troop compartment has vision devices and firing ports so that the embarked troops can use their personal weapons from inside the vehicle; there is also a mortar-carrying version with a 120-mm (4·72-in) mortar located at the rear of the troop compartment in such a fashion that it can be readily dismounted for ground use
ABAL: battlefield ammunition resupply version armed with a single 7·62-mm (0·3-in) machine-gun for local defence, and with its rear compartment modified to carry 64 rounds of 100-mm (3·94-in) or 104 rounds of 76-mm (3-in) ammunition in lockers accessed from the outside

Abdallah Al-Faris Al Jazirah

(Saudi Arabia)
Type: wheeled armoured personnel carrier
Crew: 2 + 10
Combat weight: 16,000 kg (35,273 lb)
Dimensions: length overall 6·99 m (22·93 ft); width 2·94 m (9·65 ft); height to hull top 2·05 m (6·73 ft)
Armament system: not revealed
Armour: welded steel
Powerplant: one 255-kW (342-hp) Mercedes-Benz diesel engine with an unrevealed quantity of internal fuel, and driving a 6 × 6 layout
Performance: not revealed

Variant
Al Jazirah: this has been developed as a private venture since 1977, and amongst its features are variable suspension, power steering and a central tyre pressure-regulation system

Sandock-Austral Ratel 20

(South Africa)
Type: wheeled infantry fighting vehicle
Crew: 4 + 7
Combat weight: 18,500 kg (40,785 lb)
Dimensions: length, hull 7·212 m (23·66 ft); width 2·516 m (8·25 ft); height overall 2·915 m (9·56 ft)
Armament system: one 20-mm GIAT M693 (F2) cannon with 1,200 rounds, two 7·62-mm (0·3-in) machine-guns (one co-axial and one AA) with 6,000 rounds, and two smoke-dischargers on each side of the turret; there is also a 7·62-mm (0·3-in) AA and local defence machine-gun at the hull rear; the turret is manually powered, the main gun lacks stabilization in either elevation (− 8° to + 38°) or azimuth (360°), and an optical fire-control system is fitted
Armour: welded steel varying in thickness from 6 to 20 mm (0·24 to 0·79 in)
Powerplant: one 210-kW (282-hp) D 3256 BTXF diesel engine with 430 litres (94·5 Imp gal) of internal fuel, and driving a 6 × 6 layout
Performance: speed, road 105 km/h (65·2 mph); range, road 1000 km (621 miles); fording 1·2 m (3·9 ft); gradient 60%; side slope 30%; vertical obstacle 0·35 m (13·8 in); trench 1·15 m (3·8 ft); ground clearance 0·34 m (13·4 in)

Variants
Ratel 20: this infantry fighting vehicle is notable

for its good range, good firepower, modest maintenance requirements and excellent cross-country mobility combined with first-class anti-mine protection; as with other variants of the Ratel, the embarked troops can fire their personal weapons from inside the hull via eight ports (four in each side of the troop compartment); the embarked troops use three doors (one in each side and one in the rear), and optional equipment includes night vision devices and an air-conditioning system

Ratel 60: Ratel 20 version with a 60-mm (2·36-in) breech-loading mortar (plus some 50 bombs) in place of the 20-mm cannon and its ammunition

Below: The Ratel 20 has 6 × 6 drive, a turreted 20-mm cannon, two machine-guns and ports for troops to fire their personal weapons.

Ratel 90: 19,000-kg (41,887-lb) baseline model that entered service in 1976 as a fire-support vehicle designed to the exacting requirements of the South African army; this model is armed with a 90-mm (3·54-in) GIAT CN-90 (F1) rifled gun in exactly the same turret as used on the Eland armoured car, and 69 rounds of ammunition are carried; some 6,000 rounds of ammunition are carried for the three 7·62-mm (0·3-in) machine-guns (one co-axial, one turret AA and one hull AA); the crew is 4+6, one infantryman being dropped to allow the carriage of 40 90-mm (3·54-in) rounds in the hull; the current **Ratel 90 Mk 3** incorporates modifications dictated by the hard lessons of South Africa's internal and external military operations, and the earlier **Ratel 90 Mk 1** and **Ratel 90 Mk 2** vehicles are being brought up to this improved standard

Ratel Command: 18,000-kg (39,683-lb) command post model featuring a two-man turret fitted with one 0·5-in (12·7-mm) Browning M2HB heavy machine-gun with 300 rounds and a 7·62-mm (0·3-in) AA machine-gun; there is also a rear-mounted 7·62-mm (0·3-in) machine-gun, and 3,600 small-calibre rounds are carried; the crew is 3+6, and a mass of command equipment is fitted

Ratel Logistic: 29,000-kg (63,933-lb) logistic support model of the Ratel series, a much developed 8 × 8 model lengthened to 8·739 m (28·67 ft) and fitted with a 239-kW (320-hp) ADE 423 T diesel; the crew is three including a gunner for the 0·5-in machine-gun with 600 rounds; designed to support the Ratel IFV and FSV, the logistic model has the same cross-country mobility and can carry water, fuel, ammunition and supplies of several other types

Daewoo Korean Infantry Fighting Vehicle

(South Korea)
Type: tracked infantry fighting vehicle
Crew: 3+7
Combat weight: 12,900 kg (28,439 lb)
Dimensions: length overall 5·486 m (18·00 ft); width 2·846 m (9·33 ft); height to hull top 2·93 m (9·61 ft) and overall 2·518 m (8·26 ft)
Armament system: one 0·5-in (12·7-mm) Browning M2HB cupola-mounted heavy machine-gun with an unrevealed number of rounds, one 7·62-mm (0·3-in) pintle-mounted machine-gun with an unrevealed number of rounds, and six smoke-dischargers on the hull front; the cupola is manually powered, the gun lacks stabilization in either elevation (an unrevealed arc) or azimuth (360°), and simple optical sights are fitted
Armour: welded aluminium with an appliqué layer of laminate steel
Powerplant: one 210-kW (282-hp) MAN D-2848M diesel engine with 400 litres (88 Imp gal) of internal fuel
Performance: speed, road 74 km/h (46 mph) and water 6 km/h (3·7 mph) driven by its tracks; range, road 480 km (298 miles); fording amphibious; gradient 60%; side slope not revealed; vertical obstacle 0·63 m (24·8 in); trench 1·7 m (5·6 ft); ground clearance 0·41 m (16·1 in)

Variants
KIFV: this is essentially the South Korean adaptation of the FMC Armored Infantry Fighting Vehicle; the main armament is merely a 0·5-in (12·7-mm) heavy machine-gun, but this is fitted with a shield as well as with lateral and rear protection for the gunner; the troops embark by

means of a large rear ramp/door, and can fire their personal weapons from inside the vehicle via six ports (two in each side and two in the ramp); the vehicle is fitted as standard with an NBC protection system; the KIFV can also be used as a mortar-carrier, command vehicle, ammunition carrier and recovery vehicle
KIFV 25: basic KIFV with its 0·5-in (12·7-mm) heavy machine-gun cupola replaced by a one-man turret fitted with a 25-mm cannon; it is also possible to fit the type with turreted 75- or 90-mm (2·95- or 3·54-in) guns, or with a launcher for BGM-71 TOW heavy anti-tank missiles
KIFV Vulcan: South Korean equivalent of the M163 self-propelled AA cannon mounting with a 20-mm Vulcan cannon

Autocamiones BMR-600

(Spain)
Type: wheeled infantry fighting vehicle
Crew: 2+11
Combat weight: 14,000 kg (30,864 lb)
Dimensions: length overall 6·15 m (20·18 ft); width 2·50 m (8·20 ft); height including armament 2·36 m (7·74 ft)
Armament system: one 0·5-in (12·7-mm) Browning M2HB cupola-mounted machine-gun with 2,500 rounds (130 on the gun and 2,370 in the hull); the turret is manually powered, the gun lacks stabilization in either elevation (−15° to +40°) or azimuth (360°), and simple optical sights are fitted
Armour: welded aluminium
Powerplant: one 230-kW (308-hp) Pegaso modelo 9157/8 diesel engine with 400 litres (88

Imp gal) of internal fuel, and driving a 6 × 6 layout
Performance: speed, road 103 km/h (64 mph) and water 9 km/h (5·6 mph) driven by two water-jets; range, road 1000 km (621 miles); fording amphibious; gradient 68%; side slope 30%; vertical obstacle 0·8 m (31·5 in); trench 1·2 m (3·9 ft); ground clearance 0·4 m (15·75 in)

Variants
BMR-600: this is the Spanish army's infantry fighting vehicle, designed in the early 1970s and built from 1979 as the **Pegaso 3560/50**; the troops can in most models fire their personal weapons from inside the hull via six ports (three on each side of the troop compartment), and use a large rear ramp; there is a rear-mounted winch, and options include an air-conditioning system, deletion of amphibious capability and wheel-propelled amphibious capability; the basic vehicle can also be fitted out as an ambulance, and can carry the HCT turret with twin launchers for HOT heavy anti-tank missiles
Pegaso 3560/51: command model with additional equipment such as mapboards and extra radios
Pegaso 3560/53: mortar-carrier model with an 81-mm (3·2-in) mortar firing from the rear hull
Pegaso 3560/54: ambulance model with a crew of two and two medical attendants, and the ability to carry four litters or two litters and four seated casualties
Pegaso 3560/55: recovery and maintenance model with specialized equipment
Pegaso 3560/56: radio communications model
Pegaso 3564: fire-support model with a GIAT TS 90 turret carrying a 90-mm (3·54-in) GIAT CS Super (F4) rifled gun

Below: The BMR-600 has a CETME TC-3 cupola with a remotely controlled 0·5-in (12·7-mm) machine-gun.

Bottom: The Pegaso 3560/53's mortar can be fired from inside, or dismounted for use with the baseplate and tripod carried externally.

Above: Visible on the rear of this BLR's rear hull are stowed ditch-crossing channels.

Santa Barbara BLR

(Spain)

Type: wheeled armoured personnel carrier
Crew: 1 + 12
Combat weight: 12,000 kg (26,455 lb)
Dimensions: length overall 5·65 m (18·54 ft); width 2·50 m (8·20 ft); height to hull top 1·99 m (6·53 ft)
Armament system: one 7·62-mm (0·3-in) cupola-mounted machine-gun with an unrevealed number of rounds; the cupola is manually powered, the gun lacks stabilization in either elevation (an unrevealed arc) or azimuth (360°), and simple optical sights are fitted

Armour: welded steel
Powerplant: one 125-kW (168-hp) Pegaso modelo 9220 or 165-kW (221-hp) Pegaso modelo 9100/41 diesel engine with 200 litres (44 Imp gal) of internal fuel, and driving a 4 × 4 layout
Performance: speed, road 93 km/h (57·8 mph); range, road 570 km (354 miles); fording 1·1 m (3·6 ft); gradient 75%; side slope 30%; vertical obstacle not revealed; trench not revealed; ground clearance 0·32 m (12·6 in)

Variant

BLR: this private-venture design is a comparatively simple vehicle better suited to internal security than front-line operations; the embarked troops have the use of four doors (one in each side and two in the rear) but cannot fire their personal weapons from inside the vehicle

Hagglund & Soner Pansarbandvagn 302

(Sweden)

Type: tracked infantry fighting vehicle
Crew: 2 + 10
Combat weight: 13,500 kg (29,762 lb)
Dimensions: length overall 5·35 m (17·55 ft); width 2·86 m (9·38 ft); height to turret top 2·50 m (8·20 ft)
Armament system: one 20-mm Hispano-Suiza cannon with 505 rounds, and six smoke-dischargers; the turret is manually powered, the gun lacks stabilization in either elevation (−10° to +50°) or azimuth (360°), and simple optical sights are fitted
Armour: welded steel
Powerplant: one 210-kW (282-hp) Volvo-Penta THD 100B diesel engine with 285 litres (63 Imp gal) of internal fuel
Performance: speed, road 66 km/h (41 mph) and water 8 km/h (5 mph) driven by its tracks; range, road 300 km (186 miles); fording amphibious; gradient 60%; side slope not revealed; vertical obstacle 0·61 m (24 in); trench 1·8 m (5·9 ft); ground clearance 0·4 m (15·75 in)

Variants

Pbv 302A: this pioneering infantry fighting vehicle was designed in the early 1960s and produced between 1966 and 1971; this type is still viable, but it now has operational disadvantages in its lack of NBC protection and the inability of the embarked troops to fire their personal weapons from inside the vehicle (though there are long roof hatches for semi-exposed firing); access to the troop compartment is provided by two doors in the rear of the hull; the basic model can also be used to carry 2000 kg (4,409 lb) of cargo or as an ambulance (four litters, or six litters with the aid of a special kit)

Left: The Pbv 302 lacks features such as an NBC system considered essential for any more modern infantry fighting vehicle.

97

Pbv 302B: improved version of the Pbv 302A with a rear-mounted observation cupola for the embarked troops' commander, two Lyran launchers for illumination flares, and spaced armour over the front of the vehicle; the 20-mm cannon can be replaced by a 25-mm Oerlikon-Bührle KBA weapon if desired, and this is one of the features (together with powered turret functions and gun stabilization) proposed by Hagglund & Soner for its **Product-Improved Pbv 302**, which would have revised accommodation for a smaller number of infantrymen, who would have the ability to use their personal weapons from inside the vehicle via six ports (three in each side); the vehicle would also have a more powerful engine in the form of a 230-kW (308-hp) Volvo THD 100C diesel

Bplpbv 3023: fire-direction post model with extra radios and a ranging group of seven men in addition to the crew of three

Epbv 3022: observation post model with the commander's hatch replaced by an observation cupola with rangefinder

Stripbv 3021: command post model with mapboards and extra radios

Right: The Pbv 302 has no provision for personal weapons to be fired.

Above and left: The Tornado and Improved Tornado are impressive and versatile infantry combat vehicles that can be fitted with any of several armament turrets and a remotely controlled machine-gun at the rear.

MOWAG Improved Tornado

(Switzerland)
Type: tracked mechanized infantry combat vehicle
Crew: 3 + 7
Combat weight: 22,300 kg (49,162 lb)
Dimensions: length overall 6·70 m (21·98 ft); width 3·15 m (10·33 ft); height to hull top 1·75 m (5·74 ft)
Armament system: one 25-mm Oerlikon-Bührle KBA cannon with an unrevealed number of rounds (including 120 HE and 80 APDS) and one 7·62-mm (0·3-in) co-axial machine-gun with an unrevealed number of rounds, two 7·62-mm (0·3-in) remotely-controlled machine-guns in an optional installation at the rear of the hull, and smoke-dischargers; the turret is manually powered, the main gun lacks stabilization in either elevation (− 12° to + 52°) or azimuth (360°), and an optical fire-control system is fitted
Armour: welded steel
Powerplant: one 465-hp (347-kW) Detroit Diesel 8V-71TA diesel engine with 500 litres (110 Imp gal) of internal fuel
Performance: speed, road 66·1 km/h (41·1 mph); range, road 400 km (249 miles); fording 1·3 m (4·27 ft) without preparation and 1·7 m (5·6 ft) with preparation; gradient 60%; side slope 40%; vertical obstacle 0·85 m (33·5 in); trench 2·2 m (7·2 ft); ground clearance 0·45 m (17·7 in)

Variant
Improved Tornado: this is a very capable mech-

anized infantry combat vehicle based on the company's **Tornado** prototype, developed during the 1970s from the Marder (also designed by MOWAG) but fitted with a lower-rated Detroit Diesel 6V-71T engine; the embarked troops can fire their personal weapons from inside the vehicle via two ports in each side of the troop compartment, which is entered by a large rear ramp; standard equipment includes an NBC protection system and night vision devices; the type can be fitted with a variety of one- and two-man turrets carrying 25-mm cannon, the specification above describing the one-man Oerlikon-Bührle GBD-COA turret

---

MOWAG Piranha 8 × 8

(Switzerland)
Type: wheeled armoured personnel carrier
Crew: 15
Combat weight: 12,300 kg (27,116 lb)
Dimensions: length overall 6·365 m (20·88 ft); width 2·50 m (8·20 ft); height to turret top 1·85 m (6·07 ft)
Armament system: see Variants (below)
Armour: welded steel
Powerplant: one 300-hp (224-kW) Detroit Diesel 6V-53T diesel engine with 300 litres (66 Imp gal) of internal fuel, and driving an 8 × 8 layout
Performance: speed, road 100 km/h (62·1 mph) and water 10·5 km/h (6·5 mph) driven by two propellers; range, road 780 km (485 miles); fording amphibious; gradient 70%; side slope 35%; vertical obstacle 0·5 m (19·7 in); trench not revealed; ground clearance 0·5 m (19·7 in)

Variants
Piranha 4 × 4: possessing a combat weight of 7800 kg (17,196 lb), a length of 5·32 m (17·45 ft) and

a crew of 10, this 4 × 4 version is powered by a 216-hp (161-kW) Detroit Diesel 6V-53 diesel and can be fitted with turrets armed with one or two 7·62-mm (0·3-in) machine-gun(s), or with one externally mounted 0·5-in (12·7-mm) Browning M2HB heavy machine-gun, or with one 20-mm Oerlikon-Bührle KAA-001 cannon; the series was designed in the early 1970s for the export market, and deliveries began in 1976; alternative roles are anti-tank warfare with missiles, command post, cargo-carrying, ambulance, mortar carrying, reconnaissance and recovery, and standard features such as an NBC protection system and air conditioning can be supplemented by active or passive night vision devices
Piranha 6 × 6: possessing a combat weight of 10,500 kg (23,148 lb), a length of 5·97 m (19·59 ft) and a crew of 14, this 6 × 6 version is essentially a lengthened version of the 4 × 4 model powered by the 300-hp (224-kW) Detroit Diesel 6V-53T diesel and able to carry more infantrymen and a more advanced turret; as in the 4 × 4 model the embarked troops can fire their personal weapons from inside the hull, in this instance via two ports in each side of the troop compartment, and the turret options are the Oerlikon-Bührle GAD-AOA with a 20-mm cannon, the Oerlikon-Bührle GBD-COA with a 25-mm cannon, the British Scorpion turret with a 76-mm (3-in) L23 rifled gun, and the Belgian CM 90 turret with a Cockerill 90-mm (3·54-in) rifled gun; other armament options are an internally mounted 81-mm (3·2-in) mortar and anti-tank missiles, the latter being either two ready-to-fire TOWs in a Norwegian one-man Thun-Eureka turret, or two ready-to-fire TOWs in a US TOW 2 elevating launcher; the options available on the 4 × 4 model are also available on the 6 × 6 variant, and other models are an ambulance and a battlefield surveillance model fitted with RASIT radar; derivatives of the Piranha 6 × 6 include the Canadian Cougar, Grizzly and Husky,

and a number of Chilean models built by Card-
oen, which has also adapted the type with the Brazilian ET-90 turret and 90-mm (3·54-in) rifled gun;
a version of the Piranha 6 × 6 in service with the
Swiss army is the **Panzerjager 90** anti-tank
vehicle with the Thun-Eureka Armoured Launch-
ing Turret for two TOW 2 heavy anti-tank missiles; the vehicle has a five-man crew and carries,
in addition to the two ready-to-fire missiles, eight
reload rounds inside the vehicle

Piranha 8 × 8: stretched model with superior
cross-country and load-carrying capabilities; the
armament options are the same as those for the
6 × 6 model with the addition of AA turrets armed
with two 20- or 30-mm cannon, a towed 120-mm
(4·72-in) mortar and a launcher with two banks of
15 81-mm (3·2-in) rockets; the Piranha 8 × 8 is also
the basis of the US Marine Corps' Canadian-
developed LAV-25 vehicle

Piranha AFV-90: version of the 8 × 8 Piranha
fitted with a KEnerga Weapons Station; this is a
two-man powered turret accommodating a
90-mm (3·54-in) MECAR KEnerga 90/46 low-
recoil rifled gun and 7·62-mm (0·3-in) co-axial
machine-gun; the 90-mm (3·54-in) ammunition
stowage amounts to 44 rounds (34 in the hull and
10 in the turret); the turret can be used with either
the Texas Instruments Lightweight Modular Thermal Sight or the OIP LRS 5 with image-intensifying
optics; as an alternative to the KEnerga Weapons
Station, the Piranha AFV-90 can be fitted with the
GIAT TS 90 turret carrying a GIAT CN-90 (F1)
rifled gun; the Piranha AFV-90 can also be
upgraded with a number of optional packages
such as a land navigation system, additional fuel
capacity for a range of 1000 km (621 miles), an
additional hatch and an 8000-kg (17,637-lb) capacity winch; the variant weighs 13,000 kg
(28,660 lb), and its primary dimensions include a
length of 6·79 m (22·28 ft) with gun forward and a
height of 2·70 m (8·86 ft)

**Below: This 8 × 8 Piranha has a CM-90 turret
with 90-mm (3·54-in) Cockerill Mk III gun,
7·62-mm (0·3-in) co-axial machine-gun and
electrically operated smoke-dischargers.**

MOWAG Grenadier

(Switzerland)
Type: wheeled armoured personnel carrier
Crew: 1 + 8
Combat weight: 6100 kg (13,448 lb)
Dimensions: length overall 4·84 m (15·88 ft);
width 2·30 m (7·55 ft); height to turret top 2·12 m
(6·96 ft)
Armament system: see Variant (below)
Armour: welded steel
Powerplant: one 150-kW (201-hp) petrol engine
with 180 litres (40 Imp gal) of internal fuel, and
driving a 4 × 4 layout
Performance: speed, road 100 km/h (62·1 mph)
and water 10 km/h (6·2 mph) driven by a single
propeller; range, road 550 km (342 miles); fording amphibious; gradient 60%; side slope 30%;
vertical obstacle 0·4 m (15·75 in); trench not
revealed; ground clearance 0·25 m (9·8 in)

**Below: Grenadier with an overhead weapon
mount and remotely controlled 7·62-mm
(0·3-in) machine-gun and smoke-dischargers.**

Variant
Grenadier: designed as a second-line armoured
personnel carrier, the Grenadier entered service in 1967 and can be fitted with a number of
armament types, including a single machine-gun,
or a 20- or 25-mm cannon, or an anti-tank missile
system, or an 81-mm (3·2-in) rocket-launcher
system; the embarked troops have only limited
provision for firing their weapons from inside the
vehicle

MOWAG Roland

(Switzerland)
Type: wheeled armoured personnel carrier
Crew: 3 + 3
Combat weight: 4900 kg (10,802 lb)
Dimensions: length overall 4·73 m (15·52 ft);
width 2·05 m (6·73 ft); height to turret top 2·10 m
(6·89 ft)
Armament system: one 7·62-mm (0·3-in)
machine-gun with an unrevealed number of

rounds; the turret is manually powered, the gun lacks stabilization in either elevation (an unrevealed arc) or azimuth (360°), and simple optical sights are fitted

Armour: welded steel

Powerplant: one 150-kW (201-hp) petrol engine with 170 litres (37·4 Imp gal) of internal fuel, and driving a 4 × 4 layout

Performance: speed, road 110 km/h (68·4 mph); range 570 km (354 miles); fording 1·0 m (3·3 ft); gradient 60%; side slope 30%; vertical obstacle 0·4 m (15·75 in); trench not revealed; ground clearance 0·42 m (16·5 in)

Variant

Roland: designed as a private venture in the 1960s, the Roland has sold well to African and Latin American countries, mainly in the internal security role; the basic vehicle can also be fitted with manual transmission, with a useful saving in weight (200 kg/441 lb) and overall dimensions (length drops to 4·44 m/14·57 ft) at the expense of driver fatigue; many optional items are offered, including night vision devices, an obstacle-clearing blade and provision for the embarked troops to fire their personal weapons from inside the vehicle

Above: Roland with a remotely controlled 7·62-mm (0·3-in) machine-gun above the roof.

Below: The BMP-2 is a much revised and improved development of the limited BMP-1.

BMP-2

(USSR)

Type: tracked mechanized infantry combat vehicle

Crew: 3 + 7

Combat weight: 14,600 kg (32,187 lb)

Dimensions: length overall 6·858 m (22·50 ft); width 3·089 m (10·135 ft); height 2·077 m (6·81 ft)

Armament system: one 30-mm 2A42 cannon with 500 rounds, one 7·62-mm (0·3-in) PKT co-axial machine-gun with 2,000 rounds, one launcher for an unrevealed number of AT-5 'Spandrel' anti-tank missiles and three smoke-dischargers on each side of the turret; the turret is electrically powered, the main gun lacks stabilization in either elevation (unrevealed depression to +74°) or azimuth (360°), and an optical fire-control system is fitted; the type can also generate smoke by injecting fuel into the exhaust system

Armour: welded steel with appliqué steel on the turret sides

Powerplant: one 300-kW (402-hp) Model 5D20 diesel engine with 460 litres (101 Imp gal) of internal fuel

Performance: speed, road 80 km/h (49·7 mph) and water 7 km/h (4·3 mph) driven by its tracks; range, road 500 km (311 miles); fording amphibious; gradient 60%; side slope not revealed; vertical obstacle 0·7 m (27·6 in); trench 2·5 m (8·2 ft); ground clearance not revealed

Variant

BMP-2: developed from the baseline BMP-1, the BMP-2 entered service in the late 1970s and is a considerable advance on its predecessor in that the commander is located in the turret rather than behind the driver, that a more powerful diesel is used, and that the low-velocity 73-mm (2·87-in) gun in a one-man turret is replaced by a powerful high-velocity 30-mm cannon in a two-man turret; it is also believed that the frontal arc has been uparmoured; the embarked infantry can use their personal weapons from inside the vehicle via six ports (two in each side and one in each of the two rear doors), and the anti-tank system fitted is the advanced AT-5 'Spandrel', for which a ground launcher is additionally carried; standard equipment includes an NBC protection system and night vision devices; the 30-mm turret of the BMP-2 has also been fitted to the hull of the 2S1 (SO-122 Gvozdika) self-propelled howitzer to produce a vehicle whose precise role is as yet uncertain, but which offers greater buoyancy and thus better amphibious capability than the BMP-2 that is only marginally amphibious when fully laden; the type lacks the extensive armour protection of the BMP-2 and is probably intended for the reconnaissance role with the Warsaw Pact and export customers reluctant to bear the cost of the better defended BMP-2; the type's exact designation remains unknown

BMP-1

(USSR)

Type: tracked mechanized infantry combat vehicle

Crew: 3 + 8

Combat weight: 13,500 kg (29,762 lb)

Dimensions: length overall 6·74 m (22·11 ft); width 2·94 m (9·65 ft); height over searchlight 2·15 m (7·05 ft)

Armament system: one 73-mm (2·87-in) 2A28 smooth-bore gun with 40 rounds in an automatic loader, one 7·62-mm (0·3-in) PKT co-axial machine-gun with 2,000 rounds, and one launcher for five AT-3 'Sagger' anti-tank missiles; the turret is electrically powered, the main gun lacks stabilization in either elevation (−4° to +33°) or azimuth (360°), and an optical fire-control system is fitted; the type can generate smoke by injecting fuel into the exhaust system

Armour: welded steel varying in thickness from 6 to 33 mm (0·24 to 1·3 in)

Powerplant: one 225-kW (301-hp) Model 5D20 diesel engine with 460 litres (101 Imp gal) of internal fuel

Performance: speed, road 80 km/h (49·7 mph) and water 8 km/h (5 mph) driven by its tracks; range, road 500 km (311 miles); fording amphibious; gradient 60%; side slope 30%; vertical

Below: Polish troops disembark from the rear doors of their BMP infantry fighting vehicle.

obstacle 0·8 m (31·5 in); trench 2·2 m (7·2 ft); ground clearance 0·39 m (15·4 in)

Variants

BMP-1: developed in the early 1960s as the primary armoured personnel carrier for the infantry units within Soviet tank divisions (and thus the counterpart of the wheeled BTR-60 developed for the infantry of motor rifle divisions), the BMP-1 was at first known in the West as the **M1967** and then as the **BMP-76PB**, and was developed via an interim vehicle designated **BMP M1966** in the US system of terminology to the definitive **BMP M1970** with better amphibious capabilities and a small snorkel; the BMP-1 is a very useful mechanized infantry combat vehicle let down by its generally poor armament, the 73-mm (2·87-in) low-pressure gun in the one-man turret having so mediocre a muzzle velocity that its projectile is highly susceptible to crosswinds; the embarked infantrymen can use their personal weapons from inside the vehicle via eight ports (three in each side and one in each of the two rear doors), and the BMP-1 has full NBC protection plus night vision devices; variations on this basic theme include a model with a rear ramp in place of the two doors, a launcher for AT-4 'Spigot' rather than AT-3 'Sagger' anti-tank missiles, and additions on

the turret (such as the 30-mm AGS-17 grenade-launcher or six smoke-dischargers) and hull (appliqué armour as proved necessary by operations in Afghanistan)

BMP-1K: command model designated **BMP M1974** in the US system of terminology; the vehicle retains armament but has a revised interior with mapboards, extra radios etc; a later **BMP-1KSh** model is used for the command and staff role, and is designated **BMP M1978** in the US system of terminology; the variant has extra radios but no armament

BRM: known as the **BMP-R** or **BMP M1976** in the US system of terminology, this reconnaissance version has a 73-mm (2·87-in) gun in a two-man turret; the **BMP M1976/2** improved model has a parabolic antenna above the turret

BVP-1: Czech-developed armoured recovery vehicle with a 1500-kg (3,309-lb) capacity crane in place of the turret

PRP-3: artillery fire-control version known in the US system of terminology as the **BMP M1975** with a crew of five, a two-man turret, radar above the hull rear, and armament of one 7·62-mm (0·3-in) machine-gun

BMP-PPO: training model with eight roof cupolas for trainees, but no turret

IRM: 17,000-kg (37,478-lb) amphibious engineer

The BMP-1 has four roof hatches for its troops.

reconnaissance derivative designed for beach reconnaissance; the vehicle is 8·22 m (26·97 ft) long and is fully amphibious, using a snorkel and two shrouded propellers in the water

NORINCO WZ 501: 13,300-kg (29,321-lb) Chinese copy of the BMP-1, identical with the Soviet original apart from very slightly reduced combat weight, a slightly reduced road speed of 65 km/h (40·4 mph), and the installation of the Chinese Red Arrow 73 anti-tank missile (Chinese copy of the AT-3 'Sagger') over the 73-mm (2·87-in) main gun

NORINCO/FMC NFV-1: hull of the WZ 501 fitted with the American FMC One Man Electric Drive Enclosed Weapon Station, a turret carrying a 25-mm McDonnell Douglas M242 Bushmaster cannon with 165 rounds and a 7·62-mm (0·3-in) co-axial machine-gun with 230 rounds; the turret can be traversed through 360°, and the armament elevated in an arc from −7° to +47°, and additional ammunition is carried in the hull; the variant weighs 13,600 kg (29,982 lb), and is powered by a 220-kW (295-hp) NORINCO 6V-150 diesel for a maximum speed of 65 km/h (40·4 mph) and a road range of 460 km (286 miles) on a fuel capacity of 460 litres (101 Imp gal)

BMD-1

(USSR)

Type: tracked airborne forces combat vehicle
Crew: 7
Combat weight: 6700 kg (14,771 lb)
Dimensions: length overall 5·40 m (17·72 ft); width 2·63 m (8·63 ft); height 1·97 m (6·46 ft)
Armament system: one 73-mm (2·87-in) 2A28 smooth-bore gun with 40 rounds in an automatic loader, one 7·62-mm (0·3-in) PKT co-axial machine-gun with 2,000 rounds, and one launcher rail for two AT-3 'Sagger' anti-tank missiles in the turret, and two 7·62-mm (0·3-in) PKT bow-mounted machine-guns with an unrevealed number of rounds; the turret is electrically powered, the main gun lacks stabilization in either elevation (−4° to +33°) or azimuth (360°), and an optical fire-control system is fitted; the type can generate smoke by injecting fuel into the exhaust system
Armour: welded steel varying in thickness from 7 mm (0·28 in) to 23 mm (0·91 in)
Powerplant: one 225-kW (301-hp) Model 5D20 diesel engine with 300 litres (66 Imp gal) of internal fuel plus provision for an unknown quantity of auxiliary fuel in the troop compartment
Performance: speed, road 70 km/h (43·5 mph) and water 10 km/h (6·2 mph) driven by two water-

jets; range, road 320 km (199 miles); fording amphibious; gradient 60%; side slope not revealed; vertical obstacle 0·8 m (31·5 in); trench 1·6 m (5·25 ft); ground clearance 0·45 m (17·7 in)

Variants

BMD-1: originally known in the US system of terminology as the **M1970**, the BMD-1 was designed specially for the Soviets' large airborne arm, and is a useful vehicle within its limitations of small size, comparatively light protection and the same turret as the BMP-1 with its indifferent 73-mm (2·87-in) low-pressure gun; troop accommodation is cramped even for three men, who enter and depart the troop compartment by means of a forward-opening concertina hatch; the embarked troops cannot use their personal weapons from inside the vehicle, but extra firepower is provided by two flexible bow-mounted machine-guns; standard equipment includes an NBC protection system and night vision devices; variants of the basic model include the **BMD-1M** of 1980 with a revised ventilation system to reduce the chances of crew asphyxiation when the weapons are fired, the **BMD-1M/9K111** with the 'Sagger' installation over the 73-mm (2·87-in) gun replaced by an AT-4 'Spigot' launcher on the right of the turret, the **BMD-1 M1981/1** with a 30-mm 2A42 cannon in

place of the 73-mm (2·87-in) gun, and the **BMD-1M (30-mm)** paralleling the BMD-1 M19801/1 in its main armament
BMD-1 Mortar: mortar-carrier model with an 82-mm (3·2-in) mortar in the troop compartment
BMD-2: originally designated **BMD M1979** in the US system of terminology, this is a slightly lengthened version with six rather than five road wheels; the type was developed concurrently with the BMD-1 as a transport rather than assault vehicle, and has appeared in several subtypes such as the **BMD-2 M1979/1** armoured personnel carrier with two 7·62-mm (0·3-in) bow machine-guns, and rear accommodation for two 30-mm AGS-17 grenade launchers plus their crews, and the **BMD-2KSh** (in the US system of terminology **BMD M1979/3**) command post model without the bow machine-guns and turret, but carrying extra radios and 'Clothes Rail' folding antenna round the superstructure; the BMD-2 has a crew of 1 + 9, a combat weight of 7500 kg (16,534 lb) and an overall length of 5·95 m (19·52 ft); power is provided by one 224-kW (300-hp) Model 5D20 diesel for a road speed of 60 km/h (37·3 mph) and a road range of 500 km (311 miles); the type's maximum armour thickness is 16 mm (0·63 in)

Below: The BMD-1 is only lightly protected to ensure a high measure of air portability.

BTR-70

(USSR)

Type: wheeled armoured personnel carrier

Crew: 2 + 9

Combat weight: 11,500 kg (25,353 lb)

Dimensions: length overall 7·535 m (24·72 ft); width 2·80 m (9·19 ft); height overall 2·235 m (7·33 ft)

Armament system: one 14·5-mm (0·57-in) KPVT heavy machine-gun with 500 rounds and one 7·62-mm (0·3-in) PKT co-axial machine-gun with 2,000 rounds; the turret is manually operated, the main gun lacks stabilization in either elevation (−5° to +30°) or azimuth (360°), and simple optical sights are fitted

Armour: welded steel

Powerplant: two 90-kW (121-hp) ZMZ-4905 petrol engines with about 350 litres (77 Imp gal) of internal fuel plus provision for an unrevealed quantity of auxiliary fuel, and driving an 8 × 8 layout

Performance: speed, road 80 km/h (49·7 mph) and water 10 km/h (6·2 mph) driven by one water-jet; range, road 400 km (249 miles) on internal fuel and 600 km (373 miles) with external tanks; fording amphibious; gradient 60%; side slope 40%; vertical obstacle 0·5 m (19·7 in); trench 2·0 m (6·6 ft); ground clearance 0·475 m (18·7 in)

Variants

BTR-70: designed in the 1970s as successor to the BTR-60P but not judged to be wholly successful, the BTR-70 entered service in the late 1970s and initially received the Western designations **SPW-70** and in the US system of terminology **BTR M1970**; the embarked infantry can use their personal weapons from inside the vehicle via three ports in each side of the troop compartment, which has only poor means of access and egress through a small door between the second and third wheels on each side of the vehicle; there are two rectangular hatches, each fitted with a firing port, in the roof of the troop compartment, the forward hatch opening forward, and the rear hatch opening rearward; standard equipment includes an RPG-7 rocket-launcher, two 30-mm

AGS-17 grenade-launchers, a front-mounted winch, a central tyre pressure-regulation system, and an NBC protection system

BTR-70/AGS-17: extemporized version seen in Afghanistan with a 30-mm AGS-17 grenade-launcher on its roof

BTR-70MS: turretless version optimized for communications

BTR-70KShM: command post and staff version

BREM: armoured recovery vehicle with a bow-mounted crane and other items of specialized equipment

BTR-80: the new designation indicates that this is an updated and considerably improved development of the BTR-70 designed to overcome the earlier type's principal operational failings of modest range and a comparatively inaccessible troop compartment; the two petrol engines of the earlier model are replaced by one 195-kW (262-hp) V-8 diesel engine, and this boosts not only reliability and range but improves speed marginally and reduces the fire risk, which is also countered by the installation of a fire-suppression system; the one-man turret of the BTR-70 is retained, though the 14·5-in (0·57-in) heavy

Above: The BTR-70 8 × 8 wheeled APC.

machine-gun can be elevated to +60° rather than +30° for improved capability against low-flying aircraft and battlefield helicopters; located on the rear of the turret is a bank of six smoke-dischargers; other improvements include better firing ports and larger hatches for the embarked troops

TAB-77: Romanian version of the BTR-70 with a single diesel engine rather than two petrol engines, and fitted with the same turret as the Romanian TAB-72 version of the Soviet BTR-60PB; this turret is a manually powered unit containing one 14·5-mm (0·57-in) KPV heavy machine-gun with 500 rounds and one 7·62-mm (0·3-in) PKT co-axial machine-gun with 2,000 rounds; like the Soviet unit, the Romanian turret has 360° traverse, but the guns can be elevated in an arc between −5° and +85°, the higher elevation limit providing improved capability against battlefield helicopters

Below: The BTR-80 is similar to the BTR-70 with larger side doors and a single diesel.

BTR-60PB

(USSR)

Type: wheeled armoured personnel carrier
Crew: 2 + 14
Combat weight: 10,300 kg (22,207 lb)
Dimensions: length overall 7·56 m (24·80 ft); width 2·825 m (9·27 ft); height to turret top 2·13 m (6·99 ft)
Armament system: one 14·5-mm (0·57-in) KPV heavy machine-gun with 500 rounds and one co-axial 7·62-mm (0·3-in) PKT machine-gun with 2,000 rounds; the turret is manually powered, the main gun lacks stabilization in either elevation (−5° to +30°) or azimuth (360°), and simple optical sights are fitted.
Armour: welded steel varying in thickness from 5 to 9 mm (0·20 to 0·35 in)
Powerplant: two 67-kW (90-hp) GAZ-49B petrol engines with 290 litres (64 Imp gal) of internal fuel, and driving an 8 × 8 layout

Performance: speed, road 80 km/h (49·7 mph) and water 10 km/h (6·2 mph) driven by one water-jet; range, road 500 km (311 miles); fording amphibious; gradient 60%; side slope 40%; vertical obstacle 0·4 m (15·75 in); trench 2·0 m (6·6 ft); ground clearance 0·475 m (18·7 in)

Variants

BTR-60P: this vehicle was developed in the 1950s as successor to the BTR-152 as the primary armoured personnel carrier for motor rifle divisions, and entered service in 1961; though clearly better than the non-amphibious BTR-152, the BRT-60P has an open-topped crew and troop compartment (with three firing ports in each side so that the embarked troops can fire their personal weapons from inside the vehicle), and the armament is a single 7·62-mm SGMB or PKB pintle-mounted machine-gun, sometimes replaced by a 12·7-mm (0·5-in) DShKM heavy machine-gun

BTR-60PA: much improved 9980-kg (22,022-lb) model introduced in 1961 and featuring an enclosed troop compartment with NBC protection; the variant can carry 2 + 16 men (though 2 + 12 is more common), and is 2·055 m (6·74 ft) high to the top of the hull
BTR-60PB: essentially the BTR-60PA fitted with the same turret and armament as used on the BRDM-2, BTR-70 and SKOT; the nominal troop capacity is seldom used, a more normal complement being 2 + 8; there is also a forward air control version of this model, the armament being removed from the turret and replaced by a transparent cover so that the FAC officer can undertake forward observation and call in aircraft by means of the additional radio equipment carried in the troop compartment
BTR-60PU: command post version of the BTR-60P with mapboards and extra radio equipment
BTR-60PU-12: improved command post version of the BTR-60PA with an additional generator in a box over the roof; the type is generally used with air-defence gun and missile units
BTR-60MS: radio communications version with a telescopic aerial
TAB-71: Romanian version of the BTR-60P, first seen in 1971 and similar to the baseline Soviet version in lacking overhead armour and a turret
TAB-72: Romanian version of the Soviet BTR-60PB, first seen in 1972 and differing from the Soviet baseline vehicle in having two 105-kW (141-hp) rather than 67-kW (90-hp) petrol engines; the vehicle has a combat weight of 11,000 kg (24,250 lb) and its performance includes road and water speeds of 95 and 10 km/h (59 and 6·2 mph) and a road range of 500 km (311 miles) on 290 litres (64 Imp gal) of internal fuel; the only external difference is the Romanian version's different turret, a manually powered unit containing one 14·5-mm (0·57-in) KPV heavy machine-gun with 500 rounds and one 7·62-mm (0·3-in) PKT co-axial machine-gun with 2,000 rounds; like the Soviet unit, the Romanian turret has 360° traverse, but the guns can be elevated in an arc between −5° and +85°, the higher elevation limit providing improved capability against battlefield helicopters
TAB-73: Romanian mortar-carrier based on the TAB-72 but without the turret and fitted with an 82-mm (3·2-in) mortar in the rear compartment, which has outward-opening overhead hatches and is also adapted for the carriage of up to 100 bombs

Above and below: The BTR-60PB has the same turret as the BRDM-2 and is fully amphibious, with one waterjet (integral rudder) in the hull rear.

BTR-50PK

(USSR)

Type: tracked armoured personnel carrier
Crew: 2 + 20
Combat weight: 14,200 kg (31,305 lb)
Dimensions: length overall 7·08 m (23·23 ft); width 3·14 m (10·30 ft); height to hull top 1·97 m (6·46 ft)
Armament system: one 7·62-mm (0·3-in) SGMB pintle-mounted machine-gun with 1,250 rounds; the mounting is manually powered, the gun lacks stabilization in either elevation (−6° to +23·5°) or azimuth (90° as 45° left and 45° right of the centreline), and simple optical sights are fitted
Armour: welded steel varying in thickness from 6 to 10 mm (0·24 to 0·39 in)
Powerplant: one 180-kW (241-hp) diesel engine with 400 litres (88 Imp gal) of internal fuel
Performance: speed, road 44 km/h (27·3 mph) and water 11 km/h (6·8 mph) driven by two waterjets; range, road 400 km (249 miles); fording amphibious; gradient 70%; side slope 40%; vertical obstacle 1·1 m (43·3 in); trench 2·8 m (9·2 ft); ground clearance 0·37 m (14·6 in)

Variants

BTR-50P: developed in the middle of the 1950s on the chassis of the PT-76 amphibious light tank, the BTR-50P was the Soviet army's standard tracked armoured personnel carrier until the advent of the BMP-1; the type suffers from the major tactical limitation of an open-topped crew compartment, the troops being exposed not only to the elements but to the NBC threat, and moreover having to embark and disembark over the sides; standard equipment includes limited night-vision equipment; ramps at the hull rear allow a 57-mm (2·24-in) ZIS-2 anti-tank gun or 85-mm (3·35-in) D-44 field gun to be loaded onto the vehicle
BTR-50PA: version without loading ramps and often armed with the 14·5-mm (0·57-in) KVPT machine-gun
BTR-50PK: improved model with a covered troop compartment and NBC protection system; the troops have to embark and disembark via two roof hatches; the type has two ports in each side of the hull through which the embarked troops can fire their personal weapons
BRT-50PU: command post model with extra radios and mapboards etc in the troop compartment; there are two subvariants, the **BTR-50PU Model 1** with a single projecting bay at the rear, and the **BTR-50PU Model 2** with two projecting bays
MTK: mineclearing model of the BTR-50PK with a launcher to fire explosive-filled tubes designed to clear paths through minefields
MTP: technical support model of the BTR-50PK with a workshop built onto the rear, and also used for the front-line delivery of fuel
OT-62A: armoured personnel carrier built in Czechoslovakia and Poland, also known as the **TOPAS** and similar in appearance to the BTR-50PU; this model is unarmed though there is provision for the type to carry the 82-mm (3·2-in) vz 59A recoilless rifle
OT-62B: improved 15,000-kg (33,069-lb) Czech and Polish model fitted with a small turret (on the right) housing a 7·62-mm (0·3-in) vz 59T machine-gun plus 1,250 rounds and accommodating on its right an 82-mm (3·2-in) T-21 recoilless rifle plus 12 rounds; the turret is manually powered, the gun lacks stabilization in either elevation (−10° to +20°) or azimuth (360°), and simple optical sights are fitted; this variant is also known as the **TOPAS-2A**; the variant has a crew of 2 + 18, and the principal dimensions include an overall length of 7·08 m (23·23 ft), a width of 3·14 m (10·30 ft) and an overall height of 2·23 m (7·32 ft); the powerplant is a 225-kW (302-hp) PV-6 diesel with 417 litres (92 Imp gal) of fuel, sufficient for a maximum road speed of 58·4 km/h (36·3 mph) and a maximum road range of 460 km (286 miles)
OT-62C: 16,390-kg (36,133-lb) version used only by the Polish army and also known as the **TOPAS-2AP**; it has a centrally mounted turret for one 14·5-mm (0·57-in) KVPT heavy machine-gun plus 500 rounds and one 7·62-mm (0·3-in) KPT machine-gun plus 2,000 rounds; the manually powered turret provides 360° traverse, and the guns can be elevated from −4° to +89·5°; the type can also carry two four-man mortar teams each with its 82-mm (3·2-in) mortar and bombs; the variant has a crew of 3 + 12, and the principal dimensions include an overall length of 7·00 m (22·97 ft), a width of 3·225 m (10·58 ft) and an overall height of 2·725 m (8·94 ft); the powerplant is a 225-kW (302-hp) PV-6 diesel with 520 litres (114 Imp gal) of fuel, sufficient for a maximum road speed of 60 km/h (37·3 mph) and a maximum road range of 570 km (354 miles)
OT-62 Ambulance: Czech and Polish ambulance model
OT-62 Command: simple development of the basic OT-62 vehicle with additional radios
WPT-TOPAS: Polish recovery vehicle development of the OT-62A with a 2500-kg (5,511-lb) capacity winch, a hand-operated crane capable of lifting 1000 kg (2,205 lb) and one 7·62-mm (0·3-in) PK machine-gun in additional to personal weapons and an RPG-7 anti-tank rocket-launcher

Below: Though structurally and automotively similar to the baseline BTR-50, the BTR-50PK has an NBC system and full overhead cover for the embarked infantry.

NORINCO Type 77: Chinese armoured personnel carrier clearly based on the BTR-50PK, but is slightly larger and possesses better performance than its Soviet counterpart thanks to the installation of a 300-kW (402-hp) Type 12150L-2A diesel with 416 litres (91·5 Imp gal) of fuel, sufficient for a road range of 370 km (230 miles) and a water range of 120 km (75 miles); the Type 77 turns the scales at 15,500 kg (34,171 lb), but has maximum road and water speeds of 60 and 12 km/h (37·3 and 7·5 mph) respectively; water propulsion is by two rear-mounted waterjets; the main armament is a roof-mounted 12·7-mm (0·5-in) machine-gun with 500 rounds, and in addition to its crew of two the vehicle can carry 16 troops or 3000 kg (6,614 lb) of freight; the primary dimensions include an overall length of 7·40 m (24·28 ft), a width of 3·20 m (10·50 ft) and an overall height of 2·436 m (7·99 ft); the basic vehicle is available in two variants, namely the **Type 77-1** with three removable ramps at the rear, and the **Type 77-2** baseline infantry personnel carrier

Right: The BTR-50PK's two rectangular roof hatches are also the troops' only means of entry and exit.

MT-LB

(USSR)

Type: tracked multi-purpose vehicle
Crew: 2+11
Combat weight: 11,900 kg (26,235 lb)
Dimensions: length overall 6·454 m (21·17 ft); width 2·85 m (9·35 ft); height to turret top 1·865 m (6·12 ft)
Armament system: one 7·62-mm (0·3-in) PKT machine-gun with 2,500 rounds; the turret is manually powered, the gun lacks stabilization in either elevation (−5° to +30°) or azimuth (360°), and simple optical sights are fitted
Armour: welded steel varying in thickness from 7 to 14 mm (0·28 to 0·55 in)
Powerplant: one 180-kW (241-hp) YaMZ 238 V diesel engine with 450 litres (99 Imp gal) of internal fuel
Performance: speed, road 61·5 km/h (38·2 mph) and water 6 km/h (3·7 mph) driven by its tracks; range, road 500 km (311 miles); fording amphibious; gradient 60%; side slope 30%; vertical obstacle 0·7 m (27·6 in); trench 2·7 m (8·9 ft); ground clearance 0·4 m (15·75 in)

Variants

MT-LB: developed from the MT-L unarmoured carrier in the later part of the 1960s as successor to the AT-P tracked artillery tractor, the MT-LB was initially known as the **M1970** in the US system of terminology and has since been seen in a number of roles including that of armoured personnel carrier in snowy or marshy conditions, ambulance, artillery tractor, cargo carrier, command vehicle, engineer vehicle (with rear-mounted plough for use in reverse) and artillery fire-control vehicle; standard equipment includes an NBC protection system and night vision devices, but there is only limited capability for the embarked troops to use their personal weapons from inside the vehicle via four ports; these are located as one in each side of the troop compartment and one in each of the two rear doors, the embarked troops' only means of access to and egress from the troop compartment; there are also two forward-opening hatches in the roof of the troop compartment
MT-LBV: MT-LB fitted with tracks 565 mm (22·24 in) wide rather than the standard 350 mm (13·78 in) wide to reduce ground pressure (by

Below: The multi-role MT-LB is an 11-man APC; also an artillery tractor for equipments like this 100-mm (3·94-in) T-12 anti-tank gun.

almost half) and so facilitate operation in snowy or marshy conditions

MT-LBU: command post version with extra radios, land navigation system and a tented rear extension

MT-SON: artillery fire-control version with 'Pork Trough' radar mounted on the roof

MT-LB/'Big Fred': artillery- and mortar-locating version with 'Big Fred' radar mounted on the roof

MT-LB/Sani: unlike the 82-mm (3·2-in) mortar-carrier listed below, this is a fully engineered model mounting the 120-mm (4·72-in) 2S12 Sani mortar

MT-LB/Vasilek: version of the basic MT-LB fitted with the 82-mm (3·2-in) 2B9 Vasilek mortar; this mortar installation is located on an assembly of ammunition boxes above the rear decking, and comprises the standard wheeled mounting for this mortar with its wheels removed

MT-LB/WAT: Polish version of the basic vehicle fitted with the same WAT turret as used on the OT-62C armoured personnel carrier derivative of the Soviet BTR-50PK, and fitted with one 14·5-mm (0·57-in) and one 7·62-mm (0·3-in) machine-gun

MTP-LB: turretless repair version with a front-mounted A-frame capable of lifting 1500 kg (3,307 lb), a crane, a 6700-kg (14,770-lb) capacity winch and many items of specialized repair kit

RKhM: chemical reconnaissance vehicle with a redesigned superstructure and dispenser for lane-marking

Below: Like other Soviet ASPCs of its time, the BTR-152 was designed without overhead cover, a failing remedied in the BTR-152K model seen here.

BTR-152V1

(USSR)

Type: wheeled armoured personnel carrier
Crew: 2 + 17
Combat weight: 8950 kg (19,731 lb)
Dimensions: length overall 6·83 m (22·41 ft); width 2·32 m (7·61 ft); height to hull top 2·05 m (6·73 ft)
Armament system: one 12·7-mm (0·5-in) DShKM pintle-mounted heavy machine-gun with an unrevealed number of rounds, or one 7·62-mm (0·3-in) SGMB pintle-mounted machine-gun with 1,250 rounds; the main mounting is manually powered, the gun lacks stabilization in either elevation (−6° to +23·5°) or azimuth (90° as 45° left and 45° right of the centreline), and simple optical sights are fitted
Armour: welded steel varying in thickness from 4 to 13·5 mm (0·16 to 0·53 in)
Powerplant: one 82-kW (110-hp) ZIL-123 petrol engine with 300 litres (66 Imp gal) of internal fuel, and driving a 6 × 6 layout
Performance: speed, road 75 km/h (46·6 mph); range, road 780 km (485 miles); fording 0·8 m (2·6 ft); gradient 55%; side slope not revealed; vertical obstacle 0·6 m (23·6 in); trench 0·69 m (2·25 ft); ground clearance 0·295 m (11·6 in)

Variants

BTR-152: introduced in 1951, this was the Soviet army's first armoured personnel carrier developed after World War II, and is based on the chassis and automotive system of the ZIL-151 truck; the type is still in limited service but suffers the grave disadvantages on the modern battlefield of lacking NBC protection, amphibious capability, and overhead cover for the embarked troops who can, however, use their personal weapons from inside the vehicle via eight ports (three in each side and one in each of the two rear doors); the vehicle's machine-gun can be supplemented by two side-mounted 7·62-mm (0·3-in) SGMB machine-guns

BTR-152V: 1955 development of the BTR-152 with a central tyre pressure-regulation system; there is also an artillery command derivative of this model designated **BTR-152I**

BTR-152V1: 1962 improved model based on the chassis and automotive system of the ZIL-157 truck; the variant features a 5000-kg (11,023-lb) capacity front-mounted winch and a central tyre pressure-regulation system with external air lines

BTR-152V2: BTR-152V1 without a winch

BTR-152V3: model with internal air lines, winch and IR driving lights

BTR-152K: much improved BTR-152V3 with overhead protection for the troop compartment; there are two hatches in the troop compartment roof, one fitted with a single firing port and the other with two ports

BTR-152A: AA vehicle with a ZTPU-2 turret for two 14·5-mm (0·57-in) KPV machine-guns; the turret is manually powered, the guns lack stabilization in either elevation (−5° to +80°) or azimuth (360°), and simple optical sights are fitted; variations include Egyptian vehicles with a Czech M53 mounting for four 12·7-mm (0·5-in) DShKM machine-guns, and Palestine Liberation Organization vehicles with a Soviet ZU-23 mounting for two 23-mm cannon

BTR-152U: command post model with raised superstructure and windows

BTR-40

(USSR)
Type: wheeled armoured personnel carrier
Crew: 2 + 8
Combat weight: 5300 kg (11,684 lb)
Dimensions: length overall 5·00 m (16·40 ft); width 1·90 m (6·23 ft); height without armament 1·75 m (5·74 ft)
Armament system: one 7·62-mm (0·3-in) SGMB pintle-mounted machine-gun with 1,250 rounds; the mounting is manually powered, the gun lacks stabilization in either elevation (−6° to +23·5°) or azimuth (90° as 45° left and 45° right of the centre-line), and simple optical sights are fitted
Armour: welded steel to a maximum thickness of 8 mm (0·315 in)
Powerplant: one 60-kW (80-hp) GAZ-40 petrol engine with 120 litres (26·4 Imp gal) of internal fuel, and driving a 4 × 4 layout
Performance: speed, road 80 km/h (49·7 mph); range, road 285 km (177 miles); fording 0·8 m (2·6 ft); gradient 60%; side slope 30%; vertical obstacle 0·47 m (18·5 in); trench 0·7 m (2·3 ft) with channels; ground clearance 0·275 m (10·8 in)

Variants

BTR-40: developed shortly after the BTR-152, the BTR-40 was based on the GAZ-63 truck and designed primarily for reconnaissance and command post duties, entering service in 1951; the type is still widely used by Soviet clients in the Middle East and Africa despite the fact that it lacks amphibious capability, overhead cover for the troop compartment, night-vision devices and even the central tyre pressure-regulation system otherwise standard on Soviet front-line vehicles; the troop compartment has three firing ports in each side and two in the rear, the latter to each side of the twin doors used by the embarked troops for access and egress
BTR-40A: AA version in a manually-operated turret for two 14·5-mm (0·57-in) KPV heavy machine-guns with 2,400 rounds; the turret is manually powered, the guns lack stabilization in either elevation (−5° to +80°) or azimuth (360°), and simple optical sights are fitted
BTR-40B: improved armoured personnel carrier with overhead cover for the troop compartment; the roof is fitted with two outward-opening hatches on each side, each fitted with a firing port
BTR-40Kh: chemical reconnaissance version with provision for the fixing of marker poles
BTR-40/'Sagger': East German training version with an overhead triple launcher for AT-3 'Sagger' anti-tank missiles

AT-P

(USSR)
Type: tracked artillery tractor and armoured personnel carrier
Crew: 3 + 6
Combat weight: 6000 kg (13,228 lb)
Dimensions: length overall 4·45 m (14·60 ft); width 2·50 m (8·20 ft); height 1·83 m (6·00 ft)
Armament system: one 7·62-mm (0·3-in) SGMT bow-mounted machine-gun with an unrevealed number of rounds
Armour: welded steel to a maximum thickness of 12 mm (0·47 in)
Powerplant: one 82-kW (110-hp) ZIL-123F petrol engine with an unrevealed quantity of internal fuel
Performance: speed, road 50 km/h (31·1 mph); range, road 500 km (311 miles); fording 0·7 m (2·3 ft); gradient 60%; side slope 30%; vertical obstacle 0·7 m (27·6 in); trench 1·22 m (4·0 ft); ground clearance 0·3 m (11·8 in)

Variants

AT-P: this vehicle was introduced in the 1950s as a tractor for artillery pieces of up to 122-mm (4·8-in) calibre; it can also carry a 1200-kg (2,645-lb) payload, but as it lacks overhead cover, NBC protection and amphibious capability it has generally been replaced by the MT-LB
AT-P (Command): improved version with a commander's cupola, overhead protection and extra radio equipment
AT-P (Reconnaissance): artillery reconnaissance version with full-width rear compartment and specialized equipment

Above: The AT-P lacks overhead and NBC protection and is now only of limited use even as a tractor.

GKN Defence MCV-80 Warrior

(UK)
Type: tracked infantry combat vehicle
Crew: 3 + 7
Combat weight: 54,000 lb (24,494 kg)
Dimensions: length overall 20·80 ft (6·34 m); width 9·95 ft (3·034 m); height to hull roof 6·33 ft (1·93 ft) and overall 8·97 ft (2·735 m)
Armament system: one 30-mm ROF L21A1 RARDEN cannon with an unrevealed number of rounds, one co-axial 7·62-mm (0·3-in) ROF/ McDonnell Douglas Helicopters EX-34 Chain Gun with an unrevealed number of rounds, and four smoke-dischargers on each side of the turret; the turret is electrically powered, the main gun lacks stabilization in either elevation (an unrevealed arc) or azimuth (360°) , and an optical fire-control system is fitted
Armour: welded aluminium (hull) and welded steel (turret)
Powerplant: one 550-hp (410-kW) Perkins (Rolls-Royce) Condor CV8 TCA diesel engines with 170 Imp gal (772 litres) of internal fuel
Performance: speed, road 47 mph (75·6 km/h); range, road 310 miles (499 km); fording 4·25 ft (1·3 m); gradient 60%; side slope 40%; vertical obstacle 30 in (0·76 m); trench 8·25 ft (2·5 m); ground clearance 19·25 in (0·49 m)

Variants

MCV-80 Warrior: having entered service with the British army in the second half of the 1980s, the Warrior is the UK's first true mechanized infantry combat vehicle, and though it features good armament, protection and performance, the type has no provision for the embarked troops to use their personal weapons from inside the vehicle, and also lacks amphibious capability; the embarked troops are provided with a large power-operated rear door; standard equipment includes an NBC protection system and night vision devices; the manufacturer has proposed a whole series of derivatives, and the most significant of these are the types itemized below, for which the British army has a perceived need
MCV/C: command post vehicle with extra radios and specialized equipment
MCV/CRV: combat repair vehicle armed with a

Left: The BTR-40 is an obsolete type without overhead protection and possessing only limited mobility and payload.

Above: The Warrior Desert Fighting Vehicle is seen during Mid-Eastern trials with open crew hatches.

7·62-mm (0·3-in) L7 machine-gun and fitted with an extending-jib crane
MCV/MOR: mortar-carrier version with a 7·62-mm (0·3-in) L7 machine-gun and a rear-mounted 81-mm (3·2-in) mortar
MCV/MRV: mechanized recovery vehicle
MCV/P: platoon command vehicle armed with a 7·62-mm (0·3-in) L7 machine-gun

GKN Defence FV432

(UK)
Type: tracked armoured personnel carrier
Crew: 2 + 10
Combat weight: 33,685 lb (15,280 kg)
Dimensions: length overall 17·23 ft (5·25 m); width 9·19 ft (2·80 m); height including machine-gun 7·50 ft (2·29 m)
Armament system: one 7·62-mm (0·3-in) L7A2 cupola-mounted machine-gun with 1,600 rounds and three smoke-dischargers on each side of the hull front; an alternative fit is one 7·62-mm (0·3-in) L7A2 machine-gun with 1,600 rounds and four smoke-dischargers on each side of an electrically powered lightweight turret; the turret is electrically powered, the gun lacks stabilization in either elevation (− 15° to + 50°) or azimuth (360°), and simple optical sights are fitted
Armour: welded steel varying in thickness from 6 to 12 mm (0·24 to 0·47 in)
Powerplant: one 240-hp (179-kW) Rolls-Royce K60 Mo·4 Mk 4F multi-fuel engine with 100 Imp gal

Right: An FV432 brings up the rear of a column behind a Chieftain, two Scorpions and a Sultan.

(454 litres) of internal fuel

Performance: speed, road 32·5 mph (52·3 km/h) and water 4·1 mph (6·6 km/h) driven by its tracks and supported by a flotation screen; fording 3·5 ft (1·07 m) without preparation and amphibious with preparation; gradient 60%; side slope not revealed; vertical obstacle 24 in (0·61 m); trench 6·75 ft (2·06 m); ground clearance 16 in (0·41 m)

Variants

FV432: evolved from the FV420 series of armoured vehicles which failed to enter production in the 1950s, the FV432 armoured personnel carrier appeared in the early 1960s, production beginning in 1963 of the **FV432 Mk 1** with a highly noticeable exhaust on the left of the vehicle; successive models were the **FV432 Mk 1/1** and **FV432 Mk 2** with exhausts running over the roof, and the current **FV432 Mk 2/1** with a flush rather than protruding NBC pack; the type has night vision devices, and can be made amphibious with a simple kit; there is no provision for the embarked troops to use their personal weapons from inside the vehicle, or even to survey the terrain before disembarking; access to the troop compartment is provided by a large door mounted in the rear of the hull; a few FV432s with the 30-mm RARDEN cannon-armed turret of the FV721 Fox were produced, and these unwieldy vehicles serve with the British army's Berlin Brigade; other variants (often without formal designation) are itemized below

FV432 Ambulance: unarmed model with provision for a crew of two plus four litters or two litters and five seated casualties

FV432 Cargo: cargo model with a payload of 8,100 lb (3674 kg)

FV432 Carl Gustav: simple anti-tank model with a bar above the troop compartment for the 84-mm (3·31-in) Carl Gustav rocket-launcher; a comparable model carries the Milan medium anti-tank missile system, the launcher and missiles being disembarked for firing

FV432 Command: 34,170-lb (15500-kg) command version with a crew of seven, two mapboards, extra radio equipment and a tented rear extension

FV432 Minelayer: tow vehicle for the Bar minelayer, and able to lay anti-tank mines at the rate of 600 per hour; a Ranger anti-personnel minelayer can be fitted on the hull roof so that combined anti-tank/anti-personnel minefields can be laid

FV432 Mortar: 36,155-lb (16,400-kg) carrier for the 81-mm (3·2-in) L16 mortar, a crew of six and 160 bombs

FV432 Radar: carrier for either the Marconi ZB 298 short-range battlefield surveillance radar or the EMI Cymbeline medium-range mortar-locating radar

FV432 Recovery: battlefield recovery vehicle with a rear-mounted winch of 40,340-lb (18,298-kg) capacity

FV432 Royal Artillery: fire-control vehicle fitted with Marconi Field Artillery Computer Equipment (FACE) and a Plessey sound ranging system; as with other Royal Artillery-operated members of the series, the armament is a single 7·62-mm (0·3-in) Bren Gun

FV432 Royal Engineers: tow vehicle for the Giant Viper mine-clearing system

FV434: maintenance carrier version operated by REME and designed for the field changing of main battle tank powerpacks with the aid of a crane

FV438: anti-tank variant with two launchers and 16 Swingfire heavy anti-tank missiles

FV439: specialized Royal Signals communications model with additional equipment including parts of the Ptarmigan and Wavell systems

Alvis Stormer

(UK)

Type: tracked armoured personnel carrier

Crew: 3 + 8

Combat weight: 28,000 lb (12,701 kg)

Dimensions: length overall 17·50 ft (5·33 m); width 8·825 ft (2·69 m); height to top of machine-gun 7·45 ft (2·27 m)

Armament system: one 7·62-mm (0·3-in) L7A2 cupola-mounted machine-gun with an unrevealed number of rounds (200 in the cupola and an unrevealed number in the hull); the cupola is manually powered, the gun lacks stabilization in

either elevation (− 10° to + 55°) or azimuth (360°), and simple optical sights are fitted

Armour: welded aluminium

Powerplant: one 250-hp (186-kW) Perkins T6·3544 diesel engine with 88 Imp gal (400 litres) of internal fuel

Performance: speed, road 50 mph (80·5 km/h) and water 6 mph (9·6 km/h) driven by one propeller or 4 mph (6·4 km/h) driven by its tracks; range, road 400 miles (644 km); fording 3·6 ft (1·1 m) without preparation and amphibious with preparation; gradient 60%; side slope not revealed; vertical obstacle 18 in (0·46 m); trench 5·75 ft (1·75 m); ground clearance 16·5 in (0·42 m)

Variants

Stormer: this is the Alvis development of the FV4333 armoured vehicle designed in the late 1970s by the Military Vehicles and Engineering Establishment, the development being centred on the incorporation of proved components from the Scorpion CVR(T) series and the evolution of the type as the core of a large number of variants including an air-defence vehicle (with the General Electric Modular Weapon System turret carrying a 25- or 30-mm rotary cannon, two FIM-92 Stinger SAMs and Electronique Serge Dassault RA-20S radar plus a FLIR/laser sighting system), mortar carrier, anti-tank vehicle, missile launcher, maintenance and recovery vehicle, engineer vehicle, electronic warfare vehicle, command vehicle, logistics vehicle, ambulance, squad carrier, mobile protected gun/light assault vehicle, assault gun, low-profile 75-mm (2·95-in) gun vehicle and low-profile 90-mm (3·54-in) gun vehicle; of the vehicles ordered by Malaysia some have the Helio FVT-900 turret armed with a 20-mm Oerlikon-Bührle KAA cannon and 7·62-mm (0·3-in) co-axial machine-gun, and the others the Thyssen Henschel TH-1 turret with twin 7·62-mm (0·3-in) machine-guns; the British army has ordered a variant fitted with the new Shorts Starstreak hypervelocity SAM for the defence of first-line field formations

Below: The Starstreak is the SAM system based on the Stormer tracked APC.

Alvis FV603 Saracen

(UK)
Type: wheeled armoured personnel carrier
Crew: 2 + 10
Combat weight: 22,420 lb (10,170 kg)
Dimensions: length overall 17·17 ft (5·23 m); width 8·33 ft (2·54 m); height to turret top 8·08 ft (2·46 m)
Armament system: two 7·62-mm (0·3-in) machine-guns (one L3A3 in the turret and one Bren Gun on the hull-rear ring mounting) with 3,000 rounds, and three smoke-dischargers on each side of the hull front; the turret is manually powered, the gun lacks stabilization in either elevation (−12° to +45°) or azimuth (360°), and simple optical sights are fitted
Armour: welded steel varying in thickness from 8 to 16 mm (0·315 to 0·63 in)
Powerplant: one 160-hp (119-kW) Rolls-Royce B80 Mk 6A petrol engine with 44 Imp gal (200 litres) of internal fuel, and driving a 6 × 6 layout
Performance: speed, road 45 mph (72·4 km/h); range, road 250 miles (402 km); fording 3·5 ft (1·07 m) without preparation and 6·5 ft (1·98 m) with preparation; gradient 42%; side slope not revealed; vertical obstacle 18 in (0·46 m); trench 5·0 ft (1·52 m); ground clearance 17 in (0·43 m)

Variants
FV603: designed in the late 1940s as part of the British army's first post-war generation of light armoured fighting vehicles, the Saracen entered production in 1952 and has since seen extensive worldwide service; the type lacks an NBC protection system and night vision devices, and must be regarded as obsolete by modern standards despite the fact that the crew can fire their personal weapons from inside the vehicle (three on each side and one in each of the two rear doors), unlike the situation in later British APCs; the initial **FV603A Saracen Mk 1** vehicles had the B80 Mk 3A engine, but by the time of the **FV603B Saracen Mk 2** the B80 Mk 6A had become standard, and this engine was retained in the **FV603C Saracen Mk 3** with reverse-flow cooling for hot-climate operations; Saracens used in Northern Ireland for security operations are generally fitted with wire screens to defeat the HEAT warheads of RPG-7 anti-tank rockets, and often have water cannon or other riot-control weapons in place of the machine-guns
FV604: command post version with mapboards, extra radio equipment and a tented rear extension for a six-man crew
FV610(A): Royal Artillery command vehicle with specialist Royal Artillery equipment and a tented rear extension for its six-man crew
FV611: ambulance model with a crew of two and accommodation for 10 seated casualties, or three litters and two seated casualties, or two litters and six seated casualties

A Saracen with boxed Swingfire missiles.

Alvis FV103 Spartan

(UK)
Type: tracked armoured personnel carrier
Crew: 3 + 4
Combat weight: 18,015 lb (8172 kg)
Dimensions: length overall 16·81 ft (5·125 m); width 7·40 ft (2·26 m); height 7·48 ft (2·28 m)
Armament system: one 7·62-mm (0·3-in) L37A1 cupola-mounted machine-gun with 3,000 rounds, and four smoke-dischargers mounted on each side of the hull front; the cupola is manually powered, the gun lacks stabilization in either elevation (−10° to +55°) or azimuth (360°), and simple optical sights are fitted
Armour: welded aluminium
Powerplant: one 190-hp (142-kW) Jaguar J60 No·1 Mk 100B petrol engine with 85 Imp gal (386 litres) of internal fuel
Performance: speed, road 50 mph (80·5 km/h); range, road 300 miles (483 km); fording 3·5 ft (1·07 m) without preparation and amphibious with preparation; gradient 60%; side slope not revealed; vertical obstacle 19·75 in (0·5 m); trench 6·75 ft (2·06 m); ground clearance 14 in (0·36 m)

Variants
FV102 Striker: having entered service in 1975, the 18,400-lb (8346-kg) Striker is the specialist anti-tank missile variant of the Scorpion CVR(T) family, and is based on the hull of the FV103; this version has a crew of three, and an armament of one cupola-mounted L37A1 machine-gun and one

quintuple launcher with 10 Swingfire heavy anti-tank missiles; the type's overall length is 15·83 ft (4·826 m) and height 7·50 ft (2·28 m), and the fuel capacity is reduced to 77 Imp gal (350 litres)

FV103 Spartan: armoured personnel carrier variant of the Scorpion CVR(T) family, and entered service in 1978 for specialist transport tasks such as the carriage of Blowpipe SAM teams and Royal Engineer assault pioneer teams, and for the resupply of the FV102 Striker with Swingfire anti-tank missiles; other projected variants on the Spartan theme include an AA model (mounting a turret with two 20-mm cannon or four Blowpipe-type missiles) and an anti-tank model (with a TOW launcher and nine missiles, or an HCT turret with four HOT missiles, or an MCT turret with 10 Milan missiles)

FV104 Samaritan: 19,100-lb (8664-kg) ambulance variant of the Scorpion CVR(T) family and entered production in 1978; the hull is basically similar to that of the FV105 Sultan, and can carry a crew of two plus four litters, or two litters and three seated casualties, or five seated casualties; the type's principal dimensions include an overall length of 16·62 ft (5·067 m) and a height of 7·93 ft (2·416 m); the fuel capacity is 87 Imp gal (395 litres)

FV105 Sultan: 19,100-lb (8664-kg) command variant of the Scorpion CVR(T) family with a crew of five or six; two radios are carried, and the raised superstructure carries map boards and other command equipment; there is a 7·62-mm (0·3-in) L37A1 cupola-mounted machine-gun for local defence, and the type's principal dimensions include an overall length of 15·75 ft (4·80 m) and a height of 8·40 ft (2·559 m); the fuel capacity is 87 Imp gal (395 litres)

FV106 Samson: 19,265-lb (8739-kg) armoured recovery variant of the Scorpion CVR(T) family; the type entered service in 1978, and specialist equipment includes a 26,500-lb (12,020-kg) capacity winch, an A-frame and role-dedicated tools and appliances; the type's principal dimensions include an overall length of 15·71 ft (4·778 m) and a height of 7·40 ft (2·254 m); the fuel capacity is 89 Imp gal (404 litres)

Streaker HMLC: private-venture high-mobility load-carrier variant of the Scorpion CVR(T) family, able to carry a load of 6,615 lb (3001 kg); the type has a flat rear deck and the option of a light unarmoured or heavier armoured cab; the type can be powered by the standard Jaguar petrol engine, though the 200-hp (149-kW) Perkins T6·3544 diesel can be installed; the maximum road speed is 52 mph (83·7 km/h) and the maximum road range 300 miles (483 km); the Streaker has also been proposed as the basis of a whole series of armed or unarmed vehicles for the whole gamut of battlefield roles

Above and below: The FV103 Spartan is the APC member of the CVR(T) Scorpion family of light AFVs and can be fitted (below) with the ZB 298 ground surveillance radar.

Performance: speed, road 62 mph (99·8 km/h); range, road 400 miles (644 km); fording 3·25 ft (0·99 m); gradient 60%; side slope 40%; vertical obstacle 17·75 in (0·45 m); trench not revealed; ground clearance 17·75 in (0·45 m)

Variants

Simba APC: designed as a private venture by GKN Defence, the Simba Light Combat Vehicle family was evolved for export to countries requiring an integrated combat vehicle series capable of mounting guns up to 90 mm (3·54 in) in calibre, comparatively cheap to buy and operate, and simple to maintain in the field; the armoured personnel carrier is the baseline model of the series, and in its simpler form can carry a maximum of 10 men; the armament comprises a turret-mounted 0·5-in (12·7-mm) Browning M2HB heavy machine-gun or 7·62-mm (0·3-in) medium machine-gun, and the embarked troops can fire their personal weapons from inside the vehicle

via ports in the vehicle's sides; access to the troop compartment is provided by two doors (one in the rear and the other on the left side), each fitted with a firing port; the **Simba Low-Profile APC** has only a cupola in the roof, and can carry a maximum of 12 men

Simba AIFV: armoured infantry fighting vehicle offered with the capability to accept most 20- or 25-mm cannon-armed turrets

Simba AT: anti-tank vehicle offered with the choice of the Emerson TUA (TOW Under Armor) or Euromissile HCT turrets respectively for the BGM-71 TOW or HOT heavy anti-tank missiles

Simba FSV: fire-support vehicle able to accept any of the several 90-mm (3·54-in) gun turrets currently available

Simba IS: internal security vehicle offered with a wide assortment of specialist riot-control and other equipment

Simba Mortar: carrier for the 81-mm (3·2-in) mortar on a turntable in the rear of the vehicle

GKN Defence Simba APC

(UK)
Type: wheeled armoured personnel carrier
Crew: 2 + 10
Combat weight: 21,825 lb (9900 kg)
Dimensions: length overall 17·55 ft (5·35 m); width 8·20 ft (2·50 m); height to hull top 7·19 ft (2·19 m)
Armament system: see Variants (below)
Armour: welded steel
Powerplant: one 212-hp (158-kW) Perkins TV8·540 diesel engine with 53 Imp gal (241 litres) of internal fuel, and driving a 4 × 4 layout

Above: The Simba Fire Support Vehicle is seen here with the CM-90 turret complete with 90-mm (3·54-in) Cockerill Mk III gun and co-axial machine-gun.

GKN Defence AT105-P Saxon

(UK)

Type: wheeled armoured personnel carrier
Crew: 2 + 8/10
Combat weight: 25,700 lb (11,658 kg)
Dimensions: length overall 16·96 ft (5·169 m); width 8·17 ft (2·489 m); height to commander's cupola 8·62 ft (2·629 m)
Armament system: one 7·62-mm (0·3-in) L7A1 cupola-mounted machine-gun with an unrevealed number of rounds; the cupola is manually powered, the gun lacks stabilization in either elevation (−15° to +50°) or azimuth (360°), and simple optical sights are fitted
Armour: welded steel
Powerplant: one 164-hp (122-kW) Bedford 600 diesel engine with 35 Imp gal (160 litres) of internal fuel, and driving a 4 × 4 layout
Performance: speed, road 60 mph (96·6 km/h); range, road 315 miles (507 km); fording 3·67 ft (1·12 m); gradient 60%; side slope not revealed; vertical obstacle 16 in (0·41 m); trench not revealed; ground clearance 11·5 in (0·29 m)

Variants

AT105-A Saxon: the Saxon family was evolved from the limited-production AT104 type with greater protection to the automotive system, improved protection to the personnel from mines, and greater performance; the AT105-A is the ambulance model based on the AT-105P and able to carry four litters with a crew of four, or two litters and four seated casualties with a crew of three

AT105-E Saxon: upgraded version of the AT105-P with a turret-mounted 7·62-mm (0·3-in) machine-gun and optional riot-control equipment

AT105-P Saxon: basic rifle section transport model derived from the internal-security AT104, and entered service in 1985; a large number of optional fits are possible, including night vision devices, internal-security equipment and revised armament

AT105-Q Saxon: command version of the AT105-P with interior fitted out as a command post, and armed with one or two turret-mounted 7·62-mm (0·3-in) machine-guns

AT105/ARWEN Saxon: internal security version with a turret-mounted ARWEN 37V riot-control weapon, grenade-launchers and other items of internal security equipment

AT105 Recovery Saxon: recovery version with a side-mounted winch and specialist equipment

Below: The AT105-A version of the Saxon is a wholly unexceptional 4 × 4 wheeled APC.

Humber FV1611 'Pig'

(UK)

Type: wheeled armoured personnel carrier
Crew: 2 + 6/8
Combat weight: 12,765 lb (5790 kg)
Dimensions: length overall 16·16 ft (4·93 m); width 6·71 ft (2·04 m); height 6·96 ft (2·12 m)
Armament system: generally none
Armour: welded steel
Powerplant: one 120-hp (89-kW) Rolls-Royce B60 Mk 5A petrol engine with 32 Imp gal (145 litres) of internal fuel, and driving a 4 × 4 layout
Performance: speed, road 40 mph (64 mph);

range, road 250 miles (402 km); other details not revealed

Variants

FV1609: produced as an interim vehicle pending deliveries of the FV603 Saracen, the open-topped FV1609 was produced in the late 1940s by converting FV1601A 1-ton trucks to the armoured personnel carrier role with armoured bodies
FV1611: definitive model whose troop compartment is provided with overhead cover; although obsolete by front-line standards, these vehicles have a useful internal-security role in Northern Ireland as they are less overtly military than later

vehicles; FV1611s have thus been fitted with a wide assortment of internal-security equipment and uparmoured to a weight of some 15,435 lb (7001 kg) to make their bodies impenetrable by high-velocity rifle rounds
FV1612: radio vehicle with crew of three
FV1613: ambulance model with a crew of two and accommodation for three litters, or one litter and four seated casualties, or eight seated casualties

---

Below: In appearance the M2 and M3 versions of the Bradley fighting vehicle are identical, the vehicles differing only in armament and capacity.

FMC M2 Bradley

(USA)

Type: tracked infantry fighting vehicle
Crew: 3 + 7
Combat weight: 49,800 lb (22,590 kg)
Dimensions: length overall 21·17 ft (6·453 m); width 10·50 ft (3·20 m); height to turret roof 8·42 ft (2·565 m)
Armament system: one 25-mm McDonnell Douglas Helicopters M242 Bushmaster cannon with 900 rounds, one 7·62-mm (0·3-in) M240C co-axial machine-gun with 2,340 rounds, one retractable two-tube launcher with seven TOW missiles, and two smoke-dischargers on each side of the turret; the turret is electrically powered, the main gun is stabilized in elevation (−10° to +60°) and azimuth (360°), and a day/night optical fire-control system is fitted in addition to the TOW sight and control unit; the type can also generate smoke by injecting fuel into the exhaust system
Armour: welded aluminium, aluminium appliqué and laminate
Powerplant: one 500-hp (373-kW) Cummins VTA-903 diesel engine with 175 US gal (662 litres) of internal fuel
Performance: speed, road 41 mph (66 km/h) and water 4·5 mph (7·2 km/h) driven by its tracks; range, road 300 miles (483 km); fording amphibious; gradient 60%; side slope 40%; vertical obstacle 36 in (0·91 m); trench 8·33 ft (2·54 m); ground clearance 17 in (0·43 m)

Variants

M2 Bradley: designed as a mechanized infantry combat vehicle for the US Army from the early 1960s, this series originated with the XM701 experimental vehicle of 1965 and the Armored Infantry Fighting Vehicle of 1967 onwards; neither these types nor their derivatives found favour with the US Army, which issued its definitive specification in 1972, and this resulted in the XM723 prototype that eventually led via tortuous development and political programmes to the Fighting Vehicles System comprising the M2 Infantry Fighting Vehicle, the M3 Cavalry Fighting Vehicle, and the launch vehicle for the General-Support Rocket System (now known as the Multiple-Launch Rocket System); the first XM2 prototypes were built in 1978 and in December 1979 the type was standardized as the M2, with production deliveries beginning in 1981; the M2 and M3 are designed to scout for and support the M1 Abrams main battle tanks on advanced-technology battlefields, and are thus designed for maximum crew protection and decisive offensive firepower; standard equipment includes night vision devices, an NBC protection system and provision for the embarked troops to fire their personal weapons from inside the vehicle via six ports (two in each side and two in the rear); the troops enter and leave the vehicle by means of a large power-operated ramp (with inset emergency door) in the hull rear, and over the troop compartment is a rearward-opening hatch; offensive punch is augmented by the embarked troops' three Light Anti-tank Weapons
M2A1 Bradley: introduced in May 1986, this is the basic vehicle upgraded with the improved TOW 2 launcher, better 25-mm ammunition, improved armour, the addition of an anti-spall lining and several detail modifications, while future plans call for improved navigation and night vision capability, and superior protection against biological/chemical agents and electro-magnetic pulse effects; current thinking is devoted to a High-Survivability Bradley with weight increased to a figure between 55,000 and 60,000 lb (24,948 and 27,216 kg) by the addition of bolt-on reactive armour panels; performance will be maintained by the use of a 600-hp (447-kW) VTA-903T engine, and other possible improvements include new high-performance 25-mm ammunition
M2A2 Bradley: introduced in April 1989, this production variant results from the high-Survivability Bradley programme, and in its Phase I includes additional armour, brackets for armour tiles, internal spall liners, modified ammunition stowage, and a reduction in the numbers of firing ports from six to two; the Phase II improvements will include the VTA-903T engine with an uprated power train, extra armour, and protection for the vision blocks
M2A3 Bradley: due for introduction in the mid-1990s, this variant will mark a major improvement in the series with improved optics, a new main gun of 40-mm or possibly 50-mm calibre in a new turret, a new type of anti-tank missile, a hybrid NBC protection system, system survivability improvements with emphasis on protection against mines, a full-solution fire-control system, and an improved electronic system with a databus and automatic information processing

Below: The Bradley's turret houses the stabilized 25-mm cannon, co-axial machine-gun, TOW launcher, eight smoke-dischargers and fire-control system.

FMC M3 Bradley

(USA)

Type: tracked cavalry fighting vehicle
Crew: 3 + 2
Combat weight: 49,480 lb (22,444 kg)
Dimensions: length overall 21·17 ft (6·453 m); width 10·50 ft (3·20 m); height to turret roof 8·42 ft (2·565 m)
Armament system: one 25-mm McDonnell Douglas Helicopters M242 Bushmaster cannon with 1,500 rounds, one 7·62-mm (0·3-in) M240C co-axial machine-gun with 4,540 rounds, one retractable two-tube launcher for 12 TOW anti-tank missiles, and two smoke-dischargers on each side of the turret; the turret is electrically powered, the main gun is stabilized in elevation (−10° to +60°) and azimuth (360°), and a day/night optical fire-control system is fitted in addition to the TOW sight and control unit; the type can also generate smoke by injecting fuel into the exhaust system
Armour: welded aluminium and laminate
Powerplant: one 500-hp (373-kW) Cummins VTA-903 diesel engine with 175 US gal (662 litres) of internal fuel
Performance: speed, road 41 mph (66 km/h) and water 4·5 mph (7·2 km/h) driven by its tracks; range, road 300 miles (483 km); fording amphibious; gradient 60%; side slope 40%; vertical obstacle 36 in (0·91 m); trench 8·33 ft (2·54 m); ground clearance 17 in (0·43 m)

Variant

M3 Bradley: this counterpart of the M2 in the Fighting Vehicle System is designed for reconnaissance with enhanced anti-tank capability, and carries two rather than seven embarked infantrymen; as a result more ammunition of all types can be carried, but the embarked infantry have no provision to fire their personal weapons from inside the vehicle; other modifications include lack of anti-mine appliqué armour, but the same improvements being made to (and under investigation for) the M2 are also being made to the M3 to produce the **M3A1 Bradley**, the **M2A2 Bradley** and ultimately the **M3A3 Bradley**

FMC Armored Infantry Fighting Vehicle

(USA)

Type: tracked armoured infantry fighting vehicle
Crew: 3 + 7
Combat weight: 30,175 lb (13,687 kg)
Dimensions: length overall 17·25 ft (5·26 m); width 9·25 ft (2·82 m); height to turret roof 8·60 ft (2·62 m)
Armament system: one 25-mm Oerlikon-Bührle KBA-BO2 cannon with 324 rounds and one 7·62-mm (0·3-in) FN-MAG co-axial machine-gun with 1,940 rounds, and six smoke-dischargers on the hull front; the turret is electro-hydraulically powered, the main gun has optional stabilization in elevation (−10° to +50°) and azimuth (360°), and an optical fire-control system is fitted
Armour: welded aluminium and spaced laminate steel
Powerplant: one 350-hp (261-kW) Detroit Diesel 6V-53T diesel engine with 110 US gal (416 litres) of internal fuel
Performance: speed, road 38 mph (61·2 km/h) and water 3·9 mph (6·3 km/h) driven by its tracks; range, road 305 miles (491 km); fording amphibious; gradient 60%; side slope 30%; vertical obstacle 25 in (0·635 m); trench 5·33 ft (1·625 m); ground clearance 17 in (0·43 m)

Variants

AIFV (Belgium): Belgium was the second country to adopt the AIFV, which is essentially the M113 armoured personnel carrier revised into a true Armored Infantry Fighting Vehicle; the proper designation of this series is **AIFV-B**, which is operated by the Belgian forces in a number of forms alongside the closely related M113A1-B; the major differences in the Belgian series are the individual NBC air supply, suspension modelled on that of the M113A1-B, an engine compartment fire-extinguishing system, and a troop compartment heater; the three models of the AIFV-B are the **AIFV-B-25 mm** squad transport (with a turret-mounted 25-mm Oerlikon-Bührle KBA-BO2 cannon, a crew of seven, provision for a launcher for Milan medium anti-tank missiles, and two Lyran flare launchers), the **AIFB-B-·50** squad transport (with a 0·5-in/12·7-mm Browning M2HB pintle-mounted heavy machine-gun), and the **AIFV-B-CP** command post model (with a 0·5-in/12·7-mm Browning M2HB pintle-mounted heavy machine-gun and troop compartment fitted out for command post operations with a crew of seven); the turret of the AIFV-B-25 mm is the FMC Enclosed Weapons Station, otherwise known as the FMC 25-mm One-Man Turret; this has ready-use supplies of 180 25-mm and 230 7·62-mm (0·3-in) rounds
AIFV (Netherlands): the Netherlands was the first country to adopt the AIFV, which was developed by FMC in the mid-1960s on the basis of the M113 armoured personnel carrier with a power-operated turret and five firing ports (two in each side and one in the power-operated rear ramp) for the embarked infantry, who also have access to a rearward-opening hatch in the troop compartment roof; this XM765 led to the Product Improved M113A1 of 1970 with a centrally mounted turret and the commander's cupola behind it; trials confirmed the unsuitability of this arrangement, and the type was redesigned as the AIFV with side-by-side turret and commander's cupola (the former on the right and the latter on the left); the first Dutch order was placed in 1975, and deliveries of what the Dutch designate the **YPR 765 PRI** began in 1977; this is the standard AIFV, and variants are the **YPR 765 PRCO-B** command post model with a crew of nine and combat weight

of 30,200 lb (13699 kg), the **YPR 765 PRCO-C** multi-role version armed with a 0·5-in (12·7-mm) M2HB and possessing a nine-man crew at a combat weight of 27,335 lb (12,399 kg), the **YPR 765 PRCO-C1** for battalion command, the **YPR 765 PRCO-C2** for battalion gunnery control, the **YPR 765 PRCO-C3** for mortar fire-control, the **YPR 765 PRCO-C4** for AA fire-control and the **YPR 765 PRCO-C5** for observation post duties, the **YPT 765 PRRDR** battlefield surveillance model with ZB 298 radar, the **YPR 765 PRRDR-C** radar and command model, the **YPR 765 PRGWT** ambulance with provision for four litters, the 10-man **YPR 765 PRI/I** squad vehicle with cupola-mounted 0·5-in (12·7-mm) M2HB heavy machine-gun, the **YPR 765 PRMR** tractor for the 120-mm (4·72-in) Thomson Brandt mortar and 51 bombs, the **YPR 765 PRVR** 4,500-lb (2041-kg) payload cargo vehicle, the **YPR 765 PRAT** anti-tank vehicle with Emerson TUA launcher system for BGM-71 TOW heavy anti-tank missiles, and the **YPR 806 PRBRG** armoured recovery vehicle with roof-mounted crane
AIFV (Philippines): basically similar to the Dutch YPR 765 PRI but with a 0·5-in (12·7-mm) M2HB heavy machine-gun instead of the Oerlikon-Bührle cannon

FMC M113A1

(USA)

Type: tracked armoured personnel carrier
Crew: 2 + 11
Combat weight: 24,595 lb (11,156 kg)
Dimensions: length overall 15·95 ft (4·863 m); width 8·81 ft (2·69 m); height 8·20 ft (2·50 m)
Armament system: one 0·5-in (12·7-mm) Browning M2HB cupola-mounted heavy machine-gun with 2,000 rounds (100 on the weapon and 1,900 in the hull); the cupola is manually powered, the gun lacks stabilization in either elevation (−21° to +53°) or azimuth (360°), and simple optical sights are fitted
Armour: welded aluminium varying in thickness from 0·5 to 1·5 in (12·7 to 38·1 mm)
Powerplant: one 210-hp (157-kW) Detroit Diesel

Right: The M113 series is the most important APC of Western origins, and has also been the starting point for a large number of derived vehicles.

Below: An Armoured Infantry Fighting Vehicle (Netherlands).

6V-53N diesel engine with 95 US gal (360 litres) of internal fuel

Performance: speed, road 42 mph (67·6 km/h) and water 3·6 mph (5·8 km/h) driven by its tracks; range, road 300 miles (483 km); fording amphibious; gradient 60%; side slope not revealed; vertical obstacle 24 in (0·61 m); trench 5·5 ft (1·68 m); ground clearance 16 in (0·41 m)

Variants

M113: development of this most important Western armoured personnel carrier began in 1956 to a US Army requirement for a tracked armoured personnel carrier that would be amphibious and air-portable, yet well protected and possessing good cross-country performance, and also capable of development into a variety of other forms; in 1960 the T113E1 trials vehicle was standardized as the 22,615-lb (10,258-kg) M113 with the 209-hp (156-kW) Chrysler Model 75M petrol engine and 80 US gal (302 litres) of fuel for a range of 200 miles (322 km) and a maximum road speed of 40 mph (64·4 km/h); there is no provision for the embarked troops to fire their personal weapons from inside the vehicle; US Army procurement was in the order of 4,975 vehicles compared with foreign military sales of 9,840 vehicles, and many experimental and/or trials developments have been made (in the USA and elsewhere) of the basic model and its developments

M113A1: standardized in 1963, the M113A1 has a diesel engine and increased fuel capacity for greater range with less danger of fire; US Army procurement was in the order of 16,160 vehicles compared with foreign military sales of 7,415 vehicles

M113A2: designed as the **Product Improved M113A1**, this 25,000-lb (11,341-kg) variant was produced in the period up to 1989 by converting some 18,000 M113s and M113A1s and procuring 2,660 new-build vehicles; in this variant the main alterations are improvement of engine cooling and exhaust, and the strengthening and improvement of the suspension and shock-absorption systems to give greater ground clearance (17 in/0·43 m) and better cross-country performance

M113A2 Recovery Vehicle: simple derivative of the M113A2 with a small roof-mounted crane, a rear-mounted winch, and two or three rear-mounted spades; this model was originally known as the **M806**, and there was also an **M806A1** based on the M113A1

M113A3: from 1987 M113A1s and M113A2s have been further upgraded to M113A3 standard with developments for greater reliability and performance; these derive mainly from the use of the 275-hp (205-kW) 6V-53T turbocharged diesel with a more modern transmission system, though other improvements are armoured external fuel tanks and anti-spall linings in the crew compartments; the RISE (Reliability Improvement of Selected Equipment) of key components in the automotive system provides much enhanced cross-country performance, and also reduces fuel consumption by about 22%, adding significantly to vehicle range even without the additional fuel capacity; other improvements being considered or implemented are appliqué armour and a hull lengthened by 26 in (0·66 m); the latter requires the addition of a sixth road wheel on each side, and provides for a payload of 9,300 lb (4218 kg) at a combat weight of 33,000 lb (14,968 kg), which in the standard armoured personnel carrier role converts to a capacity of 2 + 14 carried over 300 miles (483 km) at a maximum road speed of 40 mph (64·4 km/h); like other members of the M113 series the M113A2 can be fitted with a front-mounted dozer blade of inher-

ently buoyant construction, allowing M113 vehicles thus equipped to clear obstacles and to improve access to and egress from rivers

M48 Chaparral: this is a light AA missile-launch vehicle using a chassis derived from that of the M548 cargo carrier fitted at the rear with a turntable-mounted four-arm launcher (for a total of 12 MIM-72 SAMs derived from the widely-deployed IR-homing AIM-9 Sidewinder air-to-air missile) and the gunner's turret; once alerted by the MPQ-49 forward-area alerting radar or by a visual sighting, the gunner slews the missile mounting to follow the target until an aural bleep indicates that the missile seeker has locked-on, whereupon the missile is fired for autonomous homing; the engagement envelope includes a maximum range of 6,500 yards (5945 m) and minimum/maximum altitudes of 150/10,000 ft (46/3050 m)

M106: mortar-carrier version with a 107-mm (4·2-in) M30 mortar, mounted on a turntable in the erstwhile troop compartment, and 93 bombs; there is also a 26,445-lb (11,995-kg) **M106A1** version with 88 bombs and an **M106A3** version with RISE improvements; the M30 is to be replaced by a 120-mm (4·72-in) mortar when such a weapon has been standardized for US service; all three models have the M2HB cupola-mounted heavy machine-gun but only 1,000 rounds

M125: mortar-carrier version with an 81-mm (3·2-in) M29 mortar, mounted on a turntable in the erstwhile troop compartment, with 114 bombs and the same machine-gun armament as the M106; there are also **M125A1** and **M125A2** versions, the former having a combat weight of 24,825 lb (11,261 kg) and the latter featuring the RISE improvement package

M132: flamethrower variant of the M113 series, and was based on the M113 and M113A1 chassis, the use of the latter resulting in the designation **M132A1**

M163: AA version fitted with an M168 Vulcan 20-mm cannon on a powered mounting and provided with 2,100 rounds, lead-computing sight and VPS-2 range-only radar; this model weighs 27,140 lb (12,311 kg), has a height of 8·98 ft (2·74 m) including the turret, and has a four-man crew; the cannon has two rates of fire, 1,000 rounds per minute for the surface-to-surface role to a range of 3,300 yards (3020 m), and 3,000 rounds per minute for the AA role to an effective range of 5,250 ft (1600 m); the limitations of the type are lack of gun range, and restriction to clear-weather operation by lack of search and tracking radar; there are several add-on improvement packages to produce the **Autotrack Vulcan Air Defense System**, the **Product Improved Vulcan Air Defense System** and the **Improved Fire-Control System/Vulcan Air Defense System**

M548: unarmoured cargo-carrier version based on the M113A1 with a payload of 12,000 lb (5443 kg); the equivalent of the M113A2 is the **M548A1**, and currently under investigation is a stretched model with a payload of 16,000 lb (7258 kg); the M548 chassis is also used as the launcher for the SLUFAE (Surface-Launched Unit, Fuel/Air Explosive) mineclearing system, and as the basis for the **M727** chassis for the MIM-23 Improved HAWK SAM system's triple launcher, **M730** and RISE-improved **M730A1** chassis for the M48 Chaparral SAM system, **Tracked Rapier** SAM system, **MSM-Fz** anti-tank minelayer for the West German army, **M752** launch vehicle for the Lance battlefield missile, and **M688** loader/transporter support vehicle (with two reload missiles) for the M752

M577: five-man command post version which

entered service in 1962; this variant has a higher roof over the previous troop compartment, extra radios and generating capacity, and a tented rear extension; the armament is a single 7·62-mm (0·3-in) machine-gun with 1,000 rounds, and improved models are the 25,380-lb (11,513-kg) **M577A1** and the RISE-improved **M577A2**; the US Army is currently considering a further improved model proposed by the builder as the **M577A3** with a lengthened hull (indicated by the introduction of a sixth road wheel on each side), a 275-hp (205-kW) 6V-53T turbocharged engine, bolt-on armour packages for increased overhead and flank protection, internal anti-spall lining, and fuel tankage relocated to the rear of the vehicle in twin tanks attached outside the area of the rear ramp

M806: recovery vehicle variant of the M113 series, and is fitted with rear-mounted spades and a rear-mounted winch

M901 Improved TOW Vehicle: anti-tank model that entered service in 1979 as an M113A2 fitted with a sighting cupola, a retractable two-tube launcher/sight assembly and 12 TOW missiles; local defence is entrusted to a single 7·62-mm (0·3-in) machine-gun with 1,000 rounds; the **M901A1 Improved TOW Vehicle** has the RISE upgrade package

M981 Fire Support Team Vehicle: support vehicle for the M901 Improved TOW Vehicle, and like its partner developed largely by Emerson Electric

M1059 Smoke Generating System: M113A2 derivative fitted with two M54 smoke generators with 120 US gal (454 litres) of fog oil

Lynx: 19,345-lb (8775-kg) Canadian development of the basic M113A1 with a lower superstructure and equipment suiting it for the command and reconnaissance roles with a crew of three; armament comprises one 0·5-in (12·7-mm) M2HB heavy machine-gun with 1,000 rounds mounted externally on a small forward turret and one 7·62-mm (0·3-in) machine-gun with 2,000 rounds pintle-mounted at the rear of the roof; there are three smoke-dischargers on each side of the turret; the Dutch use a similar vehicle under the designation **M113 C & R**, though many of these vehicles have been retrofitted with an Oerlikon-Bührle GBD-AOA turret carrying a 25-mm KBA-B cannon with 200 rounds; the performance of these two variants is usefully better than that of the basic M113 series, with a maximum speed of 44 mph (70·8 km/h) and a range of 325 miles (523 km)

M113 (Australia): the Australian army uses many M113 models, most of them with slight modifications to suit local conditions and requirements; the model most different from the US main sequence is the **M113A1 FSV (Scorpion)** fire-support vehicle fitted with the turret and 76·2-mm (3-in) L23 gun of the British Scorpion reconnaissance vehicle; this variant is 15·96 ft (4·86 m) long, and is fitted with extra buoyancy aids; others of the M113 series are fitted with the Cadillac Gage T50 turret armed with two 7·62-mm (0·3-in) machine-guns plus 5,000 rounds or one 0·5-in (12·7-mm) and one 7·62-mm (0·3-in) machine-gun plus 2,500 and 3,000 rounds respectively; the Australian designations include **M113A1 APC(A)** for the ambulance version, **M113A1 APC(F)** for the fitters' repair carrier, **M113A1 APC/LRV** for the armoured personnel carrier and light reconnaissance vehicle, **M125A1 APC(M)** for the mortar-carrier, **M113A1 FSV (Saladin)** for the fire-support vehicle with turret and 76·2-mm (3-in) gun of the Saladin armoured car, **M548 TLC** for the tracked load carrier, **M577 ACV** for the armoured command vehicle, and **M806A1**

ARV(L) for the light armoured recovery vehicle

M113 (Belgium): Belgium uses the M113A1 under the designation **M113A1-B** with local modifications such as an engine compartment fire-extinguishing system, suspension to M113A2 standard, individual NBC-protected air supply to each crew member, and a different heater/air-conditioning system; the variants in Belgian service are the **M113A1-B-AMB** ambulance with a crew of three and accommodation for four litters, or six seated casualties, or two litters and three seated casualties, the **M113A1-B-ATK** anti-tank and squad transport vehicle with a crew of 10, provision for an anti-tank missile launcher, and a 0·5-in (12·7-mm) cupola-mounted heavy machine-gun plus a 7·62-mm (0·3-in) pintle-mounted machine-gun, the **M113A1-B-CP** command post vehicle with a crew of five, mapboards and a tented rear extension, the **M113A1-B-ENG** assault pioneer vehicle with a crew of eight, demolition charges and a self-recovery winch, the **M113A1-B-MIL** dedicated anti-tank vehicle with a crew of five, provision for a Milan anti-tank launcher, and a 0·5-in (12·7-mm) cupola-mounted heavy machine-gun, the **M113A1-B-MTC** maintenance vehicle with a crew of five, a roof-mounted crane and a winch, the **M113A1-B-REC** recovery vehicle with a crew of four, a roof-mounted crane, specialist equipment and a self-recovery winch, and the **M113A1-B-TRG** training model with two clear canopies

M113 (Brazil): Brazil's 700 M113 series vehicles are being re-engined with the Mercedes-Benz OM 352A diesel

M113 (Canada): the Canadian Armed Forces use the standard M113A1, of which many are being modified to M113A2 standard, possibly with the addition of a Delco two-man turret fitted with a 25-mm McDonnell Douglas Helicopters M242 Bushmaster cannon and 7·62-mm (0·3-in) co-axial machine-gun; other vehicles are being modified to **M113A1 EVSEV** (Engineering Variant Specially Equipped Vehicle) standard as combat engineer vehicles with a front-mounted dozer blade, hydraulically-powered earth auger and other engineer features

M113 (Egypt): Egypt plans a total of 500 M113-series vehicles with additional armour of the appliqué type

M113 (Israel): Israeli M113 series vehicles have been extensively modified to remove amphibious capability, allow the carriage of up to four 0·5-in (12·7-mm) or 7·62-mm (0·3-in) machine-guns, and permit the carriage of personal kit in hull-side baskets; other modifications are appliqué armour to resist HEAT warheads, and different armament including a 60-mm (2·36-in) Soltam mortar or TOW/Mapats anti-tank missile launcher

M113 (New Zealand): many of New Zealand's M113A1s are fitted with the same T50 turret as the Australian vehicles

M113 (Norway): Norway's variant is the **NM-135**, essentially the M113A1 fitted with a Swedish Hagglund & Soner turret containing a 20-mm Rheinmetall MK 20 Rh 202 cannon and 7·62-mm (0·3-in) co-axial machine-gun

M113 (Singapore): these vehicles have been modified locally into carriers for 81- and 120-mm (3·2- and 4·7-in) mortars

M113 (Spain): these are generally similar to their US counterparts, though the mortar-carriers use Spanish weapons

M113 (Switzerland): Swiss **Schützenpanzer 63** vehicles are similar to the M113A1, though the installation of a Hagglund & Soner turret with a 20-mm cannon results in the designation **Schützenpanzer 63/73**; 316 of these vehicles are being upgraded to **Schützenpanzer 63/89** standard after the installation of an FMC upgrade package that includes new frontal and side armour, armoured external fuel tanks, a new diesel engine and smoke-dischargers; other Swiss vehicles in the series are the **Feuerleitpanzer 63** artillery command vehicle, the **Géniepanzer 63** armoured bulldozer, the **Kommandopanzer 63** and upgunned **Kommandopanzer 63/73** higher-echelon command vehicles of which 66 are to be upgraded to **Kommandopanzer 63/69** standard with the same upgrade package as the Schützenpanzer 63/89, the **Kranpanzer 63** repair vehicle, the **Minenwerferpanzer 64** mortar-carrier, the **Schützenpanzer Kommando 63** low-echelon command vehicle, and the **Ubermittlungspanzer 63** radio vehicle

M113 (Taiwan): the M113A1 has been used as the basis for the development of an armoured infantry fighting vehicle in Taiwan; this new vehicle combines the basic hull and systems of the M113 with a 215-hp (160-kW) Perkins TV8·640 diesel engine driving a Taiwanese transmission system, additional armour (a laminate steel layer over the front and sides of the vehicle, sandwiching polyurethane foam for additional buoyancy), and a shielded 0·5-in (12·7-mm) Browning M2HB heavy machine-gun at the front; the result has the basic capabilities of the M113A2; the type is also being developed as a true AIFV with 20- or 30-mm cannon, rocket-launch vehicle with the Kung Feng IV 126-mm (4·96-in) multiple launcher, anti-tank vehicle with US or Taiwanese missiles, mortar carrier (81-, 107- and 120-mm/3·2-, 4·2- and 4·7-in types), and command post vehicle

M113 (West Germany): West Germany uses large numbers of the M113 series, most of them brought up to M113A1 standard, and substantial quantities locally modified for special tasks such as mortar location (Green Archer radar), battlefield surveillance (RATAC radar) and mortar-carrying (120-mm/4·7-in Tampella mortar); the German designations include **ABRA** for the artillery observation vehicle, **BeobPzArt** for the armoured artillery observation vehicle, **FlgltPz** for the armoured FAC vehicle, **FltPzArt** for the armoured artillery fire-control vehicle, **KrKw** for the armoured ambulance and **PzM** for the self-propelled mortar

Below: The M113A2 is the basis of the fire-control unit of the Franco-Egyptian Nile 23 AA system.

FMC M59

(USA)

Type: tracked armoured personnel carrier
Crew: 2 + 10
Combat weight: 42,600 lb (19,323 kg)
Dimensions: length overall 18·42 ft (5·61 m); width 10·71 ft (3·26 m); height to top of cupola 9·08 ft (2·77 m)
Armament system: one 0·5-in (12·7-mm) Browning M2HB cupola-mounted heavy machine-gun with 2,205 rounds; the cupola is manually powered, the gun lacks stabilization in either elevation (− 10° to + 58°) or azimuth (360°), and simple optical sights are fitted
Armour: welded steel varying in thickness from 10 to 16 mm (0·39 to 0·63 in)
Powerplant: two 127-hp (95-kW) General Motors Model 302 petrol engines with 137 US gal (518 litres) of internal fuel
Performance: speed, road 32 mph (51·5 km/h) and water 4·3 mph (6·9 km/h) driven by its tracks; range, road 102 miles (164 km); fording amphibious; gradient 60%; side slope not revealed; vertical obstacle 18 in (0·46 m); trench 5·5 ft (1·68 m); ground clearance 18 in (0·46 m)

Variants

M59: produced as successor to the M75 and standardized in December 1953, the M59 is a massive and decidedly under-powered and under-ranged vehicle; it is amphibious only in calm water, and lacks the capability for the embarked troops to use their personal weapons from the inside of the vehicle, which is entered via a power-operated rear ramp; the shortcomings of this vehicle prompted the development of the far more satisfactory M113
M84: mortar-carrier version carrying the 107-mm (4·2-in) M30 mortar and 88 bombs
Moto Pecas Charrua XMP-1: Brazilian reworked version of the M59 with more modern equipment and the 300-kW (402-hp) Saab-Scania DSI 11 diesel for greater range and a maximum road speed of 70 km/h (43·5 mph); the type has a combat weight of 20,000 kg (44,092 lb), and has a crew of 2 + 12

FMC/International Harvester M75

(USA)

Type: tracked armoured personnel carrier
Crew: 2 + 10
Combat weight: 41,500 lb (18,824 kg)
Dimensions: length overall 17·04 ft (5·19 m); width 9·33 ft (2·84 m); height to top of commander's cupola 9·10 ft (2·78 m)
Armament system: one 0·5-in (12·7-mm) Browning M2HB pintle-mounted heavy machine-gun with 1,800 rounds; the mounting is manually powered, the gun lacks stabilization in either elevation (an unrevealed arc) or azimuth (360°), and simple optical sights are fitted
Armour: welded steel varying in thickness from 0·375 to 1 in (9·5 to 25·4 mm)
Powerplant: one 295-hp (220-kW) Continental AO-895-4 petrol engine with 150 US gal (568 litres) of internal fuel
Performance: speed, road 44 mph (71 km/h); range, road 115 miles (185 km); fording 4·0 ft (1·22 m) without preparation and 6·67 ft (2·03 m) with preparation; gradient 60%; side slope not revealed; vertical obstacle 18 in (0·46 m); trench 5·5 ft (1·68 m); ground clearance 18 in (0·46 m)

Variant

M75: designed in the late 1940s on the basis of the M41 light tank, the M75 APC was not regarded as a great success because of its height and lack of performance; there is no provision for the embarked troops to fire their personal weapons from inside the vehicle, and no provision for NBC protection is available

Cadillac Gage Commando V-300

(USA)

Type: multi-role wheeled armoured vehicle
Crew: 3 + 9
Combat weight: 32,000 lb (14,515 kg)
Dimensions: length 21·00 (6·40 m); width 8·33 ft (2·54 m); height to hull top 6·50 ft (1·98 m)
Armament system: see Variants (below)
Armour: welded steel
Powerplant: one 235-hp (175-kW) Cummins VT-504 diesel engine with 70 US gal (265 litres) of internal fuel, and driving a 6 × 6 layout
Performance: speed, road 57 mph (92 km/h) and water 3 mph (4·8 km/h) driven by its wheels; range, road 435 miles (700 km); fording amphibious; gradient 60%; side slope 30%; vertical obstacle 24 in (0·61 m); trench not revealed; ground clearance 14 in (0·36 m)

Variants

Commando V-300: a logical development of the 4 × 4 Commando V-150 series, the 6 × 6 Commando V-300 offers greater capabilities plus superior cross-country performance with a basic hull and automotive system capable of accepting a number of armament options; development began in the late 1970s, and the first production vehicles were delivered to Panama in 1983; other options are an NBC protection system, night vision devices, heating and air-conditioning; the current armament options are a series of Cadillac Gage one- and two-man turrets mounting a

Below: The Commando V-300 has several armament options including this 25-mm M242 cannon in a Cadillac-Gage two-man turret.

90-mm (3·54-mm) Cockerill Mk III rifled gun, or a 76·2-mm (3-in) Royal Ordnance L23A1 rifled gun, or a 25-mm McDonnell Douglas Helicopters M242 Bushmaster cannon plus two 7·62-mm (0·3-in) machine-guns (one co-axial and one AA) and smoke-dischargers, or a 20-mm Oerlikon-Bührle 204 GK cannon, or twin 0·5-in (12·7-mm) Browning M2HB or 7·62-mm (0·3-in) machine-guns (or one of each); other options under development are an anti-tank version with TOW missiles, a mortar-carrier with an 81-mm (3·2-in) mortar and 60 bombs, an ambulance, a recovery vehicle, an AA vehicle and a command vehicle; the embarked troops use two doors in the rear of the hull, and can fire their personal weapons from inside the vehicle via eight ports (three on each side and one in each of the doors)

Cadillac Gage Commando V-150/20-mm Turret

(USA)

Type: multi-role wheeled armoured vehicle
Crew: 3 + 9
Combat weight: 21,800 lb (9888 kg)
Dimensions: length overall 18·67 ft (5·69 m); width 7·41 ft (2·26 m); height to hull top 6·50 ft (1·98 m)
Armament system: see Variants (below)
Powerplant: one 202-hp (151-kW) Cummins VT-504 diesel engine with 80 US gal (303 litres) of internal fuel, driving a 4 × 4 layout
Performance: speed, road 55 mph (88·5 km/h) and water 3 mph (4·8 km/h) driven by its wheels; range, road 400 miles (644 km); fording amphibious; gradient 60%; side slope 30%; vertical obstacle 24 in (0·61 m); trench not revealed; ground clearance 15 in (0·38 m)

Variants

Commando V-100: this original model appeared in 1963, with deliveries beginning in the following year; this 12-man model weighed 16,250 lb (7371 kg) and could attain 62 mph (100 km/h) on its 200-hp (149-kW) Chrysler 362 petrol engine
Commando V-200: 28,065-lb (12,730-kg) stretched version of the V-100 produced in very

Above and below: The Commando V-150 is also offered with several turreted armament options, including this one-man unit with a 20-mm cannon.

small numbers, the Commando V-200 can attain 60 mph (96 km/h) on its 275-hp (205-kW) Chrysler 440 CID engine

Commando V-150: 1971 model that replaced both the V-100 and V-200 series in production; the type can be used as a standard armoured personnel carrier with front and rear pintle-mounted machine-guns (0·5-in/12·7-mm Browning M2HB heavy machine-gun and/or 7·62-mm/0·3-in medium machine-gun), and optional equipment includes an NBC protection system, smoke-dischargers, troop compartment firing ports, winch etc; the current production model is the **V-150S**, which is slightly heavier (23,590 lb/10,700 kg) and longer (20·14 ft/6·14 m) as well as featuring a number of automotive improvements, and the type can also be fitted with a number of turreted armament options as detailed below

Commando V-150/MG Turret: 19,800-lb (8981-kg) version with a one-man Cadillac Gage turret fitted with two 7·62-mm (0·3-in) machine-guns or one 0·5-in (12·7-mm) and one 7·62-mm (0·3-in) machine-gun; this version carries a crew of 3+7, and has an overall height 8·33 ft (2·54 m)

Commando V-150/1-m MG Turret: 19,300-lb (8754-kg) version with a Cadillac Gage 1-metre turret fitted with two 0·5-in (12·7-mm) or 7·62-mm (0·3-in) machine-guns, or with one of each calibre; this version carries a crew of 3+7, and has an overall height of 8·50 ft (2·59 m)

Commando V-150/1-m Cannon Turret: 20,000-lb (9072-kg) version with a one-man Cadillac Gage turret fitted with one 20-mm Oerlikon-Bührle 204 GK cannon with 400 rounds and a 7·62-mm (0·3-in) co-axial machine-gun with 3,200 rounds; this version carries a crew of 3+5, and has an overall height of 9·50 ft (2·90 m)

Commando V-150/20-mm Turret: 21,800-lb (9888-kg) version with a two-man Cadillac Gage turret armed with one 20-mm Oerlikon-Bührle 204 GK cannon with 400 rounds and two 7·62-mm (0·3-in) machine-guns (one co-axial and one AA) with 3,200 rounds; this version carries a crew of 3+2, and has an overall height of 8·33 ft (2·54 m)

Commando V-150/25-mm Turret: 23,000-lb (10,433-lb) version with a two-man turret armed with one 25-mm McDonnell Douglas Helicopters M242 Bushmaster cannon with 630 rounds and two 7·62-mm (0·3-in) M240C machine-guns (one co-axial and one AA) with 1,600 rounds; delivered as the **Commando V-150S** for the Light Armored Vehicle competition, this version carries a crew of 3+9, and has a length of 10·14 ft (6·14 m)

Commando V-150/40-mm Turret: version with a one-man turret armed with a Mk 19 40-mm grenade-launcher, a 0·5-in (12·7-mm) co-axial heavy machine-gun and four smoke-dischargers mounted on each side of the turret

Commando V-150 ADV: AA version with a 20-mm Vulcan rotary-barrel cannon system

Commando V-150/76-mm Turret: 21,800-lb (9888-kg) version with the two-man turret of the British Scorpion CVR(T) with its 76-mm (3-in) L23A1 gun and 41 rounds, plus two 7·62-mm (0·3-in) machine-guns (one co-axial and one AA) and 3,200 rounds; this version carries a crew of 3+3

Commando V-150/90-mm Turret: 21,800-lb (9888-kg) version with a two-man turret fitted with a 90-mm (3·54-mm) Cockerill Mk III gun and 39 rounds, plus two 7·62-mm (0·3-in) machine-guns (one co-axial and one AA) and 3,200 rounds; the crew is 3+4

Commando V-150/81-mm Mortar: 19,500-lb (8845-kg) version with turntable-mounted M29 81-mm (3·2-in) mortar with 62 bombs in the erstwhile troop compartment now fitted with concertina roof-top hatches; the crew is five

Commando V-150/TOW: 19,750-lb (8958-kg) anti-tank version similar to the mortar-carrier version but with a TOW launcher and seven missiles; provision is made for the location of a 7·62-mm (0·3-in) machine-gun (2,000 rounds) on any of four positions; the crew is 4+2

Commando V-150/Command: variation on the standard model with a pod located over the roof opening, with provision for the location of a 7·62-mm (0·3-in) machine-gun (2,000 rounds) in any of the four sides; the crew is 3+7 and the overall height 7·58 ft (2·31 m)

Commando V-150/Base Security: 20,000-lb (9072-kg) version similar to the mortar-carrier in having concertina roof hatches, and carrying a crew of 3+8; a 7·62-mm (0·3-in) machine-gun (3,000 rounds) or 40-mm grenade-launcher can be located at any of four positions

Commando V-150/ERV: 20,200-lb (9162-kg) police emergency rescue vehicle with a crew of 3+9 and a roof pod possessing eight gun ports and provision on the roof hatch for a 7·62-mm (0·3-in) or 0·5-in (12·7-mm) machine-gun

Commando V-150/Recovery: winch-fitted recovery vehicle of the series with an armament of a 7·62-mm (0·3-in) or 0·5-in (12·7-mm) machine-gun plus 2,200 rounds

Vulcan-Commando: 22,500-lb (10,206-kg) version of the Commando V-150 fitted with a 20-mm Vulcan cannon turret (the same as that fitted to the M163 derivative of the M113 APC) and three internally controlled stabilizing jacks; the type has a crew of four

---

Cadillac Gage Commando Ranger

(USA)
Type: wheeled armoured personnel carrier
Crew: 2+6
Combat weight: 10,000 lb (4536 kg)
Dimensions: length overall 15·42 ft (4·70 m); width 6·62 ft (2·02 m); height 6·50 ft (1·98 m)
Armament system: see Variant (below)
Armour: welded steel
Powerplant: one 180-hp (134-kW) Dodge 360 CID petrol engine with 32 US gal (121 litres) of internal fuel, and driving a 4 × 4 layout
Performance: speed, road 70 mph (113 km/h); range, road 345 miles (556 km); fording not revealed; gradient 60%; side slope 30%; vertical obstacle 10 in (0·25 m); trench not revealed; ground clearance 8 in (0·20 m)

Variant
Commando Ranger: this vehicle was designed in the late 1970s as a low-cost security vehicle, and deliveries to the US Air Force began in 1980; the type can be used as a normal armoured personnel carrier (with the option for one or two turreted 7·62-mm/0·3-in or 0·5-in/12·7-mm machine-guns), or as a command, ambulance or reconnaissance vehicle

---

Verne Dragoon 300

(USA)
Type: multi-role wheeled armoured vehicle
Crew: 3+6
Combat weight: 28,000 lb (12,701 kg)
Dimensions: length overall 18·33 ft (5·59 m); width 8·00 ft (2·44 m); height to turret periscopes 8·67 ft (2·64 m)

Armament system: see Variants (below)
Armour: welded steel
Powerplant: one 300-hp (224-kW) Detroit Diesel 6V-53T diesel engine with 90 US gal (341 litres) of internal fuel, and driving a 4 × 4 layout
Performance: speed, road 72 mph (116 km/h) and water 3 mph (4·8 km/h) driven by its wheels; range, road 650 miles (1046 km); fording amphibious; gradient 60%; side slope 30%; vertical obstacle 39 in (0·99 m); trench not revealed; ground clearance 15 in (0·38 m)

Variants
Dragoon 300 APC: this basic armoured personnel carrier type designed and produced by the Verne Corporation can also be used as a reconnaissance, command, recovery and escort vehicle with a 7·62-mm (0·3-in) or 0·5-in (12·7-mm) pintle- or ring-mounted machine-gun; as with the other variants, there is a wide range of optional equipment such as NBC protection, night vision devices and the like, and the manufacturer has proposed a large family of associated vehicle types offering the customer great commonality of parts and operating techniques, with consequent logistical and training advantages

Dragoon 300 LWC: light weapons carrier type armed with one or two 7·62-mm or 0·5-in machine-guns

Dragoon 300 SWC: special weapons carrier type armed with an 81-mm (3·2-in) mortar, TOW anti-tank missile launcher and other such weapons

Dragoon 300 HWC: heavy weapons carrier type armed with turreted weapons such as 20-, 25- and 30-mm cannon, or 76-mm (3-in) and 90-mm (3·54-in) rifled guns together with co-axial and AA machine-guns

---

Autocar/Diamond T/ International Harvester/ White M2A1

(USA)
Type: halftrack armoured personnel carrier
Crew: 2+8
Combat weight: 19,600 lb (8891 kg)
Dimensions: length with winch 10·13 ft (6·14 m); width with mine racks 7·29 ft (2·22 m); height overall 8·83 ft (2·69 m)
Armament system: one 0·5-in (12·7-mm) Browning M2HB pintle-mounted heavy machine-gun with 700 rounds, and one 7·62-mm (0·3-in) pintle-mounted machine-gun with 7,750 rounds; each mounting is manually powered, the gun lacks stabilization in either elevation (−15° to +45°) or azimuth (360°), and simple optical sights are fitted
Armour: welded and bolted steel varying in thickness from 0·25 to 0·5 in (6·4 to 12·7 mm)
Powerplant: one 128-hp (95-kW) White 160 AX petrol engine with 60 US gal (227 litres) of internal fuel
Performance: speed, road 40 mph (64 km/h); range, road 175 miles (282 km); fording 2·67 ft (0·81 m); gradient 60%; side slope not revealed; vertical obstacle 12 in (0·30 m); trench not revealed; ground clearance 9·2 in (0·23 m)

Variants
M2: this halftrack armoured personnel carrier and reconnaissance vehicle was produced in the late 1930s by combining the chassis and automotive system of the M2 unarmoured halftrack with the armoured body of the M3A1 scout car, and the result was one of the most important vehicle types of World War II, many of whose examples are still

in widespread service to this day despite their obsolescence by first-division standards; the total complement is 10, and the armament single 7·62-mm (0·3-in) and 0·5-in (12·7-mm) machine-guns on a skate mounting round the open-topped troop compartment

M2A1: as M2 but with a ring-mounted 0·5-in (12·7-mm) machine-gun; instead of the front-mounted winch the variant can be fitted with a roller to help cross-country mobility, this reducing overall length to 19·56 ft (5·96 m)

M3: similar to the M2 but developed by Diamond T with a longer body, pedestal mount for 7·62-mm (0·3-in) machine-gun, and accommodation for 13 men

M3A1: as M3 but with ring mount

M3A2: successor to the M2, M2A1, M3 and M3A1 with accommodation for a maximum of 12, and armament comprising four pintle-mounted machine-guns in the troop compartment, and a ring-mounted machine-gun in the front right-hand side of the compartment

M5: similar to the M3 built by International Harvester

M5A1: equivalent of the M3A1

M5A2: equivalent of the M3A2

M9A1: International Harvester equivalent of the M2A1

M4: mortar-carrier version of the M2 with an 81-mm (3·2-in) mortar designed to be dismounted before firing; 97 bombs are carried

M4A1: mortar-carrier with the 81-mm (3·2-in) mortar designed for onboard firing

M13: M3 fitted with an AA mounting for two 0·5-in (12·7-mm) machine-guns

M14: M5 fitted with an AA mounting for two 0·5-in (12·7-mm) machine-guns

M15: M3 fitted with a turreted AA installation of one 37-mm M1A2 gun and two 0·5-in (12·7-mm) machine-guns

M15A1: lightened version of the M15

M16: M3 fitted with an AA mounting for four 0·5-in (12·7-mm) machine-guns and 5,000 rounds

M16A1: lightened version of the M16

M17: M5 fitted with an AA mounting for four 0·5-in (12·7-mm) machine-guns and 5,000 rounds

M21: 81-mm (3·2-in) mortar-carrier version of the M3

M2/M3/M5/M9 (Israel): Israel still uses a large number of halftracks, most of them rebuilt to a common standard with the 172-hp (128-kW) Detroit Diesel 6V-53 diesel engine; these Israeli vehicles are used for 120-mm (4·72-in) mortar-carrying, for AA defence (pedestal or turreted 20-mm cannon), for anti-tank operations (106-mm/4·17-in recoilless rifle, SS.11 missile or 90-mm/3·54-in gun) and as ambulances, command vehicles, ammunition carriers and electronic warfare vehicles

Above and below: The LVTP7A1 (now AAVP7A1) is a much improved version of the LVTP7 whose many improvements include a new diesel engine.

FMC LVTP7A1

(USA)
Type: tracked amphibious assault vehicle
Crew: 3 + 25
Combat weight: 52,890 lb (23,991 kg)
Dimensions: length overall 26·06 ft (7·943 m); width 10·73 ft (3·27 m); height to turret roof 10·25 ft (3·12 m)
Armament system: one 0·5-in (12·7-mm) Browning M85 heavy machine-gun with 1,000 rounds; the turret is electro-hydraulically powered, the gun lacks stabilization in either elevation (−15° to +60°) or azimuth (360°), and simple optical sights are fitted

Armour: welded aluminium varying in thickness from 0·26 to 1·77 in (6·7 to 45 mm)
Powerplant: one 400-hp (298-kW) Cummins VT-400 diesel engine with 171 US gal (647 litres) of internal fuel
Performance: speed, road 44 mph (72·4 km/h) and water 8·2 mph (13·2 km/h) driven by two waterjets or 4·5 mph (7·2 km/h) driven by its tracks; range, road 300 miles (483 km); endurance, water 7 hours; fording amphibious; gradient 60%; side slope 60%; vertical obstacle 36 in (0·91 m); trench 8·0 ft (2·44 m); ground clearance 16 in (0·41 m)

Variants
LVTP7: this 50,350-lb (22,839-kg) vehicle was developed from 1964 as successor to the US Marine Corps' LVTP5 series of amphibious assault vehicles, which were troublesome to maintain and possessed generally inadequate performance; deliveries began in 1971, and since that time several variants have been produced; the type is not fitted with an NBC protection system, and the amphibious role precludes the provision of firing ports in the troop compartment, to which access is provided by a power-operated rear ramp; the type is powered by a 400-hp (298-kW) Detroit Diesel 8V-53T diesel with 180 US gal (681 litres) of fuel, providing road and water speeds of 40 mph (64·4 mph) and 8·4 mph (13·5 km/h) respectively; the type can be fitted out as an ambulance with accommodation for six litters or as a cargo carrier with a payload of 10,000 lb (4536 kg); in 1985 the type was redesignated **AAVP7**

LVTP7A1: the US Marine Corps' surviving

vehicles have been modernized in the period 1982-85 to this upgraded standard, initially designated **LVT7A1** and since 1985 designated **AAVP7A1**, with a Cummins VT-400 turbocharged diesel engine and 171 US gal (647 litres) of fuel, smoke-generating capability, passive night vision devices, secure radio, improved fire-extinguishing systems, better ventilation, and updated electric and hydraulic systems; the type is also undergoing trials with revised armament, in the form of a new electrically powered turret fitted with a 40-mm Mk 19 grenade-launcher as well as the 0·5-in (12·7-mm) machine-gun, and is to be fitted with appliqué armour

LVTC7: 44,110-lb (20,008-kg) command version with the turret replaced by a hatch, and a crew of 12 including four command staff and five radio operators in a revised troop compartment; this version has as armament a single pintle-mounted 7·62-mm (0·3-in) M60D machine-gun with 1,000 rounds; the type is being upgraded to **LVTC7A1** standard, since redesignated **AAVC7A1**

LVTR7: 51,440-lb (23,333-kg) recovery version with the same hatch and armament as the LVTC7; this version has much specialist recovery and repair equipment, a roof-mounted hydraulic crane with extending jib and a high-capacity winch; the crew is five; the type is being upgraded to **LVTR7A1** standard, since redesignated **AAVR7A1**

Ingersoll (Borg-Warner) LVTP5A1

(USA)
Type: tracked amphibious assault vehicle
Crew: 3 + 34
Combat weight: 82,500 lb (37,422 kg)
Dimensions: length overall 29·67 ft (9·04 m); width 11·70 ft (3·57 m); height to turret top 9·58 ft (2·92 m)
Armament system: one 0·3-in (7·62-mm) Browning M1919A4 machine-gun with 2,000 rounds; the turret is manually powered, the gun lacks stabi-

lization in either elevation (−15° to +60°) or azimuth (360°), and simple optical sights are fitted
Armour: welded steel varying in thickness from 0·25 to 0·62 in (6·37 to 15·87 mm)
Powerplant: one 810-hp (604-kW) Continental LV-1790-1 petrol engine with 456 US gal (1726 litres) of internal fuel
Performance: speed, road 30 mph (48 km/h) and water 6·8 mph (10·9 km/h) driven by its tracks; range, road 190 miles (306 km); fording amphibious; gradient 70%; side slope 60%; vertical obstacle 36 in (0·91 m); trench 12·0 ft (3·66 m); ground clearance 18 in (0·46 m)

Variants
LVTP5A1: in the 1960s all surviving LVTP5 amphibious assault vehicles (produced between 1952 and 1957) of the US Marine Corps were upgraded to this standard with a small snorkel and other improvements, the LVTP5 clearly having inadequate freeboard when fully loaded; the type can also be fitted out as an ambulance with accommodation for 12 litters; Taiwan is assessing the feasibility of re-engining its LVTP5A1s with a diesel powerplant for better range and reduced fire risk
LVTC5: command vehicle with the troop compartment outfitted as a command post with mapboards, extra radios etc
LVTE1: engineer vehicle fitted with a front-mounted dozer blade and rocket-propelled mineclearing system
LVTH6: fire-support version with a turret-mounted M49 105-mm (4·13-in) howitzer and 100 rounds, plus a 0·3-in (7·62-mm) co-axial machine-gun with 1,000 rounds and a 0·5-in (12·7-mm) AA machine-gun with 1,050 rounds
LVTR1: recovery version with a roof-mounted crane and winch, plus many items of specialist equipment

Below: The LVTP5A1 is an obsolete amphibious vehicle with inadequate full-load freeboard for operation in any but the calmest conditions.

BVP M80A

(Yugoslavia)
Type: tracked mechanized infantry combat vehicle
Crew: 2 + 8
Combat weight: 14,000 kg (30,864 lb)
Dimensions: length overall 6·42 m (21·06 ft); width 2·995 m (9·83 ft); height over missile launcher 2·67 m (8·76 ft)
Armament system: one 20-mm Oerlikon-Bührle HS 804 cannon with 1,400 rounds, one 7·62-mm (0·3-in) co-axial machine-gun with 2,000 rounds, and one twin-rail launcher for four AT-3 'Sagger' anti-tank missiles; the turret is manually powered, the gun lacks stabilization in either elevation (−10° to +65°) or azimuth (360°), and simple optical sights are fitted
Armour: welded steel varying in thickness from 8 to 30 mm (0·315 to 1·18 in)
Powerplant: one 235-kW (315-hp) diesel engine with 510 litres (112 Imp gal) of internal fuel; the type can generate smoke by injecting diesel fuel into the exhaust
Performance: speed, road 64 km/h (39·8 mph) and water 7·8 km/h (8·5 mph) driven by its tracks; range, road 500 km (311 miles); fording amphibious; gradient 60%; side slope 40%; vertical obstacle 0·8 m (31·5 in); trench 2·4 m (7·9 ft); ground clearance 0·4 m (15·75 in)

Variants
BVP M80A: introduced in 1984, this is a development of the M-980 with slightly greater weight and a larger hull; the type has a more powerful engine, ensuring slightly improved all-round performance, and other features are passive night vision equipment, a fire detection and suppression system, and an NBC system
BVP M80AK: revealed in 1989, this is an improved BVP M80A with a 30-mm M86 long-barrel cannon in a power-operated turret that provides full main armament stabilization in both elevation and azimuth; the M86 is the same weapon as used in the BOV anti-aircraft vehicle,

Above: The M80A is a development of the M-980 with greater dimensions and a more powerful engine for improved habitability and better performance.

and its projectile can penetrate 60 mm (2·36 in) of armour at 1000 m (1,095 yards); the extra mass of the cannon and turret (the latter carrying the same machine-gun/missile armament as the BVP M80A's turret) increases combat weight to 14,400 kg (31,746 lb)

M-980: this Yugoslav mechanized infantry combat vehicle appeared in the early 1970s, and its powerplant (195-kW/262-hp Hispano-Suiza HS 115-2 diesel) and automotive system are related closely to those of the French AMX-10P; the type is fitted as standard with an NBC protection system, and the embarked troops can fire their personal weapons from inside the vehicle via eight ports (three on each side and one in each of the two rear doors); the M-980 has a crew of 2 + 8 and a combat weight of 13,700 kg (30,203 lb), and its principal dimensions include an overall length of 6·40 m (21·00 ft), a width of 2·59 m (8·50 ft) and an overall height of 2·50 m (8·20 ft); the type's performance includes maximum road and water speeds of 60 and 7·5 km/h (37·3 and 4·7 mph) respectively, and though its cross-country capability is comparable to that of the BVP M80A, the trench-crossing capability is slightly inferior at 2·2 m (7·2 ft)

M-60P

(Yugoslavia)
Type: tracked armoured personnel carrier

Right: The M-60P was unadventurous in design even by the standards of its day, and is now obsolete. In common with other such vehicles, the M-60P was also developed in models for other roles.

Crew: 3 + 10
Combat weight: 11,000 kg (24,250 lb)
Dimensions: length overall 5·02 m (16·47 ft); width 2·77 m (9·09 ft); height including machine-gun 2·385 m (7·82 ft)
Armament system: one 0·5-in (12·7-mm) Browning M2HB cupola-mounted heavy machine-gun with an unrevealed number of rounds, and one 7·92-mm (0·312-in) bow-mounted machine-gun with an unrevealed number of rounds; the cupola is manually powered, the gun lacks stabilization in either elevation (an unrevealed arc) or azimuth (360°), and simple optical sights are fitted
Armour: welded steel varying in thickness from 10 to 25 mm (0·39 to 0·98 in)
Powerplant: one 105-kW (141-hp) FAMOS diesel engine with 150 litres (33 Imp gal) of internal fuel
Performance: speed, road 45 km/h (28 mph);

range, road 400 km (249 miles); fording 1·35 m (4·4 ft); gradient 60%; side slope 40%; vertical obstacle 0·6 m (23·6 in); trench 2·0 m (6·6 ft); ground clearance 0·4 m (15·75 in)

Variants

M-60P: developed in the early 1960s, the M-60P is an unremarkable armoured personnel carrier lacking amphibious capability and NBC protection, though there is provision for the embarked troops to fire their personal weapons from inside the vehicle via eight ports (three on each side and one in each of the two rear doors); the type also exists in ambulance, command, radio and recovery forms

M-60PB: anti-tank version with two 82-mm (3·23-in) recoilless rifles on a traversing mount above the left-hand side of the roof

NORINCO Type 83 152-mm SP gun/howitzer

(China)
Type: tracked self-propelled gun/howitzer
Crew: 5
Combat weight: 30,000 kg (66,138 lb)
Dimensions: length, gun forward 7·33 m (24·05 ft) and hull 6·882 m (22·58 ft); width 3·236 m (10·62 ft); height 3·502 m (11·49 ft)
Armament system: one 152-mm (6-in) modified Type 66 gun/howitzer with 30 rounds of ready-use ammunition, one 12·7-mm (0·5-in) Type 54 AA heavy machine-gun with 650 rounds, one 7·62-mm (0·3-in) co-axial machine-gun with 650 rounds, and one Type 40 rocket-launcher with 4 rounds in a hydraulically powered turret; direct- and indirect-fire sights are fitted
Armour: welded steel
Powerplant: one 390-kW (523-hp) Type 12150L diesel engine with 885 litres (195 Imp gal) of internal fuel
Performance: speed, road 55 km/h (34·2 mph); range, road 450 km (280 miles); fording 1·3 m (4·27 ft) without preparation; gradient 32°; side slope 30°; vertical obstacle 0·7 m (27·6 in); trench 2·7 m (8·86 ft); ground clearance 0·45 m (17·7 in)

Variant
Type 83: first revealed in 1984, this useful piece of self-propelled ordnance is thought to have entered service some years before that date; the hull is a purpose-designed unit also used by a 122-mm (4·8-mm) self-propelled multiple rocket-launcher, and is notable for having the four central units of its six road wheels grouped in pairs; the ordnance appears to be a derivative of the Type 66 towed gun/howitzer fitted with a fume extractor, and can be elevated in an arc between −5° and +65°, while the turret can be traversed

Below: The Type 83 uses a chassis developed specially for this application, and has power-operated turret functions.

through 360°; assuming that this ordnance has the same performance as the Type 66, the Type 83 can fire HE and smoke rounds, the HE projectile having a muzzle velocity of 655 m (2,149 ft) per second for a maximum range of 17,230 m (18,845 yards); the maximum rate of fire is four rounds per minute

---

NORINCO Type 54-1 122-mm SP howitzer

(China)
Type: tracked self-propelled howitzer
Crew: 7
Combat weight: 15,300 kg (33,730 lb)
Dimensions: length overall 5·60 m (18·37 ft); width 3·07 m (10·07 ft); height to top of gun 2·685 m (8·81 ft)

Above: The Type 54-1 later model has five rather than four road wheels on each side, while the howitzer is located on an open mounting.

Armament system: one 122-mm (4·8-in) Type 54-1 howitzer with 40 rounds of ready-use ammunition, and one 7·62-mm (0·3-in) Type 67 machine-gun with 1,000 rounds on a limited-traverse mounting; direct- and indirect-fire sights are fitted
Armour: welded steel to a maximum thickness of 12 mm (0·47 in)
Powerplant: one 195-kW (262-hp) Type 6150L diesel engine with ? litres (? Imp gal) of internal fuel
Performance: speed, road 56 km/h (34·8 mph); range, road 450 km (280 miles); fording not revealed; gradient 25°; side slope not revealed; vertical obstacle 0·6 m (23·6 in); trench 2·0 m (6·56 ft); ground clearance 0·45 m (17·7 in)

Variants
Type 54-1: this simple self-propelled howitzer is based on the chassis of the Type 531 (YW531) armoured personnel carrier, and has been pro-

duced in two forms; the earlier variant uses the standard Type 531 chassis while the later variant uses a chassis lengthened by the addition of an extra road wheel on each side; the ordnance is a copy of the Soviet M-30 (Model 1983) weapon, and is carried in an open mounting above the rear of the hull with its original shield forming the frontal armour; the ordnance can be elevated in an arc between −2·5° and +63°, and the mounting can be traversed a total of 45° (22·5° left and 22·5° right of the centreline); separate-loading ammunition is used, projectile types being HE, smoke and illuminating; the HE projectile weighs 21·76 kg (47·97 lb), and is fired with a muzzle velocity of 515 m (1,690 ft) per second to reach a maximum range of 11,800 m (12,905 yards)
New 122-mm SP howitzer: it is thought that a similar main ordnance is used on a new Chinese self-propelled howitzer with a chassis that features six road wheels on each side; the ordnance is carried in a fully enclosed turret located at the rear of the chassis, and it is thought that a 12·7-mm (0·5-in) heavy machine-gun is carried on the turret roof for AA defence

Right: The wheeled DANA is cheaper than tracked equivalents, but cramped in its fighting compartment, divided by the ordnance.

DANA 152-mm SP howitzer

(Czechoslovakia)

Type: wheeled self-propelled howitzer
Crew: probably 3
Combat weight: 23,000 kg (50,705 lb)
Dimensions: length, gun forward 10·40 m (34·12 ft) and hull 8·87 m (29·10 ft); width, turret 2·97 m (9·74 ft) and hull 2·722 m (8·93 ft); height to top of machine-gun 3·525 m (11·56 ft)
Armament system: one 152-mm (6-in) 2S3 (Model 1973) howitzer with an unrevealed quantity of ready-use ammunition, and one 12·7-mm (0·5-in) DShKM AA heavy machine-gun in a hydraulically powered turret; direct- and indirect-fire sights are fitted
Armour: welded steel
Powerplant: one 260-kW (349-hp) Tatra T-928 (T3-930) multi-fuel engine with an unrevealed quantity of internal fuel, and driving an 8 x 8 layout
Performance: speed, road 80 km/h (50 mph); range, road 1000 km (621 miles); fording 1·4 m (4·6 ft) without preparation; gradient 60%; side slope not revealed; vertical obstacle not revealed; trench 2·0 m (6·6 ft); ground clearance not revealed

Variant

DANA: this very useful SP howitzer was introduced into service in 1981, and is based on the chassis and automotive system of the Tatra 815 8 x 8 high-mobility truck, which offers the same type of cross-country mobility as a tracked chassis at considerably less cost; the DANA has a central tyre pressure-regulation system so that the best pressure can be selected for each type of terrain

encountered; the howitzer crew and ammunition are carried in a separate vehicle, the ordnance having automatic loading powered by a hydraulic motor which also traverses the turret through 360° and provides power for elevation between −3° and +60°; for firing the vehicle is stabilized by three hydraulically actuated jacks, the location of these (one at each side and the third at the rear) suggesting that the DANA may be designed to fire only over the frontal arc despite the 360° traverse available to the turret, which is located centrally and accommodates the ordnance in a central slot that removes the need for a bore evacuator as the crew are accommodated in the two compartments to the sides of the ordnance; the ordnance is based on the Soviet 2S3 weapon and can fire a 43·51-kg (95·92-lb) HE-FRAG projectile to 17,410 m (19,040 yards); other ammunition types are HE RAP (fired to a range of some 24,000 m/26,245 yards), AP HE, illuminating and smoke

---

Royal Ordnance SP122 SP howitzer

(Egypt/UK)

Type: tracked self-propelled howitzer
Crew: 5
Combat weight: 44,092 lb (20,000 kg)
Dimensions: length 25·25 ft (7·70 m); width 9·25 ft (2·82 m); height 8·83 ft (2·69 m)
Armament system: one 122-mm (4·8-in) D-30 howitzer with 80 rounds of ready-use ammunition, and one 0·5-in (12·7-mm) Browning M2HB AA

heavy machine-gun with 500 rounds on a limited-traverse mounting; direct- and indirect-fire sights are fitted
Armour: welded steel
Powerplant: one 300-hp (224-kW) Perkins TV8·540 diesel engine with an unrevealed quantity of internal fuel
Performance: speed, road 34 mph (55 km/h); range, road 186 miles (300 km); fording 3·25 ft (1·0 m) without preparation; gradient 60%; side slope 30%; vertical obstacle 30 in (0·76 m); trench 7·55 ft (2·3 m); ground clearance not revealed

Variant

SP122: this is a competitor in an Egyptian army competition for a new SP howitzer carrying the locally built version of the Soviet D-30 howitzer; the other competitor is an American entry from BMY based on the chassis of the M109 series of SP weapons; the SP122 has a fixed superstructure with the ordnance projecting through the front, allowing elevation from −5° to +70° and total traverse of 60° (30° left and 30° right of the centreline); the two main types of ammunition available for the ordnance are HE-FRAG and HEAT-FS, the 21·76-kg (47·97-lb) projectile of the former being fired at a muzzle velocity of 690 m (2,264 ft) per second to reach a maximum range of 15,300 m (16,730 yards) and the 21·63-kg (47·7-lb) projectile of the latter being fired at a muzzle velocity of 740 m (2,428 ft) per second to pierce 460 mm (18·1 in) of armour at any range; other projectile types are HE RAP, chemical, illuminating and smoke; the basic chassis is also being considered for a number of other vehicle types, including an ammunition carrier, ambulance, command post and recovery vehicle

BMY ARE 122-mm SP howitzer

(Egypt/USA)

Type: tracked self-propelled howitzer
Crew: 5
Combat weight: 50,885 lb (23,182 kg)
Dimensions: length, gun forward 22·82 ft (6·957 m) and hull not revealed; width 10·33 ft (3·15 m); height 9·33 ft (2·84 m)
Armament system: one 122-mm (4·8-in) D-30 howitzer with 85 rounds of ready-use ammunition, and one 0·5-in (12·7-mm) Browning M2HB AA heavy machine-gun with 500 rounds on a limited-traverse mounting; direct- and indirect-fire sights are fitted
Armour: welded steel
Powerplant: one 405-hp (302-kW) Detroit Diesel 8V-71T diesel engine with 135 US gal (511 litres) of internal fuel
Performance: speed, road 35 mph (56·3 km/h); range, road 215 miles (346 km); fording 3·5 ft (1·7 m) without preparation; gradient 60%; side slope 40%; vertical obstacle 21 in (0·53 m); trench 6·0 ft (1·83 m); ground clearance not revealed

Variant

ARE: this is the equipment competing with the British-designed SP122 for an Egyptian order, and though based on the chassis of the Field Artillery Ammunition Support Vehicle (the ammunition supply vehicle for the M109 SP howitzer series and using the same basic chassis) is conceptually similar to the British equipment with a fixed superstructure that allows ordnance elevation in an arc between −5° and +70°, and traverse through a total of 60° (30° left and 30° right of the centreline); the ordnance fires the same range of separate-loading ammunition as the British-developed vehicle, the standard loading being 80 HE-FRAG and 5 HEAT-FS projectiles

GIAT GCT 155-mm SP gun

(France)

Type: tracked self-propelled gun
Crew: 4
Combat weight: 42,000 kg (92,593 lb)
Dimensions: length, gun forward 10·25 m (33·63 ft) and hull 6·70 m (21·98 ft); width 3·15 m (10·33 ft); height to turret top 3·25 m (10·66 ft)
Armament system: one 155-mm (6·1-in) GIAT gun with 42 rounds of ready-use ammunition, one 7·62-mm (0·3-in) or 0·5-in (12·7-mm) AA machine-gun with 2,050 or 800 rounds, and two smoke-dischargers on the front of the hydraulically powered turret; direct- and indirect-fire sights are fitted
Armour: welded steel
Powerplant: one 535-kW (718-hp) Hispano-Suiza HS 110 multi-fuel engine with 970 litres (213 Imp gal) of internal fuel
Performance: speed, road 60 km/h (37·3 mph); range, road 450 km (280 miles); fording 2·1 m (6·9 ft) without preparation; gradient 60%; side slope 30%; vertical obstacle 0·93 m (36·6 in); trench 1·9 m (6·2 ft); ground clearance 0·42 m (16·5 in)

Variant

GCT: designed to replace obsolescent 105- and 155-mm (4·13- and 6·1-in) self-propelled weapons based on the chassis of the AMX-13 light tank, the GCT (Grande Cadence de Tir, or great rate of fire) is based on the chassis of the AMX-30 MBT and entered service in 1978 initially with Saudi Arabia; the vehicle replaces the MBT's low-silhouette turret with a voluminous unit accommodating the ordnance, ammunition and an automatic loading system; this last makes possible a high rate of fire using the onboard ammunition supply (a burst capability of six rounds in 45 seconds); reloading of the ammunition supply can be undertaken while the gun is in action, four men accomplishing a complete reload in 15 minutes; optional equipment includes an NBC protection system and specialized artillery items; the French designation is **155 AU F1**, and the L/40 ordnance can be elevated in an arc between −4° and +66° in the 360° traverse turret; projectile types are HE-FRAG, HE RAP, anti-tank mine, smoke and illuminating; typical range is 21,200 m (23,185 yards) with the 43·75-kg (96·45-lb) HE-FRAG projectile, though the 42·5-kg (93·7-lb) HE RAP attains 30,500 m (33,355 yards); the type can also fire the US Copperhead cannon-launched guided projectile

Below: France's most modern item of self-propelled artillery, the GCT is based on the chassis of the AMX-30 tank. The large turret provides a big space for the crew, ready-use ammunition supply and automatic loading system. The GCT has full NBC protection.

Creusot-Loire Mk F3
155-mm SP gun/howitzer

(France)
Type: tracked self-propelled gun/howitzer
Crew: 2
Combat weight: 17,400 kg (38,360 lb)
Dimensions: length, overall 6·22 m (20·41 ft); width 2·72 m (8·92 ft); height 2·085 m (6·84 ft)
Armament: one 155-mm (6·1-in) ATS gun/howitzer with no ready-use ammunition on a limited-traverse mounting; direct- and indirect-fire sights are fitted
Armour: welded steel varying in thickness from 10 to 20 mm (0·39 to 0·79 in)
Powerplant: one 185-kW (248-hp) SOFAM 8Gbx petrol engine or one 280-hp (209-kW) Detroit Diesel 6V-53T diesel engine with 450 litres (99 Imp gal) of internal fuel
Performance: speed, road 60 km/h (27·3 mph) with petrol engine or 64 km/h (40 mph) with diesel engine; range, road 300 km (186 miles) with petrol engine or 400 km (249 miles) with diesel engine; fording 1·0 m (3·3 ft) without preparation; gradient 40%; vertical obstacle 0·6 m (23·6 in); trench 1·5 m (4·9 ft); ground clearance 0·48 m (18·9 in)

Variant
Mk F3: this self-propelled gun is based on the shortened chassis of the AMX-13 light tank, and since its introduction in the later 1950s has been offered in petrol- or diesel-engined models; kits are available to permit the operators of petrol-engined versions to convert their guns to diesel power; on its unprotected rear-mounted position the gun can be traversed a total of 50° (20° left and 30° right of the centreline) at elevation angles between 0° and +50°, and a total of 46° (16° left and 30° right of the centreline) at elevation angles between +50° and +67°; the vehicle is stabilized while firing by twin spades at the rear; the eight-man gun crew and 25 rounds are carried in an accompanying VCA tracked vehicle; the L/33 ordnance fires HE-FRAG, HE RAP, smoke and illuminating projectiles, the 43·75-kg (96·45-lb) HE-FRAG type being fired with a muzzle velocity of 725 m (2,379 ft) per second to reach a maximum range of 20,050 m (21,925 yards)

Above: the ordnance of the Mk F3 is carried on an open mounting on a chassis derived from that of the AMX-13 light tank. The crew and 25 rounds of ammunition are carried in the accompanying VTT/VCA support vehicle based on the same chassis.

Creusot-Loire Mk 61
105-mm SP howitzer

(France)
Type: tracked self-propelled howitzer
Crew: 5
Combat weight: 16,500 kg (36,357 lb)
Dimensions: length, overall 5·70 m (18·70 ft); width 2·65 m (8·69 ft); height to top of cupola 2·70 m (8·86 ft)
Armament system: one 105-mm (4·13-in) Modèle 50 howitzer with 56 rounds of ready-use ammunition on a manually powered limited-traverse mounting, and one or two 7·5- or 7·62-mm (0·295- or 0·3-in) machine-guns (one for AA defence and one optional for local defence) with 2,000 rounds; direct- and indirect-fire sights are fitted
Armour: welded steel varying in thickness from 10 to 20 mm (0·39 to 0·79 in)
Powerplant: one 185-kW (248-hp) SOFAM 8Gbx petrol engine with 415 litres (91 Imp gal) of internal fuel
Performance: speed, road 60 km/h (37·3 mph); range, road 350 km (217 miles); fording 0·8 m (2·6 ft) without preparation; gradient 60%; side slope 30%; vertical obstacle 0·65 m (25·6 in); trench 1·6 m (5·2 ft); ground clearance 0·275 m (10·8 in)

Variant
Mk 61: designed in the late 1940s, the Mk 61 is now obsolescent in terms of chassis (derived from that of the AMX-13 light tank) and ordnance, and was accepted for French service in 1958; the type lacks NBC protection and amphibious capability, and the ordnance can be traversed a total of only 40° (20° left and 20° right of the centreline) at elevation angles between −4·5° and +66° on its mounting in the rear-mounted armoured fighting compartment; the L/23 or L/30 ordnance fires HE-FRAG or HEAT projectiles, the former weigh-

ing 16 kg (35·3 lb) and attaining a range of 15,000 m (16,405 yards) after being fired at a muzzle velocity of 670 m (2,198 ft) per second, and the latter being capable of penetrating 350 mm (13·78 in) of armour at any range after being fired at a muzzle velocity of 700 m (2,297 ft) per second

Catapult 130-mm SP gun

(India)
Type: tracked self-propelled gun
Crew: not revealed
Combat weight: not revealed
Dimensions: length, gun forward not revealed and hull not revealed; width 3·168 m (10·39 ft); height not revealed
Armament system: one 130-mm (5·12-in) M1946 gun with 30 rounds of ready-use ammunition on a limited-traverse mounting; direct- and indirect-fire sights are fitted
Armour: welded steel to a maximum thickness of 63·5 mm (2·5 in)
Powerplant: one 650-hp (485-kW) Leyland L60 Mk 4B multi-fuel engine with 1000 litres (220 Imp gal) of internal fuel
Performance: speed, road 48·3 km/h (30 mph); range, road not revealed; fording 1·143 m (3·75 ft) without preparation; gradient 60%; side slope 30%; vertical obstacle 0·91 m (36 in); trench not revealed; ground clearance not revealed

Variant
Catapult: this Indian equipment is a comparatively simple combination of the Vijayanta MBT chassis (lengthened by the addition of an extra road wheel on each side) and the Soviet-supplied M1946 gun; the latter is located in place of the MBT's turret on a limited-traverse mounting that allows fire over the vehicle rear; the L/55 barrel can fire several types of separate-loading ammunition including a 33·4-kg (73·6-lb) HE-FRAG projectile fired at a muzzle velocity of 1050 m (3,445 ft) per second to reach a maximum range of 27,150 m (29,690 yards), and an APC-T projectile fired at the same muzzle velocity to pierce 230 mm (9·06 in) of armour at a range of 1000 m (1,095 yards); the ordnance can also fire HE RAP, smoke and illuminating projectiles

Al Fao 155-mm SP howitzer

(Iraq)
Type: wheeled self-propelled howitzer
Crew: probably 3 or 4
Combat weight: 48,000 kg (105,820 lb)
Dimensions: not revealed
Armament system: one 210-mm (8·27-in) howitzer with an unrevealed quantity of ready-use ammunition in a hydraulically powered turret; direct- and indirect-fire sights are fitted
Armour: welded steel
Powerplant: one Mercedes-Benz diesel engine of unrevealed power with an unrevealed quantity of internal fuel, and driving a 6 x 6 layout
Performance: speed, road 90 km/h (55·9 mph); range, road not revealed; fording not revealed; gradient 60%; side slope not revealed; vertical obstacle not revealed; trench not revealed; ground clearance not revealed

Variant

Al Fao: first revealed in 1989, this weapon bears a conceptual similarity to the South African G6 system but is based on an articulated chassis comprising a forward section with the engine and driver's cab, and a rear section with the turret and fighting compartment; the L/53 ordnance can fire its 109·4-kg (241·2-lb) ERFF-BB projectile to a maximum range of 57,340 m (62,710 yards), a truly prodigious performance that can be maintained at the rate of 1 round per minute for sustained fire or 4 rounds per minute for burst fire; the system was developed with the aid of European industrial concerns, most particularly several in France

Majnoon 155-mm SP howitzer

(Iraq)
Type: wheeled self-propelled howitzer
Crew: probably 3 or 4
Combat weight: 43,000 kg (94,797 lb)
Dimensions: not revealed
Armament system: one 155-mm (6·1-in) howitzer with an unrevealed quantity of ready-use ammunition in a hydraulically powered turret; direct- and indirect-fire sights are fitted
Armour: welded steel
Powerplant: one Mercedes-Benz diesel engine of unrevealed power with an unrevealed quantity of internal fuel, and driving a 6 x 6 layout
Performance: speed, road 90 km/h (55·9 mph); range, road not revealed; fording not revealed; gradient 60%; side slope not revealed; vertical obstacle not revealed; trench not revealed; ground clearance not revealed

Variant

Majnoon: first revealed in 1989, this weapon is apparently related quite closely to the Al Fao system but uses a smaller-calibre L/51·65 weapon; the ordnance can fire its 45·5-kg (100·3-lb) ERFB-BB projectile to a maximum range of 38,000 m (41,555 yards); the rates of fire are identical to those of the Al Fao system

Iraqi 120-mm 155-mm SP mortar

(Iraq)
Type: tracked self-propelled mortar
Crew: 5
Combat weight: not revealed
Dimensions: length overall not revealed and hull not revealed; width 2·85 m (9·35 ft); height not revealed
Armament system: four 120-mm (4·72-in) mortars with 104 rounds of ready-use ammunition; indirect-fire sights are fitted
Armour: welded steel
Powerplant: one 180-kW (241-hp) YaMZ-238 V diesel engine with 450 litres (99 Imp gal) of internal fuel
Performance: speed, road not revealed; range, road not revealed; fording amphibious; gradient 60%; side slope 30%; vertical obstacle 0·7 m (27·6 in); trench 2·7 m (8·9 ft); ground clearance 0·4 m (15·75 in)

Variant

Iraqi 120-mm SP mortar: this weapon was first revealed in 1989, and the proper designation has not yet been released; the weapon is an adaptation of the Soviet MT-LB multi-purpose tracked vehicle's chassis modified to carry a bank of four mortars on a frame hinged to lie horizontally over the roof of the vehicle for travel before being swung back through 90° to the vertical firing position; in firing position the vehicle is stabilized by two hydraulically operated outriggers lowered to the ground at the sides of the hull rear; the mortars can be elevated between + 40° and + 80°, and can be traversed a total of 20° (10° left and 10° right of the centreline); the mortars can be fired individually or collectively, and use two types of bombs, the 12-kg (26·46-lb) type being delivered to a maximum range of 10,000 m (10,935 yards) and the 16-kg (35·27-lb) type being delivered to a maximum range of 8000 m (8,750 yards)

Soltam 'Slammer' 155-mm SP howitzer

(Israel)
Type: tracked self-propelled howitzer
Crew: 4
Combat weight: not revealed
Dimensions: length, gun forward not revealed and hull 7·45 m (24·44 ft); width 3·70 m (12·14 ft); height to turret top not revealed
Armament system: one 155-mm (6·1-in) Soltam howitzer with 75 rounds of ready-use ammunition in an electro-hydraulically powered turret; direct- and indirect-fire sights are fitted
Armour: cast and welded steel
Powerplant: one 900-hp (671-kW) Teledyne Continental Motors AVDS-1790-6A diesel engine with 900 litres (198 Imp gal) of internal fuel
Performance: speed, road 46 km/h (28·6 mph); range, road 400 km (249 miles); fording 1·38 m (4·5 ft) without preparation and 2·0 m (6·6 ft) with preparation; gradient 60%; side slope 38%; vertical obstacle 0·95 m (37·4 in); trench 3·0 m (9·8 ft); ground clearance 0·47 m (18·5 in)

Variant

'Slammer': introduced in 1990, this is an Israeli development on the basis of the Merkava MBT chassis and hull; a prototype was produced in the 1980s, but remained nothing more than this until Israel perceived serious development problems with the HIP (Howitzer Improvement Program) update of the US M109 series; the initial model is fitted with an L/45 ordnance, though an L/52 barrel is also available, and all standard types of 155-mm (6·1-in) ammunition can be fired

Soltam M-72 155-mm SP gun/howitzer

(Israel)
Type: tracked self-propelled gun/howitzer
Crew: 5
Combat weight: not revealed
Dimensions: length, gun forward not revealed and hull 7·823 m (25·67 ft); width 3·39 m (11·12 ft); height not revealed
Armament system: one 155-mm (6·1-in) Soltam gun/howitzer with an unrevealed quantity of ready-use ammunition in a hydraulically operated turret, and one 0·5-in (12·7-mm) Browning M2HB AA machine-gun or one 7·62-mm (0·3-in) AA machine-gun with an unrevealed number of rounds; direct- and indirect-fire sights are fitted
Armour: welded steel varying in thickness between 17 and 76 mm (0·67 and 3 in)
Powerplant: one 750-hp (559-kW) Teledyne Continental Motors AVDS-1790-2A diesel engine with an unrevealed quantity of internal fuel
Performance: speed, road 48 km/h (26·7 mph); range, road about 600 km (373 miles); fording 1·45 m (4·75 ft) without preparation; gradient 60%; side slope 30%; vertical obstacle 0·91 m (36 in); trench 3·35 m (11·0 ft); ground clearance 0·51 m (20 in)

Variant

M-72: this may be regarded as the modern equivalent of the L-33 weapon using a similar L/33 ordnance though the type is also offered with a more modern L/39 ordnance; the hull is basically that of the British Centurion MBT as updated and improved by the Israelis with a diesel-engined powerplant and other features, including the relocation of the driver to the right of the hull front allowing the fitment of a large left-hand door through which ammunition can be loaded even as the equipment is in action; the neat and comparatively small turret weighs 14,000 kg (30,864 lb) complete with ammunition, and in action is generally traversed to fire over the rear of the vehicle; the turret can be traversed through 360°, and the ordnance elevated in an arc between − 3° and + 65°; a moderately high rate of fire is made possibly by the use of a pneumatically operated rammer that allows loading at all angles of elevation, and the L/33 ordnance uses standard NATO types of ammunition, including a 43·7-kg (96·34-lb) HE-FRAG projectile fired with a muzzle velocity of 725 m (2,379 ft) to a maximum range of 20,500 m (22,420 yards); the equivalent figures for the L/39 ordnance with the same projectile are a muzzle velocity of 820 m (2,690 ft) per second and a maximum range of 23,500 m (25,700 yards); the complete equipment is offered with a number of optional features including full NBC protection, and the turret can also be installed on a number of other MBT chassis

Soltam L-33 155-mm SP gun/howitzer

(Israel)
Type: tracked self-propelled gun/howitzer
Crew: 8
Combat weight: 41,500 kg (91,490 lb)
Dimensions: length, gun forward 8·47 m (27·79 ft) and hull 6·47 m (21·23 ft); width 3·50 m (11·48 ft); height 3·45 m (11·32 ft)
Armament system: one 155-mm (6·1-in) Soltam

Above: The ordnance of the L-33 is located in a massive superstructure of armour plate on the chassis of the M4A3E8 version of the World War II Sherman medium tank, and this restricts total traverse to 60° on the mounting.

M-68 gun/howitzer with 60 rounds of ready-use ammunition on a manually powered limited-traverse mounting, and one 7·62-mm (0·3-in) AA machine-gun; direct- and indirect-fire sights are fitted

Armour: welded steel varying in thickness between 16 and 64 mm (0·63 to 2·5 in)

Powerplant: one 460-hp (343-kW) Cummins VT8-460-Bi diesel engine with 820 litres (180 Imp gal) of internal fuel

Performance: speed, road 38 km/h (23·6 mph); range, road 260 km (162 miles); fording 0·9 m (3·0 ft) without preparation; gradient 60%; side slope 30%; vertical obstacle 0·91 m (36 in); trench 2·3 m (7·5 ft); ground clearance 0·43 m (17 in)

Variant

L-33: this simple yet effective Israeli development locates an M-68 gun/howitzer in a massive fixed fighting compartment on the chassis of an obsolete M4A3E8 Sherman medium tank (horizontal-volute rather than vertical-volute spring suspension type); the ordnance is installed in a tall slab-sided fighting compartment built upwards from the basic hull of the vehicle; the ordnance can be traversed through a total of 60° on its mounting, and can be elevated in an arc between −3° and +52°; the type has proved operationally successful since it entered Israeli service in 1973; the L/33 ordnance can use all types of NATO ammunition in its calibre, including a 43·7-kg (96·3-lb) HE-FRAG projectile fired at a muzzle velocity of 725 m (2,379 ft) per second to a maximum range of 20,000 m (21,870 yards)

EEFA Bourges M-50 155-mm SP howitzer

(Israel/France)
Type: tracked self-propelled howitzer
Crew: 8
Combat weight: 31,000 kg (68,342 lb)
Dimensions: length overall 6·10 m (20·01 ft); width 2·98 m (9·78 ft); height 2·80 m (9·19 ft)
Armament system: one 155-mm (6·1-in) Modèle 50 howitzer with an unrevealed quantity of ready-use ammunition on a manually operated limited-traverse mounting; direct- and indirect-fire sights are fitted
Armour: welded steel
Powerplant: one 450-hp (336-kW) Ford GAA petrol engine with 168 US gal (636 litres) of internal fuel
Performance: speed, road about 45 km/h (28 mph); range, road 160 km (100 miles); fording 0·9 m (3·0 ft) without preparation; gradient 60%; side slope not revealed; vertical obstacle 0·61 m (24 in); trench 2·26 m (7·4 ft); ground clearance 0·43 m (17 in)

Variant

M-50: this self-propelled howitzer was developed in France during the 1950s to meet an Israeli requirement, and combines a French Modèle 50 howitzer with an open-topped fighting compartment built onto the chassis and lower hull of an M4 Sherman medium tank (vertical-volute rather than horizontal-volute spring suspension type) reworked to move the engine forward; the maximum elevation of the rear-mounted ordnance is +69°; ammunition types include HE, this projectile weighing 43 kg (94·8 lb) and reaching a range of 17,600 m (19,250 yards) after being fired at a muzzle velocity of 650 m (2,133 ft) per second

OTO Melara Palmaria 155-mm SP howitzer

(Italy)
Type: tracked self-propelled howitzer
Crew: 5
Combat weight: 46,000 kg (101,411 lb)
Dimensions: length, gun forward 11·474 m (37·74 ft) and hull 7·40 m (24·28 ft); width 3·386 m (11·11 ft); height without machine-gun 2·874 m (9·43 ft)
Armament system: one 155-mm (6·1-in) OTO Melara L/41 howitzer with 30 rounds of ready-use ammunition, and one 0·5-in (12·7-mm) or 7·62-mm (0·3-in) AA machine-gun in a hydraulically powered turret; direct- and indirect-fire sights are fitted
Armour: welded steel and aluminium
Powerplant: one 535-kW (718-hp) MTU MB 837 Ea diesel engine with 900 litres (198 Imp gal) of internal fuel
Performance: speed, road 60 km/h (37·3 mph); range, road 400 km (249 miles); fording 1·2 m (3·9 ft) without preparation and 4·0 m (13·1 ft) with preparation; gradient 60%; side slope 30%; vertical obstacle 1·0 m (39·3 in); trench 3·0 m (9·8 ft); ground clearance 0·4 m (15·75 in)

Variant

Palmaria: this is the chassis of the OF-40 MBT with a lower-powered engine and modified to take a turret accommodating an OTO Melara howitzer with an automatic loader permitting a rate of fire of three rounds in 20 seconds, or one round per minute for 1 hour, or one round every 3 minutes indefinitely; the turret can be traversed through 360°, and the ordnance can be elevated in an arc between −4° and +70°, firing a 43·5-kg (95·9-lb) HE-FRAG projectile to a maximum range of 24,700 m (27,010 yards) or a 43·5-kg (95·9-lb) HE RAP round to a maximum range of 30,000 m (32,810 yards); other projectile types are smoke and illuminating; the Palmaria turret has also been fitted to the hull of the Argentine TAM medium tank.

Mitsubishi Type 75 155-mm SP howitzer

(Japan)
Type: tracked self-propelled howitzer
Crew: 6
Combat weight: 25,300 kg (55,776 lb)
Dimensions: length, gun forward 7·79 m (25·56 ft) and hull 6·64 m (21·78 ft); width 3·09 m (10·14 ft); height to turret roof 2·545 m (8·35 ft)
Armament system: one 155-mm (6·1-in) NSJ howitzer with 28 ready-use rounds and one 0·5-in (12·7-mm) Browning M2HB AA heavy machine-gun with 1,000 rounds in a hydraulically powered turret; direct- and indirect-fire sights are fitted
Armour: welded aluminium
Powerplant: one 335-kW (449-hp) Mitsubishi 6ZF diesel engine with 650 litres (143 Imp gal) of internal fuel
Performance: speed, road 47 km/h (29·2 mph); range, road 300 km (186 miles); fording 1·3 m (4·25 ft); gradient 60%; side slope 30%; vertical obstacle 0·7 m (27·6 in); trench 2·5 m (8·2 ft); ground clearance 0·4 m (15·75 in)

Variant
Type 75: this Japanese self-propelled howitzer

Below: The Type 75 is a modestly advanced equipment with full NBC protection.

entered service in 1978, and resembles the US M109 series in layout, with the L/30 ordnance located in a rear-mounted turret that can traverse through 360° and permits ordnance elevation in an arc between −5° and +70°; projectile types include HE fired to a maximum range of 19,000 m (20,770 yards), and HE RAP fired to a maximum range of 24,000 m (26,245 yards); an NBC protection system is fitted

Komatsu/Japan Steel Works Type 74 105-mm SP howitzer

(Japan)
Type: tracked self-propelled howitzer
Crew: 5
Combat weight: 16,500 kg (36,376 lb)
Dimensions: length 5·90 m (19·36 ft); width 2·90 m (9·51 ft); height 2·39 m (7·84 ft)
Armament system: one 105-mm (4·13-in) NSJ howitzer with an unrevealed number of ready-use rounds and one 0·5-in (12·7-mm) Browning M2HB AA heavy machine-gun in a hydraulically powered turret; direct- and indirect-fire sights are fitted
Armour: welded steel
Powerplant: 225-kW (302-hp) Mitsubishi 4ZF diesel engine with an unrevealed quantity of internal fuel
Performance: speed, road 50 km/h (31 mph); range, road 300 km (186 miles); fording 1·2 m (3·9 ft) without preparation and amphibious with preparation; gradient 60%; vertical obstacle 0·61 m (24 in); trench 2·0 m (6·6 ft); ground clearance 0·4 m (15·75 in)

Variant
Type 74: based on the chassis and automotive system of the Type 73 APC, the Type 74 self-propelled howitzer began to enter service in 1975; the rear-mounted turret traverses through 360°; no details of ammunition types or performance have been revealed; it is thought that the type has an NBC protection system

'Koksan' 175-mm SP gun

(North Korea)
Type: tracked self-propelled gun
Crew: not revealed
Combat weight: not revealed
Dimensions: length, gun forward not revealed and hull 6·243 m (20·48 ft); width 3·298 m (10·82 ft); height not revealed
Armament system: one 175-mm (6·89-in) rifled gun with ready-use rounds on the electro-hydraulically powered mounting; direct- and indirect-fire sights are fitted
Armour: cast and welded steel
Powerplant: one 435-kW (583-hp) Model 12150L-7BW diesel engine with an unrevealed quantity of internal fuel
Performance: speed, road not revealed; range, road not revealed; fording 1·4 m (4·6 ft); gradient 60%; side slope 40%; vertical obstacle 0·8 m (31·5 in); trench 2·7 m (8·9 ft); ground clearance 0·425 m (16·75 in)

Variant
'Koksan': known in the West only by its American reporting name, this North Korean equipment combines the chassis and hull of the Chinese Type 59 MBT with a powerful gun probably supplied by the USSR during the 1950s as a coast-defence

weapon; the turret aperture is plated over to provide a basis for the open gun mounting, which has only limited traverse; the ordnance is fitted with a multi-baffle muzzle brake, and in firing position the vehicle is stabilized by two rear-mounted spades; space limitations mean that the crew and ammunition have to be carried in a supporting vehicle

Armscor G6 Renoster 155-mm SP howitzer

(South Africa)
Type: wheeled self-propelled howitzer
Crew: 6
Combat weight: 47,000 kg (103,263 lb)
Dimensions: length, gun forward 10·335 m (33·91 ft) and hull 9·20 m (30·18 ft); width 3·40 m (1·15 ft); height to turret top 3·20 m (10·5 ft)
Armament system: one 155-mm (6·1-in) Armscor G5 howitzer with 47 ready-use rounds, one 0·5-in (12·7-mm) Browning M2HB AA machinegun with 900 rounds, and four 81-mm (3·2-in) grenade-launchers on each side of the hydraulically powered turret; direct- and indirect-fire sights are fitted
Armour: welded steel
Powerplant: one 391-kW (525-hp) diesel engine with 700 litres (154 Imp gal) of fuel, driving a 6 × 6 layout
Performance: speed, road 90 km/h (56 mph); range, road 600 km (373 miles); fording 1·0 m (3·3 ft); gradient 50%; side slope 30%; vertical obstacle 0·45 m (17·7 in); trench 1·0 m (3·3 ft); ground clearance 0·45 m (17·7 in)

Variant
G6 Renoster: this self-propelled howitzer, whose name is the Afrikaans word for rhinoceros, was inspired by a Canadian idea but realized entirely in South Africa as a long-range weapon able to support other armoured vehicles in all types of terrain; the type entered service in the mid-1980s; the rear-mounted turret is capable of 360° traverse, and the L/45 ordnance can be elevated in an arc between − 5° and + 75°, firing a range of extended-range full-bore projectiles that includes HE-FRAG, HE BB, HE RAP, smoke and illuminating; the HE-FRAG projectile weighs 45·5 kg (100·3 lb) and reaches 30,000 m (32,810 yards), while the 47-kg (103·6-lb) HE base-bleed projectile attains a highly capable 40,000 m (43,745 yards)

Fabrica de Artilleria de Sevilla SB 155/39 ATP 155-mm SP howitzer

(Spain)
Type: tracked self-propelled howitzer
Crew: 5
Combat weight: 38,000 kg (83,774 lb)
Dimensions: length, gun forward 9·80 m (32·15 ft) and hull not revealed; width 3·20 m (10·50 ft); height to turret top not revealed
Armament system: one 155-mm (6·1-in) Santa Barbara 155/39 howitzer with 28 ready-use rounds, and one 0·5-in (12·7-mm) Browning M2HB AA machine-gun in an electro-hydraulically

powered turret; direct- and indirect-fire sights are fitted
Armour: welded steel
Powerplant: one 912-hp (680-kW) Detroit Diesel 12V-71QTA diesel engine with 1300 litres (286 Imp gal) of internal fuel
Performance: speed, road 70 km/h (43·5 mph); range, road 550 km (342 miles); fording 0·9 m (2·95 ft); gradient 60%; side slope 30%; vertical obstacle 0·9 m (35·4 in); trench 2·8 m (9·2 ft); ground clearance 0·46 m (18·1 in)

Variant
SB 153/39 ATP: this comparatively simple self-propelled equipment is under final development based on a new chassis with a rear mounting for the turret accommodating a standard Santa Barbara L/39 howitzer; the turret can be traversed through 360°, and the ordnance can be elevated through an unrevealed arc; the turret has twin loading doors in its rear, and the complete equipment is stabilized for firing by twin jacks, the ammunition range including the full range of NATO types in this calibre; the standard HE projectile can be fired to a maximum range of 24,000 m (26,245 yards) while the HE RAP type attains a maximum range of 30,000 m (32,810 yards)

Bofors Bandkanon 1A 155-mm SP gun

(Sweden)
Type: tracked self-propelled gun

The Bandkanon 1A has a large automatic loader.

Crew: 5
Combat weight: 53,000 kg (116,843 lb)
Dimensions: length, overall 11·00 m (36·08 ft) and hull 6·55 m (21·49 ft); width 3·37 m (11·06 ft); height over machine-gun 3·85 m (12·63 ft)
Armament system: one 155-mm (6·1-in) Bofors gun with 14 ready-use rounds and one 7·62-mm (0·3-in) AA machine-gun in an electrically powered turret; direct- and indirect-fire sights are fitted
Armour: welded steel varying in thickness between 10 and 20 mm (0·39 and 0·79 in)
Powerplant: one 240-hp (179-kW) Rolls-Royce K60 diesel engine and one 300-shp (224-kW) Boeing Model 502/10MA gas turbine with 1445 litres (318 Imp gal) of internal fuel
Performance: speed, road 28 km/h (17·4 mph); range, road 230 km (143 miles); fording 1·0 m (3·3 ft); gradient 60%; side slope 30%; vertical obstacle 0·95 m (37·4 in); trench 2·0 m (6·6 ft); ground clearance 0·37 m (14·6 in)

Variant
Bandkanon 1A: entering service in 1966, this self-propelled gun is a massive and fairly slow equipment that uses many automotive components from the Strv 103 MBT, but has an automatic loader that permits a high rate of fire and its 14-round clip can be recharged in a mere two minutes; the L/50 ordnance is located in a large turret at the rear of the vehicle, and can be traversed through a total of 30° (15° left and 15° right of

the centreline) above an elevation angle of 0°, the figures declining to a total of 19° (15° left and 4° right of the centreline) below an elevation angle of 0°; the ordnance elevation limits are − 3° and + 40° in powered mode, and + 2° to + 38° in manual mode; the 48-kg (105·8-lb) HE-FRAG projectile is fired at a muzzle velocity of 865 m (2,838 ft) per second to attain a maximum range of 25,600 m (27,995 yards)

T-34/122 122-mm SP howitzer

(Syria)
Type: tracked self-propelled howitzer
Crew: 6
Combat weight: 29,000 kg (63,933 lb)
Dimensions: length overall 6·01 m (19·70 ft); width 2·99 m (9·81 ft); height 2·70 m (8·86 ft)
Armament system: one 122-mm (4·8-in) D-30 howitzer with 40 ready-use rounds mounted on a manually operated turntable; direct- and indirect-fire sights are fitted
Armour: welded and cast steel
Powerplant: one 370-kW (496-hp) Model V-2 diesel engine with 560 litres (123 Imp gal) of internal fuel
Performance: speed, road 60 km/h (37·3 mph); range, road 300 km (186 miles); fording 1·3 m

(4·3 ft); gradient 35%; side slope not revealed; vertical obstacle 0·7 m (27·6 in); trench 2·29 m (7·5 ft); ground clearance 0·4 m (15·75 in)

Variant
T-34/122: introduced in the early 1970s, the T-34/122 is a conversion of the elderly T-34 medium tank to mount an exposed 122-mm (4·8-in) Soviet howitzer in place of the turret, 10 four-round ammunition boxes being attached to the hull sides; the mounting has a practical traverse limit of 120° (60° left and 60° right of the centreline to the rear), and the L/40 ordnance can be elevated in an arc between − 7° and + 70°; the projectile types that can be fired are HE-FRAG, HEAT and smoke, the normal complements of these types being 32, 4 and 4; the 21·76-kg (49·97-lb) HE-FRAG projectile is fired at a muzzle velocity of 690 m (2,264 ft) per second to attain a maximum range of 15,400 m (16,840 yards), while the 25-kg (55·1-lb) HEAT-FS projectile is fired at a muzzle velocity of 740 m (2,428 ft) per second to penetrate 460 mm (18·1 in) of armour at any range

2S4 Self-propelled 240-mm mortar

(USSR)
Type: tracked self-propelled mortar
Crew: not revealed
Combat weight: not revealed
Dimensions: length overall not revealed and hull 6·454 m (21·17 ft); width 2·85 m (9·35 ft); height not revealed
Armament system: one 240-mm (9·45-in) M-240 mortar with an unrevealed number of ready-use rounds in a hydraulically powered rear mounting; indirect-fire sights are fitted
Armour: welded steel varying in thickness between 7 and 14 mm (0·28 and 0·55 in)
Powerplant: one 180-kW (241-hp) YaMZ 238 V diesel engine with 450 litres (99 Imp gal) of internal fuel
Performance: speed, road 61·5 km/h (38·2 mph); range, road 500 km (311 miles); fording not revealed; gradient 60%; side slope 30%; vertical obstacle 0·7 m (27·6 in); trench 2·7 m (8·9 ft); ground clearance 0·4 m (15·75 in)

Variant
2S4: this powerful equipment is based on the chassis of the GMZ tracked minelayer, and carries at its rear the M-240 breech-loading mortar; the mortar is essentially similar to the towed equipment apart from the vehicle mounting attachments on the baseplate, allowing the weapon to be pivoted by a hydraulic system round the vehicle rear so that the baseplate is firmly embedded in the ground under the vehicle rear for firing; the mortar can fire HE, chemical, concrete-piercing or tactical nuclear projectiles between minimum and maximum ranges of 800 and 12,700 m (875 and 13,890 yards); the HE bomb weighs 130 kg (286 lb), and the maximum rate of fire is probably one round per minute, possibly with the use of an assisted-loading device; this equipment has the Soviet military and industrial designations **SM-240** and 2S4, and in the US system of terminology is known as the **M1975**

Left: The 2S4 has its breech-loaded mortar at the rear of a chassis derived from that of the GMZ on a hinged mounting that allows the baseplate to be lowered to the ground as a stable firing platform.

2S7 203-mm SP gun

(USSR)

Type: tracked self-propelled gun
Crew: 4
Combat weight: 40,000 kg (88,183 lb)
Dimensions: length overall 12·80 m (42·00 ft) and hull 10·50 m (34·45 ft); width 3·50 m (11·48 ft); height 3·50 m (11·48 ft)
Armament system: one 203-mm (8-in) gun with an unrevealed number of ready-use rounds in a powered limited-traverse mounting; direct- and indirect-fire sights are fitted
Armour: welded steel
Powerplant: one 335-kW (449-hp) diesel engine with an unrevealed quantity of internal fuel
Performance: not revealed

Variant

2S7: this impressive item of equipment is probably the largest AFV in the Warsaw Pact's current inventory; the chassis appears to combine features of the SA-12 self-propelled SAM launcher and T-72 MBT, and has the massive but unprotected gun mounted at its rear with a powered loading system; it is unlikely that any more than two ready-use rounds are carried on the vehicle, which has the Soviet service designation **SO-203** and US designation **M1975**; the bulk of the equipment's ready-use ammunition supply is carried on an accompanying vehicle; the 2S7 has a large rear-mounted stabilizing spade, and its maximum rate of fire is probably two rounds per minute, the sustained rate being one round every two minutes; the weapon is deployed at front (army group) level, and the gun can be elevated to +60° to deliver projectiles (100-kg/220·5-lb conventional and 2/5-kiloton nuclear) to a maximum range of 30,000 m (32,810 yards)

Above right: The 2S7 is designed for very long-range fire, and thus has its powerful ordnance on an open mounting at the rear of the chassis.

Above, left and right: Very little is known of the 2S5 equipment, which is based on the chassis of the GMZ minelayer with an open mounting for its long-range ordnance.

Below: The ordnance of the 2S5 does not have a fume extractor, and the whole equipment is stabilized in firing position by a large rear-mounted spade that is lowered into the earth.

2S5 Giatsint self-propelled 152-mm gun

(USSR)

Type: tracked self-propelled gun
Crew: not revealed
Combat weight: not revealed
Dimensions: not revealed
Armament system: one 152·4-mm (6-in) gun with an unrevealed number of ready-use rounds and one 12·7-mm (0·5-in) NSV heavy machine-gun in a powered limited-traverse mounting; direct- and indirect-fire sights are fitted
Armour: welded steel varying in thickness betwen 7 and 14 mm (0·28 and 0·55 in)
Powerplant: one diesel engine of unrevealed power with an unrevealed quantity of internal fuel
Performance: not revealed

Variant

2S5: known in the West by the US designation **M1979**, this is a powerful equipment based on the chassis of the GMZ minelaying vehicle; the ordnance mounted at the rear of the hull is that of the 2A26 (M1976) towed howitzer, and is able to fire substantial rounds (2/5-kiloton tactical nuclear, chemical, concrete-piercing and HE) to a maximum range of 27,000 m (29,530 yards); the type can also fire an HE RAP type to a maximum range of about 37,000 m (40,465 yards); the type is known in Soviet service as the **Giatsint** (hyacinth)

2S3 Akatsiya 152-mm SP gun/howitzer

Above: The 2S3 uses the well proved chassis of the SA-4 'Ganef' self-propelled SAM system.

Below: The 2S1's chassis uses many MT-LB components, featuring full NBC protection.

(USSR)

Type: tracked self-propelled gun/howitzer
Crew: 6
Combat weight: 23,000 kg (50,705 lb)
Dimensions: length, gun forward 7·78 m (25·52 ft) and hull 7·14 m (23·43 ft); width 3·20 m (10·50 ft); height 2·72 m (8·92 ft)
Armament system: one 152·4-mm (6-in) modified D-20 gun/howitzer with 46 ready-use rounds and one 7·62-mm (0·3-in) AA machine-gun in a powered turret; direct- and indirect-fire sights are fitted
Armour: welded steel
Powerplant: one 390-kW (523-hp) diesel engine with 500 litres (110 Imp gal) of internal fuel
Performance: speed, road 55 km/h (34 mph); range, road 300 km (186 miles); fording 1·1 m (3·6 ft); gradient 60%; side slope 30%; trench 2·8 m (9·2 ft); ground clearance 0·45 m (17·7 in)

Variant

2S3: originally known in the West as the **M1973**, and possessing the Soviet service designation **SO-152** and name **Akatsiya** (acacia), this useful self-propelled gun/howitzer combines the well-tried D-20 ordnance in a neat turret on a chassis/automotive system combination based on that of the self-propelled launcher for the SA-4 'Ganef' SAM; the type has night vision devices and an NBC protection system, but is not amphibious; the turret traverses through 360°, and the L/34 ordnance can be elevated in an arc between −3° and +65°; ammunition types are HE-FRAG with a 43·5-kg (95·9-lb) projectile fired to a maximum range of 18,500 m (20,230 yards), HE RAP with a projectile fired to a maximum range of 24,000 m (26,245 yards), HEAT, AP-T, smoke, illuminating and nuclear with a sub-kiloton to 5-kiloton selectable yield; it is believed that an automatic loader may be fitted

2S1 Gvozdika 122-mm SP howitzer

(USSR)
Type: tracked self-propelled howitzer
Crew: 4
Combat weight: 16,000 kg (35,273 lb)
Dimensions: length overall 7·30 m (23·95 ft); width 2·85 m (9·35 ft); height 2·40 m (7·87 ft)
Armament system: one 122-mm (4·8-in) modified D-30 howitzer with 40 ready-use rounds in an electrically powered turret; direct- and indirect-fire sights are fitted
Armour: welded steel up to a maximum thickness of 20 mm (0·79 in)
Powerplant: one 180-kW (241-hp) YaMZ 238 V diesel engine with 550 litres (121 Imp gal) of internal fuel
Performance: speed, road 60 km/h (37·3 mph) and water 4·5 km/h (2·8 mph) driven by its tracks; range, road 500 km (311 miles); fording amphibious; gradient 60%; side slope 30%; vertical obstacle 1·1 m (43·3 in); trench 2·7 m (8·9 ft); ground clearance 0·46 m (18·1 in)

Variants

2S1: originally known in the West as the **M1974** and in Soviet service as the **SO-122** with the name **Gvozdika** (carnation), this vehicle uses a modified version of the D-30 ordnance in a new turret on a hull based on that of the MT-LB multi-role vehicle, at least in its chassis and automotive

system; the type is amphibious, and has night vision devices and an NBC protection system; the turret traverses through 360°, and the L/40 ordnance can be elevated in an arc between −3° and +70° ; the main ammunition types are HE-FRAG with a 21·72-kg (47·9-lb) projectile fired at a muzzle velocity of 690 m (2,264 ft) per second to a maximum range of 15,300 m (16,730 yards), HE RAP with a projectile fired to a maximum range of 21,900 m (23,950 yards), HEAT-FS with a 21·63-kg (47·7-lb) projectile fired at a muzzle velocity of 680 m (2,231 ft) per second to penetrate 460 mm (18·1 in) of armour at any range, smoke and illuminating
M1974-1 ACRV: artillery command and reconnaissance vehicle with a large superstructure and issued at battalion level; this is armed with a 12·7-mm (0·5-in) DShK heavy machine-gun; the crew is five and the combat weight 14,000 kg (30,864 lb)
M1974-2 ACRV: battery command model with a laser rangefinder
M1974-3 ACRV: battalion staff vehicle with additional communications gear
M1974 ACRV/'Big Fred': version fitted with 'Big Fred' artillery- and mortar-locating radar
M1979 MCV: mineclearing vehicle with a turret and three rockets for the discharge of explosive-filled hose

Below: the 2S9 was developed for use mainly by the Soviet army's airborne divisions.

2S9 self-propelled gun/ mortar

(USSR)
Type: tracked airborne forces assault self-propelled gun/mortar
Crew: 4
Combat weight: 9000 kg (19,841 lb)
Dimensions: length, gun forward 6·02 m (19·75 ft); width 2·63 m (8·63 ft); height 2·30 m (7·55 ft)
Armament system: one 120-mm (4·72-in) L/15 gun/mortar with 60 ready-use rounds in a powered turret; direct- and indirect-fire sights are fitted
Armour: welded steel varying in thickness between 7 and 16 mm (0·28 and 0·63 in)
Powerplant: one 225-kW (302-hp) Model 5D-20 diesel engine with an unrevealed quantity of internal fuel
Performance: speed, road 60 km/h (37·3 mph) and water 9 km/h (5·6 mph) driven by two water-jets; range, road 500 km (311 miles) and water 90 km (56 miles); fording amphibious; gradient 32°; side slope 18°; vertical obstacle 0·8 m (31·5 in); trench not revealed; ground clearance variable between 0·1 and 0·45 m (3·94 and 17·7 in)

Variant

2S9: also known in Soviet service terminology as the **SO-120**, this is an important new light support vehicle introduced in 1984 and based on the

lengthened chassis of the BMD-2 tracked carrier; the vehicle is designed to provide Soviet airborne formations with powerful direct and indirect fire support using a turret-mounted 120-mm (4·72-in) gun/mortar of hybrid type using a clip feed mechanism to generate a maximum rate of fire approaching 30 rounds per minute, the sustained rate being between 6 and 8 rounds per minute; there appears to be no physical limitation to 360° traverse for the turret, the apparent operational limitation to a total of 70° (35° left and 35° right of the centreline) probably reflecting stability problems with the light chassis; the weapon can be elevated in an arc between −4° and +80°, and is a useful multi-role type able to fire a HEAT projectile capable of penetrating some 600 mm (23·6 in) of conventional armour at any range; it can also fire indirectly to a range of perhaps 8800 m (9,625 yards) with projectiles such as HE, phosphorus and smoke

Vickers AS-90 155-mm SP howitzer

(UK)
Type: tracked self-propelled howitzer
Crew: 4
Combat weight: 79,365 lb (36,000 kg)
Dimensions: length, gun forward 31·82 ft (9·70 m) and hull 25·25 ft (7·70 m); width 10·82 ft (3·30 m); height overall 9·84 ft (3·00 m)

Armament system: one 155-mm (6·1-in) Royal Ordnance Nottingham howitzer with 40 ready-use rounds, and one 7·62-mm (0·3-in) L37A1 AA machine-gun with 400 rounds in an electrically powered turret; direct- and indirect-fire sights are fitted
Armour: welded steel to a maximum thickness of 17 mm (0·67 in)
Powerplant: one 660-hp (492-kW) Cummins VTA-903T diesel engine with 155 Imp gal (705 litres) of internal fuel
Performance: speed, road 34 mph (54·7 km/h); range, road 220 miles (354 km); fording 4·9 ft (1·5 m) without preparation; gradient 60%; side slope 30%; vertical obstacle 29·5 in (0·75 m); trench 9·85 ft (3·0 m); ground clearance 16 in (0·41 m)

Variant
AS-90: this equipment was selected in 1989 as the British army's replacement for the elderly and now undergunned Abbot; the AS-90 (Artillery System for the 1990s) was developed as a private venture by Vickers and the Brazilian company Verolme, the latter being responsible for the chassis, and amongst the many advanced features of the complete equipment are modest overall weight and dimensions, a high power-to-weight ratio for good performance and battlefield agility, an NBC protection system, night vision devices, and fully automatic fire capability as a result of the advanced fire-control and land navigation systems; the turret can be traversed

through 360°, and the L/39 ordnance can be elevated in an arc between −5° and +70°; the ordnance is an extremely capable one able to fire all types of NATO ammunition in this calibre, and the use of a flick rammer allows a burst rate of three rounds in 10 seconds, or six rounds per minute for a short period, or two rounds per minute indefinitely; the ready-use ammunition supply of 40 rounds is accommodated as 11 rounds in the hull and 29 rounds in the turret bustle, these latter being moved forward into line with the breech by two conveyors; power-assisted or automatic loading are available as options; with standard ammunition the ordnance can fire the HE-FRAG projectile to a maximum range of 27,000 yards (24,690 m) and the ERFB projectile to a maximum range of 35,000+ yards (32,005+ m)

Vickers FV433 Abbot 105-mm SP gun

(UK)
Type: tracked self-propelled gun
Crew: 4
Combat weight: 36,500 lb (16,556 kg)
Dimensions: length, gun forward 19·16 ft (5·84 m) and hull 18·07 ft (5·709 m); width 8·67 ft

Below: The Abbot is very reliable, but is thought to be undergunned for the modern battlefield.

(2·64 m); height without AA machine-gun 8·17 ft (2·18 m)

Armament system: one 105-mm (4·13-in) L13A1 gun with 40 ready-use rounds, one 7·62-mm (0·3-in) L4A4 AA machine-gun with 1,200 rounds, and three smoke-dischargers on each side of the powered turret; direct- and indirect-fire sights are fitted

Armour: welded steel varying in thickness between 6 and 12 mm (0·24 and 0·47 in)

Powerplant: one 240-hp (179-kW) Rolls-Royce K60 Mk 4G multi-fuel engine with 85 Imp gal (386 litres) of internal fuel

Performance: speed, road 29·5 mph (47·5 km/h) and water 3 mph (4·8 km/h) driven by its tracks; range, road 240 miles (386 km); fording 4·0 ft (1·22 m) without preparation and amphibious with preparation; gradient 60%; side slope 30%; vertical obstacle 24 in (0·61 m); trench 6·75 ft (2·06 m); ground clearance 16 in (0·41 m)

Variants

FV433 Abbot: this is a member of the FV430 series of AFVs, and uses many of the same automotive components as the FV432 armoured personnel carrier with consequent advantages in training, maintenance and spares holdings; the type entered service in 1964, and features night vision devices and NBC protection; the turret provides 360° traverse, and the comparatively small-calibre ordnance can be elevated between −5° and +70°; the ammunition types are HE with a 35·5-lb (16·1-kg) projectile fired to a maximum

range of 18,600 yards (17,010 m), HESH, smoke and illuminating; the maximum rate of fire is 12 rounds per minute (a rate aided by the provision of a powered rammer), and ammunition is brought up by the Alvis Stalwart 6 × 6 high-mobility truck

Value Engineered Abbot: export version bought by India, and differs in having no night vision or NBC gear, a generally reduced standard of equipment, no AA machine-gun and smoke-dischargers and a diesel-only 213-hp (159-kW) version of the K60 engine; this version weighs 35,050 lb (15,899 kg) and has slightly shorter lengths

---

Pacific Car and Foundry M110A2 8-in SP howitzer

(USA)

Type: tracked self-propelled howitzer
Crew: 5
Combat weight: 62,500 lb (28,350 kg)
Dimensions: length, gun forward 35·21 ft (10·73 m) and hull 18·75 ft (5·72 m); width 10·33 ft (3·149 m); height to top of barrel (travelling position) 10·31 ft (3·14 m)
Armament system: one 8-in (203-mm) M201 howitzer with 2 ready-use rounds in a hydraulically powered limited-traverse mounting; indirect-fire sights are fitted

Armour: welded steel
Powerplant: one 405-hp (302-kW) Detroit Diesel 8V-71T diesel engine with 260 US gal (984 litres) of internal fuel
Performance: speed, road 34 mph (54·7 km/h); range, road 325 miles (523 km); fording 3·5 ft (1·07 m); gradient 60%; side slope 30%; vertical obstacle 42 in (1·07 m); trench 6·25 ft (1·91 m); ground clearance 15·5 in (0·39 m)

Variants

M110: this initial model entered service in 1962, and as the type was conceived as a long-range delivery system for massive shells, no NBC protection system was fitted and the ordnance was mounted in an exposed position above the rear of the vehicle, only two ready-use rounds being carried; most of the 13-man crew is accommodated in the accompanying M548 support vehicle, which also carries most of the ready-use ammunition; the M2A2 ordnance has a short L/25 barrel producing an overall length of 24·50 ft (7·47 m) and a combat weight of 58,500 lb (26,536 kg), and the mounting over the rear of the hull provides total traverse of 60° (30° left and 30° right of the centreline) together with an elevation arc between −2° and +65°; a hydraulically powered loading and ramming system is fitted, and ammunition types include HE with a 204-lb (92·53-kg)

Below: Designed for long-range intervention on the battlefield, the M110 has its ordnance on an exposed rear mounting.

projectile fired at a muzzle velocity of 1,925 ft (587 m) per second to a maximum range of 18,400 yards (16,825 m), HE grenade-launching, chemical and nuclear (the M422 projectile with 0·5- or 10-kiloton W33 warhead); the standard rate of fire is one round in two minutes

M110A1: improved model introduced in 1977 with a longer-barreled L/37 M201 ordnance for greater propellant load and improved projectile range including the standard M106 HE projectile fired at a muzzle velocity of 2,333 ft (711 m) per second to a maximum range of 23,300 yards (21,305 m); in this model the fuel capacity was reduced from the 300 US gal (1137 litres) of the M110, thus reducing range, though the extra weight of the longer ordnance also adversely affected speed, trench-crossing capability and ground clearance, aspects in which the M110 equalled the M107

M110A2: definitive version of the M110A1 introduced in 1978 with a double-baffle muzzle brake; this variant fires the same rounds as the M110 together with an HE RAP projectile fired to a maximum range of 31,825 yards (29,100 m) and the M753 nuclear RAP with a 0·5-, 1- or 2-kiloton selectable yield W79-1 warhead fired to a maximum range of 31,825 yards (29,100 m)

M578: armoured recovery vehicle of the type, using the same chassis and automotive system but fitted with a winch and other specialized equipment

Pacific Car and Foundry M107 175-mm SP gun

(USA)

Type: tracked self-propelled gun
Crew: 5
Combat weight: 62,100 lb (28,169 kg)
Dimensions: length, gun forward 36·93 ft (11·26 m) and hull 18·75 ft (5·72 m); width 10·33 ft (3·15 m); height to top of barrel (travelling position) 12·07 ft (3·68 m)
Armament system: one 175-mm (6·89-in) M113 gun with 2 ready-use rounds in a hydraulically powered limited-traverse mounting; direct- and indirect-fire sights are fitted

Armour: welded steel

Powerplant: one 405-hp (302-kW) Detroit Diesel 8V-71T diesel engine with 300 US gal (1137 litres) of internal fuel

Performance: speed, road 35 mph (56 km/h); range, road 450 miles (724 km); fording 3·5 ft (1·07 m); gradient 60%; side slope 30%; vertical obstacle 42 in (1·07 m); trench 7·5 ft (2·3 m); ground clearance 18·3 in (0·47 m)

Variant

M107: this was designed as the partner for the M110 howitzer, and intended to deliver heavy fire over very long ranges; one of the main features of the system was the use of identical chassis and ordnance mounting, allowing the rapid change of the M107 into the M110 and vice versa, and the type entered service in 1962; the ordnance mounting over the rear of the hull provides for a total traverse of 60° (30° left and 30° right of the centreline), and the L/60 ordnance can be elevated in an arc between −2° and +65°, firing a 147·25-lb (66·8-kg) HE projectile at a muzzle velocity of 2,992 ft (912 m) per second to a maximum range of 35,750 yards (32,690 m); like the M110 the M107 is stabilized for firing by two rear-mounted spades, and normally fires at the rate of one round every two minutes, though one round per minute can be achieved for short periods thanks to the provision of a hydraulically powered loading and ramming system; the gun crew and the bulk of the ready-use ammunition are carried in an M548 support vehicle

Below: In firing position the M107 is stabilized by two hydraulically operated spades located at the rear of the chassis.

Cleveland Army Tank Plant/Bowen-McLaughlin-York M109A2 155-mm SP howitzer

(USA)
Type: tracked self-propelled howitzer

Crew: 6

Combat weight: 55,000 lb (24,948 kg)

Dimensions: length, gun forward 29·92 ft (9·12 m) and hull 20·31 ft (6·19 m); width 10·17 ft (3·10 m); height including machine-gun 10·75 ft (3·28 m)

Armament system: one 155-mm (6·1-in) M126 howitzer with 36 ready-use rounds, and one 0·5-in (12·7-mm) Browning M2HB AA heavy machine-gun with 500 rounds in a hydraulically powered turret; direct- and indirect-fire sights are fitted

Armour: welded aluminium

Powerplant: one 405-hp (302-kW) Detroit Diesel 8V-71T diesel engine with 135 US gal (511 litres) of internal fuel

Performance: speed, road 35 mph (56·3 km/h); range, road 215 miles (346 km); fording 3·25 ft (1·0 m); gradient 60%; side slope 40%; vertical obstacle 21 in (0·53 m); trench 6·0 ft (1·83 m); ground clearance 17·75 in (0·45 m)

Variants

M109: this type entered service late in 1962, and the series has since been built and developed extensively as successor to the M44 series with greater operational capabilities combined with better crew protection; the basic model weighs 44,200 lb (20,049 kg) and has IR driving lights but no NBC protection system; the fording capability is 6·0 ft (1·83 m) without preparation, though the addition of nine air bags gives the type a limited amphibious capability at a track-propelled water speed of 4 mph (6·4 km/h); the turret is fitted at the rear of the vehicle and provides 360° traverse, while the L/20 ordnance can be elevated in an arc between −3° and +75°; the vehicle is stabilized for firing by two rear-mounted spades, and the ammunition stowage amounts to 28 rounds; the ammunition types available include HE with a

M109A2 with armoured hood for optical fire-control equipment.

94·6-lb (42·9-kg) projectile fired at a muzzle velocity of 1,845 ft (562 m) per second to a maximum range of 16,000 yards (14,630 m), HE grenade- and mine-launching, HE RAP, illuminating, smoke, chemical, M454 nuclear (with a 0·1/1-kiloton W48 warhead) and laser-guided Copperhead (two of these 22,000-yard/20,115-m ranged cannon-launched guided projectiles generally being carried in place of other rounds); the standard rate of fire is one round per minute, though three rounds per minute can be achieved

M109A1: improved M109 with longer L/33 M185 ordnance and new charge system extending HE range to 19,800 yards (18,105 m) at a muzzle velocity of 2,245 ft (684 m) per second, and RAP range to 26,250 yards (24,005 m); the type was produced by M109 conversion, and entered service in 1973; the variant weighs 53,065 lb (24,070 kg) and has an overall length of 29·67 ft (9·04 m)

M109A2: having entered service in 1979, this is the definitive M109 model based on the M109A2 but with many detail improvements over earlier types and a turret bustle for greater ammunition capacity; the version proposed for Thailand by BMY and Rheinmetall is the **M109A2T** with a new ordnance combining features of the FH-170 and M198 to provide a range of 24,700 m (27,000 yards) with the standard projectile and 30,000 m (32,810 yards) with the base-bleed projectile

M109A3: earlier vehicles brought up to M109A2 standard

M109A4: earlier vehicles upgraded in the Howitzer Extended Life Program (HELP) with the RAM-D (Reliability, Availability, Maintainability - Durability) package, improved battlefield survivability features and the addition of an NBC protection system

M109A5: M109A1 and M109A2 vehicles upgraded from the late 1980s onwards in the Howitzer Improvement Program (HIP) with the RAM-D package of reliability developments, plus

extended range, an automatic fire-extinguishing system, an aluminium/Kevlar turret, a full-width turret bustle with storage for 36 charges, an ordnance loading-assist device, and an improved fire-control system (including an onboard ballistic computer and inertial reference system); the nature of the ordnance is as yet uncertain, the choice still lying between the current M185 or a new ordnance with an L/39 or L/53 barrel for significantly improved range; the type is capable of firing a new nuclear round with a W82 warhead

M109A6: under development as a joint Israeli-American programme based on the M109A5, this variant offers the ability to engage targets at a range of 33,000 yards (30,175 m) and to fire the first aimed round within 30 seconds of the vehicle coming to a halt; the type has a Honeywell computerized fire-control system

M109AL: Israeli M109A1 version with stowage racks to permit the external carriage of personal kit, so boosting internal ammunition capacity

M109G: West German version of the M109 with a revised breech boosting range to 18,500 m (20,230 yards) with the standard HE projectile, a new muzzle brake, tracks with features of the Leopard 1's tracks and a 7·62-mm (0·3-in) MG3 AA machine-gun; the type also has three smoke-dischargers on each side of the turret, and German fire-control equipment; existing equipments are being upgraded to **M109A3G** standard with a new L/39 ordnance based on that of the FH-70 towed howitzer; this allows the full range of FH-70 and NATO projectiles to be fired, the standard HE type reaching a maximum range of 24,700 m (27,010 yards) and the base-bleed HE type attaining 30,000 m (32,810 yards); the new ordnance can also fire the latest types of carrier projectiles; the ordnance is supplied from a new projectile magazine in the turret bustle; this has outward-opening doors for reloading purposes, and accommodates 22 projectiles for a vehicle total of 34

M109L: Italian M109 version carrying an OTO Melara L/39 ordnance with a double-baffle muzzle brake (essentially that of the ordnance used in the M109G) and fume extractor, able to fire the ammunition range of the FH-70 howitzer to ranges of between 24,000 m (26,245 yards) with standard projectiles and 30,000 m (32,810 yards) with RAPs; other modifications are an armoured hood for the roof-mounted sight, and a revised bustle to allow the carriage of extra ammunition

M109U: Swiss version, the original **Panzerhaubitze 66** type being the M109, which was followed by the **Panzerhaubitze 74** (M109A1) and **Panzerhaubitze 66/74** (Pzh 66 upgraded to Pzh 74 standard); these Swiss vehicles have a revised electrical system and a loading system that operates at all angles of ordnance elevation

M109 (Netherlands): the Dutch army uses a number of turretless M109s for driver training

M109 (Norway): the Norwegian army's fleet of M109 self-propelled howitzers is to be upgraded by Norsk Forsvarateknologi with a new L/37 ordnance (supplied by Rheinmetall) and other modifications to improve battlefield capability

M109 (Taiwan): under the local designation **XT-69**, Taiwan has combined the chassis and automotive system of the M109 with an exposed mounting for an ordnance derived from the US 155-mm M114 towed howitzer but fitted with a multi-baffle muzzle brake; the crew is five, and it is believed that some 25 rounds of ammunition are carried, the ordnance having a maximum range of some 15,000 m (16,405 yards)

M992: field artillery ammunition support vehicle derived from the M109 with a large superstructure in place of the turret; in this superstructure is an extending conveyor system for the movement of 155-mm (6·1-in) ammunition, stowage amounting to 93 projectiles, 99 propellant charges and 104 fuses; the type can also be used for 175- and 203-mm (6·89- and 8-in) ammunition, stowage of the latter being 98 projectiles, 53 charges and 56 fuses; it has also been proposed that the M992 be used as the basis of a whole family of self-propelled artillery support vehicles including fire-direction centre, command post, ambulance, rearmament, and maintenance assistance vehicles

Massey Harris M44A1 155-mm SP howitzer

(USA)

Type: tracked self-propelled howitzer
Crew: 5
Combat weight: 64,000 lb (29,030 kg)
Dimensions: length 20·21 ft (6·16 m); width 10·62 ft (3·24 m); height over tarpaulin cover 10·20 ft (3·11 m)
Armament system: one 155-mm (6·1-in) M45 howitzer with 24 ready-use rounds, and one 0·5-in (12·7-mm) Browning M2HB AA heavy machine-gun with 900 rounds in a manually powered limited-traverse mounting; direct- and indirect-fire sights are fitted
Armour: welded steel to a standard thickness of 0·5 in (12·7 mm)
Powerplant: one 500-hp (373-kW) Continental AOSI-895-5 petrol engine with 150 US gal (568 litres) of internal fuel
Performance: speed, road 35 mph (56·3 km/h); range, road 82 miles (132 km); fording 3·5 ft (1·07 m); gradient 60%; vertical obstacle 30 in (0·76 m); trench 6·0 ft (1·83 m); ground clearance 19 in (0·48 m)

Variants

M44A1: this weapon uses the same basic chassis and automotive system as the 105-mm (4·13-in) M52, which are very similar to those of the M41 light tank; this was the last US self-propelled artillery equipment with an open-topped fighting compartment; the original **M44** had a normally aspirated engine, but was replaced in the mid-1950s by the M44A1 with a fuel-injected engine; the turret has a total traverse of 60° (30° left and 30° right of the centreline) and the L/20 ordnance can be elevated in an arc between −5° and +65°; the ammunition types are HE, HE grenade-launching, smoke, illuminating and chemical, and maximum range with the 94·6-lb (42·9-kg) HE projectile is 16,000 yards (14,630 m); the normal rate of fire is one round per minute with the vehicle stabilized by two rear-mounted spades

Rheinmetall M44: West German upgrade of the original weapon; the revised vehicle is powered by a 335-kW (450-hp) MTU 883 Aa diesel for a range of 600 km (373 miles), and has many detail modifications; the main armament is a Rheinmetall 155-mm (6·1-in) L/39 howitzer based on the FH-70 ordnance, and the mounting allows ordnance elevation in an arc between −5° and +65°; 30 rounds of ammunition can be carried, and maximum projectile ranges are 24,000 m (26,245 yards) with standard ammunition, and 30,000 m (32,810 yards) with extended-range ammunition

Cadillac (General Motors) M108 105-mm SP howitzer

(USA)

Type: tracked self-propelled howitzer
Crew: 5
Combat weight: 49,500 lb (22,453 kg)
Dimensions: length 20·06 ft (6·11 m); width 10·81 ft (3·295 m); height including machine-gun 10·35 ft (3·155 m)
Armament system: one 105-mm (4·13-in) M103 howitzer with 87 ready-use rounds, and one 0·5-in (12·7-mm) Browning M2HB AA heavy machine-gun with 500 rounds in a manually powered turret; direct- and indirect-fire sights are fitted
Armour: welded aluminium
Powerplant: one 405-hp (302-kW) Detroit Diesel 8V-71T diesel engine with 135 US gal (511 litres) of internal fuel
Performance: speed, road 35 mph (56·3 km/h) and water 4 mph (6·4 km/h) driven by its tracks; range, road 240 miles (386 km); fording 6·0 ft (1·83 m) without preparation and amphibious with preparation; gradient 60%; vertical obstacle 21 in (0·53 m); trench 6·0 ft (1·83 m); ground clearance 17·75 in (0·45 m)

Variant

M108: introduced in 1964, the M108 shares a common chassis and automotive system with the M109 155-mm (6·1-in) self-propelled howitzer, and like that vehicle can be fitted with flotation bags to provide a measure of amphibious capability; the type lacks an NBC protection system, but has IR driving lights; the turret traverses through 360°, and the ordnance can be elevated in an arc between −4° and +74°; the ammunition types available are HE, HE grenade-launching, illuminating, smoke and chemical, and typical performance includes a maximum range of 12,600 yards (11,520 m) with an HE round that weighs 39·9 lb (18·1 kg) complete

Detroit Arsenal M52A1 105-mm SP howitzer

(USA)

Type: tracked self-propelled howitzer
Crew: 5
Combat weight: 53,000 lb (24,041 kg)
Dimensions: length 19·00 ft (5·80 m); width 10·33 ft (3·15 m); height including machine-gun 10·88 ft (3·32 m)
Armament system: one 105-mm (4·13-in) M49 howitzer with 102 ready-use rounds, and one 0·5-in (12·7-mm) Browning M2HB AA heavy machine-gun with 900 rounds in a manually powered turret; direct- and indirect-fire sights are fitted
Armour: welded steel to a standard thickness of 0·5 in (12·7 mm)
Powerplant: one 500-hp (373-kW) Continental AOSI-895-5 petrol engine with 180 US gal (681 litres) of internal fuel
Performance: speed, road 42 mph (67·6 km/h); range, road 100 miles (161 km); fording 4·0 ft (1·22 m); gradient 60%; vertical obstacle 36 in (0·91 m); trench 6·0 ft (1·83 m); ground clearance 19·33 in (0·49 m)

Variant

M52A1: this is the 105-mm (4·13-in) equivalent of the 155-mm (6·1-in) M44, introduced in 1954 and possessing the same basic characteristics as the M44 apart from its different primary armament and associated ammunition in a turret capable of 360° traverse; the ordnance can be elevated in an arc between −10° and +65°, and the ammunition types include HE with a projectile fired to a maximum range of 12,325 yards (11,270 m), HEAT, HE grenade-launching, smoke, illuminating and chemical; the original normally aspirated AOS-895-3 engine of the **M52** was soon supplanted by the fuel-injected AOSI-895-5; this version has no need of rear-mounted spades

American Locomotive/ Federal Machine/Pressed Steel Car M7 Priest 105-mm SP howitzer

(USA)

Type: tracked self-propelled howitzer
Crew: 7
Combat weight: 50,634 lb (22,967 kg)
Dimensions: length 19·75 ft (6·02 m); width 9·42 ft (2·87 m); height 9·58 ft (2·92 m)
Armament system: one 105-mm (4·13-in) M1A2 howitzer with 69 ready-use rounds, and one 0·5-in (12·7-mm) Browning M2HB AA heavy machine-gun with 300 rounds in a manually powered limited-traverse mounting; direct- and indirect-fire sights are fitted
Armour: cast and welded steel varying in thickness between 0·5 and 4·5 in (12·7 and 114·3 mm)
Powerplant: one 340-hp (254-kW) Continental R-975-C1 petrol engine with 179 US gal (678 litres) of internal fuel
Performance: speed, road 26 mph (42 km/h); range, road 125 miles (201 km); fording 4·0 ft (1·22 m); gradient 60%; vertical obstacle 24 in (0·61 m); trench 7·5 ft (2·3 m); ground clearance 17·1 in (0·43 m)

Variants

M7: introduced in 1942 on the basis of the M3

medium tank with an M1A2 howitzer, the M7 series found immediate favour as a reliable and hard-hitting front-line support weapon; the howitzer is located at the front of the fighting compartment, can be traversed through a total of 38° (12° left and 26° right of the centreline) and can be elevated in an arc between −5° and +33°, firing the standard 33-lb (14·97-kg) HE projectile to a maximum range of 12,000 yards (10,975 m)

M7B1: later production standard based on the chassis of the M4A3 medium tank with the 500-hp (373-kW) Ford GAA engine and fitted with the improved M2 howitzer

M7B2: refined version of the M7B1 with higher 'pulpit' for the AA machine-gun

CITEFA Model 77 155-mm howitzer

(Argentina)
Type: towed howitzer
Calibre: 155 mm (6·1 in)
Barrel length: 33 calibres
Muzzle brake: double-baffle type
Carriage: split-trail type with two road wheels and two castors; no shield
Weight: 8000 kg (17,637 lb) in travelling order
Dimensions: length 10·15 m (33·30 ft); width 2·67 m (8·76 ft); height 2·2 m (7·22 ft)
Traverse/elevation: 70° total/0° to +67°
Rate of fire: 1 round per minute (normal) and 4 rounds per minute (maximum)
Maximum range: 22,000 m (24,060 yards) with standard round and 25,300 m (27,670 yards) with RAP
Crew: not revealed

Variants
Model 77: this is the ordnance of the French Mk F3 self-propelled howitzer mounted on a bottom carriage of Argentine design and manufacture; the type fires separate-loading HE, HE RAP, smoke and illuminating rounds, the HE projectile weighing 43 kg (94·8 lb) and having a muzzle velocity of 765 m (2,510 ft) per second
Model 81: updated version with Argentine-built ordnance and detail modifications

NORICUM GH N-45 155-mm gun/howitzer

(Austria)
Type: towed gun/howitzer
Calibre: 155 mm (6·1 in)
Barrel length: 45 calibres
Muzzle brake: multi-baffle type
Carriage: split-trail type with four road wheels and two castors; no shield
Weight: 10,070 kg (22,200 lb) in travelling and firing orders
Dimensions: length, travelling with muzzle forward 13·97 m (45·83 ft) and with muzzle to rear 9·72 m (31·89 ft), and firing 11·40 m (37·40 ft); width, travelling 2·50 m (8·20 ft) and firing 9·931 m (32·58 ft); height, travelling 2·05 m (6·73 ft)
Traverse/elevation: 70° total (30° left and 40° right of the centreline)/−5° to +69°
Rate of fire: 3 rounds in 16 seconds (burst), 2 rounds per minute (normal), and 7 rounds per minute (maximum)
Maximum range: 30,300 m (33,135 yards) with normal round and 39,600 m (43,305 yards) with base-bleed round
Crew: 6

Variant
GHN-45: developed by Voerst-Alpine in Austria and marketed by NORICUM, this is an improved GC 45 with features designed to ease manufacture and to aid field reliability and handling; the most important modification is the optional addition of an auxiliary power unit for battlefield mobility; the APU is a 90-kW (121-hp) Porsche unit with 60 litres (13·2 Imp gal) of fuel, permitting a maximum speed of 30 km/h (18·6 mph) and a range of 150 km (93 miles) in an equipment weighing 12,382 kg (27,297 lb); the dimensions are also slightly different, with a travelling width of 2·75 m (9·02 ft); the barrel has a semi-automatic breech with a pneumatically operated rammer, and optional features on the powered version are a powered traverse and elevation system, a six-round ammunition bracket, and ammunition-handling device and tracks to increase the traction of the wheels

NORICUM ATG N 105 105-mm anti-tank gun

(Austria)
Type: towed anti-tank gun
Calibre: 105 mm (4·13 in)
Barrel length: 56·1 calibres
Muzzle brake: none
Carriage: split-trail type with two road wheels; shield
Weight: 3600 kg (7,937 lb) in travelling and firing orders
Dimensions: length, travelling with muzzle over trails 7·20 m (23·62 ft) and in firing position 9·50 m (31·17 ft); width, travelling 2·50 m (8·20 ft) and firing 4·90 m (16·08 ft); height, travelling not revealed
Traverse/elevation: not revealed
Rate of fire: not revealed
Maximum range: not revealed
Crew: not revealed

Variant
ATG N 105: this equipment was developed initially as a mobile trials mount for NORICUM's LRN 105 long-recoil tank gun using the range of ammunition developed for the L7/M68 series of rifled tank guns, and was then evolved into a production version for countries wishing a potent anti-tank gun; details are still sparse, but the equipment is of standard configuration with an ordnance that can be turned through 180° to lie of the trail legs while being towed; the type can also fire a special NP 105 A2 APDSFS round whose projectile weighs 19·3 kg (42·55 lb) and, leaving the muzzle at 1485 m (4,872 ft) per second, can penetrate 150 mm (5·91 in) of armour inclined at 60° at a range of 5800 m (6,345 yards)

SRC International GC 45 155-mm gun/howitzer

(Belgium)
Type: towed gun/howitzer
Calibre: 155 mm (6·1 in)
Barrel length: 45 calibres
Muzzle brake: multi-baffle type
Carriage: split-trail type with four road wheels and two castors; no shield
Weight: 8222 kg (18,126 lb) in travelling and firing orders

Dimensions: length, travelling with muzzle to rear 13·614 m (44·67 ft), travelling with muzzle over trails 9·144 m (30·00 ft) and firing 10·82 m (35·50 ft); width, travelling 2·692 m (8·83 ft) and firing 10·364 m (34·00 ft); height, travelling 3·28 m (10·75 ft)
Traverse/elevation: 80° total/−5° to +69°
Rate of fire: 4 rounds per minute (burst rate for 15 minutes) and 2 rounds per minute (normal)
Maximum range: 30,000 m (32,810 yards) with normal round and 38,000 m (41,560 yards) with base-bleed round
Crew: 8

Variant
GC 45: designed in Belgium and Canada by PRB and the Space Research Corporation, the GC 45 is an advanced weapon designed to fire separate-loading ammunition (including all standard NATO 155-mm/6·1-in ammunition types) and fitted with an automatic breech and pneumatic rammer; the type is notable for the fact that its extended-range full-bore projectile reaches 30,000 m (32,810 yards) without rocket assistance; the ERFB Mk 10 projectile weighs 45·4 kg (100 lb), contains 8·8 kg (19·4 lb) of HE and has a maximum muzzle velocity of 897 m (2,943 ft) per second

MECAR KEnerga 90/46 90-mm anti-tank gun

(Belgium)
Type: towed anti-tank gun
Calibre: 90 mm (3·54 in)
Barrel length: 46 calibres
Muzzle brake: double-baffle type
Carriage: split-trail type with two road wheels; optional shield
Weight: 1000 kg (2,205 lb) in travelling and firing orders
Dimensions: not revealed
Traverse/elevation: 54° total/not revealed
Rate of fire: 10 rounds per minute (maximum) and 7 rounds per minute (normal)
Maximum range: not revealed
Crew: 3-4

Variant
KEnerga 90/46: this is a simple development of the KEnerga low recoil force rifled gun designed for use in light AFVs; the ordnance can fire nine types of fixed ammunition including APDSFS, HEAT (three varieties including one practice), HE, HESH, smoke (two varieties) and canister; the 2·73-kg (6·02-lb) projectile of the M603 APDSFS round leaves the muzzle at 1430 m (4,692 ft) per second and can penetrate the NATO standard target armour at a range of 2000 m (2,185 yards), the 4·085-kg (9·01-lb) projectile of the M644 HV-HEAT round leaves the muzzle at 1020 m (3,346 ft) per second and can penetrate the NATO standard target armour at a range of 1200 m (1,315 yards), and the 5·1-kg (11·24-lb) projectile of the M656 HESH round leaves the muzzle at 800 m (2,625 ft) per second; the M629 canister round releases 1,100 lead balls with a muzzle velocity of 775 m (2,543 ft) per second

MECAR Field Mount 90-mm anti-tank gun

(Belgium)
Type: towed anti-tank gun

Calibre: 90 mm (3·54 in)
Barrel length: 32·2 calibres
Muzzle brake: none
Carriage: three-leg (tripod) type with two road wheels; shield
Weight: 880 kg (1,940 lb) in travelling and firing orders
Dimensions: length, travelling 3·50 m (11·48 ft); width, travelling 1·25 m (4·10 ft); height, travelling 1·36 m (4·46 ft)
Traverse/elevation: 360° total/ − 10° to + 12°
Rate of fire: 18 rounds per minute (maximum) and 10 rounds per minute (normal)
Maximum range: see Variant (below)
Crew: 3-4

Variant
Field Mount: this is the MECAR 90-mm (3·54-in) anti-tank gun that was designed for installation in light armoured vehicles but, in this application, fitted on a towed carriage with twin road wheels that lift to allow the folding tripod legs to be opened out for 360° traverse; the fixed ammunition options are HEAT-CAN-90 anti-tank (a 2·44-kg/5·4-lb projectile with a muzzle velocity of 633 m/2,077 ft per second and the ability to defeat 375 mm/14·76 in of armour at 1000 m/1,095 yards), HE-CAN-90 anti-personnel (4-kg/8·8-lb projectile with a muzzle velocity of 338 m/1,109 ft per second and a range of 3000 m/3,280 yards), CNT-CAN-90 canister (effective range 250 m/275 yards), and smoke

NORINCO Type WAC 21 155-mm gun/howitzer

(China)
Type: towed gun/howitzer
Calibre: 155 mm (6·1 in)
Barrel length: 45 calibres
Muzzle brake: multi-baffle type
Carriage: split-trail type with four road wheels and two castors; no shield
Weight: 9700 kg (21,384 lb) in travelling and firing orders

Dimensions: length, travelling with muzzle forward 13·512 m (44·33 ft) and with muzzle to rear 9·068 m (29·75 ft), and firing 11·40 m (37·40 ft); width, travelling 2·67 m (8·76 ft) and firing 9·931 m (32·58 ft); height, travelling with muzzle forward 3·048 m (10·00 ft) and with muzzle to rear 2·23 m (7·32 ft)
Traverse/elevation: 70° total (30° left and 40° right of the centreline)/ − 5° to + 72°
Rate of fire: 4-5 rounds per minute (maximum) and 2 rounds per minute (normal)
Maximum range: 30,000 m (32,810 yards) with normal round and 39,000 m (42,650 yards) with base-bleed round
Crew: 6

Variant
Type WAC 21: this appears to be a Chinese development of the GH N-45, and the two types are so similar that the ordnance of the Austrian weapon can be accommodated without change on the Chinese carriage; the type has a flick rammer, and it is believed than an auxiliary power unit can be installed to provide modest battlefield mobility without a towing vehicle

NORINCO Type 83 152-mm gun

(China)
Type: towed gun
Calibre: 152 mm (6 in)
Barrel length: about 45 calibres
Muzzle brake: single-baffle type
Carriage: split-trail type with four road wheels (including a two-wheel limber) and two castors; shield
Weights: 10,500 kg (23,148 lb) in travelling order and 9700 kg (21,384 lb) in firing position
Dimensions: length, travelling 9·40 m (30·84 ft); width, travelling 2·67 m (8·76 ft); height, travelling 1·865 m (6·12 ft)
Traverse/elevation: 50° total (24° left and 26° right of the centreline)/ − 2° to + 45°
Rate of fire: 3-4 rounds per minute (normal)
Maximum range: 30,370 m (33,215 yards)
Crew: not revealed

Variant
Type 83: comparatively little is known of this thor-

oughly orthodox equipment, which apparently uses the carriage of the Type 66 152-mm (6-in) gun/howitzer; the ordnance fires a 48-kg (105·8-lb) HE projectile with a muzzle velocity of 955 m (3,133 ft) per second

NORINCO Type 66 152-mm gun/howitzer

(China)
Type: towed gun/howitzer
Calibre: 152 mm (6 in)
Barrel length: about 34 calibres
Muzzle brake: double-baffle type
Carriage: split-trail type with two road wheels and two castors; optional shield
Weight: 5720 kg (12,610 lb) in travelling and in firing orders
Dimensions: length, travelling 8·69 m (28·51 ft); width, travelling 2·42 m (7·94 ft); height, travelling 2·52 m (8·27 ft)
Traverse/elevation: 58° total/ − 5° to + 45°
Rate of fire: 6-8 rounds per minute (normal)
Maximum range: 17,230 m (18,845 yards)
Crew: 10-12

Variant
Type 66: this is the Chinese version of the Soviet D-20 equipment, and is notable for its light weight, comparatively large crew and, for its calibre, relatively short range; the ordnance uses a variable six-charge propellant system, and can attain its maximum normal range with the 43·56-kg (96-lb) HE and smoke projectiles; the type can also fire a RAP of the same weight, range with this projectile being 21,880 m (23,930 yards) without any loss of accuracy

NORINCO Type 59-1 130-mm gun

(China)
Type: towed gun
Calibre: 130 mm (5·12 in)
Barrel length: about 58·5 calibres
Muzzle brake: double-baffle type
Carriage: split-trail type with two road wheels and two castors; shield

Above: The Type 59-1 in firing position. Note the raised castors on the spread trail legs.

Weight: 6300 kg (13,889 lb) in travelling and firing orders
Dimensions: length, travelling 10·80 m (35·43 ft); width, travelling 2·42 m (7·94 ft); height, travelling 2·75 m (9·02 ft)
Traverse/elevation: 58° total/−2·5° to +45°
Rate of fire: 8-10 rounds per minute (normal)
Maximum range: 27,490 m (30,065 yards) with normal round, 32,000 m (34,995 yards) with base-bleed round, and 34,260 m (37,575 yards) with RAP
Crew: 8-10

Variants
Type 59: this is the Chinese copy of the Soviet M-46 equipment, and differs from the Soviet original in no significant details
Type 59-1: simple combination of the Type 59 with features of the Type 60 (Chinese copy of the Soviet D-74) to produce an equipment that is handier than the Type 59; the Type 59-1 uses a scaled-up version of the Type 60's muzzle brake, recoil system and breech on a carriage with a number of Type 60 features; in combination with a lighter shield this produces an equipment that is usefully lighter and has the additional advantage of not requiring the Type 59's two-wheel limber; the Type 59-1 fires a 33·4-kg (73·6-lb) HE projectile with a muzzle velocity of 930 m (3,051 ft) per minute, a RAP of the same weight, a 32·4-kg (71·45-lb) RAP, and an illuminating projectile

Right: The Type 54-1 is the Type 54 adapted for ease of manufacture in Chinese factories.

NORINCO Type 54-1 122-mm howitzer

(China)
Type: towed howitzer
Calibre: 121·92 mm (4·8 in)
Barrel length: about 23 calibres

Muzzle brake: none
Carriage: split-trail type with two road wheels; shield
Weight: 2500 kg (5,511 lb) in travelling and firing orders
Dimensions: length, travelling 5·90 m (19·36 ft); width, travelling 1·975 m (6·48 ft); height, travelling 1·82 m (5·97 ft)

Traverse/elevation: 49° total/−3° to +60·5°
Rate of fire: 5-6 rounds per minute (normal)
Maximum range: 11,800 m (12,905 yards)
Crew: 8

Variants

Type 54: this is the Chinese copy of the Soviet M-30 (Model 1938) equipment, and differs from the Soviet original in no significant details
Type 54-1: development of the baseline Type 54 equipment with modifications to suit Chinese industrial practices; the ordnance uses a variable nine-charge propellant system; the 21·76-kg (47·97-lb) HE projectile is fired with a muzzle velocity of 515 m (1,690 ft) per second, and the other projectile types available are smoke, illuminating, incendiary and leaflet

---

NORINCO Type 59 100-mm gun

(China)
Type: towed gun
Calibre: 100 mm (3·94 in)
Barrel length: 92 calibres
Muzzle brake: double-baffle type
Carriage: split-trail type with two double road wheels; shield
Weight: about 3450 kg (7,606 lb) in travelling and firing orders
Dimensions: length, travelling 9·37 m (30·74 ft); width, travelling 2·15 m (7·03 ft); height, travelling 1·50 m (4·92 ft)
Traverse/elevation: about 50° total/−5° to +45°
Rate of fire: 7 rounds per minute
Maximum range: maximum 20,000 m (21,720 yards)
Crew: 6

Variants

Type 59: the designation of this equipment remains unconfirmed, but not in doubt is the type's derivation quite closely from the Soviet BS-3 (Model 1944) weapon, which is still a useful dual-role counter-battery and heavy anti-tank gun; the ordnance can fire a 15·6-kg (34·4-lb) FRAG-HE round in the counter-battery role, or an AP-T in the anti-tank role; the AP-T projectile can penetrate 170 mm (6·7 in) of armour at 500 m (545 yards), declining to 157 mm (6·18 in) at 1000 m (1,095 yards)
Abu Zabal Engineering Industries Type 59: Egyptian version of the Type 59 with no significant alterations from the Chinese norm

---

NORINCO Type 86 100-mm anti-tank gun

(China)
Type: towed anti-tank gun
Calibre: 100 mm (3·94 in)
Barrel length: not revealed
Muzzle brake: multi-baffle
Carriage: split-trail type with two road wheels; shield
Weight: 3660 kg (8,069 lb) in travelling and firing orders
Dimensions: length, travelling 9·52 m (31·23 ft); width, travelling 2·12 m (9·96 ft); height, travelling 1·838 m (6·03 ft)
Traverse/elevation: 50° total /−4° to +38°
Rate of fire: 8-10 rounds per minute
Maximum range: 13,650 m (14,930 yards)
Crew: not revealed

Variant

Type 86: introduced in 1987, this is a simple yet effective anti-tank gun, apparently based on the combination of a new smooth-bore ordnance on the carriage of the Type 56 field gun; the weapon is designed primarily for the direct-fire role, but indirect-fire sights are fitted for fire to a maximum range limited by the equipment's low maximum elevation; the type can also be fitted with a night vision device; no details of the ammunition have yet been revealed; the Type 86 can be towed at up to 50 km/h (31·1 mph)

NORINCO Type 56 85-mm gun

(China)
Type: towed gun
Calibre: 85 mm (3·35 in)
Barrel length: 55·2 calibres
Muzzle brake: double-baffle type
Carriage: split-trail type with two road wheels and (on some equipments) one castor; shield
Weight: 1750 kg (3,858 lb) in travelling order
Dimensions: length, travelling 8·34 m (27·36 ft); width, travelling 1·73 m (5·68 ft); height, travelling 1·42 m (4·66 ft)
Traverse/elevation: 54° total/−7° to +35°
Rate of fire: 15-20 rounds per minute
Maximum range: 15,650 m (17,115 yards)
Crew: 6-8

Variant

Type 56: this is essentially the Soviet D-44 gun built with slight modification in China; the ordnance can fire HE, HEAT and HESH rounds, and is thus used mainly as a support and anti-tank weapon; the HEAT projectile weighs 7 kg (15·43 lb), and at a range of 970 m (1,060 yards) can penetrate 100 mm (3·94 in) of armour inclined at 65°

Right and below: The Type 53 is an unexceptional equipment optimized for the dual anti-tank and field gun roles.

M53 100-mm field and anti-tank gun

(Czechoslovakia)
Type: towed field and anti-tank gun
Calibre: 100 mm (3·94 in)
Barrel length: 67·35 calibres (including muzzle brake)
Muzzle brake: double-baffle type
Carriage: split-trail type with two road wheels and two castors; shield
Weights: 4280 kg (9,436 lb) in travelling order and 4210 kg (9,281 lb) in firing position
Dimensions: length, travelling 9·10 m (29·86 ft); width, travelling 2·36 m (7·74 ft); height, travelling 2·606 m (8·55 ft)
Traverse/elevation: 60° total/−6° to +42°
Rate of fire: 8-10 rounds per minute
Maximum range: 21,000 m (22,965 yards)
Crew: 6

Variant

M53: introduced in the early 1950s, the M53 is a dual-purpose field and anti-tank gun firing fixed ammunition, including a 16-kg (35·3-lb) APC-T projectile at 1000 m (3,281 ft) per second to penetrate 185 mm (7·28 in) of armour at 1000 m (1,095 yards), a 12·36-kg (27·25-lb) HEAT-FS projectile at 900 m (2,953 ft) per second to penetrate 380 mm (14·96 in) of armour at any range, a 5·69-kg (12·54-lb) HVAPDS-T projectile at 1415 m (4,642 ft) per second to penetrate 200 mm (7·87 in) of armour at 1000 m (1,095 yards), and a 15·59-kg (34·37-lb) FRAG-HE projectile at 900 m (2,953 ft) per second

M52/55 85-mm field and anti-tank gun

(Czechoslovakia)
Type: towed field and anti-tank gun
Calibre: 85 mm (3·35 in)
Barrel length: 59·65 calibres
Muzzle brake: double-baffle type
Carriage: split-trail type with two road wheels; shield
Weights: 2168 kg (4,780 lb) in travelling order and 2111 kg (4,654 lb) in firing position
Dimensions: length, travelling 7·52 m (24·67 ft); width, travelling 1·98 m (6·50 ft); height, travelling 1·515 m (4·97 ft)
Traverse/elevation: 60° total/−6° to +38°
Rate of fire: 20 rounds per minute
Maximum range: 16,160 m (17,675 yards)
Crew: 7

Variants

M52: introduced in 1952, this is a dual-purpose field and anti-tank gun, and among the fixed ammunition types available are AP-T (a 9·2-kg/20·28-lb projectile with a muzzle velocity of 820 m/2,690 ft per second to penetrate 123 mm/4·84 in of armour at 1000 m/1,095 yards), HEAT-FS, HVAP-T and HE
M52/55: improved model of 1955 with the slightly greater weights of 2168 kg (4,780 lb) in travelling order and 2111 kg (4,654 lb) in firing position

Tampella M-74 155-mm gun/howitzer

(Finland)
Type: towed gun/howitzer
Calibre: 155 mm (6·1 in)
Barrel length: 38·65 calibres
Muzzle brake: single-baffle type
Carriage: split-trail type with four road wheels; no shield
Weight: 9500 kg (20,944 lb) in travelling and firing orders
Dimensions: length, travelling 7·50 m (24·61 ft); width, travelling 2·58 m (8·46 ft); height, travelling 21·0 m (6·56 ft)
Traverse/elevation: 90° total/−5° to +52°
Rate of fire: 4 rounds per minute (bursts) and 2 rounds per minute (normal)
Maximum range: 24,000 m (26,245 yards) with normal round and 30,000 m (32,810 yards) with base-bleed round
Crew: 8

Variant

M-74: this useful weapon, currently entering service with the Finnish army under the designation **155K83**, is apparently a development of the Israeli Soltam M-68 with a longer barrel, no barrel counterweight, provision for an extra propellant charge and a number of detail modifications; the ammunition is of the separate-loading type, and the 43·6-kg (96·12-lb) HE projectile leaves the muzzle with a velocity of 850 m (2,789 ft) per second

Tampella M-60 122-mm field gun

(Finland)
Type: towed field gun

Calibre: 122 mm (4·8 in)
Barrel length: 53 calibres
Muzzle brake: single-baffle type
Carriage: split-trail type with four road wheels; no shield
Weight: 8500 kg (18,739 lb) in travelling and firing orders
Dimensions: length, travelling 7·20 m (23·62 ft); width, travelling 2·58 m (8·46 ft); height, travelling 2·00 m (6·56 ft)
Traverse/elevation: 90° total/−5° to +50°
Rate of fire: 4 rounds per minute
Maximum range: 25,000 m (27,340 yards)
Crew: 8

Variant

M60: entering service in 1964, this powerful equipment has a semi-automatic breech and fires separate-loading ammunition; the 25-kg (55·1-lb) HE projectile has a muzzle velocity of 950 m (3,117 ft) per second; the four-wheel bogie can be powered hydraulically from the towing vehicle for improved cross-country mobility

Tampella M-61/37 105-mm light field howitzer

(Finland)
Type: towed light field howitzer
Calibre: 105 mm (4·13 in)
Barrel length: not revealed
Muzzle brake: single-baffle type
Carriage: split-trail type with two road wheels; shield
Weight: 1800 kg (3,968 lb) in travelling and firing orders
Dimensions: not revealed
Traverse/elevation: 53° total/−6° to +45°
Rate for fire: 7 rounds per minute
Maximum range: 13,400 m (14,655 yards)
Crew: 6

Variants

M61/37: this is a Finnish-designed ordnance fitted on the carriage of the obsolete M-37 field howitzer, and firing separate-loading ammunition with a muzzle velocity of 600 m (1,969 ft) per second for the 14·9-kg (32·8-lb) HE projectile
M37/10: another hybrid equipment with a Tampella ordnance on the carriage of the Soviet M-10 field howitzer

GIAT TR 155-mm gun

(France)
Type: towed gun
Calibre: 155 mm (6·1 in)
Barrel length: 40 calibres
Muzzle brake: double-baffle type
Carriage: split-trail type with two road wheels; no shield
Weight: about 10,650 kg (23,479 lb) in travelling order
Dimensions: length, travelling with muzzle over trails 8·75 m (28·71 ft) and firing 10·00 m (32·81 ft); width, travelling 3·09 m (10·14 ft) and firing 8·40 m (27·56 ft); height, firing 1·65 m (5·41 ft)
Traverse/elevation: 65° total (27° left and 38° right of the centreline)/−5° to +66°
Rate of fire: 3 rounds in 18 seconds (with cold barrel), 6 rounds per minute (for 2 minutes), and 2 rounds per minute (normal)
Maximum range: 24,000 m (26,245 yards) with hollow-base projectile and 33,000 m (36,090 yards) with RAP
Crew: 8

Variant

TR: entering production in 1984, the TR is a modern equipment designed for the support of motorized divisions; a hydraulically powered rammer is standard to reduce crew fatigue, and helps the equipment to generate a high initial rate of fire with its standard French separate-loading ammunition; types include HE with a projectile weight of 43·25 kg (95·35 lb) and a muzzle velocity of 830 m (2,723 ft) per second for a range of 24,000 m (26,245 yards), HE RAP with a projectile weight of 43·5-kg (95·9 lb) and a muzzle velocity of 830 m (2,723 ft) per second for a range of 33,000 m (36,090 yards), anti-tank mine-launching with a projectile weight of 46 kg (101·4 lb) and a load of six 0·55-kg (1·2-lb) mines, smoke and illuminating; the TR can also fire the US M107 round and the ammunition of the FH-70 series; a measure of battlefield mobility is provided by the 29-kW (39-hp) auxiliary power unit, which offers a road speed of 8 km/h (5 mph)

Below: The TR 155-mm (6·1-in) gun.

Modèle 50 155-mm howitzer

(France)
Type: towed howitzer
Calibre: 155 mm (6·1 in)
Barrel length: 28·45 calibres including muzzle brake
Muzzle brake: multi-baffle type
Carriage: split trail with four road wheels; no shield
Weights: 9000 kg (19,841 lb) in travelling order and 8100 kg (17,857 lb) in firing position
Dimensions: length, travelling 7·80 m (25·59 ft) and firing 7·15 m (23·46 ft); width, travelling 2·75 m (9·02 m) and firing 6·80 m (22·31 ft); height, travelling 2·50 m (8·20 ft) and firing 1·65 m (5·41 ft)
Traverse/elevation: 80° total/− 4° to + 69°
Rate of fire: 3-4 rounds per minute
Maximum range: 18,000 m (19,685 yards) with standard ammunition or 23,300 m (25,480 yards) with RAP
Crew: 11

Variant

Modèle 50: developed in the period immediately after World War II, this equipment is now verging on the obsolete but is still in limited service; the type fires separate-loading ammunition including a 43-kg (94·8-lb) HE projectile with a muzzle velocity of 650 m (2,133 ft) per second

M 18/49 howitzer

(Germany/Czechoslovakia)
Type: towed field howitzer
Calibre: 105 mm (4·13 in)
Barrel length: 28 calibres
Muzzle brake: double-baffle type
Carriage: split-trail type with two wheels; shield
Weight: 1750 kg (3,858 lb) in travelling and firing orders
Dimensions: length, travelling 5·86 m (19·62 ft); width, travelling 2·10 m (6·89 ft); height, travelling 1·80 m (5·91 ft)
Traverse/elevation: 60° total/− 5° to + 42°
Rate of fire: 6-8 rounds per minute
Maximum range: 12,320 m (13,475 yards) with HE round
Crew: 8

Variants

M 18: current designation for the weapon developed in 1928/9 by the Germans as the **leichte Feldhaubitze 18**; this is now an obsolete weapon that nonetheless remains in fairly widespread service, and weighs 1985 kg (4,376 lb); the type has no muzzle brake and fires a 14·8-kg (30·86-lb) separate-loading HE projectile at a muzzle velocity of 470 m (1,542 ft) per second to 10,675 m (11,675 yards); the crew is six and the maximum traverse is 56°
M 18M: improved version originally known as the **leichte Feldhaubitze 18M** (or as the **leichte Feldhaubitze 18/40** when fitted on the tubular split-trail carriage of the PaK 40 anti-tank gun for a weight of 1800 kg/3,968 lb) with a double-baffle muzzle brake, a weight of 2040 kg (4,497 lb) and a muzzle velocity of 540 m (1,772 ft) per second to fire a 14·8-kg projectile to 12,320 m (13,475 yards); the crew is 10
M 18/49: version produced after World War II in Czechoslovakia with modern wheels and possessing the same improved traverse arc as the M 18/40

Rheinmetall/OTO Melara/Vickers FH-70 155-mm field howitzer

(West Germany/Italy/UK)
Type: towed field howitzer
Calibre: 155 mm (6·1 in)
Barrel length: 38·85 calibres
Muzzle brake: single-baffle type
Carriage: split-trail type with auxiliary power unit, two road wheels and two castors; no shield
Weight: 9300 kg (20,503 lb) in travelling and firing orders
Dimensions: length, travelling 9·80 m (32·15 ft) and firing 12·43 m (40·78 ft); width, travelling 2·204 m (7·23 ft) and firing 9·80 m (32·15 ft); height, travelling 2·56 m (8·40 ft) and firing 2·192 m (7·19 ft)
Traverse/elevation: 56° total/− 5° to + 70°
Rate of fire: 3 rounds in 8 seconds (with optional flick loader), 3 rounds in 13 seconds (bursts), 6 rounds per minute (normal) and 2 rounds per minute (sustained fire)
Maximum range: 24,000 m (26,245 yards) with standard projectile and 30,000 m (32,810 yards) with RAP
Crew: 8

Variants

FH-70: developed jointly by West Germany, Italy and the UK in the late 1960s and entering service from 1978, the FH-70 is an advanced field howitzer firing its own special separate-loading ammuni-

Below: The FH-70 is a highly capable weapon that fires all NATO standard ammunition and has been adopted by several major armies.

tion as well as standard NATO types and the Copperhead cannon-launched guided projectile; the type uses a semi-automatic breech and loader for reduced crew fatigue and high rates of fire (with a flick loader optional for higher rates still), while the addition of an 1800-cc (110-cu in) Volkswagen petrol-engined auxiliary power unit provides power for getting the equipment into and out of action, and also gives good battlefield mobility at speeds of up to 16 km/h (10 mph), gradients of 34% and a fording depth of 0·75 m (2·5 ft);

included in the ammunition types are FRAG-HE (43·5-kg/95·9-lb projectile with 11·3 kg/24·9 lb of HE), HE RAP, smoke and illuminating; the use of an eight-charge propellant system allows muzzle velocities between 213 and 827 m (700 and 2,715 ft) per second

FH-70J: Japanese version of the FH-70 produced by Rheinmetall; Japan is also developing a self-propelled weapon using the same ordnance under the designation **Type 75 155-mm SPH Kai**
FH-70R: improved model developed as a private

venture by Rheinmetall; this version has an L/46 barrel, making possible ranges of 30,000 m (32,810 yards) with the standard projectile and of 36,000 m (39,370 yards) with a base-bleed projectile; Rheinmetall is also developing combustible charge containers for this weapon and other 155-mm (6·1-in) types

Below: This illustration of the FH-70 firing at high elevation shows propellant gas diverted sideways by the double-baffle muzzle brake.

Indian Ordnance Factories Jabalpur 105-mm Indian Field Gun Mk 1

(India)

Type: towed gun/howitzer
Calibre: 105 mm (4·13 in)
Barrel length: not revealed
Muzzle brake: double-baffle type
Carriage: split-trail type with two road wheels; no shield
Weight: 3450 kg (7,606 lb) in travelling and firing orders
Dimensions: not revealed
Traverse/elevation: 360° total/not revealed
Rate of fire: 5 rounds per minute
Maximum range: 17,400 m (19,030 yards)
Crew: 6

Variant

105-mm Indian Field Gun Mk 1: this weapon was designed and produced in India as replacement for the British 25-pdr gun/howitzer, and has adequate performance though only at considerable weight; the standard HE round weighs 16·56 kg (36·5 lb), and other types of projectile used with this equipment include HESH and smoke

Indian Ordnance Factories Jabalpur 105-mm Light Field Gun Mk 2

(India)

Type: towed gun/howitzer
Calibre: 105 mm (4·13 in)
Barrel length: 36·3 calibres
Muzzle brake: double-baffle type
Carriage: bow type with two road wheels; no shield
Weight: 2250 kg (4,960 lb) in firing position
Dimensions: length, travelling 7·216 m (23·675 ft) and firing 5·054 m (16·58 ft); width, travelling 1·82 m (9·57 ft); height, travelling 1·494 m (4·90 ft)
Traverse/elevation: 360° on platform and 10° total on carriage/−5° to +73°
Rate of fire: 6 rounds per minute (10-minute bursts), 4 rounds per minute (normal), and 1 round per 2 minutes (sustained)
Maximum range: 17,425 m (19,055 yards)
Crew: not revealed

Variant

105-mm Light Field Gun Mk 2: evolved to overcome the IFG's weight problem, the LFG Mk 2 weighs 2040 kg (4,497 lb) excluding the firing platform and is carefully balanced to reduce loads; the type is easily air-transportable (it being possible to turn the barrel through 180° over the trails to reduce length) and can be helicopter-carried or para-dropped; the type has physical and conceptual similarities to the British Light Gun, and this is attributable to the fact that both weapons were evolved on the basis of the ordnance used in the FV433 Abbot self-propelled gun, which is employed by the British and Indian armies; the ordnance fires separate-loading ammunition and has an eight-charge propellant system

Right: The modello 56 pack howitzer is seen in its field rather than anti-tank configuration, allowing a maximum ordnance elevation of 65° rather than 25°.

Soltam Model 839P 155-mm gun/howitzer

(Israel)

Type: towed gun/howitzer
Calibre: 155 mm (6·1 in)
Barrel length: 43 calibres
Muzzle brake: single-baffle type
Carriage: split-trail type with auxiliary power unit, four road wheels and two castors; no shield
Weight: 10,850 kg (23,920 lb) in travelling and firing orders
Dimensions: length, travelling 7·50 m (24·61 ft) and firing at 0° elevation 10·80 m (35·43 ft); width, travelling 2·58 m (8·46 ft) and firing 8·00 m (26·25 ft); height, travelling 2·10 m (6·89 ft) and firing at 70° elevation 7·20 m (23·62 ft)
Traverse/elevation: 78° total/−3° to +70°
Rate of fire: 4 rounds per minute (short periods) and 2 rounds per minute (sustained fire)
Maximum range: 23,500 m (25,700 yards)
Crew: 8

Variants

Model 839P: this version of the M-71 gun/howitzer entered service in 1984 and uses the same ordnance on a revised carriage fitted with a 60-kW (80-hp) Deutz diesel-engined auxiliary power unit; this provides a road speed of 17 km/h (10·6 mph), a range of 70 km (43·5 miles) and a gradient capability of 34%, as well as power for trail-spreading/opening, wheel lifting/lowering and firing platform lowering/lifting; a pneumatically operated rammer eases crew fatigue and increases rate of fire, and the ordnance fires separate-loading ammunition of various types including FRAG-HE (43·5-kg/95·9-lb projectile with 8·5 kg/18·74 lb of HE) and HE RAP (4·5 kg/9·9 lb of HE)
Model 845P: entering service in 1985, this is a version of the Model 839P with an L/45 barrel and a range of 28,500 m (31,170 yards) with a 'special projectile'

Soltam M-71 155-mm gun/howitzer

(Israel)

Type: towed gun/howitzer
Calibre: 155 mm (6·1 in)
Barrel length: 39 calibres
Muzzle brake: single-baffle type
Carriage: split-trail type with four road wheels; no shield
Weights: 9200 kg (20,282 lb) in travelling order

Dimensions: length, travelling 7·50 m (24·61 ft); width, travelling 2·58 m (8·46 ft); height, travelling 2·115 m (6·94 ft)
Traverse/elevation: 84° total/−3° to +54°
Rate of fire: 4 rounds per minute (short periods) and 2 rounds per minute (sustained fire)
Maximum range: 23,500 m (25,700 yards)
Crew: 8

Variant

M-71: this is a development of the same company's M-68 equipment with a longer ordnance and a compressed-air rammer for rapid reloading at all angles of elevation; the ammunition types used with the M-71 are those detailed for the M-68

Soltam M-68 155-mm gun/howitzer

(Israel)

Type: towed gun/howitzer
Calibre: 155 mm (6·1 in)
Barrel length: 33 calibres
Muzzle brake: single-baffle type
Carriage: split-trail type with four road wheels; no shield
Weights: 9500 kg (20,944 lb) in travelling order and 8500 kg (18,739 lb) in firing position
Dimensions: length, travelling 7·20 m (23·62 ft); width, travelling 2·58 m (8·46 ft); height, travelling 2·00 m (6·56 ft)
Traverse/elevation: 90° total/−5° to +52°
Rate of fire: 4 rounds per minute (short periods) and 2 rounds per minute (sustained fire)
Maximum range: 21,000 m (22,965 yards) with NATO ammunition and 23,500 m (25,700 yards) with Tampella ammunition
Crew: 8

Variant

M-68: this baseline variant of Israel's important 155-mm (6·1-in) gun/howitzer family combined an Israeli ordnance on a locally developed adaptation of the carriage of the Finnish M-60; development of the M-68 was undertaken in the 1960s, final trials being completed in 1968 for the equipment to enter service in 1970; the ordnance fires all standard NATO projectiles of this calibre, the 43·7-kg (96·3-lb) HE projectile leaving the muzzle at 725 m (2,379 ft) per second to attain a maximum range of 21,000 m (22,965 yards); the weapon can also use the more capable range of 155-mm (6·1-in) ammunition developed by Tampella, using a nine-charge propellant system to attain a maximum range of 23,500 m (25,700 yards)

OTO Melara Modello 56 105-mm pack howitzer

(Italy)
Type: towed pack howitzer
Calibre: 105 mm (4·13 in)
Barrel length: 14·08 calibres
Muzzle brake: multi-baffle type
Carriage: split-trail type with two road wheels; optional shield
Weight: 1290 kg (2,844 lb) in travelling and firing orders
Dimensions: length, travelling 3·65 m (11·98 ft) and firing 4·80 m (15·75 ft); width, travelling 1·50 m (4·92 ft) and firing 2·90 m (9·51 ft); height, travelling and firing 1·93 m (6·33 ft)
Traverse/elevation: 36° total/− 5° to + 65°
Rate of fire: 4 rounds per minute (30-minute period) and 3 rounds per minute (1-hour period)
Maximum range: 10,575 m (11,565 yards) with standard ammunition
Crew: 7

Variant
Modello 56: this widely used pack howitzer entered production in 1957, and amongst its attractions is the fact that it can be broken down into 11 sections, the heaviest weighing 122 kg (269 lb) for animal or light helicopter transport; in the field role the Modello 56's wheels are over-slung, but for the dedicated anti-tank role they are underslung to reduce height to 1·55 m (5·09 ft), increase traverse to 56° total, and reduce elevation to an arc between − 5° and + 22°; in the anti-tank role the rate of fire is 8 rounds per minute with the semi-fixed 16·7-kg (36·8-lb) HEAT round, whose projectile leaves the muzzle at a velocity of 387 m (1,270 ft) per second to penetrate 102 mm (4 in) of armour; the standard HE round has a weight of 16·7 kg (36·8 lb) and its projectile leaves the muzzle with a velocity of 472 m (1,550 ft) per second

Left: Italian mountain troops with a modello 56 pack howitzer in field configuration with its wheels underslung but without a shield.

RDM M139 155-mm howitzer

(Netherlands)
Type: towed howitzer
Calibre: 155 mm (6·1 in)
Barrel length: 38·8 calibres excluding muzzle brake
Muzzle brake: double-baffle type
Carriage: split-trail type with two road wheels; optional shield
Weight: 7500 kg (16,534 lb) in travelling and firing orders
Dimensions: length, travelling 10·00 m (332·81 ft); width, travelling 2·44 m (8·01 ft); height, travelling 2·31 m (7·58 m)
Traverse/elevation: 49° total (24° left and 25° right of the centreline)/− 2° to + 63°
Rate of fire: 4 rounds per minute (maximum) and 2 rounds per minute (normal)
Maximum range: 18,100 m (19,795 yards) with standard HE, 24,600 m (26,905 yards) with extended-range projectile, and 32,400 m (35,435 yards) with extended-range base-bleed projectile
Crew: 11

Variants
M114/39: this is the designation of the US-built

M114 equipment upgraded with a number of modern features as well as a new ordnance that allows the firing of the latest 155-mm (6·1-in) ammunition types including the extended-range projectile varieties; the programme was initiated by SRC International of Canada but brought to fruition by RDM Engineering that sees a large world market for the kit, which features a new ordnance supplied by Bofors

M139: new-build weapon identical in all significant respects to the M114/39; a recent development (also applicable to the M114/39), is the optional installation of a 45-kW (60-hp) auxiliary power unit on the forward part of the carriage; this provides the equipment with a fair measure of battlefield autonomy, allowing independent movement at up to 10 km/h (6·1 mph)

Romanian 100-mm mountain gun/howitzer

(Romania)
Type: mountain gun/howitzer
Calibre: 100 mm (3·94 in)
Barrel length: not revealed
Muzzle brake: multi-baffle type
Carriage: split-trail type with two road wheels and an optional castor; no shield
Weight: 1500 kg (3,307 lb) in firing position
Dimensions: not revealed
Traverse/elevation: 50° total/−5° to +65°
Rate of fire: not revealed
Maximum range: 10,000 m (10,935 yards)
Crew: 7

Variant
Romanian 100-mm mountain gun/howitzer: this is a conventional equipment resembling the Italian Modello 56 pack howitzer, and its most distinctive feature is the fact that each trail leg can be folded to shorten overall transport length; the ordnance fires an HE projectile in the longer-range indirect role, and a HEAT projectile in the shorter-range direct role to an effective maximum of 600 m (655 yards)

Ordnance Development and Engineering FH-88 155-mm gun/howitzer

(Singapore)
Type: towed gun howtizer
Calibre: 155 mm (6·1 in)
Barrel length: 39 calibres
Muzzle brake: double-baffle type
Carriage: split-trail type with four road wheels; no shield
Weight: 13,200 kg (29,101 lb) in travelling and firing orders
Dimensions: length, travelling with muzzle over the trails 8·81 m (28·9 ft) and firing 9·49 m (31·135 ft); width, travelling 2·80 m (9·19ft); height, travelling 2·30 m (7·55 ft)
Traverse/elevation: 60° total/°3° to +70°
Rate of fire: 3 rounds in 15 seconds (bursts), 8 rounds per minute (20-minute period), and 2 rounds per minute (normal)
Maximum range: 19,000 m (20,780 yards) with standard NATO ammunition, 24,000 m (26,245 yards) with M56 HE projectile, and 30,000 m (32,810 yards) with extended-range full-bore projectile
Crew: 6

Variant
FH-88: in production since 1986, this Singaporean ordnance is a useful but unexceptional item of equipment attractive to Third World buyers mainly for its comparatively low cost; the type can be fitted with a 70-kW (94-hp) Deutz diesel-engined auxiliary power unit for independent movement at road and cross-country speeds of 16 and 6 km/h (10 and 3·7mph) respectively; the APU has a 50-litre (11-Imp gal) fuel tank, sufficient for a range of 60 km (37·3 miles); the flick rammer is independently powered

Armscor G5 155-mm gun/howitzer

(South Africa)
Type: towed gun/howitzer
Calibre: 155 mm (6·1 in)
Barrel length: 45 calibres
Muzzle brake: single-baffle type
Carriage: split-trail type with auxiliary power unit, four road wheels and two castors; no shield
Weight: 15,500 kg (29,762 lb) in travelling and firing orders
Dimensions: length, travelling 9·10 m (29·86 ft) and firing 11·20 m (36·75 ft); width, travelling 2·50 m (8·20 ft) and firing 8·60 m (28·22 ft); height, travelling 2·30 m (7·55 ft)
Traverse/elevation: 84° total up to +15° elevation and 65° total above +15° elevation/−3° to +75°
Rate of fire: 3 rounds per minute (15-minute period) and 2 rounds per minute (normal)
Maximum range: 30,000 m (32,810 yards) with standard ammunition, and 37,500 m (41,010 yards) with HE base-bleed ammunition
Crew: 8

Variant
G5: this extremely potent piece of equipment was developed from 1975 on the basis of the GC 45, though the process altered virtually every feature of the Canadian/Belgian weapon; the type entered South African service in 1983 and has proved very successful in terms of range, accuracy and cross-country mobility; battlefield capabilities are considerably aided by the installation of a 51-kW (68-hp) Magirus-Deutz diesel-engined auxiliary power unit for hydraulic functions such as lowering/raising the firing platform and castors, and for opening/closing the trails; crew fatigue is reduced by the provision of a pneumatically operated rammer; a three-charge propellant system is used for muzzle velocities between 250 and 897 m (820 and 2,943 ft) per second, and the projectile types are a 45·5-kg (100·3-lb) HE, 47-kg (103·6-lb) base-bleed HE, smoke, illuminating and white phosphorus; a cargo-carrying round is under development

Kia Machine Tool KH179 155-mm howitzer

(South Korea)
Type: towed howitzer
Calibre: 155 mm (6·1 in)
Barrel length: 39·33 calibres
Muzzle brake: double-baffle type
Carriage: split-trail type with two road wheels; no shield
Weight: 6890 kg (15,190 lb) in travelling and firing orders

Dimensions: length, travelling 10·39 m (34·09 ft); width, travelling 2·438 m (8·00 ft); height, travelling 2·77 m (9·09 m)
Traverse/elevation: 48·7° total (23·5° left and 25·2° right of the centreline)/0° to +68·6°
Rate of fire: 4 rounds per minute (maximum) and 2 rounds per minute (normal)
Maximum range: 22,000 m (24,060 yards) with standard HE and 30,000 m (32,810 yards) with RAP
Crew: 11

Variant
KH179: just as the KH178 is a reworking of the US M101, the KH179 is an updating of the US M114 with a longer barrel and detail improvements; the type fires all standard NATO separate-loading 155-mm (6·1-in) ammunition

Kia Machine Tool KH178 105-mm howitzer

(South Korea)
Type: towed light howitzer
Calibre: 105 mm (4·13 in)
Barrel length: 39 calibres
Muzzle brake: double-baffle type
Carriage: split-trail type with two road wheels; optional shield
Weight: 2650 kg (5,842 lb) in travelling and firing orders
Dimensions: length 7·56 m (24·80 ft); width 2·146 m (7·04 ft); height not revealed
Traverse/elevation: 45·5° total/−5° to +65°
Rate of fire: 15 rounds per minute (maximum) and 5 rounds per minute (normal)
Maximum range: 14,700 m (16,075 yards) with standard ammunition and 18,000 kg (19,685 yards) with RAP
Crew: 8

Variant
KH178: this new South Korean equipment is derived from the US M101A2 howitzer with a longer barrel, and incorporates features of the British Light Gun and the West German Rheinmetall conversion of the M101; the weapon fires the semi-fixed ammunition types of the M101 with a muzzle velocity of 663 m (2,175 ft) per second

Santa Barbara SB 155/39 155-mm howitzer

(Spain)
Type: towed howitzer
Calibre: 155 mm (6·1 in)
Barrel length: 39 calibres
Muzzle brake: double-baffle type
Carriage: split-trail type with two road wheels and two castors; no shield
Weight: 9000 kg (19,841 lb) in travelling order
Dimensions: length, travelling 9·20 m (30·18 ft) with the muzzle over the trails and firing 12·00 m (39·37 ft); width, travelling 2·50 m (8·20 ft); height, travelling 2·40 m (7·87 ft) and firing 1·525 m (5·00 ft)
Traverse/elevation: 60° total (30° left and 30° right of the centreline)/−5° to +70°
Rate of fire: 4 rounds per minute (bursts), 3 rounds per minute (30-minute period), 2 rounds per minute (60-minute period), and 1 round per minute (sustained)
Maximum range: 24,000 m (26,245 yards) with standard ammunition
Crew: 6

SB 155/39: entering service in the later 1980s, this is a conventional but useful equipment firing the full range of NATO separate-loading ammunition, and for towing the barrel is turned through 180° to rest over the closed trails

SB 155/39 REMA: entering Spanish service in the later 1980s, this REMA (Remolccado con motor auxiliar) variant is a useful equipment fitted with 48·8-kW (65·5-hp) Citroen auxiliary power unit for battlefield mobility with a speed of 12 km/h (7·5 mph) and a gradient capability of 30%, and for the generation of hydraulic power for functions such as wheel lowering/raising and trail opening/closing

Reinosa R-50/26 105-mm field howitzer

(Spain)
Type: towed field howitzer
Calibre: 105 mm (4·13 in)
Barrel length: 31·9 calibres
Muzzle brake: double-baffle type
Carriage: split-trail type with two road wheels; no shield
Weight: 1950 kg (4,299 lb) in travelling and firing orders
Dimensions: length, travelling 6·08 m (19·95 ft); width, travelling 2·10 m (6·89 ft); height, travelling 2·20 m (7·22 ft)
Traverse/elevation: 50° total/−5° to +45°
Rate of fire: 6 rounds per minute
Maximum range: 11,450 m (12,520 yards)
Crew: 6

Variant
R-50/26: introduced in 1950, this Spanish weapon was designed to fire its own range of semi-fixed ammunition as well as standard US ammunition; the latter is slightly lighter than the Spanish type, has less muzzle velocity and thus less range; the Spanish HE projectile weighs 15·27 kg (33·66 lb) and has a muzzle velocity of 504 m (1,654 ft) per second, and the HEAT projectile can penetrate 85 mm (3·35 in) of armour at 1000 m (1,095 yards); later versions of this weapon are designated **R-50/53**, **R-58** and **NR-61**

Bofors FH-77A 155-mm field howitzer

(Sweden)
Type: towed field howitzer
Calibre: 155 mm (6·1 in)
Barrel length: 38 calibres
Muzzle brake: pepperpot type
Carriage: split-trail type with an auxiliary power unit, two road wheels and two castors; no shield

Weights: 11,500 kg (25,353 lb) in travelling and firing orders
Dimensions: length, travelling 11·60 m (38·06 ft) and firing 11·20 m (36·75 ft); width, travelling 2·64 m (8·66 ft) and firing 7·18 m (23·56 ft); height,

Below: The FH-77B in fire position with projectiles and bagged charges ready for loading.
Bottom: The FH-77B can be towed at speeds up to 70 km/h (43·5 mph).

travelling 2·75 m (9·02 ft) and firing at 50° elevation 6·75 m (22·15 ft)

Traverse/elevation: 50° total up to +5° elevation and 60° total over +5° elevation/−3° to +50°
Rate of fire: 3 rounds in 6-8 seconds or 6 rounds in 20-25 seconds (bursts), and 6 rounds every other minute (20-minute period)
Maximum range: 22,000 m (24,060 yards)
Crew: 6

Variants
FH-77A: the FH-77A entered production in 1975, and is a highly capable equipment though only at great cost and considerable size; one of the main features of the equipment is its use of a Volvo B20 auxiliary power unit for a hydraulic system that drives the road wheels and castors, providing good battlefield mobility (at a maximum speed of 8 km/h; 5 mph) and competent into/out of action times; elevation and traverse are also hydraulically powered, and a powered rammer is used in conjunction with crane-supplied loading table (the crane delivering three projectiles at a time) and semi-automatic breech to make possible very high burst rates of fire; the FH-77A fires particularly potent separate-loading ammunition, the HE projectile weighing 42·2 kg (93 lb); the weapon uses a six-charge propellant system offering muzzle velocities between 310 and 774 m (1,017 and 2,539 ft) per second with projectiles that include HE, base-bleed HE, smoke and illuminating
FH-77B: export version of the FH-77A with a longer L/39 barrel, a screw rather than vertical sliding wedge breech mechanism, a fully automatic ammunition-handling system, elevation to +70°, and improvements to cross-country mobility (including power take-off from the tractor to provide full 8 × 8 drive for the tractor/ordnance combination); weight is increased to 11,900 kg (26,235 lb), and a bagged rather than cartridge charge propellant system is used; the standard range of the FH-77B is 24,000 m (26,245 yards) rising to 30,000 m (32,810 yards) with an extended-range full-bore round; the FH-77B can also be fitted with the Ferranti FIN 1150 gyrostabilized land navigation system to permit autonomous positioning of the equipment: trials have confirmed the utility of such a system for 'shoot-and-scoot' tactics, one equipment (with a crew of four men) in a period of 5 minutes 10 seconds coming into action, firing four rounds, moving 50 m (55 yards) and firing another three rounds
Karin: version of the FH-77A with 120-mm (4·72-in) calibre and intended for the coastal role; this uses a conveyor-type loading system, a modified laying system so that moving ship targets can be followed, and remote-control facilities so that the weapon can be used in conjunction with a fire-control centre accommodated in a container-type body with radar, optronic director and computers
CD-77: mobile coast-defence development of the FH-77, using the same elevating mass and loading system but fitted with a specially developed laying system, Philips Elektronikindustrier fire-control computer and communications system for the accurate engagement of moving targets at long ranges

Bofors m/39 150-mm field howitzer

(Sweden)
Type: towed field howitzer

Calibre: 150 mm (5·9 in)
Barrel length: 24 calibres
Muzzle brake: pepperpot type
Carriage: split-trail type with two road wheels; no shield
Weight: 5720 kg (12,610 lb) in travelling order
Dimensions: length, travelling with barrel forward 7·37 m (24·18 ft), travelling with barrel out of battery 6·55 m (21·49 ft) and firing 7·27 m (23·85 ft); width, travelling 2·50 m (8·20 ft) and firing 5·53 m (18·14 ft); height, travelling 2·50 m (8·20 ft)
Traverse/elevation: 45° total/−5° to +66°
Rate of fire: 4-6 rounds per minute
Maximum range: 14,600 m (15,965 yards)
Crew: 8

Variant
m/39: now an obsolescent weapon, the m/39 uses separate-loading ammunition with a 41·5-kg (91·5-lb) HE projectile fired at a muzzle velocity of 580 m (1,903 ft) per second; the m/39 has solid wheels, the improved **m/39b** having pneumatic tyres

Bofors Tp 4140 105-mm field howitzer

(Sweden)
Type: towed field howitzer
Calibre: 105 mm (4·13 in)
Barrel length: 32 calibres
Muzzle brake: single-baffle type
Carriage: four-leg split-trail type with two road wheels; no shield
Weights: 3000 kg (6,614 lb) in travelling order and 2800 kg (6,173 lb) in firing position
Dimensions: length, travelling 6·80 m (22·31 ft) and firing 5·52 m (18·11 ft); width, travelling 1·81 m (5·94 ft) and firing 4·90 m (16·08 ft); height, travelling 1·85 m (6·07 ft) and firing 1·20 m (3·94 ft)
Traverse/elevation: 360° total/−5° to +60°
Rate of fire: 25 rounds per minute
Maximum range: 15,600 m (17,060 yards)
Crew: 4

Variant
Tp 4140: this Swedish equipment was developed after World War II and bears strong conceptual relationships to an inter-war Czech design; the four-trail carriage opens into a cruciform firing platform allowing 360° traverse, and the type fires fixed ammunition to make possible a very high rate of fire; the HE projectile weighs 15·3 kg (33·7 lb) at a muzzle velocity of 640 m (2,100 ft) per second

Federal Construction M46 105-mm field howitzer

(Switzerland)
Type: towed field howitzer
Calibre: 105 mm (4·13 in)
Barrel length: 22 calibres
Muzzle brake: multi-baffle type
Carriage: split-trail type with two road wheels and one castor; shield
Weight: 1840 kg (4,056 lb) in firing position
Dimensions: not revealed
Traverse/elevation: 56° to 72° total depending on elevation/−5° to +67°
Rate of fire: 6-10 rounds per minute
Maximum range: 10,000 m (10,935 yards)
Crew: 7

Variant
M46: designed in Sweden by Bofors and built in Switzerland up to 1953, this is an obsolescent weapon that fires separate-loading HE ammunition, the 15·1-kg (33·3-lb) projectile being fired at a muzzle velocity of 490 m (1,080 ft) per second

Federal Construction M35 105-mm field gun

(Switzerland)
Type: towed field gun
Calibre: 105 mm (4·13 in)
Barrel length: 42 calibres
Muzzle brake: double-baffle type
Carriage: split-trail type with two road wheels; shield
Weight: 4245 kg (9,358 lb) in firing position
Dimensions: not revealed
Traverse/elevation: 60° total/−3° to +45°
Rate of fire: 6 rounds per minute
Maximum range: 17,500 m (19,140 yards) with old ammunition and 21,000 m (22,965 yards) with new ammunition
Crew: 9

Variant
M35: designed in Sweden by Bofors but built in Switzerland, the M35 is an obsolete equipment whose utility has been improved by the adoption of a new separate-loading ammunition type with greater muzzle velocity (800 rather than 785 m/2,625 rather than 2,575 ft per second for the 15·15-kg/33·4-lb HE projectile); other projectiles are AP and illuminating

Federal Construction M57 90-mm anti-tank gun

(Switzerland)
Type: towed anti-tank gun
Calibre: 90 mm (3·54 in)
Barrel length: 33·7 calibres
Muzzle brake: multi-baffle type
Carriage: split-trail type with two road wheels; shield
Weights: 600 kg (1,323 lb) in travelling order and 570 kg (1,257 lb) in firing position
Dimensions: not revealed
Traverse/elevation: 70° total up to +11° elevation and 44° total over +11° elevation/−15° to +23°
Rate of fire: 20 rounds per minute (maximum) and 6 rounds per minute (normal)
Maximum range: 3000 m (3,280 yards) overall, or 900 m (985 yards) against a static target, or 700 m (765 yards) against a moving target
Crew: 5

Variant
M57: introduced in 1958, this light anti-tank equipment fires a 2·7-kg (5·95-lb) HEAT projectile at a muzzle velocity of 600 m (1,969 ft) per second to penetrate 250 mm (9·84 in) of armour

Federal Construction M50 90-mm anti-tank gun

(Switzerland)
Type: towed anti-tank gun
Calibre: 90 mm (3·54 in)
Barrel length: 32·2 calibres

M-240 240-mm towed mortar

(USSR)
Type: towed mortar
Calibre: 240 mm (9·45 in)
Barrel length: 22·25 calibres
Muzzle brake: none
Carriage: box type with two road wheels; no shield
Weight: 4150 kg (9,149 lb) in firing position
Dimensions: length, travelling 6·51 m (21·36 ft); width, travelling 2·49 m (8·17 ft); height, travelling 2·21 m (7·25 ft)
Traverse/elevation: 18° total/ + 45° to + 65°
Rate of fire: 1 round per minute
Maximum range: 9700 m (10,610 yards)
Crew: 9-11

Variant
M-240: designed primarily for the destruction of fortifications and buildings that cannot be engaged successfully by other ordnance, the M-240 was first revealed publicly in 1953 and was at the time allocated the designation **M1953** in the US system of nomenclature; the type is generally fielded in heavy artillery brigades deployed at front level, the brigade comprising two batteries with the M-240 mortars and two batteries with the 203-mm (8-in) B-4M (M1931) howitzer; the M-240 is towed muzzle-first on a two-wheel carriage that also incorporates the boom used to translate the ordnance from its travelling position to its firing position with the large baseplate firmly embedded in the earth; the ordnance has a minimum range of 800 m (875 yards), and is breech-loaded with an HE bomb weighing 130 kg (286·6 lb) including 34 kg (74·96 lb) of explosive

S-23 180-mm towed gun

(USSR)
Type: towed gun
Calibre: 180 mm (7·09 in)
Barrel length: 48·88 calibres
Muzzle brake: pepperpot type
Carriage: split-trail type with four road wheels and a two-wheel limber; no shield
Weight: 21,450 kg (47,288 lb) in firing position
Dimensions: length, travelling 10·485 m (34·40 ft); width, travelling 2·996 m (9·83 ft); height, travelling 2·621 m (8·60 ft)
Traverse/elevation: 44° total/ − 2° to + 50°
Rate of fire: 1 round per minute (bursts) and 1 round per 2 minutes (sustained fire)
Maximum range: 30,400 m (33,245 yards) with normal ammunition and 43,800 m (47,900 yards) with RAP
Crew: 16

Variant
S-23: originally thought by Western analysts to be a 203-mm (8-in) weapon, the S-23 was at first

Muzzle brake: none
Carriage: split-trail type with two road wheels; shield
Weights: 600 kg (1,323 lb) in travelling order and 556 kg (1,226 lb) in firing position
Dimensions: not revealed
Traverse/elevation: 66° total up to + 11° elevation and 34° total over + 11° elevation/ − 10° to + 32°
Rate of fire: 20 rounds per minute (maximum) and 6 rounds per minute (normal)
Maximum range: 3000 m (3,280 yards) overall, or 700 m (765 yards) against a static target or 500 m (550 yards) against a moving target
Crew: 5

Variant
M50: introduced in 1953, this light anti-tank equipment fires a 1·95-kg (4·3-lb) HEAT projectile at a muzzle velocity of 600 m (1,969 ft) per second to penetrate 250 mm (9·84 in) of armour

Though elderly, the M-240 mortar is still in service as its bomb is devastating against fortifications, especially in built-up areas.

Below: The S-23's length can be reduced by pulling the ordnance out of battery over the trails.

known in US terminology as the **M1955** and originated as a naval weapon in the early 1950s; to facilitate towed transport the ordnance can be withdrawn from battery and the ends of the trails supported on a two-wheel limber; the type fires separate-loading ammunition with variable bag charges, and the projectiles include an 84·09-kg (185·4-lb) HE type fired at a muzzle velocity of 790 m (2,592 ft) per second, an HE RAP type fired at a muzzle velocity of 850 m (2,789 ft) per second, a 97·7-kg (215·4-lb) concrete-piercing type, and a nuclear type with a yield of 0·2 kilotons

2A36 152-mm field gun

(USSR)
Type: towed field gun
Calibre: 152·4 mm (6 in)
Barrel length: not revealed
Muzzle brake: multi-baffle type
Carriage: split-trail type with four road wheels; shield
Weight: about 8800 kg (19,400 lb) in travelling and firing orders
Dimensions: length, travelling 12·93 m (42·42 ft) and in firing position 12·30 m (40·35 ft); width, travelling 2·788 m (9·15 ft); height, travelling 2·76 m (9·06 ft)
Traverse/elevation: 50° total (25° left and 25° right of the centreline)/−2° to +57°
Rate of fire: 5-6 rounds per minute
Maximum range: 27,000 m (29,530 yards) with standard projectile and 37,000 m (40,465 yards) with RAP
Crew: 10

Below: The D-20 is a well-established gun/howitzer in service with many Soviet-allied states.

Variant

2A26: known in the West as the **M1976**, its designation in the US system of terminology, this equipment began to enter service in 1981 and is apparently the modern replacement for the 130-mm (5·12-in) M-46 gun in the counter-battery role with army-level artillery divisions and brigades; the ordnance can fire HE, RAP, HEAT, chemical and nuclear projectiles of the separate loading type, and the 46-kg (101·4-lb) HE fragmentation projectile is fired at a muzzle velocity of 800 m (2,625 ft) per second; other details of this undoubtedly impressive weapon are woefully lacking; the same ordnance is fitted on the 2S5 self-propelled mounting

D-20 152-mm gun/howitzer

(USSR)
Type: towed gun/howitzer
Calibre: 152·4 mm (6 in)
Barrel length: 37 calibres
Muzzle brake: double-baffle type
Carriage: split-trail type with two road wheels and two castors; shield
Weights: 5700 kg (12,566 lb) in travelling order and 5650 kg (12,456 lb) in firing position
Dimensions: length, travelling 8·69 m (28·51 ft);

Below: The 2A36 replaces the counter-battery M-46, combining accuracy and long range.

width, travelling 2·32 m (7·61 ft); height, travelling 1·925 m (6·32 ft)
Traverse/elevation: 360° on firing platform and 58° total on carriage/−5° to +63°
Rate of fire: 5-6 rounds per minute
Maximum range: 17,400 m (19,030 yards) with standard projectile and 24,000 m (26,245 yards) with RAP
Crew: 10

Variant
D-20: developed after World War II for a service debut in the early 1950s, the D-20 was initially called the **M1955** in the West and designed as successor to the ML-20; the recoil system and carriage are identical to those of the D-74 field gun though supporting a shorter and considerably fatter ordnance; the equipment fires separate-loading case ammunition with several projectiles, including a 43·51-kg (95·9-lb) HE-FRAG type at a muzzle velocity of 655 m (2,149 ft) per second, an HE RAP type to a maximum range of 24,000 m (26,245 yards), a 48·78-kg (107·5-lb) AP-T type at a muzzle velocity of 600 m (1,969 ft) per second to penetrate 124 mm (4·88 in) of armour at 1000 m (1,095 yards), a HEAT type, a concrete-piercing type, a smoke type, an illuminating type, a chemical type and a nuclear type with a yield of 0·2 kilotons
M84: Yugoslav-made version of the D-20; this uses the same carriage as the D-20 but possesses a number of improved features including a longer barrel and two hydraulic pumps used to locate the weapon on its circular firing platform and raise the wheels clear of the ground; maximum rate of fire is 6 rounds per minute, and the Yugoslav ordnance can fire the same ammunition as the Soviet weapon, including the OF-540 HE-FRAG projectile, but can also fire the new Yugoslav M84 HE projectile; this is fired with a muzzle velocity of 810 m (2,657 ft) per second to attain a maximum range of 24,000 m (26,245 yards); also available are an illuminating projectile and the new HE/ICM (High Explosive/Improved Conventional Munition), the latter carrying 63 KB-2 bomblets to a range of 22,500 m (24,605 yards); each of these top-attack anti-armour bomblets weighs 0·25 kg (0·55 lb), and its dimensions include a length and diameter of 85 and 40 mm (3·35 and 1·575 in) respectively
Type 66: Chinese-made copy of the D-20

Below: The D-1 was introduced in World War II, and now serves mainly with Soviet client states.

D-1 152-mm howitzer

(USSR)
Type: towed howitzer
Calibre: 152·4 mm (6 in)
Barrel length: 25 calibres
Muzzle brake: double-baffle type
Carriage: split-trail type with two road wheels; shield
Weights: 3640 kg (8,025 lb) in travelling order and 2600 kg (5,732 lb) in firing position
Dimensions: length, travelling 7·558 m (24·80 ft); width, travelling 1·994 m (6·54 ft); height, travelling 1·854 m (6·08 ft)
Traverse/elevation: 35° total/−3° to +63·5°
Rate of fire: 3-4 rounds per minute
Maximum range: 12,400 m (13,560 yards)
Crew: 10

Variants
D-1: developed for service in 1943 as the **M1943**, this equipment combines the recoil system and carriage of the M-30 (M1938) 122-mm (4·8-in) howitzer and the ordnance of the M-10 (M1938) 152-mm (6-in) howitzer with a double-baffle muzzle brake; it was itself the replacement for the M-10, and is currently being replaced in service by the M1973 self-propelled howitzer; separate-loading case-type ammunition is used, and projectiles include two 40-kg (88·2-lb) HE-FRAG types fired at a muzzle velocity of 508 m (1,667 ft) per second, and chemical, HEAT, semi-AP, smoke and illuminating types
Type 54: Chinese-made copy of the D-1

ML-20 152-mm gun/howitzer

(USSR)
Type: towed gun/howitzer
Calibre: 152·4 mm (6 in)
Muzzle brake: multi-baffle type
Carriage: split-trail type with two twin road wheels and a two-wheel limber; shield
Weights: 8073 kg (17,798 lb) in travelling order and 7270 kg (16,027 lb) in firing position
Dimensions: length, travelling 7·21 m (23·65 ft); width, travelling 2·312 m (7·59 ft); height, travelling 2·26 m (7·41 ft)
Traverse/elevation: 58° total/−2° to +65°
Rate of fire: 4 rounds per minute
Maximum range: 17,265 m (18,880 yards)
Crew: 9

Variant
ML-20: introduced in 1938 as the **M1937**, this equipment uses the carriage of the A-19 (M1931/37) gun, the ordnance being pulled back out of battery for towed transport; the ML-20 has been replaced in front-line Soviet service by the D-20 but remains in valuable service elsewhere; the ordnance fires separate-loading case-type ammunition, and amongst the projectiles are a 43·51-kg (95·9-lb) HE type fired at a muzzle velocity of 655 m (2,149 ft) per second and an AP-T type fired at a muzzle velocity of 600 m (1,969 ft) per second to penetrate 124 mm (4·88 in) of armour at 1000 m (1,095 yards), as well as HEAT, concrete-piercing, smoke and illuminating types

Above: The ML-20 is an obsolete weapon introduced in 1937 and now only in limited service.

M-46 130-mm field gun

(USSR)
Type: towed field gun
Calibre: 130 mm (5·12 in)
Barrel length: 55 calibres
Muzzle brake: pepperpot type
Carriage: split-trail type with two road wheels and a two-wheel limber; shield
Weights: 8450 kg (18,629 lb) in travelling order and 7700 kg (16,975 lb) in firing position
Dimensions: length, travelling 11·73 m (38·48 ft); width, 2·45 m (8·04 ft); height, travelling 2·55 m (8·37 ft)
Traverse/elevation: 50° total/−2·5° to +45°
Rate of fire: 5-6 rounds per minute
Maximum range: 27,150 m (29,690 yards)
Crew: 9

Above and right: The M-46 is a standard field gun in Soviet artillery divisions and brigades, and for travelling can be shortened by pulling the ordnance out of battery.

Variants

M-46: introduced in the early 1950s as successor to the A-19 (M1931/37) gun, the M-46 has its ordnance pulled right back out of battery for towed transport; the type's ordnance is essentially similar to 130-mm (5·12-in) guns used in warships of the Soviet navy, and fires separate-loading case-type ammunition with projectiles such as a 33·4-kg (73·6-lb) HE-FRAG type fired at a muzzle velocity of 1050 m (3,445 ft) per second and an APC-T type fired at the same muzzle velocity to penetrate 230 mm (9·06 in) of armour at 1000 m (1,095 yards), as well as HE RAP, smoke and illuminating types

M-46 (Mod): upgraded version with a longer barrel, cradle and recuperator

M-46 (Israel): sufficient M-46 equipments have been captured from the Arabs in various wars to make it worthwhile putting this weapon into Israeli service with a carriage modified (amongst other features) with four wheels

---

SM-4-1 130-mm coastal gun

(USSR)

Type: towed coast-defence gun
Calibre: 130 mm (5·12 in)
Barrel length: 58·46 calibres
Muzzle brake: modified pepperpot type
Carriage: four-leg split-trail type with two four-wheel axles; no shield
Weights: 19,000 kg (41,887 lb) in travelling order and 16,000 kg (35,273 lb) in firing position
Dimensions: length, travelling 12·80 m (42·00 ft); width, travelling 2·85 m (9·35 ft); height, travelling 3·05 m (10·01 ft)
Traverse/elevation: 360° total/−5° to +45°

Rate of fire: 5 rounds per minute
Maximum range: 29,500 m (32,260 yards)
Crew: not revealed

Variant

SM-4-1: developed soon after World War II, this is still a powerful coast-defence equipment when used in conjunction with a radar fire-control system for engagement of moving targets in all weather conditions; in the firing position the carriage's axles are removed and the four stabilizing legs extended and staked down; the ordnance fires separate-loading ammunition, and the projectiles in service are a 33·4-kg (73·6-lb) HE type fired at a muzzle velocity of 1050 m (3,445 ft) per second, and a 33·6-kg (74·1-lb) APHE type fired at the same muzzle velocity to penetrate 250 mm (9·84 in) of armour at 1000 m (1,095 yards)

D-74 122-mm field gun

(USSR)

Type: towed field gun
Calibre: 121·92 mm (4·8 in)
Barrel length: 47 calibres
Muzzle brake: double-baffle type
Carriage: split-trail type with two road wheels and two castors; shield
Weights: 5550 kg (12,235 lb) in travelling order and 5500 kg (12,125 lb) in firing position
Dimensions: length, travelling 9·875 m (32,40 ft); width, travelling 2·35 m (7·71 ft); height, travelling 2·745 m (9·01 ft)
Traverse/elevation: 58° total/−5° to +45°
Rate of fire: 6-7 rounds per minute
Maximum range: 24,000 m (26,245 yards)
Crew: 10

Variants

D-30: having entered service in the early 1960s as successor to the M-30, this equipment offers useful advantages such as 360° traverse (on its three-leg firing platform) and greater range; the weapon is towed by its muzzle and fires separate-loading case-type ammunition; among the projectiles available are a 21·76-kg (47·97-lb) HE-FRAG type fired at a muzzle velocity of 690 m (2,264 ft) per second and a 21·63-kg (47·7-lb) HEAT-FS type fired at a muzzle velocity of 740 m (2,428 ft) per second to penetrate 460 mm (18·1 in) of armour at any range, as well as HE RAP, chemical, illuminating and smoke types

Saddam: Iraqi-made version of the D-30 with weights of 3440 and 3335 kg (7,584 and 7,352 lb) in travelling order and firing position respectively; the type fires a 22-kg (48·5-lb) projectile to a maximum range of 17,135 m (18,740 yards) at the rate of 6 to 8 rounds per minute

Type 83: Chinese-made version of the D-30

M-30 122-mm howitzer

(USSR)
Type: towed howitzer
Calibre: 121·92 mm (4·8 in)

Above: The D-74 was produced for export, and in firing position traverses on a firing pedestal.

Variants

D-74: designed in the late 1940s as a possible successor to the A-19 (M1931/37) gun, the D-74 was at first known in the West as the **M1955** but not adopted by the Soviet army, which instead accepted the 130-mm (5·12-in) M-46; the D-74 uses the same carriage as the D-20 152-mm (6-in) gun/howitzer, and was widely produced for export; the type is installed on a circular firing platform for operation, and fires separate-loading case-type ammunition; among the projectiles available are a 27·3-kg (60·2-lb) HE-FRAG type fired at a muzzle velocity of 885 m (2,904 ft) per second and a 25-kg (55·1-lb) APC-T type fired at the same muzzle velocity to penetrate 185 mm (7·28 in) of armour at 1000 m (1,095 yards), as well as chemical, illuminating and smoke types

Type 60: Chinese-made copy of the D-74

D-30 122-mm howitzer

(USSR)
Type: towed howitzer
Calibre: 121·92 mm (4·8 in)
Barrel length: 35·5 calibres
Muzzle brake: multi-baffle type
Carriage: three-leg split-trail type with two road wheels; shield
Weights: 3210 kg (7,077 lb) in travelling order and 3150 kg (6,944 lb) in firing position
Dimensions: length, travelling 5·40 m (17·72 ft); width, travelling 1·95 m (6·40 ft); height, travelling 1·66 m (5·45 ft)
Traverse/elevation: 360° total/−7° to +70°
Rate of fire: 7-8 rounds per minute
Maximum range: 15,400 m (16,840 yards) with standard ammunition and 21,900 m (23,950 yards) with RAP
Crew: 7

Right: The D-30 is a standard weapon for artillery battalions in tank and motorized rifle divisions.

Barrel length: 22·7 calibres
Muzzle brake: none
Carriage: split-trail type with two road wheels; shield
Weight: 2450 kg (5,401 lb) in travelling and firing orders
Dimensions: length, travelling 5·90 m (19·36 ft); width, travelling 1·975 m (6·48 ft); height, travelling 1·82 m (5·97 ft)
Traverse/elevation: 49° total/−3° to +63·5°
Rate of fire: 5-6 rounds per minute
Maximum range: 11,800 m (12,905 yards)
Crew: 8

Variants
M-30: introduced in 1939 as the **M1938**, this remained the Soviet army's basic divisional howitzer until the advent of the D-30; the equipment uses the same carriage as the D-1 (M1943) 152-mm (6-in) howitzer, and fires separate-loading case-type ammunition; the projectile variants include a 21·76-kg (47·97-lb) HE-FRAG type fired at a muzzle velocity of 515 m (1,690 ft) per second and a 13·3-kg (29·3-lb) HEAT type fired at a muzzle velocity of 570 m (1,870 ft) per second to penetrate 200 mm (7·87 in) of armour at 1000 m (1,095 yards), as well as chemical, illuminating and smoke types
Type 54: Chinese-made copy of the M-30

The M-30 with sponge rubber filled tyres.

A-19 122-mm gun

(USSR)
Type: towed gun
Calibre: 121·92 mm (4·8 in)
Barrel length: 46 calibres
Muzzle brake: none
Carriage: split-trail type with two road wheels

and a two-wheel limber; shield
Weights: 8050 kg (17,747 lb) in travelling order and 7250 kg (15,983 lb) in firing position
Traverse/elevation: 58° total/−2° to +65°
Rate of fire: 5-6 rounds per minute
Maximum range: 20,800 m (22,745 yards)
Crew: 8

Variant
A-19: introduced in the late 1930s as the **M1931/37** updated version of the M1931, the A-19 was designed as a corps-level weapon and has been

replaced in front-line Soviet service by the M1946 and D-74 guns, though it continues in widespread service with Soviet clients; the ordnance fires separate-loading case-type ammunition, and the projectile variants include a 25-kg (55·1-lb) HE-FRAG type fired at a muzzle velocity of 800 m (2,625 ft) per second and an AP-T type of the same weight and fired at the same muzzle velocity to penetrate 160 mm (6·3 in) of armour at 1000 m (1,095 yards), as well as concrete-piercing and smoke types

Below: The M-30 has been in service since 1939, and is obsolete but still widely used.

Above: The T-12 is exclusively an anti-tank weapon, and still in limited service.

T-12 100-mm anti-tank gun

(USSR)
Type: towed anti-tank gun
Calibre: 100 mm (3·94 in)
Barrel length: 84·8 calibres
Muzzle brake: pepperpot type
Carriage: split-trail type with two road wheels; shield
Weight: 3000 kg (6,614 lb) in travelling and firing orders
Dimensions: length, travelling 9·162 m (30·06 m); width, travelling 1·70 m (5·58 ft); height, travelling 1·448 m (4·75 ft)
Traverse/elevation: 27° total/ − 10° to + 20°
Rate of fire: 10 rounds per minute
Maximum range: 8500 m (9,295 yards)
Crew: 6

Variants
T-12: designed as successor to the 85-mm (3·35-in) D-48 anti-tank gun, the T-12 was introduced in the mid-1960s and uses fixed ammunition of two types, namely APFSDS with a 5·5-kg (12·13-lb) projectile fired at a muzzle velocity of 1500 m (4,921 ft) per second to penetrate 406 mm (16 in) of armour at 500 m (550 yards), and HEAT with a 9·5-kg (20·94-lb) projectile fired at a muzzle velocity of 990 m (3,248 ft) per second to penetrate 400 mm (15·75 in) of armour at any range up to 1200 m (1,310 yards)
T-12A: modified version with larger wheels, a weight of 3100 kg (6,834 lb) and an overall length of 9·64 m (31·63 ft)

BS-3 100-mm field and anti-tank gun

(USSR)
Type: towed field and anti-tank gun
Calibre: 100 mm (3·94 in)

Barrel length: 60·7 calibres
Muzzle brake: double-baffle type
Carriage: split-trail type with two twin road wheels; shield
Weight: 3650 kg (8,047 lb) in travelling and firing orders
Dimensions: length, travelling 9·37 m (30·74 ft); width, travelling 2·15 m (17·05 ft); height, travelling 1·50 m (4·92 ft)
Traverse/elevation: 58° total/ − 5° to + 45°
Rate of fire: 8-10 rounds per minute
Maximum range: 21,000 m (22,965 yards)
Crew: 6

Variants
BS-3: introduced in 1944 as the **M1944**, this powerful weapon was derived from a naval ordnance and fires fixed ammunition; among the projectiles are a 15·6-kg (34·4-lb) HE-FRAG type fired at a muzzle velocity of 900 m (2,953 ft) per second, a 16-kg (35·3-lb) APC-T type fired at a muzzle velocity of 1000 m (3,281 ft) per second to penetrate 185 mm (7·28 in) of armour at 1000 m (1,095 yards), a 5·69-kg (12·54-lb) HVAPDS-T type fired at a muzzle velocity 1415 m (4,642 ft) per second to penetrate 200 + mm (7·87 + in) of armour at 1000 m (1,095 yards), and a 12·36-kg (27·25-lb) HEAT-FS type fired at a muzzle velocity of 900 m (2,953 ft) per second to penetrate 380 mm (14·96 in) of armour at any range up to 1000 m (1,095 yards)
Type 59: provisional designation of the Chinese copy of the BS-3 being adopted as successor to the 85-mm (3·35-in) Type 56 as an anti-tank and counter-battery weapon; the equipment's weight is estimated at 3450 kg (7,606 lb), and the AP-T projectile's penetration is thought to be 157 mm (6·18 in) of armour at 1000 m (1,095 yards); maximum range with the 15·6-kg (34·4-lb) HE-FRAG projectile is believed to be 20,000 m (21,870 yards)

Below: The BS-3 is obsolescent, but because of its dual field gun and anti-tank roles and its ready availability it remains in service with a number of Soviet allies and client states.

SD-44 85-mm field and anti-tank gun

(USSR)
Type: towed field and anti-tank gun
Calibre: 85 mm (3·35 in)
Barrel length: 53 calibres
Muzzle brake: double-baffle type
Carriage: split-trail type with an auxiliary power unit, two road wheels and one castor; shield
Weight: 2250 kg (4,960 lb) in travelling and firing orders
Dimensions: length, travelling 8·22 m (26·97 ft); width, travelling 1·78 m (5·84 ft); height, travelling 1·42 m (4·66 ft)
Traverse/elevation: 54° total/−7° to +35°
Rate of fire: 15 rounds per minute (bursts) and 10 rounds per minute (sustained fire)
Maximum range: 15,650 m (17,115 yards)
Crew: 7

Variant

SD-44: this equipment is essentially the D-44 divisional gun fitted with a 10·4-kW (14-hp) M-72 petrol-engined auxiliary power unit to provide airborne formations with a relatively powerful ordnance possessing limited self-mobility at a maximum road speed of 25 km/h (15·5 mph); the ordnance fires fixed ammunition, and the projectiles include a 9·6-kg (21·2-lb) HE-FRAG type fired at a muzzle velocity of 792 m (2,598 ft) per second, a 9·2-kg (20·3-lb) AP-T type fired at the same muzzle velocity to penetrate 125 mm (4·92 in) of armour at 1000 m (1,095 yards), a 5·06-kg (11·16-kg) HVAP-T type fired at 1030 m (3,379 ft) per second to penetrate 180 mm (7·09 in) of armour at 1000 m (1,095 yards), and a 7·34-kg (16·2-lb) HEAT-FS type fired at a muzzle velocity of 840 m (2,756 ft) per second to penetrate 300 mm (11·8 in) of armour at any range

D-48 85-mm anti-tank gun

(USSR)
Type: towed anti-tank gun
Calibre: 85 mm (3·35 in)
Barrel length: 74 calibres
Muzzle brake: pepperpot type
Carriage: split-trail type with two road wheels and one castor; shield
Weight: 2350 kg (5,181 lb) in travelling and firing orders
Dimensions: (estimated) length, travelling 8·717 m (28·60 ft); width, travelling 1·585 m (5·20 ft); height, travelling 1·89 m (6·20 ft)
Traverse/elevation: 54° total/−6° to +35°
Rate of fire: 15 rounds per minute (bursts) and 8 rounds per minute (sustained fire)
Maximum range: 18,970 m (20,745 yards)
Crew: 6

Variant

D-48: this was originally thought in the West to be a 100-mm (3·94-in) weapon when introduced in the mid-1950s, and it does indeed use a 100-mm type of fixed round, though necked down in this application for an 85-mm (3·35-in) projectile, either a 9·7-kg (221·4-lb) APHE type fired at a muzzle velocity of 1000 m (3,281 ft) per second to penetrate 190 mm (7·48 in) of armour at 1000 m (1,095 yards) or a 9·3-kg (20·5-lb) HVAP type fired at a muzzle velocity of some 1200 m (3,937 ft) per second to penetrate 240 mm (9·45 in) of armour at the same range; the type began to leave Soviet front-line service in the later 1960s

D-44 85-mm field and anti-tank gun

(USSR)
Type: towed field and anti-tank gun
Calibre: 85 mm (3·35 in)
Barrel length: 55·2 calibres including muzzle brake
Muzzle brake: double-baffle type
Carriage: split-trail type with two road wheels and one castor; shield
Weights: 1725 kg (3,803 lb) in travelling order and 1703 kg (3,754 lb) in firing position
Dimensions: length, travelling 8·34 m (27·36 ft); width, travelling 1·78 m (5·84 ft); height, travelling 1·42 m (4·66 ft)
Traverse/elevation: 54° total/−7° to +35°
Rate of fire: 20 rounds per minute (bursts) and 15 rounds per minute (sustained fire)
Maximum range: 16,560 m (18,110 yards)
Crew: 8

Variant

D-44: introduced in the late 1940s as successor to the ZIS-3 (M1942) 76·2-mm (3-in) divisional gun, the D-44 is no longer in first-line Soviet service but remains a widely encountered piece of equipment elsewhere; the same ordnance is used in the SD-44, and the D-44 thus fires the same ammunition types
Type 56: Chinese-made copy of the D-44 with only very slight modifications; the anti-armour performance is generally comparable to that of the Soviet equipment

Below: Seen in an Israeli park of captured Arab weapons, the D-44 is no longer in Soviet service but still used in many other countries.

Vasilyek 82-mm automatic mortar

(USSR)
Type: towed automatic mortar
Calibre: 82 mm (3·2 in)
Barrel length: not revealed
Muzzle brake: none
Carriage: split-trail type with two road wheels; no shield
Weight: not revealed
Dimensions: not revealed
Traverse/elevation: 10° total/0° to +80°
Rate of fire: 4 rounds in 2 seconds (bursts) and 40-60 rounds per minute (cyclic)
Maximum range: 5000 m (5,470 yards)
Crew: not revealed

Variant

Vasilyek: this interesting weapon has been known for some time, but details remain sparse; the Vasilyek (cornflower) can be towed, but is generally transported on a truck flatbed before being brought into firing position on its wheels; in firing position the equipment is stabilized on its spread trail legs and a forward leg that is hand-cranked down to lift the wheels off the ground; the weapon is breech-loaded, recoil-operated and fed with four-round clips for high burst and sustained rates over indirect-fire minimum and maximum ranges of 100 to 5000 m (110 and 5,470 yards), and a direct-fire maximum range of 1000 m (1,095 yards); nothing is known of bomb types, though these presumably include HE-FRAG, smoke and illuminating

Above right: The Vasilyek is a very important Soviet tactical weapon.

Variant

M1966: otherwise known as the **M1969** in the Western provisional terminology, this mountain howitzer appeared in the second half of the 1960s; the type can fire all the ammunition types available to the ZIS-3 76·2-mm (3-in) divisional gun, and with the HEAT-FS round the M1966 can penetrate 280 mm (11·02 in) of armour; it is believed that the weapon can be broken down in components small enough for animal or light helicopter transport

---

ZIS-3 76-mm field gun

(USSR)

Type: towed field gun
Calibre: 76·2 mm (3 in)
Barrel length: 45 calibres including muzzle brake
Muzzle brake: double-baffle type
Carriage: split-trail type with two road wheels; shield
Weight: 1116 kg (2,460 lb) in travelling and firing orders
Dimensions: length, travelling 6·095 m (20·00 ft); width, travelling 1·645 m (5·40 ft); height, travelling 1·375 m (4·51 ft)
Traverse/elevation: 54° total/−5° to +37°
Rate of fire: 20 rounds per minute (bursts) and 15 rounds per minute (sustained fire)
Maximum range: 13,290 m (14,535 yards)
Crew: 7

Variants

ZIS-3: although no longer in first-line service with any major element of the Warsaw Pact armies, this **M1942** weapon is still widely used elsewhere in the world despite its age; the ordnance fires fixed ammunition, including HE-FRAG, AP-T, HVAP-T, HEAT and smoke types
Type 54: Chinese-made copy of the ZIS-3

M1966 76-mm mountain howitzer

(USSR)

Type: towed mountain howitzer
Calibre: 76·2 mm (3 in)
Barrel length: not revealed
Muzzle brake: none
Carriage: split-trail type with two road wheels; shield
Weight: 780 kg (1,720 lb) in travelling order
Dimensions: length, travelling 4·80 m (15·75 ft); width, travelling 1·50 m (8·20 ft); height, travelling not revealed
Traverse/elevation: 50° total/−5° to +65°
Rate of fire: 15 rounds per minute
Maximum range: about 11,000 m (12,030 yards)
Crew: 6

Left: The M1966 mountain gun.

Below: The ZIS-3 field gun displayed at the 1990 Moscow Army parade.

Above: The ZIS-3 is another obsolete weapon still in widespread Warsaw Pact and Third-World service.

Ch-26 57-mm anti-tank gun

(USSR)
Type: towed anti-tank gun
Calibre: 57 mm (2·24 in)
Barrel length: 71·4 calibres including muzzle brake
Muzzle brake: double-baffle type
Carriage: split-trail type with an auxiliary power unit and three road wheels; shield
Weight: 1250 kg (2,756 lb) in travelling and firing orders
Dimensions: length, travelling 6·112 m (20·05 ft); width, travelling 1·80 m (5·91 ft); height, travelling 1·22 m (4·00 ft)
Traverse/elevation: 56° total/−4° to +15°
Rate of fire: 12 rounds per minute
Maximum range: 6700 m (7,325 yards)
Crew: 5

Variant
Ch-26: designed for use by airborne formations, the Ch-26 remains in second-line service with a few countries, and features a 10·4-kW (14-hp) petrol-engined auxiliary power unit to provide a maximum road speed of 40 km/h (25 mph); the ordnance uses fixed ammunition whose projectiles include a 3·75-kg (8·27-lb) HE-FRAG type fired with a muzzle velocity of 695 m (2,280 ft) per second, a 3·14-kg (6·92-lb) AP-T type fired with a muzzle velocity of 980 m (3,215 ft) per second to penetrate 106 mm (4·17 in) of armour at 500 m (550 yards), and a 1·76-kg (3·88-lb) HVAP-T type fired at a muzzle velocity of 1255 m (4,117 ft) per second to penetrate 140 mm (5·51 in) of armour at 500 m (550 yards)

ZIS-2 57-mm anti-tank gun

(USSR)
Type: towed anti-tank gun
Calibre: 57 mm (2·24 in)
Barrel length: 73 calibres
Muzzle brake: none
Carriage: split-trail type with two road wheels; shield
Weight: 1150 kg (2,535 lb) in travelling and firing orders
Dimensions: length, travelling 6·795 m (22·29 ft);

width, travelling 1·70 m (5·58 ft); height, travelling 1·37 m (4·49 ft)
Traverse/elevation: 56° total/−5° to +25°
Rate of fire: 25 rounds per minute
Maximum range: 8400 m (9,185 yards)
Crew: 7

Variants
ZIS-2: introduced in 1943, this **M1943** equipment is obsolescent but remains in widespread service with Soviet clients; it fires the same ammunition types as the Ch-26 and has comparable anti-armour performance
Type 55: Chinese-made copy of the ZIS-2

5·5-in Medium Gun

(UK)
Type: towed gun
Calibre: 5·5 in (139·7 mm)
Barrel length: 29·9 calibres
Muzzle brake: none

Carriage: split-trail type with two road wheels; no shield
Weight: 12,900 lb (5851 kg) in travelling and firing orders
Dimensions: length, travelling 24·67 ft (7·52 m); width, travelling 8·33 ft (2·54 m); height, travelling 8·58 ft (2·62 m)
Traverse/elevation: 60° total/−5° to +45°
Rate of fire: 2 rounds per minute
Maximum range: 16,200 yards (14,815 m) with 100-lb (45·36-kg) HE projectile and 18,000 yards (16,460 m) with 80-lb (36·29-kg) HE projectile
Crew: 10

Variant
5·5-in Medium Gun: introduced in 1942 and now obsolescent, this is a moderately powerful equipment that fires separate-loading ammunition with two types of HE projectile, with smoke and illuminating projectiles also available; in South Africa the equipment is designated the **G2**

Below: A World War II type, the 5·5-in remains in modest worldwide service.

L118A1 105-mm Light Gun

(UK)
Type: towed field gun
Calibre: 105 mm (4·13 in)
Barrel length: 29·2 calibres
Muzzle brake: double-baffle type
Carriage: split trail type with two road wheels; no shield
Weight: 4,100 lb (1860 kg) in travelling and firing orders
Dimensions: length, travelling with gun forward 20·75 ft (6·32 m), travelling with barrel over trails 16·00 ft (4·88 m) and in firing position with barrel horizontal 23·00 ft (7·01 m); width, travelling and in firing position 5·83 ft (1·78 m); height, travelling with barrel forward 8·63 ft (2·63 ft)
Traverse/elevation: 360° on firing platform and 11° total on carriage/−5·5° to +70°

Rate of fire: 8 rounds in 60 seconds (bursts), 6 rounds per minute (3-minute period) and 3 rounds per minute (sustained fire)
Maximum range: 18,800 yards (17,190 m)
Crew: 6

Variants

L118A1: introduced in 1974, the L118A1 is the basic electrically fired British version of the Light Gun and is a thoroughly modern piece of equipment designed to fulfil the pack howitzer and gun roles while being airportable under medium-lift helicopters; the ordnance fires semi-fixed ammunition with a seven-charge propellant system offering ranges between 2,750 and 18,800 yards (2515 and 17,190 m); the projectile types available are 35·5-lb (16·1-kg) HE, 23·1-lb (10·49-kg) HESH, illuminating and three smoke varieties
L118F1 Hamel: version of the L118A1 built under licence in Australia for the Australian and New Zealand armies
L119A1 Hamel: the version developed for the US M1 ammunition series with different rifling, a single-baffle muzzle brake, percussion firing and a maximum range of 12,000 yards (10,975 m); the type is used by Australia and New Zealand as a training weapon for the L118F1, using existing stocks of US-supplied ammunition and being better suited, because of its shorter range, for operational training in battle areas
L127A1: version developed for Switzerland with different rifling, a double-baffle muzzle brake and percussion firing

Below: The Light Gun is transportable as a slung load under many medium helicopters, and is a capable equipment that is still securing useful orders for the export market.

25-pdr Mk 3 field gun

(UK)
Type: towed field gun
Calibre: 87·6 mm (3·45 in)
Barrel length: 28·3 calibres
Muzzle brake: double-baffle type
Carriage: box-type with two road wheels; shield
Weight: 3,970 lb (1801 kg) in travelling and firing positions
Dimensions: length, travelling 26·00 ft (7·92 m); width, travelling 6·96 ft (2·12 m); height, travelling 5·41 ft (1·65 m)
Traverse/elevation: 360° on firing platform and 8° total on carriage/−5° to +40°
Rate of fire: 10 rounds per minute (bursts) and 5 rounds per minute (sustained fire)
Maximum range: 13,400 yards (12,255 m)
Crew: 6

Variant
25-pdr Mk 3: a classic weapon introduced in 1939 as the **25-pdr Mk 1** (or **18/25-pdr**) with an 18-pdr ordnance on a 25-pdr carriage and entering definitive service in 1940 as the **25-pdr Mk 2** before being developed into the 25-pdr Mk 3 of 1942 with a muzzle brake to make feasible the firing of armour-piercing rounds at a high muzzle velocity; now obsolete, the type still serves in some numbers with smaller armies and fires separate-loading ammunition, including a 25-lb (11·34-kg) HE projectile fired at a muzzle velocity of 1,700 ft (518 m) per second, a 20·3-lb (9·2-kg) AP projectile fired at a muzzle velocity of 2,000 ft (609 m) per second and able to penetrate 2·75 in (70 mm) of armour at 400 yards (365 m), an illuminating projectile and a smoke projectile

Below: The 25-pdr (seen with its firing platform) is an obsolete weapon still used in many ex-British colonies and dependencies.

17-pdr anti-tank gun

(UK)
Type: towed anti-tank gun
Calibre: 76·2 mm (3 in)
Barrel length: 58·3 calibres
Muzzle brake: double-baffle type
Carriage: split-trail type with two road wheels; shield
Weights: 6,700 lb (3039 kg) in travelling order and 6,445 lb (2923 kg) in firing position
Dimensions: length, travelling 24·75 ft (7·54 m); width, travelling 7·30 ft (2·225 m); height, travelling 5·50 m (1·68 m)
Traverse/elevation: 60° total/−6° to +16·5°
Rate of fire: 10 rounds per minute
Maximum range: 10,000 yards (9145 m)
Crew: 6

Variant
17-pdr: introduced in 1943, this obsolete equipment is still in service with smaller armies, and fires fixed ammunition; the 15·4-lb (6·98-kg) HE projectile is fired at a muzzle velocity of 2,875 ft (876 m) per second, the 17-lb (7·7-kg) AP projectile is fired at a muzzle velocity of 2,900 ft (884 m) per second to penetrate 4·3 in (109 mm) of armour at 1,000 yards (915 m), the 17-lb APC projectile is fired at the same muzzle velocity to penetrate 4·65 in (118 mm) of armour at 1,000 yards (915 m), and the 7·6-lb (3·4-kg) APDS projectile is fired at a muzzle velocity of 3,945 ft (1203 m) per second to penetrate 9·1 in (231 mm) of armour at 1,000 yards (915 m); the maximum effective anti-tank range is 1,650 yards (1510 m)

M115 8-in howitzer

(USA)
Type: towed howitzer
Calibre: 8 in (203·2 mm)
Barrel length: 25 calibres
Muzzle brake: none
Carriage: split-trail type with four twin road wheels and a two-wheel limber; no shield
Weights: 32,000 lb (14,515 kg) in travelling order and 29,700 lb (13,472 kg) in firing position
Dimensions: length, travelling 36·00 ft (10·97 m); width, travelling 9·33 ft (2·84 m) and in firing position 22·50 ft (6·86 m); height, travelling 9·00 ft (2·74 m)
Traverse/elevation: 60° total/−2° to +65°
Rate of fire: 1 round per minute (bursts) and 1 round per 2 minutes (sustained fire)
Maximum range: 18,375 yards (16,800 m)
Crew: 14

Variant
M115: introduced in 1940 as the M1 and redesignated M115 after World War II, this is the largest-calibre towed equipment in current Western service; the ordnance fires separate-loading ammunition with a seven-charge propellant system; the projectiles include a 204-lb (92·53-kg) HE type fired at a muzzle velocity of 1,925 ft (587 m) per second to the weapon's maximum range, a 200-lb (90·72-kg) HE grenade-launching type fired at the same muzzle velocity and carrying 104 M43 grenades to the maximum range, a 206·5-kg (93·66-kg) HE grenade-launching type fired at a muzzle velocity of 1,950 ft (594 m) per second and carrying 195 M42 grenades to a range of 17,500 yards (16,000 m), a 204-lb (92·53-kg) chemical type fired at a muzzle velocity of 1,925 ft (587 m) per second to the maximum range, an M422 nuclear type carrying a W33 warhead of 0·5- or 10-kiloton yield, and an M753 nuclear type carrying a W79-1 warhead of 0·5-, 1- or 2-kiloton yield

102·57-lb/46·53-kg type with 88 dual-purpose grenades and a 95-lb/43·09-kg type with 60 anti-personnel grenades), a 96-lb (43·54-kg) HE RAP type fired at a muzzle velocity of 2,710 ft (826 m per second), two types of HE mine-launcher each weighing 103 lb (46·72 kg) with nine anti-tank mines, the Copperhead laser-guided anti-tank projectile, three chemical/gas types, two illuminating types, two smoke types and the M454 nuclear type with a 0·1-kiloton W48 warhead (to be replaced by the W82 enhanced-radiation 'neutron' warhead)

Above: The M115 fires a very substantial projectile, but only over a short range.

M198 155-mm howitzer

(USA)
Type: towed howitzer
Calibre: 155 mm (6·1 in)
Barrel length: 39·3 calibres
Muzzle brake: double-baffle type
Carriage: split-trail type with two road wheels; no shield
Weight: 15,790 lb (7162 kg) in travelling and firing orders
Dimensions: length, travelling with barrel forward 40·50 ft (12·34 m), travelling with barrel over trails 24·41 ft (7·44 m) and in firing position 36·08 ft (11·00 m); width, travelling 9·17 ft (2·794 m) and in firing position 28·00 ft (8·534 m); height, travelling with barrel forward 9·50 ft (2·90 m), travelling with barrel over trails 6·96 ft (2·121 m) and in firing position with barrel horizontal 5·92 ft (1·803 m)
Traverse/elevation: 45° total/−5° to +72°
Rate of fire: 4 rounds per minute
Maximum range: 19,850 yards (18,150 m) with HE grenade-launching projectile and 32,800 yards (29,995 m) with HE RAP
Crew: 11

Variant
M198: intended as successor to the M114 series,

the M198 towed howitzer began to enter US service in 1978; the type is designed to fire the full range of standard NATO separate-loading ammunition, and projectiles that can be used are two types of HE mine-launcher each weighing 102·5 lb (42·5 kg) and carrying 36 anti-personnel mines, two types of HE grenade-launcher (a

M59 155-mm gun

(USA)
Type: towed gun
Calibre: 155 mm (6·1 in)
Barrel length: 45 calibres
Muzzle brake: none
Carriage: split-trail type with four twin road wheels and a two-wheel limber; no shield
Weights: 30,600 lb (13,880 kg) in travelling order and 27,780 lb (12,601 kg) in firing position
Dimensions: length, travelling 36·17 ft (11·024 m); width, travelling 8·25 ft (2·512 m); height, travelling 8·92 ft (2·718 m)
Traverse/elevation: 60° total/−2° to +63°
Rate of fire: 4 rounds per minute (bursts), 2 rounds per minute (short period) and 1 round per minute (sustained fire)
Maximum range: 24,000 yards (21,945 m)
Crew: 14

Variants
M59: introduced as the M1 series in 1938 and redesignated M59 after World War II, this 'Long Tom' is a cumbersome but still notably accurate weapon; the M59 fires separate-loading ammunition, the three basic projectiles being a 95·7-lb (43·4-kg) HE type fired at a muzzle velocity of 2,745 ft (837 m) per second, a 99-lb (44·9-kg) AP type fired at a muzzle velocity of 2,800 ft (854 m) per second to penetrate 3 in (76 mm) of armour, and a smoke type

Below: Though an old design, the M59 has impressive accuracy over medium ranges.

M114A1 howitzer

(USA)

Type: towed howitzer
Calibre: 155 mm (6·1 in)
Barrel length: 20 calibres
Muzzle brake: none
Carriage: split-trail type with two road wheels; shield
Weights: 12,785 lb (5799 kg) in travelling order and 12,700 lb (5761 kg) in firing position
Dimensions: length, travelling 24·00 ft (7·315 m); width, travelling 8·00 ft (2·438 m); height, travelling 5·92 ft (1·803 m)
Traverse/elevation: 49° total (24° left and 25° right of the centreline)/−2° to +63°
Rate of fire: 2 rounds in 30 seconds, 8 rounds in 4 minutes and 16 rounds in 10 minutes (bursts), and 40 rounds per hour (sustained fire)
Maximum range: 16,000 yards (14,630 m)
Crew: 11

Variants

M114: introduced in 1941 as the M1 series, this type was redesignated M114 after World War II, and though obsolescent in its basic form it is still in very widespread service firing much of the standard NATO separate-loading ammunition; typical projectiles are the 94·6-lb (42·91-kg) HE type fired at a muzzle velocity of 1,850 ft (564 m) per

Left and below: The M114 howitzer has a firing jack operated by a rack and pinion mechanism.

second, the 95-lb (43·1-kg) HE grenade-launcher type with 60 anti-personnel grenades fired at the same muzzle velocity, three chemical/gas types, two illuminating types, two smoke types and the nuclear M454 type with the 0·1-kiloton W48 warhead (to be replaced by the W82 enhanced-radiation 'neutron' warhead)

M114A1: version of the M114 on the M1A2 rather than M1A1 carriage with a screw- rather than rack/pinion-operated firing jack

M114A2: US M114A1 fitted with the ordnance of the M198

M114F: M114 with a French-produced conversion kit to allow the ordnance to fire extended-range rounds

M65: Yugoslav-made copy of the M114A1 differing only in detail from the US original

OTO Melara 155/39TM: upgraded version of the M114 developed in Italy by OTO Melara with an L/39 ordnance possessing identical ballistic performance to the ordnance of the M109L self-propelled howitzer in Italian service; the new ordnance has a double-baffle muzzle brake, revised breech and a weight of 2450 kg (5,401 lb) compared with the 1700 kg (3,748 lb) of the original ordnance; the use of a semi-automatic breech alters the weapon's traverse limits, traverse up to an elevation of +45° remaining unaltered at a total of 49° (24° left and 25° right of the centreline), but at elevation angles between +45° and +60° reducing to a total of 42° (17° left and 25° right of the centreline); the barrel of the revised ordnance is essentially identical to that of the FH-70 howitzer, and can fire an M107 HE projectile to 18,200 m (19,905 yards), an L15A1 HE projectile to 18,500 m (20,230 yards) and an M549A1 RAP to 30,000 (32,810 yards)

Rheinmetall FH155(L): updated version proposed in West Germany, with an improved shield, a new barrel and breech offering superior

firing and wear characteristics, and a double-baffle muzzle brake

SITECSA M114: updated version of the M114 offered by the Spanish company SITECSA; the type is offered in variants with L/39 or L/45 barrels based on that of the same company's 155/45 ST 012 equipment, which is fitted with a multi-baffle muzzle brake and an automatic breech; other modifications include the ability to fire most modern NATO ammunition types, a pneumatically operated rammer, a hydraulically operated jack/float system, and a device to pull the ordnance back out of battery as a means of reducing travelling length; key data for the L/45 version include a weight of 7350 kg (16,204 lb), a travelling length of 9·761 m (32·02 ft), a travelling width of 2·438 m (8·00 ft), a firing width of 4·7 m (15·42 ft), total traverse of 49° (24° left and 25° right of the centreline), elevation between −2° and +60°, normal and maximum rates of fire of 2 and 5 rounds per minute, and a maximum range of 39,600 m (43,305 yards)

T65: M114A1 made under licence in Taiwan, and generally similar to the US original apart from a weight of 5000 kg (11,023 lb) and a range of 15,000 m (16,405 yards)

M102 105-mm howitzer

(USA)

Type: towed howitzer
Calibre: 105 mm (4·13 in)
Barrel length: 32 calibres
Muzzle brake: none
Carriage: box-type with two road wheels and a longitudinal roller for traverse; no shield
Weight: 3,300 lb (1497 kg) in travelling and firing orders

Dimensions: length, travelling 17·00 ft (5·182 m); width, travelling 6·44 ft (1·964 m); height, travelling 5·23 ft (1·594 m)
Traverse/elevation: 360° total on baseplate/−5° to +75°
Rate of fire: 10 rounds per minute
Maximum range: 12,575 yards (11,500 m) with standard ammunition and 16,500 yards (15,090 m) with HE RAP
Crew: 8

Variant

M102: designed as a lightweight successor to the M101 for service with airborne and air-mobile formations, the M102 entered the inventory in 1966 and is notable for its compact design and aluminium box trail; the type fires the same semi-fixed ammunition as the M101, but its longer barrel allows a slightly higher muzzle velocity and thus enhanced range

---

M101A1 105-mm howitzer

(USA)

Type: towed field howitzer
Calibre: 105 mm (4·13 in)
Barrel length: 22·5 calibres
Muzzle brake: none
Carriage: split-trail type with two road wheels; shield
Weight: 4,980 lb (2259 kg) in travelling and firing orders
Dimensions: length, travelling 19·67 ft (5·991 m); width, travelling 7·08 ft (2·159 m) and in firing pos-

Below: Part of an M101 105-mm (4·13-in) battery in firing position. The type still serves with the armies of many smaller countries.

ition 12·00 ft (3·657 m); height, travelling 5·16 ft (1·574 m)
Traverse/elevation: 46° total/−5° to +66°
Rate of fire: 10 rounds per minute (bursts) and 3 rounds per minute (sustained fire)
Maximum range: 12,325 yards (11,270 m) with standard ammunition and 15,965 yards (14,600 m) with HE RAP
Crew: 8

Variants

M101: introduced in 1940, the M2 series was redesignated M101 after World War II; though it is an obsolescent equipment by modern standards it is still in widespread service; the equipment weighs 4,475 lb (2030 kg) in travelling and firing orders, and has a travelling height of 5·00 ft (1·524 m); the ordnance fires a wide range of NATO standard semi-fixed ammunition, the projectiles including one HE, two HE grenade-launching, one HE RAP, one HEP, one anti-personnel, one chemical, two smoke and one illuminating types; these have complete round weights varying from 33·45 to 46·4 lb (15·17 to 21·06 kg), and muzzle velocities ranging from 1,400 to 1,800 ft (427 to 549 m) per second
M101A1: improved version using the M2A2 rather than M2A1 carriage
FH105(L): improved version of the M101A1 developed in West Germany by Rheinmetall; this has an L/35·5 barrel and a single-baffle muzzle brake, the effect being an increase in the muzzle velocity of the standard HE round from 1,550 to 1,970 ft (472 to 600 m) per second and a lengthening of the range from 12,325 to 15,420 yards (11,270 to 14,100 m) at the expense of an additional 280 kg (617 lb) of weight and a weapon difficult to tow because it is unbalanced
105-mm Howitzer C1: Canadian licence-built version of the M101A1 with an improved ordnance and breech

M116 75-mm pack howitzer

(USA)
Type: towed pack howitzer
Calibre: 75 mm (2·95 in)
Barrel length: 15·9 calibres
Muzzle brake: none
Carriage: box-type with two road wheels; shield
Weight: 1,440 lb (653 kg) in travelling and firing orders
Dimensions: length, travelling 12·00 ft (3·658 m); width, travelling 3·91 ft (1·194 m); height, travelling 3·08 m (0·94 m)
Traverse/elevation: 6° total/−5° to +45°
Rate of fire: 6 rounds per minute (bursts) and 3 rounds per minute (sustained fire)
Maximum range: 9,600 yards (8780 m)
Crew: 5

Variant

M116: introduced in 1927 as the M1 series, this equipment became the M116 after World War II, and was designed for pack animal transport (eight mule-transportable loads), paradropping (nine loads), or towing by a light vehicle; the type fires either fixed ammunition in the form of the HEAT-T type with a 15·65-lb (7·1-kg) projectile fired at a muzzle velocity of 1,000 ft (304 m) per second or semi-fixed ammunition in the form of the HE type with a 18·25-lb (8·27-kg) projectile fired at a muzzle velocity of 1,250 ft (381 m) per second, and the smoke type

M56 105-mm howitzer

(Yugoslavia)
Type: towed howitzer
Calibre: 155 mm (6·1 in)
Barrel length: 27·9 calibres
Muzzle brake: multi-baffle type
Carriage: split-trail type with two road wheels; shield
Weights: 2100 kg (4,630 lb) in travelling order and 2060 kg (4,541 lb) in firing position
Dimensions: length, travelling 6·17 m (20·24 ft); width, travelling 2·15 m (7·05 ft); height, travelling 1·56 m (5·12 ft)
Traverse/elevation: 52° total/−12° to +68°
Rate of fire: 16 rounds per minute

Maximum range: 13,000 m (14,215 yards)
Crew: 7

Variant

M56: this Yugoslav equipment was introduced in the second half of the 1950s and is based loosely on the German leFH 18/40 but firing US M1 ammunition; the ordnance fires semi-fixed ammunition such as HE, AP-T, HESH-T, illuminating and smoke

M48(B-1) 76-mm mountain gun

(Yugoslavia)
Type: towed mountain gun
Calibre: 76·2 mm (3 in)
Barrel length: 15·45 calibres
Muzzle brake: multi-baffle type
Carriage: folding split-trail type with two road wheels; shield
Weights: 720 kg (1,587 lb) in travelling order and 705 kg (1,554 lb) in firing position
Dimensions: length, travelling 2·42 m (7·94 ft); width, travelling 1·46 m (4·79 ft); height, travelling 1·22 m (4·00 ft)
Traverse/elevation: 50° total/−15° to +45°
Rate of fire: 25 rounds per minute
Maximum range: 8750 m (9,570 yards)
Crew: 6

Variant

M48: designed after World War II to meet the special requirements of Yugoslav mountain units, this equipment entered service in the late 1940s and has proved moderately successful; there are four subtypes, namely the **M48(B-1)** basic model that can be broken down into eight mule loads, the **M48(B-1A1-1)** that cannot be broken down for pack transport, the **M48(B-1A2)** with alloy wheels and solid tyres, and the **M48B-2** updated version; the ordnance fires semi-fixed HE, HEAT and smoke rounds

Below: The M48 is suited to Yuogoslavia's particular needs, and can be towed by an animal.

NORINCO Type 80 SP 57-mm twin AA gun mounting

(China)

Type: tracked self-propelled twin 57-mm AA gun mounting

Crew: 6

Combat weight: 31,000 kg (68,342 lb)

Dimensions: length, guns forward 8·42 m (27·62 ft) and hull 6·243 m (20·48 ft); width 3·307 m (10·85 ft); height 2·748 m (9·016 ft)

Armament system: two 57-mm Type 59 guns with 300 rounds of ready-use ammunition; the turret is electro-hydraulically powered, the guns lack stabilization in either elevation (−5° to +85° in powered mode and −1° to +81° in manual mode) or azimuth (360°), and an optical fire-control system is fitted

Armour: cast and welded steel varying in thickness between 12 and 45 mm (0·47 and 1·77 in)

Powerplant: one 435-kW (583-hp) Model 12150L-7BW diesel engine with an unrevealed quantity of internal fuel

Performance: speed, road 50 km/h (31·1 mph); range, road 440 km (273 miles); fording 1·4 m (4·6 ft); gradient 60% ; side slope 40% ; vertical obstacle 0·8 m (31·5 in); trench 2·7 m (8·9 ft); ground clearance 0·425 m (16·75 in)

Variants

Type 80: introduced in the mid-1980s, and based on the Soviet ZSU-57-2 but using the hull of the Chinese Type 69-II; the turret of the original is replaced by a more angular unit carrying two 57-mm guns; like its Soviet counterpart, the Type 80 is limited to clear-weather operations by its

Below: The Type 80 has good protection, mobility and firepower, though it lacks an all-weather fire-control system.

optical sights; no other details of the system have been revealed, though it is clear that the tactical role intended for the Type 80 is the defence of China's armoured and mechanized divisions against low-level air attack; the guns have a maximum horizontal range of 12,000 m (13,125 yards) and an effective slant range of 5500 m (6,015 yards), and fire two types of round each with a muzzle velocity of 1000 m (3,281 ft) per second; the vehicle has storage for 300 6·47-kg (14·26-lb) HE-T and 6·45-kg (14·22-lb) APC-T rounds for use against aircraft and lightly armoured targets respectively, and these are supplied to the guns in clips of four, reducing the rate of fire per barrel from a cyclic 120 to a practical 70 rounds per minute.

Chinese 37-mm SP AA gun mounting: the Chinese have also developed a twin 37-mm AA mounting on the same chassis, though the designation for this useful system remains unknown; the two-man power-operated turret has an optronic fire-control system for the twin Type P793 Type B cannon, each with a cyclic rate of 380 rounds per minute and muzzle velocity of 1000 m (3,281 ft) per second using belt-fed ammunition; the guns have a single-feed arrangement, and can thus fire only one type of ammunition in any engagement; the practical slant range is 4000 m (4,375 yards), and the effective horizontal range 3500 m (3,830 yards); the combat weight of this variant is 34,200 kg (75,397 lb), and the powered traverse and elevation are respectively 360° and an arc between −7° and +87°

NORINCO Type 63 SP 37-mm twin AA gun mounting

(China)

Type: tracked self-propelled 37-mm twin AA gun mounting

Crew: 6

Combat weight: 32,000 kg (70,547 lb)

Dimensions: length, guns forward 6·432 m (20·10 ft) and hull 6·19 m (20·31 ft); width 3·27 m (10·73 ft); height to turret top 2·995 m (9·83 ft)

Armament system: two 37-mm guns with an unrevealed number of rounds of ready-use ammunition; the turret is manually powered, the guns lack stabilization in either elevation (−5° to +85°) or azimuth (360°), and an optical fire-control system is fitted

Armour: cast and welded steel varying in thickness betwen 16 and 47 mm (0·63 and 1·85 in)

Powerplant: one 375-kW (503-hp) Model V-2-34 diesel engine with 590 litres (130 Imp gal) of internal fuel

Performance: speed, road 55 km/h (34·2 mph); range, road 300 km (186 miles); fording 1·32 m (4·33 ft); gradient 60% ; side slope 30% ; vertical obstacle 0·73 m (29 in); trench 2·5 m (8·2 ft); ground clearance 0·41 m (16 in)

Variant

Type 63: this was the first Chinese-designed self-propelled anti-aircraft equipment to enter service, and is based on the chassis of the obsolete Soviet T-34 medium tank: the tank turret has been removed, the gap inside the turret ring being plated over to provide the support necessary for the twin 37-mm cannon mounting, essentially the Type 63 wheeled mounting located on the tank-mounted platform; protection of a limited nature for the cannon and gun crew is provided by a tall slab-sided, open-topped turret of 16-mm (0·63-in) armour bolted to the gun mounting; the turret carries a small quantity of ready-use ammunition, but most of the vehicle's ammunition is carried in wooden boxes stored inside metal containers welded to the sides of the hull; tactical limitations are the vehicle's lack of any NBC protection, night

vision equipment and amphibious capability; the two basic ammunition types used by the Type 63 are FRAG-T (two types) and AP-T, which are loaded in five-round clips and replenished in the turret's ready-use supply from the hull-side reserve supply below the turret; fire-control is of the basic optical type, and the cannon have cyclic and practical rates (per barrel) of 180 and 80 rounds per minute respectively to an effective slant range of 3000 m (3,280 yards) with the FRAG-T ammunition types; the cannon have a maximum horizontal range of 9500 m (10,390 yards)

Avia M53/59 SP 30-mm twin AA gun mounting

(Czechoslovakia)
Type: wheeled self-propelled 30-mm twin AA gun mounting
Crew: 5
Combat weight: 10,300 kg (22,707 lb)
Dimensions: length overall 6·92 m (22·70 ft); width 2·35 m (7·71 ft); height including magazines 2·95 m (9·68 ft)
Armament system: two 30-mm cannon with 800 rounds of ready-use ammunition; the mounting is

Below: An unusual perspective of the M53/59 with the overhead vertical magazines for the two 30-mm cannon on their hydraulically powered mounting.

hydraulically powered, the guns lack stabilization in either elevation (−10° to +85°) or azimuth (360°), and optical sights are fitted
Armour: welded steel to a maximum thickness of 10 mm (0·39 in)
Powerplant: one 82-kW (110-hp) Tatra T 212-2 diesel engine with 120 litres (26 Imp gal) of internal fuel, and driving a 6 × 6 layout
Performance: speed, road 60 km/h (37·3 mph); range, road 500 km (311 miles); fording 0·8 m (2·6 ft); gradient 60% ; side slope 30% ; vertical obstacle 0·46 m (18·1 in); trench 0·69 m (2·25 ft); ground clearance 0·4 m (15·75 in)

Variants
M53/59: introduced to service in 1959, this is a simple equipment combining the chassis and automotive system of the Praga V3S truck with an armoured body and, mounted at the very rear of the vehicle behind the rear axle, turntable-mounted twin 30-mm cannon; the cannon can be elevated in an arc from −10° to +85°, though depression is limited to +2° over the crew compartment; the cannon are conventional weapons, their ammunition feed comprising a large 50-round magazine over each weapon (fed by 10-round clips of HEI and API ammunition) for cyclic and practical rates of 500 and 150 rounds per minute respectively; the maximum horizontal range of the cannon is 9700 m (10,610 yards), and the maximum vertical range 6300 m (20,670 ft), but within this context the effective slant range is 3000 m (3,280 yards) using API ammunition; the system is provided with only a simple optical fire-

control system, and is thus limited to clear-weather operations; the complete system suffers the disadvantages of lacking NBC protection and night vision devices, and while the hull is well protected by nicely sloped armour the gunner (seated to the left of the cannon) is only modestly protected to his front, sides and back, with overhead protection absent
M53/70: version introduced in 1970 for the export market; it appears identical to the M53/59 other than being fitted with a slightly improved fire-control system

GIAT/Thomson-CSF Shahine SP surface-to-air missile system

(France)
Type: tracked self-propelled surface-to-air missile system
Crew: 3
Combat weight: 38,800 kg (85,538 lb)
Dimensions: length overall 6·59 m (21·62 ft); width 3·10 m (10·17 ft); height not revealed
Armament system: six launchers (three on each side of the central weapon/sensor pedestal) with six R.460 missiles; the pedestal is electrically powered but lacks stabilization in either elevation (an unrevealed arc) or azimuth (360°), and a radar-directed fire-control system is fitted
Armour: welded steel

Above: The firing unit of the Shahine system has fire-control radar and six R.460 missiles.

Below: The acquisition unit of the Shahine system with its 360° scan surveillance radar.

Powerplant: one 460-kW (617-hp) Hispano-Suiza HS 110 multi-fuel engine with 970 litres (213 Imp gal) of internal fuel

Performance: speed, road 65 km/h (40·4 mph); range, road 600 km (373 miles); fording 2·2 m (7·2 ft) with preparation; gradient 60% ; side slope 30% ; vertical obstacle 0·93 m (36·6 in); trench 2·9 m (9·5 ft); ground clearance 0·45 m (17·7 in)

Variants

Shahine: in 1975 Saudi Arabia ordered a gun-armed anti-aircraft vehicle (the AMX-30 SA) based on the chassis of the AMX-30 main battle tank and at the same time ordered a missile-armed counterpart as the Shahine; this is based on the same GIAT AMX-30 chassis, but given the importance of the missile and radar systems the prime contractor is the electronics giant Thomson-CSF, with Matra subcontracted for the R.460 missile, which is essentially an upgraded version of the R.440 used in the Crotale systems; the standard Shahine firing battery comprises one acquisition vehicle and four missile vehicles, all using a modified AMX-30S chassis; the acquisition unit weighs 32,700 kg (72,090 lb) and is tasked with surveillance, target detection and interrogation using a Thomson-CSF pulse-Doppler radar; the missile system on the firing unit has a vertical bank of three missile container/launchers on an elevating mounting on each side of the central pedestal; the pedestal accommodates the antennae for the Thomson-CSF monopulse target-acquisition and missile-guidance radar; initial target data are received by the appropriate firing unit over a microwave data-link, allowing the firing unit's target-acquisition radar to pick up the target as soon as it enters the radar's search range; the firing unit's onboard fire-control system uses radar data to generate a fire-control solution, and automatically fires one or two missiles as soon as the target is within range

Shahine 2: upgraded standard with modest but useful improvements: the range of the main search radar is increased by 1000 m (1,095 yards) to 19,500 m (21,325 yards), the missile has been provided with alternative radar and IR proximity fuses, and a revised SHADL (SHAhine Data-Link) has been introduced to allow the system to be linked into high command levels

---

Thomson-CSF/Matra Crotale SP surface-to-air missile system

(France)

Type: wheeled self-propelled surface-to-air missile system

Crew: 2

Combat weight: 14,800 kg (32,628 lb)

Dimensions: length overall 6·22 m (20·41 ft); width 2·65 m (8·69 ft); height 2·04 m (6·69 ft)

Armament system: four launchers (two on each side of the the central weapon/sensor pedestal) with four R.440 missiles; the pedestal is electrically powered but lacks stabilization in either elevation (an unrevealed arc) or azimuth (360°), and a radar-directed fire-control system is fitted

Armour: welded steel varying in thickness between 3 and 5 mm (0·12 and 0·2 in)

Powerplant: one petrol engine of unrevealed power with an unrevealed quantity of internal fuel, and driving a 4 × 4 layout

Performance: speed, road 70 km/h (43·5 mph); range, road 500 km (311 miles); fording 0·68 m (2·25 ft); gradient 40% ; side slope not revealed ; vertical obstacle 0·3 m (11·8 in); trench not revealed; ground clearance 0·45 m (17·7 in)

Variants

Cactus: the origins of this Crotale system lie with South Africa, which was in 1964 refused permission by the British government to obtain a British SAM system; South Africa thus turned to Thomson-Houston (now Thomson-CSF) for the development of an all-weather anti-aircraft system using the Matra R.440 missile for low-altitude defence of mobile forces; the result was the Cactus system, which entered service in 1971

Crotale: standard version used by other countries; this comes as a battery of one acquisition vehicle and two or three firing units, each based on a P4R 4 × 4 vehicle; the acquisition vehicle has a crew of two, and weighs 12,500 kg (27,557 lb); the vehicle has the same dimensions and performance as the firing vehicle, and is tasked with surveillance, target acquisition, target identification and target designation with the Thomson-CSF Mirador IV pulse-Doppler radar; a two-way data-link system is then used to pass information to the best placed firing vehicle, which keeps the acquisition vehicle fully informed about its own status over the same link; the firing vehicle has a mono-pulse radar for the tracking of one target and two missiles out to a range of 17,000 m (18,590 yards), a command transmitter for the control of two missiles despatched, with a 3-second interval between them, against a single target, an IR gathering system, a TV back-up tracking system, an optical sighting system and a digital fire-control system for use in conjunction with the four R.440 missiles carried in vertical pairs on each side of the pedestal for the sensor and guidance systems; the Crotale has gone through a number of marks characterized by electronic and mechanical improvements; the original **Crotale 1000** entered service in 1969, the **Crotale 2000** in 1973, the **Crotale 3000** in 1975 and the current **Crotale 4000** in 1983; up to the Crotale 3000 the system was limited by a slow into-action time, for the battery's units had to be cable-connected after coming to a halt; with the Crotale 4000, however, this delay was removed by the incorporation of the LIVH radio data-link system that also allows the separation of vehicles by as much as 3000 m (3,280 yards); entering service in the second half of the 1980s is the **Crotale 5000** with a number of detail improvements and modifications and (perhaps) Matra Mistral short-range SAMs for additional capability in handling saturation attacks

Left: Firing unit of the Crotale system with R.440 missiles in containerized launch tubes.

Above: An R.440 missile departs the upper left-hand launcher of its Crotale system firing unit.

GIAT AMX-13 DCA SP 30-mm twin AA gun system

(France)

Type: tracked self-propelled 30-mm twin AA gun mounting

Crew: 3

Combat weight: 17,200 kg (37,919 lb)

Dimensions: length, guns forward 5·40 m (17·72 ft) and hull 4·88 m (16·01 ft); width 3·80 m (12·47 ft); height with radar lowered 3·00 m (9·84 ft)

Armament system: two 30-mm Hispano-Suiza HSS 831A cannon with 600 rounds of ready-use ammunition, and two smoke-dischargers on each side of the turret; the turret is electro-hydraulically powered, the guns lack stabilization in either elevation (−5° to +85°) or azimuth (360°), and a radar-directed fire-control system is fitted

Armour: welded steel varying in thickness between 10 and 20 mm (0·39 and 0·79 in)

Powerplant: one 185-kW (248-hp) SOFAM 8Gxb petrol engine with 415 litres (91 Imp gal) of internal fuel

Performance: speed, road 60 km/h (37·3 mph); range, road 300 km (186 miles); fording 0·6 m (2·0 ft); gradient 60% ; side slope 30% ; vertical obstacle 0·65 m (25·6 in); trench 1·7 m (5·6 ft); ground clearance 0·43 m (16·9 in)

Variants

AMX-13 DCA: AMX-13/Mk 61 light tank/SP howitzer chassis fitted with the SAMM S401A twin 30-mm AA turret carrying two 30-mm cannon, Thomson-CSF Oeil Noir 1 search and ranging radar, Sagem optical sights and a fire-control system; the first vehicle ran in 1960 without radar, and complete vehicles were evaluated between 1964 and 1966, allowing production for the French army between 1968 and 1969; the cannon are belt fed, and the ammunition types are HEI, HEI-T, SAPHEI-T, TP-T and TP; the maximum effective slant range is 3500 m (3,830 yards), and the cannon can be used for single shots, or bursts of 5 or 15 rounds, or fully automatic fire using left- or right-hand weapon, or both together

AMX-30 SA: version of the AMX-30S with an improved version of the S401A turret, the SAMM TG230A, and thus the gun-armed equivalent to the Shahine; in addition to the 600 rounds of ready-use ammunition in the turret, the cannon can call on an additional 900 rounds stowed in the hull; the greatest advance incorporated in the TG230A turret is the more capable Oeil Vert 1 radar which is capable of target detection at any altitude between 0 and 3000 m (0 and 9,845 ft) out to optional ranges of 6500 and 15,000 m (7,110 and 16,405 yards), it being possible to extend the latter to 20,000 m (21,870 yards)

Panhard AML/S530 SP 20-mm AA gun mounting

(France)

Type: wheeled self-propelled 20-mm twin AA gun mounting

Crew: 3

Combat weight: 5500 kg (12,125 lb)

Dimensions: length, guns forward 3·95 m (12·96 ft) and hull 3·79 m (12·43 ft); width 1·97 m (6·46 ft); height to turret top 2·24 m (7·35 ft)

Armament system: two 20-mm GIAT M621 cannon with 600 rounds of ready-use ammunition, and two smoke-dischargers on each side of the turret; the turret is powered, the guns lack stabi-

lization in either elevation (−10° to +75°) and azimuth (360°), and optical sights are fitted

Armour: welded steel

Powerplant: one 67-kW (90-hp) Panhard 4 HD petrol engine with 156 litres (34 Imp gal) of internal fuel, and driving a 4 × 4 layout

Performance: speed, road 90 km/h (55·9 mph); range, road 600 km (373 miles); fording 1·1 m (3·6 ft) or amphibious with a special kit; gradient 60% ; side slope 30% ; vertical obstacle 0·3 m (11·8 in); trench 0·8 m (2·6 ft) with one channel; ground clearance 0·33 m (13 in)

Variants

AML/S530: this was developed on the basis of the AML light armoured car specifically for the important export market; in common with other French turrets, the SAMM S530 twin 20-mm AA turret used on the AML has its two 20-mm cannon located centrally in the front plate; the 20-mm M621 cannon each possess a cyclic rate of 740 rounds per minute, and the gunner can select single-shot, burst or sustained fire; there are several types of ammunition available for the M621 cannon, those most commonly used being AP, HE and HEI

ERC 20 Kriss: the latest variant of the turret is the TAB 220, originally known as the S530F and introduced in 1983 as a versatile turret suitable for installation on a number of chassis types; the use of this turret on the 6 × 6 chassis of the Panhard ERC produces the ERC 20 Kriss

Below: Both ESD Radar system and raised outriggers are displayed here on the Panhard M3 20-mm VDA.

Panhard M3 VDA SP 20-mm twin AA gun system

(France)

Type: wheeled self-propelled 20-mm twin AA gun system

Crew: 3

Combat weight: 7200 kg (15,873 lb)

Dimensions: length overall 4·45 m (14·60 ft); width 2·40 m (7·87 ft); height with radar lowered 2·995 m (9·83 ft)

Armament system: two 20-mm Hispano-Suiza HS 820 SL cannon with 650 rounds of ready-use ammunition, one 7·62-mm (0·3-in) machine-gun with 200 rounds, and two smoke-dischargers on each side of the turret; the turret is hydraulically powered, the guns lack stabilization in either elevation (−5° to +85°) or azimuth (360°), and a radar-directed fire-control system is fitted

Armour: welded steel varying in thickness between 8 and 12 mm (0·315 and 0·47 in)

Powerplant: one 67-kW (90-hp) Panhard 4 HD petrol engine with 165 litres (36 Imp gal) of internal fuel, and driving a 4 × 4 layout

Performance: speed, road 90 km/h (55·9 mph); range, road 1000 km (621 miles); fording amphibious; gradient 60% ; side slope 30% ; vertical obstacle 0·3 m (11·8 in); trench 3·1 m (10·2 ft) with four channels; ground clearance 0·35 m (13·75 in)

Variants

Panhard M3 VDA: this was developed in collaboration with Electronique Serge Dassault, VDA standing for Véhicule de Défense Anti-aérienne (air-defence vehicle); development was undertaken in the early 1970s, allowing production to begin in 1975; the M3 vehicle is modified only

slightly, the main alteration being the addition of four hydraulically actuated outriggers to provide stability by lifting the vehicle clear of the ground, though the system can be used without its stabilizers so long as the cannon are fired at their lower rate of fire (200 rounds per minute); on top of the hull is a Hispano-Suiza CNMP H20 R AA 20-mm twin AA gun turret, which is alternatively designated Electronique Serge Dassault TA 20 AA by Hispano-Suiza's partner in the programme, and this unit accommodates the two cannon and the Officine Galileo P56T sight system; the HS 820 SL cannon fire a range of APHEI, API and HEI ammunition to a maximum effective slant range of 2500 m (2,735 yards) and a maximum effective altitude of 1500 m (4,920 ft); fire capabilities are single-shot, burst or full automatic at gunner-selected cyclic rates of 200 or 1,000 rounds per minute per barrel; additional capability can be added with the incorporation at the rear of the turret of ESD RA-20 surveillance radar; additional options are an IFF unit, a TV tracking system and a laser rangefinder

Steyr 4K 7FA FLA 1/2·20: the Austrian 4K 7FA armoured personnel carrier chassis fitted with the same CNMP H 20-series turret; the turret can also be installed on other APCs such as the Belgian SIBMAS and Brazilian ENGESA EE-11 Urutu, and also on the French AMX VCI infantry combat vehicle

Electronique Serge Dassault Sinai 23: further development of the same basic concept to produce a self-propelled twin 23-mm AA gun/SAM, and designed in response to the competitive requirement issued by Egypt during 1984 for a self-propelled anti-aircraft gun system using two Soviet-designed AZP-23 23-mm cannon and the chassis of the American-designed FMC M113A2 tracked armoured personnel carrier; the Sinai 23 system uses two vehicle types of which one is the radar-equipped 'leader' and the other is the armament-fitted 'satellite', of which four can be controlled by a single leader out to a maximum separation distance of 2000 m (2,185 yards); the leader carries ESD RA-20S pulse-Doppler surveillance radar, and the satellite vehicle is fitted with the Electronique Serge Dassault TA 23E powered turret, a development of the M3 VDA's TA 20 turret with revision to allow the carriage of a hybrid armament of two AZP-23 cannon and six Ayn as-Sakr short-range SAMs; the system provides two layers of defence (the cannon to an effective slant range of 2500 m/2,735 yards and the missiles to a range of 4400 m/4,810 yards); the cannon are each provided with 300 rounds of ammunition, the two most important types being API and HEI

Renault/ESD VDAA SP 20-mm twin AA gun mounting

(France)

Type: wheeled self-propelled 20-mm twin AA gun mounting
Crew: 3
Combat weight: 14,200 kg (31,305 lb)
Dimensions: length overall 5·98 m (19·62 ft); width 2·49 m (8·17 ft); height to hull top 2·06 m (6·76 ft)
Armament system: two 20-mm Hispano-Suiza HS 820 SL cannon with 650 rounds of ready-use ammunition, one 7·62-mm (0·3-in) machine-gun with 200 rounds, and two smoke-dischargers on each side of the turret; the turret is hydraulically powered, the guns lack stabilization in either elevation (−5° to +85°) and azimuth (360°), and a radar-directed fire-control system is fitted
Armour: welded steel
Powerplant: one 175-kW (235-hp) MAN D 2356 HM72 or one 170-kW (228-hp) Renault VI MIDS 06·20·45 diesel engine with 165 litres (36 Imp gal) of internal fuel, and driving a 4 × 4 or 6 × 6 layout
Performance: speed, road 92 km/h (57·2 mph) and water 7·5 km/h (4·7 mph) driven by two waterjets; range, road 1000 km (621 miles); fording amphibious; gradient 50% ; side slope 30% ; vertical obstacle 0·4 m (15·75 in); trench not revealed; ground clearance 0·4 m (15·75 in)

Variants

VDAA: this consists of the 4 × 4 or 6 × 6 version of the basic VAB armoured personnel carrier fitted with the Hispano-Suiza CNMP H 20 R AA 20-mm twin AA gun turret (otherwise known as the Electronique Serge Dassault TA 20 AA) complete with two 20-mm Hispano-Suiza HS 820 SL cannon, Officine Galileo P56T sight system and optional radar; the standard practice is for a firing battery to consist of two vehicles, one carrying radar for the control of both vehicles; the HS 820 SL cannon fire a range of APHEI, API and HEI ammunition to a maximum effective horizontal range of 2500 m (2,735 yards) and a maximum effective altitude of 1500 m (4,920 ft); fire capabilities are single-shot, burst or full automatic at gunner-selected cyclic rates of 200 or 1,000 rounds per minute per barrel; in its basic form the turret offers limited anti-aircraft capability under normal daylight conditions; extra capability is added on some vehicles by the incorporation at the rear of the turret of an ESD RA-20S coherent pulse-Doppler surveillance and target-acquisition radar

Renault/Mata SATCP: a system using a basically similar turret adapted for the carriage of missiles rather than cannon, this is based on the 6 × 6 Panhard ERC chassis and hull to accommodate the SANTAL turret, SANTAL standing for Systeme ANTi-aérien Autonomme Léger (light autonomous anti-aircraft system) and SATCP for Système Anti-aérienne a Très Courte Portée (very short-range anti-aircraft system); the armament comprises six Matra Mistral short-range IR-homing SAMs, and the fire-control system can be any of one IR or two radar systems with the optical head or antenna on the turret rear; the turret is also fitted with two smoke-dischargers on each side, and can be provided with a 7·62-mm (0·3-in) local-defence machine-gun on the single-piece hatch cover

Thomson-CSF Mygale/Aspic: this is another self-propelled SAM system using the Mistral missile; the system is of the modular type based on the Mygale warning and fire-control system (generally carried on the Panhard VBL 4 × 4 light vehicle, though another possibility is the Peugeot P4 4 × 4 vehicle) and the Aspic weapon system; data are automatically relayed to the Aspic weapon system, which can be deployed between 3000 and 5000 m (3,280 and 5,470 yards) from the Mygale vehicle; the Aspic system is generally mounted on the same type of chassis as the Mygale, and comprises a 360° traverse pedestal mount for up to six missiles in two laterally-mounted banks that can be elevated by the operator from his remote firing console up to 30 m (33 yards) from the vehicle; still greater capability is provided by the allocation of a Crouzet DALDO helmet-pointing system (giving the chance of engaging targets of opportunity) to the other member of the Aspic's two-man crew. The system can also be upgraded with a laser rangefinder, an IFF system, and a FLIR sensor

Euromissile Roland/Marder SP surface-to-air missile system

(West Germany/France)

Type: tracked self-propelled surface-to-air missile system
Crew: 3
Combat weight: 32,500 kg (71,649 lb)
Dimensions: length overall 6·195 m (22·69 ft); width 3·24 m (10·63 ft); height with radar lowered 2·92 m (9·58 ft) and with radar raised 4·62 m (15·16 ft)
Armament system: two launchers (one on each side of the central weapon/sensor pedestal) with 10 Roland missiles, and one 7·62-mm (0·3-in) MG3 machine-gun with an unrevealed number of rounds; the pedestal is electro-hydraulically powered, the launchers lack stabilization in either elevation (an unrevealed arc) and azimuth (360°), and a radar-directed fire-control system is fitted
Armour: welded steel
Powerplant: one 450-kW (604-hp) MTU MB 833 Ea-500 diesel engine with 652 litres (143 Imp gal) of internal fuel
Performance: speed, road 70 km/h (43·5 mph); range, road 600 km (373 miles); fording 1·5 m (4·9 ft) with preparation; gradient 60% ; side slope 30% ; vertical obstacle 1·15 m (45·3 in); trench 2·5 m (8·2 ft); ground clearance 0·44 m (17·3 in)

Variants

Roland/AMX-30: designated **AMX-30R** by the French army, this is based on the hull of the AMX-30 main battle tank, and accommodates the standard Roland weapon/sensor turret in place of the standard gun turret; having entered service in 1977-78, the Roland system is intended for the engagement of low-level targets ranging from hovering helicopters to supersonic aircraft; the project was inaugurated in 1964 as a Franco-German undertaking to replace weapons such as the 40-mm Bofors L/70 gun, with Aérospatiale responsible for the initial Roland 1 clear-weather variant and MBB for the later Roland 2 all-weather variant; from the start of the programme it was envisaged that the missile would be developed in parallel with its automatic launcher system, a turret that could be fitted on different chassis and with varying sensor fits and equipment; each lateral launcher arm carries one or (on some later variants) two missile launch tubes complete with a missile; when a missile has been fired, the empty tube is discarded, and a loaded tube is automatically lifted from the launcher's associated four-round rotary magazine onto the horizontal launcher arm; the Roland/AMX-30 has the standard turret/weapon assembly accommodating the operator in the central pedestal, and has a combat weight of 35,000 kg (77,160 lb); French units were originally designed for the use of the Roland 1 missile, but later-production examples were completed for Roland 2 compatibility and earlier vehicles were upgraded to this standard

Roland/Marder: designated **FlaRakPz Roland** by the West German army, this variant is based on the hull of the Thyssen Henschel Marder tracked mechanized infantry combat vehicle for a weight of 32,500 kg (71,649 lb); both the French and West German vehicles have the advantages of a comparatively advanced chassis designed for operations on the high-technology European battlefield; both are well protected, and offer the advantages of NBC protection and night vision equipment; in both these current baseline sys-

Above: Launch of a Roland SAM from a West German FlaRakPz Roland based on the Marder chassis.

tems the turret accommodates above its rear portion the retractable antenna for a coherent pulse-Doppler surveillance and target detection radar, the Siemens MPDR 16; once a missile has been launched, the operator keeps his sight aligned on the target and the digital fire-control computer uses an IR system for automatic gathering and tracking of the missile before using its computer-run command to line of sight guidance system to direct the missile up the periscope's line of sight until it impacts the target; the Roland 2 system adds a Thomson-CSF tracking radar to the optical system

US Roland: in 1974 the US Army decided to buy the Roland 2 system to meet its SHORADS (SHOrt-Range Air-Defense System) requirement and a Boeing Aerospace/Hughes Aircraft consortium was formed to produce the system (MIM-115 SAM and associated items) under licence in the USA, the chosen chassis being the M975, derived very closely from that of the M109 self-propelled 155-mm (6·1-in) howitzer; the project ran into severe problems of cost, technology transfer and 'Americanization' of the complete system (including a more powerful tracking radar with enhanced ECCM capability); the development programme was completed successfully at a technical level, but the delays meant that the first US Roland missile was not fired until February 1978 and it was then decided that the total procurement would amount to only 27 palletized launcher units and 595 missiles, for use by an air-defence battalion of the Army National Guard in the continental USA (three batteries each equipped with nine launcher units); these launchers are intended for use in emplaced positions or as movable units on M812A1 5-ton truck; the complete pallet weighs 22,925 lb (10,399 kg) fully loaded with 10 missiles and fuel for 37 hours of continuous operation

Shelter Roland: European system comparable in many respects to the US Roland, and developed for various types of 6 × 6 and 8 × 8 wheeled trucks; the most successful of these has been the **Fla-RakRad Roland** developed in West Germany for the protection of US and West German air bases,

as well as other high-value fixed targets in West Germany; this system weighs 11,800 kg (26,014 lb) complete with its onboard power generator, and possesses a fair measure of land mobility when carried on the back of a MAN 10-tonne 8 × 8 truck

Krauss-Maffei/Contraves 5PFZ-B2 Gepard SP 35-mm twin AA gun system

(West Germany/Switzerland)

Type: tracked self-propelled 35-mm twin AA gun system

Crew: 3

Combat weight: 47,300 kg (104,277 lb)

Dimensions: length, guns forward 7·68 m (25·20 ft) and hull 6·85 m (22·47 ft); width without skirts 3·27 m (10·73 ft); height with radar lowered 3·29 m (10·79 ft) and with radar raised 4·03 m (13·22 ft)

Armament system: two 35-mm Oerlikon-Bührle KDA cannon with 680 rounds of ready-use ammunition, and four smoke-dischargers on each side of the turret; the turret is hydraulically powered, the guns lack stabilization in either elevation (−10° to +85°) or azimuth (360°), and a radar-directed fire-control system is fitted

Armour: welded steel

Powerplant: one 620-kW (832-hp) MTU MB 838 Ca-M500 diesel engine with 985 litres (217 Imp gal) of internal fuel

Performance: speed, road 65 km/h (40·4 mph); range, road 550 km (342 miles); fording 2·5 m (8·2 ft) with preparation; gradient 60% ; side slope 30% ; vertical obstacle 1·15 m (45·3 in); trench 3·0 m (9·84 ft); ground clearance 0·44 m (17·3 in)

Variants

5PFZ-B2: this was ordered into production in 1973, with Contraves as prime contractor and Krauss-Maffei as chief constructor; the first production-standard vehicle, known in West German service as the **Flakpanzer Gepard**, entered service late in 1976, and in 1980 production was completed of 195 baseline and 225 **5PFZ-2BL** vehicles, the latter being of an improved

standard with a Siemens laser rangefinder; the Gepard is an extremely capable all-weather low-level air-defence system based on the hull and automotive system of the Leopard 1 main battle tank, though slightly lengthened and carrying thinner armour in this application and fitted, in place of the tank's massive main turret, with an Oerlikon-Bührle GDP-CO2 35-mm twin AA gun turret with its two crew members (commander and gunner), the twin 35-mm Oerlikon-Bührle KDA belt-fed cannon, the Contraves fire-control system (based on an analog computer) and the two Siemens radars; these last are the MPDR 12 coherent pulse-Doppler search radar and a Siemens-Albis pulse-Doppler tracking radar; the turret is driven hydraulically from the main engine, with electrical back-up from a 66-kW (88·5-hp) Daimler Benz OM 314 multi-fuel auxiliary power unit; the Gepard has a land navigation system, and this is used to keep the radar screen oriented to the north; the MPDR 12 radar has its antenna above the rear of the turret (being swivelled to lie flat on its back when not in use), and can be operated with the vehicle on the move, sweeping continuously through 360° for rapid detection of all potential targets within its surveillance range; any target identified as hostile is designated by the commander to the tracking radar, whose antenna is located on the turret front on a swivelling mount so that it can be turned inwards when not in use; this Siemens-Albis equipment is designed for automatic tracking of targets within a 200° arc; for the solution of the fire-control problem, the tracking radar's data are fed into the fire-control system together with climatic data (updated on a daily basis), continually-monitored muzzle velocity and vehicle inclination. When the target is between 3000 and 4000 m (3,280 and 4,375 yards) distant the cannon open fire, target engagement generally occurring at a range of between 2000 and 3000 m (2,185 and 3,280 yards) with the arrival of a typical burst of between 20 and 40 rounds; the KDA gas-operated cannon have a cyclic rate of 550 rounds per minute per barrel, and are provided with APDS, HEI, SAPHEI and practice ammunition, most of the types being available without tracer; the Gepard's capability on the modern battlefield is enhanced by its possession of an NBC system, a comprehensive testing and

Above: Based on the Leopard 1 chassis, the Gepard is the West's most potent self-propelled AA gun system currently in service.

monitoring unit (capable of switching in the fire-control system's stand-by computer if required) and a special coating on exterior surfaces to reduce the vehicle's IR detectability; Belgium operates 55 vehicles similar in all essential respects to the West German equipments

5PFZ-C CA1 Caesar: the same basic type was also ordered by the Dutch, whose 95 vehicles (delivered between 1977 and 1979) are to a slightly different standard with Hollandse Signaalapparaten monopulse-Doppler integrated search and tracking radars; this revised radar fit results in a very short reaction time, allows track-while-scan through 360°, permits search on the move with compensation for vehicle speed, provides excellent performance against ECM and in the clutter conditions of low-angle search/tracking, and has integrated IFF capability; the system also reduces overall height to 3·70 m (12·14 ft) with the radar antenna erected; the other major external modification is the installation of six smoke-dischargers on each side of the turret; the vehicle is designated **PRTL** (Pantser Rups Tegen Luchtdoelen) by the Dutch army

T-55/Marksman: the same basic weapon fit is used in the Marconi Command and Control Systems Marksman 35-mm twin AA gun turret, ordered by Finland for installation on the T-55 tank chassis; this extremely impressive installation was developed as a private venture, and is designed for installation on the chassis of many main battle tanks to provide a high degree of battlefield mobility and protection matched to the logistic infrastructure of armoured divisions; the

turret weighs some 24,250 lb (11,000 kg), and can be located with minimal modification on the chassis of American tanks (most notably the M47, M48 and M60), British tanks (the Centurion, Chieftain, Challenger and Vickers Mk 3), French tanks (the AMX-30) and Soviet tanks (most notably the T-54, T-55 and T-62); the turret is electrically powered, and there is provision for the installation of a diesel-powered electrical generator in the hull so that full firing capability can be retained even with the main engine shut down; power traverse through 360° is complemented by cannon elevation in an arc between −10° and +85°; the ammunition supply for each cannon is held in a container (so reducing reload time to between 5 and 10 minutes), and comprises 20 rounds of APDS and 230 rounds of HEI; located above the turret rear is the antenna for the Marconi 400-series lightweight radar, an equipment that uses a single antenna for surveillance and target-tracking

OTO Melara SIDAM 25 SP 25-mm quadruple AA gun system

(Italy)

Type: tracked self-propelled 25-mm quadruple AA gun mounting
Crew: 3
Combat weight: 12,500 kg (27,557 lb)
Dimensions: length overall 5·041 m (16·539 ft); width 2·686 m (8·81 ft); height not revealed
Armament system: four 25-mm Oerlikon-

Bührle KBA-B cannon with 630 rounds of ready-use ammunition; the turret is hydraulically powered, the guns lack stabilization in either elevation (−10° to +75°) and azimuth (360°), and an optronic fire-control system is fitted
Powerplant: one 215-hp (160-kW) Detroit Diesel 6V-53N diesel engine with 360 litres (79 Imp gal) of internal fuel
Performance: speed, road 64·4 km/h (40 mph) and water 5 km/h (3·1 mph) driven by its tracks; range, road 550 km (342 miles); fording amphibious; gradient 60% ; side slope 30% ; vertical obstacle 0·61 m (24 in); trench 1·68 m (5·5 ft); ground clearance 0·406 m (16 in)

Variant

SIDAM 25: in the early 1980s the Italian army contracted with OTO Melara for the design and development of a turreted air-defence system that could be installed without difficulty on the chassis of the VCC-1 infantry armoured fighting vehicle, an Italian development of the M113A1 armoured personnel carrier, and its use in the SIDAM 25 system provides a high degree of performance and mechanical compatibility within Italian mechanized formations; the SIDAM 25 system can also be installed on other variants of the basic M113 family; the core of the system is a welded aluminium armour turret weighing some 3200 kg (7,055 lb) and accommodating the gunner, armament and fire-control system; the system is designed for the engagement of attack aircraft and helicopters operating at low altitude in clear daylight weather conditions, with optional upgrade to night through the addition of a video-compatible thermal imaging system to the baseline optronic system; the ADNOT fire-control system is therefore of the limited type,

range, road 300 km (186 miles); fording 1·0 m (3·3 ft) without preparation and 2·0 m (6·6 ft) with preparation; gradient 60% ; side slope 40% ; vertical obstacle 1·0 m (39·4 in); trench 2·7 m (8·85 ft); ground clearance variable between 0·2 and 0·65 m (7·9 and 25·6 in)

Variant

Type 87: developed by Mitsubishi (hull and fire-control system) and Nippon (armament system) as the AW-X, this equipment is based on the hull of the Type 74 main battle tank with its hull sides heightened and made vertical to accept the deeper basket of the new turret, which is modelled on the Oerlikon-Bührle GDP-C02 turret used in the 5PFZ Gepard and Caesar of the Belgian, Dutch and West German armies; the turret accommodates the tactical crew of two (commander and gunner), the advanced fire-control system, and the armament; this last comprises a pair of Oerlikon-Bührle KDA 35-mm cannon cradle-mounted one on each side of the traverse turret; details as yet unreleased are the elevation arc of the cannon, and also the ammunition capacity; the cannon have a cyclic rate of 550 rounds per minute per barrel, and are provided with APDS, HEI, SAPHEI and practice ammunition, most of the types being available without tracer; the all-weather fire-control system depends on two radars (for 360° surveillance and for tracking) with their antennae located above the rear of the turret roof; these primary sensors are complemented by an optical tracking system, a laser rangefinder, possibly a low-light-level TV and an advanced digital computer; the first AW-X prototype was completed in 1984, and the Type 87 should enter service in the early 1990s

Daewoo SP 30-mm twin AA gun system

(South Korea)

Type: tracked self-propelled 30-mm twin AA gun mounting

Crew: 3

Combat weight: not revealed

Dimensions: not revealed

Armament system: two 30-mm cannon with an unrevealed number of ready-use rounds, and three smoke-dischargers on each side of the turret; the turret is electrically powered, the guns lack stabilization in either elevation (an unrevealed arc) and azimuth (360°), and a radar-directed fire-control system is fitted

Armour: welded aluminium

Powerplant: one 210-kW (282-hp) MAN D 2848M diesel engine with 400 litres (88 Imp gal) of internal fuel

Performance: speed, road 74 km/h (46 mph) and water 6 km/h (3·7 mph) driven by its tracks; range, road 480 km (298 miles); fording amphibious; gradient 60% ; side slope 30% ; vertical obstacle 0·63 m (24·8 in); trench 1·7 m (5·8 ft); ground clearance 0·41 m (16·1 in)

Variant

Daewoo SP 35-mm twin AA gun system: South Korean air-defence weapon currently under development by Daewoo Heavy Industries; in essence it comprises the lengthened chassis of the Korean Infantry Fighting Vehicle (produced by Daewoo in the basis of the FMC Armored Infantry Fighting Vehicle) fitted with a derivative of the Emerson Electric EMERLEC-30 turret, as used on South Korean (and other) warships, and

Above: The SIDAM 25 quadruple 25-mm AA gun system on an M113 series chassis APC.

though possessing an autotrack facility; the ADNOT has an IFF subsystem for interrogation of potential targets, and can receive external data through a TADDS (Target Alert Display Data Set); the cannon are mounted in vertical pairs on lateral cradles outside the body of the turret, and have a dual-feed arrangement so that armour-piercing ammunition can be introduced at any point in an engagement; the cannon installation has a cyclic rate of 600 rounds per minute per barrel, and the maximum effective range is 2000 m (2,185 yards); the standard ammunition supply is sufficient for eight 2-second bursts, and the gunner can select single shots, 15-round bursts, 25-round bursts or continuous fire; trials of the SIDAM 25 were started in 1983, and the type began to enter Italian service in 1989; being based on the chassis of the M113 series, the SIDAM 25 series has NBC protection and is amphibious, driven in the water by its tracks; the SIDAM 25 turret can also be employed on the chassis of the Italian VCC-80 and Brazilian EE-11 Urutu armoured personnel carriers

Mitsubishi/Nippon Type 87 SP 35-mm twin AA gun system

(Japan)

Type: tracked self-propelled 35-mm twin AA gun system

Crew: 3

Combat weight: not revealed

Dimensions: not revealed

Armament system: two 35-mm Oerlikon-Bührle KDA cannon with an unrevealed number of ready-use rounds, one 7·62-mm (0·3-in) machine-gun with an unrevealed number of rounds, and three smoke-dischargers on each side of the turret; the turret is hydraulically powered, the guns lack stabilization in either elevation (an unrevealed arc) or azimuth (360°), and a radar-directed fire-control system is fitted

Armour: welded steel

Powerplant: one 560-kW (751-hp) Mitsubishi 10ZF Type 33 WT diesel engine with 950 litres (209 Imp gal) of internal fuel

Performance: speed, road 53 km/h (32·9 mph);

two KCB cannon licence-made by the Tong Il Industry Company; other than Daewoo (chassis and turret), the other major contractors involved in this little known self-propelled AA cannon mounting are Samsung Precision Instruments (optronic tracker) and the Goldstar Electric Company (licence-built derivative of the Siemens MPDR 18/X radar); the cannon each fire at a cyclic rate of 650 rounds per minute to a maximum horizontal range of 10,000 m (10,935 yards) and to an effective slant range of 3500 m (3,830 yards), and use the standard range of Oerlikon-Bührle ammunition for the KCB, in the form of three operational (HEI, HEI-T and SAPHEI) and two practice types

Hagglund & Soner Lvrbv 701 SP surface-to-air missile system

(Sweden)

Type: tracked self-propelled surface-to-air missile system
Crew: 4
Combat weight: 9700 kg (21,384 lb)
Dimensions: length overall 4·81 m (15·78 ft); width 2·54 m (8·33 ft); height with missile launcher lowered 2·00 m (6·56 ft) and with missile launcher raised 2·98 m (9·78 ft)
Armament system: one elevating launcher with an unrevealed number of Rbs 70 Rayrider ready-use missiles; the launcher is powered but lacks stabilization in either elevation (an unrevealed arc) or azimuth (360°), and an optical fire-control system is fitted
Armour: welded steel
Powerplant: one 136-hp (101-kW) Ford Model 2658E petrol engine with 260 litres (57 Imp gal) of internal fuel
Performance: speed, road 41 km/h (25·5 mph); range, road 350 km (217 miles); fording 0·9 m (3·0 ft); gradient 60% ; side slope 30% ; vertical obstacle not revealed; trench 1·5 m (4·9 ft); ground clearance 0·33 m (13 in)

Variant

Lvrbv 701: entering service in the mid-1980s, this is a conversion of obsolete Ikv 102 and Ikv 103 infantry cannon vehicles to low-altitude air-defence vehicles, which are grouped into specialized companies allocated to armoured and mechanized brigades for air-defence against helicopters and other low-flying attack aircraft; the infantry cannon hulls have been rebuilt: on each the gun aperture in the glacis has been plated over, the crew compartment lengthened, the powerplant and transmission replaced, and the communications equipment upgraded; a large hatch (with outward opening twin covers) has been cut into the hull roof, and under this is located the elevating launcher surmounted by an IFF device; the launcher is stowed inside the hull until required, when it can be erected rapidly, and is essentially similar to the standard ground-based unit; reload missiles are carried in a magazine located over the engine/transmission space, with access by means of the magazine's front, which hinges up; the Rbs 70 system is extremely capable and also virtually unjammable because of its laser beam-riding guidance, but can be used to best effect only when supported by some type of early-warning system; this allows the missile to be readied and traversed onto the right bearing so that the operator can acquire the target at maximum stand-off range

Oerlikon/Bührle/Martin Marietta ADATS/M113A2 SP surface-to-air missile system

(Switzerland/USA)

Type: tracked self-propelled surface-to-air missile system
Crew: 3-4
Combat weight: about 33,000 lb (14,969 kg)
Dimensions: length overall 18·78 ft (5·725 m); width 9·25 ft (2·82 m); height to top of launcher 8·83 ft (2·692 m) and with radar raised 12·59 ft (3·838 m)
Armament system: eight launchers (four on each side of the central weapon/sensor pedestal) with 16 ADATS missiles; the pedestal is powered but lacks stabilization in either elevation (− 10° to + 90°) or azimuth (360°), and a radar-directed fire-control system is fitted
Armour: welded aluminium varying in thickness between 0·5 and 1·5 in (13 and 38 mm)
Powerplant: one 215-hp (160-kW) Detroit Diesel 6V-53N diesel engine with 95 US gal (360 litres) of internal fuel
Performance: speed, road 42 mph (67·6 km/h); range, road 300 miles (483 km); fording amphibious; gradient 60% ; side slope 30% ; vertical obstacle 36 in (0·91 m); trench 5·5 ft (1·68 m); ground clearance 17 in (0·43 m)

Variant

ADATS/M113A2: this dual-role SAM and anti-tank missile system is one of the most interesting weapon systems currently available, ADATS standing for Air Defense Anti-Tank System; the company initially worked to produce a missile system effective against the whole gamut of battlefield air targets, but the company soon appreciated that many operators could profit from combining the air-defence role with an anti-tank capability in a single dual-role missile and associated launcher/fire-control system that could be carried on any of several chassis types; such a system would offer significant advantages such as the operator's need to purchase a smaller number of chassis and fire-control systems, while the selection of a single missile type would reduce unit costs and missile holdings; develop-

ment began in 1979, with Martin Marietta Orlando Aerospace as subcontractor charged with the design and development of the missile, in which a potent anti-tank capability was added without extra hardware or system cost; the trials vehicles were based on the chassis of the M113A2 armoured personnel carrier (and it is this chassis that has been selected by Canada, the first customer for the system): this has an overall length of 18·78 ft (5·725 m) and a height of 12·60 ft (3·838 m) with the radar raised; the manufacturers soon proposed other tracked units such as those of the American M2/M3 Bradley fighting vehicle, and various wheeled units; the core of the system is the powered turret, which accommodates the optronic sensor package in a stabilized mounting at the front of the central pedestal, and the two four-tube launcher units on a yoke assembly projecting from its sides; the whole ADATS system weighs some 4500 kg (9,921 lb) excluding the vehicle and, as noted above, the central pedestal locates the sensors for the ADATS system: these include a Contraves Italiana surveillance radar, a tracking system using a FLIR sensor and TV camera, a neodymium-YAG laser rangefinder and a carbon dioxide missile-guidance laser; the turret is itself unmanned, the two-man tactical crew of the system being located at individual consoles inside the hull of the vehicle; as soon as the commander designates a target for engagement, the turret trains onto the required bearing and the missile operator begins his search with the FLIR sensor and TV camera of the Martin Marietta optronic module; once he has acquired the target, the missile operator makes his decision between the FLIR or TV sensors, locks onto the target and initiates the automatic tracking process, bearing and elevation data being fed into the fire-control system's computer, together with range data from the neodymium-YAG laser and, if thought necessary, from the track-while-scan facility of the radar; a fire-control solution is rapidly calculated and the launchers elevated to the correct angle; as soon as the target is within range a missile is launched, thereafter riding the carbon dioxide laser's beam, which is initially aligned off the target to avoid alerting any laser warning system and only brought to bear precisely on the

Below: The ADATS on the chassis of an M113A2 APC with eight ready-to-launch missiles.

target in the closing stages of the missile's flight; the use of a laser beam-riding system (especially with the offset guidance facility) makes the system all but unjammable; once a missile has been fired, its spent container can be removed from the pedestal's lateral mounting and discarded, a fresh container being loaded manually from the reserve carried in the hull of the launch vehicle; in 1986 the ADATS (in a package with the Contraves Skyguard radar fire-control system and Oerlikon-Bührle GDF-005 twin 35-mm towed cannon mounting) won the difficult Canadian Low-Level Air Defense competition against offerings from Bofors (a combination of the 40-mm Trinity gun system and the Rbs 70 Rayrider SAM with Ericsson HARD radars on the M113A2 chassis) and Contraves (the ATAK-35 twin 35-mm self-propelled cannon mounting, Sparrow SAM and GDF-005 towed cannon, and Ericsson Super Giraffe Mk IV and Skyguard radars); a development of the basic ADATS was entered in a US Army air-defence competition, and late in 1987 this Oerlikon-Bührle contender was declared winner over three other candidates

ZRK Strela-10 (SA-13) SP surface-to-air missile system

(USSR)

Type: tracked self-propelled surface-to-air missile system
Crew: 3
Combat weight: 12,500 kg (27,557 lb)
Dimensions: length overall 6·60 m (21·65 ft); width 2·90 m (9·51 ft); height in travelling order 2·30 m (7·55 ft) and in firing position 3·80 m (12·47 ft)
Armament system: four launchers (two on each side of the central weapon/sensor pedestal) with 20 SA-13 'Gopher' ready-use missiles; the pedes-

tal is manually powered, the launchers lack stabilization in either elevation (an unrevealed arc) or azimuth (360°), and an optical fire-control system is fitted
Armour: welded steel to a maximum thickness of 14 mm (0·55 in)
Powerplant: one 180-kW (241-hp) YaMZ 238 V diesel engine with 450 litres (99 Imp gal) of internal fuel
Performance: speed, road 55 km/h (34·2 mph); range, road 450 km (280 miles); fording amphibious; gradient 60%; side slope 30%; vertical obstacle 0·7 m (27·6 in); trench 2·7 m (8·9 ft); ground clearance 0·4 m (15·75 in)

Variant

ZRK Strela-10: this system was introduced to Soviet service from the late 1970s as a more mobile successor to the SA-9 'Gaskin' system with the less limited SA-13 'Gopher' missile; the equipment is based on the hull of the MT-LB multi-role vehicle, and as such is fully amphibious and fitted with complete NBC protection; the hull has its crew compartment at the front, the powerplant immediately to the rear of this forward compartment, and stowage for reload missiles and other equipment in the rear compartment; over this last section of the hull is located a radar/missile launcher assembly similar to that of the SA-9 system, with a central cab and large transparency (for the missile operator) surmounted by an elevating arm topped by the radar antenna and two lateral pairs of missile container-launchers; six SA-9 missiles can be carried on the SA-13 vehicle instead of four of the later weapon, but the SA-13 offers superior tactical and operational capabilities, especially in conjunction with the ranging radar whose antenna is located centrally between the two missile pairs; there are two subvariants of the

Below: The TELAR-2 version of the ZRK Strela-10 (SA-13 'Gopher') SAM system is identifiable by its lack of 'Hat Box' passive radar detection units.

system, designated **SA-13 TELAR-1** and **SA-13 TELAR-2** by the USA and NATO with TELAR standing for Transporter Erector Launcher And Radar; the former has four 'Hat Box' passive radar-warning receivers (two facing outward on the rear decking, one facing aft on the tail of the vehicle and one facing forward on the nose) and the latter none; it is also possible that these 'Hat Box' antennae serve as a radar link with the B-76 'Gun Dish' radar of ZSU-23-4 self-propelled anti-aircraft cannon system or other fire-control radars; in both variants the spent containers are removed after an action, fresh containers from the vehicle being used for manual reloading; in 1987 there was revealed a variant with containers attached to the side of the vehicle, these probably carrying two reload missiles each, increasing the vehicle's total missile complement to 20 (four on the launcher assembly, 12 in the hull and another four in the external panniers); the SA-13's engagement envelope includes minimum and maximum ranges of 500 and 10,000 m (550 and 10,935 yards), and minimum and maximum altitudes of 10 and 10,000 m (33 and 32,810 ft), though the effective ceiling is thought to be 3200 m (10,500 ft); the use of a range radar on the launcher is a useful and comparatively simple method of reducing wastage by preventing rounds from being fired outside their engagement capability, and additional capability has recently been added to the Strela-10/ZSU-23-4 combination by the deployment of one 'Dog Ear' early warning radar to each battery

ZRK ? (SA-12) SP surface-to-air missile system

(USSR)

Type: tracked self-propelled surface-to-air missile system
Crew: 4

Combat weight: 30,000 kg (66,138 lb)
Dimensions: length overall 12·50 m (41·01 ft); width 3·50 m (11·48 ft); height with missiles horizontal 3·80 m (12·47 ft)
Armament system: one four-tube launcher with four SA-12 'Gladiator' missiles; the launcher is powered for elevation to +90°, and a radar-directed fire-control system is fitted
Armour: none
Powerplant: one 390-kW (523-hp) D12A diesel engine with an unrevealed quantity of internal fuel
Performance: speed, road 50 km/h (31·1 mph); range, road 450 km (280 miles); other details not revealed

Variant

ZRK ? (SA-12): introduced in 1986 but still very little known or appreciated in the West, the self-propelled system using the SA-12A 'Gladiator' was designed from the mid-1970s to succeed the Krug as an extremely capable vertical-launch system for the all-altitude engagement of all tactical- and operational-level air targets at medium and long ranges; the system has two or four missiles mounted singly or in two pairs, together with the associated guidance radar, on a tracked transporter/erector/launcher (TEL) vehicle derived from the MT-T heavy tractor (itself derived ultimately from the T-64 main battle tank, and thus providing a high level of cross-country and battlefield mobility); the type probably operates in a battery of three TELs, one reload vehicle (carrying four missiles and, in place of the TEL's radar, a hydraulic crane), one command and control vehicle (based on the TEL but carrying a large shelter on its flatbed), and one phased-array engagement radar vehicle, all based on the same MT-T chassis and data-linked for the real-time transfer of fire-control information and decisions; it has been suggested that the powerful SA-12A system, whose Soviet designation remains unrevealed, is deployed in specialized air-defence divisions, each with 48 launchers, allocated at the rate of one division per front, rather than as specialized air-defence brigades (as is the case with 27-launcher Krug units) allocated at army level; the two subordinate brigade HQs each possess perhaps two major phased-array target-acquisition radar vehicles (again using the MT-T chassis) as well as a number of command and control vehicles, while each of the launcher battalion HQs has one target-acquisition radar vehicle and some command and control vehicles; it is also likely that a data-link system is used for real-time communication between the three unit levels; there is also a version of the basic system using the SA-12B 'Giant' (an improved missile with greater range), making it suitable for the operational- or perhaps even strategic-level tasks of defending ICBM launcher fields against attack by cruise and ballistic missiles; this SA-12B system carries two rather than four missiles, each carried in a six-hoop elevating support frame rather than the four-hoop frame associated with the four-missile SA-12A system; the system weighs 20,000 kg (44,092 lb), and estimates for its primary dimensions include a length of 9·50 m (31·17 ft), a considerably narrower width of 2·90 m (9·51 ft) and a height of 3·30 m (10·83 ft)

ZRK ? (SA-11) SP surface-to-air missile system

(USSR)

Type: tracked self-propelled surface-to-air missile system
Crew: 4
Combat weight: 16,000 kg (35,273 lb)
Dimensions: length overall 9·40 m (30·84 ft); width 3·10 m (10·17 ft); height 3·70 m (12·14 ft)
Armament system: four launchers (two on each side of the central weapon/sensor pedestal) with four SA-11 'Gadfly' missiles; the pedestal is powered but lacks stabilization in elevation (an unrevealed arc) and azimuth (360°), and a radar-directed fire-control system is fitted
Armour: welded steel to a maximum thickness of 9 mm (0·35 in)
Powerplant: one 210-kW (282-hp) Model V-6R diesel engine with an unrevealed quantity of internal fuel
Performance: speed, road 50 km/h (31·1 mph); range, road 300 km (186 miles); other details not revealed

Variant

ZRK ? (SA-11): having entered development in the early 1970s for service from the mid-1980s, the self-propelled system using the SA-11 'Gadfly' weapon is an important part of the Soviets' tactical armoury, but its proper designation remains unknown; the system is designed for essentially the same role as the Kub system with its SA-6 missile, namely the medium-range area defence of Soviet first-line divisions against low/medium-altitude air attack; however, the tactical limitations of the Kub system prompted an early start on a successor system in which each launch vehicle was provided with its own engagement radar; initial Western reports of the 'Gadfly' system suggested that it was modelled closely on the Kub system it was designed to complement and then to succeed; the Soviets realized from an early stage of the programme that the Kub system's chassis was too small and light to support the new missile system and its associated radar, and therefore evolved a new chassis with a longer track length and considerably greater internal volume; development of this vehicle and its associated radar moved ahead more swiftly than did that of the missile, and as an interim step the Soviets were able to produce the hybrid SA-6B 'Gainful' Mod 1 variant of the Kub system with the 'Gainful' launcher/missile combination on the SA-11's chassis and supported by the new radar; the definitive SA-11 system began trials in 1979, and began to supplement the SA-6 system in Soviet tank and motor rifle divisions from 1983; it is likely that the allocation of the SA-11 follows that of the SA-6 with each division having an organic regiment of SA-11 equipments; the regiment comprises a regimental HQ (with a new type of long-range early-warning radar whose NATO reporting name has not yet been revealed) and five SA-11 batteries; each battery comprises a central radar vehicle, four (peace) or six (war) SA-11 launchers, and an unknown number of reloading vehicles; each launcher carries four rather than three missiles; the basic layout of the SA-11 system is very similar to that of the SA-6 system with the tracked chassis accommodating the crew in a forward compartment, the electronics in the centre and the powerplant in the rear, with the launcher/radar assembly located on a turntable above the hull; the turntable supports a large rectangular platform with the launcher at its rear and the radar at its front; the launcher is hinged at its rear to allow the complete launcher to be elevated, and carries rails for four missiles; the radar is similar to the 'Front Dome' equipment of the SA-N-7 system; it is likely that early warning is provided by the regimental-level radar equipment, probably a new type of advanced surveillance radar which transmits preliminary target data by data-link to the SA-11 battery's central radar vehicle; each target is probably engaged by two SA-11 missiles, the use of monopulse semi-active homing by the missile making the enemy's task in implementing effective ECM that much more difficult, especially as the missile's high speed produces a short flight time; the flexibility of the system is great, and offers the tactical advantage that the regimental- and battery-level radars are not absolutely essential, the launcher vehicle's radar being in itself sufficient for a complete engagement, albeit with reduced target detection range; the engagement envelope of the SA-11 system includes minimum and maximum ranges of 3000 and 30,000 m (3,280 and 32,810 yards), and minimum and maximum altitudes of 30 and 15,000 m (100 and 49,215 ft).

ZRK ? (SA-10) SP surface-to-air missile system

(USSR)

Type: wheeled self-propelled surface-to-air missile system
Crew: 4
Combat weight: 20,000 kg (44,092 lb)
Dimensions: length overall 9·40 m (30·84 ft); width 3·10 m (10·17 ft); height 3·70 m (12·14 ft)
Armament system: one four-tube launcher with four SA-10 'Grumble' missiles; the launcher is powered for elevation to +90°, and a radar-directed fire-control system is fitted
Armour: probably none
Powerplant: one 390-kW (523-hp) D12A diesel engine with an unrevealed quantity of internal fuel, and driving an 8 × 8 layout
Performance: speed, road 85 km/h (52·8 mph); range, road 650 km (404 miles); other details not revealed

Variant

ZRK ? (SA-10): the self-propelled system using the SA-10 'Grumble' is an extremely important new weapon in the Soviet arsenal, but its Soviet designation remains unknown; the system apparently began to enter service in 1980 with so wide a range of capabilities that the missile can be tasked with the whole gamut of air defence roles including the interception of cruise missiles and the destruction of tactical and theatre ballistic missiles; the SA-10A missile was designed for use on fixed launch sites, but the SA-10B is the missile used since 1985 in a mobile version based on a development of the MAZ-9310 8 × 8 wheeled tractor; this carries a bank of four missile launch tubes at its rear; with the system on the move the missiles lie in a horizontal position on the rear of the launch vehicle, but in firing position are hydraulically elevated to the vertical position; the fire-control system associated with the SA-10B has a continuous-wave pulse-Doppler target-tracking and fire-control radar based on a similar vehicle for compatibility of transport; the radar has a planar array about 2·5 m (8·2 ft) square; the SA-10B is used by batteries that probably comprise one radar vehicle, three transporter/erector/launcher vehicles and perhaps two missile-reload vehicles

ZRK Strela-1 (SA-9) SP surface-to-air missile system

(USSR)

Type: wheeled self-propelled surface-to-air missile system

Crew: 3

Combat weight: 7000 kg (15,432 lb)

Dimensions: length overall 5·80 m (19·02 ft); width 2·40 m (7·87 ft); height in travelling order 2·30 m (7·55 ft)

Armament system: four launchers (two on each side of the central weapon/sensor pedestal) with eight SA-9 'Gaskin' missiles; the pedestal is manually powered but lacks stabilization in either elevation (an unrevealed arc) or azimuth (360°), and an optical fire-control system is fitted

Armour: welded steel varying in thickness between 2 and 14 mm (0·08 and 0·55 in)

Powerplant: one 105-kW (141-hp) GAZ-41 petrol engine with 290 litres (64 Imp gal) of internal fuel, and driving a 4 × 4 layout

Performance: speed, road 100 km/h (62·1 mph) and water 10 km/h (6·2 mph) driven by one waterjet; range, road 750 km (466 miles); fording amphibious; gradient 60%; side slope 30%; vertical obstacle 0·4 m (15·75 in); trench 1·25 m (4·1 ft); ground clearance 0·43 m (16·9 in)

Variant

ZRK Strela-1: this is the standard point defence missile system of Soviet tank and motor rifle regiments, and uses the SA-9 'Gaskin' IR-homing missile; the system was developed in parallel with the ZSU-23-4 self-propelled cannon mounting, and each Soviet regiment has a nicely balanced air-defence battery comprising four ZSU-23-4 self-propelled cannon mountings and four self-propelled SA-9 missile mountings; the system entered service in 1968, and has only a limited point-defence capability as, in its basic form, it is limited to clear-weather engagements; the equipment is based on the chassis of the BRDM-2 reconnaissance vehicle, and presumably retains that vehicle's amphibious capability and NBC protection; despite the limitations imposed by what is apparently a 4 × 4 drive layout, the chassis does in fact possess moderately good cross-country performance, for under the belly are two retractable pairs of chain-driven wheels which can be lowered in adverse conditions to produce an 8 × 8 configuration; the BRDM-2's machine-gun turret is replaced by a powered turret assembly accommodating the missile operator (behind a large transparency) and four missiles, located as two containerized pairs on the sides of an elevating launcher arm just behind the operator's position; the launcher is generally lowered onto the vehicle's rear decking when the system is on the move, this feature reducing height very considerably; the system uses the simple optical target-acquisition procedure (visual search by the operator), though warning can be provided by a central command post or from a radar-equipped vehicle to allow the turret to be trained onto the correct bearing; as the SA-9 system operates with the ZSU-23-4, the B-76 'Gun Dish' radar of this system is the most likely source of early warning. Some export customers of the SA-9 have used the system in association with the 'Gun Dish' radar located on the flatbed of a truck; once he has sighted the target, the operator brings the turret onto precisely the right bearing and elevates the missiles to the right attitude and, when informed that the seekers have secured a positive lock onto the target, fires a salvo of two missiles, generally at an interval of 5 seconds; the missiles home entirely automatically; two or four reloads can be carried on the frames on the vehicle's upper sides, and these containerized rounds can be manually attached to the launcher when the spent containers have been discarded, a process taking about five minutes; the whole system is highly limited, especially as the operator has to traverse the whole turret assembly as he searches for a target; Soviet divisions have in the first half of the 1980s been provided with an upgraded version that accommodates four 'Hat Box' passive radar-warning receivers (two above the front wheels and two on the sides of the operator's position) for early warning (and possibly direction) of radar-equipped attack aircraft

---

ZRK Romb (SA-8) SP surface-to-air missile system

(USSR)

Type: wheeled self-propelled surface-to-air missile system

Crew: 3

Combat weight: 9000 kg (19,841 lb)

Dimensions: length overall 9·14 m (30·00 ft); width 2·90 m (9·51 ft); height with radar lowered 4·20 m (13·78 ft)

Armament system: one quadruple launcher with four SA-8 'Gecko' missiles; the turret is manually powered but lacks stabilization in either elevation (an unrevealed arc) or azimuth (360°), and an optical fire-control system is fitted

Armour: none

Powerplant: one 130-kW (174-hp) ZIL-375 diesel engine with 350 litres (77 Imp gal) of internal fuel, and driving a 6 × 6 layout

Performance: speed, road 60 km/h (37·3 mph) and water 5 km/h (3·1 mph) driven by two waterjets; range, road 500 km (311 miles); fording amphibious; gradient not revealed; side slope not revealed; vertical obstacle 0·5 m (19·7 in); trench 1·2 m (3·9 ft); ground clearance 0·4 m (15·75 in)

Variant

ZRK Romb: first revealed publicly in November 1975, having entered full-scale service in 1974 after a fairly protracted development programme that began as early as 1959, this is an equipment of considerable historical as well as tactical importance; on the historical side, this was the world's first operational self-propelled SAM system to be fitted with its own engagement radar equipment; on the tactical side, the Romb system appears to have been developed within the Soviets' overall concept of a layered battlefield air defence system covering all ranges and all altitudes; the Romb system is in many respects the Soviet counterpart to the Raytheon MIM-23 HAWK in US service, though tactically the Soviet system is far superior as a result of its concentration of the whole outfit on a single vehicle, with all

Below: The SA-8 'Gecko' Model 1 variant of the ZRK Romb system has six, not four, missiles.

the battlefield mobility advantages that such concentration confers; the Romb system was evaluated from 1967 and entered limited service in 1970, but the fact that full-scale service did not follow until 1974 suggests that there remained considerable problems to be ironed out; like that of the Kub, the vehicle of the Romb launcher provides its crew with night vision equipment and NBC protection, plus the advantages of amphibious capability without extensive preparation; the Romb regiment comprises a regimental headquarters (with two 'Long Track' surveillance radars and one 'Thin Skin-B' height-finding radar) and five launcher batteries, each made up of four (peace) or six (war) launcher vehicles and two support vehicles; the support vehicle is based on the same chassis as the Romb launcher for compatibility of battlefield mobility, and carries 32 reload missiles plus, in place of the radar/missile system, a hydraulically powered crane; the availability of 64 missiles (four missiles per rail) for immediate reload provides the Romb battery with a decided tactical advantage over the Kub battery (six reload missiles for 12 rails), and this adds significantly to the benefits of multiple target engagement capability and superior system performance in face of the enemy's ECM; the Romb launcher vehicle has a distinctive appearance, and is divided into three compartments (crew at the front, electronics in the centre, and powerplant at the rear together with the two waterjets for waterborne propulsion); on the vehicle's centre of gravity, just above the central pair of wheels, is the Romb's radar/missile-launcher assembly, located on a hydraulically powered turntable; the whole radar assembly has the NATO reporting name 'Land Roll' and is derived from the 'Pop Group' radar used with the naval SA-N-4 missile; at the rear of the turntable is the pedestal for the surveillance radar, which has

a rotating antenna at the top of the assembly for search out to a range of some 30,000 m (32,810 yards); the surveillance radar's pedestal also accommodates the missile launchers proper: on the original Romb variant, these launchers comprise two lateral pairs of elevating rails, giving a ready-use complement of four SA-8A missiles; at the front of the turntable is located the guidance group: the primary components of this assembly are a target-tracking monopulse radar (in the centre) operating to a range of some 25,000 m (27,340 yards), flanked by two limited-traverse monopulse missile-tracking/guidance radars with two command-link missile-gathering horns; the other features in this group are designed for use in ECM conditions: they comprise two rectangular electronic tracking devices (just outside the horns) and two low-light-level TV cameras (above the missile-guidance antennae); this last feature is of considerable importance in giving the Romb system a continued operational capability under adverse electronic and/or weather conditions, and allows limited operations to continue with the radar shut down for fear of anti-radiation missiles; the Romb system can operate entirely autonomously, but is aided considerably when used in association with the regimental-level radar facility for early warning of likely targets, allowing the Romb's radar to be primed with initial target data; target detection at ranges of more than 100 km (62 miles) is tasked to the separate regimental-level 'Long Track' surveillance and radar. This is located on a modified AT-T tracked artillery tractor, and operates in the E-band purely for the detection of targets at maximum range, and 'Thin Skin-B' height-finding radars; as soon as the target is detected by the Romb's surveillance radar (either independently or with the aid of warning and preliminary data from the 'Long Track/Thin Skin-B' combination)

and identified as hostile by the IFF system, the turntable is trained onto the target's bearing and the target acquired by the tracking radar; this allows the generation of a solution to the fire-control problem by the Romb's computer, with the missile launched as soon as the target is within range; it is likely that a salvo of two missiles is launched at a single target to maximize the chances of a kill; in 1980 the Soviets revealed a new version of the Romb system, with a total of six SA-8B missiles in two banks of three ribbed containers which, apart from any other considerations, provide the missiles with better environmental protection. This latter is of considerable importance given the generally adverse conditions likely to be encountered on the battlefield. The SA-8B missile variant may be more closely related than the SA-8A to the SA-N-4, and almost certainly has folding fins to allow stowage inside the container; the Romb with four SA-8A missiles is often designated **SA-8A 'Gecko' Model 0** in the Western literature, the designation **SA-8B Model 1** being used for the variant with six containerized missiles; the engagement envelope for the system includes minimum and maximum ranges of 1600 and 12,000 m (1,750 and 13,125 yards), and minimum and maximum altitudes of 50 and 13,000 m (164 and 42,650 ft)

ZRK Kub (SA-6) SP surface-to-air missile system

(USSR)

Type: tracked self-propelled surface-to-air missile system

Below: The ZRK Kub system carries its three SA-6 'Gainful' SAMs in an exposed position.

Crew: 3
Combat weight: 14,000 kg (30,864 lb)
Dimensions: length overall 7·389 m (24·24 ft) and hull 6·79 m (22·28 ft); width 3·18 m (10·43 ft); height including missiles 3·45 m (11·32 ft)
Armament system: one three-missile launcher with three SA-6 'Gainful' missiles; the launcher is powered but lacks stabilization in either elevation (to +85°) or azimuth (360°), and a radar-directed fire-control system is fitted
Armour: welded steel varying in thickness between 10 and 15 mm (0·39 and 0·59 in)
Powerplant: one 210-kW (282-hp) Model V-6R diesel engine with 250 litres (55 Imp gal) of internal fuel
Performance: speed, road 44 km/h (27·3 mph); range, road 260 km (162 miles); fording 1·0 m (3·3 ft); gradient 60%; side slope 30%; vertical obstacle 1·1 m (43·3 in); trench 2·8 m (9·2 ft); ground clearance 0·4 m (15·75 in)

Variant

ZRK Kub: using the same basic chassis as the ZSU-23-4, this is the mobile launcher for the SA-6 'Gainful' missile and was designed for the medium-range protection of Soviet first-line divisions against low- and medium-altitude air threats; the type entered full operational service in 1970 after being revealed publicly for the first time in November 1967. The system's early career was beset by a number of severe technical problems, but from an early point in its service career the Kub has proved a highly successful system that has since been exported with the designation **Kvadrat**; given its planned divisional deployment level the Kub is rightly provided with night vision equipment though, oddly enough, it lacks any amphibious capability; in common with other Soviet tactical systems, the Kub has NBC protection; in Soviet and Warsaw Pact service the Kub system is now deployed at divisional level, each tank and motor rifle division having an organic regiment of Kub equipments; the regiment comprises a regimental HQ (with two 'Long Track' surveillance radars and one 'Thin Skin-B' height-finding radar) and five Kub batteries; each battery comprises one 'Straight Flush' fire-control vehicle, four (peace) or six (war) Kub launchers, and two ZIL-131 6 × 6 trucks each carrying three reload missiles and a hydraulic crane; as noted above, the Kub system is based on the chassis of the ZSU-23-4 with the crew in a front compartment, the missile launcher on a turntable above the centre of the vehicle, and the powerplant at the rear; the turntable provides the launcher with 360° traverse, and the launcher can elevate its three rails to a maximum of 85°; for travelling the turntable is normally traversed to the rear, with the launcher lying in the horizontal position; the tactical mode of operation for the Kub system is akin to that for the Krug, using the 'Long Track' surveillance and 'Thin Skin' height-finding radars for initial target detection; target detection at ranges of more than 100 km (62 miles) is tasked to one of the separate regimental-level 'Long Track' surveillance radars; once a target has been determined at regimental level, its data are passed to the Kub battery's 60/90-km (37/56-mile) range 'Straight Flush' fire-control system, which is mounted on the same type of chassis as the Kub launcher and with the aid of two separate turret-mounted antennae undertakes surveillance, low-level target detection and acquisition, target tracking and illumination, missile tracking (as a secondary role) and missile command guidance; as soon as the illuminator has locked onto the target one or more missiles (up to a maximum of three, with short intervals between each launch, against a single target) are fired and the illuminator switches to continuous-wave mode; on the missile one of the fins accommodates a beacon transmitter and another a command-link receiver, allowing the 'Straight Flush' to know the position of the missile with great accuracy and to pass microwave guidance commands; in the terminal phase of the engagement the missile(s) switch to semi-automatic homing; to overcome the system's rapidly proved susceptibility to ECM, the SA-6B missile was developed to supplant the original SA-6A; and the limitation to single-target engagement has been mitigated by the development of a hybrid system, with SA-6B missiles on the standard triple launcher mounted on the tracked launcher vehicle of the SA-11 'Gadfly', which has its own tracking radar; each Kub battery has replaced one SA-6 launcher vehicle with one hybrid SA-6B/SA-11 launcher/radar vehicle, thereby doubling its simultaneous engagement capability to two targets. This also reduces the previous problem inherent in having only a single radar vehicle per battery

ZRK Krug (SA-4) SP surface-to-air missile system

(USSR)

Type: tracked self-propelled surface-to-air missile system
Crew: 5
Combat weight: 25,000 kg (55,115 lb)
Dimensions: length overall 9·46 m (31·04 ft) and hull 7·30 m (23·95 ft); width 3·20 m (10·50 ft); height including missiles 4·472 m (14·67 ft)
Armament system: one two-missile launcher with two SA-4 'Ganef' missiles; the launcher is powered but lacks stabilization in either elevation

Below: The reload vehicles for the ZRK Krug system each carry two SA-4 'Ganef' SAMs.

ZSU-57-2 SP 57-mm twin AA gun mounting

(USSR)
Type: tracked self-propelled 57-mm twin AA gun mounting
Crew: 6
Combat weight: 28,100 kg (61,949 lb)
Dimensions: length, guns forward 8·48 m (27·82 ft) and hull 6·22 m (20·41 ft); width 3·27 m (10·73 ft); height 2·75 m (9·02 ft)
Armament system: two 57-mm S-68 guns with 316 rounds of ready-use ammunition; the turret is hydraulically powered, the guns lack stabilization in either elevation (−5° to +85°) or azimuth (360°), and an optical fire-control system is fitted
Armour: welded steel varying in thickness between 10·6 and 15 mm (0·42 and 0·59 in)
Powerplant: one 390-kW (947-hp) Model V-54 diesel engine with 812 litres (179 Imp gal) of internal fuel plus provision for 400 litres (88 Imp gal) of external fuel
Performance: speed, road 50 km/h (31·1 mph); range, road 420 km (261 miles) on internal fuel and 595 km (370 miles) with auxiliary fuel; fording 1·4 m (4·6 ft); gradient 60%; side slope 30%; vertical obstacle 0·8 m (31·5 in); trench 2·7 m (8·9 ft); ground clearance 0·425 m (16·75 in)

Variant
ZSU-57-2: though now obsolete, at the time of its introduction in the mid-1950s this was an extremely potent air-defence weapon; the hull is that of the T-54 main battle tank (though the armour has been thinned and the hull thus made considerably lighter), the standard low-silhouette turret with a single 100-mm (3·94-in) rifled gun being replaced by a substantially larger and lighter turret accommodating two 57-mm S-68 guns, which are essentially similar to the S-60 towed equipment of the same calibre, and offer the same performance with the same ammunition; the ZSU-57-2 was soon in widespread production for service as the primary air-defence equipment of the Soviet army's tank and motorized rifle regiments but has now been relegated to second-line service in Soviet service, though it remains amongst the first-line inventory of many Eastern bloc and Soviet client states; the driver is located at the front of the vehicle on the right, and the rest of the hull comprises the fighting compartment in the centre and the powerplant at the rear; it is believed that the ZSU-57-2 lacks any NBC protection, is not amphibious and, unlike the vast majority of Soviet armoured fighting vehicles, is not equipped to produce a smoke-screen by injecting fuel into the engine exhaust system; more important, however, is the ZSU-57-2's lack of anything but a simple optical fire-control system ill-suited to the engagement of modern battlefield aircraft in all but the most perfect weather conditions; the ZSU-57-2's tactical crew is located in the turret, and comprises the commander to the rear on the right, the gunner to the rear on the left, the fuse setter at the very back to the right of the gunner, and two loaders to the front on the left and right; manual controls are fitted for emergency use, but hydraulic power is normally used for turret traverse and gun elevation, both at rates too slow for the realistic engagement of modern battlefield aircraft; the field in which the ZSU-57-2 still has a formidable capability is in its secondary role against armoured fighting vehicles through the use of two types of potent APC round; these both fire a 2·82-kg (8·22-lb) projectile at a muzzle velocity of 1000 m (3,281 ft) per second to pierce 96 mm

(to +45°) or azimuth (360°), and a radar-directed fire-control system is fitted
Armour: welded steel to a maximum thickness of 15 mm (0·59 in)
Powerplant: one 450-kW (604-hp) diesel engine with 850 litres (187 Imp gal) of internal fuel
Performance: speed, road 50 km/h (31·1 mph); range, road 450 km (280 miles); fording 1·5 m (4·9 ft); gradient 30%; side slope not revealed; vertical obstacle 1·0 m (3·3 in); trench 2·5 m (8·2 ft); ground clearance 0·44 m (17·3 in)

Variant
ZRK Krug: the SA-4 'Ganef' high/medium-altitude area-defence missile was developed in the late 1950s to provide major Soviet ground formations with area defence against high- and medium-altitude air attack; the missile was developed as part of the ZRK Krug mobile weapon system, which entered service in the early 1960s and was initially revealed in public during May 1964; the brigade comprises a brigade HQ, three missile battalions and one technical battalion; the technical battalion is tasked with providing the missile battalions with early warning of attack, and is thus equipped with one 'Long Track' surveillance radar and one 'Thin Skin' height-finding radar; each battalion has three Krug battalions and, for local defence, eight ZU-23-2 towed twin or ZSU-23-4 self-propelled quadruple 23-mm cannon equipments; the battalion is the basic Krug unit, and comprises three batteries each fielding three (peace) or four (war) Krug launchers, one 'Pat Hand' fire-control vehicle and four Ural-375 6×6 4-tonne trucks each carrying one reload missile; as it is designed to operate just behind the front line, the Krug has little need of amphibious and night vision capabilities, but is similar to other tactically important Soviet systems in being fitted with an NBC system; the launcher is carried on a tracked chassis developed specifically for this application, but since adopted (with modification) for the GMZ armoured minelayer and for the 2S3 152-mm (6-in) self-propelled howitzer; at the front of the vehicle, to left and right, are located the driver and powerplant; to the rear of this mobility sec-

Above: The ZRK Kub system firing unit is based on a purpose-designed tracked chassis since adopted for several other equipments.

tion the available chassis volume is devoted to the tactical crew and electronics; on the vehicle's centre of gravity is the missile launcher, which is based on a hydraulically actuated turntable; the launcher has two arms (that on the left carrying its missile about 0·35 m/9·8 in higher than that on the right) and the launcher arms can be elevated through an angle of 45°; target detection at ranges of more than 100 km (62 miles) is tasked to separate brigade-level 'Long Track' surveillance and 'Thin Skin' height-finding radars; data are passed to the Krug battery's 'Pat Hand' fire-control and missile-guidance radar, which assumes control of the engagement once it has acquired the designated target; the 'Pat Hand' is mounted on the same type of chassis as the Krug launcher, ensuring compatibility of battlefield mobility; the 'Pat Hand' system's computer produces a fire-control solution and allocates the target to the Krug launcher best positioned for an interception; the 'Pat Hand' system provides the Krug launcher's onboard system with the appropriate training and elevation details; the missile is then launched, tracked by the 'Pat Hand' system using the continuous-wave radar transponder fixed to one of the missile's fins, and provided with command guidance until its onboard semi-active guidance system takes over; from the late 1960s, low-altitude interception has become more important than the Krug's original mission, and the launcher can accept the SA-4B missile optimized for this role, as well as the original SA-4A missile; unconfirmed reports suggest that the SA-4 missile may also possess a secondary surface-to-surface capability, but this seems unlikely; the system's engagement envelope includes minimum and maximum ranges of 9·3 and 72 km (5·8 and 44·7 miles), plus altitude limits of 1100 and 24,000 m (3,610 and 78,740 ft); the Krug system is now obsolescent in terms of mobility and electronics, and remains tactically fettered (as it always has been) by the allocation of only one 'Pat Hand' fire-control vehicle to each battery

(3·7 in) of armour inclined at 0° at a range of 1000 m (1,095 yards); in the anti-aircraft role the guns fire two types of FRAG projectile at a muzzle velocity of 1000 m per second; one weighs 2·81 kg (6·2 lb) and the other weighs 2·85 kg (6·28 lb); of the total ammunition complement, 264 are stored in the turret for ready use, and are loaded by the two gunners in clips of four; the guns each have cyclic and practical firing rates of 120 and 70 rounds per minute, and their maximum horizontal range is 12,000 m (13,125 yards) while the effective slant range is 4000 m (4,375 yards), with a maximum ceiling of 8800 m (28,870 ft) attainable

Left: The ZSU-57-2 is tactically unimpressive because of its slow traverse and elevation rates and its restriction to clear-weather engagements.

ZSU-30-4 (2S6 Tunguska) SP 30-mm twin AA gun/ surface-to-air missile system

(USSR)

Type: tracked self-propelled surface-to-air missile/30-mm quadruple AA gun system
Crew: 4
Combat weight: 34,000 kg (74,596 lb)
Dimensions: length overall 7·84 m (25·72 ft); width 3·47 m (11·38 ft); height with radar lowered 3·08 m (10·105 ft) and with radar raised 3·89 m (12·76 ft)
Armament system: four 30-mm 2A42 cannon with between 500 and 700 rounds of ready-use ammunition, eight SA-19 surface-to-air missiles, and six smoke-dischargers on each side of the turret; the turret is electrically powered, the guns lack stabilization in either elevation (an unrevealed arc) or azimuth (360°), and a radar-directed fire-control system is fitted
Armour: welded steel
Powerplant: one 390-kW (523-hp) modified Model V-59 diesel engine with an unrevealed quantity of internal fuel
Performance: speed, road 65 km/h (40·4 mph); range, road 500 km (311 miles); other details not revealed

Variant
ZSU-30-4: little of a concrete nature is known about this equipment, which is a new Soviet point defence tactical AA cannon mounting, other than the fact that it is designated **2S6** in Soviet production terminology and has the service name **Tunguska;** it is a self-propelled gun/missile system using a chassis related to that of the MT-S tracked command vehicle and carrying four 30-mm cannon (related to the 2A42 weapon of the BMP-2 mechanized infantry combat vehicle but with a longer barrel for higher muzzle velocity and longer range) and eight short-range SAMs; the cannon are mounted on each side of the turret in two closely grouped pairs, and are believed to possess an effective slant range of 3800 m (4,155 yards); the external positioning of the cannon ensures that no fumes enter the turret to disrupt the tactical crew, and each weapon is fitted with a muzzle velocity-measuring device and a cooling system; located outside each of the cannon is a quartet of SAMs, believed to be designated SA-19 in the US system of terminology, and these

Below: The 2S6 is an extremely capable AA system with an all-weather fire-control system for its cannon and SAMs.

weapons traverse and elevate with the cannon, the gunner being able to select the weapon more appropriate for any particular engagement; the power-operated turret contains or mounts the fighting crew and the main elements of the 'Hot Shot' radar fire-control system including the large antenna for the surveillance radar above the turret rear, and the circular antenna for the tracking radar on the turret front; the use of twin radars is a marked improvement over the ZSU-23-4's single-radar arrangement in allowing continued surveillance once the tracking radar has been allocated a target; the fire-control system also possesses an optronic input

ZSU-23-4 SP 23-mm quadruple AA gun system

(USSR)

Type: tracked self-propelled 23-mm quadruple AA gun system
Crew: 4
Combat weight: 19,000 kg (41,887 lb)
Dimensions: length overall 6·54 m (21·46 ft); width 2·95 m (9·68 ft); height with radar lowered 2·25 m (7·38 ft) and with radar raised 3·80 m (12·47 ft)
Armament system: four 23-mm AZP-23 cannon with 2,000 rounds of ready-use ammunition; the turret is electrically powered, the guns lack stabilization in either elevation (−4° to +85°) or azimuth (360°), and a radar-directed fire-control system is fitted
Armour: welded steel varying in thickness betwen 10 and 15 mm (0·39 and 0·59 in)
Powerplant: one 210-kW (282-hp) Model V-6R diesel engine with 250 litres (55 Imp gal) of internal fuel

Performance: speed, road 44 km/h (27·3 mph); range, road 260 km (162 miles); fording 1·07 m (3·5 ft); gradient 60% ; side slope 30% ; vertical obstacle 1·1 m (43·3 in); trench 2·8 m (9·2 ft); ground clearance 0·4 m (15·75 in)

Variant

ZSU-23-4: by the late 1950s it was clear that the days of the ZSU-57-2's useful operational capability were numbered; what was needed was a new air-defence system offering the same levels of battlefield mobility and protection as the ZSU-57-2, but optimized for the short-range protection of Soviet first-line combat formations in all weather conditions by day and night; this called for a tracked chassis carrying a lightweight turret fitted with a multiple battery of fast-firing cannon, the combination of lighter weapons and powerful motors providing the rapid traverse and elevation rates required for the sustained engagement of high-speed manoeuvring targets, especially when supported by a radar-directed fire-control system for adequate target detection and fast processing of a fire-control solution; the

resulting ZSU-23-4 was designed in the early 1960s, and began entering service in the mid-1960s with the Soviet army name **Shilka**; the ZSU-23-4 is based on components of the PT-76 light amphibious tank, and the hull is all but identical with that used for the SA-6 'Gainful' SAM system; the vehicle is divided into three compartments, with the driver's position at the front (on the left), the fighting compartment in the centre and the powerplant at the rear; the core of the fighting compartment is the large rectangular turret, which has an admirably low silhouette and accommodates the other three crew members (the commander on the left under a 360° traverse cupola fitted with three periscopes, with the radar operator/gunner and range operator to his right); these three are separated from the armament section of the turret by a gas-tight bulkhead; the radar used in the ZSU-23-4 is the 'Gun Dish' type, which has its downward-folding antenna above the rear of the turret; this is designated B-76 in Soviet service and can detect targets at a range of 20,000 m (21,875 yards) and track them at 8000 m (8,750 yards); the rest of the fire-control

system comprises an optical sight (for use when the enemy is using ECM) and a fire-control computer; the four water-cooled 23-mm cannon are stabilized in elevation (the turret being stabilized in azimuth), and each gas-operated cannon has a cyclic rate of between 800 and 1,000 rounds per minute, translating to a practical rate of 3,400 rounds per minute with all cannon firing; each cannon fires HEI and API projectiles, the ammunition being loaded as one API and three HEI rounds, with a muzzle velocity of 970 m (3,182 ft) per second; the API projectile can pierce 25 mm (1 in) of armour at 500 m (545 yards), declining to 19·3 mm (0·76 in) at 1000 m (1,095 yards); in general, 3-, 5- or 10-round bursts are fired, though a 30-round burst can also be fired; the maximum range in the surface-to-surface role is 3000 m (3,280 yards), and in the anti-aircraft role the effective slant range is 2500 m (2,735 yards) with an effective ceiling of 1000 m (3,280 ft); an additional 3,000 rounds of ammunition can be

Below: The ZSU-23-4 is still a formidable weapon with a quartet of hard-hitting cannon.

towed in a special limber, though it is more common for each vehicle to be followed, some 1500 to 2500 m (1,640 to 2,735 yards) to the rear, by a supply truck carrying 3,000 rounds; standard equipment includes an NBC system and night-vision devices; there are at least nine variants of the basic ZSU-23-4, most of them featuring alterations to the cooling and stowage facilities (the latter adding a pannier for two ammunition boxes to each side of the turret). The most important of these variants are the pre-production and initial production **ZSU-23-4 Model 1965**, the full-production **ZSU-23-4V Model 1968** and **ZSU-23-4V1 Model 1972**, and the latest **ZSU-23-4M Model 1977**; this last features panniers for three rather than two ammunition boxes, an armoured cover for the cannon, an improved 'Gun Dish' radar that is not slaved to the gun barrels (allowing independent radar search), and a digital rather than analog fire-control system that can be linked electronically to off-set radars and fire-control systems; in 1985 there appeared a subvariant of the ZSU-23-4M with revised radar

BTR-152A

(USSR)

Type: wheeled self-propelled 14·5-mm (0·57-in) twin AA gun mounting
Crew: 4
Combat weight: 9600 kg (21,164 lb)
Dimensions: length overall 6·83 m (22·41 ft); width 2·32 m (7·61 ft); height 2·80 m (9·19 ft)
Armament system: two 14·5-mm (0·57-in) KPV heavy machine-guns with 2,000 rounds of ready-use ammunition; the mounting is manually powered, the guns lack stabilization in either elevation (−5° to +80°) or azimuth (360°), and optical sights are fitted
Armour: welded steel varying in thickness between 4 and 13·5 mm (0·16 and 0·53 in)
Powerplant: one 80-kW (107-hp) ZIL-123 petrol engine with 300 litres (66 Imp gal) of internal fuel, and driving a 6 × 6 layout
Performance: speed, road 65 km/h (40·4 mph); range, road 780 km (485 miles); fording 0·8 m (2·6 ft); gradient 55%; side slope not revealed; vertical obstacle 0·6 m (23·6 in); trench 0·69 m (2·25 ft); ground clearance 0·295 m (11·6 in)

Variants

BTR-152A: introduced in the mid-1950s, this equipment is based on the Soviet army's first armoured personnel carrier to have entered service after World War II, namely the BTR-152V that appeared in 1951 after development on the chassis and automotive system of the ZIL-157 truck; the BTR-152A is still in limited service, but suffers the grave disadvantages on the modern battlefield of lacking NBC protection and amphibious capability; the BTR-152A anti-aircraft vehicle is modelled closely on the BTR-152V series, but is fitted with a ZTPU-2 manually operated turret for two 14·5-mm (0·57-in) KPV machine-guns; the use of a manual system limits traverse and elevation rates, thereby reducing the system's capability against all but the slowest crossing targets, and this factor is compounded by the fact that the turret is provided with only the simplest of optical sight systems; the KPV is one of the standard Soviet heavy machine-guns, and has several ammunition options, including an API round that fires its projectile with a muzzle velocity of 1000 m (3,281 ft) per second for an armour-penetration capability of 32 mm (1·26 in) at 500 m (545 yards); the guns are credited with

maximum horizontal and vertical ranges of 8000 m (8,750 yards) and 5000 m (16,405 ft) respectively, but the effective horizontal and slant ranges are 2000 and 1400 m (2,185 and 1,530 yards) respectively; the cyclic rate of the KPV is 600 rounds per minute, reduced in practical circumstances to 150 rounds per minute, and the projectiles have increasingly marginal capability against all but light tactical aircraft; variations on this BTR-152A theme include Egyptian vehicles with a Czech M53 mounting for four 12·7-mm (0·5-in) DShKM machine-guns, and Palestine Liberation Organization vehicles with a Soviet ZU-23-2 mounting for two 23-mm cannon

BTR-40A: the same ZPTU-2 turret with its armament of two 14·5-mm (0·57-in) KPV heavy machine-guns is also carried in this equipment, a variant of the BTR-40 armoured personnel carrier; this vehicle has a crew of five, and its ammunition capacity is 2,400 rounds; the performance of the turret and machine-guns is identical with that of the installation on the BTR-152A; basic data for the BTR-40A include a combat weight of about 6000 kg (13,228 lb), a length of 5·00 m (16·40 ft), a width of 1·90 m (6·23 ft), a height of 2·50 m (8·20 ft) and, on the power of a 60-kW (80-hp) GAZ-40 petrol engine driving a 4 × 4 layout, road performance slightly inferior to the BTR-40's maximum speed of 80 km/h (49·7 mph) and range of 285 km (177 miles)

Below: The Tracked Rapier has eight ready-to-launch missiles on a variant of the M113 chassis.

British Aerospace Tracked Rapier SP surface-to-air missile system

(UK)

Type: tracked self-propelled surface-to-air missile system
Crew: 3
Combat weight: 30,885 lb (14,009 kg)
Dimensions: length overall 21·00 ft (6·40 m); width 9·19 ft (2·80 m); height for air transport 8·20 ft (2·50 m) and with tracker raised 9·12 ft (2·78 m)
Armament system: eight launchers (four on each side of the central weapon/sensor pedestal) with eight Rapier missiles, and 20 smoke-dischargers; the pedestal is electrically powered but lacks stabilization in either elevation (an unrevealed arc) or azimuth (360°), and a radar-directed fire-control system is fitted
Armour: welded aluminium to a maximum thickness of 1 in (25 mm)
Powerplant: one 210-hp (157-kW) Detroit Diesel 6V-53N diesel engine with 87·5 Imp gal (398 litres) of internal fuel
Performance: speed, road 30 mph (48 km/h) and water 3·5 mph (5·6 km/h) driven by its tracks; range, road 185 miles (298 km); fording amphibious with screen; gradient 60%; side slope 30%; vertical obstacle 24 in (0·61 m); trench 5·5 ft (1·68 m); ground clearance 16 in (0·41 m)

Variants

Tracked Rapier Mk 1A: introduced to service in

1983, this is the high-mobility version of the Towed Rapier SAM system and is based on the hull of the US M548 cargo carrier; the system is designed for the short-range defence of armoured and mechanized divisions against low-altitude air threats, the need for such a system having been appreciated from early in the Rapier programme though implemented only from 1974 after expressions of strong interest from the Iranian army; first prototype trials were carried out in 1976 using the missile launcher vehicle, which was joined during the following year by the FAST (Forward Area Support Team) reload vehicle on the same chassis; initial orders were placed by Iran and the UK, though the Iranian order was cancelled after the overthrow of the Shah of Iran in 1979; in British service the Tracked Rapier is allocated to light air-defence regiments, each supporting a high-value ground formation; each regiment operates both the towed and tracked versions of the Rapier, being based on four batteries each operating 12 firing units (and thus giving the regiment 24 Tracked Rapier and 24 Towed Rapier launchers); the chassis of the Tracked Rapier is a variant of the FMC M548 designated RCM 748 in this application; the RCM 748 comprises a front-mounted cab of aluminium armour for the crew of three (driver on the left, commander in the centre and operator on the right), the powerplant, diesel generator and air-conditioner in the centre, and the missile-launcher and associated electronics at the rear; this last is an assembly capable of powered traverse, and the missiles are located in two lateral four-round bins made of 1-in (25-mm) armour; apart from the eight Rapiers, this rear-mounted launcher assembly contains the antenna for the pulse-Doppler surveillance radar, operating to a range of 12,500 yards (11,430 m), and mounts the elevating antenna for the missile guidance system: this latter uses a microwave link for automatic command-to-line-of-sight guidance using a cab-mounted periscopic optical (TV) tracker, the elevation of the antenna on a special pantograph ensuring that the guidance system's beam clears the top of the crew cab. In common with the Towed Rapier, the Tracked Rapier has a very useful performance capability right down to the horizon, or even below it, as a result of its optical tracking and command guidance system; the system operates in exactly the same way as the Towed Rapier and has the same engagement envelope, including minimum and maximum ranges of 900 and 7,100+ yards (825 and 6490+ m), and minimum and maximum altitudes of 0 and 10,000 ft (0 and 3050 m); the Rapier Mk 2 and Rapier Mk 3 missiles will be integrated into the Tracked Rapier system as they become available, so maintaining the viability of the system into the next century; each Towed Rapier launch vehicle is backed by a Tracked Rapier Support Vehicle (again using the M548 chassis) with a crew of two and 20 reload missiles, and the FAST vehicles are used for battlefield support with test equipment, replacement components and a front-mounted crane.

Tracked Rapier Mk 1B: the initial Tracked Rapier Mk 1A was produced in limited numbers as it is capable only of clear-weather operations, while the main production version is the Tracked Rapier Mk 1B with TOTE (Tracker Optical Thermally Enhanced) for adverse-weather and night capability: Mk 1A equipments are being upgraded to Mk 1B standard; time into action from the move is about 15 seconds, and time out of action about 20 seconds; the reaction time (between target detection and missile launch) is five seconds, the second missile following two

seconds later; single-shot kill probability is quoted at 70%

Alvis/Shorts Stormer Starstreak SP surface-to-air missile system

(UK)
Type: tracked self-propelled surface-to-air missile system
Crew: 3
Combat weight: about 26,500 lb (12,020 kg)
Dimensions: length overall 17·67 ft (5·38 m); width 7·87 ft (2·40 m); height not revealed
Armament system: eight launchers (four on each side of the central weapon/sensor pedestal) with 20 Starstreak missiles, and four smoke-dischargers on each side of the hull; the pedestal is electrically powered but lacks stabilization in either elevation (an unrevealed arc) or azimuth (360°), and an optical fire-control system is fitted
Armour: welded aluminium
Powerplant: one 250-hp (186-kW) Perkins T6·3544 diesel engine with 73 Imp gal (332 litres) of internal fuel
Performance: speed, road 45 mph (72 km/h) and water 6 mph (9·6 km/h) driven by one propeller or 4 mph (6·4 km/h) driven by its tracks; range, road 330 miles (531 km); fording 3·6 ft (1·1 m) without preparation and amphibious with preparation; gradient 60%; side slope 30%; vertical obstacle 18 in (0·46 m); trench 5·9 ft (1·8 m); ground clearance 16·75 in (0·43 m)

Variant
Stormer Starstreak: the Alvis Stormer is the company's private-venture development of the FV4333 armoured vehicle designed in the late 1970s by the Military Vehicles and Engineering Establishment, the Alvis development being centred on the incorporation of proved components from the Scorpion CVR(T) series and the evolution of the type as the core of a large number of variants; the British army has ordered the Stormer Starstreak as a self-propelled SAM system fitted with the new and exceptionally impressive Shorts Starstreak high-velocity missile for the point defence of first-line field formations; the basic hull of the Stormer is retained, with the driver and powerplant at the front (to the left and right respectively) and the two-man tactical crew plus the armament in the compartment to the rear; the core of the system is the combination of missiles and guidance system; the missiles are fired from an eight-round powered pedestal above the rear of the vehicle: this pedestal allows powered traverse as well as elevation to the launch angle indicated by the operator's combined optronic sight/guidance unit, which is a periscopic unit farther forward along the tactical compartment, with the commander's cupola to its left; a maximum of 12 reload missiles can be carried in the hull of the vehicle

Ford Aerospace/FMC M48 Chaparral SP surface-to-air missile system

(USA)
Type: tracked self-propelled surface-to-air missile system
Crew: 4-5

Combat weight: 25,350 lb (11,499 kg)
Dimensions: length overall 19·88 ft (6·06 m); width 8·83 ft (2·69 m); height over tarpaulin cover 8·79 ft (2·68 m)
Armament system: four launchers (two on each side of the central weapon/sensor pedestal) with 12 MIM-72 Chaparral missiles; the pedestal is electrically powered but lacks stabilization in either elevation (−5° to +90°) or azimuth (360°), and an optronic fire-control system is fitted
Armour: none
Powerplant: one 202-hp (151-kW) Detroit Diesel 6V-53N diesel engine with 106 US gal (401 litres) of internal fuel
Performance: speed, road 38 mph (61·2 km/h) and water 3·5 mph (5·6 km/h) driven by its tracks; range, road 313 miles (504 km); fording amphibious; gradient 60%; side slope 30%; vertical obstacle 24 in (0·61 m); trench 5·5 ft (1·68 m); ground clearance 16 in (0·41 m)

Variants
M48 Chaparral: this was developed as an interim measure to provide US divisions with a high-mobility SAM system in substitution for the originally planned system using the Convair MIM-46 Mauler missile cancelled in 1965; the replacement system uses the Ford Aerospace MIM-72 Chaparral missile, the M54 turret and launcher unit, and the M730 chassis derived from the FMC M548 tracked carrier; the complete system was developed between 1965 and 1969, and is used as part of the composite air-defence battalion organic to each first-line division of the US Army; this battalion has four firing batteries, two equipped with the M48 Chaparral and two with the M163 cannon mounting: each battery has 12 self-propelled equipments; when the vehicle halts at a firing position the men remove the tarpaulin cover and supporting bows from over the Chaparral system, and fit blast screens over the closed-down vehicle cab; a mechanical system is then used to elevate the M54 launcher unit for the Chaparral, which is a palletized system accommodated over the flatbed rear of the vehicle; the base structure of the M54 accommodates the system's support equipment including a 10-hp (7·46-kW) petrol-engined generator, the air compressor that supplies the air used to cool the missile seekers, the master control panel, communications equipment and, in two lateral groups of four, eight manually reloaded missiles; the missiles are stored without their fins and control surfaces, which must be attached before the missiles are ready for use; the base also supports the hydraulically actuated turret/launcher assembly in which the operator sits on an adjustable seat under a curved top transparency in a cab that is air-conditioned with cleaned air, and commands the operation with two hand controllers and a number of panel displays and switches; the turret can be traversed through 360°, and the launcher arms can be elevated from −5° to +90° in the **M54A1** baseline version or from −9° to +90° in the improved **M54A2** version, on which each launcher rail is fitted with an IFF interrogator unit; the complete M54 launcher unit weighs 10,700 lb (4854 kg); once he has acquired the target visually, the operator tracks it with the complete turret, and selects one of the four missiles carried in pairs on the two lateral twin-rail launcher units; the selected missile then locks onto the target using its high-discrimination cooled seeker, and the operator is informed of the lock by an audible signal. He can then fire the missile, which homes automatically; the M48 system is limited basically to clear-weather operations, and this is clearly a distinct tactical

The M48 Chaparral system has four MIM-72 SAMs but only an optical fire-control system.

limitation for units tasked with operations in areas such as Europe where such weather is far from the norm. The US army has therefore undertaken a development programme to fit M48 Chaparral systems with a FLIR sensor, such thermal imaging serving to provide an autotrack capability. The sensor has optional wide- and narrow-angle fields of vision (for target acquisition and target tracking respectively), and the system provides a useful increase in capability by making possible operations at night and in adverse day conditions such as haze or smoke; at the same time other features of the launcher are being upgraded, most notably the replacement of the 10-hp (7·46-kW) petrol engine with a 30-hp (22·4-kW) diesel engine as the launcher's power unit; the M730 is also being improved in reliability and performance by the adoption of the RISE modifications developed for the basic M113 series; the implementation of the RISE modification results in the designation M730A2

Cadillac (General Motors) M42A1 Duster SP 40-mm twin AA gun mounting

(USA)
Type: tracked self-propelled 40-mm twin AA gun mounting

Crew: 6
Combat weight: 49,500 lb (22,453 kg)
Dimensions: length, guns forward 20·85 ft (6·36 m) and hull 19·09 ft (5·82 m); width 10·58 ft (3·23 m); height 9·33 ft (2·84 m)
Armament system: two 40-mm M2A1 guns with 480 rounds of ready-use ammunition; the turret is hydraulically powered, the guns lack stabilization in either elevation (−3° to +85°) or azimuth (360°), and an optical fire-control system is fitted
Armour: welded steel varying in thickness between 0·35 and 1·2 in (9 and 31 mm)
Powerplant: one 500-hp (373-kW) Continental AOSI-895-5 petrol engine with 140 US gal (530 litres) of internal fuel
Performance: speed, road 45 mph (72·4 km/h); range, road 100 miles (161 km); fording 3·33 ft (1·02 m); gradient 60%; side slope 30%; vertical obstacle 28 in (0·71 m); trench 6·0 ft (1·83 m); ground clearance 17·25 in (0·44 m)

Variants
M42 Duster: this was developed in the early 1950s to replace the self-propelled twin 40-mm cannon mounting which had equipped the US ground forces at the end of World War II, namely the M19 based on the chassis of the M24 light tank; an extensive development of gun and fire-control vehicles designed to operate as a team was then cancelled for reasons of cost, and the M42 was rapidly produced as a development of the M19 system, using the same turret and armament but now carried on the chassis of the M41 light tank;

the original M42 was fitted with the normally aspirated AOS-895-5 engine and was introduced in 1952, but this was replaced from 1956 by the **M42A1** with the fuel-injected AOSI-895-3 engine, and most M42s were improved to this standard; the type was designed for the low-level defence of armoured and mechanized divisions, and is now thoroughly obsolete as it lacks armament protection, radar search and control, an NBC system and other modern essentials; the US licence-built Bofors guns each have a practical fire rate of 120 rounds per minute (with single shots as an option), and the system possesses very useful horizontal and slant ranges that cannot, however, be fully exploited for lack of an effective fire-control system: the maximum horizontal range is 10,350 yards (9465 m) and the maximum slant range 5,500 yards (5030 m)

General Electric/FMC M163 SP 20-mm multi-barrel AA gun mounting

(USA)
Type: tracked self-propelled 20-mm multi-barrel AA gun mounting
Crew: 4
Combat weight: 27,140 lb (12,311 kg)
Dimensions: length overall 15·94 ft (4·86 m); width 9·35 ft (2·85 m); height 8·98 ft (2·736 m)
Armament system: one 20-mm M168 Vulcan

cannon with 2,100 rounds of ready-use ammunition; the turret is electrically powered, the gun lacks stabilization in either elevation ($-5°$ to $+80°$) or azimuth ($360°$), and an optronic/radar-directed fire-control system is fitted

Armour: welded aluminium varying in thickness between 0·5 and 1·5 in (13 and 38 mm)

Powerplant: one 215-hp (160-kW) Detroit Diesel 6V-53N diesel engine with 95 US gal (360 litres) of internal fuel

Performance: speed, road 42 mph (67·6 km/h) and water 3·5 mph (5·6 km/h) driven by its tracks; range, road 300 miles (483 km); fording amphibious; gradient 60%; side slope 30%; vertical obstacle 24 in (0·61 m); trench 5·5 ft (1·68 m); ground clearance 16 in (0·41 m)

Variants

M163: designed by Rock Island Arsenal in the mid-1960s (the programme starting in 1964 and including the M167 towed version) but produced by an industrial contractor, this is a point-defence weapon limited to clear-weather engagements at short ranges as successor to the obsolete M42 mounting; the type was accepted for service in 1968, and has since been produced in considerable numbers as the **M163A1** for the home and export markets; the equipment's main deficiencies are its limitation to clear-weather operation and its lack of effective protection against shell splinters and the weather as well as the NBC threat; the M163 is deployed in composite air-defence battalions with the M48 Chaparral missile system, each such battalion having two M163 and two Chaparral batteries, each with 12 M163 and 12 Chaparral systems respectively; the M163's effective anti-aircraft range is a mere 1,750 yards (1600 m), and this means that the use of the Sanders MPQ-49 FAAR (Forward-Area Alerting Radar) is essential to cue the M163 equipments onto the right bearing for an anticipated attacker; the M163 is based on a simple development of the M113 armoured personel carrier's chassis, in this application designated M741, carrying lateral and nose packs for additional buoyancy, and fitted with a suspension-locking system to provide the cannon with a stable firing platform; the cannon is the 20-mm General Electric M168 Vulcan, a rotary-action weapon with an assembly of six barrels turning on its axis to produce a very high rate of fire (two rates being possible with the M163's weapon) and considerable reliability using a linkless feed arrangement from a 1,100-round drum that can be replenished from the 1,000-round reserve in the hull; the cannon is generally fired at 1,000 rounds per minute at ground targets, in which the maximum range is 5,000 yards (4570 m) and the effective range 3,250 yards (2970 m), and at 3,000 rounds per minute against aerial targets; this cannon is located in an open-topped mounting on the hull roof; when warned by radar of an imminent target, the gunner trains his turret to the appropriate bearing and searches visually for the target; having acquired the target, the gunner then tracks it with the aid of his gyro lead-computing sight; the coherent pulse-Doppler range radar is boresighted onto the optical line of sight and provides range and range-rate data to the sight generator, which receives angular tracking data from the gyro sight

Autotrack Vulcan Air Defense System: though comparatively sophisticated for what it is, the M163 is still limited to clear-weather operation, and attempts have been made to overcome this limitation in the Autotrack Vulcan Air Defense System, which adds to the basic M163 an automatic tracking capability, a helmet sight for better visual acquisition of the target, an option for automatic search, more powerful servos for faster traverse and elevation rates, enhanced solution of the fire-control problem, and an internal self-test facility

Product-Improved Vulcan Air Defense System: this is a General Electric programme that adds the Mk 149 APDS round to the Vulcan's repertoire of ammunition types; the new round has an effective range of 2,850 yards (2605 m), and modifications to the fire-control system include rate-aided tracking for the director sight, and linking a digital computer into the ranging radar to produce more accurate range and range-rate data; these modifications are being retrofitted to in-service M163A1 equipments to produce the **M163A2** variant

---

General Electric/Cadillac Gage Vulcan-Commando SP 20-mm multi-barrel AA gun mounting

(USA

Type: wheeled self-propelled 20-mm multi-barrel AA gun mounting

Crew: 4

Combat weight: 22,500 lb (10,206 kg)

Dimensions: length overall 18·67 ft (5·689 m); width 7·41 ft (2·26 m); height to hull top 6·50 ft (1·98 m)

Armament system: one 20-mm M168 Vulcan cannon with 1,300 rounds of ready-use ammunition; the turret is electrically powered, the gun lacks stabilization in either elevation ($-5°$ to $+85°$) or azimuth ($360°$), and an optronic/radar-directed fire-control system is fitted

Armour: welded steel

Powerplant: one 202-hp (151-kW) Cummins V-504 diesel engine with 80 US gal (303 litres) of internal fuel, and driving a 4 × 4 layout

Performance: speed, road 55 mph (88·5 km/h) and water 3 mph (4·8 km/h) driven by its wheels; range, road 400 miles (643 km); fording amphibious; gradient 60%; side slope 30%; vertical obstacle 36 in (0·914 m); trench not revealed; ground clearance 15 in (0·381 m)

Below: The BOV-3 has the unusual AA armament of three 20-mm cannon in a powered turret.

Variant

Vulcan-Commando: 'off-the-shelf' combination of the Cadillac Gage V-150 Commando light armoured personnel carrier and the General Electric M61A1 Vulcan armament system as used in the M163 tracked self-propelled AA mounting; the only major modification to the chassis is the addition of three hydraulically operated stabilizing jacks to make the vehicle a steady gun platform, and otherwise the Vulcan-Commando has the same characteristics and improvement options as the M163; four modes of operation are possible with the Vulcan-Commando: radar, manual, external (which is essentially the same as manual, but with an external observer keying in his estimates of target range and speed) and ground (in which the gyro sight is not used)

BOV-3/20-mm SP 20-mm triple AA gun mounting

(Yugoslavia)

Type: wheeled self-propelled 20-mm triple AA gun mounting

Crew: 4

Combat weight: 9400 kg (20,723 lb)

Dimensions: length overall 5·791 m (19·00 ft); width 2·525 m (8·28 ft); height 3·21 m (10·53 ft)

Armament system: three 20-mm Hispano-Suiza HSS 666 cannon with 1,500 rounds of ready-use ammunition; the turret is hydraulically powered, the guns lack stabilization in either elevation ($-4·5°$ to $+83°$) or azimuth ($360°$), and an optical fire-control system is fitted

Armour: welded steel

Powerplant: one 110-kW (148-hp) Deutz F 6L 413 F diesel engine with an unrevealed quantity of internal fuel, and driving a 4 × 4 layout

Performance: speed, road 93·4 km/h (58 mph) and water unrevealed driven by its wheels; range, road 500 km (311 miles); fording amphibious; gradient 55%; side slope 30%; vertical obstacle 0·54 m (21·25 in); trench 0·64 m (2·1 ft); ground clearance 0·325 m (12·8 in)

Variants

BOV-3/20-mm: this is a simple wheeled anti-aircraft mounting with three 20-mm cannon on the open-topped turret together with a neat but simple optical fire-control system; the mounting was developed on the basis of the BOV-1 anti-tank

vehicle, and the BOV-3 has a trim basic design, with the driver at the front, a crew/ammunition compartment at the rear, and the powerplant at the rear; the BOV-3/20-mm is designed for clear-weather operation, and is thus a limited system; the open-topped turret is located above the hull, with access only from the outside; the armament installation is based on that of the M55 A4 B1 towed mounting with triple 20-mm cannon, and each barrel has cyclic and practical rates of 750 and 150 rounds per minute respectively, the gunner being able to select between single shots, 10-round bursts, 10/20-round bursts or sustained fire; the ammunition feed system comprises a 60-round drum over each barrel, the drums being changed manually by the loader, who stands on a hull extension on each side of the vehicle forward of the turret; the maximum horizontal range of the cannon is some 2000 m (2,185 yards), and the effective anti-aircraft range about 1500 m (1,640 yards) with the aid of the J-171 optical sight

BOV-30: introduced in 1985, this is a self-propelled twin 30-mm AA gun mounting based on the BOV-3's hull but carrying a smaller and more vertical turret with the gunner seated in a small cupola at its rear; the two 30-mm cannon are externally cradle-mounted, and belt-fed with ammunition from inside the turret; the cannon are probably Hispano-Suiza HSS 831 (Oerlikon-Bührle KCB) weapons with local modifications

FAMIL FAM-2M 20-mm twin AA gun mounting

(Chile)
Type: towed twin 20-mm AA gun mounting
Calibre: 20 mm
Barrel length: 95·3 calibres overall
Carriage: two-wheel platform with outriggers; shield
Weights: 1600 kg (3,527 lb) in travelling order and 1250 kg (2,756 lb) in firing position
Dimensions: not revealed
Traverse/elevation: 360° total/not revealed
Rate of fire (per barrel): 1,000 rounds per minute (cyclic)
Horizontal range: 6500 m (7,110 yards) maximum
Slant range: 1500 m (1,640 yards) effective
Crew: 2–3

Variant
FAM-2L: this mounting was designed primarily for airfield defence, and originally mounted 20-mm cannon removed from de Havilland Vampire jet fighters; these HS 820 weapons have since been replaced by an improved version of this basic ordnance, the Oerlikon-Bührle KAD fed from a box holding 200 belted rounds; the mounting has a small petrol engine for hydraulically powered traverse and weapon elevation, and a gyro sight is fitted; a battery comprises four such equipments linked into a central fire-direction post

NORINCO Type 59 57-mm AA gun mounting

(China)
Type: towed 57-mm AA gun mounting
Calibre: 57 mm
Barrel length: about 77 calibres overall
Carriage: four-wheel carriage with outriggers; optional shield

Weight: 4780 kg (10,538 lb) in travelling and firing orders
Dimensions: length, travelling 8·60 m (28·22 ft); width, travelling 2·07 m (6·79 ft); height, travelling 2·46 m (8·07 ft)
Traverse/elevation: 360° total/−5° to +87°
Rate of fire: 100-120 rounds per minute (cyclic)
Horizontal range: 12,000 m (13,125 yards) maximum
Slant range: 6000 m (6,560 yards) effective
Crew: 7-8

Variant
Type 59: in essence this is the Chinese copy of the Soviet S-60 towed equipment, a recoil-operated type fed from four-round clips; the mounting carries a small petrol-engined generator for its electrically powered functions

NORINCO Type 74 37-mm twin AA gun mounting

(China)
Type: towed twin 37-mm AA gun mounting
Calibre: 37 mm
Barrel length: about 73·8 calibres overall

Carriage: four-wheel carriage with outriggers; no shield
Weight: 2835 kg (6,250 lb) in travelling and firing orders
Dimensions: length, travelling 6·205 m (20·36 ft); width, travelling 1·816 m (5·96 ft); height, travelling 2·28 m (7·48 ft)
Traverse/elevation: 360° total/−5° to +87° in manual mode and 0° to +81·5° in electrically powered mode
Rate of fire (per barrel): 220-240 rounds per minute (cyclic)
Horizontal range: 8500 m (9,295 yards) maximum
Slant range: 3500 m (3,830 yards) effective
Crew: not revealed

Variants
Type 74: this is the Chinese development of the Type 65, itself a copy of the Soviet M1939 twin mounting adapted for optional use with a radar fire-control system; the guns fire the same type of ammunition as the type 65, namely a 1·416-kg (3·12-lb) HE round firing its 0·732-kg (1·614-lb) projectile at a muzzle velocity of 865 m (2,838 ft)

The Type 59 is a simple clear-weather AA gun copied with minimal alteration from the widely used Soviet S-60 equipment.

Above: The Type 65 Chinese copy of a Soviet gun, a variant of the 37-mm M1939.

NORINCO 23-mm twin AA gun mounting

(China)

Type: towed twin 23-mm AA gun mounting
Calibre: 23 mm
Barrel length: 87·4 calibres overall
Carriage: two-wheel platform with outriggers; no shield
Weight: 950 kg (2,094 lb) in travelling and firing orders
Dimensions: length, travelling 4·57 m (14·99 ft); width, travelling 1·83 m (6·00 ft); height, travelling 1·87 m (6·135 ft)
Traverse/elevation: 360° total/−10° to +90°
Rate of fire (per barrel): 800-1,000 rounds per minute (cyclic) and 200 rounds per minute (practical)
Horizontal range: 7000 m (7,655 yards) maximum
Slant range: 2500 m (2,735 yards) effective
Crew: 5

Below: The Chinese twin-barrel 23-mm AA gun is a reverse-engineered version of the Soviet ZU-23-2 with detail modifications.

per second; this ammunition is fed in five-round clips
P793: 3100-kg (6,834-lb) upgraded version of the Type 74 with superior powered functions and a C335 optronic sight (perhaps a Chinese copy of the Officine Galileo VANTH unit); the mounting is available in two forms as the **Type P793 Type A** and **Type P793 Type B**, the former with barrels each offering a cyclic rate of between 220 and 240 rounds per minute at a muzzle velocity of 880 m (2,887 ft) per second, and the latter with barrels each offering a cyclic rate of 270-300 rounds per minute at a muzzle velocity of 1000 m (3,281 ft) per second; in addition to the basic HE round these equipments can also fire a new 1·44-kg (3·18-lb) AP type whose 0·758-kg (1·67-lb) projectile is fired at a muzzle velocity of 880 m (2,887 ft) per second to penetrate 40 mm (1·575 in) of armour

NORINCO WA 709 25-mm twin AA gun mounting

(China)

Type: towed twin 25-mm AA gun mounting
Calibre: 25 mm
Barrel length: not revealed
Carriage: two-wheel platform with outriggers; no shield
Weight: 1500 kg (3,307 lb) in travelling and firing orders
Dimensions: length, travelling 4·68 m (15·35 ft); width, travelling 2·04 m (6·69 ft); height, travelling 2·08 m (6·82 ft)
Traverse/elevation: 360° total/−10° to +90°
Rate of fire (per barrel): 600-700 rounds per minute (cyclic)
Horizontal range: not revealed
Slant range: 3200 m (3,500 yards) effective
Crew: 3

Variant

WA 709: introduced in the first half of the 1980s, this is a useful mounting about which very little of a concrete nature is known; the installation appears very similar to that of the Chinese reverse-engineered version of the Soviet ZU-23-2

23-mm mounting: this is a reverse-engineered version of the Soviet ZU-23-2 equipment designed to be towed behind a 4 × 4 truck

M53 30-mm twin AA gun mounting

(Czechoslovakia)
Type: towed twin 30-mm AA gun mounting
Calibre: 30 mm
Barrel length: 81 calibres overall
Carriage: four-wheel platform with outriggers; no shield
Weights: 2100 kg (4,630 lb) in travelling order and 1750 kg (3,858 lb) in firing position
Dimensions: length, travelling 7·587 m (24·89 ft); width, travelling 1·758 m (5·77 ft); height, travelling 1·575 m (5·17 ft)
Traverse/elevation: 360° total/− 10° to + 85°
Rate of fire (per barrel): 450-500 rounds per minute (cyclic) and 100 rounds per minute (practical)
Horizontal range: 9700 m (10,610 yards) maximum
Slant range: 3000 m (3,280 yards) effective
Crew: 4

Variant
M53: this weapon entered service in the late 1950s, and offers considerable range advantages over Soviet towed 23-mm equipments; the M53 suffers from lack of radar fire-control, and is thus limited to clear-weather operation; ammunition is fed by 10-round clips and the two basic ammunition types are HEI (with a 0·45-kg/0·99-lb projectile) and AP-T (with a 0·54-kg/1·2-lb projectile able to pierce 55 mm/2·16 of armour at 500 m/550 yards); both types are fired at a muzzle velocity of 1000 m (3,281 ft) per second

M53 12·7-mm quadruple AA gun mounting

(Czechoslovakia)
Type: towed quadruple AA gun mounting
Calibre: 12·7 mm (0·5 in)
Barrel length: 125 calibres overall
Carriage: two-wheel platform with outriggers; no shield
Weights: 2830 kg (6,239 lb) in travelling order and 628 kg (1,384 lb) in firing position
Dimensions: length, travelling 2·90 m (9·51 ft); width, travelling 1·57 m (5·15 ft); height, travelling 1·78 m (5·84 ft)
Traverse/elevation: 360° total/− 7° to + 90°
Rate of fire (per barrel): 550-600 rounds per minute (cyclic) and 80 rounds per minute (practical)
Horizontal range: 6500 m (7,110 yards) maximum
Slant range: 1000 m (1,095 yards) effective
Crew: 6

Variant
M53: introduced in the mid-1950s, this equipment combines four Soviet DShK heavy machine-guns with a Czech mounting and carriage; the machine-guns are fed from 50-round belts, and fire a 49·5-g (1·75-oz) API projectile at a muzzle velocity of 840 m (2,756 ft) per second, sufficient to penetrate 20 mm (0·79 in) of armour at 500 m (550 yards)

GIAT 76T2 Cerbère 20-mm twin AA gun mounting

(France)
Type: towed twin AA gun mounting
Calibre: 20 mm
Barrel length: 103·25 calibres overall
Carriage: two-wheel platform with outriggers; shield
Weights: 2019 kg (4,451 lb) in travelling order without ammunition and 1513 kg (3,336 lb) in firing position with ammunition
Dimensions: length, travelling 5·05 m (16·57 ft) and in firing position 4·02 m (13·19 ft); width, travelling 2·39 m (7·84 ft) and in firing position 2·06 m (6·76 ft); height, travelling 2·075 m (6·81 ft) and in firing position 2·06 m (6·76 ft)
Traverse/elevation: 360° total/− 3·5° to + 81·5° in powered mode and − 5° to + 83° in manual mode
Rate of fire (per barrel): 900 rounds per minute (cyclic) and 200-240 rounds per minute (cyclic)
Horizontal range: 6000 m (6,560 yards) maximum
Slant range: 2000 m (2,185 yards) effective
Crew: 3

Variant
76T2 Cerbère: this is a French development of the West German MK 20 Rh 202 mounting with the original cannon replaced by two French GIAT M693 (F2) weapons; the type can be operated in the powered or manual modes, and there is a selectable dual-feed mechanism, ammunition supply amounting to 270 rounds per barrel; the Cerbère can be used with its on-mounting sight, or in conjunction with a radar fire-control system, or with a helmet-mounted target-indicator system

GIAT 53T2 Tarasque 20-mm AA gun mounting

(France)
Type: towed single 20-mm AA gun mounting
Calibre: 20 mm
Barrel length: 103·25 calibres overall
Carriage: two-wheel platform with outriggers; shield
Weights: 840 kg (1,852 kg) in travelling order with ammunition and 660 kg (1,455 lb) in firing position with ammunition
Dimensions: length, travelling 4·15 m (13·62 ft); width, travelling 1·90 m (6·23 ft); height, travelling 1·70 m (5·58 ft)
Traverse/elevation: 360° total/− 8° to + 83°
Rate of fire: 740-900 rounds per minute (cyclic) and 200-240 rounds per minute (practical)
Horizontal range: 6000 m (6,560 yards) maximum
Slant range: 2000 m (2,185 yards) effective
Crew: 3

Variant
53T2 Tarasque: introduced in 1982, the Tarasque is a light AA mounting (with secondary anti-AFV and anti-personnel capabilities) designed for rapid cross-country movement; the M693 (F2) weapon is hydraulically powered, and is dual-fed by belts for 100 HEI and 40 APDS rounds, the former having a muzzle velocity of 1050 m (3,445 ft) per second and the latter of 1293 m (4,242 ft) per second; the APDS projectile can penetrate 20 mm (0·79 in) of armour at 1000 m (1,095 yards)

GIAT 53T1 20-mm AA gun mounting

(France)
Type: towed single 20-mm AA gun mounting
Calibre: 20 mm
Barrel length: 103·25 calibres overall
Carriage: two-wheel platform with outriggers; shield
Weights: 635 kg (1,400 kg) in travelling order with ammunition and 480 kg (1,058 lb) in firing position with ammunition
Dimensions: length, travelling 3·25 m (10·66 ft); width, travelling 1·76 m (5·77 ft); height, travelling 1·60 m (5·25 ft)
Traverse/elevation: 360° total/− 3° to + 83°
Rate of fire: 740-900 rounds per minute (cyclic) and 200-240 rounds per minute (practical)
Horizontal range: 6000 m (6,560 yards) maximum
Slant range: 2000 m (2,185 yards) effective
Crew: 2

Variant
53T1: introduced in the early 1960s, this is a light AA equipment with a useful secondary capability against vehicles and light armoured fighting vehicles; the cannon is the M621 fed with ammunition from a box holding 20 disintegrating-linked rounds, either AP or HEI

Rheinmetall MK 20 Rh 202 20-mm twin AA gun mounting

(West Germany)
Type: towed twin 20-mm AA gun mounting
Calibre: 20 mm
Barrel length: 130·5 calibres overall
Carriage: two-wheel platform with outriggers; shield
Weights: 2160 kg (4,762 lb) in travelling order without ammunition and 1640 kg (3,616 lb) in firing position with ammunition
Dimensions: length, travelling 5·035 m (16·52 ft) and in firing position 4·05 m (13·29 ft); width, travelling 2·36 m (7·74 ft) and in firing position 2·30 m (7·55 ft); height, travelling 2·075 m (6·81 ft) and in firing position 1·67 m (5·48 ft)
Traverse/elevation: 360° total on mounting/ − 3·5° to + 81·6° in powered mode and − 5·5° to + 83·5° in manual mode
Rate of fire (per barrel): 880-1,030 rounds per minute (cyclic)
Horizontal range: 3000 m (3,280 yards) maximum
Slant range: 2000 m (2,185 yards) effective
Crew: 3-4

Variant
MK 20 Rh 202: this twin-barrel light AA equipment was produced to a West German specification, but has also been one of the most successful export weapons of its type as the designers found an excellent combination of accuracy (using a computerized optical sight), ammunition supply and rates of traverse and elevation using an onboard power supply (a small petrol engine driving a hydraulic system); each barrel has its own 270-round ammunition box, and there are another 10 rounds in the feed mechanism, the ammunition types being APDS-T, API-T, HEI and HEI-T fired at muzzle velocities between 1045 and 1150 m (3,428 and 3,773 ft) per second; it is planned that West German equipments be upgunned with the 25-mm Mauser Model E cannon

RAMTA TCM Mk 3 20-, 23- or 25-mm twin AA gun mounting

(Israel)
Type: towed twin 20-, 23- or 25-mm AA gun mounting
Calibre: 20 mm, 23 mm or 25 mm
Barrel length: dependent on specific cannon type
Carriage: two-wheel platform with outriggers; shield
Weight: (with 20-mm Hispano-Suiza HS 404 cannon) 1350 kg (2,976 lb) in towed configuration
Dimensions: length, travelling 3·27 m (10·73 ft); width, travelling 1·70 m (5·58 ft); height 1·63 m (5·35 ft)
Traverse/elevation: 360° total/−6° to +85° in electrically powered mode and −10° to +90° in manual mode
Rate of fire (per barrel): (with HS-404 cannon) 700 rounds per minute (cyclic) and 150 rounds per minute (practical)
Horizontal range: (with HS 404 cannon) 5700 m (6,235 yards) maximum
Slant range: (with HS 404 cannon) 1200 m (1,315 yards) effective
Crew: 3

Variant
TCM Mk 3: this equipment entered service in 1984, and is essentially a product-improved TCM-20 with more modern assemblies (for greater reliability and less maintenance) plus a more advanced sight, the option of a night sight and control by a computerized fire-control system with laser ranger; the same type of electric drive is used, and the accommodation of the weapons on special adaptors means that most types of 20-, 23- and 25-mm cannon can be installed; the mounting can also be fitted on the back of light armoured vehicles of the halftrack type still so favoured by the Israelis

RAMTA TCM-20 20-mm twin AA gun mounting

(Israel)
Type: towed twin 20-mm AA gun mounting
Calibre: 20 mm
Barrel length: not revealed
Carriage: two-wheel platform with outriggers; shield
Weight: 1350 kg (2,976 lb) in travelling order with two loaded magazines
Dimensions: length, travelling 3·27 m (10·73 ft); width, travelling 1·70 m (5·58 ft); height, travelling 1·63 m (5·35 ft)
Traverse/elevation: 360° total/−10° to +90°
Rate of fire (per barrel): 700 rounds per minute (cyclic) and 150 rounds per minute (practical)
Horizontal range: 5700 m (6,235 yards) maximum
Slant range: 1200 m (1,315 yards) effective
Crew: 3

Variant
TCM-20: developed in Israel during the late 1960s, the TCM-20 is in essence an updated version of the US M55 mounting armed with two 20-mm Hispano-Suiza HS 404 cannon rather than four 0·5-in (12·7-mm) Browning M2HB heavy machine-guns; the mounting is traversed and the weapon elevated by electric motors powered by two 12-volt batteries, the charge of the batteries being topped up by a small petrol engine; the

Above: The MK 20 Rh 202 is a light but modestly sophisticated clear-weather AA gun mounting.

HAI Artemis 30 30-mm twin AA gun system

(Greece)
Type: towed twin 30-mm AA gun system
Calibre: 30 mm
Barrel length: 86·25 calibres overall
Carriage: four-wheel platform with outriggers; no shield
Weights: 7100 kg (15,653 lb) in travelling order and 5600 kg (12,346 lb) in firing position
Dimensions: length, travelling 7·85 m (25·75 ft); width, travelling 2·38 m (7·81 ft); height, travelling 2·39 m (7·84 ft)
Traverse/elevation: 360° total/−5° to +85°
Rate of fire (per barrel): 800 rounds per minute (cyclic) and an unrevealed number of rounds per minute (practical)
Horizontal range: 5000 m (5,470 yards) effective
Slant range: 3500 m (3,830 yards) effective
Crew: not revealed

Variant
Artemis 30: though co-ordinated and built in Greece by Hellenic Arms Industries, this impressive system is in reality a co-operative venture, the guns and carriage being West German and the fire-control system Swedish; the on-carriage optronic fire-control system allows useful performance in the standard powered and emergency unpowered modes, though the equipment is designed for battery use under the remote control of a computerized fire-control centre using a Siemens target acquisition and tracking radar; the circular tanks in the central pedestal hold 250 rounds for each barrel, the ammunition being of the type developed in the USA for the powerful GAU-8 Avenger tank-busting aircraft cannon, but made under licence in West Germany for the Mauser Model F (MK 30) cannon used in this and other applications
Kuka Arrow: West German equipment designed to a Thai requirement, and modelled on the Artemis system, but using two 30-mm Mauser MK 30 Model F cannon (firing Aerojet-produced ammunition) on a powered mounting designed by Kuka; the associated fire-control system is the Contraves Skyguard

type has built up an enviable combat record against low-flying aircraft, helicopters and light armoured vehicles, and can also be installed on the back of vehicles such as the M2 and M3 halftracks still widely employed by the Israelis; the two HS-404 cannon have been modified to use HS-804 ammunition (fed from 60-round drums) including APHE-T, APDS-T and HE-T; the type is optically controlled, but is often used with a radar warning system

Breda Twin 40L70 Field Mounting 40-mm twin AA gun mounting

(Italy)

Type: towed twin 40-mm AA gun mounting
Calibre: 40 mm
Barrel length: 70 calibres
Carriage: four-wheel platform with outriggers; glassfibre gunhouse
Weight: 11,500 kg (25,353 lb) in firing position with ammunition
Dimensions: length, travelling 8·20 m (26·90 ft); width, travelling 3·155 m (10·35 ft); height, travelling 3·47 m (11·385 ft)
Traverse/elevation: 360° total/−13° to +85°
Rate of fire (per barrel): 300 rounds per minute (cyclic)
Horizontal range: 12,500 m (13,670 yards) maximum
Slant range: 4000 m (4,375 yards) effective
Crew: 0

Variant

Twin 40L70 Field Mounting: this is a land mounting developed from the successful Breda 40L70 Compact naval installation, and is designed for fully automatic operation with an external power source and control from a radar fire-control system; the circular magazine in the bottom of the firing platform holds 444 rounds, which are loaded in 4-round clips and fed automatically to the breeches; the standard range of Bofors 40-mm ammunition is used

Breda Sentinel 30-mm twin AA gun mounting

(Italy)

Type: towed twin 30-mm AA gun mounting
Calibre: 30 mm
Barrel length: 81·9 calibres without muzzle brake
Carriage: four-wheel platform with outriggers; shield
Weight: 5000 kg (11,023 lb) in firing position with ammunition
Dimensions: length, travelling 6·46 m (21·19 ft); width, travelling 1·76 m (5·77 ft); height, travelling 1·94 m (6·36 ft)
Traverse/elevation: 360° total/−5° to +85°
Rate of fire (per barrel): 800 rounds per minute (cyclic)
Horizontal range: 5000 m (5,470 yards) maximum
Slant range: 3500 m (3,830 yards) effective
Crew: 3

Variant

Sentinel: this is a capable equipment developed from a naval installation (the Twin 30 Compact) and fitted with the same pair of Mauser MK 30 Model F cannon; the carriage is fitted with an onboard electrical power generator for traverse, elevation and the Officine Galileo P75D optronic fire-control system; located outboard of the cannon are two 500-round ammunition boxes that contain APDS and HEI rounds fed to the weapons via a dual-feed arrangement that permits instantaneous supply of either ammunition type; the 0·707-kg (1·56-lb) APDS round fires its subcalibre penetrator at a muzzle velocity of 1250 m (4,101 ft) per second, and the 0·811-kg (1·79-lb) HEI round fires its 0·363-kg (0·8-lb) projectile at a muzzle velocity of 1100 m (3,609 ft) per second

Kongsberg FK 20-2 20-mm AA gun mounting

(Norway)

Type: towed single 20-mm AA mounting
Calibre: 20 mm
Barrel length: 130·5 calibres overall
Carriage: two-wheel platform with tripod legs; shield
Weights: 660 kg (1,455 lb) in travelling order and 440 kg (970 lb) in firing position
Dimensions: length, travelling 4·00 m (13·12 ft); width, travelling 1·86 m (6·10 ft); height, travelling 2·20 m (7·22 ft)
Traverse/elevation: 360° total/−8° to +83°
Rate of fire: 880–1,030 rounds per minute (cyclic)
Horizontal range: 3000 m (3,280 yards) effective
Slant range: 2000 m (2,185 yards) effective
Crew: 3

Variant

FK 20-2: designed to meet a West German and Norwegian requirement, this neat manually-operated light mounting is intended for operation in the surface-to-air and surface-to-surface roles with APDS-T, API-T, HEI and HEI-T ammunition carried in two 75-round side magazines plus 10 rounds in the feed mechanism and fired from the MK 20 Rh 202 cannon at muzzle velocities between 1045 and 1150 m (3,428 and 3,773 ft) per second

Romanian 30-mm twin AA gun mounting

(Romania)

Type: towed twin 30-mm AA mounting
Calibre: 30 mm
Barrel length: not revealed
Carriage: four-wheel platform with outrigger legs; no shield
Weight: 3000 kg (6,614 lb) in travelling order
Dimensions: not revealed
Traverse/elevation: 360° total/not revealed
Rate of fire (per barrel): 500 rounds per minute (cyclic)
Horizontal range: not revealed
Slant range: 3500 m (3,830 yards) effective
Crew: 3

Variant

Romanian 30-mm AA gun mounting: very little is known of this equipment, which was first revealed in 1989; mounted to the left of the weapons is a tracking and ranging radar with a range of 15,000 m (16,405 yards), and the cannon are each fed with ammunition from boxes mounted on the outside of the breeches; the cannon have a secondary capability against ground targets, and this suggests a dual-feed arrangement

Bofors 40L70 Type B 40-mm AA gun mounting

(Sweden)

Type: towed single 40-mm towed AA gun mounting
Calibre: 40 mm
Barrel length: 70 calibres
Carriage: four-wheel platform with outriggers; shield
Weight: 5150 kg (11,354 lb) in travelling order
Dimensions: length, travelling 7·29 m (23·92 ft); width, travelling 2·23 m (7·30 ft); height, travelling 2·35 m (7·71 ft)
Traverse/elevation: 360° total/−4° to +90°
Rate of fire: 240 or 300 rounds per minute (cyclic) in earlier and later models respectively
Horizontal range: 12,500 m (13,670 yards) maximum
Slant range: 4000 m (4,375 yards) effective
Crew: 4-6

Below: The Bofors 40L70 is still the most important light AA gun, though often updated with a more capable fire-control system and an improved ammunition supply (either greater capacity or an automatic system).

Variants

40L70 Type A: introduced after World War II, this remains one of the most powerful light weapons in the world (in both the surface-to-air and surface-to-surface roles) thanks to its high rate of fire (resulting from the use of an automatic breech and the ramming of each round during the run-out), good range and excellent ammunition; the Type A is the original model without on-carriage power, and weighs 4800 kg (10,582 lb) in travelling order; ammunition types are APC-T, HCHE, HE-T and PFHE fired at muzzle velocities between 1005 and 1030 m (3,297 and 3,379 ft) per second, and the ammunition is fed in 4-round clips into an optional overhead stay holding 26 rounds and from two 48-round racks at the rear of the carriage

40L70 Type B: improved model with on-carriage power generator, but otherwise similar to the Type A and operated in local control by a gunner on the left of the ordnance

40L70 BOFI Fair Weather: development of the Type B with Bofors Optronic Fire-control Instrument and proximity-fused ammunition; this model weighs 5500 kg (12,125 lb) in travelling order, and the BOFI equipment uses a laser rangefinder, a day/night image-intensifying sight and a fire-control computer to generate aiming and firing instructions for the gunner, with early warning provided optionally by an off-carriage radar system

40L70 BOFI All Weather: development of the 40L70 BOFI Fair Weather system with the addition of a pulse-Doppler radar for automatic target acquisition and tracking capability; this model has a travelling weight of 5700 kg (12,566 lb)

Breda 40L70: 40L70 built under licence in Italy, where Breda has developed an optional automatic feeding device, which takes ammunition in groups of three from a magazine pre-loaded with 144 rounds in 4-round clips; the travelling weight of the Breda equipment is 5300 kg (11,684 lb) and there are some other detail differences in dimensions

Bofors m/36 40L60 40-mm AA gun mounting

(Sweden)
Type: towed single 40-mm AA gun mounting
Calibre: 40 mm
Barrel length: 56 or 60 calibres
Carriage: four-wheel platform with outriggers; no shield
Weight: 2400 kg (5,291 lb) in travelling and firing orders
Dimensions: length, travelling 6·38 m (20·93 ft); width, travelling 1·72 m (5·64 ft); height, travelling 2·00 m (6·56 ft)
Traverse/elevation: 360° total/−5° to +90°
Rate of fire: 120-140 rounds per minute (cyclic) and 70 rounds per minute (practical)
Horizontal range: 4750 m (5,195 yards) maximum
Slant range: 2500 m (2,735 yards) effective
Crew: 4-6

Variants

40L60: introduced in 1936 as the **m/36**, this manually operated equipment is still in widespread service as it uses a powerful round and is still effective in regions of less advanced technology; it is found on three carriages, the m/38 for a weight of 2150 kg (4,740 lb), the m/39 as described above, and the m/49e for a weight of 2050 kg (4,519 lb); the ordnance fires AP or HE projectiles at a muzzle velocity of 850 m (2,788 ft) per second

Automatic Anti-Aircraft Gun Mk 1: British licence-made version with a different carriage, a travelling weight of 5,045 lb (2288 kg) and a number of detail modifications

Automatic Anti-Aircraft Gun M1: US licence-made with a different carriage travelling weight of 5,855 lb (2656 kg), and other modifications.

Oerlikon-Bührle GDF-005 35-mm twin AA gun mounting

(Switzerland)
Type: towed twin 35-mm AA gun mounting
Calibre: 35 mm
Barrel length: 90 calibres
Carriage: four-wheel platform with outriggers; shield
Weight: 7700 kg (16,975 lb) in travelling order with ammunition
Dimensions: length, travelling 7·80 m (25·59 ft) and in firing position 8·83 m (28·97 ft); width, travelling 2·26 m (7·41 ft) and in firing position 4·49 m (14·73 ft); height, travelling 2·60 m (8·53 ft) and in firing position 1·72 m (5·64 ft)
Traverse/elevation: 360° total/−5° to +92°
Rate of fire (per barrel): 550 rounds per minute (cyclic)
Horizontal range: 9500 m (10,390 yards) maximum
Slant range: 4000 m (4,375 yards) effective
Crew: 3

Variants

GDF-001: introduced in the early 1960s as the **2 ZLA 353 MK**, this is the heavyweight of the Oerlikon AA series, and an exceptionally potent weapon capable of effective use in the surface-to-air and surface-to-surface roles with its HEI, HEI-T and SAPHEI-T ammunition fired at a muzzle velocity of 1175 m (3,855 ft) per second from the two KDB (formerly 353 MK) cannon, which are fed automatically from two 56-round containers replenished in 7-round clips from the two 63-round reserve containers carried on the carriage; the mounting has three operating modes, namely remote electric control from the Super Fledermaus or Skyguard fire-control radar, local electric control with the Xaba optical sight, and local manual control with handwheels

GDF-002: updated version available from 1980 with Ferranti Type GSA Mk 3 sights and digital data transmission; the type is also available with optional packages such as camouflage, automatic reloaders, a gunner's cab, and integrated power source, and a Minisight Gun King incorporating a laser rangefinder

GDF-003: GDF-002 equipment built with the full upgrade package

GDF-005: most modern version with Gun King optronic sight system incorporating all the updating features available on the earlier marks

Below: The potent combination of a Skyguard fire-control and a GDF-002 twin 35-mm gun mounting.

Oerlikon-Bührle GBF-BOB Diana 25-mm twin AA gun system

(Switzerland)
Type: towed twin 25-mm AA gun system
Calibre: 25 mm
Barrel length: 92 calibres
Carriage: two-wheel platform with outriggers; gunner's cab
Weights: 2955 kg (6,515 lb) in travelling order without ammunition and 3340 kg (7,364 lb) in firing position with ammunition
Dimensions: length, travelling 4·295 m (14·09 ft); width, travelling 2·10 m (6·89 ft); height, travelling 2·13 m (6·99 ft)
Traverse/elevation: 360° total/−5° to +85°
Rate of fire (per barrel): 800 rounds per minute (cyclic)
Horizontal range: 6000 m (6,560 yards) maximum
Slant range: 2500 m (2,735 yards) effective
Crew: 4-5

Variants

GBF-BOB Diana: introduced in the mid-1980s, this is an advanced AA weapon with secondary capability against light AFVs, and provides a capability between Oerlikon's twin 20-mm and twin 35-mm weapons; the carriage has its own electrical and hydraulic power, but the system can also be operated manually in emergencies; the cannon are two Oerlikon KBB weapons with dual-feed capability for the 250 ready-use APDS-T and HEI rounds, which have muzzle velocities of 1355 and 1160 m (4,446 and 3,806 ft) per second respectively; the system can be used in conjunction with the Skyguard radar fire-control or Alerter surveillance radar systems, but is designed principally for autonomous operation with its own Contraves Gun King optical fire-control system incorporating a laser rangefinder and digital computer
GBF-AOA Diana: this version has twin Oerlikon KBA cannon, each with a cyclic rate of 570 rounds per minute and firing APDS-T, HEI and SAPHEI-T ammunition; this equipment has a lower muzzle velocity than the GBF-BOB and is fitted with an Officine Galileo P75 optronic sight

Oerlikon-Bührle ILTIS 25-mm AA gun mounting

(Switzerland)
Type: towed single 25-mm AA gun mounting
Calibre: 25 mm
Barrel length: 92 calibres
Carriage: two-wheel carriage with three outriggers; no shield
Weight: 240 kg (529 lb) in travelling order
Dimensions: not revealed
Traverse/elevation: 360° total on normal mounting or 120° total (60° left and 60° right of the centreline) on low-profile mounting/−10° to +45°
Rate of fire: 800 rounds per minute (cyclic)
Horizontal range: 6000 m (6,560 yards) maximum
Slant range: 2500 m (2,735 yards) effective
Crew: 3

Variant

ILTIS: this interesting mounting is a dual-purpose type designed for infantry use against low-flying aircraft and against light armoured fighting vehicles, the provision of a low mounting

and a prone operator's position (with a sight connected to the boresighted type by a fibre-optic cable) providing exceptional concealment at the expense of elevation angle; the equipment's cannon is the Oerlikon-Bührle KBB, which fires its own range of potent ammunition including one APDS and two HEI types; the 0·615-kg (1·36-lb) APDS round fires its 0·15-kg (0·33-lb) penetrator at a muzzle velocity of 1355 m (4,446 ft) per second to penetrate 30 mm (1·18 in) of armour angled at 30° at a range of 2000 m (2,185 yards); the 0·625-kg (1·38-lb) HEI types fired their 0·23-kg (0·51-lb) projectiles at a muzzle velocity of 1160 m (3,806 ft) per second; ammunition feed is from dual magazines when the normal mounting is employed, and from special 10- and 15-round strip magazines when the low-profile mounting is employed

Oerlikon-Bührle GBI-A01 25-mm AA gun mounting

(Switzerland)
Type: towed single 25-mm AA gun mounting
Calibre: 25 mm
Barrel length: 80 calibres without muzzle brake
Carriage: two-wheel platform with tripod legs; no shield
Weights: 666 kg (1,468 lb) in travelling order with ammunition and 506 kg (1,116 lb) in firing position with ammunition
Dimensions: length, travelling 4·72 m (15·49 ft) and in firing position 4·17 m (13·68 ft); width, travelling 1·80 m (5·91 ft) and in firing position 1·79 m (5·87 ft); height, travelling 1·65 m (5·41 ft) and in firing position 1·45 m (4·76 ft)
Traverse/elevation: 360° total/−10° to +70°
Rate of fire: 570 rounds per minute (cyclic) and 170 rounds per minute (practical)
Horizontal range: 6000 m (6,560 yards) maximum
Slant range: 2500 m (2,735 yards) effective
Crew: 3

Variant

GBI-A01: though designed primarily for AA use, the manually operated GBI-A01 mounting can be used against battlefield targets such as light AFVs, the Oerlikon KBA-C cannon being able to fire APDS-T projectiles at a muzzle velocity of 1335 m (4,380 ft) per second, plus HEI, HEI-T, SAPHEI and SAPHEI-T projectiles at 1100 m (3,609 ft) per second; these rounds are accommodated in two 40-round containers (one on each side of the weapon), a dual-feed mechanism allowing selection of round type

Oerlikon-Bührle GAI-D01 20-mm twin AA gun mounting

(Switzerland)
Type: towed twin 20-mm AA gun mounting
Calibre: 20 mm
Barrel length: 95·3 calibres including flash suppressor
Carriage: two-wheel platform with outriggers; shield
Weights: 1800 kg (3,968 lb) in travelling order with ammunition and 1330 kg (2,932 lb) in firing position with ammunition
Dimensions: length, travelling 4·59 m (15·06 ft) and in firing position 4·555 m (14·94 ft); width, travelling 1·86 m (6·10 ft) and in firing position

1·81 m (5·94 ft); height, travelling 2·34 m (7·68 ft) and in firing position 1·48 m (4·86 ft)
Traverse/elevation: 360° total/−3° to +81° in powered mode and −5° to +85° in manual mode
Rate of fire (per barrel): 1,000 rounds per minute (cyclic)
Horizontal range: 5700 m (6,235 yards) maximum
Slant range: 1500 m (1,640 yards) effective
Crew: 5

Variant

GAI-D01: designed in the mid-1970s as the **HS 666A** and available from 1978, this equipment has successfully bridged the tactical gap between Oerlikon's single-barrel 20-mm weapons and more capable equipments such as the twin 35-mm GDF-002; the equipment is hydraulically powered, with reversion to manual operation in emergencies, and though intended primarily for AA use can also be deployed for a number of battlefield roles; the two Oerlikon KAD-B cannon can fire AP-T, HEI, HEI-T, SAPHEI and SAPHEI-T ammunition (the first at a muzzle velocity of 1150 m/3,773 ft per second and the other four at a muzzle velocity of 1100 m/3,609 ft per second) fed from a 120-round magazine on the side of each weapon; the GAI-D01 can also be tied into a fire-control system and early warning radar

Oerlikon-Bührle GAI-C04 20-mm AA gun mounting

(Switzerland)
Type: towed single 20-mm AA gun mounting
Calibre: 20 mm
Barrel length: 95·3 calibres including flash suppressor
Carriage: two-wheel platform with tripod legs; no shield
Weight: 589 kg (1,299 lb) in travelling order with ammunition and 435 kg (959 lb) in firing position with ammunition
Dimensions: length, in firing position 3·87 m (12·70 ft); width, in firing position 1·70 m (5·58 ft); height, in firing position 1·45 m (4·76 ft)
Traverse/elevation: 360° total/−7° to +83°
Rate of fire: 1,050 rounds per minute (cyclic)
Horizontal range: 5700 m (6,235 yards) maximum
Slant range: 1500 m (1,640 yards) effective
Crew: 3

Variants

GAI-C01: developed as the **HS 639-B3·1** and fitted with an Oerlikon KAD-B13-3 (formerly HS-820-SL7° A3-3) cannon, this manually operated equipment has weights (in travelling order and in firing position respectively, each with ammunition) of 534 and 370 kg (1,177 and 816 lb); the type fires the same ammunition as the GAI-D01, and is single-fed by a 75-round magazine on the right of the weapon, so limiting the type's utility in dual-role operations
GAI-C03: developed as the **HS 639-B4·1** and fitted with an Oerlikon KAD-AO1 (formerly HS-820 SAA1) cannon, this equipment fires the same ammunition as the GAI-D01, though rounds are fed to the cannon from an overhead drum containing 50 rounds; the type has weights (in travelling order and in firing position respectively, complete with ammunition) of 510 and 432 kg (1,124 and 952 lb)
GAI-C04: developed as the **HS 639-B5** and fitted with an Oerlikon KAD-B14 (formerly HS-820-SL7 A4) cannon, this is an improved version of the GAI-C01 with a dual-feed mechanism and two 75-

round magazines for greater surface-to-air and secondary surface-to-surface capability

Oerlikon-Bührle GAI-B01 20-mm AA gun mounting

(Switzerland)

Type: towed single 20-mm AA gun mounting
Calibre: 20 mm
Barrel length: 120 calibres
Carriage: two-wheel platform with tripod legs; no shield
Weights: 547 kg (1,206 lb) in travelling order and 405 kg (893 lb) in firing position
Dimensions: length, travelling 3·85 m (12·63 ft) and in firing position 4·71 m (15·45 ft); width, travelling and in firing position 1·55 m (5·09 ft); height, travelling 2·50 m (8·20 ft) and in firing position 1·50 m (4·92 ft)
Traverse/elevation: 360° total/−5° to +85°
Rate of fire: 1,000 rounds per minute (cyclic)
Horizontal range: 5700 m (6,235 yards) maximum
Vertical range: 1500 m (1,640 yards) effective
Crew: 3

Variant

GAI-B01: the lightweight of the Oerlikon AA family, this equipment was designed as the **10 ILa/5TG** and is fitted with an Oerlikon KAB-001 cannon; the equipment is manually operated, and the cannon fires the same type of ammunition as the GAI-D01, fed from a 50- or a 20-round drum, or from an 8-round box

KS-30 130-mm AA gun mounting

(USSR)

Type: towed 130-mm AA gun mounting
Calibre: 130 mm (5·12 in)
Barrel length: 64·7 calibres overall
Muzzle brake: none
Carriage: eight-wheel platform with outriggers; no shield
Weight: 29,500 kg (65,035 lb) in travelling order and 24,900 kg (54,894 lb) in firing position
Dimensions: length, travelling 11·52 m (37·80 ft); width, travelling 3·03 m (9·95 ft); height, travelling 3·05 m (10·00 ft)
Traverse/elevation: 360° total/−5° to +80°
Rate of fire: 10-12 rounds per minute
Horizontal range: 27,000 m (29,530 yards) maximum

Below: The KS-130 is a heavy but obsolete towed AA gun generally used with 'Fire Wheel' radar.

Slant range: 13,700 m (14,985 yards) effective
Crew: 15-20

Variant

KS-30: introduced in the early 1950s as the initial Soviet response to the threat of high-flying US strategic bombers, the KS-30 is an obsolete weapon that can be used in the AA (33·4-kg/73·6-lb HE projectile) and anti-tank (33·4-kg/73·6-lb APHE projectile) roles; the ammunition is of the separate-loading type and fired at a muzzle velocity of 970 m (3,182 ft) per second with the aid of a semi-automatic breech, an automatic fuse setter and a power rammer; the type has on-carriage sights, but is generally operated in conjunction with 'Fire Wheel' radar and the appropriate director

KS-19 100-mm AA gun mounting

(USSR)

Above: The KS-19 is another obsolete AA gun, in this instance generally used with the 'Fire Can' or 'Whiff' fire-control radars.

Type: towed 100-mm AA gun mounting
Calibre: 100 mm (3·94 in)
Barrel length: 57·4 calibres overall
Muzzle brake: multi-baffle type
Carriage: four-wheel platform with outriggers; no shield
Weight: 9550 kg (21,054 lb) in travelling order
Dimensions: length, travelling 9·45 m (31·00 ft); width, travelling 2·35 m (7·71 ft); height, travelling 2·20 m (7·22 ft)
Traverse/elevation: 360° total/−3° to +85°
Rate of fire: 15 rounds per minute
Horizontal range: 21,000 m (22,965 yards) maximum

Slant range: 13,700 m (14,985 yards) with proximity-fused ammunition
Crew: 15

Variants
KS-19: introduced in the late 1940s as successor to the USSR's standard 85-mm (3·35-in) AA guns, the KS-19 is obsolescent but still in widespread service with Soviet clients; the type has a semi-automatic breech, an automatic fuse setter and a power rammer for the fixed ammunition, and is designed for dual-role operation against aircraft (HE, HE-FRAG and FRAG projectiles fired at a muzzle velocity of 900 m/2,953 ft per second) and tanks (AP-T and APC-T projectiles fired at muzzle velocities of 100 m/3,281 ft and 900 m (2,953 ft) per second respectively); the weapon has on-carriage fire-control, but is generally used with 'Fire Can' or 'Whiff' radars and appropriate directors
Type 59: Chinese-made copy of the KS-19

KS-18 85-mm AA gun mounting

(USSR)
Type: towed 85-mm AA gun mounting
Calibre: 85 mm (3·35 in)
Barrel length: 67·6 calibres overall
Muzzle brake: T-shape type
Carriage: four-wheel platform with outriggers; shield
Weight: 5000 kg (11,023 lb) in travelling and firing orders
Dimensions: length, travelling 8·20 m (26·90 ft); width, travelling 2·15 m (7·05 ft); height, travelling 2·25 m (7·38 ft)
Traverse/elevation: 360° total/−3° to +82°
Rate of fire: 15-20 rounds per minute
Horizontal range: 18,000 m (19,685 yards) maximum
Slant range: 10,000 m (10,935 yards)
Crew: 7

Variants
KS-12: introduced in 1939 as the **M1939** with a 55·2-calibre barrel, this equipment is still in limited service with Soviet clients; it fires fixed FRAG anti-aircraft ammunition at a muzzle velocity of 792 m (2,598 ft) per second or HVAP anti-tank ammunition at 1030 m (3,379 ft) per second, and a good rate of fire is ensured by the use of a semi-automatic breech; this weapon has a weight of 4300 kg (9,480 lb) in travelling and firing orders, and a travelling length of 7·05 m (23·13 ft); the type has a multi-baffle muzzle brake
KS-18: much developed model introduced as the **M1944** and generally used in conjunction with 'Fire Can' radar and appropriate director; the longer barrel of this ordnance increases standard muzzle velocity to 900 m (2,953 ft) per second, with consequent improvements in effective and maximum ranges
Type 56: Chinese-made copy of the KS-12

S-60 57-mm AA gun mounting

(USSR)
Type: towed single 57-mm AA gun mounting
Calibre: 57 mm
Barrel length: 77 calibres overall
Muzzle brake: pepperpot type

Above: The S-60 weapon still serves in large numbers, and can be used with radar.

Carriage: four-wheel platform with outriggers; no shield
Weights: 4660 kg (10,273 lb) in travelling order and 4500 kg (9,921 lb) in firing position
Dimensions: length, travelling 8·50 m (27·89 ft); width, travelling 2·05 m (6·74 ft); height, travelling 2·37 m (7·78 ft)
Traverse/elevation: 360° total/−4° to +85°
Rate of fire: 110 rounds per minute (cyclic) and 70 rounds per minute (practical)
Horizontal range: 12,000 m (13,125 yards) maximum
Slant range: 4000 m (4,375 yards) with on-carriage control and 6000 m (6,560 yards) with off-carriage control
Crew: 7

Variant
S-60: introduced in the late 1940s as a heavy tactical AA weapon to replace the 37-mm M1939, this equipment fires FRAG and APC ammunition (of the fixed type and fed in four-round clips) at a muzzle velocity of 1000 m (3,281 ft) per second; the weapon can be used with its on-carriage fire-control system, but is far more capable when used with 'Fire Can' or 'Flap Wheel' radar and appropriate director; night vision sights have also been seen on the type, which can be operated manually or with servo-assistance

M1939 37-mm AA gun mounting

(USSR)
Type: towed single 37-mm AA gun mounting
Calibre: 37 mm
Barrel length: 73·75 calibres overall
Carriage: four-wheel platform with outriggers; optional shield
Weight: 2100 kg (4,630 lb) in firing position without shield
Dimensions: length, travelling 6·04 m (19·80 ft); width, travelling without shield 1·94 m (6·35 ft); height, travelling without shield 2·11 m (6·91 ft)
Traverse/elevation: 360° total/−5° to +85°
Rate of fire: 170 rounds per minute (cyclic) and 80 rounds per minute (practical)

Horizontal range: 9500 m (10,390 yards) maximum
Slant range: 3000 m (3,280 yards) effective
Crew: 8

Variants
M1939: a clear-weather system now thoroughly obsolete, the manually-operated M1939 is still widely used by Soviet clients, and fires fixed ammunition (fed in 5-round clips) of the FRAG-T and AP-T types at a muzzle velocity of 880 m (2,887 ft) per second
Type 55: Chinese-made copy of the M1939

ZU-23-2 23-mm twin AA gun mounting

(USSR)
Type: towed twin 23-mm AA gun mounting
Calibre: 23 mm
Barrel length: 87·4 calibres overall
Carriage: two-wheel triangular platform with screw jacks; no shield
Weight: 950 kg (2,094 lb) in travelling and firing orders with ammunition
Dimensions: length, travelling 4·57 m (14·99 ft);

Below: The ZU-23-2 is a light yet potent AA mounting with a capability against light vehicles.

width, travelling 1·83 m (6·00 ft); height, travelling 1·87 m (6·14 ft)

Traverse/elevation: 360° total/− 10° to + 90°
Rate of fire (per barrel): 800-1,000 rounds per minute (cyclic) and 200 rounds per minute (practical)
Horizontal range: 7000 m (7,655 yards) maximum
Slant range: 2500 m (2,735 yards) effective
Crew: 5

Variant
ZU-23-2: introduced in the mid-1960s as successor to the ZPU series, the ZU-23 is the most important towed AA equipment in the Soviet armoury, and has been widely exported to client states, many of whom have installed the equipment on vehicles; the equipment is manually operated and designed only for clear-weather operations with two types of ammunition (API-T and HEI-T) fired at a muzzle velocity of 970 m (3,182 ft) per second and delivered from boxes (one on the side of each barrel) containing 50 belted rounds

ZPU-4 14·5-mm quadruple AA gun mounting

(USSR)
Type: towed quadruple 14·5-mm AA gun mounting
Calibre: 14·5 mm (0·57 in)
Barrel length: 93 calibres overall
Carriage: four-wheel platform with outriggers; no shield
Weight: 1810 kg (3,990 lb) in travelling and firing orders
Dimensions: length, travelling 4·53 m (14·86 ft); width, travelling 1·72 m (5·64 ft); height, travelling 2·13 m (6·99 ft)
Traverse/elevation: 360° total/− 10° to + 90°
Rate of fire (per barrel): 600 rounds per minute (cyclic) and 150 rounds per minute (practical)
Horizontal range: 8000 m (8,740 yards) maximum
Slant range: 1400 m (1,530 yards) effective
Crew: 5

Below: The ZPU-4 is the four-barrel version of the ZPU series using the 14·5-mm (0·57-in) KPV heavy machine-gun.

Variants
ZPU-1: single-barrel version on a two-wheel carriage, introduced soon after World War II and based on the KPV heavy machine-gun with 150 rounds of belted ammunition (API, API-T and I-T) in a side-mounted magazine; like the later ZPUs this is a clear-weather weapon and has a weight of 413 kg (910 lb) in travelling and firing orders
ZPU-2: introduced from 1949, this is the twin-barrel weapon of the series and was produced in early and late models, the former having travelling and firing weights of 994 and 639 kg (2,191 and 1,409 lb) respectively, and the latter of 649 and 621 kg (1,431 and 1,369 lb) respectively
ZPU-4: introduced in 1949, this is the four-barrel model of the ZPU series
Type 56: Chinese-made copy of the ZPU-4
Type 58: Chinese-made copy of the ZPU-2

M118 90-mm AA gun mounting

(USA)
Type: towed 90-mm AA gun mounting
Calibre: 90 mm (3·54 in)
Barrel length: 50 calibres overall
Muzzle brake: none
Carriage: four-wheel platform with outriggers; shield
Weight: 32,300 lb (14,651 kg) in travelling order
Dimensions: length, travelling 29·50 ft (8·99 m); width, travelling 8·60 ft (2·62 m); height, travelling 10·08 ft (3·07 m)
Traverse/elevation: 360° total/− 10° to + 80°
Rate of fire: 28 rounds per minute (burst fire) and 23 rounds per minute (sustained fire)
Horizontal range: 20,750 yards (18,975 m) maximum
Slant range: 9,300 yards (8505 m) effective
Crew: 10-12

Variants
M117: introduced in 1940 as the M1 and redesignated after World War II, this was in its time a capable AA weapon weighing 19,015 lb (8625 kg) in travelling order and 14,650 lb (6645 kg) in firing position; it was deleted from US service in the 1960s but still serves with a number of other countries
M118: developed from the M1 during World War II as the M2, this weapon was produced for the object of equipping the US field forces with a multi-role (AA, anti-tank and field) gun offering significantly better AA and tactical capabilities than those of the M1; the type was redesignated after World War II, and is still used by some American allies; the weapon fires three types of projectile, namely APHE at a muzzle velocity of 2,800 ft (853 m) per second, HE at a muzzle velocity of 2,700 ft (823 m) per second and HVAP-T at a muzzle velocity of 3,355 ft (1023 m) per second, the fixed ammunition being loaded by a power rammer; the type is generally used with the M33 radar fire-control system

M167 Vulcan 20-mm multi-barrel AA gun system

(USA)
Type: towed sextuple-barrel 20-mm AA gun system
Calibre: 20 mm
Barrel length: 76·2 calibres overall
Carriage: two-wheel platform with outriggers; no shield
Weights: 3,500 lb (1588 kg) in travelling order and 3,450 lb (1565 kg) in firing position
Dimensions: length, travelling 16·09 ft (4·91 m); width, travelling 6·50 ft (1·98 m); height, travelling 6·69 ft (2·04 m)
Traverse/elevation: 360° total/− 5° to + 80°
Rate of fire: selectable 1,000 (surface-to-surface) or 3,000 (surface-to-air) rounds per minute (cyclic)
Horizontal range: 6,500 yards (5,945 m) maximum
Slant range: 1,300 yards (1190 m) effective
Crew: 1

Variants
M167: this is the towed version of the M163 self-propelled AA mounting, and though it features a capable fire-control system (with range-only radar and a lead-computing sight) and the formidable Vulcan six-barrel cannon plus 500 rounds of ammunition (AP and HEI fired at a muzzle velocity of 3,380 ft/1030 m per second), the equipment is limited by the need for external power and its lack of all-weather capability; the type has been improved in reliability and cross-country mobility by the addition of an extra wheel on each side
M167A1: improved M167
Basic Vulcan: export version of the M167 with a range-updating computer instead of the range radar and other modifications

Kimberly-Clark/Bowen and McLaughlin M55 0·5-in quadruple AA gun mounting

(USA)
Type: towed quadruple 0·5-in AA gun mounting
Calibre: 0·5 in (12·7 mm)
Barrel length: 90 calibres overall
Carriage: two-wheel platform; shield
Weight: 2,950 lb (1338 kg) in travelling order
Dimensions: length, travelling 9·48 ft (2·89 m); width, travelling 6·86 ft (2·09 m); height, travelling 5·27 ft (1·61 m)

Weight: 1100 kg (2,425 lb) in travelling and firing orders with ammunition
Dimensions: length, travelling 4·30 m (14·11 ft); width, travelling 1·27 m (4·17 ft); height, travelling 1·47 m (4·82 ft)
Traverse/elevation: 360° total/−5° to +83°
Rate of fire (per barrel): 700 rounds per minute (cyclic)
Horizontal range: 5500 m (6,015 yards) maximum
Slant range: 2000 m (2,185 yards) effective
Crew: 6

Variants
M55 A2: introduced in 1955, this is the basic model of a three-equipment series, and uses three licence-built Hispano-Suiza HS 804 cannon on a variation of the HS 630-3 carriage; the type is manually operated, and the weapons fire HEI and HEI-T ammunition at a muzzle velocity of 850 m (2,789 ft) per second, or API and API-T ammunition at 840 m (2,756 ft) per second; each barrel is fed from a 60-round drum
M55 A3 B1: version of the M55 A2 with a 6-kW (8-hp) Wankel engine to provide hydraulic power for traverse and elevation; the weight of this variant is 1236 kg (2,725 lb)
M55 A4 B1: combination of the triple-barrel armament of the previous M55 variants with a derivative of the HS 666A (Oerlikon GAI-D01) carriage revised to accommodate a Wankel engine for powered traverse and elevation; this model weighs 1350 kg (2,976 lb) and has a licence-built Officine Galileo P56 computerized sight

SDPR 20/1 mm M75 20-mm AA gun mounting

(Yugoslavia)
Type: towed single 20-mm AA gun mounting
Calibre: 20 mm
Barrel length: 97·8 calibres overall
Carriage: two-wheel platform with tripod legs; no shield
Weight: 260 kg (573 lb) in travelling and firing orders with ammunition
Dimensions: length, travelling not revealed; width, travelling 1·51 m (4·95 ft); height, travelling not revealed
Traverse/elevation: 360° total/−10° to +83°
Rate of fire: 700 rounds per minute (cyclic)
Horizontal range: 5500 m (6,015 yards) maximum
Slant range: 2000 m (2,185 yards) effective
Crew: 4-6

Variant
M75: this is a lightweight manually operated mounting for a single Hispano-Suiza HS 804 cannon; the type fires the same ammunition as the M55 series, using either a 60-round drum (HEI and HEI-T rounds) or a 10-round box (AP-T, API and API-T rounds)

The M55 is a Yugoslav mounting with three 20-mm Hispano-Suiza (now Oerlikon-Bührle) barrels.

Traverse/elevation: 360° total/−10° to +90°
Rate of fire (per barrel): 500 rounds per minute (cyclic) and 150 rounds per minute (practical)
Horizontal range: 1,650 yards (1510 m) effective
Slant range: 1,300 yards (1190 m) effective
Crew: 4

Variants
M55: designed in World War II and now obsolete though still in widespread service, the M55 is electrically operated in azimuth and elevation, the two 6-volt batteries for the task being charged by a small petrol engine; each barrel is fed by a 210-round belt, and the ammunition types that can be used are AP, API, API-T, ball and incendiary; the mount can also be installed on the back of light armoured vehicles, halftracks and the like

Lysam M55 (Modernized): evolved as a kit in Brazil, this type has modern 12-volt electrics and other improvements designed principally to improve rates of traverse and elevation
Lysam M55 (Modernized)/20-mm: this is a simple yet useful development of the M55 (Modernized) with a pair of 20-mm Hispano-Suiza HS 404 cannon each with 160 rounds of ammunition

SDPR 20/3 mm M55 A2 20-mm AA gun mounting

(Yugoslavia)
Type: towed triple 20-mm AA gun mounting
Calibre: 20 mm
Barrel length: 97·8 calibres overall
Carriage: two-wheel platform with tripod legs; no shield

CITEFA SAPBA-1 multiple rocket system

(Argentina)
Type: 36-tube multiple rocket system
Rocket dimensions: diameter 127 mm (5 in); length 2·228 m (7·31 ft)
Rocket weights: whole round 54 kg (119·05 lb); warhead 18 kg (40 lb) HE fragmentation or anti-personnel
Rocket range: 20,000 m (21,870 yards)

Reload time: 5 minutes for all four 9-tube pods
Launcher traverse/elevation: 180° total (90° left and 90° right of the centreline)/0° to +60°
Crew: 5
Mounting: vehicle rear (generally Fiat 697 6 × 6 truck)

Variant
SAPBA-1: this is a capable area-saturation multiple rocket system whose projectiles can be fired singly or in a ripple at 0·5-second intervals; the rocket is powered by a solid-propellant rocket motor delivering 3500-kg (7,716-lb) thrust, stabilized by four fins, and has either an HE fragmentation warhead with a lethal area of 1000 m² (10,765 sq ft) or a proximity-fused anti-personnel type that disperses 4,500 steel pellets over an area of 6000 m² (64,585 sq ft)

CITEFA SLAM-Pampero multiple rocket system

(Argentina)
Type: 16-tube multiple rocket system
Rocket dimensions: diameter 105 mm (4·13 in); length 1·45 m (4·76 ft)
Rocket weights: whole round 28 kg (61·7 lb); warhead 10·5 kg (23·2 lb) HE fragmentation
Rocket range: 11,000 m (12,030 yards)
Reload time: not revealed
Launcher traverse/elevation: 180° total (90° left and 90° right of the centreline)/0° to +52°
Crew: not revealed
Mounting: Unimog 416 light truck

Variant
SLAM-Pampero: little is known of this comparatively new Argentine system, which is powered by a solid-propellant rocket and stabilized by four wrap-round fins; a 16-round salvo can be launched in 7·5 seconds, and the salvo is believed to land within 50 m (55 yards) of the aiming point

Les Forges de Zeebrugge LAU-97 multiple rocket system

(Belgium)
Type: 40-tube multiple rocket system
Rocket dimensions: diameter 69·85 mm (2·75 in); length 1·19 m (3·904 ft)
Rocket weights: whole round 8·6 to 11·9 kg (19·0 to 26·2 lb) depending on warhead; warhead 2·9 to 6·2 kg (6·4 to 13·7 lb) depending on type
Rocket range: 8000 m (8,750 yards)
Reload time: not revealed
Launcher traverse/elevation: 360° total/0° to +55°
Crew: 3
Mounting: trailer or vehicle rear (generally Land Rover or similar light truck)

Variant
LAU-97: this is a light artillery rocket system based on the US FFAR aircraft rocket and intended for saturation and holding fire at regimental level; the launcher comprises five 8-tube horizontal rows of tubes, and the rockets can be launched singly or in a 6-second salvo to saturate an area 200 m by 300 m (220 yards by 330 yards);

the type is currently qualified with the FZ-67, FZ-68 and Mk 40 rocket motors, the last providing a range of 6000 m (6,560 yards), though the new NRZ-96 rocket boosts range to 10,000 m (10,935 yards); the standard warhead types are a cargo type with nine 0·48-kg (1·06-lb) anti-tank/anti-personnel minelets, anti-armour, anti-building, white phosphorus marker/smoke, anti-personnel, anti-personnel/light armoured vehicle, smoke and chaff

AVIBRAS FGT X-40 multiple rocket system

(Brazil)
Type: 3-rail multiple rocket system
Rocket dimensions: diameter 300 mm (11·81 in); length 4·85 m (15·91 ft)
Rocket weights: whole round 654 kg (1,441·8 lb); warhead 147 kg (324 lb) HE fragmentation
Rocket range: 68,000 m (74,365 yards)
Reload time: not revealed
Launcher traverse/elevation: not revealed
Crew: 3
Mounting: launcher mounted on tracked chassis

Variant
FGT X-40: this is an exceptionally long-ranged artillery rocket based on a 7200-kg (15,873-kg) thrust solid-propellant rocket to provide a burn-out speed of 4590 km/h (2,852 mph); the type has a combat weight of 17,070 kg (37,633 lb) and is based on the chassis of the Bernardini X1A light

Below: The prototype of the FTG X-40 system, using the largest of Brazil's unguided rockets.

tank modified with a rear spade and two stabilizing jacks; the launcher assembly is controlled in azimuth by a mechanical system, and in elevation by a hydraulic system

AVIBRAS Astros II/SS-60 multiple rocket system

(Brazil)
Type: 4-tube multiple rocket system
Rocket dimensions: diameter 300 mm (11·81 in); length 5·60 m (18·37 ft)
Rocket weights: whole round 595 kg (1,312 lb); warhead 160 kg (353 lb) cluster munition
Rocket range: 60,000 m (65,615 yards)
Reload time: not revealed
Launcher traverse/elevation: not revealed
Crew: not revealed
Mounting: ASTROS launcher on rear of TECTRAN 6 × 6 vehicle

Variant
SS-60: largest of the SS series, the SS-60 has a solid-propellant rocket and wrap-round fins, and is designed to deliver a substantial load of dual-purpose anti-tank/anti-personnel bomblets over considerable range, the minimum range being 20,000 m (21,870 yards); like the other rocket-launchers in the series it uses the Contraves Fieldguard fire-control system; the size of the area sown with bomblets depends on the fused burst altitude of the rocket

AVIBRAS FGT X-20 multiple rocket system

(Brazil)
Type: 3-rail multiple rocket system
Rocket dimensions: diameter 180 mm (7·09 in); length 2·78 m (9·12 ft)
Rocket weights: whole round 120 kg (265 lb); warhead 40 kg (88·2 lb) HE fragmentation
Rocket range: 25,000 m (27,340 yards)
Reload time: not revealed
Launcher traverse/elevation: not revealed
Crew: not revealed
Mounting: launcher on a trailer or tracked chassis

Variant
FGT X-20: this is a development undertaken jointly by the army, air force and private interests, and its launcher is mounted on a development of the Bernardini X1A light tank chassis, or alternatively on a trailer towed by any suitable 4 × 4 or 6 × 6 truck; the rocket is powered by a 2100-kg (4,630-lb) thrust solid-propellant rocket to provide a burn-out speed of 4175 km/h (2,594 mph)

AVIBRAS Astros II/SS-40 multiple rocket system

(Brazil)
Type: 16-tube multiple rocket system
Rocket dimensions: diameter 180 mm (7·09 in); length 4·20 m (13·78 ft)
Rocket weights: whole round 152 kg (335 lb); warhead 54 kg (119 lb) HE or cluster munition
Rocket range: 35,000 m (38,275 yards)

Reload time: not revealed
Launcher traverse/elevation: not revealed
Crew: not revealed
Mounting: ASTROS launcher on rear of TECTRAN 6 × 6 vehicle

Variant
SS-40: designed to use another version of the TECTRAN-mounted launcher and the same Contraves Fieldguard fire-control system, the SS-40 rocket has a solid-propellant motor and wrap-round fins, but its warhead is a cluster-munition type designed to carry dual-purpose anti-tank/anti-personnel bomblets; the size of the area sown with bomblets depends on the fused burst altitude of the rocket; the rocket's minimum range is 15,000 m (16,405 yards)

AVIBRAS Astros II/SS-30 multiple rocket system

(Brazil)
Type: 32-tube multiple rocket system
Rocket dimensions: diameter 127 mm (5 in); length 3·90 m (12·80 ft)
Rocket weights: whole round 68 kg (149·9 lb); warhead 20 kg (44 lb) HE
Rocket range: 30,000 m (32,810 yards)
Reload time: not revealed
Launcher traverse/elevation: not revealed
Crew: not revealed
Mounting: ASTROS II launcher on rear of TECTRAN 6 × 6 vehicle

Variant
SS-30: designed for launch from an armoured cross-country vehicle, this rocket has a solid-propellant motor and wrap-round rear fins, and the system is designed to operate in conjunction with the Contraves Fieldguard fire-control system for maximum accuracy; the rocket's minimum range is 9000 m (9,845 yards); this is the smallest member of the ASTROS (Artillery SaTuration ROcket System) family, and all three vehicles in the family system (rocket launcher, resupply type and fire-control type) use the same TECTRAN 6 × 6 chassis

AVIBRAS SBAT-127 multiple rocket system

(Brazil)
Type: 12-rail multiple rocket system
Rocket dimensions: diameter 127 mm (5 in); length not revealed
Rocket weights: whole round 48 or 61 kg (105·8 or 134·5 lb) depending on warhead; warhead 22 or 35 kg (48·5 or 77·2 lb) HE
Rocket range: 14,000 or 12,500 m (15,310 or 13,670 yards) depending on warhead weight
Reload time: not revealed
Launcher traverse/elevation: not revealed
Crew: not revealed
Mounting: trailer or rear of vehicle

Variant
SBAT-127: developed from the 127-mm (5-in) air-craft rocket, the SBAT-127 is powered by a solid-propellant rocket motor and stabilized by fins

AVIBRAS FGT108-RA1 multiple rocket system

(Brazil)
Type: 16-tube multiple rocket system
Rocket dimensions: diameter 108 mm (4·25 in); length 0·967 m (3·17 ft)
Rocket weights: whole round 17 kg (37·5 lb); warhead 3 kg (6·6 lb) HE
Rocket range: 7000 m (7,655 yards)
Reload time: not revealed
Launcher traverse/elevation: 24° total (12° left and 12° right of the centreline)/− 1° to + 50°
Crew: 4
Mounting: two-wheel trailer

Variant
FGT108-RA1: this neat little system is fired at a maximum rate of two rounds per second, and is normally grouped in batteries of four launchers each with 64 reloads (four 16-round containers); the rocket is powered by a solid-propellant rocket motor delivering 1250-kg (2,755-lb) thrust, and spin-stabilized by six canted rocket nozzles; the loaded trailer weighs 802 kg (1,768 lb)

AVIBRAS SBAT-70 multiple rocket system

(Brazil)
Type: 36-tube multiple rocket system
Rocket dimensions: diameter 70 mm (2·76 in); length not revealed
Rocket weights: whole round 9 kg (19·8 lb); warhead 4 kg (8·8 lb) of various types
Rocket range: 7500 m (8,200 yards)
Reload time: not revealed
Launcher traverse/elevation: 24° total (12° left and 12° right of the centreline)/0° to + 50°
Crew: 4
Mounting: two-wheel trailer

Variant
SBAT-70: this rocket is powered by a solid-propellant rocket motor and stabilized by four folding fins, and the trailer has a loaded weight of some 1000 kg (2,205 lb); the warhead types are HEAT, HE fragmentation, HE anti-tank/anti-personnel, flechette, white phosphorus smoke, and three practice types

Type 762 multiple rocket system

(China)
Type: single-cradle rocket system
Rocket dimensions: diameter 425 mm (16·73 in); length 4·70 m (15·42 ft)
Rocket weights: whole round about 760 kg (1,676 lb); warhead 600 kg (1,323 lb) fuel/air explosive
Rocket range: 10,000 m (10,935 yards)
Reload time: not revealed
Launcher traverse/elevation: not revealed
Crew: not revealed
Mounting: launcher on a tracked chassis

Variant
Type 762: this is a mineclearing rocket type, the single launcher being carried on what appears to be a derivative of the chassis used for the Type 83 self-propelled gun/howitzer; the payload appears to be a number of FAE containers, and

the rocket is boosted to a maximum speed of 360 km/h (224 mph) by a 150-kg (331-lb) solid-propellant rocket section

CPMIEC WS-1 multiple rocket system

(China)
Type: four-tube multiple rocket system
Rocket dimensions: diameter 320 mm (12·6 in); length 4·52 m (14·83 ft)
Rocket weights: whole round 520 kg (1,146 lb); warhead 150 kg (331 lb) cluster type
Rocket range: 80 km (49·7 miles)
Reload time: not revealed
Launcher traverse/elevation: not revealed
Crew: not revealed
Mounting: launcher on a wheeled chassis

Variant
WS-1: revealed in 1989, this Chinese system is designed to bridge the gap between conventional multiple-launch rocket systems and battlefield missiles; the type is fired from a four-round launcher located on the rear of a 6 × 6 truck and probably fitted with a powered traverse/elevation system; the minimum range of the Mach 3·6 rocket is between 20,000 and 30,000 m (21,870 and 32,810 yards), and it is likely that a cluster-munition warhead is carried

Type 74 multiple rocket system

(China)
Type: 10-rail multiple rocket system
Rocket dimensions: diameter 284 mm (11·18 in); length 2·47 m (8·10 ft)
Rocket weights: whole round 127 kg (280·0 lb); warhead not revealed (but comprising 10 Type

Below: The Type 74 is a Chinese system, each rocket carrying 10 anti-tank mines.

69 or Type 79 anti-tank mines)
Rocket range: 1500 m (1,640 yards)
Reload time: not revealed
Launcher traverse/elevation: 90° total (45° left and 45° right of the centreline)/+7° to +48°
Crew: 6
Mounting: rear of CA-30A 6 × 6 truck

Variant
Type 74: this Chinese system is designed for the laying of anti-tank minefields, each rocket having a solid-propellant motor and fixed cruciform fins; the rockets are mounted in an over-and-under arrangement on a launcher frame based on that of the Soviet BM-13 equipment, and a battery of four launchers can lay a minefield of 400 m² (478 sq yards) with a single salvo; the combat weight of each launcher vehicle is 8780 kg (19,356 lb), and a 10-rocket salvo is fired in 15 seconds

Type 83 multiple rocket system

(China)
Type: 4-cell multiple rocket system
Rocket dimensions: diameter 273 mm (10·75 in); length 4·73 m (15·52 ft)
Rocket weights: whole round 484 kg (1,067·0 lb); warhead not revealed
Rocket range: 40,000 m (43,745 yards)
Reload time: not revealed
Launcher traverse/elevation: 20° total (10° left and 10° right of the centreline)/+5° to +56°
Crew: 5
Mounting: rear of Type 60-1 tracked artillery tractor

Variant
Type 83: this is the largest conventional MRS in Chinese service, and the complete salvo of four rockets can be fired in 7·5 seconds; each rocket is propelled by a solid-propellant rocket that generates a burn-out speed of 2915 km/h (1,811 mph); the launch vehicle is a simple modification of an

existing type, and the combat weight of the complete system is 15,134 kg (33,364 lb)

Type 82 multiple rocket system

(China)
Type: 30-tube multiple rocket system
Rocket dimensions: diameter 130·7 mm (5·15 in); length not revealed
Rocket weights: whole round not revealed; warhead (Type 63) HE or (Type 82) HE fragmentation
Rocket range: 10,215 m (11,170 yards)
Reload time: not revealed
Launcher traverse/elevation: 170° total (32° left and 138° right of the centreline)/0° to +50°
Crew: 7
Mounting: rear of 6 × 6 truck or YW 531H armoured personnel carrier chassis

Variant
Type 82: this useful MRS has a combat weight of 9000 kg (19,841 lb) complete with two sets of rockets; the launcher comprises three 10-tube horizontal rows, and a launcher's complete complement of 60 rockets (two salvoes) can be fired in 5 minutes; the Type 63 rocket has a standard HE warhead, while the Type 82 rocket has increased lethality against soft-skinned targets through the provision of a casing of steel balls over an HE core

Type 70 multiple rocket system

(China)
Type: 19-tube multiple rocket system
Rocket dimensions: diameter 130·65 mm (5·14 in); length 1·048 m (3·44 ft)
Rocket weights: whole round 32·8 kg (72·3 lb); warhead 14·7 kg (32·5 lb) HE fragmentation
Rocket range: 10,370 m (11,340 yards)
Reload time: not revealed
Launcher traverse/elevation: 180° total (90° left and 90° right of the centreline)/0° to +50°
Crew: 6
Mounting: rear of YW 531 armoured personnel carrier chassis

Variants
Type 63: this system is used by the Chinese as a replacement for the Soviet BM-13-16, and the solid-propellant fin-stabilized rockets are thought to have a performance comparable to that of the Soviet 140-mm (5·51-in) types; the launch tubes are disposed as a row of 10 over a row of nine; in this variant the launcher is carried on the rear of an NJ-230 2·5-ton 4 × 4 truck, and the type has been seen in two subvariants with open and enclosed cabs; the type is generally grouped in batteries of six launcher vehicles for the support of infantry divisions
Type 70: this has the same launcher and rockets as the Type 63, but in this application located above the hull of the YW 531 APC for the support of tank divisions; the combat weight of the system is 13,400 kg (29,542 lb)

Opposite page, top: The type 70 multiple-launch rocket system is based on the chassis of the YW 531 armoured personnel carrier, and is designed for saturation attacks on high-value targets such as armour concentrations.

122-mm multiple rocket system

(China)

Type: 40-tube multiple rocket system
Rocket dimensions: diameter 122·4 mm (4·82 in); length 2·87 m (9·42 ft)
Rocket weights: whole round 66·9 kg (147·4 lb); warhead 19·25 kg (42·4 lb) HE fragmentation
Rocket range: 20,580 m (22,505 yards)
Reload time: not revealed
Launcher traverse/elevation: 168° total (102° left and 66° right of the centreline)/0° to +50°
Crew: 5
Mounting: rear of Type 83 self-propelled gun/howitzer chassis

Variant

122-mm MRS: this is a useful MRS whose designation remains unknown; the type is clearly modelled on the Soviet BM-21 system, and its location on the chassis of an SP gun/howitzer indicates that it is tasked with support of mechanized formations; the rockets can be fired individually or in a 20-second salvo, whereupon the launcher is replenished from the pack of 40 reload rockets carried over the forward part of the top decking

Type 81 multiple rocket system

(China)

Type: 12-tube multiple rocket system
Rocket dimensions: diameter 106·7 mm (4·2 in); length 0·841 m (2·76 ft) for HE type and 0·915 m (3·0 ft) for incendiary type
Rocket weights: whole round 18·8 kg (41·45 lb) for HE type and 18·74 kg (41·31 lb) for incendiary type; warhead 8·33 kg (18·4 lb) HE fragmentation and 7·5 kg (16·6 lb) incendiary
Rocket range: 7900 m (8,640 yards) for HE type and 8500 m (9,295 yards) for incendiary type
Reload time: 3 minutes
Launcher traverse/elevation: 360° total/−3° to +57°
Crew: 4
Mounting: rear of 4 × 4 truck

Variants

Type 63: designed in the late 1950s, this system

Above: The Type 81 is the truck-mounted counterpart to the towed Type 63 system.

has three four-round horizontal rows of launch tubes, and is generally carried on a towed two-wheel trailer for a combat weight of 602 kg (1,327·2 lb); this model has a crew of five and 32° traverse; the launcher can also be installed on the back of light vehicles; the rocket is spin-stabilized and powered by a solid-propellant motor
Type 63-1: lightened version of the Type 63 with smaller, spoked wheels and four rows of three tubes for a combat weight of 466 kg (1,027·3 lb)
Type 81: truck-mounted variant for greater tactical mobility; 12 reload rockets are carried on the truck

M51 multiple rocket system

(Czechoslovakia)

Type: 32-tube multiple rocket system
Rocket dimensions: diameter 130 mm (5·12 in); length 0·80 m (2·62 ft)

Rocket weights: whole round 24·2 kg (53·4 lb); warhead not revealed
Rocket range: 8200 m (8,970 yards)
Reload time: 2 minutes
Launcher traverse/elevation: 120° total/0° to +50°
Crew: 6
Mounting: rear of Praga V3S or ZIL-151/157 6 × 6 trucks (Czech and most export models) or Steyr 680 M3 6 × 6 truck (Austrian model)

Variant

M51: developed in the 1950s, this system uses a solid-propellant spin-stabilized rocket, 64 reload rounds being carried in the launcher base structure and in boxes on the sides of the truck; the system has a combat weight of 8900 kg (19,621 lb); the rocket has a burn-out speed of 1495 km/h (929 mph), and it is thought that Czechoslovakia has recently introduced an uprated version of the rocket with greater range; the system is sometimes designated the **RM-130**, and is allocated at the rate of one 18-launcher battalion to each motor rifle division

SAKR-30 multiple rocket system

(Egypt)
Type: 40-tube multiple rocket system
Rocket dimensions: diameter 122 mm (4·8 in); length 2·58 m (8·46 ft) with HE warhead and 3·18 m (10·43 ft) with cluster munition warheads
Rocket weights: whole round 55 kg (121·25 lb) with HE warhead, 61·5 kg (135·6 lb) with anti-tank mine warhead and 63 kg (138·9 lb) with anti-tank/anti-personnel minelet warhead; warhead 18·5 kg (40·79 lb) HE fragmentation and 27·5 kg (60·63 lb) cluster munition warhead
Rocket range: 30,000 m (32,810 yards)
Reload time: probably 10 minutes
Launcher traverse/elevation: 240° total (120° left and 120° right of the centreline)/0° to +50°
Crew: 6
Mounting: rear of Ural-375D 6 × 6 truck

Variant
SAKR-30: this is essentially the Soviet BM-21 launcher system fitted with a rocket designed and produced in Egypt, and using an advanced solid-propellant motor for very good range with all three rocket types; the system also uses (in its larger forms) two types of indigenously produced submunition warhead; one of these can hold either 100 anti-vehicle/anti-personnel minelets or 35 larger anti-personnel bomblets, while the other contains six anti-tank mines; the role of the SAKR-30 is area-saturation of defended territory

---

VAP multiple rocket system

(Egypt)
Type: 12-tube multiple rocket system
Rocket dimensions: diameter 80 mm (3·15 in); length 1·50 m (4·92 ft)
Rocket weights: whole round 12 kg (26·5 lb); warhead not revealed
Rocket range: 8000 m (8,750 yards)
Reload time: not revealed
Launcher traverse/elevation: 360° total/not revealed
Crew: 2-3
Mounting: rear of light truck or AFV

Variant
VAP: this lightweight Egyptian rocket is powered by a solid-propellant motor and fin-stabilized, and designed to carry an HE fragmentation or illuminating warhead; the pedestal-mounted system can be installed in most light trucks and AFVs, thus providing the Egyptian armed forces with a potent weapon of great tactical flexibility

---

LARS-2 multiple rocket system

(West Germany)
Type: 36-tube multiple rocket system
Rocket dimensions: diameter 110 mm (4·33 in); length 2·263 m (7·424 ft)
Rocket weights: whole round 35 kg (77·2 lb); warhead 17·3 kg (38·14 lb)
Rocket range: 14,000 m (15,310 yards)
Reload time: 15 minutes
Launcher traverse/elevation: 190° total (95° left and 95° right of the centreline)/−9° to +55°
Crew: 5
Mounting: rear of MAN 7-ton 6 × 6 truck

Above: Reload rockets loaded into the 32-tube launcher of the Czech M51 rocket launcher, on the back of Praga V3S truck chassis.

SAKR-18 multiple rocket system

(Egypt)
Type: 21-, 30- and 40-tube multiple rocket system
Rocket dimensions: diameter 122 mm (4·8 in); length 3·25 m (10·66 ft)
Rocket weights: whole round 67 kg (147·7 lb); warhead 21 kg (46·3 lb) cluster munition
Rocket range: 18,000 m (19,685 yards)
Reload time: not revealed
Launcher traverse/elevation: not revealed
Crew: not revealed
Mounting: back of light AFV or truck

Variants
SAKR-18: available in three types of launcher configuration, this system is based on a simple rocket designed to carry a payload of 21 anti-tank bomblets or 28 anti-personnel bomblets for area saturation purposes
PRL-111: tripod-mounted single-tube launcher intended for the use of special forces; overall length is 2·4 m (7·87 ft), width 1·5 m (4·9 ft) and height 2·5 m (8·2 ft); the traverse is 14° total (7° left and 7° right of the centreline), and the elevation from −10° to +40°; the standard 122-mm rocket can be fired to minimum and maximum range of 3000 and 10,800 m (3,280 and 11,810 yards); the rate of fire is 1 round per minute
PRL-113: a tripod-mounted triple-tube launcher intended for the use of special forces; overall length is 2·5 m (8·2 ft), width 1·5 m (4·9 ft) and height 2·8 m (9·19 ft); the traverse is 14° total (7° left and 7° right of the centreline), and the elevation from −10° to +40°; the standard 122-mm rocket can be fired to minimum and maximum range of 3000 and 10,800 m (3,280 and 11,810 yards); the rate of fire is 3 rounds per minute

Above: The West German LARS is one of today's most powerful multiple-launch rocket systems.

Variant

LARS-2: developed in the mid- to late 1960s for the West German army as the LARS-1, the Light Artillery Rocket System was in the 1980s upgraded to LARS-2 standard with improved rockets, a new fire-control system and a MAN rather than Magirus-Deutz truck for improved cross-country capability; the solid-propellant rockets are fin-stabilized, and are fired singly or in ripples at 0·5-second intervals, a full salvo being launched in 17·5 seconds; the weight of the entire truck-mounted system is 17,480 kg (38,536 lb); the LARS-2 is used in conjunction with the Contraves Fieldguard fire-control system, and a diversity of rocket types is available, the most important being the dispenser (with five AT2 hollow-charge anti-tank mines) and the radar target (used to calibrate the system before full fire is opened); less important types are HE fragmentation, smoke and a dispenser type with eight AT1 anti-tank mines; in recent years two improved rockets have been introduced, these keeping the original rocket casing, dimensions and weights but adding new propellant filling for maximum ranges of 19,000 and 25,000 m (20,780 and 27,340 yards); improved warheads are under final development, including a type that releases a single anti-tank weapon with infra-red terminal guidance; there is also a 15-tube version of the LARS-2 carried on a towed two-wheel trailer

Nazeat multiple rocket system

(Iran)

Type: multi-tube multiple rocket system
Rocket dimensions: diameter 355 mm (13·98 in); length 5·90 m (19·36 ft)
Rocket weights: whole round 950 kg (2,094 lb); warhead 150 kg (330·7 lb)
Rocket range: not revealed
Reload time: not revealed
Launcher traverse/elevation: not revealed
Crew: not revealed
Mounting: rear of truck chassis

Variant

Nazeat: developed for use in the Gulf War, this is a rocket produced specifically to meet Iranian requirements and now available on the export market

Shahin 2 multiple rocket system

(Iran)

Type: multi-tube multiple rocket system
Rocket dimensions: diameter 333 mm (13·1 in); length 3·87 m (12·70 ft)
Rocket weights: whole round 580 kg (1,279 lb); warhead 180 kg (397 lb)
Rocket range: not revealed
Reload time: not revealed
Launcher traverse/elevation: not revealed
Crew: not revealed
Mounting: rear of truck chassis

Variant

Shahin 2: developed for use in the Gulf War, this is a rocket produced specifically to meet Iranian requirements and now available on the export market

Oghab multiple rocket system

(Iran)

Type: multi-tube multiple rocket system
Rocket dimensions: diameter 230 mm (9·06 in); length 4·82 m (15·81 ft)
Rocket weights: whole round 360 kg (793·7 lb); warhead 70 kg (154·3 lb)
Rocket range: not revealed
Reload time: not revealed
Launcher traverse/elevation: not revealed
Crew: not revealed
Mounting: rear of truck chassis

Variant

Oghab: developed for use in the Gulf War, this is a rocket produced specifically to meet Iranian requirements and now available on the export market

IMI MAR-290 multiple rocket system

(Israel)

Type: 4-tube multiple rocket system
Rocket dimensions: diameter 290 mm (11·4 in); length 5·45 m (17·88 ft)
Rocket weights: whole round 600 kg (1,323 lb); warhead 320 kg (705·5 lb)
Rocket range: 25,000 m (27,340 yards)
Reload time: 10 minutes
Launcher traverse/elevation: 360° total/0° to +60°
Crew: 4
Mounting: chassis of Centurion MBT

Variants

MAR-290: this system was developed by Israel Military Industries during the 1960s, and entered service on the chassis of Sherman medium tanks modified to accept a quadruple frame rack for this exceptionally powerful solid-propellant fin-stabilized rocket; in the early 1980s the system was developed onto the chassis of the Centurion with a four-tube launcher fitted onto the turret ring for 360° traverse; in this guise the whole system weighs 50,800 kg (111,993 lb), and the four rockets can be salvoed in 10 seconds; the reloading process is controlled by a single man making extensive use of hydraulics to manoeuvre the heavy rockets from the reload vehicle into the launch tube
MAR-350: larger version of the MAR-290 and designed for use with the same launch vehicle and system; the rocket has a diameter of 350 mm (13·78 in) and a maximum range in the order of 70,000 m (76,550 yards)

IMI BM-24 multiple rocket system

(Israel)

Type: 12-rack multiple rocket system
Rocket dimensions: diameter 240 mm (945 in); length 1·29 m (4·23 ft)
Rocket weights: whole round 110·5 kg (243·6 lb); warhead 48·3 kg (106·5 lb)
Rocket range: 10,700 m (11,700 yards)
Reload time: 4 minutes
Launcher traverse/elevation: 140° total/0° to +55°
Crew: 6
Mounting: rear of ZIL-157 6 × 6 truck

Variant

IMI BM-24: Israel has captured from various Arab combatants in recent years sufficient Soviet BM-24 equipments to take the type into her own inventory and to undertake manufacture of an Israeli development of the Soviet rocket; this is a solid-propellant type with spin stabilization, and on detonation the rocket breaks into some 12,000 steel fragments that cover an area of 12,000 m² (14,352 sq yards); a salvo blankets an area of 125,000 m² (149,505 sq yards)

IMI LAR-160 multiple rocket system

(Israel)

Type: 36-tube multiple rocket system
Rocket dimensions: diameter 160 mm (6·3 in); length 3·311 m (10·86 ft)

Rocket weights: whole round 110 kg (242·5 lb); warhead 50 kg (110 lb) cluster munition
Rocket range: 30,000 m (32,810 yards)
Reload time: not revealed
Launcher traverse/elevation: 360° total/0° to +54°
Crew: not revealed
Mounting: rear of AMX-13 light tank chassis

Variants
LAR-160: this is a highly advanced multiple rocket system of Israeli design and manufacture, based on a solid-propellant rocket with wrap-round stabilizing fins, and currently deployed on the chassis of the obsolete AMX-13 light tank (two 18-tube pods for a combat weight of 19,200 kg/ 43,328 lb) and M548 cargo carrier (two 13-tube pods for a combat weight of 12,800 kg/28,219 lb); it could also be fitted on the M809 6 × 6 truck (two 13-tube pods for a combat weight of 14,170 kg/ 31,239 lb) or on the M47 tank chassis (two 25-tube pods for a combat weight of 45,000 kg/99,206 lb); the LARS-160 battery comprises six launcher systems and one Contraves Fieldguard or Westinghouse Quickfire radar fire-control system; the submunition payload of the rocket comprises 187 M42 bomblets, a FASCAM scatterable mine unit, a chemical or biological agent type, Skeet anti-tank weapons, a 155-mm (6·1-in) howitzer projectile, or an illuminating type; the rocket is delivered in a sealed glassfibre/aluminium container that also serves as the disposable launch tube
Lightweight LAR-160: towed by light vehicles such as the US Hummer or to be carried by medium helicopters such as the US Sikorsky UH-60 series, the Lightweight LAR-160 system can comprise a single eight-tube launcher pod (for an unloaded towed weight of 7500 kg/ 16,534 lb), or one 18-tube launcher pod (for an unloaded weight of 11,500 kg/25,353 lb towed by a 5-ton truck), or two eight-tube launcher pods; the Mk 1 rocket has a 40-kg (88-lb) HE or submunition warhead, while the Mk 2 rocket has a 50-kg (110-lb) HE or submunition warhead for a range of 30,000 m (32,810 yards)

SNIA FIROS 25 multiple rocket system

(Italy)
Type: 40-tube multiple rocket launcher
Rocket dimensions: diameter 122 mm (4·8 in); length 3·174 m (10·41 ft) with cluster munition warhead and 2·575 m (8·45 ft) with conventional warhead
Rocket weights: whole round 63 kg (138·9 lb) with cluster munition warhead and 52·5 kg (115·75 lb) with conventional warhead; warhead 27·5 kg (60·6 lb) with cluster munition and 17 kg (37·5 lb) with conventional warhead
Rocket range: 22,000 m (24,060 yards) with cluster munition warhead and 25,000 m (27,340 yards) with conventional warhead
Reload time: not revealed
Launcher traverse/elevation: 210° total (105° left and 105° right of the centreline)/0° to +60°
Crew: 3-4
Mounting: rear of most 6 × 6 trucks

Variant
FIROS 25: essentially an enlarged development of the FIROS 6 system, this equipment fires solid-propellant rockets carrying either a conventional warhead (HE, HE fragmentation or smoke) or a cluster munition warhead (seven anti-tank mines,

66 anti-personnel mines, or 84 dual-role anti-tank/anti-personnel bomblets); the launchers are grouped in batteries of six with a fire-control vehicle and six reload vehicles, the whole system being designed for the rapid saturation of large areas

SNIA FIROS 6 multiple rocket system

(Italy)
Type: 48-tube multiple rocket system
Rocket dimensions: diameter 51 mm (2 in); length 1·05 m (3·44 ft)
Rocket weights: whole round 4·8 kg (10·6 lb); warhead 2·2 kg (4·4 lb) HEI, HE fragmentation, anti-tank/anti-personnel, illuminating or smoke
Rocket range: 6550 m (7,165 yards)
Reload time: 5 minutes
Launcher traverse/elevation: 360° total/−5° to +45°
Crew: 2-3
Mounting: rear of light wheeled vehicle

Variant
FIROS 6: this system was designed by SNIA as an area-saturation equipment to be fitted on the rear of any lightweight 4 × 4 vehicle or on an APC, the type firing a developed version of the solid-propellant folding-fin aircraft rocket; the rockets are ripple-fired at the rate of 10 per second; a typical installation is the 480-kg (1,058-lb) loaded launcher assembly on a Fiat 1107 truck for a combat weight of 2670 kg (5,886 lb) with 48 reload rockets

Type 67 multiple rocket system

(Japan)
Type: two-rail multiple rocket system
Rocket dimensions: diameter 307 mm (12·09 in); length 4·50 m (14·76 ft)
Rocket weights: whole round 573 kg (1,263 lb); warhead not revealed
Rocket range: 28,000 m (30,620 yards)
Reload time: not revealed
Launcher traverse/elevation: not revealed
Crew: 2
Mounting: rear of Hino 4-ton 6 × 6 truck

Variant
Type 67: now an obsolescent system, the Type 67 launcher was designed in the mid-1960s; it fires the Type 68 rocket, which has fixed cruciform fins and a solid-propellant motor, and carries an HE fragmentation warhead; the launcher vehicle is supported by a reload vehicle with six more rockets and a hydraulic crane for a comparatively rapid reload time

Type 75 multiple rocket system

(Japan)
Type: 30-frame multiple rocket system
Rocket dimensions: diameter 131·5 mm (5·18 in); length 1·856 m (6·09 ft)
Rocket weights: whole round 43 kg (94·8 lb); warhead 15 kg (33 lb) HE
Rocket range: 15,000 m (16,405 yards)
Reload time: not revealed

Launcher elevation/traverse: 100° total (50° left and 50° right of the centreline)/0° to +50°
Crew: 3
Mounting: rear of Type 73 armoured personnel carrier chassis

Variant
Type 75: developed in the first half of the 1970s, this equipment is in Japanese service only, and can fire its rockets individually or in a 12-second ripple salvo; the rocket is fin-stabilized and powered by a solid-propellant motor; the combat weight of the complete system is 16,500 kg (36,376 lb)

WP-8 multiple rocket system

(Poland)
Type: 8-tube multiple rocket system
Rocket dimensions: diameter 140 mm (5·51 in); length 1·092 m (3·58 ft)
Rocket weights: whole round 39·6 kg (81·35 lb); warhead 18·8 kg (41·4 lb) HE fragmentation
Rocket range: 9800 m (10,715 yards)
Reload time: 2 minutes
Launcher traverse/elevation: 28° total (14° left and 14° right of the centreline)/−12° to 47°
Crew: 5
Mounting: two-wheel trailer

Variant
WP-8: this Polish equipment is designed for the use of airborne forces, and uses the same solid-propellant rocket as the Soviet RPU-14 and BM-14 launchers; the loaded weight of the trailer is 688 kg (1,517 lb), and the type can be towed by a UAZ-469 4 × 4 light truck

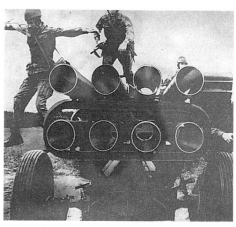

Above: The WP-8 is an eight-tube launcher for 140-mm (5·51-in) free-flight rockets.

Romanian 122-mm multiple rocket system

(Romania)
Type: 40-tube multiple rocket system
Rocket dimensions: diameter 122 mm (4·8 in); length not revealed
Rocket weights: whole round not revealed; warhead not revealed
Rocket range: 20,000 m (21,875 yards)
Reload time: 15 minutes
Launcher traverse/elevation: 180° total (100° left and 80° right of the centreline)/an unrevealed depression to +55°
Crew: 5
Mounting: rear of DAC 665 T 6 × 6 truck

Variants

Romanian 122-mm 40-tube MRS: revealed in 1989, this equipment was developed to replace the Czech M51 system carried on a ZIL-151 rather than the original Praga V3S 6 × 6 truck; the rockets can be ripple-fired in a period between 20 and 40 seconds, and a complete salvo saturates an area of 210,000 m² (251,165 sq yards); the same DAC 665 T truck is also used as the basis of the required resupply vehicle, carrying 40 rockets in two containers for reloading with the aid of a 6-tonne crane; the resupply vehicle can also tow a four-wheel trailer with another 80 rockets

Romanian 122-mm 12-tube MRS: this is a smaller equipment believed to use the same rocket but in a 12-tube arrangement carried on the back of a 4 × 4 truck that can also tow a trailer carrying 18 reload rockets; there is also a single-tube launcher for use by mountain and guerrilla forces; this is carried on a tripod for elevation/traverse arcs of 360°/−3° to +50°, and fires the rocket to a maximum range of 13,400 m (14,655 yards)

Armscor Valkyri multiple rocket system

(South Africa)

Type: 24-tube multiple rocket system
Rocket dimensions: diameter 127 mm (5 in); length 2·68 m (8·8 ft)
Rocket weights: whole round not revealed; warhead not revealed
Rocket range: 22,000 m (24,060 yards)
Reload time: 10 minutes
Launcher traverse/elevation: 104° total (52° left and 52° right of the centreline)/50° total
Crew: 2
Mounting: rear of SAMIL 20 4 × 4 truck

Variant

Valkyri: designed in direct response to the threat of Soviet-supplied BM-21 equipments in the hands of African 'freedom fighters', the Valkyri is a highly capable piece of kit designed for area saturation in bush conditions, the solid-propellant rocket being fin-stabilized to deliver a load of 3,500 steel balls to the target area, where the lethal area is 1500 m² (1,795 sq yards); the rockets

Below: Operations have confirmed the successful nature of the Valkyri rocket system.

can be fired individually or in ripples of between 2 and 24 rockets at the rate of one rocket per second, range being variable between 8000 and 22,000 m (8,750 and 24,060 yards) by the use of spoiler rings on the rockets to slow them; the launcher vehicle has a combat weight of 6440 kg (14,198 lb), and each is accompanied by a vehicle with 72 reload rockets

Kooryong multiple rocket system

(South Korea)

Type: 36-tube multiple rocket system
Rocket dimensions: diameter 130 mm (5·12 in); length 2·40 m (7·87 ft)
Rocket weights: whole round 55 kg (121·25 lb); warhead 21 kg (46·3 lb) HE fragmentation
Rocket range: 23,000 m (25,155 yards)
Reload time: not revealed
Launcher elevation/traverse: 240° total (120° left and 120° right of the centreline)/0° to +55°
Crew: 3
Mounting: rear of KM809A1 6 × 6 truck

Variant

Kooryong: designed for South Korea's extremes of terrain and climate, this useful multiple rocket system can be installed on most 5-ton 6 × 6 trucks, and the rockets can be fired individually or in a ripple of two rockets per second; the combat weight of the complete system is 16,800 kg (37,037 lb)

Santa Barbara Teruel-2 multiple rocket system

(Spain)

Type: 40-tube multiple rocket system
Rocket dimensions: diameter 140·5 mm (5·53 in); length 2·044 m (6·71 lb) with HE fragmentation warhead and 2·14 m (7·02 ft) with cluster munition warhead
Rocket weights: whole round 56 kg (123·5 lb) with HE warhead and 59 kg (130 lb) with cluster munition warhead; warhead 18·6 kg (41 lb) HE fragmentation or 21 kg (46·3 lb) cluster munition
Rocket range: 18,200 m (19,905 yards)
Reload time: 5 minutes
Launcher traverse/elevation: 240° total (120°

left and 120° right of the centreline)/0° to +50°
Crew: 2-3
Mounting: rear of Pegaso 3055 6 × 6 truck

Variants

Teruel-2: the launcher comprises two sub-assemblies each containing five horizontal rows each of four launcher tubes; the rockets have folding fins for stabilization, and are powered by solid-propellant motors; launcher batteries have six launchers, and each launcher truck is accompanied by a vehicle with 80 reload rockets; the cluster munition warhead can contain 28 impact-fused anti-tank grenades, or six anti-tank mines or 42 anti-personnel grenades; the Teruel is designed to supplant the multitude of older rockets and launchers still in Spanish service; a complete salvo can be fired in 45 seconds

Teruel-3: updated version whose rockets have a maximum range of 28,000 m (30,620 yards) through use of a new motor section with double-grain solid propellant; the rocket is 3·23 m (10·60 ft) long and weighs 76 kg (167·55 lb) with the same HE fragmentation warhead as the Teruel-2; however, the 57·4-kg (126·54-lb) core can alternatively carry a more advanced submunition warhead weighing 21 kg (46·3 lb) and filled with 42 anti-personnel minelets, or 28 hollow-charge anti-tank minelets each able to pierce 110 mm (4·33 in) of armour, or six pressure-activated anti-tank mines, or 21 smoke dispensers, or a number of anti-personnel mines; the Teruel system allows both types of rocket to be used in a single launcher, which is supported by a replenishment vehicle carrying six blocks of 20 Teruel-2 or four blocks of 20 Teruel-3 reload rockets

Oerlikon-Bührle RWK-014 multiple rocket system

(Switzerland)

Type: 30-tube multiple rocket system
Rocket dimensions: diameter 81 mm (3·12 in); length 1·80 m (5·91 ft)
Rocket weights: whole round 15·7 or 19·6 kg (34·6 or 43·2 lb) depending on warhead; warhead 7 or 11 kg (15·4 or 24·25 lb) HE fragmentation
Rocket range: 10,400 m (11,375 yards)
Reload time: not revealed
Launcher traverse/elevation: 360° total/−10° to +50°
Crew: not revealed
Mounting: most light AFVs

Variant

RWK-014: this Swiss launcher fires folding fin-stabilized solid-propellant SNORA rockets developed jointly with SNIA in Italy, and a salvo of 30 rockets is fired in 3 seconds; the loaded launcher weighs some 1410 kg (3,108 lb)

Kung Feng III and IV multiple rocket systems

(Taiwan)

Type: 40-tube multiple rocket system
Rocket dimensions: diameter 126 mm (4·96 in); length about 0·80 m (2·625 ft)
Rocket weights: whole round about 25 kg (55·1 lb); warhead not revealed
Rocket range: 9000 m (9,845 yards)
Reload time: not revealed

Launcher traverse/elevation: 0° total/not revealed
Crew: not revealed
Mounting: two-wheel trailer or M113 APC

Variants

Kung Feng III: this is the trailer-mounted version towed by a 0·75-ton truck, the launcher comprising two launcher banks, each containing five horizontal rows of four tubes; the 40 rockets are ripple-fired in 16 seconds
Kung Feng IV: vehicle-mounted version, generally carried on the back of an M113 APC but also used on LVTP7 amphibious APCs

Kung Feng VI multiple rocket system

(Taiwan)
Type: 45-tube multiple rocket system
Rocket dimensions: diameter 117 mm (4·61 in); length 1·80 m (5·91 ft)
Rocket weights: whole round 60 kg (132·3 lb); warhead not revealed
Rocket range: 15,000 m (16,405 yards)
Reload time: 15 minutes
Launcher traverse/elevation: 180° total (90° left and 90° right of the centreline)/not revealed
Crew: not revealed
Mounting: rear of M52 6 × 6 truck

Variant

Kung Feng VI: this truck-mounted system comprises five horizontal rows of nine tubes, and the rockets are ripple-fired in 22 seconds to saturate an area of 30,000 m² (35,880 sq yards)

BM-? Smerch multiple rocket system

(USSR)
Type: multi-tube multiple rocket system
Rocket dimensions: diameter 300 mm (11·81 in); length not revealed
Rocket weights: whole round not revealed; warhead not revealed
Rocket range: not revealed
Reload time: not revealed
Launcher traverse/elevation: not revealed
Crew: not revealed
Mounting: rear of 8 × 8 truck

Variant

BM-? Smerch: this important new multiple-launch rocket system, called Smerch (tornado) by the Soviets, entered service in 1989 and is thought to fire a rocket carrying as warhead several types of improved conventional munition; no details other than rocket calibre are currently available

BM-25 multiple rocket system

(USSR)
Type: 6-frame multiple rocket system
Rocket dimensions: diameter 250 mm (9·84 in); length 5·822 m (19·10 ft)
Rocket weights: whole round 455 kg (1,003 lb); warhead not revealed
Rocket range: 30,000 + m (32,810 + yards)
Reload time: 10-20 minutes

Launcher traverse/elevation: 20° total (10° left and 10° right of the centreline)/0° to +55°
Crew: 8-12
Mounting: rear of KrAZ-214 6 × 6 truck

Variant

BM-25: introduced in the 1950s, this is the largest rocket to have entered Soviet service since World War II (though a 280-mm/11·02-in type is known to be under development), and is now obsolete; the type is powered by a storable liquid-propellant rocket, and is stabilized by four fixed fins which engage in helical grooves in the launcher for imparted spin; the warhead is of the HE type; the combat weight of the whole equipment is 18,145 kg (40,002 lb)

BM-24 multiple rocket system

(USSR)
Type: 12-frame multiple rocket system
Rocket dimensions: diameter 240 mm (9·45 in); length 1·18 m (3·87 ft)
Rocket weights: whole round 112·5 kg (248 lb); warhead 46·9 kg (103·4 lb) HE fragmentation
Rocket range: 11,000 m (12,030 yards)
Reload time: 3-4 minutes
Launcher traverse/elevation: 140° total (70° left and 70° right of the centreline)/0° to +65°
Crew: 6
Mounting: rear of ZIL-157 6 × 6 truck

Variants

BM-24: this equipment was introduced to Soviet service in the early 1950s, and was one of the most important support weapons available to motor rifle divisions until the advent of the BM-21; the combat weight of the complete equipment is 9200 kg (20,282 lb); the rocket is powered by a solid-propellant motor and is spin-stabilized; each launcher is supported by a vehicle carrying 48 reload rounds

BM-24T: version with tube rather than frame launchers, and mounted on the AT-S armoured and tracked artillery tractor; the type was used for the support of tank divisions and may no longer remain in service

BM-22 Uragzy multiple rocket system

(USSR)
Type: 16-tube multiple rocket system
Rocket dimensions: diameter 220 mm (8·66 in);

length 4·80 m (15·75 ft)
Rocket weights: whole round 360 kg (793·7 lb); warhead not revealed
Rocket range: 40,000 m (43,745 yards)
Reload time: 15-20 minutes
Launcher traverse/elevation: 240° total (120° left and 120° right of the centreline)/0° to +55°
Crew: 6
Mounting: rear of ZIL-135 8 × 8 truck

Variant

BM-22 Uragzy: introduced in 1977 and at first known as the **BM-27**, this modern and highly capable cross-country equipment is known to the Soviets as the Uragzy (hurricane) and comprises a three-bank launcher (four, six and six tubes)

Above: The BM-24 system uses a steel-frame launcher on the back of a ZIL-157 truck.

Below: The BM-22 Uragzy is one of the USSR's most modern and impressive rocket systems.

firing solid-propellant rockets in support of Soviet manoeuvre formations; the rocket can deliver HE, chemical and cluster munition warheads, the last including HE fragmentation, incendiary and mine types; the combat weight of the whole equipment is 22,750 kg (50,154 kg), and each launcher vehicle is supported in the field by two ZIL-135s each carrying 16 reload rockets, a reloading crane and a power rammer; the standard unit is the battalion of one HQ battery, one support battery and three launcher batteries each equipped with six launcher vehicles and 12 reload vehicles; the type is used at every level from front down to division

BMD-20 multiple rocket system

(USSR)

Type: 4-frame multiple rocket system
Rocket dimensions: diameter 200 mm (7·87 in); length 3·11 m (10·20 ft)
Rocket weight: whole round 194 kg (427·7 lb); warhead not revealed
Rocket range: 20,000 m (21,870 yards)
Reload time: 6-10 minutes
Launcher traverse/elevation: 20° total (10° left and 10° right of the centreline)/+ 6° to + 60°
Crew: 6
Mounting: rear of ZIL-157 6 × 6 truck

Variant

BMD-20: introduced into Soviet service in the first half of the 1950s, this equipment is obsolete but still in service with some Soviet clients; the rocket is fin-stabilized (with spin imparted by guide rails in the frames) and powered by a solid-propellant motor; the combat weight of the whole equipment is 8700 kg (19,180 lb)

BM-14-17 multiple rocket system

(USSR)

Type: 17-tube multiple rocket system
Rocket dimensions: diameter 140·4 mm (5·53 in); length 1·092 m (3·58 ft)
Rocket weights: whole round 39·6 kg (87·3 lb); warhead 18·8 kg (41·45 lb) HE fragmentation
Rocket range: 9800 m (10,715 yards)
Reload time: 2 minutes
Launcher traverse/elevation: 210° total (145° left and 65° right of the centreline)/0° to + 52°
Crew: 7
Mounting: rear of GAZ-63A 4 × 4 truck

Variants

BM-14-17: this equipment was introduced to Soviet service in the mid- and late 1950s as the complement to the BM-14-16 equipment in motor rifle and tank divisions; the combat weight of the whole equipment is 5323 kg (11,735 lb), and the launcher comprises two horizontal rows, with nine tubes over eight; the rocket is spin-stabilized and powered by a solid-propellant motor
BM-14-16: introduced in the early 1950s, this equipment has a combat weight of 6432 kg (14,180 lb) including the ZIL-131 6 × 6 truck; the rocket is the same M-14-OF fired by the BM-14-17, and the type can carry smoke or chemical loads as alternatives to the HE payload; the launcher is arranged as two horizontal rows of eight tubes each; this equipment has a crew of seven, and the launcher traverse/elevation arcs are 200° total (140° left and 60° right of the centreline)/0° to + 52°
RPU-14: this is a towed equipment using the M-14-OF rocket, with four rows of four tubes on a two-wheel trailer that provides the launcher with traverse/elevation angles of 30° total/0° to + 48° ; the equipment was designed for the use of Soviet airborne formations, and thus has the comparatively light combat weight of 1835 kg (4,045 lb); the crew is five, and the normal towing vehicle is the GAZ-66 4 × 4 truck; the equipment is also operated by a number of Third World and guerrilla forces supported by the USSR

BM-13-16 multiple rocket system

(USSR)

Type: 8-rail multiple rocket system with rockets located above and below each rail
Rocket dimensions: diameter 132 mm (5·20 in); length 1·743 m (5·72 ft)
Rocket weights: whole round 42·5 kg (93·7 lb); warhead 18·5 kg (40·8 lb) HE fragmentation
Rocket range: 9000 m (9,845 yards)
Reload time: 5-10 minutes
Launcher traverse/elevation: 20° total (10° left and 10° right of the centreline)/+ 15° to + 45°
Crew: 6
Mounting: rear of ZIL-151 6 × 6 truck

Variant

BM-13-16: introduced in 1941 and now regarded as one of the decisive weapons of World War II on the Eastern Front, this 'Katyusha' system is still in service with some Soviet client states; the equipment has a combat weight of 6430 kg (14,175 lb), and the eight launcher rails each carry two rockets (one above and the other below) for a salvo time of between 7 and 10 seconds

BM-21 Grad multiple rocket system

(USSR)

Type: 40-tube multiple rocket system
Rocket dimensions: diameter 122·4 mm (4·82 in); length 1·905 m (6·25 ft) for short rocket and 3·23 m (10·60 ft) for long rocket
Rocket weight: whole round 45·8 kg (100·97 lb) for short rocket and 77 kg (169·75 lb) for long rocket; warhead 19·4 kg (42·8 lb) HE fragmentation
Rocket range: 11,000 m (12,030 yards) for short rocket and 20,380 m (22,290 yards) for long rocket
Reload time: 10 minutes
Launcher traverse/elevation: 180° total (120° left and 60° right of the centreline)/0° to + 55°
Crew: 6
Mounting: rear of Ural-375D 6 × 6 truck

Variants

BM-21 Grad: introduced in the early 1960s as known to the Soviets as the Grad (hail), this equipment is the standard area support equipment of Soviet motor rifle and tank divisions (being deployed at the rate of one battery of six equipments to the divisional artillery regiment), though the BM-27 is in the process of supplanting it; the equipment has a combat weight of 11,500 kg (25,353 lb), and the solid-propellant rocket has wrap-round fins for stabilization after initial spin has been imparted by helical grooves in the launch tube; the rocket comes in two types for medium- or long-range use, and three types of warhead are available (HE fragmentation, chemical and smoke); among the chemical loads for the warhead is the blood agent hydrogen cyanide; each launcher is supported by a vehicle carrying 40 reload rounds
M1975: NATO designation for a Soviet equipment of unknown designation, a version with 12 tubes (two six-tube horizontal rows) mounted on a GAZ-66 light truck, and is designed as the replacement for the BM-14-17 and RPU-14 within Soviet airborne formations
M1976: NATO designation for a Soviet equipment of unknown designation, essentially an improved 36-tube version (four nine-tube horizontal rows)

of the basic BM-21 mounted on a ZIL-131 3·5-ton 6 × 6 truck
BM-21/Bucegi: Romanian equipment with a 21-tube launcher mounted on a Bucegi SR-114 4 × 4 truck; the proper designation is unknown
BM-21/Isuzu: 30-tube Palestine Liberation Organization development, with two banks (each of three five-tube horizontal rows) mounted on the back of a Japanese Isuzu 2·5-ton 6 × 6 truck, and used operationally against the Israelis during the Lebanon fighting of 1982; a similar type is used by Pakistan
LRAR: Indian version of the BM-21 system using the Shaktiman 6 × 6 truck
M1972: introduced in the early 1970s as a companion to the BM-21 with improved cross-country capability, this Czech version uses the standard launcher and rocket mounted on the rear of a Tatra 813 8 × 8 truck together with a reload pack of 40 rockets located between the launcher and the armoured cab; the combat weight of the whole equipment is 33,700 kg (74,295 lb), and the type is known to bear the Czech designation **RM-70**
Type 81: Chinese version of the BM-21 system on a CQ-61 truck, the Chinese-built version of the Berliet GB4 6 × 6 truck from France
Type 83: 24-round Chinese version of the BM-21 system on a 6 × 6 truck; the launcher three eight-tube horizontal rows, can be traversed 90° left and right of the centreline, and elevated between 0° and + 55° ; the combat weight of the Type 83 is 8700 kg (19,180 lb), and the equipment can fire a full salvo in a time of between 15 and 20 seconds ; China is exporting this version to Thailand, which is developing a cargo rocket carrying anti-tank mines

Vought Multiple-Launch Rocket System

(USA)

Type: 12-tube multiple rocket system
Rocket dimensions: diameter 8·94 in (227 mm); length 12·92 ft (3·937 m)
Rocket weights: whole round 680 lb (308·4 kg); warhead 340 lb (154·2 kg) submunition type
Rocket range: 33,000+ yards (30,175 + m), but see Variant (below)
Reload time: 10 minutes
Launcher traverse/elevation: 360° total/not revealed
Crew: 3
Mounting: rear of M2 Bradley infantry fighting vehicle chassis

Variant

MLRS: this system is a key ingredient of the NATO powers' plans for the defeat of any Warsaw Pact incursion into Western Europe as it offers the possibility of generating swiftly, but at long range, large areas impassable to AFVs and men; the system is based on an existing high-mobility chassis, which carries at its rear a frame arrangement into which the accompanying Heavy Expanded Mobility Tactical Truck can fit two of its four pre-loaded six-tube rocket pods, another four loaded pods being accommodated on the HEMTT-drawn Heavy Expanded Mobility Ammunition Trailer; the rocket is a folding fin type with solid-propellant motor, and can carry any of four singularly advanced warheads currently under development or in service; these are a cluster munition with 644 M77 shaped-charge HE fragmentation dual-purpose anti-tank/anti-personnel bomblets (fired to 33,000 yards/30,175 m), a clus-

Above: The MLRS is without doubt the world's most advanced and capable multiple rocket system.

ter munition with 28 AT-2 parachute-retarded anti-tank mines (fired to a range of 43,750 yards/40,005 m), a cluster munition with six active-radar terminally-guided free-fall anti-tank shaped charge bomblets (fired to a range of 45,925 yards/41,995 m) and a chemical warhead with 92 lb (41·7 kg) of binary nerve gas agent; other warheads are under investigation for future development; the combat weight of the MRLS is 55,535 lb (25,191 kg)

LRSV M-87 multiple rocket system

(Yugoslavia)
Type: 12-tube multiple rocket system
Rocket dimensions: diameter 262 mm (10·315 in); length 4·20 m (13·78 ft)
Rocket weights: whole round 400 kg (882 lb); warhead 95 kg (209·4 lb) minelaying or cluster
Rocket range: 50,000 m (54,680 yards)
Reload time: not revealed
Launcher traverse/elevation: not revealed
Crew: 5
Mounting: rear of FAP 8 × 8 truck

Variant
LRSV M-87: revealed in 1989, this useful medium-range multiple launch rocket system is based on the FAP truck chassis whose 240-kW (322-hp) OM 403 diesel provides the 32,000-kg (70,547-lb) vehicle with a speed of 80 km/h (49·7 mph); the rear-mounted launcher assembly is powered in traverse and elevation, and the rockets can be fired individually or in salvoes

from the cabin or by a remote fire unit; each rocket is powered by a two-stage solid-propellant rocket in which the booster stage provides 8000-kg (17,637-lb) thrust for 0·2 second and the sustainer stage generates 1800-kg (3,968-lb) thrust for five seconds; the rocket can carry either of two warhead types, the mine-laying unit carrying 30 anti-tank mines and the cluster unit carrying 300 dual-purpose anti-personnel/anti-vehicle bomblets; each of these bomblets has 420 steel balls and possesses a lethal radius of 10 m (32·8 ft); there is a 12·7-mm (0·5-in) AA machine-gun on the cab, and recessed into the bumper are four smoke-dischargers; the system can be brought into action in two minutes, the bows and tarpaulin cover for the flatbed being removed and four stabilizers (one at each side of the second axle and two at the rear) lowered

M-77 Oganj multiple rocket system

(Yugoslavia)
Type: 32-tube multiple rocket system
Rocket dimensions: diameter 128 mm (5·04 in); length 2·60 m (8·53 ft)
Rocket weights: whole round 65 kg (143·3 lb); warhead 20 kg (44·1 lb) HE fragmentation
Rocket range: 20,000 m (21,870 yards)
Reload time: 2 minutes
Launcher traverse/elevation: 360° total/0° to +50°
Crew: not revealed
Mounting: rear of FAP 2020BS 6 × 6 truck

Variant
M-77 Oganj: developed for service in the mid-

1970s, this is a useful Yugoslav equipment with a combat weight of about 12,000 kg (26,455 lb) complete with a reload pack of 32 rockets, which are of the solid-propellant type and reloaded by an automatic loader after the dispatch of a full salvo from the launcher, which has four eight-tube horizontal rows; the rockets can be fired individually or in a ripple salvo of 18 seconds

M-63 Plaman multiple rocket system

(Yugoslavia)
Type: 32-tube multiple rocket system
Rocket dimensions: diameter 128 mm (5·04 in); length 0·814 m (2·67 ft)
Rocket weights: whole round 23·1 kg (50·9 lb); warhead 7·55 kg (16·6 lb) HE fragmentation
Rocket range: 8600 m (9,405 yards)
Reload time: 5 minutes
Launcher traverse/elevation: 30° total (15° left and 15° right of the centreline)/0° to +48°
Crew: 3-5
Mounting: two-wheel trailer

Variants
M-63 Plaman: this equipment uses a spin-stabilized solid-propellant rocket, and the rockets can be fired individually or in a ripple with intervals of 0·2, 0·4 or 0·6 seconds; the same rocket is also used in two export models (eight or 16 tubes)

M-71 Partisan: single-tube launcher intended for partisan (guerrilla) force; the launcher weighs 22 kg (48·5 lb) and fires the rocket to a maximum range of 8600 m (9,405 yards)

AVIBRAS SS-70

(Brazil)

Type: single-stage surface-to-surface battlefield missile

Dimensions: diameter 0·33 m (13·0 in); length not revealed

Weight: total round not revealed

Propulsion: one solid-propellant rocket delivering unrevealed thrust

Range limits: not revealed/70 km (not revealed/43 miles)

CEP: not revealed

Warhead: HE

Launch: wheeled transporter/erector/launcher vehicle

Guidance: inertial

Variant

SS-70: little is known of this new Brazilian weapon, but it may be a development of the X-40 rocket, which can carry a 146-kg (322-lb) payload over a range of 68 km (42 miles)

AVIBRAS SS-300

(Brazil)

Type: single-stage surface-to-surface battlefield missile

Dimensions: diameter 0·93 m (36·6 in); length not revealed

Weight: total round not revealed

Propulsion: one solid-propellant rocket delivering unrevealed thrust

Range limits: not revealed/300 km (not revealed/186 miles)

CEP: not revealed

Warhead: 1000-kg (2,205-lb) HE

Launch: wheeled transporter/erector/launcher vehicle

Guidance: inertial

Variant

SS-300: this Brazilian weapon entered flight test in 1987, and offers modest battlefield capability with a conventional warhead, though a submunition-dispenser type may later be developed; it is also suggested that Brazil is developing a yet-larger missile able to carry a substantial payload to a range of 1000 km (621 miles)

CPMIEC Model M

(China)

Type: single-stage surface-to-surface theatre/battlefield missile

Dimensions: diameter 1·0 m (39·37 in); length 9·10 m (29·86 ft)

Weight: total round 6200 kg (13,668 lb)

Propulsion: one solid-propellant rocket delivering unrevealed thrust

Range limits: not revealed/600 km (not revealed/373 miles)

CEP: not revealed

Warhead: HE fragmentation

Launch: wheeled transporter/erector/launcher vehicle

Guidance: inertial

Variant

Model M: this Chinese weapon is being developed for several theatre and battlefield roles with HE/fragmentation and submunition-dispenser warheads, though a tactical nuclear

warhead is also a possibility; flight trials apparently began in 1986, with service deliveries beginning in late 1988 or early 1989; ranges between 200 and 600 km (124 and 373 miles) are possible; the export version is designated **M-9**

Aérospatiale Hades

(France)

Type: single-stage surface-to-surface theatre/battlefield missile

Dimensions: diameter 0·60 m (1·97 ft); length 8·00 m (26·25 ft); span 1·50 m (4·92 ft)

Weight: total round not revealed

Propulsion: one SNPE/SEP solid-propellant rocket delivering unrevealed thrust

Range limits: not revealed/350 km (not revealed/217 miles)

CEP: not revealed

Warhead: 10/25-kiloton variable-yield nuclear

Launch: trailer-mounted vertical box

Guidance: ESD/Sagem inertial

Variant

Hades: under development for service in the late 1980s or early 1990s, the Hades is designed as the longer-range successor to the Pluton; in 1988 it was announced that France has opted for an improved version of the baseline Hades for service from 1992, this model featuring an increase in range to 500 km (311 miles) and an increase in warhead yield to 500 kilotons to allow deep strikes against operational-level targets in East Germany and farther to the east

Aérospatiale Pluton

(France)

Type: single-stage surface-to-surface battlefield missile

Dimensions: diameter 0·65 m (2·13 ft); length 7·64 m (25·07 ft); span 1·41 m (4·63 ft)

Weight: total round 2423 kg (5,342 lb)

Propulsion: one SEP/SNPE/Aérospatiale dual-thrust solid-propellant rocket delivering unrevealed thrust

Range limits: 10/120 km (6·2/75 miles)

CEP: 330 m (360 yards)

Warhead: 350-kg (772-lb) 15-kiloton nuclear or 500-kg (1,102-lb) 25-kiloton AN 51 nuclear

Launch: box on converted AMX-30 MBT chassis

Guidance: SFENA strap-down inertial

Variant

Pluton: designed in the late 1960s, the Pluton began to enter French service in 1974 and is a capable battlefield weapon with fair accuracy for use primarily against operational-level targets such as transport centres and follow-on troop concentrations; the larger warhead contains the same MR50 nuclear charge as used in the CEA-developed AN 52 free-fall store carried by French strike aircraft

Below: The Pluton is France's first-generation surface-to-surface battlefield missile. This type is relatively unsophisticated and, based on the chassis of the AMX-30 main battle tank, is designed to deliver a low-yield nuclear warhead up to a range of 120 km (75 miles).

Defence Research and Development Laboratory Prithvi

(India)

Type: single-stage surface-to-surface battlefield missile
Dimensions: not revealed
Weight: total round not revealed
Propulsion: one solid-propellant rocket delivering unrevealed thrust
Range limits: not revealed
CEP: not revealed
Warhead: HE
Launch: not revealed
Guidance: strap-down inertial

Variant

Prithvi: first revealed late in 1988, this is a weapon of odd appearance with a comparatively short and fat body, a cruciform of low-aspect-ratio wing half way down the body, and a cruciform of tiny fins indexed in line with the wings

Defence Industries Organization Iran-130

(Iran)

Type: single-stage surface-to-surface battlefield missile
Dimensions: not revealed
Weight: total round not revealed
Propulsion: one solid-propellant rocket delivering unrevealed thrust
Range limits: not revealed/130 km (not revealed/80·8 miles)
CEP: not revealed
Warhead: HE
Launch: not revealed
Guidance: strap-down inertial

Variant

Iran-130: introduced during the closing stages of the Gulf War in 1988, this is an indigenous Iranian development of which virtually nothing is known

Haft-I

(Pakistan)

Type: single-stage surface-to-surface battlefield missile
Dimensions: not revealed
Weight: total round not revealed
Propulsion: one solid-propellant rocket delivering unrevealed thrust
Range limits: not revealed/80 km (not revealed/49·7 miles)
CEP: not revealed
Warhead: HE
Launch: wheeled transporter/erector/launcher vehicle
Guidance: inertial

Variant

Haft-I: no details have been released about this 'Deadly-I' battlefield missile

Haft-II

(Pakistan)

Type: single-stage surface-to-surface tactical/

operational missile
Dimensions: not revealed
Weight: total round not revealed
Propulsion: one solid-propellant rocket delivering unrevealed thrust
Range limits: not revealed/300 km (not revealed/186 miles)
CEP: not revealed
Warhead: 500-kg (1,102-lb) HE
Launch: wheeled transporter/erector/launcher vehicle
Guidance: inertial

Variant

Haft-II: revealed in 1989, this 'Deadly-II' missile is believed to be a development of the Haft-I; no details other than range and claimed warhead weight are known, but the launcher is adapted from the carriage of the British 3·7-in (94-mm) anti-aircraft gun

Ching Feng

(Taiwan)

Type: single-stage surface-to-surface battlefield missile
Dimensions: diameter 0·60 m (23·6 in); length 7·0 m (22·97 ft)
Weight: total round 1400 kg (3,086 lb)
Propulsion: one solid-propellant rocket delivering unrevealed thrust
Range limits: not revealed/120 km (not revealed/75 miles)
CEP: not revealed
Warhead: HE
Launch: not revealed
Guidance: unknown radar-based system

Variant

Ching Feng: this Taiwanese 'Green Bee' missile appears to be based conceptually on the US Lance, though the fins are somewhat smaller and a radar guidance system is used; the weapon was revealed in 1981 and has since been claimed to be the precursor of a more formidable missile with 1000-km (621-mile) range, which may explain the apparent cancellation of the programme under

pressure from the USA, which feared the strategic and political implications of Taiwanese possession of a potentially nuclear-capable missile system able to reach targets on the Chinese mainland

FROG-3

(USSR)

Type: two-stage surface-to-surface battlefield rocket
Dimensions: diameter (warhead) 0·55 m (21·65 in) and (rocket) 0·40 m (15·75 in); length 10·50 m (34·45 ft)
Weight: total round 2250 kg (4,960 lb)
Propulsion: one non-jettisonable solid-propellant booster rocket delivering unrevealed thrust, and one solid-propellant sustainer rocket delivering unrevealed thrust
Range limits: not revealed/40 km (not revealed/25 miles)
CEP: 400 m (440 yards)
Warhead: originally provided with interchangeable 200-kiloton nuclear and 450-kg (992-lb) HE warheads, only the latter now being available to the Soviet allies still using the system
Launch: converted PT-76 amphibious light tank chassis
Guidance: none

Variant

FROG-3: the oldest of the FROG (Free Rocket Over Ground) series still in service, the FROG-3 was introduced in 1957, and now possesses little real value as its CEP is so great; the rocket has the Soviet military name **Luna 2**, but its service and production designations remain unknown

FROG-5

(USSR)

Type: two-stage surface-to-surface battlefield rocket
Dimensions: diameter 0·55 m (21·65 in); length 9·10 m (29·86 ft)
Weight: total round 3000 kg (6,614 lb)
Propulsion: one non-jettisonable solid-propellant booster rocket delivering unrevealed

Below: The FROG-3 is an unguided battlefield rocket now fielded only with an HE warhead.

thrust, and one solid-propellant sustainer rocket delivering unrevealed thrust

Range limits: not revealed/55 km (not revealed/34 miles)

CEP: 400 m (440 yards)

Warhead: originally provided with interchangeable 200-kiloton nuclear and 450-kg (992-lb) HE warheads, only the latter now being available to the Soviet allies still using the system

Launch: converted PT-76 amphibious light tank chassis

Guidance: none

Variant

FROG-5: introduced in the late 1950s or early 1960s, this is a development of the FROG-3 with a revised propulsion system, the body of the rocket being increased in diameter to that of the FROG-3's warhead, in the process being slightly shortened; like the FROG-3, the FROG-5 is now elderly and of only the smallest operational value; the rocket has the Soviet military name **Luna 2**, but its service and production designations remain unknown

FROG-7

(USSR)

Type: single-stage surface-to-surface battlefield rocket

Dimensions: diameter 0·55 m (21·65 in); length 9·10 m (29·86 ft)

Weight: total round 2300 kg (5,071 lb)

Propulsion: one solid-propellant rocket delivering unrevealed thrust

Range limits: 11/70 km (6·8/43 miles)

CEP: 450/700 m (490/765 yards) depending on range

Warhead: 550-kg (1,213-lb) 10-, 100- or 200-kiloton nuclear, or 550-kg (1,213-lb) HE, or 390-kg (860-lb) chemical

Launch: ZIL-135 8 × 8 transporter/erector/launcher vehicle

Guidance: none

Variants

FROG-7A: introduced in 1965, this is the last of a series of FROG (Free Rocket Over Ground) weapons, and is being replaced by the longer-ranged and more accurate SS-21; the rocket has the Soviet military designation **R-65** and the name **Luna M**, and its production designation is **9M21**

FROG-7B: improved version which has the Soviet service designation **R-70**

SS-1C 'Scud-B'

(USSR)

Type: single-stage surface-to-surface battlefield missile

Dimensions: diameter 0·84 m (33·07 in); length 11·40 m (37·40 ft)

Weight: total round 6370 kg (14,043 lb)

Propulsion: one storable liquid-propellant rocket delivering unrevealed thrust

Range limits: 80/180 km (50/112 miles) with nuclear warhead, or 80/280 km (50/174 miles) with HE or chemical warhead

CEP: 930 m (1,015 yards) at maximum range, reducing with shorter range

Warhead: 40/100-kiloton variable-yield nuclear, or 2000-kg (4,409-lb) HE, or chemical

Launch: MAZ-543 8 × 8 transporter/erector/launcher vehicle

Guidance: inertial

Below and above: Carried on the ZIL-135 vehicle, the FROG-7 is the ultimate development of the FROG series, being replaced by longer-ranged, more accurate missiles.

Above: An SS-1C 'Scud-B' powered onto its transporter/erector/launcher vehicle.

Variants

SS-1A 'Scunner': introduced in 1957, this original operational model is no longer in front-line service with the Warsaw Pact, and is a considerably less capable weapon than its successors, having a weight of 4400 kg (9,700 lb) and being able to carry a 40-kiloton (later an HE) warhead over a range of 130 km (81 miles) after launch from its TEL, a converted IS-III heavy tank chassis; the missile has the Soviet military designation **R-1** and the name **Yedinichka**

SS-1B 'Scud-A': introduced in 1965, this is an altogether more capable weapon; the missile has the Soviet military designation **R-11** (sometimes **R-175**) and the production designation **8K11**; the SS-1 series is now being replaced by the SS-23

SS-1C 'Scud-B': introduced in about 1970, this variant has a maximum range boosted to 450 km (280 miles) by a better propellant load, but maximum-range CEP increases to 1100 m (1,205 yards) as a consequence; the missile has the Soviet military designation **R-17E** (sometimes **R-300**) and the production designation **8K14**; with an HE rather than nuclear warhead the missile has been exported to a number of Moslem countries, and of these Iraq has produced two upgraded variants, namely the **Al Hussein** with range increased to 600 km (373 miles) by reduction of the warhead to 250 kg (551 lb), and the **Al Abas** with range increased to 860 km (534 miles) by the addition of booster(s) of local design and manufacture; the Iraqi variants have greater CEPs than the baseline Soviet missile

SS-12B 'Scaleboard-B'

(USSR)
Type: single-stage short-range ballistic missile
Dimensions: diameter 0·94 m (37·00 in); length 12·38 m (40·62 ft)
Weight: total round 9000 kg (19,841 lb); re-entry vehicle not revealed
Propulsion: four solid-propellant rockets each delivering unrevealed thrust
Range limits: 220/800 km (138/497 miles)
CEP: 30 m (33 yards)
Warhead: 1250-kg (2,756-lb) 800-kiloton nuclear

Launch: MAZ-543P 8 × 8 transporter/erector/launcher vehicle
Guidance: inertial with radar or IR terminal homing

Variants
SS-12A 'Scaleboard-A': introduced in 1969, this weapon provides the Soviet army with long-range strategic/operational capability at front (army group) level; the Soviet production and service designations are **8K84** and **RS-10** (sometimes **UR-100**) respectively
SS-12B 'Scaleboard-B': originally designated **SS-22** in Western terminology and subsequently redesignated **SS-12M** in acknowledgement of the Soviet claim that the missile is a development of the SS-12 rather than a new type, this improved SS-12 has the Soviet production designation **9M76** and entered service in 1979, and has different ranges (220 to 880 km/138 to 547 miles) combined with reduced CEP (the original figure of 320 m/350 yards having been considerably reduced in recent years as it became known that the missile has terminal guidance) and alternative 550-kiloton or 1-megaton nuclear warheads that can each be exchanged for a chemical or cluster-munition warhead; the missile has an overall weight of 10,000 kg (22,046 lb), and its dimensions include a diameter of 1·0 m (3·28 ft) and a length of 12·0 m (39·37 ft)

Right: The SS-21 is one of the most important weapons in the Soviets' tactical arsenal.

SS-21 'Scarab'

(USSR)
Type: single-stage surface-to-surface battlefield missile
Dimensions: diameter 0·46 m (18·11 in); length 9·44 m (30·84 ft)
Weight: total round 3000 kg (6,614 lb)
Propulsion: one solid-propellant rocket delivering unrevealed thrust
Range limits: 14/200 km (8·75/125 miles)
CEP: 50/100 m (55/110 yards)
Warhead: 10- or 100-kiloton nuclear, or 450-kg (992-lb) HE (unitary, anti-armour cluster, anti-personnel cluster or anti-runway), or chemical
Launch: ZIL-5937 6 × 6 transporter/erector/launcher vehicle
Guidance: inertial

Variant
SS-21 'Scarab': introduced in 1976, this system is designed to replace the FROG series, and is deployed at front (army group) level as a primary means of removing NATO defensive positions slowing or halting the main axes of Soviet advance; the type is known to the Soviets as the **Tochka** (point), though its production and service designations remain unknown; data about the missile are largely conjectural, another set of data suggesting considerably different dimensions including a diameter of 0·65 m (2·13 ft), a length of 6·2 m (20·34 ft) and a span of 1·2 m (3·94 ft), different weights including a total round mass of 1500 kg (3,307 lb) and a warhead mass of 250 kg (551 lb) and different performance including a range of 100 km (62 miles) at a speed of Mach 3; the three-man TEL is basically similar to that of the SA-8 'Gecko' land-mobile SAM system, with a weight of 15,000 kg (33,069 lb), a length of 9·55 m (31·33 ft), a width of 2·78 m (9·12 ft), a height of 2·27 m (7·45 ft), and a 60-km/h (37·3-mph) maximum speed on the power of its 130-kW (175-hp) ZIL-375 diesel engine

SS-23 'Spider'

(USSR)

Type: single-stage short-range ballistic missile
Dimensions: diameter 0·89 m (35·04 in); length 7·52 m (24·67 ft)
Weight: total round 4690 kg (10,340 lb)
Propulsion: one solid-propellant rocket delivering unrevealed thrust
Range limits: 80/500 km (50/311 miles)
CEP: 30 m (33 yards)
Warhead: 100-kiloton nuclear, or chemical or cluster munition
Launch: MAZ-543 8 × 8 transporter/erector/launcher vehicle
Guidance: inertial with radar or IR terminal homing

Variant

SS-23 'Spider': introduced in 1980, this is the Soviet replacement for the 'Scud' series, and offers significantly reduced time into action as well as better range and CEP, the latter having been reduced in Western analysis to the current figure when it became apparent that the missile is a member of the Soviet 'reconnaissance strike' family with terminal guidance; the Soviet production and service designations for the type are **9M714** and **OTR-23** respectively

Douglas MGR-1B Honest John

(USA)

Type: single-stage surface-to-surface battlefield missile
Dimensions: diameter 2·50 ft (0·76 m); length 24·84 ft (7·57 ft)
Weight: total round 4,710 lb (2136 kg)
Propulsion: one solid-propellant rocket delivering unrevealed thrust

Range limits: 4·5/23 miles (7·2/37 km)
CEP: 910 yards (830 m)
Warhead: 2-, 20- or 40-kiloton W31 nuclear, or 1,500-lb (680-kg) HE or cluster munition, or 1,243-lb (564-kg) chemical
Launch: 6 × 6 truck transporter/erector/launcher vehicle
Guidance: none

Variant

MGR-1B Honest John: introduced in 1960 to replace the 1953-vintage MRG-1A initial version, the MGR-1B is an obsolescent system combining a powerful warhead and good cross-country mobility with the accuracy and range of tube artillery, but in the non-nuclear role offering limited offensive capability only at considerable cost

Below: The MGR-1B Honest John is an obsolete battlefield rocket system.

Martin Marietta MGM-31B Pershing II

(USA)

Type: two-stage medium-range ballistic missile
Dimensions: diameter 3·28 ft (1·00 m); length 34·45 ft (10·50 m)
Weight: total round 16,000 lb (7257 kg)
Propulsion: (first stage) one Hercules XM101 solid-propellant rocket delivering unrevealed thrust, and (second stage) one Hercules solid-propellant rocket delivering unrevealed thrust
Range limits: not revealed/1,125 miles (not revealed/1810 km)
CEP: 22-49 yards (20-45 m)
Warhead: 650-lb (295-kg) 5/50-kiloton selectable-yield W85 air/surface-burst or W86 earth-penetrating nuclear
Launch: M656 truck/trailer-mounted

transporter/erector/launcher vehicle
Guidance: Singer-Kearfott inertial plus Goodyear RADAG terminal homing

Variants

MGM-31A Pershing IA: introduced in 1969 as a long-range battlefield interdiction missile, the Pershing IA is derived from the 1962-vintage MGM-31 Pershing I deployed on the M474 tracked launch vehicle; the Pershing IA changes to the M656 truck/trailer TEL, is 34·78 ft (10·60 m) long, weighs 10,140 lb (4600 kg), is powered by one Thiokol XM105 solid-propellant booster rocket delivering 26,750-lb (12,134-kg) thrust and one Thiokol XM106 solid-propellant sustainer rocket delivering 15,560-lb (7058-kg) thrust, and carries a 1,650-lb (748-kg) 60/400-kiloton variable-yield W50 air-burst nuclear warhead over a range of 100/460 miles (161/740 km) with a CEP of 400 yards (365 m) under the guidance of a Bendix inertial navigation system

MGM-31B Pershing II: introduced in 1985, the Pershing II is a modular upgrading of the Pershing IA with far greater range and other system improvements, the most important of which is the RADAG (RADar Area Guidance) terminal homing, which reduces the CEP to so low a figure that a much smaller warhead (W85 surface/air-burst or W86 earth-penetrator) can be carried; the range and extreme accuracy of the weapon mean that even with a small warhead the type has operational and limited strategic capabilities

Below: The MGM-52C Lance remains an important battlefield nuclear missile system.

Vought MGM-52C Lance

(USA)
Type: single-stage battlefield support missile
Dimensions: diameter 1·83 ft (0·56 m); length 20·25 ft (6·17 m)
Weight: total round 3,373 lb (1530 kg) with nuclear warhead or 3,920 lb (1778 kg) with conventional warhead
Propulsion: two Rocketdyne T22 dual-thrust storable liquid-propellant rockets each delivering unrevealed thrust
Range limits: 3/75 miles (4·8/121 km)
CEP: 500 yards (455 m)
Warhead: 467-lb (212-kg) 1-, 10- or 50-kiloton selectable-yield W70-1/2/3 nuclear or 0·5-kiloton enhanced-radiation W70-4 nuclear, or 1,000-lb (454-kg) M251 cluster munition
Launch: M752 tracked transporter/erector/launcher vehicle
Guidance: E-Systems/Sys-Donner/Arma simplified inertial

Variant

MGM-52C Lance: introduced in 1972 as replacement for the Sergeant and Honest John weapons, the Lance is a highly capable but obsolescent battlefield missile able to deliver an assortment of alternative warheads, including the W70-4 'neutron' type and the M251 cluster munition type with 836 0·95-lb (0·43-kg) anti-personnel/anti-materiel bomblets to saturate a circle of 900-yard (820-m) diameter; NATO is currently debating the political feasibility of a Lance replacement with greater ease of maintenance and a faster response time

Vought Tactical Missile System

(USA)
Type: single-stage battlefield support missile
Dimensions: diameter 2·00 ft (0·61 m); length 13·00 ft (3·96 m)
Weight: total round not revealed
Propulsion: one Atlantic Research solid-propellant rocket delivering unrevealed thrust
Range limits: not revealed
CEP: not revealed
Warhead: cluster munition containing 1,000 M42 or M74 anti-personnel and anti-materiel bomblets
Launch: MLRS tracked transporter/erector/launcher vehicle
Guidance: Honeywell inertial

Variant

TACMS: evolved from the US Army's wide-ranging Assault Breaker programme to deliver deep attacks on the enemy's rear echelons, the TACMS (TACtical Missile System) weapon is currently under development with a large payload of APAMB submunitions carried over twice the range possible with the Lance missile to meet the quadruple requirement of attacking rear-echelon armour formations, of destroying high-value targets (helicopter refuelling and rearming sites, fuel dumps, ammunition dumps, missile batteries etc), of destroying the enemy's rear-area headquarters and communications centres, and of suppressing the enemy's air-defence capability to open lanes for air strikes; the payload of a single missile is thought capable of destroying a company-sized target or of delaying a battalion-sized target, while the payloads of four or six TACMS weapons are believed adequate to destroy a tank battalion; other payloads being considered or developed are a Martin Marietta dedicated anti-armour warhead (probably with a terminal seeker), a unitary hard-target warhead (with enhanced guidance based on the Global Positioning System), an anti-airfield warhead using Hunting SG357 runway-cratering submunitions (again with enhanced guidance based on the GPS), and a mine-scattering warhead; the TACMS is carried by the same basic launcher as the Vought Multiple-Launch Rocket System, the launcher unit being modified to take two TACMS missiles rather than 12 MLRS rockets

CPMIEC HQ-2J

(China)
Type: area defence tactical surface-to-air missile
Dimensions: diameter (missile) 0·50 m (19·69 in) and (booster) 0·70 m (27·56 in); length overall 10·70 m (35·10 ft); span (missile) 1·70 m (5·58 ft) and (booster) 2·20 m (7·22 ft)
Weight: total round 2300 kg (5,071 lb)
Warhead: 130-kg (286·6-lb) HE fragmentation
Propulsion: one jettisonable solid-propellant booster rocket delivering an unrevealed thrust, and one liquid-propellant sustainer rocket delivering an unrevealed thrust
Performance: speed Mach 3·5; range limits not revealed/50 km (not revealed/31·1 miles); altitude limits not revealed/18,000 m (not revealed 59,055 ft)
Guidance: radar command

Variant

HQ-2: this is the Chinese version of the Soviet SA-2 'Guideline' SAM; earlier models of the HQ-2

(presumably the HQ-2A to HQ-2H versions) are essentially identical to members of the Soviet family, but while photographs of the HQ-2J show this first export-available variant to be externally close to the SA-2 system in its missile and associated radars, the Chinese claim that the missile has a new type of warhead

CPMIEC HQ-61

(China)

Type: point defence tactical surface-to-air missile
Dimensions: diameter 0·286 m (11·26 in); length 3·99 m (13·09 ft); span 1·166 m (45·9 in)
Weight: total round 300 kg (661 lb)
Warhead: HE fragmentation
Propulsion: one solid-propellant rocket delivering unrevealed thrust
Performance: speed Mach 3; range limits 3000/10,000 m (3,280/10,935 yards); altitude limits 0/8000 m (0/26,245 ft)
Guidance: strapdown inertial for midcourse phase and continuous-wave semi-active radar for terminal phase

Variant

HQ-61: this Chinese-developed SAM bears a resemblance to the American Sparrow series, but is larger and heavier than the US weapon; the weapon is associated with a twin launcher located on a 6 × 6 chassis; the missile is used with a Chinese radar based on the Soviet 'Flat Face'

Below: Fire units of the Crotale 4000 series with the R.440 short-range surface-to-air missile.

Matra R.440

(France)

Type: point defence tactical surface-to-air missile
Dimensions: diameter 0·15 m (5·9 in); length 2·89 m (9·48 ft); span 0·54 m (21·25 in)
Weight: total round 85 kg (187·4 lb)
Warhead: 15-kg (33-lb) HE fragmentation
Propulsion: one SNPE Lens solid-propellant rocket delivering 4850-kg (10,962-lb) thrust
Performance: speed Mach 2·3; range limits 500/13,000 m (545/14,215 yards) against helicopters and non-manoeuvring targets, or 500/8500 m (545/9,295 yards) against manoeuvring targets, or 500/6500 m (545/7,110 yards) against low-altitude and sea-skimming targets; altitude limits 15/5000 m (50/16,405 ft)
Guidance: Thomson-CSF radar command with IR/radar gathering and tracking

Variant

R.440: entering service in 1971 after development from 1964, the R.440 SAM is designed for use in the Cactus and Crotale land-based SAM systems, and is intended for all-weather close-range engagement of aircraft flying at up to Mach 1·2; the same basic missile is used in the Naval Crotale system; the missile has canard configuration, a powder propulsion rocket and a capable IR fuse designed to initiate warhead detonation according to intercept geometry calculations or by impact; the lethal radius of the warhead is 8 m (26·25 ft), which is apparently less by a considerable margin than the likely miss distance; single-shot kill probability is thus claimed as 80%, rising to 96% for a salvo; the missile accelerates to its maximum speed of Mach 2·3 in 2·3 seconds, and reaches 8000 m (8,750 yards) in 20 seconds

Matra R.460

(France)

Type: point defence tactical surface-to-air missile
Dimensions: diameter 0·156 m (6·14 in); length 3·15 m (10·33 ft); span 0·59 m (23·23 in)
Weight: total round 100 kg (220·5 lb)
Warhead: 14-kg (30·9-lb) HE fragmentation
Propulsion: one SNPE Lens dual-thrust solid-propellant rocket delivering unrevealed thrust
Performance: speed Mach 2·5; range limits 500/12,000 m (545/13,125 yards); altitude limits 15/6000 m (50/19,685 ft)
Guidance: Thomson-CSF radar command with IR/radar gathering and tracking

Variant

R.460: a version of the R.440 with longer range and greater speed, the R.460 entered service in 1982, and is designed for used with the Shahine AFV-based battlefield SAM system

Matra Mistral

(France)

Type: point defence tactical surface-to-air missile
Dimensions: diameter 0·90 m (3·54 in); length 1·80 m (5·91 ft); span 0·19 m (7·48 in)
Weight: total round 17 kg (37·5 lb)
Warhead: 3-kg (6·6-lb) HE fragmentation
Propulsion: one SEP solid-propellant booster rocket delivering unrevealed thrust and one SEP solid-propellant sustainer rocket delivering unrevealed thrust
Performance: speed Mach 2·6; range 500/6000 m (545/6,560 yards); altitude limits 0/3000 m (0/9,845 ft)

Guidance: SAT passive IR homing

Variant
Mistral: entering service in 1989, this lightweight SAM is designed for land and naval use (and also for the protection of battlefield helicopters in the air-to-air role)

Euromissile Roland 1 and 2

(France/West Germany)
Type: point defence tactical surface-to-air missile
Dimensions: diameter 0·16 m (6·3 in); length 2·40 m (7·87 ft); span 0·50 m (19·7 in)
Weight: total round 66·5 kg (146·6 lb)
Warhead: 6·5-kg (14·3-lb) HE fragmentation
Propulsion: one SNPE Roubaix solid-propellant booster rocket delivering 1600-kg (3,527-lb) thrust for 2 seconds, and one SNPE Lampyre solid-propellant sustainer rocket delivering 200-kg (441-lb) thrust for 13·2 seconds
Performance: speed Mach 1·6; range limits 500/ 6300 m (545/6,890 yards); altitude limits 20/5500 m (65/18,045 ft)
Guidance: IR gathering then optical (Roland 1) or radar (Roland 2 and 3) semi-automatic radar command to line of sight

Variants
Roland 1: designed from the early 1960s by the antecedents of MBB (West Germany) and Aéro-spatiale (France) working as Euromissile, the Roland 1 was intended as a clear-weather low-altitude SAM for use by France on the AMX-30R converted MBT chassis and for export; the type entered service in 1981
Roland 2: produced in parallel with the Roland 1 for the West German army, the Roland 2 is designed for all-weather operation on the chassis of the Marder MICV; this system is similar to the French Roland 1 up to the time the target is designated to the alternative poor-weather tracking

Below: The AMX-30R launch unit for the Roland 2 short-range surface-to-air missile.

system, which is in this case a Thomson-CSF monopulse radar; in US service this missile is known as the **MIM-115 Roland**, produced under licence in the USA by Hughes and Boeing with a different fuse and improved ECCM
Roland 3: introduced in 1985 on the basis of the Roland 2, the Roland 3 overcomes some of the earlier model's performance shortcomings by introducing a more powerful motor to boost maximum speed to Mach 1·9 and maximum range to 8000 m (8,750 yards); otherwise the missile is closely akin to the Roland 2, and designed like that weapon for all-weather engagements with radar guidance

Selenia Aspide 1A

(Italy)
Type: area defence tactical surface-to-air missile
Dimensions: diameter 0·203 m (8·00 in); length 3·70 m (12·14 ft); span 0·80 m (31·5 in)
Weight: total round 220 kg (485 lb)
Warhead: 35-kg (77-lb) HE fragmentation
Propulsion: one SNIA-Viscosa solid-propellant rocket delivering unrevealed thrust
Performance: speed Mach 4; range limits not revealed/15,000 m (not revealed/16,405 yards); altitude limits not revealed/5000 m (not revealed/16,405 ft)
Guidance: Selenia semi-active radar homing

Variants
Aspide 1A: this is basically similar to the Aspide air-to-air missile, in this instance differing only in the cropping of the wings to fit the surface system's quadruple or octuple launcher; a single-shot kill probability of more than 70% is claimed
Spada: this is the land-based equivalent of the Albatros naval system, and was designed for the protection of small strategic areas against satura-tion attack; the system is based on a sextuple laun-cher for Aspide missiles supported by search and interrogation radars, tracking and illuminat-ing radars and control units, all integrated into a high-level air-defence system able to deal with single or multiple, sequential or saturation attacks at all levels in conditions of heavy electronic countermeasures; at the heart of the individual system is the detection centre (one Selenia Pluto F-band search and interrogation radar, and one operational control centre with three operational consoles and a data-processing system based on two digital computers), which can designate tar-gets to three firing sections; the latter each com-prise a fire-control centre with its target acquisition and illumination radar (based on the Selenia Orion 30X), back-up optronic sensor and control equipment; each fire-control centre can co-ordinate three six-tube missile launchers

Toshiba Type 81

(Japan)
Type: point defence tactical surface-to-air missile
Dimensions: diameter 0·16 m (6·3 in); length 2·70 m (8·86 ft); span 0·60 m (23·6 in)
Weight: total round 100 kg (220 lb)
Warhead: HE fragmentation
Propulsion: one Nissan Motors solid-propellant rocket delivering 8400-kg (18,519-lb) thrust
Performance: speed Mach 2·4; range limits not revealed/7000 m (not revealed/7,655 yards); alti-tude limits not revealed/3000 m (not revealed/ 9,845 ft)

Guidance: Toshiba inertial for midcourse phase and IR for terminal phase

Variant
Type 81: developed with great delays as the **Toshiba Tan-SAM** from the 1960s, the Type 81 entered Japanese service only in 1981; the type was designed for land-mobility, and the four-round launcher is carried on the rear of a Type 73 6 × 6 truck, two launchers being accompanied by a fire-control vehicle with a phased-array pulse-Doppler 3D surveillance and acquisition radar; this radar can detect targets at a range of between 20,000 and 30,000 m (21,875 and 32,810 yards), and six targets can be tracked simultaneously, two targets being passed to each fire unit; here interception courses are loaded into the autopilot as the seeker head's search pattern is activated; the missile flies on autopilot until the target's IR signature is detected and locked into the terminal guidance system; an optronic fire-control system is built into each launcher for use in severe ECM conditions

Bofors Rbs 70 Rayrider

(Sweden)
Type: point defence tactical surface-to-air missile
Dimensions: (without booster) diameter 0·106 m (4·17 in); length 1·32 m (4·33 ft); span 0·32 m (12·6 in)
Weight: total round 15 kg (33·07 lb)
Warhead: 1-kg (2·2-lb) HE fragmentation
Propulsion: one Bofors solid-propellant booster rocket delivering unrevealed thrust, and one IMI solid-propellant sustainer rocket delivering unrevealed thrust
Performance: speed supersonic; range limits not revealed/5000 m (not revealed/5,470 yards); altitude limits 0/3000 m (0/9,845 ft)
Guidance: laser beam-riding

Variants
Rbs 70 Rayrider: developed in the late 1960s and early 1970s, the Rbs 70 comprises a stand (comprising a post with tripod legs), a sight unit and 24-kg (52·9-lb) container with preloaded missile; once fired, the missile is gathered into the sight unit's field of vision and then rides the sight's laser straight to the target, where the detonating warhead fills its lethal volume with heavy metal pellets; the empty container can then be replaced by a full one for another engagement; a time of six seconds is claimed as the minimum from target detection to missile launch
Rbs 70 APC: simplified version of the Rbs 70 ARMAD designed for location in the open hatch of armoured personnel carriers
Rbs 70 ARMAD: updated version comprising an APC-compatible turret housing the Rbs 70 system (on an elevating arm), seven missiles and an Ericsson HARD 3D pulse-Doppler surveillance and target-designation radar; a time of 4 seconds is claimed as the minimum from target detection to missile launch
Rbs 70 VL: version of the basic model designed for mounting on the rear of trucks or on the turret rings of light AFVs; six reload missiles are carried, and the system is intended for use by mobile formations with organic search and target-acquisition radars so that the Rbs 70 VL crew can be provided with target bearing and range information
Rbs 70M Nightrider: night-capable version using the same basic technology as the RBS 70 Rayrider, but featuring an updated **Rbs 70X** mis-

sile with a larger sustainer rocket and heavier warhead used on a remotely controlled launcher complete with TV and IR cameras and the laser transmitter

Chung Shan Institute of Science and Technology Tien Kung I

(Taiwan)
Type: area defence tactical surface-to-air missile
Dimensions: not revealed
Weight: total round not revealed
Warhead: HE fragmentation
Propulsion: one solid-propellant rocket delivering unrevealed thrust
Performance: speed supersonic; range limits not revealed/40 km (not revealed/24·85 miles); altitude limits not revealed
Guidance: semi-active radar

Variant
Tien Kung I: this Taiwanese weapon is based conceptually on the MIM-104 Patriot of US origin; no details have been released but it is known that this 'Sky Bow' missile was first test-fired in 1986

Chung Shan Institute of Science and Technology Tien Kung II

(Taiwan)
Type: area defence tactical surface-to-air missile
Dimensions: not revealed
Weight: total round not revealed
Warhead: HE fragmentation
Propulsion: one integral solid-propellant rocket/ramjet delivering unrevealed thrust
Performance: speed supersonic; range limits not revealed/100+ km (not revealed/62·1+ miles); altitude limits not revealed
Guidance: not revealed

Variant
Tien Kung II: due to enter service in the early 1990s, this missile resembles the MIM-14B Nike Hercules in size and performance, but is an altogether more advanced weapon of which no details have been released

ABM-1B 'Galosh'

(USSR)
Type: three-stage exoatmospheric strategic anti-ballistic missile missile
Dimensions: diameter 2·57 m (8·43 ft); length 19·80 m (64·96 ft); span not revealed
Weight: total round 32,700 kg (72,090 lb)
Warhead: 3/5-megaton thermonuclear
Propulsion: (first stage) storable liquid-propellant rocket delivering unrevealed thrust, (second stage) storable liquid-propellant rocket delivering unrevealed thrust, and (third stage) storable liquid-propellant rocket delivering unrevealed thrust
Performance: speed hypersonic; range limits not revealed/740 km (not revealed/460 miles); altitude limits not revealed
Guidance: radar command

Variant
ABM-1B 'Galosh': introduced in the early 1960s as the world's first ABM missile, the 'Galosh' has the Soviet service designation **UR-96** and was designed for exoatmospheric interception of ballistic missiles, which it destroys with the electromagnetic pulse and fast radiation effects of its substantial nuclear warhead; the type remains a truly formidable system that the Soviets are updating with new radar and command systems; the most important radars are six phased-array warning radars, and 11 'Hen House' long-range warning radars supported by 'Dog House' and 'Cat House' medium-range battle-management radars in support of the 'Try Add' engagement radars

ABM-2

(USSR)
Type: exoatmospheric strategic anti-ballistic missile missile
Dimensions: not revealed
Weight: total round not revealed
Warhead: not revealed
Propulsion: not revealed
Performance: speed hypersonic; range limits not revealed; altitude limits not revealed
Guidance: radar command

Variant
ABM-2: originally known by the temporary designation **SH-04** (derived from the test site at Sary Shagan where the type was first observed), the ABM-2 is believed to be an advanced development of the ABM-1B 'Galosh'

ABM-3 'Gazelle'

(USSR)
Type: endoatmospheric anti-ballistic missile missile
Dimensions: not revealed
Weight: total round not revealed
Warhead: not revealed
Propulsion: not revealed
Performance: speed hypersonic; range limits not revealed; altitude limits not revealed
Guidance: semi-active radar for the midcourse phase and active radar for the terminal phase

Variant
ABM-3 'Gazelle': this is a highly advanced ABM missile used in conjunction with 'Flat Twin' and 'Pawn Shop' phased-array radars; virtually nothing in the way of detail is known of this advanced complement to the ABM-1 'Galosh'; the type was formerly known in the West as the **SH-08**; it is possible, however, that the designation refers to a versatile silo-launch system able to handle an SH-04 exoatmospheric or SH-08 endoatmospheric missile

SA-1 'Guild'

(USSR)
Type: area defence tactical/operational surface-to-air missile
Dimensions: diameter 0·70 m (27·56 in); length 12·00 m (39·37 ft); span 1·10 m (43·31 in)
Weight: total round 3200 kg (7,055 lb)
Warhead: HE fragmentation
Propulsion: probably one solid-propellant

booster rocket delivering unrevealed thrust and one liquid-propellant rocket delivering unrevealed thrust
Performance: speed supersonic; range limits not revealed/50 km (not revealed/32·1 miles); altitude limits not revealed
Guidance: radio command or semi-active/active radar

Variant
SA-1 'Guild': the world's second operational surface-to-air missile when it entered service in 1954 as a high-altitude destroyer of strategic bombers, the 'Guild' was for its time a stupendous technical achievement and is still a reserve weapon in the USSR; the missile itself is capable, but the real efficiency of the system derives largely from the associated 'Yo-Yo' radar, which is very powerful and can track some 30 targets simultaneously; the missile has the Soviet service designation **R-113**

SA-2 'Guideline'

(USSR)
Type: two-stage area defence tactical surface-to-air missile
Dimensions: diameter (missile) 0·50 m (19·69 in) and (booster) 0·70 m (27·56 in); length (typical overall) 10·70 m (35·10 ft); span (missile) 1·70 m (5·58 ft) and (booster) 2·20 m (7·22 ft)
Weight: total round 2300 kg (5,071 lb)
Warhead: 130-kg (286·6-lb) HE fragmentation
Propulsion: one jettisonable solid-propellant booster rocket delivering unrevealed, and one solid-propellant (some sources claim liquid-propellant) sustainer rocket delivering unrevealed thrust
Performance: speed Mach 3·5; range limits not revealed/50 km (not revealed/31 miles); altitude limits not revealed/18,000 m (not revealed/59,055 ft)
Guidance: radar command

Variant
SA-2 'Guideline': introduced in 1958 as an aerodynamic development of the SA-1 and designed for the same high-altitude bomber-destroying role, the 'Guideline' was for some two decades the most important surface-to-air missile in the world and produced in a number of variants; the

Below: SA-2 'Guideline' surface-to-air missiles on their resupply vehicles.

missile has the Soviet service designation **V-75** (or **S-75**) and name **Dvina**, but its production designation remains unknown; the type is associated with the 'Fan Song' fire-control radar, additional warning and height information being supplied by other radars; the 'Guideline' is currently operational in **SA-2B**, **SA-2C**, **SA-2D**, **SA-2E** and **SA-2F** versions, the last being capable of engagements as low as 100 m (330 ft)

SA-5 'Gammon'

(USSR)
Type: area defence tactical/operational surface-to-air missile
Dimensions: diameter 0·85 m (33·46 in); length 10·60 m (34·78 ft); span 2·90 m (9·51 ft)
Weight: total round not revealed
Warhead: nuclear or HE fragmentation
Propulsion: four jettisonable solid-propellant booster rockets each delivering unrevealed thrust, and one liquid-propellant sustainer rocket delivering unrevealed thrust
Performance: speed Mach 4+; range limits 60/300 km (37·3/186 miles); altitude limits not revealed/29,000 m (not revealed/95,145 ft)
Guidance: probably radar command for the midcourse phase and semi-active radar for the terminal phase

Below: The SA-3 'Goa' surface-to-air missile is a two-stage weapon, the section with rectangular fins dropping away once the solid-propellant booster rocket has burned out.

Variant
SA-5 'Gammon': introduced in the early 1960s, the SA-5 (which has the Soviet service designation **S-200** and is probably called **Volga**) is the 'high' component of the SA-3/SA-5 'low/high' air-defence mix (three SA-3 battalions to two SA-5 battalions for the protection of targets within the USSR); the type has frequently been identified with the massive and often-displayed RZ-25 SAM allocated the reporting name 'Griffon' by Western analysts, but this is now believed to have been a prototype weapon revealed by the Soviets for disinformation purposes; no photograph of the SA-5 has been revealed publicly in the West, but it is known that the weapon was designed for the interception of medium- and high-altitude targets (aircraft, short/medium-range missiles and, under some circumstances, ballistic missiles); the type is thought to have the option of HE or low-yield nuclear warheads (in a terminal stage that may be powered), and the associated radar is the 'Square Pair' system for target tracking and missile guidance, target detection being provided by 'Back Net' or 'Bar Lock' radars, and height-finding by a 'Side Net' radar; the type is now thought to be obsolescent in the face of the latest Western ECM; it is possible that the type has been produced in three versions as the **SA-5A** initial-production version first deployed in 1960 with a conventional warhead, the **SA-5B** first deployed in 1970 with a nuclear warhead, and the **SA-5C** first deployed in 1975 with optional HE or nuclear warheads and enhanced terminal manoeuvring capability

SA-4B 'Ganef'

(USSR)
Type: area defence tactical surface-to-air missile
Dimensions: diameter 0·90 m (35·43 in); length 8·80 m (28·87 ft); span (wings) 2·30 m (7·74 ft) and (tail) 2·60 m (8·53 ft)
Weight: total round 1800 kg (3,968 lb)
Warhead: 135-kg (297·6-lb) HE fragmentation
Propulsion: four jettisonable solid-propellant booster rockets each delivering unrevealed thrust, and one sustainer ramjet delivering unrevealed thrust
Performance: speed Mach 2·5; range limits 9·3/50 km (5·8/31·1 miles); altitude limits 1100/24,000 m (3,610/78,740 ft)
Guidance: radio command for midcourse phase and semi-active radar for terminal phase

Variant
SA-4 'Ganef': introduced in the early 1960s, the SA-4 has the Soviet production designation **3M8**

Above: Two SA-4A 'Ganef' surface-to-air missiles on their fire unit vehicle.

(later changed to **9M8**) and the service name **Krug**, and is widely used by the Warsaw Pact forces as the rear-area SAM component within the Soviet doctrine of front-line air defence in depth; the weapons are carried in pairs on a hydraulically operated ramp/turntable on a tracked chassis derived from that of the GMZ minelayer, and are generally salvo-fired in pairs in conjunction with the 'Long Track' surveillance, 'Thin Skin' height-finding and 'Pat Hand' fire-control radars; the 'Ganef' has been produced in four versions (original 3M8, improved **3M8M**, updated **9M8M1** and definitive **9M8M2**), the last two being the current versions, with the first of them (**SA-4A**) optimized for a lower effective ceiling (down to 300 m/985 ft) and the other (**SA-4B** with a longer nose producing a length of 9·00 m/29·53 ft) for greater range and ceiling; some reports attribute a weight of 2500 kg (5,511 lb)

SA-3 'Goa'

(USSR)
Type: two-stage area defence tactical surface-to-air missile
Dimensions: diameter (missile) 0·46 m (18·1 in) and (booster) 0·701 m (27·6 in); length overall 6·70 m (21·98 ft); span (missile) 1·22 m (4·00 ft) and (booster) 1·50 m (4·92 ft)
Weight: total round 946 kg (2,085·5 lb)
Warhead: 60-kg (132-lb) HE fragmentation
Propulsion: one jettisonable solid-propellant booster rocket delivering unrevealed thrust, and one solid-propellant sustainer rocket delivering unrevealed thrust
Performance: speed Mach 2·1; range limits 6000/22,000 m (6,560/24,060 yards); altitude limits 50/15,250 m (165/50,030 ft)
Guidance: radar command

Variant
SA-3A 'Goa': introduced in 1961 as a short-range SAM intended primarily for operation against low-flying targets, the comparatively small 'Goa' has the Soviet production designations **5B24** and

5V27U, the military designations **S-125** and military name **Pechora**; the 'Goa' is a two-stage missile at first carried on a two-rail launcher on the back of 6 × 6 trucks; more recently the Yugoslavs have introduced a three-rail launcher, and the Soviets have in turn produced a four-rail type; warning and target acquisition are provided by 'Flat Face' radar, and guidance is entrusted to I/J-band 'Low Blow' radar

---

SA-6 'Gainful'

(USSR)
Type: area defence tactical surface-to-air missile
Dimensions: diameter 0·335 m (13·2 in); length 5·80 m (19·03 ft); span 1·524 m (5·00 ft)
Weight: total round 550 kg (1,212 lb)
Warhead: 80-kg (176·4-lb) HE fragmentation
Propulsion: one integral solid-propellant rocket-ramjet delivering unrevealed thrust
Performance: speed Mach 2·8; range limits 4/30 m (2·5/18·6 miles) at low altitude or 4/60 km (2·5/37·3 miles) at high altitude; altitude limits 100/12,000 m (330/39,370 ft)
Guidance: radio command for the midcourse phase and semi-active radar for the terminal phase

Variants
SA-6A 'Gainful': though a potent weapon when introduced to Soviet service in the mid-1960s and used by the Arab armies in the 1973 war with Israel, the single-stage SA-6 has the Soviet production designation **9M9** and is now obsolescent through lack of capability against Western ECM; the missiles are carried on triple launchers mounted on a chassis derived from that of the ZSU-23-4 quadruple 23-mm AA gun mounting, and are used in conjunction with the 'Long Track' surveillance radar, 'Thin Skin' height-finding radar and 'Straight Flush' fire-control radar; though the type has not been upgraded electronically, system improvements have considerable enhanced performance compared with that of early models, which had a maximum range of 22,000 m (24,060 yards) and a ceiling of 9000 m (29,530 ft)
SA-6B Mod 1 'Gainful': interim improved type (Soviet production designation **9M9M**) using the combined launcher/guidance radar vehicle of the SA-11 'Gadfly' system with a three-rail SA-6 fit

Above: The SA-6 'Gainful' surface-to-air missile at the moment of launch.

SA-7A 'Grail'

(USSR)

Type: man-portable point defence tactical surface-to-air missile

Dimensions: diameter 0·07 m (2·75 in); length 1·30 m (4·27 ft); span not revealed

Weight: total round 9·2 kg (20·3 lb)

Warhead: 2·5-kg (5·5-lb) HE fragmentation

Propulsion: one solid-propellant dual-thrust rocket delivering unrevealed thrust

Performance: speed Mach 1·5; range limits not revealed/3600 m (not revealed/3,935 yards); altitude limits 45/1500 m (150/4,920 ft)

Guidance: IR homing

Variants

SA-7A 'Grail': developed in the early 1960s, the 'Grail' is known in Soviet production terminology as the **9M32** and by the service name **Strela-2**; it is a simple weapon used by two-man teams (one carrying the firing unit and a missile, and the other carrying a reload missile) for short-range air defence of front-line units; operations soon revealed that the type was prone to chasing decoys, and was also ineffective against the faster type of tactical target

SA-7B 'Grail': improved model with an IFF system and a more powerful motor, increasing speed to Mach 1·7 and ceiling to 4800 m (15,750 ft); the type has also been seen on a four-round launcher carried on light vehicles

Ayn as-Sakr: Egyptian development of the SA-7B with a number of improvements (Rank Pullin night sight, Thomson-CSF IFF, Thomson Brandt digital electronics in place of the Soviet analog electronics, and Teledyne seeker) to increase tactical capabilities with a range of 4400 m (4,810 yards) and a ceiling of 2400 m (7,875 ft)

HN-5 Red Tassel: designation of the SA-7 made in China; the original version was the HN-5 capable only of pursuit engagement of jet aircraft (but head-on engagement of helicopters), while the improved **HN-5A** has a more powerful warhead, greater detection range by use of a cooled seeker, and better discrimination against alternative IR sources; the **HN-5C** is the version used on a mobile system introduced by the Chinese in 1986 with eight ready-to-launch missiles (four missiles on each side of the powered fire-control turret and its IR tracker, TV monitor and laser rangefinder) and eight reloads in the hull of the HRB-320 cross-country vehicle

Above: SA-7 'Grail' short-range surface-to-air missiles pedestal-mounted on light vehicles.

Above: Containerized SA-8B 'Gecko' surface-to-air missiles on their ZRK Romb fire unit vehicle.

SA-8A 'Gecko'

(USSR)

Type: point defence tactical surface-to-air missile

Dimensions: diameter 0·21 m (8·25 in); length 3·20 m (10·50 ft); span 0·64 m (25·2 in)

Weight: total round 190 kg (419 lb)

Warhead: 40-kg (88-lb) HE fragmentation

Propulsion: one solid-propellant dual-thrust rocket delivering unrevealed thrust

Performance: speed Mach 2; range limits 1600/12,000 m (1,750/13,125 yards); altitude limits 10/13,000 m (33/42,650 ft)

Guidance: radar or optical command for the midcourse phase and semi-active radar and/or IR for the terminal phase

Variants

SA-8A 'Gecko': introduced to Soviet service in the early 1970s, the single-stage SA-8 system features four ready-to-fire missiles on rail launchers carried on a 6 × 6 chassis believed to be derived from that of the ZIL-167 truck; the launcher system has a 'Land Roll' radar system with a surveillance radar and twin target tracking/missile guidance radars so that a salvo of two missiles can be fired for optimum hit probability; an optical system (including a low-light-level TV) is boresighted with the missile radars for use in conditions in which electronic countermeasures make radar command impossible or problematical; the missile has the Soviet production designation **9M33**

SA-8B 'Gecko': upgraded missile (possibly the same as that of the naval SA-N-4 system) first seen in 1980 with a revised launcher arrangement of three containers (rather than two rails) on each side of the radar group; this missile is longer than the original and has greater capabilities, but details are lacking

SA-9 'Gaskin'

(USSR)

Type: point defence tactical surface-to-air missile

Dimensions: diameter 0·12 m (4·72 in); length 1·80 m (5·91 ft); span 0·38 m (14·96 in)

Weight: total round 30 + kg (66 + lb)

Warhead: 2·6-kg (5·73-lb) HE fragmentation

Propulsion: one solid-propellant booster rocket delivering unrevealed thrust, and one solid-propellant sustainer rocket delivering unrevealed thrust

Performance: speed Mach 1·5; range limits 800/6000 m (875/6,560 yards); altitude limits 14/6000 m (46/19,685 ft)

Guidance: IR homing

Variant

SA-9 'Gaskin': this weapon entered service with the Soviet forces in the late 1960s, and was at first thought in the West to be derived from the SA-7, though more recent thinking attributes the ancestry of the 'Gaskin' to the AA-2 air-to-air missile; the single-stage weapon is normally carried as two container-boxed pairs (one pair on each side of a turret-like launch position) on a converted BRDM-2 4 × 4 reconnaissance vehicle; the weapon has severe tactical limitations in that it is restricted to clear-weather operations, and the lack of any remote-sensing apparatus entails the operator having to traverse the whole turret continuously in his search for targets; the missile has the Soviet production designation **9M31** and the service name **Strela-1**

SA-10 'Grumble'

(USSR)

Type: area defence tactical surface-to-air missile

Dimensions: diameter 0·45 m (17·72 in); length 7·00 m (22·97 ft); span 1·20 m (3·94 ft)

Weight: total round 1500 kg (3,307 lb)

Warhead: 100-kg (220-lb) HE fragmentation or (possibly) nuclear of unrevealed low-kiloton yield

Propulsion: one solid-propellant rocket delivering unrevealed thrust

Performance: speed Mach 6; range limits 9·5/100 km (5·9/62·1 miles); altitude limits 10/30,500 m (33/100,065 ft)

Guidance: semi-active radar for the midcourse phase and active radar for the terminal phase

Variant

SA-10 'Grumble': entering service in 1980, the single-stage SA-10 is a highly capable weapon at first associated (**SOA-10A** version) with three different tower-mounted surveillance radars and fixed launch sites for the interception of cruise missiles; the type has since been developed

(**SA-10B** version) for mobile operations, this high-speed missile being deployed on four-round TEL (transporter, erector and launcher) vehicles located on 8 × 8 trucks, with the associated planar-array radar located on a similar chassis

SA-11 'Gadfly'

(USSR)

Type: two-stage area defence tactical surface-to-air missile
Dimensions: diameter 0·40 m (15·75 in); length 5·60 m (18·37 ft); span 1·20 m (3·94 ft)
Weight: total round 650 kg (1,433 lb)
Warhead: 90-kg (198-lb) HE fragmentation
Propulsion: one jettisonable solid-propellant booster rocket delivering unrevealed thrust, and one solid-propellant sustainer rocket delivering unrevealed thrust
Performance: speed Mach 3; range limits 3/28 km (1·86/17·4 miles); altitude limits 30/14,000 m (100/45,930 ft)
Guidance: radar command for the midcourse phase and semi-active monopulse radar for the terminal phase

Variant
SA-11 'Gadfly': introduced in the early 1980s, this two-stage missile is the Soviet replacement for the SA-6 'Gainful', a system of severe tactical limitation as each four-vehicle launch battery (12 missiles) has only one 'Straight Flush' guidance radar, limiting the battery to single-target engagement capability; the SA-11 system uses four rather than three rails on each launch vehicle, which is also provided with its own guidance radar (probably a derivative of the 'Front Dome' radar used in the SA-N-7 naval version); the system thus offers considerably enhanced performance in terms of multiple target-engagement capability, and also features greater resistance to ECM

SA-12 'Gladiator' and 'Giant'

(USSR)

Type: area defence tactical/operational surface-to-air missile
Dimensions: diameter 0·50 m (19·685 in); length 7·20 m (23·62 ft); span 1·50 m (4·92 ft)
Weight: total round 2000 kg (4,409 lb)
Warhead: 150-kg (330·7-lb) HE fragmentation
Propulsion: one jettisonable solid-propellant booster rocket delivering unrevealed thrust, and one solid-propellant sustainer rocket delivering unrevealed thrust
Performance: speed Mach 3; range limits 5/80 km (3·1/49·7 miles) for SA-12A or 5/100 km (3·1/62·1 miles) for SA-12B; altitude limits 900/30,000 m (2,950/98,425 ft)
Guidance: semi-active radar homing

Variants
SA-12A 'Gladiator': introduced in 1986, the SA-12 was designed from the mid-1970s as successor to the SA-4 'Ganef', and is a very capable vertical-launch tactical weapon (mounted in two pairs, together with the associated guidance radar, on a tracked transporter/erector/launcher vehicle derived from the MT-T heavy transporter) able to tackle targets over every altitude band at short and medium ranges; the type is associated with a

phased-array radar able to deal with several targets simultaneously
SA-12B 'Giant': operational (perhaps even strategic) version of the SA-12 system, with greater range and a number of other modifications which have not been publicly discussed in the West; it is claimed that the SA-12B has a capability against ballistic missiles (the Americans going so far as to assert an ABM capability contrary to the provisions of the ABM Treaty which bans the development of SAMs with a capability against strategic rather than tactical/operational ballistic missiles) so the SA-12B's other modifications may involve the guidance system and/or warhead

SA-13 'Gopher'

(USSR)

Type: point defence tactical surface-to-air missile
Dimensions: diameter 0·12 m (4·72 in); length 2·20 m (7·22 ft); span 0·40 m (15·75 in)
Weight: total round 55 kg (121 lb)
Warhead: 6-kg (13·2-lb) HE fragmentation
Propulsion: one solid-propellant rocket delivering unrevealed thrust
Performance: speed Mach 2; range limits 500/10,000 m (550/10,935 yards); altitude limits 10/10,000 m (33/32,810 ft)
Guidance: IR homing

Variant
SA-13 'Gopher': a new weapon of which little is known, the one-stage SA-13 has the Soviet production designation **9M37** and the service name **Strela-10** and is successor to the SA-9 in the role of point defence of Soviet ground forces, and is based on a four-round launcher (two containers on each side of the central ranging radar) on the chassis of the MT-LB tracked carrier

Above: SA-13 'Gopher' surface-to-air missiles on their ZRK Strela-10 TELAR-2 fire unit vehicles.

SA-14 'Gremlin'

(USSR)

Type: man-portable point defence tactical surface-to-air missile
Dimensions: diameter 0·75 m (2·95 in); length 1·30 m (4·625 ft); span not revealed
Weight: total round 9·9 kg (21·285 lb)
Warhead: HE fragmentation
Propulsion: one solid-propellant rocket delivering unrevealed thrust
Performance: speed supersonic; range limits 600/6000 m (655/6,560 yards); altitude limits

10/5500 m (33/18,045 ft)
Guidance: IR homing

Variant
SA-14 'Gremlin': this system was introduced in the mid-1980s as replacement for the elderly and limited SA-7 series, and virtually nothing is known of the type; the missile can be distinguished by its conical nose, which projects from the front of the revised launcher; the missile has the Soviet service name **Strela-3**

SA-15

(USSR)

Type: point defence surface-to-air missile
Dimensions: (estimated) 0·60 m (23·6 in); length 3·50 m (11·48 ft); span not revealed
Weight: total round not revealed
Warhead: HE fragmentation
Propulsion: one solid-propellant rocket delivering unrevealed thrust
Performance: speed high supersonic; range limits not revealed/16,000 m (not revealed/17,500 yards); altitude limits 20/18,000 m (65/59,055 ft)
Guidance: radar command

Variant
SA-15: virtually nothing is known of this vertically launched short-range defence missile, which is probably under development as the replacement for the SA-8 'Gecko' on the basis of the SA-N-9 system; the type has the Soviet service name **Igla**

Bristol/Ferranti Bloodhound Mk 2

(UK)

Type: area defence tactical surface-to-air missile
Dimensions: diameter 21·5 in (0·546 m); length 25·42 ft (7·75 m); span 9·29 ft (2·83 m)
Weight: total round 5,070 lb (2300 kg)
Warhead: Royal Ordnance HE fragmentation
Propulsion: four Royal Ordnance jettisonable solid-propellant booster rockets each delivering unrevealed thrust, and two Rolls-Royce (Bristol) Thor sustainer ramjets each delivering unrevealed thrust
Performance: speed Mach 3·6; range limits not

Above: The Bloodhound Mk 2 is an elderly weapon, but retains a limited operational value.

revealed/50+ miles (not revealed/80+ km); altitude limits 325/75,500 ft (100/23,000 m)
Guidance: Ferranti semi-active radar homing

Variant
Bloodhound Mk 2: introduced in 1964 as replacement for the Bloodhound Mk 1 which had entered service in 1958, the Bloodhound Mk 2 is air-transportable and land-mobile, the complete system comprising four launchers, an I/J-band Ferranti Firelight (mobile use) or Marconi Scorpion (fixed use) continuous-wave target-illuminating radar and a launch control post, the latter two using data provided by a separate surveillance radar; the large HE warhead is detonated by a proximity fuse

British Aerospace Rapier Mk 1

(UK)
Type: point defence tactical surface-to-air missile
Dimensions: diameter 5·25 in (0·133 m); length 7·35 ft (2·24 m); span 15·0 in (0·381 m)
Weight: total round 94 lb (42·6 kg)
Warhead: 1·1-lb (0·5-kg) semi-armour-piercing HE
Propulsion: one IMI Troy dual-thrust rocket delivering unrevealed thrust
Performance: speed Mach 2+; range limits 270/7,500 yards (245/6860 m); altitude limits 0/10,000+ ft (0/3050+ m)
Guidance: Marconi/Decca/Barr & Stroud optical semi-automatic command to line of sight

Variants
Rapier Mk 1: one of the most important land-mobile SAMs yet to appear, the Rapier was conceived in the 1960s as a point-defence weapon whose extreme accuracy would ensure impact with the target, so obviating the need for a large proximity-fused warhead; the weapon entered service in 1971 and has since been developed into a number of operating forms all based on the same missile, which maintains a steady Mach 2+ speed and is capable of high-g manoeuvrability against helicopters and supersonic aircraft during interception and crossing engagements; the weapon was designed with rapid-engagement capability in mind, and can thus be used against helicopters that emerge from cover at close range, as well as faster targets at heights over 3000 m (9,845 ft); the small warhead is fitted with an impact-operated crush fuse proof against all countermeasures, and explodes only when the missile has penetrated into the target
Towed Rapier: baseline Rapier system, comprising a four-round launcher plus surveillance radar on a trailer, an optical tracker, a secondary sight, a tactical control unit and a generator; it requires two men to reload missiles, and though one man can then operate the system in simple conditions, it is more common for the operator to be supported by a tactical controller when there is a mix of friendly or hostile aircraft in the area, or in severe ECM conditions; when the Racal surveillance radar detects a possible target, the system automatically interrogates it with the inbuilt Cossor IFF before alerting the operator to a hostile target with an aural signal and by slewing the launcher and Barr & Stroud optical tracker to the correct bearing; the operator then acquires and tracks the target using a small control column; the system tells the operator when the target is within launch parameters, and the operator fires a missile while keeping the tracker on the target; the

tracker unit tracks the flares on the missile and its computer reduces to zero the angular deviation between the missile and line of sight to the target, commands being transmitted by microwave link; the launcher unit is supported by a reload vehicle carrying nine Rapier missiles
Rapier Laserfire: pallet-mounted system of greatly reduced cost and weight but only marginally degraded capability, and comprising a surveillance radar, Racal/Ferranti automatic laser tracker and missile guidance system, control post, command link and four-round launcher
Rapier Blindfire: night and all-weather derivative of the basic Towed Rapier, with a BAe/Marconi DN181 Blindfire monopulse tracker radar carried on a wheeled trailer complete with its own generator to complement the standard Towed Rapier outfit and so provide full day/night operating capability; the weapon is still being improved, largely with digital rather than analog electronics
Rapier Darkfire: system with optronic guidance system based on IR tracking of missiles fired from a six- rather than four-round launcher for enhanced tactical capability by day and night
Rapier Mk 2: updated missile under development for the **Rapier 2000** system, which is based on three towed vehicles designed for minimum radio-active contamination and maximum resistance to electro-magnetic impulse effects; one vehicle has eight ready-to-launch Rapiers and an optronic tracking system, one has Plessey 3D surveillance and target-acquisition radar, and one has improved Blindfire 2000 tracking and fire-control radar; the revised missile has a Royal Ordnance Thermopylae rocket motor for a range of 8,800 yards (8045 m), and comes in two forms as the **Rapier Mk 2A** with an HE fragmentation warhead and 'smart' proximity fuse (for the engagement of RPVs and missiles) and the **Rapier Mk 2B** with an impact-fused hollow-charge warhead (for the engagement of aircraft), and the fire-control system is capable of the simultaneous engagement of two targets with two missiles
Rapier Mk 3: variant under development for service in the next century with millimetric-frequency active radar guidance

Shorts Blowpipe

(UK)
Type: man-portable point defence tactical surface-to-air missile
Dimensions: diameter 3·00 in (0·076 m); length 4·56 ft (1·39 m); span 10·9 in (0·274 m)
Weight: total round 24·5 lb (11·1 kg)
Warhead: 4·85-lb (2·2-kg) HE fragmentation
Propulsion: one Royal Ordnance Crake two-stage solid-propellant rocket delivering unrevealed thrust
Performance: speed Mach 1·5; range limits not revealed/4,400+ yards (not revealed/4025+ m); altitude limits 0/6,600 ft (0/2010 m)
Guidance: IR gathering and radio command to line of sight

Variant
Blowpipe: a capable weapon proved in combat against targets as difficult as high-speed crossing aircraft, the Blowpipe comes in a sealed container, the whole unit weighing 28·7 lb (13 kg) and being clipped to a 19·6-lb (8·9-kg) aiming unit; the operator acquires the target visually with his monocular sight, fires the missile and then guides it to the target with a thumb controller before dis-

carding the empty 4·59-ft (1·40-m) launcher tube and clipping on another round; the Blowpipe can also be installed on a pedestal mount (land and naval applications) and on the turret ring of light AFVs

Shorts Javelin

(UK)
Type: man-portable point defence tactical surface-to-air missile
Dimensions: diameter 3·00 in (0·076 m); length 4·59 ft (1·40 m); span 10·9 in (0·277 m)
Weight: total round not revealed
Warhead: HE fragmentation
Propulsion: one Royal Ordnance two-stage solid-propellant rocket delivering unrevealed thrust
Performance: speed Mach 1·5; range limits 325/6,000 yards (300/5485 m); altitude limits 0/6,500+ ft (0/1980+ m)
Guidance: semi-automatic command to line of sight

Variant
Javelin: this is a development of the Blowpipe designed to deal more effectively with battlefield targets such as combat helicopters, which can launch their anti-tank missiles at ranges of more than 4,400 yards (4025 m); to provide the necessary range a more powerful sustainer is fitted, and destructive capability is enhanced by the provision of a new type of warhead; targeting at greater range is aided by the use of semi-automatic command to line of sight guidance, requiring the operator merely to keep the target centred in his sight

Shorts Starstreak

(UK)
Type: man-portable point defence tactical surface-to-air missile
Dimensions: not revealed
Weight: total round not revealed
Warhead: assembly of three kinetic-energy darts with HE warheads
Propulsion: one Royal Ordnance dual-thrust solid-propellant rocket delivering unrevealed thrust
Performance: speed Mach 4+; range limits 325/7,650 yards (300/6995 m); altitude limits not revealed
Guidance: semi-automatic command to line of sight

Variant
Starstreak: this is an extremely advanced short-range SAM of novel concept, and due to enter service in the early 1990s

Western Electric MIM-14B Nike Hercules

(USA)
Type: two-stage area defence tactical/operational surface-to-air missile
Dimensions: diameter 31·50 in (0·80 m); length overall 41·00 or 41·50 ft (12·50 or 12·65 m); span 6·17 ft (1·88 m)
Weight: total round 10,415 or 10,710 lb (4720 or 4858 kg) depending on specific variant

Warhead: 1,123-lb (509·4-kg) 2-, 20- or 40-kiloton W31 Mod 2 nuclear or alternative HE fragmentation

Propulsion: four jettisonable Hercules solid-propellant booster rockets each delivering unrevealed thrust, and one Thiokol M30A1 solid-propellant sustainer rocket delivering unrevealed thrust

Performance: speed Mach 3·65; range limits not revealed/90 + miles (not revealed/145 + km); altitude limits not revealed/150,000 ft (not revealed/45,720 m)

Guidance: radar command

Variants

MIM-14B Nike Hercules: introduced in 1958 as successor to the first-generation Nike Ajax, the Nike Hercules is still in service though obsolescent; its replacement in the US inventory is the MIM-104 Patriot; key features of the Nike Hercules' design are its range and altitude capability, the capable General Electric HIPAR radar, and the powerful warhead; only the USA has fielded the W31 Mod 2 nuclear warhead, which was developed at the Los Alamos National Laboratory from 1954 and entered service in 1958

MIM-14C Nike Hercules: upgraded MIM-14B

Raytheon MIM-23B Improved HAWK

(USA)

Type: area defence tactical surface-to-air missile

Dimensions: diameter 14·00 in (0·356 m); length 16·79 ft (5·12 m); span 4·00 ft (1·22 m)

Weight: total round 1,383 lb (627·3 kg)

Warhead: 120-lb (54·4-kg) HE fragmentation

Propulsion: one Aerojet M112E8 dual-thrust solid-propellant rocket delivering unrevealed thrust

Performance: speed Mach 2·5; range limits not revealed/25 miles (not revealed/40 km); altitude limits 100/49,000 ft (30/17,985 m)

Guidance: Raytheon semi-active radar homing

Variants

MIM-23A HAWK: the Homing All-the-Way Killer is one of the West's most important land-mobile air defence missiles, and was introduced during 1960 in this baseline model; the system was designed to provide maximum efficiency at low and medium altitudes against the whole spectrum of Soviet attack aircraft even under severe ECM conditions, to be fully air transportable by helicopter, and to retain full capability under the most difficult geographical and climatic regimes; the basic system was considerably enhanced in the late 1960s by delivery of each missile as a certified round requiring neither field test nor repair, and the addition of a DADP (digital automatic data processor) for target data processing, threat prioritization and fire-control computation

MIM-23B Improved HAWK: improved model introduced in the 1970s with an upgraded engine, new guidance package and larger warhead; the entire HAWK system is effective but cumbersome, being designed for limited battlefield mobility by wheeled transport in several parts, the most important being the three-round launcher on a two-wheel trailer (three launchers to a battery), the PAR (pulse-Doppler high/medium-altitude acquisition radar with moving target indication and high resistance to ECCM), the CWAR (continuous-wave low-altitude acquisition radar synchronized in azimuth with the PAR for maximum ease of target correlation), the ROR

(range-only radar), the HPI (high-power illuminator), the BCC (battery control central where the tactical control officer orders the whole engagement) and the ICC (information co-ordination central, which is the fire-control data-processing and communications centre for the battery); there are various improvement standards for the MIM-23B system, based largely on improved radar capability at low levels and the adoption of electro-optical tracking systems; Phase I of this P 4IP (Phased Pre-Planned Product Improvement Program) was completed between 1977 and 1979, and saw the upgrading of CWAR, Army Tactical Data Link and PAR moving target indicator capabilities, Phase II was undertaken from 1983 to improve reliability and upgrade the HPI with solid-state electronics, and to add the TAS (Tracking Adjunct System, a passive electro-optical tracker to complement the radar system and so provide continued operational capability under the severest ECM conditions), and Phase III in the later 1980s streamlined the HAWK battery as well as cut back manpower and logistic needs; further improvement is foreseen by the adoption of a 3D frequency-agile continuous-wave acquisition radar, leading to the possibility of midcourse guidance update, a more compact fire-control system and other developments

MIM-23C Improved HAWK: upgraded MIM-23B

MIM-23D Improved HAWK: upgraded MIM-23C

MIM-23E Improved HAWK: variant of the MIM-23C with improved guidance in a multi-jamming environment

MIM-23F Improved HAWK: variant of the MIM-23D with improved guidance in a multi-jamming environment

M727 SP HAWK: self-propelled version mounted on an M548 tracked carrier chassis

NOAH: this acronym stands for NOrway Adapted HAWK, and indicates a development of the basic weapon using Hughes LASR 3D radar to replace the HAWK battery's current array of search radars; other advantages of the LASR are good results in clutter conditions, and high resistance to ECM

General Dynamics FIM-43A Redeye

(USA)

Type: man-portable point defence tactical surface-to-air missile

Dimensions: diameter 2·75 in (0·70 m); length 4·00 ft (1·22 m); span 5·50 in (0·14 m)

Weight: total round 18 lb (8·2 kg)

Warhead: HE fragmentation

Propulsion: one Atlantic Research M99 dual-thrust solid-propellant rocket delivering unrevealed thrust

Performance: speed supersonic; range limits not revealed/3,700 yards (not revealed/3385 m); altitude limits not revealed

Guidance: IR homing

Variants

FIM-43A Redeye: developed from the late 1950s in an effort to provide US infantry units with man-portable surface-to-air capability, the Redeye entered service only in 1968 after a protracted development programme, and has never proved entirely successful; the type is notable for its comparatively short range and its restriction to pursuit-only engagements (after the target has launched its attack); the missile is carried in a

sealed container, and this is clipped to the sight unit for an engagement; the empty container is discarded after firing and replaced by another round

FIM-43B Redeye: upgraded FIM-43A with the M110 solid-propellant rocket

FIM-43C Redeye: upgraded FIM-43B with the M115 solid-propellant rocket and revised launcher

FIM-43D Redeye: upgraded FIM-43C

Ford MIM-72C/R Improved Chaparral

(USA)

Type: man-portable point defence tactical surface-to-air missile

Dimensions: 5·12 in (0·13 m); length 9·54 ft (2·91 m); span 24·76 in (0·629 m)

Weight: total round 190 lb (86·3 kg)

Warhead: 24·7-lb (11·2-kg) Picatinny Arsenal M250 HE fragmentation

Propulsion: one Bermite Mk 50 Mod 0 solid-propellant rocket delivering 3,000-lb (1361-kg) thrust

Performance: speed supersonic; range limits not revealed/6,500 yards (not revealed/5945 m); altitude limits 1,150/10,000 ft (350/3050 m)

Guidance: Ford Aerospace DAW-1 IR homing

Above: MIM-72 SAMs on a launcher upgraded with a FLIR sensor for limited all-weather capability.

Variants

MIM-72A Chaparral: this was the initial Sidewinder AAM-derived missile used in the M48 Chaparral system in the late 1960s; the weapon weighs 187 lb (85 kg) and was evolved from the US Navy's Sidewinder 1D, and the system was designed to provide US Army land formations with low-level air defence to the end of the 20th century

MIM-72B Chaparral: improved model developed in the 1970s with a more powerful warhead, more sensitive General Electric/ Raytheon seeker and better fuse; the weight of this model is 190 lb (86·3 kg), and the system is used in conjunction with the MPQ-54 surveillance radar to provide the operator with the chance to traverse the four-round turret to the bearing in which he can acquire the target visually and fire a missile, thereby reducing reaction time by a significant degree

MIM-72C/R Improved Chaparral: version of the late 1970s with a more discriminating Ford Aerospace seeker (using the rosette-scan seeker technology to provide capability for head-on engagements), an IFF system, smokeless propellant to reduce launcher detectability, and provision for use on the M48 self-propelled launcher fitted with a FLIR sensor for adverse-weather and nocturnal operation; this last is derived from US Army standard common modules, and is being added as a retrofit to all existing M48 launcher equipments; further improvement is being added in the form of system reliability and performance modifications

MIM-72D Improved Chaparral: experimental development of the MIM-72C with an improved warhead and directional Doppler fuse; the type was developed further as the **MIM-72E** and **MIM-72F** versions

MIM-72G Improved Chaparral: current production model with two-colour seeker of the rosette-scan variety for improved discrimination against decoys

Bodensee Shorad: this West German development is a trailer-based short-range air defence system using the AIM-9L Sidewinder on a four-round launcher with a remotely-controlled TV camera, and is designed for the point defence of West German airfields

M54: this is the static equivalent of the M54 designed for the protection of fixed sites and slower-moving tactical formations; the turret/launcher is identical with that of the M54, but is located on a two-axle trailer supported for firing by jacks; there is also a **Lightweight Chaparral** version with an all-up weight of 12,000 lb (5443 kg)

General Dynamics FIM-92A Stinger

(USA)

Type: man-portable point defence tactical surface-to-air missile
Dimensions: diameter 2·75 in (0·07 m); length 5·00 ft (1·52 m); span 3·6 in (0·914 m)
Weight: total round 22·3 lb (10·1 kg)
Warhead: 6·6-lb (3·0-kg) Picatinny Arsenal HE fragmentation
Propulsion: one Atlantic Research dual-thrust solid-propellant rocket delivering unrevealed thrust
Performance: speed Mach 2+; range limits not revealed/5,500 yards (not revealed/5030 m); altitude limits not revealed/15,750 ft (not revealed/4800 m)
Guidance: General Dynamics (Pomona) IR homing

Variants

FIM-92A Stinger: the Stinger was designed as successor to the Redeye with all-aspect engagement capability, greater performance and manoeuvrability, an IFF system and enhanced ECM resistance; the weapon was introduced in 1981 and has proved generally successful; the missile and launcher weigh 30 lb (13·6 kg), or 33·3 lb (15·1 kg) with the IFF system and battery
Stinger-POST: this advanced model currently in production has a Passive Optical Scanning Technique seeker to provide better discrimination between the target and the ground for low-altitude engagements

Raytheon MIM-104A Patriot

(USA)

Type: area defence tactical/operational surface-to-air missile
Dimensions: diameter 16·00 in (0·406 m); length 17·00 ft (5·18 m); span 3·00 ft (0·914 m)
Weight: total round 2,200 lb (998 kg)
Warhead: HE fragmentation
Propulsion: one Thiokol TX-486-1 solid-propellant rocket delivering unrevealed thrust
Performance: speed Mach 3; range limits not revealed/37·3 miles (not revealed/60 km); altitude limits not revealed/78,750 ft (not revealed/24,000 m)
Guidance: Raytheon radar command (track via missile) for midcourse phase and Raytheon monopulse semi-active radar for the terminal phase

Variant

MIM-104A: entering service in 1986 after a protracted development, the Patriot is a highly capable medium-range air-defence weapon designed to replace the Improved HAWK and Nike Hercules; each launcher system has four containerized missiles on a semi-trailer, and up to eight (normally five) launchers can be controlled by the MSQ-104 engagement centre working with the MPQ-53 surveillance and target-acquisition radar

CITEFA Mathogo

(Argentina)

Type: short/medium-range anti-tank missile
Dimensions: diameter 0·102 m (4·02 in); length 0·998 m (3·27 ft); span not revealed
Weight: total round 11·3 kg (24·9 lb)
Warhead: 2·8-kg (6·17-lb) HEAT
Propulsion: one solid-propellant booster rocket delivering unrevealed thrust, and one solid-propellant sustainer rocket delivering unrevealed thrust
Performance: speed 325 km/h (202 mph); range limits 350/2100 m (385/2,295 yards)
Guidance: wire command to line of sight

Variant

Mathogo: introduced in the late 1970s or early 1980s, this is a simple first-generation weapon reminiscent in concept and layout (but not in dimensions and weights of the Swedish Bantam weapon; the operator can control four missiles each separated from the firing position by 50-m (165-ft) cables; the weight of the missile and launcher is 19·5 kg (64 lb), and the missile comes in two variants with range capabilities of 2000 and 3000 m (2,185 and 3,280 yards)

NORINCO Red Arrow 8

(China)

Type: short/medium-range anti-tank missile
Dimensions: diameter 0·12 m (4·72 in); length 0·875 m (2·87 ft); span 0·32 m (12·6 in)
Weight: total round 11·2 kg (24·7 lb)
Warhead: HEAT
Propulsion: one solid-propellant rocket delivering unrevealed thrust
Performance: speed 865 km/h (538 mph); range limits 100/3000 m (110/3,280 yards)
Guidance: wire semi-automatic command to line of sight

Variant

Red Arrow 8: this indigenously designed Chinese weapon began to enter service in the mid-1980s, and may be regarded as China's counterpart to the British Swingfire and US TOW systems; the missile has wrap-round fins and is carried in a container that doubles as the launch tube when installed on the head of the firing tripod; the weight of the loaded tube is 24·5 kg (54 lb), and of the launch tripod 23 kg (50·7 lb) increased by 24 kg (52·9 lb) top-section control equipment; the weapon has a HEAT warhead with an armour penetration capability of 800 mm (31·5 in), and a hit probability of 90% is claimed; the Red Arrow 8 can also be used on a pedestal mount on 4 × 4 vehicles and tracked APCs

Aérospatiale SS.11

(France)

Type: short/medium-range anti-tank missile
Dimensions: diameter 0·164 m (6·46 in); length 1·20 m (3·94 ft); span 0·50 m (19·7 in)
Weight: total round 29·9 kg (65·9 lb)
Warhead: HEAT
Propulsion: one two-stage solid-propellant rocket delivering unrevealed thrust
Performance: speed 685 km/h (426 mph); range 500/3000 m (545/3,280 yards)
Guidance: wire command to line of sight

Variants

SS.11: entering service in 1956, the SS.11 was the first of the modern anti-tank and battlefield missiles, and though obsolescent is still in fairly widespread service; the type is launched from a rail, and can carry Type 140AC anti-tank warhead capable of penetrating 600 mm (23·62 in) of armour, the Type 140AP02 delay-action anti-tank/anti-personnel warhead capable of penetrating 100 mm (0·4 in) of armour, and the Type 140AP59 anti-personnel fragmentation warhead
SS.11B1: improved model of 1962 with transistorized electronics in the control unit

Aérospatiale Eryx

(France)

Type: man-portable short-range light anti-tank missile
Dimensions: diameter 0·16 m (6·3 in); length 0·905 m (2·97 ft); span not revealed
Weight: total round 11 kg (24·25 lb)
Warhead: 3·6-kg (7·94-lb) HEAT
Propulsion: one solid-propellant rocket delivering unrevealed thrust
Performance: speed 72 km/h (44·7 mph); range limits 50/600 m (55/655 yards)
Guidance: wire semi-automatic command to line of sight

Variant

Eryx: this is a lightweight anti-tank weapon selected for the French army in 1986 after development as the ACCP (Anti-Char Courte Portée); the type has an extremely small motor resulting in very low speed, but this tactical limitation is offset by the type's minimum backblast and ability to be fired from inside a building; the flight time to 600 m (655 yards) is 3·7 seconds, and the tandem warhead located towards the rear of the missile can penetrate 900 mm (35·4 in) of armour

Euromissile HOT

(France/West Germany)

Type: medium/long-range heavy anti-tank missile
Dimensions: diameter 0·165 m (6·5 in); length

1·275 m (4·18 ft); span 0·312 m (12·28 in)
Weight: total round 23·5 kg (51·8 lb)
Warhead: 6-kg (13·2-lb) HEAT
Propulsion: one SNPE Bugeat solid-propellant booster rocket delivering unrevealed thrust, and one SNPE Infra solid-propellant sustainer rocket delivering 24-kg (53-lb) thrust
Performance: speed 865 km/h (537 mph); range limits 75/4250 m (82/4,650 yards)
Guidance: SAT/Eltro wire semi-automatic command to line of sight

Variants

HOT: entering service in the early 1970s, the HOT (Haute subsonique Optiquement téléguide tiré d'un Tube, or high-subsonic optically-guided tube-launched) missile is sometimes designated **Hot** and is a powerful anti-tank weapon designed for static ground use, or for installation in armoured fighting vehicles and helicopters; the missile can be used from single or multiple tube launchers, and can penetrate more than 800 mm (31·5 in) of armour; the type's primary disadvantage is a modest speed, which means that the missile takes some 17 seconds to reach its maximum range even when launched from a helicopter which thus has to remain exposed for this time
HOT 2: this improved version of the basic weapon features much-enhanced armour penetration as a result of its larger 150-mm (5·9-in) warhead containing 4·1 rather than 3 kg (9·04 rather than 6·61 lb) of HE, and is also faster than its predecessor with all the consequent tactical advantages of this fact; in 1992 this HOT 2 will be delivered in the **HOT 2T** form with tandem charges to defeat reactive armour, the first charge being of the forward-projecting type to open the way for the main charge's jet of gas and vaporized metal
HOT Commando ATLAS: introduced in 1986, this is the Affût de Tir Léger Au Sol (ground-based lightweight fire equipment) version designed specifically for launch from the ground (using a tripod-mounted launcher) or from a light vehicle; the HOT 2 missile is used with the launcher developed for the SA 342 helicopter and the Thomson-CSF Castor IR tracker designed for the Renault VAB carrier; the standard anti-tank warhead can penetrate 1300 mm (51·2 in) of armour at maximum range, and a new multi-purpose warhead is being developed with a 150-mm (5·9-in) diameter HEAT charge able to defeat 350 mm (13·78 in) of armour and a casing able to fill a radius of 25 m (82 ft) with 1,000 lethal fragments

Complementary weapons from Euromissile: the HOT missile (above) and the Milan missile (below).

Euromissile MILAN

(France/West Germany)

Type: short/medium-range anti-tank missile
Dimensions: diameter 0·90 m (3·54 in); length 0·769 m (2·52 ft); span 0·265 m (10·43 in)
Weight: total round 6·65 kg (14·66 lb)
Warhead: 2·98-kg (6·57-lb) HEAT
Propulsion: one SNPE Artus dual-thrust solid-propellant rocket delivering unrevealed thrust
Performance: speed 720 km/h (447 mph); range limits 25/2000 m (28/2,185 yards)
Guidance: SAT/Eltro wire semi-automatic command to line of sight

Variants

MILAN: an advanced second-generation missile, the MILAN (Missile d'Infanterie Léger ANtichar, or light infantry anti-tank missile) is often designated the **Milan** and began to enter service in the mid-1970s; the missile was designed as the man-portable counterpart to the heavyweight HOT from the same stable; the weapon is tube fired from a single launcher on the ground or located on a pedestal, or from multiple launchers located on light vehicles; the warhead can penetrate more than 650 mm (25·6 in) of armour; like the larger HOT, the MILAN suffers the tactical disadvantages of modest speed, though this failing is in part mitigated by shorter range
MILAN 2: this improved version of the basic weapon features much-improved armour penetration as a result of its 12-mm (0·47-in) larger 115-mm (4·53-in) diameter K115 warhead with extended nose probe for optimum stand-off detonation distance, and is also faster than its predecessor; from 1992 this HOT 2 will be delivered in the form of the **MILAN 2T** with tandem charges to defeat reactive armour, the first charge in the nose probe opening the way for the main charge's jet of gas and vaporized metal

MBB Mamba

(West Germany)

Type: man-portable short/medium-range anti-tank missile
Dimensions: diameter 0·12 m (4·72 in); length 0·955 m (3·13 ft); span 0·40 m (15·75 in)
Weight: total round 11·2 kg (24·7 lb)
Warhead: 2·7-kg (5·95-lb) HEAT
Propulsion: one solid-propellant dual-thrust rocket delivering unrevealed thrust
Performance: speed 505 km/h (314 mph); range limits 300/2000 m (330/2,185 yards)
Guidance: wire command to line of sight

Variants

Mamba: introduced in 1972, the Mamba is an upgraded Cobra 2000 with a single rocket providing lift as well as propulsion; the operator can control a total of 12 missiles via a junction box, and the warhead can penetrate 500 mm (19·69 in) of armour; the type is also being evaluated with a fibre-optic guidance system
Avibras MSS-1: this is a Brazilian anti-tank missile apparently identical with the Mamba externally, but possessing a launch weight of 17·2 kg (38 lb)

MBB Bo 810 Cobra 2000

(West Germany)

Type: man-portable short/medium-range anti-tank missile

Dimensions: diameter 0·10 m (3·94 in); length 0·95 m (3·12 ft); span 0·48 m (18·90 in)
Weight: total round 10·3 kg (22·7 lb)
Warhead: 2·7-kg (5·95-lb) HEAT/anti-tank shrapnel
Propulsion: one solid-propellant booster rocket delivering unrevealed thrust, and one solid-propellant sustainer rocket delivering unrevealed thrust
Performance: speed 305 km/h (190 mph); range limits 400/2000 m (435/2,185 yards)
Guidance: wire command to line of sight

Variant

Cobra 2000: designed in the late 1950s as a first-generation man-portable missile, the Cobra 2000 has proved a successful export weapon; the missile is simply placed on the ground facing the target, and launched with the aid of a nonjettisonable booster by an operator who can be laterally displaced from the weapon by as much as 70 m (230 ft) and co-ordinate eight missiles via a junction box; the HEAT warhead is able to penetrate 500 mm (19·69 in) of armour, and the anti-tank shrapnel type 350 mm (13·78 in)

IMI Mapats

(Israel)

Type: medium/long-range heavy anti-tank missile
Dimensions: diameter 0·148 m (5·83 in); length with probe extended 1·450 m (4·76 ft); span not revealed
Weight: total round 18·5 kg (40·78 lb)
Warhead: 3·6-kg (7·94-lb) HEAT
Propulsion: one solid-propellant rocket delivering unrevealed thrust
Performance: speed 1135 km/h (704 mph); range limits ?/4000 m (?/4,375 yards)
Guidance: laser beam-riding

Variant

Mapats: this is a highly capable weapon with advanced guidance and capable of penetrating 800 mm (31·5 in) of multi-layer armour; the weapon is supplied as a round in a fibreglass container which serves as the clip-on launch tube, the missile/container assembly weighing 29 kg (63·9 lb) and measuring 1·50 m (4·92 ft) in length

OTO Melara MAF

(Italy)

Type: medium-range heavy anti-tank missile
Dimensions: diameter 0·13 m (5·12 in); length 1·38 m (4·53 ft); span 0·53 m (20·87 in)
Weight: total round 14·5 kg (31·97 lb)
Warhead: 4-kg (8·82-lb) HEAT
Propulsion: one solid-propellant booster rocket delivering unrevealed thrust, and one solid-propellant sustainer rocket delivering unrevealed thrust
Performance: speed 1045 km/h (649 mph); range limits 75/3000 m (82/3,280 yards)
Guidance: automatic command to line of sight

Variants

MAF: entering service in the late 1980s, this is a third-generation anti-tank missile initially developed as the Breda Sparviero and taken over by OTO Melara in the mid-1980s; the missile is fired from a tripod launcher which weighs 69 kg (152·1 lb) complete with encapsulated missile, and uses an advanced wireless command guidance system developed by Officine Galileo; the flight time to the maximum range of 3000 m (3,280 yards) is 16 seconds, but a more realistic range is 2000 m (2,185 yards) in all but perfect conditions

Orbita MSS 1·1: this is the Brazilian licence-produced version of the MAF, built by Orbita Sistemas Aeroespaciais which is also co-operating in the final development of the weapon

Kawasaki Type 79

(Japan)

Type: medium/long-range heavy anti-tank missile

Dimensions: diameter 0·152 m (6·00 in); length 1·565 m (5·13 ft); span 0·332 m (13·1 in)

Weight: total round 33 kg (72·75 lb)

Warhead: 1·9-kg (4·2-lb) HEAT or SAP-HE

Propulsion: one Nihon Yushi solid-propellant booster rocket delivering unrevealed thrust, and one Daicel solid-propellant sustainer rocket delivering unrevealed thrust

Performance: speed 720 km/h (447 mph); range limits not revealed/4000 m (not revealed/4,375 yards)

Guidance: Nihon Electric wire semi-automatic command to line of sight

Variant

Type 79: also known as the **KAM-9D** and introduced in 1980, this is a powerful weapon modelled conceptually on the American TOW system, and able to deal effectively with tanks (the missile's armour penetration being 500 + mm/19·67 + in) and landing craft; the containerized missile weighs 42 kg (92·6 lb) and is generally fired from a tripod launcher, two missiles being allocated to each laterally-separated firing unit; low speed is the type's worst disadvantage

Kawasaki Type 64

(Japan)

Type: short/medium-range anti-tank missile

Dimensions: diameter 0·12 m (4·72 in); length 1·00 m (3·28 ft); span 0·60 m (23·6 in)

Weight: total round 15·7 kg (34·6 lb)

Warhead: HEAT

Propulsion: one Daicel/Nippon Oil two-stage solid-propellant rocket delivering unrevealed thrust

Performance: speed 305 km/h (190 mph); range 350/1800 m (385/1,970 yards)

Guidance: Nihon Electric wire command to line of sight

Variant

Type 64: introduced in 1965 and otherwise known as the **KAM-3D**, this is a simple, slow yet effective missile now being replaced by the Type 79 weapon; the system requires a three-man crew, and the operator can control one or more laterally-separated missiles from a central firing position; the missile is launched from a small ground support/baseplate

Bofors Rbs 56 Bill

(Sweden)

Type: medium-range anti-tank missile

Dimensions: diameter 0·15 m (5·91 in); length

0·90 m (2·95 ft); span 0·41 m (16·14 in)

Weight: total containerized round 16 kg (35·3 lb)

Warhead: HEAT

Propulsion: one Royal Ordnance solid-propellant rocket delivering unrevealed thrust

Performance: speed 720 km/h (447 mph); range limits 150/2000 m (165/2,185 yards)

Guidance: wire semi-automatic command to line of sight

Variant

Rbs 56 Bill: entering service in the later 1980s, the Bill (pick) is a highly advanced missile fired from a container tube fitted with a sight unit and mounted on a tripod; the key to the Bill's capabilities is the shaped-charge warhead, which is angled to fire 30° downwards from the missile centreline as the weapon overflies the target's most vulnerable upper surfaces, thus allowing the gas/vaporized metal jet to burn through the target tank's thinnest armour

Bofors Bantam

(Sweden)

Type: man-portable short/medium-range anti-tank missile

Dimensions: diameter 0·11 m (4·33 in); length 0·85 m (2·79 ft); span 0·40 m (15·75 in)

Weight: total round 11·5 kg (25·35 lb) including container

Warhead: 1·9-kg (4·2-lb) HEAT

Propulsion: one two-stage solid-propellant rocket delivering unrevealed thrust

Performance: speed 305 km/h (190 mph); range limits 300/2000 m (330/2,185 yards)

Guidance: wire command to line of sight

Variant

Bantam: this is a first-generation anti-tank missile (carried in and launched from a small container) with simple guidance and low cruising speed, the operator being afforded a measure of protection by a separation of up to 120 m (130 yards) between the launcher and the control position; the weapon was adopted in 1963, and its warhead can penetrate 500 mm (19·68 in) of armour

AT-1 'Snapper'

(USSR)

Type: man-portable short/medium-range anti-tank missile

Dimensions: diameter 0·14 m (5·51 in); length 1·13 m (3·71 ft); span 0·78 m (30·7 in)

Weight: total round 22·25 kg (49·1 lb)

Warhead: 5·25-kg (11·5-lb) HEAT

Propulsion: one solid-propellant rocket delivering unrevealed thrust

Performance: speed 320 km/h (199 mph); range limits 500/2300 m (545/2,515 yards)

Guidance: wire command to line of sight

Below: The AT-1 'Snapper' anti-tank missile.

Variant

AT-1 'Snapper': known to the Soviets by the service designation **PUR-61** and name **Shmel**, and by the production designation **3M6**, this first-generation anti-tank missile entered service in the early 1960s, and is notable for its considerable size and slow flight; the warhead can penetrate 380 mm (14·96 in) of armour

AT-2 'Swatter'

(USSR)

Type: medium/long-range anti-tank missile

Dimensions: diameter 0·132 m (5·2 in); length 1·14 m (3·74 ft); span 0·66 m (26·00 in)

Weight: total round ('Swatter-A') 26·5 kg (54·8 lb) or ('Swatter-B') 29·5 kg (65 lb)

Warhead: HEAT

Propulsion: one solid-propellant rocket delivering unrevealed thrust

Performance: speed 540 km/h (336 mph); range limits ('Swatter-A') 500/3000 m (545/3,280 yards) or ('Swatter-B') 500/3500 m (545/3,825 yards)

Guidance: radio command to line of sight with IR terminal homing

Variants

AT-2 'Swatter-A': a first-generation vehicle-launched anti-tank missile with countermeasures-prone radio command guidance, the 'Swatter' was introduced in the mid-1960s and is known to the Soviets by the service designation **PUR-62** and name **Falanga**, and by the production designation **9M17**; the HEAT warhead can penetrate 480 mm (18·9 in) of armour

AT-2 'Swatter-B': increased-range model with an improved motor and a more capable warhead able to penetrate 510 mm (20·08 in) of armour

AT-3 'Sagger'

(USSR)

Type: man-portable medium/long-range anti-tank missile

Dimensions: diameter 0·119 m (4·69 in); length 0·883 m (2·90 ft); span 0·46 m (18·1 in)

Weight: total round 11·29 kg (24·9 lb)

Warhead: 3-kg (6·6-lb) HEAT

Propulsion: one solid-propellant dual-thrust rocket delivering unrevealed thrust

Performance: speed 430 km/h (267 mph); range limits 300/3000 m (330/3,280 yards)

Guidance: wire command to line of sight

Above: AT-3 'Sagger' anti-tank missiles on the six-rail launcher of a BRDM scout car.

Variants

AT-3 'Sagger-A': introduced in about 1970, the AT-3 is a more capable and versatile weapon than the AT-2, with a countermeasures-proof wire guidance system and more powerful motor for greater (but still comparatively slow) speed; the type has the service designation **PUR-64** and name **Malyutka** (production designation **9M14**),